W9-BZM-637

Groups

PROCESS AND PRACTICE

10e

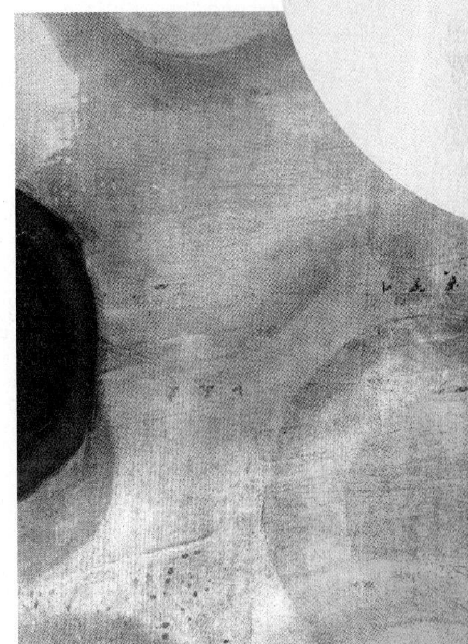

Marianne Schneider Corey
Consultant

Gerald Corey
California State University, Fullerton
Diplomate in Counseling Psychology
American Board of Professional Psychology

Cindy Corey
Licensed Clinical Psychologist
Multicultural Consultant

CENGAGE Learning®

Australia • Brazil • Mexico • Singapore • United Kingdom • United States

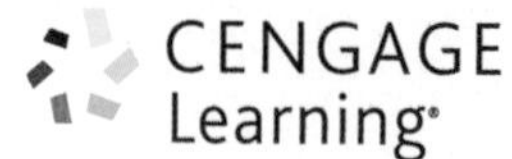

***Groups: Process and Practice*, 10th Edition**
Marianne Schneider Corey, Gerald Corey, Cindy Corey

Product Director: Marta Lee-Perriard

Product Manager: Julie Martinez

Content Developer: Alexander Hancock

Product Assistant: Kimiya Hojjat

Marketing Manager: Jennifer Levenduski

Content Project Manager: Rita Jaramillo

Digital Content Specialist: Jaclyn Hermesmeyer

Art Director: Vernon Boes

Manufacturing Planner: Judy Inouye

Production Service: Cenveo® Publisher Services

Text and Cover Designer: Jeanne Calabrese

Cover Image: Qweek/iStock /Getty Images Plus/Getty Images

Compositor: Cenveo® Publisher Services

Library of Congress Control Number: 2016941242

Student Edition:
ISBN: 978-1-305-86570-9

Loose-leaf Edition:
ISBN: 978-1-337-11185-0

Cengage Learning
20 Channel Center Street
Boston, MA 02210
USA

Cengage Learning is a leading provider of customized learning solutions with employees residing in nearly 40 different countries and sales in more than 125 countries around the world. Find your local representative at **www.cengage.com.**

Cengage Learning products are represented in Canada by Nelson Education, Ltd.

To learn more about Cengage Learning Solutions, visit **www.cengage.com.**

Purchase any of our products at your local college store or at our preferred online store **www.cengagebrain.com.**

Printed in the United States of America
Print Number: 02 Print Year: 2017

About The Authors

Marianne Schneider Corey is a licensed marriage and family therapist in California and is a National Certified Counselor. She received her master's degree in marriage, family, and child counseling from Chapman College. She is a Fellow of the Association for Specialists in Group Work and was the recipient of this organization's Eminent Career Award in 2001. She received the Lifetime Achievement Award from the American Mental Health Counselors Association in 2011 and is a member of the American Mental Health Counselors Association. She also holds memberships in the American Counseling Association, the American Group Psychotherapy Association, the Association for Specialists in Group Work, the Association for Multicultural Counseling and Development, the Association for Counselor Education and Supervision, and the Western Association of Counselor Education and Supervision.

Marianne has been involved in leading groups for different populations, providing training and supervision workshops in group process, facilitating self-exploration groups for graduate students in counseling, and cofacilitating training groups for group counselors and weeklong residential workshops in personal growth. Both Marianne and Jerry Corey have conducted training workshops, continuing education seminars, and personal-growth groups in the United States, Germany, Ireland, Belgium, Mexico, Hong Kong, China, and Korea.

In addition to *Groups: Process and Practice,* Tenth Edition (2018, with Gerald Corey and Cindy Corey), which has been translated into Korean, Chinese, and Polish), Marianne has coauthored the following books with Cengage Learning:

- *I Never Knew I Had a Choice,* Eleventh Edition (2018, with Gerald Corey and Michelle Muratori) [Translated into Chinese]
- *Becoming a Helper,* Seventh Edition (2016, with Gerald Corey) [Translated into Korean and Japanese]
- *Issues and Ethics in the Helping Professions,* Ninth Edition (2015, with Gerald Corey, Cindy Corey, and Patrick Callanan) [Translated into Japanese and Chinese]
- *Group Techniques,* Fourth Edition (2015, with Gerald Corey, Patrick Callanan, and Michael Russell) [Translated into Portuguese, Korean, Japanese, and Czech]

Marianne has made educational video programs (with accompanying student workbooks) for Cengage Learning: *Groups in Action: Evolution and Challenges DVD and Workbook* (2014, with Gerald Corey and Robert Haynes); and *Ethics in Action: DVD and Workbook* (2015, with Gerald Corey and Robert Haynes).

Marianne and Jerry have been married since 1964. They have two adult daughters, Heidi and Cindy, two granddaughters (Kyla and Keegan), and one grandson (Corey). Marianne grew up in Germany and has kept in close contact with her family and friends there. In her free time, she enjoys traveling, reading, visiting with friends, bike riding, and hiking.

To the youngest members of the Corey group:

Kyla, **Keegan**, and **Corey**.

Their creativity, compassion, energy, and curiosity keep all of us young.

Gerald Corey is Professor Emeritus of Human Services and Counseling at California State University at Fullerton. He received his doctorate in counseling from the University of Southern California. He is a Diplomate in Counseling Psychology, American Board of Professional Psychology; a licensed psychologist; and a National Certified Counselor. He is a Fellow of the American Psychological Association (Division 17, Counseling Psychology, and Division 49, Group Psychotherapy); a Fellow of the American Counseling Association; and a Fellow of the Association for Specialists in Group Work. He also holds memberships in the American Group Psychotherapy Association; the American Mental Health Counselors Association; the Association for Spiritual, Ethical, and Religious Values in Counseling; the Association for Counselor Education and Supervision; and the Western Association of Counselor Education and Supervision. Both Jerry and Marianne Corey received the Lifetime Achievement Award from the American Mental Health Counselors Association in 2011, and both of them received the Eminent Career Award from ASGW in 2001. Jerry was given the Outstanding Professor of the Year Award from California State University at Fullerton in 1991. He regularly teaches both undergraduate and graduate courses in group counseling and ethics in counseling. He is the author or coauthor of 15 textbooks in counseling currently in print, along with more than 60 journal articles and book chapters. Several of his books have been translated into other languages. *Theory and Practice of Counseling and Psychotherapy* has been translated into Arabic, Indonesian, Portuguese, Turkish, Korean, and Chinese. *Theory and Practice of Group Counseling* has been translated into Korean, Chinese, Spanish, and Russian. *Issues and Ethics in the Helping Professions* has been translated into Korean, Japanese, and Chinese.

In the past 40 years Jerry and Marianne Corey have conducted group counseling training workshops for mental health professionals at many universities in the United States as well as in Canada, Mexico, China, Hong Kong, Korea, Germany, Belgium, Scotland, England, and Ireland. In his leisure time, Jerry likes to travel, hike and bicycle in the mountains and the desert, and drive his 1931 Model A Ford. Marianne and Jerry have been married since 1964. They have two adult daughters (Heidi and Cindy), two granddaughters (Kyla and Keegan), and one grandson (Corey).

Recent publications by Gerald Corey, all with Cengage Learning, include:

- *Groups: Process and Practice*, Tenth Edition (2018, with Marianne Schneider Corey and Cindy Corey)
- *I Never Knew I Had a Choice*, Eleventh Edition (2018, with Marianne Schneider Corey and Michelle Muratori)
- *Theory and Practice of Counseling and Psychotherapy*, Tenth Edition (and *Student Manual*) (2017)
- *Theory and Practice of Group Counseling*, Ninth Edition (and *Student Manual*) (2016)
- *Becoming a Helper*, Seventh Edition (2016, with Marianne Schneider Corey)
- *Issues and Ethics in the Helping Professions*, Ninth Edition (2015, with Marianne Schneider Corey, Cindy Corey, and Patrick Callanan)
- *Group Techniques*, Fourth Edition (2015, with Marianne Schneider Corey, Patrick Callanan, and J. Michael Russell)
- *Case Approach to Counseling and Psychotherapy*, Eighth Edition (2013)
- *The Art of Integrative Counseling*, Third Edition (2013)

Jerry Corey is coauthor (with Barbara Herlihy) of *Boundary Issues in Counseling: Multiple Roles and Responsibilities*, Third Edition (2015) and *ACA Ethical Standards Casebook*, Seventh Edition (2015); he is coauthor (with Robert Haynes, Patrice Moulton, and Michelle Muratori) of *Clinical Supervision in the Helping Professions: A Practical Guide*, Second Edition (2010); he is the author of *Creating Your Professional Path: Lessons From My Journey* (2010). All four of these books are published by the American Counseling Association.

He has also made several educational DVD programs on various aspects of counseling practice: (1) *Ethics in Action: DVD and Workbook* (2015, with Marianne Schneider Corey and Robert Haynes); (2) *Groups in Action: Evolution and Challenges DVD and Workbook* (2014, with Marianne Schneider Corey and Robert Haynes); (3) *DVD for Theory and Practice of Counseling and Psychotherapy: The Case of Stan and Lecturettes* (2013); (4) *DVD for Integrative Counseling: The Case of Ruth and Lecturettes* (2013, with Robert Haynes); and (5) *DVD for Theory and Practice of Group Counseling* (2012). All of these programs are available through Cengage Learning.

Cindy Corey is a licensed clinical psychologist with a private practice in San Diego, California. She worked for over a decade as a full-time visiting professor in the Department of Counseling and School Psychology at San Diego State University in both the Community-Based Block and Marriage and Family Therapy programs. She received her master's degree in Marriage and Family Therapy from the University of San Diego and her Doctorate (PsyD) in Multicultural Community Clinical Psychology at the California School of Professional Psychology in Alhambra, California. She is a member of the American Counseling Association, the Association for Specialists in Group Work, the American Psychological Association, and the San Diego Psychological Association (SDPA). She served as the chair of the Lesbian, Gay, Bisexual, and Transgender Committee for the SDPA and has been a member of the Multicultural Committee and Women's Committee.

Cindy has focused much of her work in the area of counselor education, specializing in multicultural training, social justice, and community outreach. In addition to teaching at San Diego State University, she taught part time in the PsyD program at Alliant International University in Alhambra. Cindy has also worked as a Contracted Clinician for Survivors of Torture International, focusing primarily on helping Sudanese refugee youth adjust to life in the United States, gain employment, and attend colleges and universities.

Cindy works as a multicultural consultant and has created clinical intervention programs, training manuals, and diversity sensitive curriculum for a variety of schools, businesses, and organizations in the San Diego area. Her private practice focuses on working with women, couples, counselors, and graduate students in counseling programs.

Contents

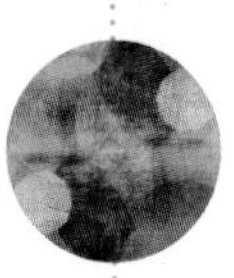

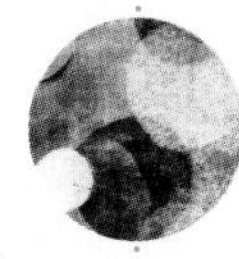

Critical Incidents

Preface

This book outlines the basic issues and key concepts of group process and shows how group leaders can apply these concepts in working with a variety of groups. In many ways this is a "how-to" book, but it is also a book about the "why" of group leadership.

When a new edition of one of our books appears, professors often ask, "What is new about this edition?" The philosophy of group work in this book has been consistent since our first edition in 1977. However, this tenth edition of *Groups: Process and Practice* contains many subtle changes in our discussion of the topics within each chapter, and many chapters have undergone considerable revision with new material added. Our thinking has been refined through our group work practice and teaching over the past 40 years (since the original edition), and we have attempted to bring each new edition in line with current practices in the field.

Beginning with the eighth edition we added the contributions of coauthor Cindy Corey, who brings her expertise in multicultural counseling to the practice of group work and to this book. Cindy has integrated current applications of diversity to the practice of group work and has expanded on the topics presented in earlier editions. Many reviewers, and the results survey by users of this book, indicated that they value the practical aspect of *Groups*, and they suggested that we add even more clinical examples to bring the topics of discussion to life. This tenth edition contains many new and expanded examples with a focus on diversity in group work.

What's New in the Tenth Edition of *Groups: Process and Practice*

For the tenth edition, each chapter has been carefully revised and updated to present the current thinking and trends in practice. The following description of the various parts of the book highlights material that has been added, updated, expanded, or revised for the tenth edition.

In Part One we deal with the basic issues in group work; these themes are addressed in the first four chapters:

- Chapter 1 (Introduction to Group Work: A Multicultural Perspective) presents an overview of various types of groups, including an updated discussion of brief groups, as well as our perspective on multicultural group work and becoming a culturally skilled group practitioner, which contains some new material.

- Chapter 2 (The Group Counselor) addresses the group counselor as a person and as a professional, and topics are illustrated with many examples. This chapter addresses the skills of group leadership and the coleadership model. There is new material on research trends in group work and ways that research can enhance one's group practice, with particular emphasis on common factors such as the therapeutic relationship.
- Chapter 3 (Ethical and Legal Issues in Group Counseling) has been revised to conform to the 2014 *ACA Ethics Code* as applied to group work. The chapter covers updated material on the ethical and legal aspects of group counseling, as well as ethical issues in training group workers with the use of experiential groups, assessing competence, and managing multiple roles and relationships in teaching group counseling courses. Featured in this chapter are social justice issues in group work and ethical concerns when using group techniques.
- Chapter 4 (Theories and Techniques of Group Counseling) highlights the relationship between theory and technique and addresses topics such as theory as a roadmap, using techniques effectively, and developing an integrative approach to group practice. This chapter is organized by four general theories: psychodynamic approaches, experiential and relationship-oriented approaches, cognitive behavioral approaches, and postmodern approaches to group counseling. Specific theoretical perspectives on the practice of group work include psychoanalytic therapy, Adlerian therapy, existential therapy, person-centered approach, Gestalt therapy, psychodrama, behavior therapy, cognitive therapy, cognitive behavior therapy, rational emotive behavior therapy, reality therapy, solution-focused brief therapy, narrative therapy, motivational interviewing, feminist therapy, and multicultural perspectives. The motivational interviewing section is new to this edition. Also included is a brief discussion of how to develop an integrative approach to group counseling.

In Part Two separate chapters deal with group process issues for each phase in the evolution of a group. These issues include designing a group and getting one started, working effectively with a coleader at each stage of a group, member roles and leader functions, problems that can occur at different times in a group, and techniques and procedures for facilitating group process. In Chapters 5 through 9 we have included a consideration of how diversity influences both the process and outcomes of groups, and new examples from a diversity perspective illustrate key challenges for each of the stages in a group's development. Special features in Chapters 5 through 9 that are new to this edition include the following:

Critical Incidents illustrates a situation associated with a stage in the group. The situation is briefly described, questions are raised, clinical reflections are given, and possible interventions to address the incident are suggested. The aim is to stimulate discussion in class on how to critically analyze the critical incident. The primary goal of this activity is to provide a clinical context for the material covered throughout the chapter.

Learning in Action presents activities integrated within the chapters that can be used with the entire class, in small groups, or at home. These activities are intended to have multiple uses in academic settings, and many are appropriate to use in clinical settings with group members as well.

Journal Prompts are a way to further the professional and personal development of the reader and may also be used with group members in a clinical setting throughout various stages of a group.

- Chapter 5 (Forming a Group) demonstrates how important careful thought and planning are in laying a solid foundation for any group. The factors we emphasize include designing a proposal for a group, attracting members, screening and selecting members, and the orientation process.
- Chapter 6 (Initial Stage of a Group) addresses specific group process concepts during the early phase of a group's development. There is a discussion of cultural considerations, dealing with a hidden agenda, the role of leader self-disclosure, and ways to create trust early in a group.
- Chapter 7 (Transition Stage of a Group) offers a reframing and reconceptualization of resistance and provides ideas related to understanding and working with difficult group behaviors therapeutically. There is more emphasis on understanding and honoring clients' resistance and new material on motivational interviewing as a way to address ambivalence and increase motivation to change. We highlight the necessity of understanding how cultural factors can account for behavioral manifestations that may appear to be problematic behavior and consider conflict and confrontation from a cultural perspective. There are more examples of both leader behavior and member behavior pertaining to dealing with mistrust in a group and how to increase trust. An expanded discussion of the role of transference and countertransference includes guidelines for dealing effectively with countertransference.
- Chapter 8 (Working Stage of a Group) includes an expanded discussion of the therapeutic factors operating in a group. Factors given special attention include member self-disclosure, guidelines for leader self-disclosure, feedback, confrontation, and group cohesion.
- Chapter 9 (Final Stage of a Group) entails a discussion on the tasks of terminating a group experience. Increased emphasis is given to dealing with emotional reactions pertaining to termination and to addressing unfinished business in a group.

Part Two includes numerous examples that illustrate a variety of leader interventions in response to the problems often encountered in facilitating a group. We tie in the theoretical approaches covered in Chapter 4 to the various topics in the stages of a group. We also have linked the group proposals described in Chapters 10 and 11 to selected topics so readers can see practical examples of the concepts being discussed. Each chapter in this section contains a summary of the characteristics of the particular stage along with member functions and leader functions at each stage of group development. The chapters conclude with several exercises that can be done either at home or in the classroom. We have integrated citations to relevant research when it was available, and we draw on our own experience in group work for personal examples and share our perspectives on the topics we explore. We have attempted to keep the reader-friendly writing style that students say they appreciate.

In Part Three we show how the basic concepts examined in Part Two can be applied to specific types of groups in the schools and in community agency settings. We offer guidelines for group leaders who want to design groups specifically for children, adolescents, adults, and older adults in different settings.

The 12 group proposals focus on the unique needs of each kind of group and how to meet those needs.

- Chapter 10 (Groups in School Settings) includes five group proposals for children and adolescents. This chapter consolidates material from two chapters in earlier editions and gives increased attention to the guidelines for group work with children and adolescents.
- Chapter 11 (Groups in Community Settings) features seven group proposals for adult groups at various developmental stages and with particular life issues. A new group proposal on treating people with substance use disorders has been added.

This edition of *Groups* is aligned with the CACREP 2016 Standards for Group Counseling and Group Work; all of the chapters address specific standards. We have added learning objectives for all of the chapters, with specific attention given to the CACREP standards identified for each chapter.

Groups: Process and Practice is intended for graduate and undergraduate students majoring in psychology, sociology, counseling, clinical mental health counseling, social work, marriage and family therapy, education, and human services who are taking courses in group counseling or group leadership. Others who may find this book useful in their work are social workers, rehabilitation counselors, teachers, pastoral counselors, correctional workers, and marriage and family therapists.

Ancillaries

We have developed a self-study DVD program and workbook combination titled *Groups in Action: Evolution and Challenges* that can be used as an integrated learning package with *Groups: Process and Practice*. This self-study program consists of three parts. The first program, *Evolution of a Group* (2 hours) depicts central features that illustrate the development of the group process and how the coleaders facilitated that process as the group moved through the various stages: initial, transition, working, and ending. The second program, *Challenges for Group Leaders* (90 minutes) demonstrates ways to work therapeutically with a variety of difficult behaviors in groups and approaches to addressing diversity issues in group counseling. The third program contains *Lecturettes on Theories and Techniques of Group Counseling* (1 hour) by Jerry Corey. An overview of the various theories and their application to techniques in group work are discussed here. The *Workbook* that accompanies this video program includes key points and questions for reflection on the lecturettes on theories and techniques of group counseling. The videos and the workbook are designed to be an integrated package. This program utilizes an interactive format and requires students to become active learners as they study the group process in action.

Groups: Process and Practice comes with MindTap, an online learning solution created to harness the power of technology to drive student success. This cloud-based platform integrates a number of learning applications ("apps") into an easy-to-use and easy-to-access tool that supports a personalized learning experience. MindTap combines student learning tools—readings, multimedia, activities, and assessments—into a singular Learning Path that guides students through the course. This MindTap includes:

- Original videos modeling specific group counseling skills in simulated group scenarios
- Self-assessments, reflection questions, discussion activities, and case studies
- Interactive Helper Studio video exercises
- Discussion questions and activities that allow students to collaborate with their peers to develop solutions and responses in an online environment
- Chapter quizzes at the end of each chapter
- A glossary and flashcards of key terms and concepts

An *Instructor's Resource Manual* for this tenth edition of *Groups: Process and Practice* is also available. It contains multiple-choice test items, essay exam questions, questions for reflection and discussion, additional exercises and activities, guidelines for using the *Groups in Action: Evolution and Challenges* program with this book, reading suggestions for instructors in preparing classes, a survey of current practices in teaching group counseling courses, power point lecture slides, and examples of course outlines. We also describe our approach to workshops in training and supervising group leaders, which can be incorporated in many group courses.

Acknowledgments

The reviewers for this tenth edition have been instrumental in our decisions regarding retaining or adding key elements. Approximately 16 professors completed a prerevision survey, providing useful feedback that we took into consideration in doing this revision. Jude Austin (Old Dominion University) and Julius Austin (Nicolls State University) served as expert reviewers for this edition. They provided their clinical and multicultural expertise to the ideas and features in this edition, class tested many of the new features of the book, and gave us feedback that was incorporated into the final manuscript. In addition, they contributed significantly to the video programs for the MindTap online program for this book.

Other faculty members who teach group counseling reviewed the revised manuscript and provided many helpful suggestions for revision and gave us specific reactions to the new material in the various chapters, especially the critical incidents, class activities, and journal prompts sections. Those who graciously volunteered their time are:

Michelle Muratori, Johns Hopkins University
Julia Whisenhunt, University of West Georgia
Elizabeth Keller-Dupree, Northeastern State University, Oklahoma
Leigh DeLorenzi, Stetson University, Florida
Kristen Dickens, Georgia Southern University
Kristin Vincenzes, Lock Haven University, Pennsylvania
Paul Blisard, University of Arkansas

Mark E. Young, of the University of Central Florida, reviewed selected chapters and invited his doctoral students to send us critical incidents they have encountered in their work as group facilitators. We appreciate the contributions of the following doctoral students from University of Central Florida: Kristina Nelson,

Elizabeth Crunk, Naomi Wheeler, Coralis Solomon, Sam Bierbrauer, Shaywanna Harris, and Christopher Belser.

The following reviewers provided us with feedback that improved this revision:

Gwen Hellon, Sinclair Community College
Petrina Fowler, Kennesaw State University
Brandie Fitch, Ivey Tech Community College
Lesley Casarez, Angelo State University
Brian Bagwell, Metropolitan State University of Denver
Paula Heller Garland, The University of North Texas
Mary Mayorga, Texas A&M University, San Antonio
Stephen Kahoe, El Paso Community College
Thomas McElfresh, Sinclair Community College
Elizabeth Andrews, Thomas Nelson Community College
Debra Giaramita, CUNY: The College of Staten Island
John Kennedy, Trevecca Nazarene University
Song Lee, California State University, Fresno
Ray Hardee, Gardner-Webb University
Ben Beitin, Seton Hall University

Guest contributors provided us with group proposals in Part Three, describing groups they had designed. Our appreciation goes to the following people for sharing a description of their groups: Lupe and Randy Alle-Corliss, Jamie Bludworth, Teresa Christensen, Kathy Elson, Alan Forrest, Paul Jacobson, Karen Kram Laudenslager, Sheila Morris, and Jason Sonnier. It is our hope that their creative group proposals inspire you to think of ways to design your own groups.

Finally, as is true of all our books, *Groups: Process and Practice* continues to develop as a result of a team effort, which includes the combined efforts of several people at Cengage Learning: Jon Goodspeed, Product Director; Julie Martinez, Product Manager, Counseling, Social Work, & Human Services; Alexander Hancock, Associate Content Developer, Sociology, Counseling, and Social Work; Vernon Boes, Art Director; Jeanne Calabrese for her work on the interior design and cover of this book; and Rita Jaramillo, Content Project Manager. Thanks to Ben Kolstad of Cenveo Publisher Services, who coordinated the production of this book. Special recognition goes to Kay Mikel, the manuscript editor of this edition, whose exceptional editorial talents continue to keep this book reader friendly. Susan Cunningham updated the *Instructor's Resource Manual* and other supplements, created and revised test items to accompany this text, and prepared the index. The efforts and dedication of all of these people have contributed to the high quality of this edition.

Marianne Schneider Corey
Gerald Corey
Cindy Corey

Groups

PROCESS AND PRACTICE

10e

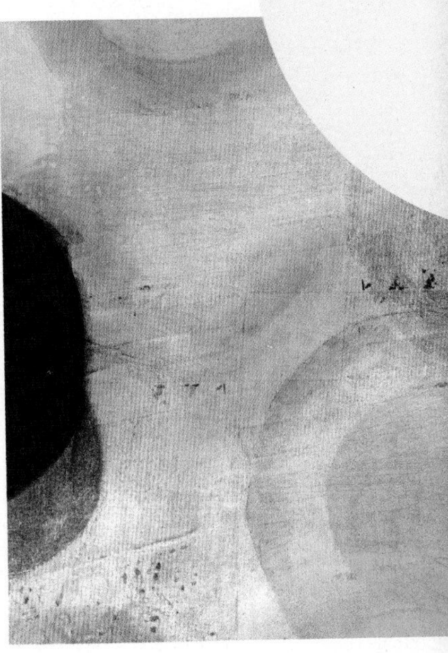

PART ONE

Introduction: Basic Issues in Group Work

The effort involved in setting up and leading groups is considerable, yet we believe this commitment is essential in facilitating successful groups. Well-run groups provide members with a place to give and receive feedback, to gain insight into their interpersonal dynamics, and to address aspects of their lives they want to change. A colleague of ours once said, "Individuals are wounded in relationships and can heal in relationships." Oftentimes, however, the people who have wounded us are not the people with whom we heal. Group counseling provides a powerful place for healing. Participants can rewrite old scripts that no longer serve them and practice new ways of being in relationship with others. A group can be either a force for healing or a force for harm. Effective group leaders provide a safe place that encourages members to participate fully and to take risks. Groups have much to offer, but designing and facilitating groups in a variety of settings is a complex undertaking. In this book we offer some blueprints for forming and conducting groups in a manner that will release the strivings for health within individuals.

Part One addresses the fundamentals of group work and provides guidelines for beginning your own work as a group leader. These chapters emphasize the importance of developing a personal style of group leadership and conceptualizing an approach to the practice of group work. In our work as group leaders we actively facilitate the group, especially during the beginning and ending phases. Most groups are time limited, and our interventions and structuring are aimed at assisting members to fully use the group process to attain their personal goals. During the initial stage we devote time to teaching members how to get the most from a group experience. Toward the end of a group we assist members in conceptualizing what they have learned so they can maximize their gains and apply new behaviors to everyday life.

1

CHAPTER

Introduction to Group Work: A Multicultural Perspective

CHAPTER LEARNING OBJECTIVES

1 Briefly introduce the major topics of group work

2 Describe the types of groups and other considerations that affect conducting groups in varied settings (CACREP, 2016, Standard F)

3 Identify the key aspects of brief group therapy

4 Introduce some basic ideas of multicultural perspectives on group work

5 Discuss what is involved in becoming a culturally skilled group worker

6 Identify ethical and culturally relevant strategies for designing and facilitating groups (CACREP, 2016, Standard G)

You are a college counselor working in the Educational Opportunity Program with students on academic probation. Several themes are emerging as reasons students tend to have difficulties with their academic performance. You have decided to form a group that will meet each week to help these students succeed academically. What kind of group will you provide—open group, closed group, short-term or long-term group, support group, psychoeducational group, collaborative leadership, structured, unstructured—how will you decide? Think about the problems a first-generation student might be facing from a sociocultural perspective and outline the methods you think would be most effective in addressing these issues in a group setting:

- What issues are these students facing, both internally and externally, at home and within the educational institution?
- Which types of groups would have the greatest impact for these students?
- What strengths do you have as a counselor in working with this population?
- What areas of growth or training might you need to pursue?

Introduction

LO1

Groups are an excellent treatment choice for numerous intrapersonal and interpersonal issues and for helping people change. Counseling groups are being offered in all kinds of settings today and for many different client groups. Most are short-term groups designed for specific client populations rather than unstructured personal-growth groups. These groups are designed to remediate specific problems or to prevent problems. Many of the problems that bring people to counseling involve difficulties in forming or maintaining intimate relationships. People often believe their problems are unique and that they have few options for making significant life changes. They may be at a loss in knowing how to live well with the ones they love. Groups provide a natural laboratory and a sense of community that demonstrates to people that they are not alone and that there is hope for creating a different life. As you will see in the chapters that follow, part of the reason groups are so powerful is because participants have the opportunity to try out different strategies for resolving their long-term problems.

An Overview of Various Types of Groups

LO2

The broad purposes of a **therapeutic group** are to increase members' knowledge of themselves and others, to help members clarify the changes they most want to make in their lives, to provide members with the tools they need to make these changes, and to support their changes. By interacting with others in a trusting and accepting environment, participants are given the opportunity to experiment with novel behavior and to receive honest feedback from others concerning the effects of their behavior. As a result, individuals learn how they affect others.

Different types of groups require different levels of leader competence and training, but all group leaders must have some common basic competencies. It is important to distinguish among group types and purposes, and to deliver those services that the group leader lists in marketing the group, so that potential group members know what kind of group they are considering joining. We identify some different types of groups in the following sections, but there is considerable overlap among these groups. The Association for Specialists in Group Work (ASGW, 2000) has identified a set of core competencies in general group work. These standards make it clear that mastery of the basic knowledge and skills all leaders need to possess does not qualify a group worker to independently practice in any group work specialty. In addition to core competencies, group practitioners must possess advanced competencies relevant to their specialty. The Association for Specialists in Group Work (ASGW, 2000) has identified four areas of advanced practice, referred to as specializations, which we consider next: (a) task groups, (b) psychoeducational groups, (c) counseling groups, and (d) psychotherapy groups.

Task Groups

Task groups (or task facilitation groups) are common in many organizations and agencies, and they include task forces, committees, planning groups, staff development groups, treatment conferences, community organizations, social action groups, discussion groups, study circles, learning groups, school groups, and other similar groups. Task groups are common in community, business, and educational settings. The task group specialist might develop skills in organizational assessment, training, program development, consultation, and program evaluation. The focus of these groups is on the application of group dynamics principles and processes to improve practice and to foster accomplishment of identified work goals.

Both leaders and participants of task groups tend to want to get down to business quickly, but focusing exclusively on the task at hand (content) can create problems for the group. A leader's failure to attend to here-and-now factors is likely to result in a group that becomes riveted on content concerns and has little appreciation for the role played by process issues in the success of a group. If interpersonal issues within the group are ignored, cooperation and collaboration will not develop, interpersonal issues may intensify, and it is unlikely that group goals will be met. It is essential that group leaders recognize that process and relationships are central to meeting the goals in this type of group. One of the leader's tasks is to assist participants in understanding how attention to this interpersonal climate directly relates to achieving the purpose and goals of the group. Learning interpersonal skills for working on a team is enhanced when participants can practice these skills in a group setting (Falco & Bauman, 2014).

Psychoeducational Groups

The psychoeducational group specialist works with relatively well-functioning group members who may have an information deficit in a certain area, such as parenting or anger management skills. **Psychoeducational groups** focus on developing members' cognitive, affective, and behavioral skills through a structured set of procedures within and across group meetings. The goal is to provide members with targeted education on a variety of psychological issues or informational deficits. This group work specialization deals with imparting, discussing, and integrating factual information. New information is incorporated through the use of planned skill-building exercises. An example of a psychoeducational group is a substance abuse prevention group. Intervention strategies based on psychoeducational formats are increasingly being applied in health care settings (see Drum, Becker, & Hess, 2011; McCarthy & Hart, 2011) and in relationship education with couples (Carlson, Barden, Daire, & Greene, 2014).

Although the topics vary, psychoeducational groups share the goals of increasing members' awareness of a life problem and providing skills training to help members cope with situations. These groups can be useful in enhancing or building on members' existing skills. Generally, sessions are 2 hours each week for 4 to 15 weeks. However, some group sessions may be as short as 30 to 45 minutes, especially with children, or for clients who have a shorter attention span or who have only basic cognitive functioning.

Psychoeducational groups fit well into today's managed health care scene because they can be designed to be brief, cost-effective treatments. For similar reasons, schools often use groups as the treatment of choice. These groups are typically time limited and have narrow goals. They often focus on symptomatic relief, teaching participants problem-solving strategies, and developing interpersonal skills that can accelerate personal changes.

Integrating counseling with psychoeducational interventions has been successful in both social and academic development groups in school settings (Steen, Henfield, & Booker, 2014). This combination of group counseling methods provides the opportunity to facilitate self-awareness and to present skills information. Examples include communication and social skills groups, friendship groups, bullying prevention groups, and groups for making decisions about careers. Psychoeducational groups provide opportunities for students to learn new information and skills, and group leaders frequently link members so they can see that others share their concerns (Falco & Bauman, 2014).

At the beginning of a psychoeducational group, members often are asked to complete a questionnaire on how well they are coping with the area of concern. The work of these groups may include structured exercises, readings, homework assignments, and contracts. When the group comes to an end, another questionnaire is completed to assess members' progress. Psychoeducational groups are useful for a broad range of problems, including stress management, substance abuse and sobriety issues, interpersonal violence, anger management, and behavioral problems. In a college setting, resident assistants (RAs) may benefit from psychoeducational groups to help them gain the knowledge and skills needed to problem solve with college students.

The emphasis on learning in psychoeducational groups provides members with opportunities to acquire and refine social skills through behavioral rehearsal, skills training, and cognitive exploration. The intervention strategies used in psychoeducational groups are largely based on the transmission of information basic to making changes and teaching a process for bringing about these changes. The leader's main tasks are to provide instruction and to create a positive and safe climate that fosters learning (Drum et al., 2011). Chapter 10 and Chapter 11 illustrate proposals for psychoeducational groups appropriate for schools and community agencies.

Counseling Groups

The group worker who specializes in counseling groups helps participants resolve the usual, yet often difficult, problems of living. Career, education, personal, social, and developmental concerns are frequently addressed. This type of group differs from a psychotherapy group in that it deals with conscious problems, is not aimed at major personality changes, is generally oriented toward the resolution of specific short-term issues, and is not concerned with treatment of the more severe psychological and behavioral disorders. These groups are often found in schools, college and university counseling centers, churches, and community mental health clinics and agencies.

Counseling groups focus on interpersonal process and problem-solving strategies that stress conscious thoughts, feelings, and behavior. Although the emphasis is on conscious material, it is not uncommon for unconscious material to emerge. The group leader needs to be prepared to deal with what emerges in a way that is congruent with the purpose and goals of the group. Counseling groups may be designed for prevention, development, or remediation purposes. They emphasize interactive group process for those who may be experiencing transitional life problems, are at risk for developing personal or interpersonal problems, or who want to enhance their relationships. A counseling group may help participants resolve problems in living or dealing with developmental concerns. This kind of group also uses interactive feedback and support methods in a here-and-now time frame. The focus of the group often is determined by the members, who are basically well-functioning individuals, and the group is characterized by a growth orientation. Members of a counseling group are guided in understanding the interpersonal nature of their problems. With an emphasis on discovering inner resources of personal strength and constructively dealing with barriers that are preventing optimal development, members expand their interpersonal skills to better cope with both current difficulties and future problems. These groups provide the support and the challenge necessary for honest self-exploration. Participants can benefit from the feedback they receive from others by comparing the perceptions they have of themselves with the perceptions others have of them, but ultimately members must decide for themselves what they will do with this information.

Counseling groups range from those with an open structure, in which participants shape the direction of the group, to those characterized by a specific theme. But they all share these goals:

- Helping people develop more positive attitudes and better interpersonal skills
- Using the group process to facilitate behavior change
- Helping members transfer newly acquired skills and behavior learned in the group to everyday life

The counselor's job is to structure the activities of the group, to see that a climate favorable to productive work is maintained, to facilitate members' interactions, to provide information that will help members see alternatives to their modes of behavior, and to encourage members to translate their insights into concrete action plans. To a large extent, counseling group leaders carry out this role by teaching members about the group process and how they can involve themselves in this process. This instruction includes understanding the norms that govern a group, the level of cohesion in the group, how trust is generated, how reluctance is manifested, how conflict emerges and can be dealt with, what forces bring about healing, how to give and receive feedback, and the various stages in a group's development. Group leaders model appropriate group behavior and help members establish personal goals that will provide direction for the group.

The counseling group becomes a microcosm of society, with a membership that is diverse but that shares common problems. The group process provides a sample of reality, with the struggles that people experience in the group resembling conflicts in their daily life. Participants learn to respect differences in cultures and values and discover that, on a deep level, they are more alike than different. Although participants' individual circumstances may differ, their pain and struggles are universal.

Counseling groups can be designed for children, adolescents, adults, and older people and are conducted in both school and community agency settings. Chapter 10 illustrates counseling groups for children who have been abused, anger management groups for high school students, and a variety of groups typically offered in college and university counseling centers. Counseling groups offered in community settings for specific client groups are organized to assist members in developing coping skills for dealing with a specific problem area. Counseling groups in school or college settings help students explore interpersonal problems, promote positive behavior, improve social skills, obtain support from others, and increase understanding of both self and others. In the college setting, these groups are particularly beneficial for first-year students who may discuss transition or identity issues. Bereavement groups assist people in expressing their grief and making connections with others who are experiencing similar grief reactions. Goals for bereavement groups in schools include normalizing the grief process, helping students to better understand their feelings about their loss, and developing positive ways of coping with loss (Falco & Bauman, 2014).

Chapter 11 includes group proposals for a women's support group for survivors of incest, a men's group in a community agency, a group for interpersonal violence offenders, a substance abuse group, a group for healthy older people, a bereavement group, and a group for institutional older people. Some groups blend features from both psychoeducational and counseling groups, such as a men's group. These groups are often structured around topics or themes designed to assist members in exploring their personal concerns, yet the group also has an educational purpose in that members learn information and can practice skills in dealing with their concerns.

Psychotherapy Groups

The group worker who specializes in **psychotherapy groups** helps individual group members remediate psychological problems and interpersonal problems of living. Group members often have acute or chronic mental or emotional problems that evidence marked distress, impairment in functioning, or both. Because the depth and extent of the psychological disturbance is significant, the goal is to aid each individual in reconstructing major personality dimensions. Exchanges among members of a therapy group are viewed as instrumental in bringing about change. This interaction provides a level of support, caring, confrontation, and other qualities not found in individual therapy. Within the group context, members are able to practice new social skills and to apply some of their new knowledge. A variety of therapy groups can be found in community mental health agencies, including groups for interpersonal violence offenders.

People generally participate in group psychotherapy in an attempt to alleviate specific symptoms or psychological problems such as depression, sexual difficulties, eating disorders, anxiety, or psychosomatic disorders. A variety of methods are employed in the conduct of therapy groups, including techniques designed to symbolically reexperience earlier experiences and methods to work with unconscious dynamics. The therapist is typically interested in creating a climate that fosters understanding and exploration of a problem area. The process of working through psychological blocks rooted in past experiences often involves exploring dreams, interpreting resistance, dealing with transference that emerges, and helping members develop a new perspective on "unfinished business" with significant others.

Brief Groups

LO3

Brief group therapy (BGT) generally refers to groups that are time limited, have a preset time for termination, have a process orientation, and are professionally led. In a time-limited group, clear ground rules are critical, and leaders provide structure for the group process (Shapiro, 2010). Many psychoeducational groups and counseling groups incorporate the characteristics of brief treatment in their groups.

The current increased interest in the various applications of BGT is largely due to the economic benefits of this approach to group work (Shapiro, 2010) and to research evidence pointing to the effectiveness and applicability of brief groups to a wide range of client problems and diverse settings (Piper & Ogrodniczuk, 2004). Brief group counseling is popular in both community agencies and school settings because of the realistic time constraints and the ability of a brief format to be incorporated into both educational and therapeutic programs. Brief groups require the group practitioner to set clear and realistic treatment goals with the members, to establish a clear focus within the group structure, to maintain an active leadership role, and to work within a limited time frame.

Most of the empirical evidence on the effectiveness of group counseling has been based on studies of time-limited, closed groups; evidence from meta-analytic studies strongly supports the value of these groups. In general, the evidence for the efficacy of brief group therapy is quite positive (Shapiro, 2010). In their review of the group literature, Fuhriman and Burlingame (1994) conclude that group therapy (including BGT) consistently results in positive outcomes with a wide range of client problems. Other reviews of the group literature lend a strong endorsement to the efficacy and applicability of BGT as well (see Burlingame, MacKenzie, & Strauss, 2004; Piper & Ogrodniczuk, 2004). BGT is often the treatment of choice for specific problems such as clients with existential concerns, complicated grief reactions, medical illnesses, personality disorders, trauma reactions, or adjustment problems (Piper & Ogrodniczuk, 2004).

Although the clinical benefits of brief group therapy are clear, this approach does have some limitations. This approach should not be thought of as a panacea or as a means of producing lasting personality change. To be effective, BGT leaders must have training in both group process and brief therapy. BGT makes unique demands on group practitioners and requires specialized skills (Piper & Ogrodniczuk, 2004).

LO4

A Multicultural Perspective on Group Work

Culture encompasses the values, beliefs, and behaviors shared by a group of people. But culture does not just delineate an ethnic or racial heritage; it also can refer to groups identified by age, gender, sexual identity, religion, or socioeconomic status. Culture is learned in groups such as families, and when individuals in a group interact, they bring their cultural learning with them. You belong to a particular cultural group (or groups), and so do your clients. Culture will influence the behavior of both you and your clients—with or without your awareness.

Culture will influence the behavior of both you and your clients—with or without your awareness.

Each person approaches participation in a group from his or her own unique perspective. DeLucia-Waack (2010) emphasizes the necessity of developing a set of tools and a way of being with others that adequately respects, addresses, and explores these differences in a therapeutic setting. Increasing your knowledge of your own cultural values and personal assumptions will help you to work effectively with culturally diverse clients. This kind of self-awareness is a necessary, but not sufficient, condition for developing competence in multicultural group work. According to DeLucia-Waack, culturally skilled group counselors need to (1) be aware of their own personal values, attitudes, biases, assumptions, and prejudices; (2) have a general knowledge about the ways the diverse backgrounds of members may affect the group process; and (3) be able to implement interventions that are appropriate for the life experiences of the members of the group.

It is important to discuss with group members how your worldview influences your beliefs and practices about groups and group process. A culturally skilled group leader engages in an ongoing process of self-reflection. Striving for competence involves examining your beliefs about how people learn and change from both a cultural and a theoretical perspective. It is necessary to think about how people from other cultures might view the group process differently. For example, a goal of the counselor may be to have members offer challenging feedback to one another. However, group members from a culture that perceives challenging feedback as a form of aggression or shaming may not be comfortable with this. The leader does not have to discourage assertive communication, but any hesitation on the part of members to use assertive communication should be examined to see if this reluctance can be explained within a cultural context.

Regardless of your ethnic, cultural, or racial background, if you hope to build bridges of understanding between yourself and group members who are different from you, it is essential to recognize your possible position of privilege and the power of your professional role in the group. We hope you will engage in critical thinking and self-exploration pertaining to your ability to connect with clients who differ from you and take steps to increase your capacity to make meaningful connections.

A useful way to think about the differences between our clients and ourselves is to consider the multiple identities each of us possess. Our identities shape the way we view others as well as the ways in which others experience us. Each of us possesses gender, sexual identity, a personality style, abilities/disabilities, socioeconomic status, relationship status, levels of privilege, and parental status. Each of these categories influences how we view the world, who we are, and how we behave, just as it informs the ways people view and interact with us. We bring these personal dimensions of ourselves to our roles as group leaders, and our identity changes and evolves at different stages in our life. Reflect on which identities are most salient for you at this point in your life and consider how they might influence the way you define your role as a group counselor.

Our identities shape the way we view others as well as the ways in which others experience us.

Learning in Action

Identity Reflection

All individuals possess multiple intersecting identities and belong to numerous cultural groups. Some of our identities change or evolve over time, but others are constant. The intersection of our multiple identities is often as powerful an influence as are the individual identities themselves. Place a check mark next to the identities that have the most impact on your life today:

_____ Gender
_____ Sexual orientation
_____ Socioeconomic status
_____ Ethnicity
_____ Cultural practices
_____ Physical ability
_____ Physical health status
_____ Mental health status
_____ Size
_____ Religious affiliation
_____ Familial affiliation (adopted, only child, etc.)
_____ Relationship status
_____ Parental status (mother, father, grandparent, etc.)
_____ Age

_____ Educational level or status

_____ Professional level or affiliation

_____ Political affiliation

_____ Other identities salient for you ______________________

Discussion

Select one salient identity for examination. Take turns answering each question before you move on to the next one, and discuss your answers in a small group.

1. What are the two most salient identities for you at this time in your life? ______________________, ______________________. (Fill in the blanks below with one of these identities.)
2. How do you see yourself as a ______________________?
3. How do others perceive you as a ______________________?
4. How much power do you feel you have as a ______________________?
5. How much power do you think others perceive that you have as a ______________________?
6. Briefly state which of your identities gives you the most and the least power or status in society. ______________________
7. The biggest misconception I feel others have about me as a ______________________ is ______________________ .
8. How do you feel your identity as a ______________________ influences your ability to connect to others similar to and different from you?
9. The most painful thing I have heard others say about people who belong to my identity as a ______________________ is ______________________.
10. The greatest privilege that comes with being a ______________________ is ______________________.

Reflection on Small Group Discussions

1. Were any of your previous beliefs about some of the identities discussed changed, challenged, or confirmed in any way?
2. How might your interactions change based on what you learned from others in your group, or from your own personal insights?

You can work toward becoming culturally responsive to the members of your groups in numerous ways. Through honest self-evaluation, supervision, and feedback from colleagues, you can begin to develop a plan for increasing your multicultural awareness, knowledge, and skills. As with any other area in counselor education, we believe that engaging in your own personal work around issues of diversity and culture is a good place to start your journey. The ideal setting in which to do this work is often one that includes a diverse population. Make a commitment to "lean into your discomfort." I (Cindy) recall feeling many growing pains as I began my work as a multicultural counselor. I was reassured by my mentors and teachers that the insecurities and sometimes great discomfort I often experienced were signs that I was indeed expanding my levels of competence.

There are advantages and limitations when using group formats with culturally diverse client populations. On the plus side, members can gain much from the power and strength of collective group feedback. They can be supportive of one another in patterns that are familiar. As members see their peers challenging themselves and making desired changes in their lives, it gives them hope that change is possible for them.

Make a commitment to "lean into your discomfort."

It is important to realize that groups are not for everyone. Some individuals may be reluctant to disclose personal material or to share family conflicts. They may see it as shameful even to have personal problems, and all the more shameful to talk about them in front of strangers. People from some cultures rely on members of their extended family, their clergy, or indigenous healers for help rather than seeking professional assistance. Some individuals may not feel comfortable in a group or even be willing to be part of a counseling group. Some may be hesitant to join a group because of their unfamiliarity with how groups work. Others may find that what is expected in a group clashes with their cultural values. Counselors and group members together can bridge these cultural divides so that people from all backgrounds benefit from group work.

Again, we want to emphasize that although it is unrealistic to expect you to have an in-depth knowledge of all cultural backgrounds, it is feasible for you to have a comprehensive grasp of the general principles for working successfully amid cultural diversity. It is equally important to have an attitude that includes an appreciation of the fact that not everyone views the world as you do. Although cognitive learning is important, this learning must be integrated with attitudinal and behavioral shifts.

LO5

Becoming a Culturally Skilled Group Counselor

In this section, we present a conceptual framework that organizes diversity, multicultural, and social justice competency into four areas: beliefs and attitudes, knowledge, skills, and action. As you read, try to become more aware of your own worldview, values, beliefs, and biases based on your cultural background. Diversity and cultural issues are important considerations for all clients. If we only examine the impact of culture when working with certain populations, we are likely to miss key elements in understanding and helping our clients. A culturally skilled counselor explores the impact of cultural factors in all aspects of the client's life.

Diversity and multicultural and social justice competence has been incorporated into the code of ethics of many professional organizations. Becoming a culturally skilled group practitioner involves understanding both the differences between people and the common ground we share. To that end, group counselors should strive to do the following:

- Understand some ways that issues pertaining to gender and sexual orientation can be productively explored within the group.

- Consider the impact of adverse social, environmental, and political factors in assessing problems and designing interventions in a group.
- Become aware of how power, privilege, social group status, and oppression influence the process of a group.
- Become aware, knowledgeable, skilled, and action-oriented in understanding the worldview of group members.
- Respect the roles of family and community hierarchies within a member's culture.
- Respect members' religious and spiritual beliefs and values.
- Acknowledge the strengths and limitations in working with individuals from privileged and marginalized groups.
- Inform members about basic values and expectations that are implicit in the group process (such as self-disclosure, reflecting on one's life, and taking risks).

A Starting Place: Understanding Your Own Culture

Effective group counselors must have some level of understanding of their own cultural conditioning, the cultural conditioning of their clients, and an awareness of the sociopolitical system of which they are a part. Translated into practice, this means that if you are raised to believe that men and women should be seen as equals, then your worldview will greatly differ from some of the clients you will encounter. If you are not able to recognize that your values are not absolute truths, but products of your cultural upbringing, then you will likely impose your own worldview and values on your group members and possibly do harm. However, we need to be careful about determining what is problematic, especially if it is based on our own standard of what we consider to be healthy and unhealthy.

DeLucia-Waack (2014) points out that each culture has its own set of beliefs about healing, honor, and family that influence group work. By examining their own beliefs about how people learn and change from a cultural perspective as well as a theoretical orientation, group leaders can begin to understand how people from diverse cultures may view group process. Effective group leadership enables members to understand themselves and others as individuals within a cultural context. Multicultural and diversity issues are inherent in all group work, and DeLucia-Waack suggests that "group leaders choose interventions and methods of change based on the interplay between individuals and their worldviews" (p. 193).

The goals and processes of the group should match the cultural values of the members of that group. If you model genuine respect for the differences among members in your groups, all the group members will benefit from this cultural diversity. Be aware of hesitation on a client's part, and do not be too quick to interpret it. We often remind our students that it is our job as therapists to remain invested in the process with our clients while maintaining an openness about the outcome of our clients' decisions and lives. They must live with the consequences of their actions, not us.

Your willingness to put yourself in situations where you can learn about different cultures outside of your role as the leader can help you recognize your blind spots and assumptions and learn where you may need to do more work.

It is important for leaders to avoid treating members in ways that make them feel as if they have to teach you all about their culture. On numerous occasions, we have heard group members talk about feeling frustrated with having to educate others about their culture or being placed in the position of being the expert on all people from their cultural background. Leaders need to strike a balance between learning from each individual about his or her specific experiences and extending themselves outside of the group to gain useful information that will make them more culturally effective leaders.

A Personal Perspective on Understanding Differences

My (Cindy's) identity development exploration has been instrumental in finding a way to successfully work with people from backgrounds much different from my own. It is crucial for me to understand how I see the world as well as how others may see the same world through a very different lens and context. I have learned that I cannot attempt to prove myself too quickly to clients who differ from me; rather, I have to trust the process and allow the relationship between us to unfold. It is much more *what I do* rather than *what I say* that gains the respect and trust of diverse group members. I am often told by my students of color that when they first see me they have a level of mistrust because they see a "privileged White woman" who is not likely to understand them or care about their causes. I am acutely aware that these students bring their past experiences with other White people to their initial interactions with me, and I know it will not be helpful for me to be defensive or take too personally their initial reactions to me. As the process of our getting to know one another unfolds, their attitudes toward me often shift as they begin to feel understood and cared for in spite of our obvious differences.

Through teaching multicultural counseling courses, I have learned that each person is at a different place with regard to her or his process of learning about diversity. My journey toward cultural effectiveness will look quite different from that of my Latino American or African American colleagues. Although we are likely to struggle with some similar issues, our histories, worldviews, and context for understanding complex diversity issues are different. Just as group members are at very different stages of their cultural awareness and identity development, so are counseling students. These differences can provide a powerful catalyst for learning if they are explored in the group.

Numerous clinicians have expressed that they face challenges in trying to develop and establish trust with diverse clients and group members. I (Cindy) too find this to be true, but there is enormous satisfaction in being able to work through these initial feelings with group members and to be a small part of helping to heal the damage that has been done to many people from diverse cultural backgrounds. The key is to be clear with myself about my own identity, its impact on others, and to continually work to keep my "isms" in check so that my personal issues do not hinder the work of group members. It is paramount that group leaders know where their blind spots are and work hard to develop those areas so that our clients do not become our main source of education around issues of diversity.

Multicultural and Social Justice Counseling Competencies 

The helping professions continue to emphasize a monocultural approach to training and practice, leaving many helpers ill prepared to deal effectively with cultural diversity (Sue & Sue, 2013). Although referral is sometimes an appropriate course of action, it is not a solution to the problem of inadequately trained practitioners. Referrals based on value conflicts between leaders and members are considered inappropriate and unethical. Moreover, the helper's limited knowledge of a cultural group is not grounds for referral, as this can be remediated through continuing education and supervision or consultation.

It is unrealistic to expect professionals to have an in-depth knowledge of all cultural backgrounds, yet it is feasible to have a comprehensive grasp of general principles for working successfully with culturally diverse clients. If you are open to the values inherent in a diversity perspective, you will find ways to avoid encapsulation. Developing competence in multicultural and social justice counseling is a lifelong endeavor.

Our views about diversity competence have been influenced by the work of a number of writers who have developed documents on multicultural counseling competence. Sue, Arredondo, and McDavis (1992) developed a conceptual framework for multicultural counseling competencies and standards in three areas. The first area deals with the helper's *self-awareness regarding their beliefs and attitudes* about race, culture, gender, and sexual orientation. The second dimension involves *knowledge and understanding* of the worldview of the helper and specific knowledge of the diverse groups with whom he or she works. The third area deals with *skills and intervention strategies* needed to serve diverse client groups. The *Multicultural and Social Justice Counseling Competencies* (Association for Multicultural Counseling and Development [AMCD], 2015) endorsed by the AMCD and the American Counseling Association in 2015 represents a revision and expansion of the original multicultural counseling competencies proposed by Sue, Arredondo, and McDavis (1992). The ASGW (1999, 2012) has adopted two documents on multicultural competence: "Principles for Diversity-Competent Group Workers" and "Multicultural and Social Justice Competence Principles for Group Workers." These standards serve as a model, reflecting the goals related to becoming culturally competent group practitioners. For an updated version of these competencies, see *Multicultural and Social Justice Counseling Competencies* (AMCD, 2015).

We have condensed the multicultural and social justice counseling competencies identified by these documents and adapted them for use by group practitioners. We prefer the term **culturally skilled group counselor** because we view effectively working with diverse individuals as a journey rather than a destination. The guidelines that follow describe areas of effective practice in *multicultural* and *diversity* settings. Use them to assess your strengths and to identify areas in which you need to acquire additional knowledge and skills.

Beliefs and Attitudes of Culturally Skilled Group Workers Effective group leaders recognize and understand their own stereotypes and preconceived notions about other racial and ethnic groups. They are aware of both direct and indirect ways in which they may communicate a lack of cultural responsiveness to diverse group members. Culturally skilled group workers:

- Acknowledge their assumptions, values, beliefs, and biases, and at the same time avoid imposing their worldview on members of their groups.
- Do not allow their personal biases, values, or problems to interfere with their ability to work with clients who are culturally different from them.
- Are aware of how their own cultural background and experiences have influenced attitudes, values, and biases about what constitutes psychologically healthy individuals.
- Have moved from being unaware to being increasingly aware of their own race, ethnic and cultural heritage, gender, socioeconomic status, social identities, sexual orientation, abilities, and spiritual beliefs, and to valuing and respecting differences.
- Seek to examine and understand the worldview of their clients. They respect clients' religious and spiritual beliefs and values.
- Recognize the sources of their discomfort with differences between themselves and others in terms of race, ethnicity, culture, and beliefs and strive to develop the knowledge of how to work through the discomfort that comes with learning about matters such as power, privilege, and oppression.
- Have awareness of and knowledge of clients' worldviews, assumptions, attitudes, values, beliefs, biases, and experiences with power, privilege, and oppression. Group leaders who welcome diverse value orientations and diverse assumptions about human behavior have a basis for sharing the worldview of their clients as opposed to being culturally encapsulated.
- Accept and value cultural diversity rather than insist that their cultural heritage is superior. They are able to identify and understand the central cultural constructs of the members of their groups, and they avoid applying their own cultural constructs inappropriately with these group members.
- Monitor their functioning through consultation, supervision, and further training or education. They realize that group counseling may not be appropriate for all clients or for all problems. They are aware of systemic barriers that create injustices in society.

We strongly encourage group leaders to increase their cultural effectiveness and responsiveness toward all of their clients by engaging in processes that challenge them intellectually, politically, emotionally, and psychologically.

Knowledge of Culturally Skilled Group Workers Culturally skilled group practitioners possess knowledge about their own racial and cultural heritage and how it affects them in their work. In addition, effective group workers:

- Understand how oppression, racism, discrimination, and stereotyping affect them personally and professionally. They do not impose their expectations on clients from differing cultural backgrounds, and they avoid stereotyping clients.
- Understand the worldview of their clients and learn about their clients' cultural backgrounds. Because they understand the basic values underlying the therapeutic group process, they know how these values may clash with the cultural values of diverse groups.
- Are aware of the institutional barriers that prevent marginalized people from actively utilizing various resources.

- Possess specific knowledge and information about the group members with whom they are working. This includes at least a general knowledge of the values, life experiences, family structures, cultural heritage, and historical background of their culturally different group members.
- Are knowledgeable about the community characteristics and the resources in the community as well as in the family.
- View diversity in a positive light, which enables them to meet and resolve challenges that arise in their work with a wide range of client populations.

Skills and Intervention Strategies of Culturally Skilled Group Workers Effective group counselors possess a wide range of skills that they are able to use with diverse client populations. Culturally skilled group workers:

- Familiarize themselves with relevant research and the latest findings regarding mental health issues that affect diverse client populations.
- Actively seek out educational experiences that foster their knowledge and skills for facilitating groups across differences.
- Are able to use methods and strategies and define goals consistent with the life experiences and cultural values of the group members. They are able to modify and adapt their interventions in a group to accommodate cultural differences.
- Are not anchored to one method or approach to group facilitation and recognize that helping styles may be culture bound. They are able to use a variety of culturally appropriate and relevant interventions, which may include consulting with traditional healers and religious and spiritual healers.
- Are able to become actively involved with clients outside the group setting (community events, celebrations, social and political functions, and neighborhood groups).
- Take responsibility for educating group members about how groups function and use sound ethical practice when facilitating groups with a diverse membership.
- Take action by collaborating with clients to identify the factors that influence the therapeutic relationship.
- Take action by inviting conversations about how culture, stereotypes, prejudice, discrimination, power, privilege, and oppression influence the therapeutic relationship with privileged and marginalized clients.

This is a good time to take an inventory of your current level of awareness, knowledge, and skills that have a bearing on your ability to function effectively in multicultural situations. Reflect on these questions:

- In what ways does your own culture influence the way you think, feel, and act?
- How prepared are you to understand and work with clients of different cultural backgrounds? Do you feel more or less comfortable working with particular groups? How might you increase your comfort level and skills with these groups?
- What kind of awareness, knowledge, and skills do you think you need to work effectively in groups with diverse client populations?

- What kinds of life experiences have you had that will better enable you to understand and counsel people who have a different worldview?
- Can you identify any areas of cultural bias that could inhibit your ability to work effectively with people who are different from you? If so, what steps might you take to challenge your biases?
- Are you familiar with how various cultural groups perceive or respond to people from your cultural group as well as those from their own cultural and ethnic identity group? How would you feel if a client shared these reactions or stereotypes with you?
- If you were to ask the people who know you most intimately, what biases, prejudices, or value judgments might they identify that could interfere with your ability to maintain neutrality in your work as a counselor?
- What specific strengths do you possess regarding understanding your own cultural background?
- How can your strengths be applied to increasing your effectiveness in working with diversity in group work?
- What are some steps you are willing to take to become a more culturally skilled group leader?

Inviting Conversations About Culture With Group Members

One way to actively incorporate a multicultural dimension into your group leadership is to initiate open discussions with the members of your groups about issues around cultural differences. Group members may be reluctant to talk with people outside of their cultural group about certain topics. Ask members if they are hesitant to raise certain topics within the group and what contributes to this reluctance. Confronting these silent issues can serve as a catalyst for meaningful and often difficult dialogue. Another way to acknowledge cultural differences is illustrated in this situation: A Persian woman is talking about feeling lonely and isolated, yet she does not mention any connection to culture. The group leader asks, "Do you think that your cultural identity or affiliation relates in any way to your feelings of loneliness or isolation?" This question invites discussion of the topic if it resonates with her, yet it also gives space for her to disagree. In addition, the leader has modeled to other members that we can talk about sensitive topics. There have been times when I (Marianne) have initiated conversations with Jewish clients about the fact that I am German, especially when I sensed they were having reactions to me. They are not likely to trust me if I represent a symbol of the atrocities inflicted upon their ancestors. Although I do not have to accept direct responsibility for these historical events, it is important that I listen nondefensively and empathically to what these clients have to say to me.

The inability to talk honestly about race and racial issues can be a major hindrance to effective multicultural counseling (D. W. Sue, 2016). When discussions about race are poorly handled, the result is often misunderstanding, increased antagonism among participants, and barriers to learning. When race talk is skillfully handled, Sue believes it can improve communication, facilitate learning and dialogue, enhance racial harmony, and expand awareness of one's racial and cultural identity. Sue identified five successful strategies to facilitate difficult conversations about culture and race:

- Understand your own racial and cultural identity.
- Recognize and be open about your racial biases.
- Encourage a discussion about feelings.
- Pay more attention to the process than to the content of race talk.
- Encourage and support people who are willing to take the risk of expressing themselves. (pp. 45–46)

Sue points out that counseling professionals can turn tricky racial and cultural conversations into teachable moments if they are willing to challenge the silence that often surrounds race and culture. Culturally skilled group leaders take the initiative to provide a safe climate for honest expression of experiences and views among people from diverse backgrounds.

Cardemil and Battle (2003) contend that conversations about culture with members enhance the therapeutic relationship and promote better treatment outcomes. We believe their recommendations can be applied to your work as a facilitator of many different kinds of groups:

- Suspend preconceptions about the race or ethnicity of clients or their family members. Avoid making incorrect assumptions about group members that could impede the development of the therapeutic relationship. During the early stage of a group, ask members how they identify culturally and ethnically.
- If you engage group members in conversations about culture and ethnicity, there is less chance of stereotyping and making faulty assumptions.
- Be aware that the more comfortable you are with conversations about race, culture, sexual orientation, and ethnicity, the more easily group members can respond appropriately to others who may be uncomfortable with such discussions.
- Address how differences between you and the members of your group might affect the process and outcomes of the group. Although it is not possible to identify every between-group difference that could surface during the course of therapy, the critical element is your willingness to consider the relevance of racial or ethnic differences with members.
- Recognize and acknowledge how power, privilege, and oppression can affect interactions with clients. Discussing these topics is invaluable in strengthening relationships within the group.
- Be open to ongoing learning about ways that cultural factors affect group work. Although acquiring knowledge about various racial and ethnic groups is important, it is not enough. It is essential that you be willing to identify and examine your own worldview, assumptions, and personal prejudices about other racial and ethnic groups. Know that this skill does not develop quickly or without effort and that you will be refining your skill throughout your career as a counselor.

Group leaders address ethnic and cultural differences between leaders and members in a variety of ways. Some ignore the difference unless members raise the concern, some ask members how they feel about the difference, and others talk directly with members about their own sense of the differences present in the room. Leaders need to be flexible in their approach to discussions of cultural differences and invite discussion on multiple levels. The initial step is to communicate verbally that you are aware of the diversity within the room and that it will likely have an impact on the relationship and connections that are formed. However, the crucial part is in your actions. Members watch what we *do* as much as they attend to what we *say.* They often pay close attention to what we communicate nonverbally as they have learned to read nonverbal language to ascertain what people really think and feel. If we miss opportunities to address cultural differences or make assumptions about gender roles, sexual identity, social identity, and cultural identity, we are communicating to members that we are not likely to understand their experiential world.

Members watch what we *do* as much as they attend to what we say.

To initiate conversations with group members about their cultural identity, it is necessary to have some fundamental understanding about the members' ethnic and cultural backgrounds. We need to carefully listen to group members as they talk about relevant differences and the meaning these differences hold for them. Again, members will provide us with the information we need to work effectively with them if we give them this opportunity and if we create a climate in which they feel safe to do so.

In working with culturally diverse individuals within a group, it helps to assess the degree of acculturation and identity development that has taken place. This is especially true for individuals who have had the experience of living in another culture. Immigrants often have allegiance to their own home culture but find certain characteristics of their new culture attractive. They may experience conflicts when integrating the values from the two cultures in which they live. These core struggles can be productively explored in an accepting group if the leader and the other members respect this cultural conflict.

One group member we worked with talked about his struggle to be more talkative during sessions. He said that he felt pressured to share himself in a way with the group that was extremely foreign and uncomfortable to him. He remarked that if he starts to open up and share his feelings, when he returns to his homeland he will not know when to stop and will likely be disapproved of by his people. This is a common struggle that members from a variety of ethnic groups might face: success in one area directly contradicts what success looks like in the member's cultural of origin.

I (Marianne) live between two cultures. When I am in Germany, I tend to use fewer words to get my message across. When I speak English, I am more verbose. Around Americans, I am more likely to disclose feelings and personal information to people other than my family. These disclosures would be frowned upon in Germany. In moving between two cultures, I am aware of making these adjustments because the consequences of what I say and how I say it differ between these two cultures. Years ago, when I participated in a therapy group as a recent immigrant, I felt very embarrassed when others disclosed personal information about their family, and I was extremely uncomfortable when asked to make myself known in a similar fashion. The challenge for both the leader and the member is to help that person find a way to define what openness might look like for him or her in both settings. How does this person want to be different, if at all?

Recognizing Our Limitations We do not always recognize when our lack of competence is coming into play, so it is crucial for us to be open to feedback from both colleagues and clients. When necessary, it is paramount that we actively seek consultation and supervision, as well as additional resources, to address our limitations, and think critically about how our own actions may be contributing to a lack of progress in a group. The most effective way of working toward cultural competence is to engage in a variety of experiential activities and personal growth opportunities that take the learning from the head to the heart. If we do not walk our talk, all the cultural knowledge in the world will not serve us or the group members with whom we work. The more able we are to immerse ourselves in culturally diverse and rich environments, the more likely we are to enhance our multicultural responsiveness.

If you are working with clients from a specific ethnic, racial, and cultural background different from your own, you can benefit from reading chapters in books and journal articles addressing group work with diverse client populations. Some resources we recommend, which are found in the References and Suggested Readings at the end of the book, are Chung and Bemak (2014); DeLucia-Waack (2010, 2014); DeLucia-Waack, Kalodner, and Riva (2014); Ivey, Pedersen, and Ivey (2008); McWhirter and Robbins (2014); Pope, Pangelinan, and Coker (2011); Salazar (2009); Singh and Salazar (2010a, 2010b, 2010c); Steen, Shi, and Hockersmith, (2014); Sue and Sue (2013); Torres Rivera, Torres Fernandez, and Hendricks (2014), and Vacha-Haase (2014).

Points to Remember

Introduction to Group Work: A Multicultural Perspective

Here are some key points to remember; many of the following chapters are built on these basic concepts.

- Groups have much to offer, but training in both core and specialty competencies is essential to design and facilitate successful groups in a variety of settings.
- There are different types of group work—task groups, psychoeducational groups, group counseling, and group psychotherapy—and each of these involves specific training in both core and specialization competencies. The goals of the group, the leader's role, and functions of members vary depending on the type of group work being considered.
- Brief group therapy is beneficial for both economic and theoretical reasons.
- Brief group counseling is popular in both community agencies and school settings because of the realistic time constraints and the ability of a brief format to be incorporated into both educational and therapeutic programs.
- Pay attention to the diversity that exists within your group, and help members recognize how their diverse backgrounds influence their values and behavior. Highlight cultural themes as they surface during a session.

- Effective delivery of group work involves taking group members' racial and cultural identity into account. Your challenge is to modify your strategies to fit the differing needs of the diverse members of your group.
- To become a culturally skilled group worker, you need to possess a range of knowledge and skills to intervene appropriately. Seek avenues for consultation and supervision as you recognize your limits in understanding diverse groups.
- Skill does not develop quickly; you will be refining your skills throughout your career as a counselor.

Exercises

The exercises at the end of each chapter can be done on your own or in class in small groups. The goal is to provide you with an opportunity to experience techniques, issues, group processes, and potential problems that can occur at various stages of a group's development. As you read the exercises at the end of each chapter, focus on those that are most meaningful to you.

Questions for Discussion

1. What experiences have you had with groups, and how might these experiences influence the attitudes you bring to this group course?
2. What kind of group would you be most interested in forming and leading?
3. What do you think are some of the advantages of a group format for delivering services?
4. Are groups suitable for all client populations? How might you modify the group structure to fit the needs of members of a particular group you are interested in designing?
5. If you were setting up a group composed of culturally diverse members, what factors would you consider?
6. What specific steps could you take to facilitate difficult conversations about race and culture that emerge in your groups?
7. How aware are you of how your cultural background is likely to influence your ability to work with a diverse range of people? What specific attitudes and beliefs might enhance or interfere with your ability to understand and work with diversity?

Guide to Groups in Action: Evolution and Challenges DVD and Workbook

1. A self-study video program and workbook combination titled *Groups in Action: Evolution and Challenges DVD and Workbook* may be used in your course as part of an integrated learning package. Throughout the book you will see an end of chapter box like this one suggesting how to make the best use of *Groups in Action*. The *Groups in Action DVD and Workbook* resources are also available in an alternative, online format through Cengage Learning's Counseling MindTap website. If you did not receive either a DVD or a Printed Access Card packaged with your book, you can purchase access to these resources at www.cengagebrain.com. Check with your professor first to find out if the online resources are required.

If you are using the *Groups in Action: Evolution and Challenges DVD and Workbook*, you can integrate some of the key ideas in this chapter with the DVD. Refer to a section in this chapter on "Becoming a Culturally Skilled Group Counselor" and review the salient issues discussed. In the *Challenges Facing Group Leaders* DVD, a program segment entitled "Challenges of Addressing Diversity Issues" illustrates various situations that most group leaders would find challenging. The scenarios that are enacted within the group provide an action-oriented picture of the skills needed to effectively address a variety of diversity themes, some of which are listed below.

- What does my culture have to do with my identity?
- I feel different from others in here.
- Sometimes I want to exclude others.
- I struggle with language.
- I resent being stereotyped.
- We are alike and we are different.
- I express myself better in my native language.
- I am colorblind.
- I know little about my culture.
- I want more answers from you leaders.

Each of the above themes is enacted in the DVD program and elaborated upon in the workbook. We suggest that you first answer the questions in the workbook dealing with each theme and then use your responses as the basis for discussion in small groups.

MindTap for Counseling

Additional resources can be found on CengageBrain.com and by logging into the MindTap course created by your professor. There you will find a variety of study tools and useful resources that include quizzes, videos, interactive exercises, and more.

CHAPTER

2 The Group Counselor

CHAPTER LEARNING OBJECTIVES

1. Explore common issues facing beginning group leaders
2. Identify the characteristics and functions of effective group leaders (CACREP, 2016, Standard D)
3. Describe the major skills required for effective group facilitation
4. Provide a rationale for and an approach to self-assessment of group leadership skills
5. Discuss some ways to select a coleader and to best work together
6. Present the advantages of coleadership of a group
7. Present the disadvantages of coleadership of a group
8. Introduce the value of a research orientation in group work
9. Consider the status of group research from an international perspective
10. Elaborate on research on common factors in group work
11. Demonstrate how research can enhance group practice
12. Illustrate the challenge of combining research and practice

You are coleading a group with adult women, and on several occasions you have felt that your coleader self-disclosed too readily and did not manage boundaries appropriately. You approach your coleader to share your concerns; he is very defensive and asserts that self-disclosure is a part of his counseling theory. He also tells you that he has many negative reactions to one of the members because she reminds him of an ex-wife. He wants to invite this group member to engage with him in a role play, asking her to take the part of his ex-wife. He believes this will help him deal more effectively with his projections.

- What might you say to your coleader about the pros and cons of his use of self-disclosure in this group?
- What kinds of self-disclosure do you think would be appropriate to share with group members?
- Would you attempt to resolve the issue with your coleader, or say nothing about your reactions?
- Would you address your thoughts and reactions with your coleader in the group? Why or why not?

Introduction

This chapter deals with the influence of the group counselor, both as a person and as a professional, on the direction a group takes. First, we consider the counselor as a person, addressing problems faced by beginning group leaders and the personal qualities of effective leadership. Then, looking at the group leader as a professional, we consider the knowledge and range of specific skills that are required for effectively leading any group. We discuss the rationale for coleadership practices, including the advantages and disadvantages of the coleadership model. We also address how research can enhance your work and the challenges of combining research with the practice of group work.

The Group Counselor as a Person

The professional practice of leading groups is a function of who the counselor is as a person. Indeed, the leader's ability to establish solid relationships with others in the group is probably the most important skill in facilitating group process. As a group leader, you bring your personal qualities, values, and life experiences to every group. For example, if you struggle with perfectionism, you may impose unrealistic standards or goals on your clients without realizing you are doing so. The more self-understanding you possess, the less likely you are to do harm to group members. In general, effective counselors have a high level of self-awareness and engage in an ongoing process of self-reflection.

We address some of the typical challenges faced by beginning group leaders, but there are many benefits to being "new" to the profession as well. We have found that our students and interns possess enormous energy, creativity, and a strong drive to be helpful to their clients. Beginning group leaders often bring a fresh perspective that can help to balance their lack of experience and skill.

If you hope to inspire others to get the most out of living, it is imperative that you attend to your own vitality and that you practice self-care throughout your career. How you deal with the stresses and anxieties of a training program have important implications for how you will function as a group counselor when you encounter various challenges in your professional work.

Problems and Issues Facing Beginning Group Leaders 

Those who are just beginning to lead groups are typically overwhelmed by the problems they face. Those new to group work often ask themselves questions such as these:

- How will I be able to get the group started?
- What techniques should I use?
- Should I wait for the group to initiate activity?
- Will I know how to follow through once something has been initiated?
- What if I don't like one of the group members?
- What if I make mistakes? Can I do harm to the members of my group?
- What do I do if there is a prolonged silence?
- Should I interrupt group members who talk too quickly or for too long?
- What should I do if a group member is not participating at all?
- How much should I participate in or involve myself in a personal way in the groups I lead?
- Will I have the knowledge and skills to work effectively with group members who are culturally different from me?
- Will I be able to address cultural issues and be sensitive to diversity in my group?
- What if a group member challenges me or doesn't like me?
- How do I know whether the group is helping people change?
- How can I work with several people at one time?
- As a group leader, should I hide feelings of anxiety or sadness?
- What do I do if I become emotionally involved and cry with my group?

Whether you are a beginning group leader or a seasoned one, successful groups cannot be guaranteed. In supervising group leaders, we hear them express their fear of making mistakes. To some degree, fear and anxiety are normal, even for seasoned practitioners. Try to harness your anxiety so that it energizes you rather than restricts you. When we are processing a group that students have facilitated in class, we ask students to share observations they had during the group work. Oftentimes trainees are very insightful, yet they keep their observations and insights to themselves because of their concern that they might say or do the wrong thing. We find that the things they are thinking, but not saying as group leaders, are often the most beneficial ideas to put into words.

We encourage you to use supervision and consultation to speak in an unedited manner and to see whether your thoughts about an intervention may have been therapeutic. After each group session, reflect on the experience by writing down the things you were thinking but chose not to say or some of the feelings you had throughout the group. With the help of a supervisor you may begin to find ways to put more of your clinical hunches into words. During a supervision session, one of my (Cindy's) students described how frustrated she was with a particular group member. LeAnn found it difficult to stay connected to the client because he spoke rapidly and often made it difficult for others to find space to share. Instead of sharing her reactions, LeAnn said nothing, and both she and the group members became increasingly frustrated. LeAnn's internal dialogue went something like this: "This guy is really annoying. He just keeps on talking. Many members look annoyed and are restless." I didn't encourage LeAnn to express her reactions in such an uncensored way, but I suggested that she could use her perceptions to give feedback to the client. I encouraged LeAnn to focus on what she was observing with this group member and to explain the impact that it had on her ability to connect with him. In this way LeAnn could use her reactions without judging him or telling him that he talked too much. Frequently our internal dialogue as counselors can be very helpful to our work with clients, with only minimal adjustments to what we are thinking. Rather than faulting the member for his behavior, tell the member how this behavior affects you. Doing so opens up a different conversation and usually results in the member being less defensive.

One problem you may face as a beginning group leader is dealing with negative reactions from members. You need to learn how to constructively confront those who have these reactions. If you become defensive, the members may, in turn, increase their defensiveness. Allowing an undercurrent of unresolved issues to continue will sabotage any further work. Later in this section and at different places in this book we suggest ways to deal with these situations.

Allowing an undercurrent of unresolved issues to continue will sabotage any further work.

It takes time to develop leadership skills, and beginning group leaders may feel like quitting after leading only a few sessions. Some struggle with the uncertainty that is a part of learning how to lead well. Nobody expects to be perfect at any other skill (skiing, playing the guitar, making pottery) in a few introductory lessons, and becoming an accomplished group leader is no different. Those who finally experience success at these endeavors have had the endurance to progress in increments.

There is probably no better teacher than experience, but unguided experience can be unsatisfactory. We cannot stress enough the importance of supervision by experienced group leaders. Immediate feedback—from a supervisor, from coleaders, or from other students in a training group—enables leaders to profit from the experience. Group supervision of group leaders offers unique opportunities for both cognitive and affective learning because it provides a way to experience group process, to observe models of group leadership, and to receive feedback from many perspectives. Because the practice of group counseling is growing rapidly, it is essential that group leaders be both competent and ethical. Group supervision is a route to the development of competent group leaders (Riva, 2014).

Personal Characteristics of the Effective Group Leader 

In our view, who the counselor is *as a person* is one of the most significant variables influencing the group's success or failure. Abundant research indicates the centrality of the *person* of the therapist as a primary factor in successful therapy, and this is inextricably intertwined with the outcome of psychotherapy (Elkins, 2016). In discussing the personality characteristics of the effective group practitioner with some of our colleagues, we have found that it is difficult to list all the traits of successful leaders and even more difficult to agree on one particular personality type associated with effective leadership. The following sections discuss some aspects of a group leader's personality that we deem to be especially important. As you read about each of these dimensions, reflect on how it applies to you. Consider the degree to which you are at least on the road to acquiring the traits essential for your success as a group leader.

Courage A critical personal trait of effective group leaders is courage. Courage is demonstrated through your willingness (a) to be vulnerable at times, admitting mistakes and imperfections and taking the same risks you expect group members to take; (b) to confront others but to stay present with them as you work out conflicts; (c) to act on your beliefs and hunches; (d) to be emotionally affected by others and to draw on your experiences to identify with them; (e) to examine your life; and (f) to be direct and honest with members in a caring and respectful way.

Willingness to Model One of the best ways to teach desired behaviors is by modeling them in the group. Through your behaviors and the attitudes conveyed by them, you can create group norms such as openness, seriousness of purpose, acceptance of others, respect for a diversity of values, and the desirability of taking risks. Remember that you teach largely by example—by doing what you expect members to do. Realize that your role differs from that of the group member, but we encourage you not to hide behind a professional facade. Engaging in honest, appropriate, and timely self-disclosure can be a way to fulfill the leadership function of modeling.

Disclosing your reactions to a member's behavior and sharing your perceptions provides feedback that the person may find very helpful. For example, consider a member who talks a great deal yet leaves out how she is feeling. You might say, "As I listen to you, I am not sure what you want us to hear. I wonder what you are feeling and what you are aware of in your body as you are telling your story." When a group member talks a lot, but says very little, other group members may no longer listen to this person and may display frustration and a lack of interest. The group leader's response challenges the talkative member and invites the member to connect to her emotions while modeling a way other members can confront people without judging them or shutting them down. The member is invited to explore her inner experience more from a place of interest and caring than from criticism.

Presence The ability to be present with group members is extremely important. Presence involves being affected by others' pain, struggles, and joys. However, it also involves not becoming overwhelmed by a member's pain. Presence implies being fully attentive to what is going on in the moment. Some members may elicit anger in a group leader, and others may evoke pain, sadness, guilt, or happiness. You become more emotionally involved with others by paying close attention to your own reactions. This does not mean that you will necessarily talk about the situation in your own life that caused you the pain or evoked the anger. It means that you will allow yourself to experience these feelings, even for just a few moments. Fully experiencing emotions gives you the ability to be compassionate and empathic with others. As you are moved by others' experiences, it is equally important to maintain your boundaries and to avoid the trap of personally identifying with your clients' situations.

Presence implies being fully attentive to what is going on in the moment.

To increase your ability to be present, spend some time alone before leading a group and block out distractions as much as possible. Prepare yourself by thinking about the people in the group and about how you might increase your involvement with them.

Goodwill, Genuineness, and Caring A sincere interest in the welfare of others is essential in a group leader. Your main job in the group is to help members get what they are coming for, not to get in their way. Caring involves respecting, trusting, and valuing people. Some members may be more difficult than others to care about, yet we hope you will at least want to care. It is vital that you become aware of what kind of people you are drawn to and what kind you find challenging. It is also helpful if you can understand what these tendencies toward connection or disconnection reveal about you.

There are various ways of exhibiting a caring attitude. One way is by inviting a client to participate and allowing that person to decide how far to go. Or you can observe discrepancies between a client's words and behavior and challenge that person in a way that doesn't intensify fear and resistance. Another way to express caring is by giving warmth, concern, and support when, and only when, you genuinely feel it toward a person. Even when you don't feel warmth, show your clients respect and concern.

Belief in Group Process We believe that a deep confidence in the value of group process is positively related to constructive outcomes. You need to believe in what you are doing and trust the therapeutic process in a group. We are convinced that our enthusiasm and convictions are powerful both in attracting a clientele and in providing an incentive to work.

It is often during the most difficult moments in group work that we are challenged to both trust the process and our ability to help group members navigate the conflicts, as well as other painful dynamics, that often arise in group work. One result of working through the rough times is that group members often describe a greater sense of closeness with one another and a deeper sense of self than they could have achieved without the growing pains involved in participating in the group.

Openness Openness means that you reveal enough of yourself to give the participants a sense of who you are as a person. It does not mean that you reveal every aspect of your personal life. Your being open can enhance group process if you appropriately reveal your reactions to the members and to how you are being affected by them. Your openness can foster a corresponding spirit of openness within the group. It will enable members to become more open about their feelings and beliefs, and it will lend fluidity to the group process.

Self-revelation is not to be used as a technique; it is best done spontaneously, when it seems appropriate. Here is an example of something we might say to a client who is typically very intellectual but at this moment is showing his emotions: "I really respect your intellect, and I know it has served you well. Yet at this moment I am so struck by the way you are sharing yourself emotionally with us. It is delightful to experience this side of you." This authentic and spontaneous statement highlights the client doing something he has expressed as a personal goal, reinforcing his efforts at emotional expression. It also acknowledges the part of the client that he values—his intellect. The compliment does not diminish one part in order to reinforce another. By sharing her perceptions and personal reactions with this member, the leader has provided another form of self-disclosure.

Nondefensiveness in Coping With Criticism Dealing frankly with criticism is related to openness. Many of the challenges you may be subjected to by group members require the clinician to develop a thick skin. Members may sometimes accuse you of not caring enough, of being selective in your caring, of structuring the sessions too much, or of not providing enough direction. Some of the criticism may be fair—and some of it may be an unfair expression of jealousy, testing authority, or projection onto you of feelings for other people. It is crucial for you to nondefensively explore with the group the feelings behind the criticism.

If members take a risk and confront the leader and are chastised for doing this, they are likely to withdraw. Furthermore, others in the group may receive the message that openness and honesty are not really valued. Even if someone verbally abuses you as a leader, it is not therapeutic for you to respond in a defensive manner. Instead, model an effective and nonaggressive way of expressing your thoughts and feelings. Maintaining a therapeutic stance with group members does not mean that you need to be unaffected by behavior that is difficult and perhaps even attacking or verbally abusive. You might say: "I don't like it when you call me offensive names. I am willing to work with you to understand what it is I do to evoke your reactions to me." As illustrated in this example, you can tell the person your reactions and let him or her know how you are affected by the confrontation. By modeling effective ways to express anger or frustration, you provide members with helpful ways of expressing these emotions in a respectful manner.

Becoming Aware of Subtle Culture Issues Most of us think of ourselves as open-minded and nonjudgmental. However, it is nearly impossible to be raised in a society filled with cultural discrimination and not to hold some degree of prejudice or misinformation about people who differ from us. Many cultural mistakes that may harm members are unconscious and are not deliberate on our part, so it is important that we increase our self-awareness and challenge our worldview and values. Becoming aware of the unconscious parts of ourselves requires deep and critical self-analysis. The harm we do is not less painful to the individual because it is not intended.

As group leaders, if we increase our awareness of our own prejudices and biases, we stand a better chance of dealing effectively with prejudicial attitudes or remarks made in a group. Even in groups of people who consider themselves open and culturally aware, racial or culturally insensitive remarks are not uncommon. Racist remarks that go unnoticed or unaddressed by leaders or the members do influence the group process. The moments in which these subtle and overt comments are made are timely opportunities for learning and for leader facilitation. If a sexist, homophobic, or racially derogatory comment is made and goes unattended, it can create a climate of mistrust and anger on the part of many members.

Being Able to Identify With a Client's Pain It is unrealistic for us to expect that we have experienced the same problems as all of our clients, but the emotions people express are common to all of us. We all experience psychological pain, even though the causes of this pain may be different. One basis for empathizing with clients is being open to the sources of pain in your own life without becoming swept up by this pain. Our willingness to engage in self-reflection can inspire our clients to explore their personal concerns.

Over the years, we have found that it is often the most difficult paths we have taken and the greatest pains we have endured that have helped to fine-tune our clinical intuition and effectiveness. It is not merely having had difficult times, but the willingness to think critically about those times that helps us use these experiences in effective ways as group leaders. For example, if you had a painful divorce, have a lot of unresolved grief, or experienced incest as a child and you have not done your personal work in these areas, it is likely that your clients' stories involving similar situations will affect you to the degree that you will not be effective with them. However, if you have engaged in your own process of healing, you will likely possess a degree of understanding and sensitivity that will show in your work with group members.

Personal Power Personal power does not entail domination of members or manipulation of them toward the leader's end. Rather, it is the dynamic and vital characteristic of leaders who know who they are and what they want. This power involves a sense of confidence in self. Such leaders' lives are an expression of what they espouse. Being self-confident is not the same as being arrogant or feeling as if you have nothing left to learn. It does not mean that we never make mistakes as leaders. Self-confidence implies trusting in our competence while continuing to fine-tune ourselves as people and professionals. In short, if we feel empowered, we have a basis for facilitating a sense of empowerment in the members of our groups.

People with a strong sense of self are congruent and can be genuine in their interpersonal relationships. Although they may be frightened by certain qualities within themselves, this fear doesn't keep them from examining these qualities. They recognize and accept their weaknesses and don't expend energy concealing them from themselves and others. In contrast, people who lack congruence may very much want to defend themselves against self-knowledge. They often act as if they are afraid that their vulnerabilities will be discovered.

Clients sometimes view leaders as perfect and undercut their own power by giving their leaders too much credit for clients' own insights and changes. We have a concern that leaders will too readily accept their clients' perceptions and admiration of them. Effective group leaders recognize the ways in which they have been instrumental in bringing about change, and at the same time they encourage clients to accept their own share of credit for their change.

Stamina Group leading can be taxing and draining as well as exciting and energizing. Therefore, you need physical and psychological stamina and the ability to withstand pressure to remain vitalized throughout the course of a group. Be aware of your own energy level and seek ways to replenish it. It is crucial to have sources other than your groups for psychological nourishment. If you depend primarily on the success level of your groups for this sustenance, you run a high risk of being undernourished and thus of losing the stamina so vital to your success as a leader. If you work primarily with very challenging groups, this is bound to have an impact on your energy level. Unrealistically high expectations can also affect your stamina. Leaders who expect immediate change are often disappointed in themselves and are too quick to judge themselves inadequate. Faced with the discrepancy between their vision of what the group *should* be and what actually occurs, leaders may lose their enthusiasm and begin to blame not only themselves but also the group members for the lack of change within the group. If your enthusiasm begins to fade, being aware of it is an excellent place to start. Examine your expectations, and if they are unrealistic, make efforts at acquiring a more realistic perspective.

Commitment to Self-Care If we hope to maintain our stamina, we need to take care of ourselves. Those of us in the helping professions have been socialized to think of others, and we often have difficulty recognizing our own needs and taking care of ourselves. At times we may give to the point of depletion and in the process neglect to care for ourselves. A growing body of research reveals the negative toll exacted from mental health practitioners in symptoms such as moderate depression, mild anxiety, emotional exhaustion, and disturbed relationships (Norcross & Guy, 2007). To be able to meet the many tasks facing us as group leaders, we need to be committed to developing effective self-care strategies. Self-care is not a luxury but an ethical mandate. The *Ethical Standards for School Counselors* (American School Counselors Association [ASCA], 2010) indicates that self-care is a prerequisite for maintaining professional competence: "Professional school counselors monitor emotional and physical health and practice wellness to ensure optimal effectiveness. They seek physical and mental health referrals when needed to ensure competence at all times" (E.1.b). The ethics code of the American Counseling Association (ACA, 2014) addresses impairment: "Counselors monitor themselves for signs of impairment from their own physical, mental, or emotional problems and refrain from offering or providing professional services when impaired" (C.2.G.).

Self-care is not a luxury but an ethical mandate.

Self-care is a basis for utilizing your strengths, which can enable you to deal effectively with the stresses of your work and prevent some of the risk factors leading to burnout. Staying alive both personally and professionally is not something that happens automatically; it is the result of a commitment to acquiring habits of thinking and action that promote wellness. Self-care involves learning to pay attention to and be respectful of our needs, which is a lifelong task. We cannot provide nourishment to those in our groups if we don't nourish ourselves. If we demonstrate a commitment to taking care of ourselves, we are modeling an important lesson of keeping vital for the members of our groups. Effective leaders express enthusiastic energy and radiate aliveness through their actions. For an excellent discussion on this topic, we recommend Norcross and Guy's (2007) book, *Leaving It at the Office: A Guide to Psychotherapist Self-Care.*

Self-Awareness A central characteristic for any therapeutic person is an awareness of self, including one's identity, cultural perspective, power and privilege, goals, motivations, needs, limitations, strengths, values, feelings, and problems. If you have a limited understanding of who you are, it is unlikely that you will be able to facilitate any kind of awareness in clients. As we've mentioned, being open to new life experiences is one way to expand your awareness. Involvement in your own personal therapy, both group and individual, is another way for you to expand your self-awareness, especially in recognizing your potential for countertransference and learning how to manage these reactions. You need to become aware of your personal characteristics; unresolved problems may either help or hinder your work as a group counselor. Awareness of why you choose to lead groups is crucial, including knowing what needs you are meeting through your work. How can you encourage others to risk self-discovery if you are hesitant to come to terms with yourself? Reflect on interactions you have had with members of your groups; this is a potentially rich source of information about yourself.

Sense of Humor We continue to find that using spontaneous wit makes us more real to the members of our groups and results in their being less intimidated by the power differential. However, everything we do and say has the power either to heal or to harm. Although using humor usually evokes positive reactions, it can elicit negative reactions from some clients. This does not mean you should avoid humor, but be cognizant of its potential impact on members. Observe members' nonverbal reactions as well as checking verbally with group members about their reactions to you, especially if you have been playful or humorous with them. When humor comes from a spontaneous place, not forced or rehearsed, it can have a positive impact. Some students have shared that when leaders are playful it can help to make them more approachable and less intimidating. It is important to maintain a sense of respect for group members when using humor; avoid language that diminishes their suffering or devalues them as people. The key is to balance being authentic and being congruent when relating to members. Refrain from overusing humor in an attempt to build rapport with the group.

Inventiveness The capacity to be spontaneous and to approach each group with fresh ideas is a most important characteristic. Freshness may not be easy to maintain, particularly if you lead groups frequently. It is important to discover new ways of approaching a group by inventing experiments that emerge from here-and-now interactions. Working with coleaders provides another source for gaining fresh ideas.

If you listen to the members in your group, you will discover opportunities to tap into their creativity. If a member is an artist or a poet, encourage the member to share some of his or her work with the group or lead the group in an activity involving creative arts. During one particularly tense session that had gone on for hours, the group members and leaders decided to step outside for some fresh air and movement. One of the members, who happened to be a soccer coach, had a ball with him and taught the other members some soccer moves. This was highly effective in releasing tension and getting unstuck, and it enabled a typically shy member to take on a leadership role. Group members were playful with one another, which had a more positive effect than continuing to talk. Preplanned exercises and activities can be useful, but often the best creativity comes from the members themselves. Create a space in which this creativity can be valued and explored.

Personal Dedication and Commitment Being a professional who makes a difference involves having ideals that provide meaning and direction in your life. This kind of dedication has direct application for leading groups. If you believe in the value of group process, and if you have a vision of how groups can empower individuals, you will be better able to ride out difficult times in a group. If you have a guiding vision, you can use it to stay focused and on track with group members when the interactions are troublesome.

Develop a stance of curiosity with group members and encourage them to do so as well. All member behavior has meaning and serves a purpose, if we choose to view it as such. Even the most difficult of members can and should be seen as approachable in spite of how challenging they may make it for others to care for them. It has been said, "Masks reveal what they are intended to conceal." We interpret this as meaning that the very things people do to keep themselves hidden tell us a lot about who they are, what they fear, what is painful, and what they desire. If individuals are striving to become more authentic, we can help them to discard their masks and to present themselves in more genuine and direct ways. We can do this only if we are invested in them both while they are wearing the mask as well as when they are not. We need to convey acceptance of and commitment to the members of our groups, especially when they are behaving in difficult ways.

Being a dedicated professional also involves humility, which means being open to feedback and ideas and being willing to explore one's self. Humility is truth. It does not mean being self-effacing. It is the opposite of the arrogance that is implied in convincing ourselves that we have nothing more to learn. The best teachers are always learning and never arrive at a place of being all-knowing. In fact, one of the great gifts of our profession is that the process of doing what we do allows us to become better human beings. In addition, professional commitment entails staying abreast of changes in the field, reading journals and books, and attending professional workshops.

The best teachers are always learning and never arrive at a place of being all-knowing.

LO3

The Group Counselor as a Professional

Overview of Group Leadership Skills

It is generally accepted that a positive therapeutic relationship is necessary but not sufficient to produce client change. Certainly it is essential that leaders possess the knowledge of how groups best function and that they have the skills to intervene in timely and effective ways. Creating a group climate that fosters interpersonal norms such as openness, directness, respect, and concern for one another will lead to therapeutic interactions among members. A leader's interpersonal skills, genuineness, empathy, and warmth are significant variables in creating the kind of climate that leads to successful outcomes. In addition to these personal characteristics, group leaders need to acquire a body of knowledge and a set of skills specific to group work. Counseling skills can be taught, but there is also an element of art involved in using these skills in a sensitive and timely way. Learning how and when to use these skills is a function of supervised experience, practice, feedback, and confidence. In Chapter 10 and Chapter 11 we describe some skills that are basic to leading groups with populations of various ages.

Several points about the skills discussed next need to be clarified. First, these skills can best be thought of as existing on a continuum of competence rather than on an all-or-nothing basis. They can be fully mastered and used in a sensitive and appropriate manner, or they can be only minimally developed. Second, these skills can be learned and refined through training and supervised experience. Participating in a group as a member is one good way to determine what a group is about. Leading or coleading a group under supervision is another excellent way to acquire and improve leadership skills. Third, group leaders must be able to multitask, continuously scanning the room, observing the verbal and nonverbal communications of multiple members, and tracking process and content issues for each member. This can be exhausting at first, but it becomes easier as you gain experience. It is helpful to have a coleader whenever possible to share these tasks. Fourth, these skills are not discrete entities; they overlap a great deal. Active listening, reflection, and clarification are interdependent. Hence, by developing certain skills, you are bound to automatically improve other skills. Fifth, these skills cannot be divorced from who you are as a person. Sixth, choosing the skills to develop and use are expressions of your personality and your leadership style.

We next consider some of the skills you will need to acquire and continue to refine as a competent group leader.

Active Listening It is most important to learn how to pay full attention to others as they communicate, and this process involves more than merely listening to the words. It involves absorbing the content, noting gestures and subtle changes in voice or expression, and sensing underlying messages. Group leaders can improve their listening skills by first recognizing the barriers that interfere with paying attention to others. Some of these roadblocks are not really listening to the other, thinking about what to say next instead of giving full attention to the other, being overly concerned about one's role or about how one will look, and judging and evaluating without putting oneself in the other person's place. Like any other therapeutic skill, active listening exists in degrees. The skilled group leader is sensitive to the congruence (or lack of it) between what a member is saying in words and what he or she is communicating through body posture, gestures, mannerisms, and voice inflections. For instance, a man may be talking about his warm and loving feelings toward his wife, yet his body may be rigid and his voice listless. A woman recalling a painful situation may be smiling and holding back tears. In addition to group leaders listening well to members, it is important that leaders teach members how to listen actively to one another.

Reflecting Reflecting, a skill that is dependent on active listening, is the ability to convey the essence of what a person has communicated so the person can see it. Many inexperienced group leaders find themselves confining most of their interactions to mere reflection. As members continue to talk, these leaders continue to reflect. Carried to its extreme, however, reflection may have little meaning; for example:

Member: I really didn't want to come to the group today. I'm bored, and I don't think we've gotten anyplace for weeks.

Leader: You didn't want to come to the group because you're bored and the group isn't getting anywhere.

There is plenty of rich material here for the leader to respond to in a personal way, with some confrontation, or by asking the person and the other members to examine what is going on in the group. Beginning on a reflective level may have value, but staying on that level does not invite deeper exploration. The leader might have done better to reply in this way:

Leader: You sound discouraged about the possibility of not getting much from this experience.

The leader would then have been challenging the member to look at the emotions that lay beneath his words and, in the process, would have been opening up opportunities for meaningful communication.

Clarifying Clarifying is a skill that can be valuably applied during the initial stages of a group. It involves focusing on key underlying issues and sorting out confusing and conflicting feelings; for example:

Member: I'm angry with my father, and I wish I didn't have to see him anymore. He hurts me so often. I feel guilty when I feel this way, because I also love him and wish he would appreciate me.

Leader: You have feelings of love and anger, and somehow having both of these feelings at once presents a problem for you.

Clarification can help the client sort out her feelings so that she can eventually experience both love and anger without experiencing overwhelming guilt. However, it may take some time before she can accept this polarity.

Summarizing The skill of summarizing is particularly useful after an initial check-in at the beginning of a group session. When the group process becomes bogged down or fragmented, summarizing is often helpful in deciding where to go next. For example, after several members have expressed an interest in working on a particular personal problem, the leader might point out common elements that connect these members.

At the end of a session the leader might make some summary statements or ask each member to summarize. For instance, a leader might say, "Before we close, I'd like each of us to make a brief statement about his or her experience in the group today." A leader might invite members to think about what they can do before the next session as a way of furthering their work. It may be useful for the leader to make the first summary statement, providing members with a model for this behavior.

Facilitating The group leader can facilitate the group process by (1) assisting members to openly express their fears and expectations, (2) actively working to create a climate of safety and acceptance in which people can trust one another and therefore engage in productive interchanges, (3) providing encouragement and support as members explore highly personal material or as they try new behavior, (4) involving as many members as possible in the group interaction by inviting and sometimes even challenging members to participate, (5) working toward lessening the dependency on the leader by encouraging members to speak directly to one another, (6) encouraging open expression of conflict and controversy, and (7) helping members overcome barriers to direct communication. The aim of most facilitation skills is to help the group members reach their own goals. Essentially, these skills involve opening up clear communication among the members and helping them increase their responsibility for the direction of their group.

Empathizing An empathic group leader can sense the subjective world of the client. This skill requires the leader to have the characteristics of caring and openness already mentioned. The leader must also have a wide range of experiences to serve as a basis for identifying with others. Further, the leader must be able to discern subtle nonverbal messages as well as messages transmitted more directly. It is impossible to fully know what another person is experiencing, but a sensitive group leader can have a sense of it. It is also important, however, for the group leader to avoid blurring his or her identity by personally identifying with group members. The core of the skill of empathy lies in being able to openly grasp another's experiences and at the same time to maintain one's separateness.

Interpreting Group leaders who are more directive are likely to make use of interpretation, which entails offering possible explanations for certain behaviors or symptoms. If interpretations are plausible and well timed, they can result in a member moving beyond an impasse. It is not necessary that the leader always make the interpretation for the client; in Gestalt therapy, clients are encouraged to make their own interpretations of their behavior. A group leader also may present an interpretation in the form of a hunch, which encourages members to assess what they are hearing. For instance, an interpretation might be stated as follows: "Jeffrey, when a person in the group talks about something painful, I've noticed that you usually intervene and become reassuring. This tends to stop the person's emotional experience and exploration. Do you have an awareness of this, and what might that say about what is going on with you?" It is important that the interpretation be presented as a hypothesis rather than as a fact and that the person has a chance to consider the validity of this hunch in the group. It is also important to consider the cultural context in making an interpretation to avoid mistakenly interpreting a member's behavior. For example, a member's silence may be related to a cultural message rather than being a sign of mistrust or resistance. This cultural message could be "Don't speak until spoken to," or "Don't draw attention to yourself." To interpret the person's silence as a sign of a lack of trust would be a mistake without understanding the cultural aspects of the behavior.

In addition to making interpretations for individuals, whole-group interpretations are appropriate. An example of this is a leader pointing out how many members may be invested in attempting to draw a particular member out. A leader might suggest that such behavior is an avoidance pattern on the part of the group as a whole. This interpretation may mean something very different during a transition stage than in a working stage. Member behavior needs to be interpreted in light of the developmental level of the group.

Questioning Questioning is overused by many group leaders. Interrogation seldom leads to productive outcomes, and more often than not it distracts the person working. If a member happens to be experiencing intense feelings, questioning is one way of reducing the intensity. Asking "Why do you feel that way?" is rarely helpful because it takes the emotional material to the cerebral level. However, appropriately timed "what" and "how" questions do serve to intensify experiencing. Examples are questions such as "What is happening with your body now, as you speak about your isolation?" "How do you experience the fear of rejection in this group?" "What are some of the things you imagine happening to you if you reveal your problems to this group?" "How are you coping with your fear that you can't trust some of the members here?" "What would your father's approval do for you?" These open-ended questions direct the person to heighten awareness of the moment. Leaders can develop the skill of asking questions like these and avoiding questions that remove people from themselves. Closed questions that are not helpful include those that search for causes of behavior, probe for information, and the like: "Why do you feel depressed?" "Why don't you leave home?"

Group leaders need to develop skills in raising questions at the group level as well as working with individual members. Group process questions such as these can be productively addressed to the group as a whole: "Where is the group with this topic now?" "I'm noticing that many of you are silent. I wonder what is not being said." "How much energy do you have at this moment?" Such questions can assist members in reflecting on what is happening in the group at different points.

Linking A group leader who has an interactional focus—that is, one who stresses member-to-member rather than leader-to-member communication—makes frequent use of linking. This is an important skill that can foster involvement by many members. This skill calls on the insightfulness of the leader in finding ways of relating what one person is doing or saying to the concerns of another person. For example, Katherine might be describing her feeling that she won't be loved unless she's perfect. If Pamela has been heard to express a similar feeling, the leader could ask Pamela and Katherine to talk with each other in the group about their fears. By being alert for cues that members have some common concern, the leader can promote member interaction and raise the level of group cohesion. Questions that can promote linking of members include "Does anyone else in the group feel connected to what Katherine is saying?" or "Who else is affected by the interchange between Pamela and Katherine, and are you willing to tell them how you are affected?"

Confronting Beginning group leaders are often afraid to challenge group members for fear of hurting them, of being wrong, or of inviting retaliation. It doesn't take much skill to attack another or to be merely critical. It does take both caring and skill, however, to confront group members when their behavior is disruptive of the group functioning or when there are discrepancies between their verbal messages and their nonverbal messages. In confronting a member, a leader should (1) specifically identify the behavior to be examined and avoid labeling the person, and (2) share how he or she feels about the person's behavior. For example, Danny has been chastising a group member for being especially quiet in the sessions. The leader might intervene: "Danny, rather than telling her that she should speak up, are you willing to let her know how her silence affects you? Will you tell her why it is important to you that she speaks?"

As is true for other skills, leaders need to learn ways to confront both individual members and the group as a whole. For example, if the group seems to be low in energy and characterized by superficial discussions, the leader might encourage the members to talk about what they see going on in the group for themselves and determine whether they want to change what is happening.

Supporting Supportive behavior can be therapeutic or counterproductive. A common mistake is offering support before a participant has had an opportunity to fully experience a conflict or some painful feelings. Although the intervention may be done with good intentions, it may abort certain feelings that the member needs to experience and express. Leaders should remember that too much support may send the message that people are unable to support themselves. Support is appropriate when people are facing a crisis, when they are facing frightening experiences, when they attempt constructive changes and yet feel uncertain about these changes, and when they are struggling to overcome old patterns that are limiting. This kind of support does not interrupt the work being done. For instance, Isaac feels very supported when several members sit close to him and listen intently as he recounts some frightening experiences as a refugee. Their presence helps him to feel less alone.

Blocking Group leaders have the responsibility to block certain activities of group members, such as questioning, probing, gossiping, invading another's privacy, breaking confidences, and so forth. Blocking helps to establish group norms and is an important intervention, particularly during the group's initial stages. If a member or members are bombarding another member with questions and pushing the member to be more personal, the leaders should comment on the process and ask the questioning members to examine the intent and consequence of their style of engagement, as well as help the member being questioned to express his reservations about disclosing. In addition, members sometimes push others to become more personal as a way for them to remain hidden. The skill here is to learn to block counterproductive behaviors without attacking the questioner. This requires both sensitivity and directness. Here are some examples of behaviors that need to be blocked:

- *Bombarding others with questions*. Members can be asked to make direct statements that involve expressing the thoughts and feelings that prompted them to ask their questions.
- *Indirect communication*. If a member talks *about* another member who is in the room, the leader can ask the person to speak directly *to* the person being spoken about.
- *Storytelling*. If lengthy storytelling occurs, a leader can intervene and ask the person to say how all this relates to present feelings and events, and why it is important that we know about a person who is not present in the group.
- *Breaking confidences*. A member may inadvertently talk about a situation that occurred in another group or mention what someone did in a prior group. The consequences and impact of breaking confidentiality need to be thoroughly discussed. Leaders need to teach members how to speak about their experiences in such a way as to maintain the confidentiality and privacy of other group members.

Assessing Assessment skills involve more than identifying symptoms and figuring out the cause of behavior. Assessment includes the ability to appraise certain behavior problems and to choose the appropriate intervention. For example, a leader who determines that a person is angry must consider the safety and appropriateness of encouraging the member to express pent-up feelings. Leaders also need to develop the skill of determining whether a particular group is indicated or contraindicated for a member and acquire the expertise necessary to make appropriate referrals. Leaders must be able to assess whether the member can be helped or harmed by the group.

Modeling One of the best ways for leaders to teach a desired behavior to members is to model it for them. If group leaders value risk-taking, openness, directness, sensitivity, honesty, respect, and enthusiasm, they must demonstrate attitudes and behaviors congruent with these values. A few specific behaviors leaders can directly model include respect for diversity, appropriate and timely self-disclosure, giving feedback in ways that others can hear and accept nondefensively, receiving feedback from members in a nondefensive manner, involvement in the group process, presence, and challenging others in direct and caring ways.

Suggesting Leaders can offer suggestions aimed at helping members develop an alternative course of thinking or action. Suggestions can take a number of forms, such as giving information, asking members to consider a specific homework assignment, asking members to create their own experiments, and assisting members in looking at a circumstance from a new vantage point. Leaders can also teach members to offer appropriate suggestions to each other. Although suggestions can facilitate change in members, there is a danger that suggestions can be given too freely and that advice can short-circuit the process of self-exploration. There is a fine line between suggesting and prescribing; the skill is in using suggestions to enhance an individual's inclination and motivation toward making his or her own decisions.

Initiating When the leader takes an active role in providing direction to members, offers some structure, and takes action when it is needed, the group is aided in staying focused on its task. These leadership skills include using catalysts to get members to focus on their personal goals, assisting members in working through places where they are stuck, helping members identify and resolve conflict, knowing how to use techniques to enhance work, providing links among the various themes in a group, and helping members assume responsibility for directing themselves. Too much leader initiation can stifle the creativity of a group, and too little leader initiation can lead to passivity on the part of the members.

Evaluating A crucial leadership skill is evaluating the ongoing process and dynamics of a group. After each group session, it is valuable for the leader to evaluate what happened, both within individual members and within the whole group, and to think about what interventions might be used next time with the group. Leaders need to get in the habit of asking themselves these questions: "What changes are resulting from the group?" "What are the therapeutic and non-therapeutic forces in the group?"

The leader has the role of teaching participants how to evaluate, so they can appraise the movement and direction of their own group. Once the group has evaluated a session or series of sessions, its members can decide what, if any, changes need to be made. For example, during an evaluation at the close of a session, perhaps the leader and the members agree that the group as a whole has not been as productive as it could be. The leader might say, "Each one of us might reflect on our participation to determine our degree of responsibility for what is happening in our group. What is each one of us willing to change to make this group more successful?"

Terminating Group leaders need to learn when and how to terminate their work with both individuals and groups. They need to develop the ability to tell when a group session should end, when an individual is ready to leave a group, and when a group has completed its work, and they need to learn how to handle each of these types of termination. Of course, at the end of each session it is helpful to create a climate that will encourage members to make contracts to do work between sessions. This will help members build the skills they will need when the group itself is coming to an end. By focusing members on the ending of each session, they are better prepared to deal with the final termination of their group.

Helping members bring closure to a particular group experience involves (1) providing members with suggestions for transferring what they have learned in the group to the environment they will return to without the continuing support of the group, (2) preparing people for the psychological adjustments they may face on leaving a group, (3) arranging for a follow-up group, (4) telling members where they can get additional therapy, and (5) being available for individual consultation at the termination of a group. Follow-up and evaluation activities are particularly important as a way for the leader to learn of the effectiveness of the group.

It is important for group leaders to have examined their own history with loss and to be aware of the issues that may be triggered for them during the ending stage of a group. In Chapter 9 we explore some creative ways leaders can facilitate positive and healthy termination for group members.

An Integrated View of Leadership Skills

Some counselor-education programs focus on developing counseling skills and assessing competencies; other programs stress the personal qualities that underlie these skills. Ideally, training programs for group leaders should give due attention to both of these aspects. In the discussion of professional standards for training group counselors in Chapter 3, we go into more detail about specific areas of knowledge and the skills group workers need.

You are likely to feel somewhat overwhelmed when you consider all the skills that are necessary for effective group leadership. It may help to remember that, as in other areas of life, you will become frustrated if you attempt to focus on all aspects of this field at once. You can expect to gradually refine your leadership style and gain confidence in using these skills effectively.

Learning in Action

Self-Assessment of Group Leadership Skills

This self-inventory will help you identify your areas of strengths and weaknesses as a group leader. Read the brief description of each skill and then rate yourself on each dimension. Think about the questions listed under each skill. These questions are designed to aid you in assessing your current level of functioning and in identifying specific ways you can enhance your learning of skills.

You can profit from this checklist by reviewing it before and after group sessions. If you are working with a coleader, he or she can provide you with a separate rating. These questions also provide a framework for exploring your level of skill development with fellow students and with your supervisor or instructor.

To what degree do you demonstrate the following? (One space is for you to rate yourself early in the term and the other space for later on.) On each skill, rate yourself using this 3-point scale:

3 = I do this most of the time with a *high degree* of competence.

2 = I do this some of the time with an *adequate degree* of competence.

1 = I do this occasionally with a *relatively low level* of competence.

_____ _____ **1. Active listening.** Hearing and understanding both subtle and direct messages, and communicating that one is doing this.

a. Am I able to hear both overt and subtle messages?

b. Do I teach members how to listen and respond?

_____ _____ 2. **Reflecting.** Capturing the underlying meaning of what is said or felt and expressing this without being mechanical.

a. Do my restatements add meaning to what was said by a member?

b. Am I able to reflect both thoughts and feelings?

_____ _____ 3. **Clarifying.** Focusing on the underlying issues and assisting others to get a clearer picture of what they are thinking or feeling.

a. Do my clarifying remarks help others sort out conflicting feelings?

b. Does my clarification lead to a deeper level of member self-exploration?

_____ _____ 4. **Summarizing.** Identifying key elements and common themes and providing a picture of the directional trends of a group session.

a. Am I able to tie together several themes in a group session?

b. Do I attend adequately to summarizing at the end of a session?

_____ _____ 5. **Facilitating.** Helping members to express themselves clearly and to take action in a group.

a. Am I able to help members work through barriers to communication?

b. Am I successful in teaching members to focus on themselves?

_____ _____ 6. **Empathizing.** Adopting the internal frame of reference of a member.

a. Can I maintain my separate identity at the same time as I empathize with others?

b. Do I promote expressions of empathy among the members?

_____ _____ 7. **Interpreting.** Explaining the meaning of behavior patterns within some theoretical framework.

a. Do I present my interpretations in the form of hunches?

b. Do I encourage members to provide their own meaning for their behavior?

_____ _____ 8. **Questioning.** Using questions to stimulate thought and action but avoiding question/answer patterns of interaction between leader and member.

a. Do I ask "what" and "how" questions instead of "why" questions?

b. Do I keep myself hidden through asking questions?

_____ _____ 9. **Linking.** Promoting member-to-member interaction and facilitating exploration of common themes in a group.

a. Do my interventions enhance interactions between members?

b. Do I foster a norm of member-to-member interactions or leader-to-member interactions?

_____ _____ 10. **Confronting.** Challenging members to look at some aspects of their behavior.

a. Do I model caring and respectful confrontation?

b. Am I able to confront specific behaviors without being judgmental?

_____ _____ 11. **Supporting.** Offering some form of positive reinforcement at appropriate times in such a way that it has a facilitating effect.

a. Do I balance challenge and support?

b. Does my providing support sometimes get in the way of a member's work?

_____ _____ 12. **Blocking.** Intervening to stop counterproductive behaviors in the group or to protect members.

a. Am I able to intervene when necessary without attacking a member?

b. Do I block a member's behavior that is disruptive to the group?

_____ _____ 13. **Assessing.** Getting a clear sense of members without labeling them.

a. Do I help members to assess their own problematic behavior?

b. Can I create interventions that fit with my assessment?

_____ _____ 14. **Modeling.** Demonstrating to members desired behaviors that can be practiced both during and between group sessions.

a. Am I able to model effective self-disclosure?

b. Can I model caring confrontations?

_____ _____ 15. **Suggesting.** Offering information or possibilities for action that can be used by members in making independent decisions.

a. Do my suggestions encourage members to take initiative?

b. How do I determine when to give suggestions and when to avoid doing so?

_____ _____ 16. **Initiating.** Demonstrating an active stance in intervening in a group at appropriate times.

a. Do I take active steps to prevent a group from floundering in unproductive ways?

b. Do I teach members how to initiate their own work in the sessions?

_____ _____ 17. **Evaluating.** Appraising the ongoing group process and the individual and group dynamics.

a. What criteria do I use to assess the progress of my groups?

b. What kinds of questions do I pose to members to help them evaluate their own gains as well as their contributions to the group?

_____ _____ 18. **Terminating.** Creating a climate that encourages members to continue working after sessions.

a. Do I prepare members for termination of a group?

b. Do I help members transfer what they learn in group to daily life?

Once you complete this self-assessment, circle the items where you most need improvement (any items that you rated as "1" or "2"). Circle the letter of the questions that are the most meaningful to you, as well as the questions that indicate a need for attention. Think about specific strategies you can design to work on the skills where you see yourself as being most limited. It is a good idea to take this inventory at least twice—once at the beginning of the course and then again later.

The Coleadership Model

The Basis of Coleadership

LO5

Many who educate and train group leaders have come to favor the coleadership model of group practice. This model has a number of advantages for all concerned: group members can gain from the perspectives of two leaders; coleaders can confer before and after a group and learn from each other; and supervisors can work closely with coleaders during their training and can provide them with feedback.

We prefer coleadership both for facilitating groups and for training and supervising group leaders, and we usually work as a team. Although each of us has independent professional involvements (including leading groups alone at times), we enjoy coleading and continue to learn from each other as well as from other colleagues with whom we work. Nevertheless, we do not want to give the impression that coleadership is the only acceptable model; many people facilitate a group alone very effectively. As we discussed earlier, group leaders preparing to meet their first group tend to experience self-doubt and anxiety. The task seems far less monumental if they meet their new group with a coleader whom they trust and respect.

In training group workers using a coleadership model, we find it is useful to observe the trainees as they colead so we can discuss what they are actually doing as they facilitate a group. Then, as we offer feedback to them, we frequently ask them to talk with each other about how they felt as they were coleading and what they think about the session they have just led. The feedback between coleaders can be both supportive and challenging; exchanging perceptions can enhance their ability to function effectively as coleaders.

Some mistakes students often make as they begin their coleadership duties include the following:

- Not sitting across from one another or making continuous eye contact with their coleader
- Having a plan or goal for the group but not communicating that to their coleader
- Being competitive with their coleader
- Asserting power over their coleader
- Trying to be right as a leader at the expense of making their coleader wrong
- Taking turns leading rather than cofacilitating
- Remaining quiet and letting the coleader do most of the work

These behaviors may be subjects for discussion between new coleaders as well as being addressed during supervision sessions.

The choice of a coleader is a critical variable. Careful selection of a coleader and time devoted to meeting together are essential. If the two leaders are incompatible, their group is bound to be negatively affected. For example, power struggles between coleaders will have the effect of dividing the group. If coleaders are in continual conflict with each other, they are providing a poor model of interpersonal relating, which will influence the group process. Such conflict typically leads to unexpressed reactions within the group, which get in the way of effective work. Certainly coleaders will have differences of opinion or conflicts from time to time. Resolving these disputes in a respectful manner provides coleaders with an opportunity to model ways of coping with interpersonal conflict for group members. If a conflict between coleaders occurs in a group, it should be addressed in the group.

We think it is important that the two leaders have some say in deciding to work as a team. Otherwise, there is a potential for harm for both the group members and the coleaders. Not being able to choose your coleader can be problematic. If you find the relationship with your coleader is not productive, consider the following steps:

- Identify the specific characteristics or behaviors that bother you about your coleader and examine why these are problematic for you.
- Seek supervision and consultation to enable you to work through these issues.
- Communicate your feelings to your coleader in an open and nonjudgmental way, and discuss what you each need to develop a more effective working relationship.
- Increase the amount of time you spend preparing for and debriefing group sessions with your coleader.
- If you, your coleader, or your supervisor determine that these conflicts are likely to cause harm to the group members, consider changing coleaders.

Luke and Hackney (2007) summarize some potential problems with coleadership and note that problems often involve relationship difficulties between leaders: interpersonal conflicts, competition between the leaders, overdependence on the coleader, and unresolved conflicts between the leaders. If these matters are addressed and resolved by the leaders, their relationship will be strengthened, which will have a positive effect on the group. If coleaders are unable to work out their relationship problems or achieve an understanding of their different perspectives, they will not be effective in facilitating their group.

To avoid negatively affecting a group, coleaders need to monitor and discuss their working relationship. A key part of their coleadership relationship involves an awareness of their personal issues that could lead to competitiveness, performance anxiety, and power and control struggles between them in the group. If they are concerned with the welfare of their group, then coleaders must be committed to exploring and resolving conflicts or any difficulties that may arise between them.

To avoid negatively affecting a group, coleaders need to monitor and discuss their working relationship.

A major factor in selecting a coleader involves mutual respect. Two or more leaders working together will surely have their differences in leadership style, and they will not always agree or share the same perceptions or interpretations. If there is mutual respect and trust between them, however, they will be able to work cooperatively instead of competitively, and they will be secure enough to be free of the constant need to prove themselves.

It is not necessary that you be best friends with your coleader, but you need a good working relationship, which you can achieve by taking time to talk with each other. Although we take delight in our personal and professional relationship, we are also willing to engage in the hard work necessary to be a successful team. We encourage those who colead groups to spend some time both *before* and *after* each session discussing their reactions to what is going on in the group as well as their working relationship as coleaders.

Advantages of the Coleadership Model

Having acknowledged our clear preference for coleading groups, here is a summary of the major advantages of using the coleadership method.

1. The chance of burnout can be reduced by working with a coleader. This is especially true if you are working with a demanding population, such as the psychologically impaired who often simply get up and leave, who hallucinate

during sessions, and who may be withdrawn or be acting out. In such groups one leader can attend to problematic behavior while the other attempts to maintain the work going on in the group.

2. If intense emotions are being expressed by one or more members, one leader can pay attention to those members while the other leader scans the room to note the reactions of other members, who can later be invited to share their reactions. Or, if appropriate, the coleader can find a way to involve members in the work of someone else. Many possibilities exist for linking members, for facilitating interaction between members, and for orchestrating the flow of a group when coleaders are sensitively and harmoniously working as a team.
3. Coleader peer supervision is clearly beneficial. The coleader can be used as a sounding board, can check for objectivity, and can offer useful feedback. There is no problem of breaking confidentiality in such instances, for the coleader was also present in the sessions. However, we do want to emphasize that it is often necessary for leaders to express and deal with such feelings in the session itself, especially if they were aroused in the group setting. For example, if you are aware that you are perpetually annoyed by the behavior of a given member, you might need to deal with your annoyance as a group matter. This is a time when a competent and trusted coleader is especially important.
4. An important advantage of coleading emerges when one of the leaders is affected by a group member to the degree that countertransference is present. Countertransference can distort one's objectivity so that it interferes with leading effectively. For example, your coleader may typically react with annoyance or some other intense feeling to one member who is seen as a problem. Perhaps you are better able to make contact with this member, and so you may be the person who primarily works with him or her. You can be of valuable assistance by helping your coleader talk about, and perhaps even resolve, reactions toward such a client.

   Likewise, if a group leader becomes the target for a member's anger or frustration, the coleader can assist in facilitating the discussion between the group member and that leader. Although it is not impossible to be both a part of the "problem" and also part of the solution, it can be beneficial not to have to manage all of these roles at once. It is advantageous to have a coleader who can assist in the process.
5. Another advantage of the coleadership model relates to differences in power and privilege based on culture, ethnicity, religious/spiritual orientation, or sexual identity. If one of the leaders represents a position of power and privilege that may affect members in a particular way, the other leader can help process this, especially if he or she does not possess the same social status position.

Disadvantages of the Coleadership Model

LO7

Even with a coleader you choose, one whom you respect and like, there are likely to be occasional disagreements. This difference of perspective and opinion need not be a disadvantage or a problem. Instead, it can be healthy for both of you because you can keep yourself professionally alert through constructive challenges and differences. Most of the disadvantages in coleading groups have to do with poor selection of a coleader, random assignment to another leader, or failure of the two leaders to meet regularly. Here are some other issues you and your coleader may have to work out.

1. Problems can occur if coleaders rarely meet with each other. The results are likely to be a lack of synchronization or even a tendency to work at cross purposes instead of toward a common goal. Leaders need to take time to discuss their differences. For example, we have observed difficulties when one group leader thought all intervention should be positive, supportive, and invitational, whereas the other leader functioned on the assumption that members need to be pushed and directly confronted. The group became fragmented and polarized as a result of these incompatible leadership styles.
2. A related issue is competition and rivalry. For example, one leader may have an exaggerated need to have center stage, to be dominant at all times, and to be perceived as the one in control. Obviously, such a relationship between coleaders is bound to have a negative effect on the group. In some cases members may develop negative reactions toward groups in general, concluding that all that ever goes on in them is conflict and the struggle for power.
3. If coleaders do not have a relationship built on trust and respect or if they do not value each other's competence, they may not trust each other's interventions. Each leader may insist on following his or her own hunches, convinced that the other's are not of value.
4. One leader may side with members against the other leader. For example, assume that Alta confronts a male leader with strong negative reactions and that his coleader (a woman) joins Alta in expressing her reactions and even invites the members to give feedback to the coleader. This practice can divide the group, with members taking sides about who is "right." It is especially problematic if one leader has not previously given negative reactions to the other and uses the situation as a chance to "unload" feelings.
5. Coleaders who are involved in an intimate relationship with each other can get into some problematic situations if they attempt to use time in the session to deal with their own relationship struggles. Although some members may support the coleaders' working on their own issues in the group, most clients are likely to resent these coleaders for abdicating their leadership functions and using the group for their own needs.

LO8 LO9

Developing a Research Orientation to Practice

We now turn to a consideration of what researchers can tell us about factors that are associated with positive outcomes in groups. Barlow, Fuhriman, and Burlingame (2004) state that "the efficacy of group psychotherapy has been undeniably established in the research literature" (p. 5). They traced the research trends in group counseling and psychotherapy and concluded that a set of recognizable factors—such as skilled leaders, appropriately referred group members, and defined goals—create positive outcomes in groups. A survey of more than 40 years of research provides abundant evidence that group approaches are associated with clients' improvement in a variety of settings and situations (Barlow et al., 2004; Burlingame, Fuhriman, & Johnson, 2004a).

Group therapy is no longer viewed as a second-choice form of treatment but instead is viewed as a potent source of change. Group therapy has been shown to be as effective as individual treatment and, in some cases, is more effective (Barlow, 2008). Practitioners need to be able to assess whether clients are better served by being in a group rather than being in individual therapy. Practitioners should know about the availability of groups and the suitability of a group for a particular client.

Weber and Weinberg (2015) were interested in how group therapy was being used worldwide, and they gathered contributions on the status of group therapy from 14 countries. They asked about the ways research informs group practice and found that the theoretical model for group therapy most often investigated by international researchers was cognitive behavior therapy. However, with the exception of Germany, Norway, and Canada, Weber and Weinberg concluded that research on group therapy is scarce to almost nonexistent internationally.

Cognitive behavior therapy and psychodynamic therapy are the models most in use worldwide, although groups were based on a number of other theoretical approaches as well. In both Sweden and Norway, cognitive behavior therapy is the main theoretical orientation. In Israel, group therapy is influenced primarily by the psychodynamic tradition. Germany emphasizes inpatient group therapy, and German group researchers and clinicians have developed a strong research network over the last 20 years. Norway has completed several significant projects comparing short-term and long-term psychodynamic group therapy outcomes using randomized control research designs. Weber and Weinberg were guest editors for the October 2015 issue of the *International Journal of Group Psychotherapy*, and this special issue contains a detailed review of how group therapy is being used around the world.

Research on Common Factors

Having a solid theoretical foundation is critical in guiding our work as group practitioners (see Chapter 4), because theory can help practitioners decide on ways to make effective interventions in a group. However, the common factors among the theories are thought to be far more important in accounting for therapeutic outcomes than the unique factors that differentiate one theory from another. The **common factors approach** focuses on the value of common elements across different theoretical systems such as empathic listening, support, warmth, developing a working alliance, opportunity for catharsis, practicing new behaviors, feedback, positive expectations of clients, working through one's own conflicts, understanding interpersonal and intrapersonal dynamics, change that occurs outside of the therapy office, client factors, therapist effects, and learning to be self-reflective about one's work (Norcross & Beutler, 2014; Prochaska & Norcross, 2014). Specific treatment techniques make relatively little difference in outcome when compared with the value of common factors, especially the human elements such as the therapeutic relationship (Elkins, 2016).

None of the common factors has received more attention and confirmation than a facilitative therapeutic relationship (Lambert, 2011). The importance of the therapeutic alliance is a well-established critical component of effective therapy. Research confirms that the client–therapist relationship is central to therapeutic change and is a significant predictor of both effectiveness and retention of therapy outcomes (Elkins, 2016; Miller, Hubble, & Seidel, 2015). Brain-imaging technology in the emerging field of interpersonal neurobiology confirms that healing changes can occur in the brain when clients experience a warm, nonjudgmental, empathic relationship with a caring counselor (Badenoch, 2008; Fosha, Siegel, & Solomon, 2009).

How Research Can Enhance Your Group Practice

With the current emphasis on short-term treatments that provide symptom relief or solve specific client problems, familiarity with research in the group work field is becoming an essential part of practice. Along with follow-up group sessions and individual interviews of members of your groups, research can help you come to a better understanding of the specific factors that contributed to the successful outcomes or the failures of your groups. In school and agency settings, you will often be expected to demonstrate accountability for the groups you conduct, which can involve some form of research on the process and outcomes of the group. Make systematic observation and assessment basic parts of your practice of group work. Applied research can help you refine your interventions and identify factors that interfere with group effectiveness.

Instead of thinking exclusively in terms of rigorous empirical research, practitioners can begin to consider alternatives to traditional scientific methods. Miller, Hubble, Duncan, and Wampold (2010) emphasize the importance of enlisting the client's active participation in the therapeutic venture. They suggest that it is useful to systematically gather and use formal client feedback to inform, guide, and evaluate treatment. Monitoring the progress of each group member through systematic data collection on how each member is experiencing the group can help leaders make adjustments to their interventions and enhance the group process.

Jensen and colleagues (2012) recommend that group practitioners integrate **practice-based evidence (PBE)** into their therapy groups to supplement clinical judgment. For example, asking members to complete a brief form at the end of each group session rating specific items can provide the group leader with a sense of the progress of the group as a whole. Collecting data directly from members about their group experience is a significant part of developing practice-based evidence. The PBE approach can help therapists assess the value of a group for its members throughout the life of the group as well as provide a tool to aid evaluation of the group experience during the termination phase. Group workers have an ethical responsibility to determine how well a group is working and should be willing to use the feedback they receive from group participants to refine their interventions.

The Challenge of Combining Research and Practice 

Ideally, theory informs your practice, and practice refines your approach to group work. Combining research and practice takes knowledge and skill, but it can reap dividends. Clinical work can be greatly aided by research findings, and clinical work can also inform research (Stockton & Morran, 2010). A commitment to be both a group practitioner and a researcher is demanding. If you do not have the time or the expertise required to conduct research, you can benefit by integrating the research findings of others into your group practice.

Whether or not group workers conduct research with their groups may be less important than their willingness to keep themselves informed about the practical applications of research on group work. At the very least, group counselors need to be up to date with the research implications for practice. Yalom (2005b) claims that group trainees need to know more than how to implement techniques in a group—they also need to know how to learn. According to Yalom, a research orientation allows group therapists, throughout their career, to remain flexible and responsive to new evidence. Practitioners who lack a research orientation will have no basis to critically evaluate new developments in the field of group work. Without a consistent framework to evaluate evidence of the efficacy of innovations in the field, practitioners run the risk of being unreasonably unreceptive to new approaches.

A gap exists between research and practice in group counseling, and closing it involves overcoming some major obstacles. One of the key problems is the lack of collaboration between researchers and practitioners. Researchers often do not really understand what can be learned from clinical experience, and practitioners often perceive research as being irrelevant to clinical practice. Only a small percentage of group practitioners use research findings in any consistent manner or engage in research of their own. Often research findings are not integrated into clinical practice due to the constraints of experimental research that limit the applicability of findings to a real-world context. Although experimental studies may have internal validity, they may have little practical value to group workers. If this knowledge gap is to be bridged, practitioners and researchers need to develop mutual respect for what each can offer and increase their collaboration (Stockton & Morran, 2010). In reporting on the status of research on group therapy in Italy, Giannone, Giordano, and Di Blasé (2015) identify methodological issues and clinicians' distrust of research as factors accounting for the limited empirical research on the effectiveness of groups. To address this challenge, researchers and group clinicians in Italy have sought ways to collaborate with each other. Practitioners can benefit from researchers by gaining useful information concerning the efficacy of the groups they conduct in their agencies. Researchers stand to benefit by collaborating with practitioners and gaining access to a variety of real-world groups that can be studied. For more on research evidence on group therapy, see G. Corey and M. Corey (2016).

Points to Remember

The Group Counselor

Concepts and Guidelines for Group Practitioners

- Personality and character are important variables of effective group leaders. Techniques and skills cannot compensate for the shortcomings of leaders who lack self-knowledge, who are not willing to do what they ask group members to do, or who are poorly trained. Think about your personal characteristics and try to decide which will be assets and which liabilities to you as a group leader.
- Effective group leaders are knowledgeable about group dynamics and possess leadership skills. Use the self-evaluation inventories at the end of this chapter as a means of thinking about skills you might need to improve and skills you might need to develop.
- As a group leader, you need to decide how much responsibility for what goes on in the group belongs to the members and how much to you, how much and what type of structuring is optimal for a group, what kind of self-disclosure is optimal, what role and function you will assume, and how you will integrate both support and confrontation into group practice.
- In a therapeutic group, participants can learn more about themselves, explore their conflicts, learn new social skills, get feedback on the impact they have on others, and try out new behaviors. The group becomes a microcosm of society in which members can learn more effective ways of living with others. Depending on the type of group, there are some clear advantages to constituting a group that is diverse with respect to age, gender, sexual orientation, cultural background, race, and philosophical perspectives.
- Develop behavioral guidelines and teach them to group members. Some of the behaviors you might stress are keeping the group's activities confidential, respecting the differences that characterize the members, taking responsibility for oneself, working hard in the group, listening, and expressing one's thoughts and feelings.
- Groups should be thought of as the treatment of choice rather than as a second-rate approach to helping people change.
- Look for ways to meaningfully combine a research perspective with your practice when leading groups.

Exercises

We encourage you to complete these exercises before you begin leading and then again toward the end of the semester. The comparison will give you a basis for seeing how your attitudes and ideas may evolve with experience.

Attitude Questionnaire on Group Leadership

This inventory does not lend itself to objective scoring. It is meant to assist you in clarifying your own attitudes concerning group leadership matters. Comparing your results with those of your coleader will help you understand each other and may lead to fruitful discussions about working together. Read these statements concerning the role and functions of a group leader. Indicate your position on each statement using the following scale:

1 = strongly agree
2 = slightly agree

3 = slightly disagree
4 = strongly disagree

_____ **1.** It is the leader's job to actively work at shaping group norms.
_____ **2.** Leaders should teach group members how to observe their own group as it unfolds.
_____ **3.** The best way for a leader to function is by becoming a participating member of the group.
_____ **4.** It is generally wise for leaders to reveal their private lives and personal problems in groups they are leading.
_____ **5.** A group leader's primary task is to function as a technical expert.
_____ **6.** It is extremely important for good leaders to have a definite theoretical framework that determines how they function in a group.
_____ **7.** A group leader's function is to draw people out and make sure that silent members participate.
_____ **8.** Group leaders influence group members more through modeling than through the techniques they employ.
_____ **9.** It is generally best for the leader to give some responsibility to the members but also to retain some.
_____ **10.** A major task of a leader is to keep the group focused on the here and now.
_____ **11.** It is unwise to allow members to discuss the past or to discuss events that occurred outside the group.
_____ **12.** It is best to give most of the responsibility for determining the direction of the group to the members.
_____ **13.** It is best for leaders to limit their self-disclosures to matters that have to do with what is going on in the group.
_____ **14.** If group leaders are basically open and disclose themselves, transference by members will not occur.
_____ **15.** A leader who experiences countertransference is not competent to lead groups.
_____ **16.** Group leaders can be expected to develop a personalized theory of leadership based on ideas drawn from many sources.
_____ **17.** To be effective, group leaders need to recognize their reasons for wanting to be leaders.
_____ **18.** Part of the task of group leaders is to determine specific behavioral goals for the participants.
_____ **19.** A leader's theoretical model has little impact on the way people actually interact in a group.
_____ **20.** If group leaders have mastered certain skills and techniques, it is not essential for them to operate from a theoretical framework.
_____ **21.** Leaders who possess personal power generally dominate the group and intimidate the members through this power.
_____ **22.** There is not much place for a sense of humor in conducting groups because group work is serious business.
_____ **23.** Group leaders should not expect the participants to do anything that they, as leaders, are not willing to do.
_____ **24.** Group leaders have the responsibility for keeping written documentation summarizing group sessions.

_____ **25.** For coleaders to work effectively with each other, it is essential that they share the same style of leadership.

_____ **26.** In selecting a coleader, it is a good idea to consider similarity of values, philosophy of life, and life experiences.

_____ **27.** If coleaders do not respect and trust each other, there is the potential for negative outcomes in the group.

_____ **28.** It is best that those who colead a group be roughly equal in skills, experiences, and status.

_____ **29.** Coleaders should never openly disagree with each other during a session, for this may lead to a division within the group.

_____ **30.** The group is bound to be affected by the type of modeling that the coleaders provide.

After you have completed this self-inventory, we suggest that your class break into small groups to discuss the items. This questionnaire provides a basis for discussion in meetings with coleaders.

Questions for Discussion

1. What knowledge and group leadership skills do you already possess?
2. What specific skills do you most need to acquire or improve? What are some ways you can work on these skills?
3. To what extent might the fear of making mistakes prevent you from being as creative as you could be in facilitating a group?
4. When you think of designing and leading groups, what major potential problems do you anticipate you will encounter? How might you deal with this challenge?
5. In leading a group characterized by many forms of diversity, what would be your main challenges? To what degree are you confident of your ability to conduct groups characterized by culturally diverse membership?
6. What specific knowledge and skills do you most need to acquire to enhance your effectiveness when working with group members who are culturally different from you? What are a few steps you can take to become a culturally skilled group leader?
7. What are some advantages and disadvantages of coleadership of a group, both for the members and for the coleaders?
8. In choosing a coleader, what specific qualities of that person would be most important to you?
9. How can developing a research orientation enhance your work as a group practitioner?
10. What are some ways to combine research and practice in group work?

MindTap for Counseling

Additional resources can be found on CengageBrain.com and by logging into the MindTap course created by your professor. There you will find a variety of study tools and useful resources that include quizzes, videos, interactive exercises, and more.

CHAPTER 3

Ethical and Legal Issues in Group Counseling

CHAPTER LEARNING OBJECTIVES

1. Identify the major ethical issues pertaining to group membership
2. Define and explore the role of informed consent in a group
3. Identify and discuss some psychological risks of group participation
4. Define and explore the role of confidentiality in a group
5. Explain the role of a leader's values in group work
6. Discuss ways to ethically deal with a conflict of values
7. Explore ethical issues addressing diversity in groups
8. Explain the social justice approach to group work
9. Identify ethical issues pertaining to sexual orientation in groups
10. Describe some ethical issues in using group techniques
11. Identify key aspects of competence and training in group work
12. Identify ethical and culturally relevant strategies for designing and facilitating groups (CACREP, 2016, Standard G)
13. Describe some ways students can get direct experience by participating as members in a small group activity (CACREP, 2016, Standard H)
14. Discuss key ethical issues in training group counselors
15. Explain legal liability and malpractice
16. List legal safeguards to practicing group work

You have been coleading a group for college students for 10 weeks. During one of the sessions you realize that one of the group members works with a friend of yours. Your friend is getting married, and you learn that both you and the group member have been invited to attend the wedding. What are the key issues you need to be aware of in this situation? In reflecting on what you might do, consider these questions:

- Do you tell the client that you are friends with the same person and that you too are invited to the wedding?
- Do you say anything to your friend who has invited you and your client? If so, what do you say? If not, what is your reasoning?
- If you go to the wedding, would you consider bringing your partner or a guest?
- Would you be inclined to talk to the group member at the wedding?
- Would you drink alcohol at the reception?
- How would you resolve any ethical conflicts you may have in this scenario?

Introduction

Throughout this chapter we refer to ethical, legal, clinical, and cultural issues. **Ethical issues** pertain to the standards that govern the conduct of professional members. These standards can be found in the ethics codes of the various professional organizations. **Legal issues** define the minimum standards society will tolerate, which are enforced by the rule of law at the local, state, or federal level. For example, there is a legal obligation for mental health professionals to report suspected child abuse. All of the codes of ethics contain a clause stating that practitioners must act in accordance with relevant federal and state statutes and government regulations. It is essential that practitioners be able to identify legal problems as they arise in their work because many of the situations they encounter that involve ethical and professional judgment will also have legal implications (Corey, Corey, Corey, & Callanan, 2015). **Clinical issues** involve using your professional judgment to act in accordance with ethical and legal mandates. For example, when reporting child abuse that involves your client, following the law is not enough. It is essential that you develop the clinical skills necessary to help the client as well. Cultural dynamics often come into play when addressing clinical issues. **Cultural issues** are factors such as a person's ethnic background, gender, sexual orientation, religious affiliation, values, or other differences that affect the way we understand and intervene with clients' problems. Cultural issues must be managed in clinically relevant ways. For example, bartering for services, gift giving, and interacting with group members in a nonprofessional setting may be seen as unethical in one culture but not in another. The ethical guidelines of our profession cannot take into account all cultural differences. You are likely to encounter clinical and cultural issues that raise ethical and legal dilemmas throughout your professional career.

Our aim in this chapter is to highlight the ethical issues of central significance to group workers. Major ethical issues in group counseling that have been consistently identified in the literature since the 1980s include leader values, screening and orientation of group members, informed consent, voluntary and involuntary group membership, group leader preparation and behaviors, confidentiality, multiple relationships in group work, diversity and multiculturalism, record keeping, and billing (Rapin, 2010, 2014).

Groups have unique therapeutic power that can be used to empower clients in their life-changing journeys, but groups also have the potential to do harm to participants. As a group counselor, your skill, style, personal characteristics, and competence in group work are crucial dimensions that contribute to the quality of the outcomes of a group you might lead. Groups designed around ethically and legally sound principles have a far greater chance of being effective than groups designed without such thought and facilitated inadequately.

For those who are preparing to become group leaders, a thorough grounding in ethics is as essential as a solid base of psychological knowledge and skills. Professionals and student-trainees must know the ethical standards of their professional specialization. They must learn to make ethical decisions, a process that can be taught both in group courses and in supervised practicum experiences. Learning to think critically about complex ethical dilemmas produces clinicians who are more clinically competent and culturally sensitive. Teaching students to think ethically, legally, clinically, and culturally is a form of social justice. This inclusive approach to ethical and legal decision making can raise the bar on our profession's effectiveness as we strive for aspirational practice. Being an ethical practitioner involves far more than a basic knowledge of the legal standards of our profession. Practicing ethically demands a high level of consciousness on our part, both personally and professionally.

Practicing ethically demands a high level of consciousness on our part, both personally and professionally.

In studying ethics, students have an opportunity to apply critical thinking to what may appear to be straightforward rules and to broaden the way the profession looks at ethical issues, especially from a cultural point of view. Although we have noticed a trend toward teaching ethics from a rule-based perspective emphasizing right and wrong actions, we believe it is important to encourage students to wrestle with the complexities and the gray areas they will confront in their work. For example, it is overly simplistic to say that multiple relationships are unethical and should be avoided. Instructors find themselves in multiple roles with students as teachers and advisers; counselors working in rural communities may find themselves customers of or members of the same church as their clients. The real world is complex and ever-changing, and counselors will wrestle with many issues that cannot be resolved by following a simple rule. We are not suggesting that you ignore the basic rules and guidelines of the profession; these are a good place to begin your inquiry. But to practice ethically and improve you clinical and cultural effectiveness, you need to develop the skills of looking deeper into ethical issues.

As a group leader, you will need to learn how to apply the established ethics codes of your profession to a range of practical problems. The "Best Practice Guidelines" (ASGW, 2008) contains useful ideas for group workers in planning, conducting, and evaluating their groups, but such ethics codes and practice guidelines typically provide only broad guidelines for responsible practice. Personal integrity is a key asset in becoming an ethical practitioner. Examining your own ethical conduct and intentions in your everyday life as well as in your professional life is a good place to start. Being aware of your personal biases and your decision-making style in challenging situations will help you guard against unethical practices in your group work.

Ethical decision making is a continuous process. Part of the decision-making process involves learning about the available resources you can draw on when you are struggling with an ethical question. Although you are ultimately responsible for making ethical decisions, you do not have to do so in a vacuum. Consult with colleagues, get continued supervision and training during the early stages of your development as a leader, keep up with recent trends, and attend relevant conventions and workshops.

Beginning group leaders are prone to burdening themselves with the expectation that they should always know the "right" thing to do in every possible situation. There is room for several appropriate responses in most situations. We hope you will gradually refine your position on the issues we raise in this chapter, a process that demands a willingness to remain open and to adopt a questioning yet responsible attitude. We do not think these topics can be resolved once and for all; these complex issues take on new dimensions as you gain experience as a group leader.

Ethical Issues in Group Membership

LO1

To begin the discussion of ethics as it pertains to group work, we suggest that you take time to reflect on the questions at the beginning of each section to increase your appreciation for what your members might experience. These questions for self-reflection can assist you in thinking about your position on each of the topics explored.

Informed Consent

LO2

Think back to a time when you were a member of a group or beginning a course in which you were required to share personal information and explore interpersonal dynamics in an open manner. What concerns did you have as a member of a group? What questions did you have about confidentiality? What did you want to know in order to feel safe in making personal disclosures to the group members and leaders?

Informed consent is a process of presenting basic information about a group to potential group participants to assist them in deciding whether to enter the group and how to participate in it. It is sound policy to provide a professional disclosure statement to group members that includes information on a variety of topics pertaining to the nature of the group. This information typically includes therapist qualifications, techniques that are often used in the group, and risks and benefits of participating in the group. It is important to convey information in a timely manner about other topics such as alternatives to group treatment; policies regarding appointments, fees, and insurance; and the nature and limitations of confidentiality in a group. This can be done at a level that is best comprehended by those who are being considered for a group. In addition, informed consent contains information about a client's right to confidentiality as well as limits of confidentiality.

It is a good idea to explain that informed consent is an ongoing process rather than a one-time event. Although it is an ethical and a legal requirement to secure informed consent at the outset of a member's participation in a group, various aspects of the consent process may need to be revisited at different phases of a group. When informed consent is done effectively, it helps promote individual autonomy, engages members in a collaborative process, and reduces the likelihood of exploitation or harm (Barnett, Wise, Johnson-Greene, & Bucky, 2007; Wheeler & Bertram, 2015).

When individuals have adequate information, they are in a position to determine whether they want to join a particular group. Other relevant information pertaining to this issue can be found in Chapter 5 (see "Guidelines for Announcing a Group and Recruiting Group Members"). A more complete discussion of informed consent can be found in Corey, Corey, Corey, and Callanan (2015).

Involuntary Membership

You have been told that you are required to participate in a group. What are your immediate reactions? What information would you expect to receive?

Ideally, participation in a group is voluntary, but this is not always the case. Especially when group participation is mandatory, much effort needs to be directed toward clearly and fully informing members of the nature and goals of the group, procedures that will be used, the rights of members to decline certain activities, the limitations of confidentiality, and ways active participation in the group may affect their life outside the group. On this topic the American Psychological Association (APA, 2010) has the following guideline: "When psychological services are court ordered or otherwise mandated, psychologists inform the individual of the nature of the anticipated services, including whether the services are court ordered or mandated and any limits of confidentiality, before proceeding" (3.10.c).

Leading groups takes considerable skill and knowledge even when the group is composed of participants who are highly motivated and who have chosen to be in the group. Leading groups composed of involuntary members makes the task even more difficult and creates new dynamics to address in the group process. Informed consent involves leaders' making members aware of both their rights and their responsibilities as group participants. Thus, in mandatory groups or in required groups that emphasize self-disclosure and personal exploration, leaders are advised to take special care to inform members of what is involved in being part of the group. If they attend a group but do not participate, members should be informed that this will be documented in their record or clinical file. Group leaders should strive to help involuntary members understand their choices and the consequences of lack of compliance with the treatment program (Rapin, 2014).

Showing involuntary members how they could personally benefit from a group can increase voluntary participation. Sometimes members are reluctant to become involved because of misinformation or stereotyped views about the nature of therapy. They may not trust the group leaders or the process involved.

Many of them have reservations about opening themselves up to others, and they are likely to be concerned about how the information they disclose will be used or possibly abused. A major factor of success in leading a group with involuntary participants involves not allowing negative attitudes of some members to contaminate the entire group experience.

Perceptive leaders deal with the reactions of members openly. Although group leaders may not be able to give members the option of dropping out of the group, leaders can provide the support necessary to enable members to fully come to grips with their fears and resistances without turning the group into a mere gripe session. Group members can be given the freedom to decide how to use the session time. Group leaders can reassure members that it is up to them to decide what personal topics they will discuss and what areas they will keep private. In other words, they should be clearly informed that they have the same rights as the members of any group—with the exception of the right not to attend.

It is critical that leaders not start out with the assumption that a mandatory group will automatically be composed of unmotivated clients, for this belief is bound to have a negative effect on group members. Instead, any initial distrust must be treated with respect as this can be the very material for exploration that leads to increased trust. It is possible for people who attend mandated groups to make significant changes in their lives. A group proposal for those mandated to attend a domestic violence group appears in Chapter 11, along with some therapeutic benefits of such a group.

Freedom to Withdraw From a Group

In a group you are leading, one member suddenly and unannounced gets up and walks out. How would you be affected? What would you say or do? In what ways might you react differently if you were a member of the group rather than the leader?

Adequate preparation and screening can reduce the risk of members leaving a group prematurely. Leaders must be clear about their policies pertaining to attendance, commitment to remaining in a group for a predetermined number of sessions, and leaving a particular session if members do not like what is going on in the group. It is a good policy for a leader to begin the initial session with a discussion of the possible risks involved in leaving the group prematurely. Ideally, both the leader and the member work in a cooperative fashion to determine whether a group experience is productive or counterproductive for each individual. Although members have the right to leave a group, it is important that they inform both the group leader and the members before making their final decision.

Group leaders must intervene if other members use undue pressure to force any member to remain in the group. It is important to consider why members may want to leave a group. Many times the behaviors we see members exhibiting in a group are indicative of how they behave in their daily lives. Some people have difficulty handling conflict or dealing with intense emotions, and these members are likely to talk about leaving the group, or may actually leave. Some participants will be physically in the group but emotionally absent from the process. The reasons for the member's behavior should be explored. If you are too quick to allow a member to quit, you may miss an excellent opportunity for insight and personal growth on the part of that member.

We are not in favor of forcing members to remain in a group regardless of the circumstances. During the individual screening interview and the orientation session, we take great care to inform prospective members about the nature of the group. In time-limited, closed groups we also stress to participants the importance of a careful commitment to carrying out their responsibilities. We emphasize how important it is for members to verbalize any doubts or concerns they are having about the group rather than keeping these reactions to themselves. Members need to know that the best way to work through interpersonal conflicts or dissatisfactions with a group is often to stay and talk. If members simply stop coming to a group, it is extremely difficult to develop a working level of trust or to establish group cohesion.

Furthermore, if a person leaves without careful consideration and explanation, the consequences could be negative for the members remaining as well as for the departing member. Some members may feel burdened with guilt and may blame themselves for saying or doing "the wrong thing" and contributing to an individual's decision to quit. And the person who leaves may have unexpressed and unresolved feelings that could have been worked through with some discussion. With a commitment to discuss the factors related to leaving, there is an opportunity for everyone concerned to express and explore unfinished business.

Occasionally unforeseen circumstances such as a family emergency may result in a member having to leave a group suddenly, either for a time or permanently. If the member is unable to explain this to the group and does not contact the leader, the leader could take the initiative and contact the person to inquire about his or her absence. Taking such steps is useful not just for the group member who must leave but also to ease the minds of the remaining members who would be wondering why the member is no longer a part of the group.

Psychological Risks for Members

LO3

What particular risks would concern you as a member of a group? As a group leader, what risks might you explore with potential members during a screening interview?

The forces at work in a therapeutic group are powerful. They can be constructive, bringing about positive change, but their unleashing always entails some risk. It is unrealistic to expect that a group will not involve risk, yet it is the ethical responsibility of the group leader to ensure that prospective group members are aware of the potential risks and to take every precaution against them and to consider ways of reducing potential risks.

The American Counseling Association (ACA, 2014) ethical standard specifies: "In a group setting, counselors take reasonable precautions to protect clients from physical, emotional, or psychological trauma" (A.9.b). This includes discussing the impact of potential life changes and helping group members explore their readiness to deal with such changes. A minimal expectation is that group leaders discuss with members the advantages and disadvantages of a given group, that they prepare the members to deal with any problems that might grow out of the group experience, and that they be alert to the fears and reservations members might have but are not expressing. Members who come from backgrounds in which conflict was harmful and abusive may find healing by learning new ways to resolve difficulties with others. They also may gain a sense of confidence in their own ability to cope with a wide range of emotions.

Group leaders must have a broad and deep understanding of the forces that operate in groups and how to mobilize those forces in an ethical fashion. Unless leaders exert caution, members not only may miss the benefits of a group but also could be psychologically harmed by it. Ways of reducing these risks include knowing members' limits, respecting their requests, developing an invitational style as opposed to a pushy or dictatorial style, avoiding assaultive verbal confrontations, describing behavior rather than making judgments, and presenting hunches in a tentative way rather than forcing interpretations on members. These risks should be discussed with the participants during the initial session. For example, a leader of a group for women who have been survivors of incest might say, "As you begin to uncover painful memories of your childhood and the abuse that took place, you may feel more depressed and anxious for a time than before you entered this group. It is very important to talk about these feelings in the group, especially if you have thoughts about quitting." Group leaders could also help members explore the concerns they have about transferring what they are learning in the group to their everyday lives.

After an intense group experience, participants may be inclined to make rash decisions that affect not only their own lives but also the lives of members of their families. For example, a woman who has been married for 20 years and who becomes aware of her extreme alienation from her husband may leave the group with a resolve to get a divorce. The group leader could caution her against making decisions too soon after an intense group session. If this woman has changed in the group, she may be able to relate to her husband differently; if she acts too soon, she may not give this behavioral change a chance to happen. It is not the leader's responsibility to stand in the way of members' decisions, but the leader is responsible for cautioning members against acting prematurely without carefully considering potential consequences. It is also a good practice to caution members who have done significant cathartic work to refrain from leaving a session and saying in person everything they may have symbolically said to a significant other in a therapeutic context. The group leader can assist members in determining what they most want to communicate and also in finding ways to express their thoughts and feelings in a manner that shows concern and is most likely to lead to a successful encounter.

Sometimes members imagine concerns of their own about the group experience and are very fearful. For example, they may believe that if they allow themselves to feel their pain they will sink into a deep depression and won't be able to recover. Some are convinced that if they give up their self-control they will not be able to function. Others are frightened of letting people know them because they expect they will be rejected. Such fears should be explored early so members can determine how realistic they are and how they can best deal with these fears in the group. The leader should stress that group members have the right to decide for themselves what to explore and how far to go. Leaders need to be alert to group pressure and block any attempts by members to get others to do something they choose not to do.

A somewhat different risk involved in group work is the reality that members can misuse the purpose of a group. For example, when I (Cindy) was facilitating an eating disorder group in college, I noticed that the members were learning self-destructive behaviors from each other by sharing tips regarding ways to burn calories and keep weight off. This kind of misuse is not common, but it calls attention to the need for screening group members to determine whether they would be better served by individual counseling rather than working in a group setting.

We expand our treatment of these issues in Chapter 6, providing guidelines to help participants get the maximum benefit from a group experience. For now, let's look briefly at some possible risks of therapeutic groups, a topic that can be addressed with participants as part of informed consent.

1. *Misuse of power* is a significant risk factor. Group leaders can do a great deal toward preventing damaging group experiences. Group leaders need to be aware of both the overt and subtle ways in which they utilize their power. For example, a leader's gender or cultural identity is likely to have an effect on how much power group members ascribe to the leader. Group therapists have legitimate power by virtue of their leadership expertise and specialized knowledge and skills. Ideally, group leaders will use their power to empower the members of their groups by helping them to discover their inner resources and capacities. This power is used to the members' good, and it can be shared. This is what collaborative relationships are about.
2. *Self-disclosure* is sometimes misused by group members. The group norm has sometimes been misunderstood to mean the more disclosure that takes place, the better. But privacy can be violated by indiscriminately sharing one's personal life. Self-disclosure is an essential aspect of any working group, but it is a means to the end of fuller self-understanding and should not be promoted in its own right. It is important to keep in mind prohibitions against self-disclosure within certain ethnic and cultural groups. Some members may have been harmed by past self-disclosure, and others may be hesitant to make any personal disclosures. Group members may avoid participating by remaining quiet and allowing other members to talk and do work.
3. *Maintaining confidentiality* is a potential risk in every group. Some of the disclosures made during a session may not remain in the group. Group leaders need to continually emphasize the importance of maintaining confidentiality. Even when they do so, however, the possibility remains that some members will talk inappropriately about what was discussed in the group.
4. *Scapegoating* may occur. Occasionally an individual member may be singled out as the scapegoat of the group. Other group members may "gang up" on this person, making the member the focus of hostile and negative confrontation. Clearly, the group leader should take firm steps to eliminate this behavior and explore what is happening within the group. Generally, it is a good practice for the leader to explore what is going on with the person doing the scapegoating before focusing on the person being scapegoated.
5. *Confrontation*, a valuable and powerful tool in any group, can be misused, especially when it is done in a destructive manner. Intrusive interventions, overly confrontive leader tactics, and pushing members beyond their limits

often produce negative outcomes. Here, again, leaders (and members as well) must be on guard against behavior that can pose serious psychological risks for group participants. To lessen the risks of nonconstructive confrontation, leaders can model the type of confrontation that focuses on specific behaviors and avoids judgments of members. This type of confrontation is a direct challenge that comes from a place of support and empathy.

It is not realistic to expect that all personal risks can be eliminated, and to imply that they can be is to mislead prospective members. But it is essential that members be made aware of the major risks, that they have an opportunity to discuss their willingness and ability to deal with them, and that as many safeguards as possible be built into the structure of the group.

One way to minimize psychological risks in groups is to use a contract, in which the leader specifies his or her responsibilities and the members specify their commitment by stating what they are willing to explore and do in the group. A contract can reduce the chances that members will be exploited or will leave the group feeling that they have had a negative experience.

LO4

Confidentiality

You are a member of a group, and the group leader tells you that "anything said in this group stays in here." Does this satisfy any potential concern you may have regarding confidentiality?

One of the keystone conditions for effective group work is confidentiality. It is especially important because in leading a group you must not only keep the confidences of members but also get the members to keep one another's confidences. You must be concerned with your own ability to act ethically, but you also must respond to ethical dilemmas that may arise, sometimes outside of your control, between group members. In group therapy it may not be possible to prevent some members from disclosing personal information about others in the group. In a group, you have less control over how sessions progress, the nature and depth of disclosures, and what happens between sessions, particularly with respect to maintaining confidentiality (Lasky & Riva, 2006).

An ethical breach might involve a member disclosing personal information or details about one's personal history to someone not in the group. An example of a more subtle breach of confidentiality can occur when members come from a group of individuals that know each other from work or school. One member might say to another group member in front of colleagues or peers that she will see him at group. This casual breach of confidentiality may be unintended, yet it breaks the confidentiality of a member who may not want others to know he or she is in group counseling.

Wheeler and Bertram (2015) point out that the risk of breach of confidentiality is heightened when members of a counseling group engage in social media. Group counselors should address the parameters of online behavior through informed consent and are advised to establish ground rules whereby members agree not to post pictures, comments, or any type of confidential information about other members online. Developing rules that address the use of online discussion outside of the group should be part of the informed consent process and part of the discussion about group norms governing the group. One way for members to share their experience with others outside the group is for them to talk about their own experience, reactions, and insights without describing other members or mentioning others in the group by name. Members can be educated to talk about themselves rather than tell stories about other group members. For example, a member might say, "One thing I noticed about myself during group is that I tend to wait for the group leader to call on me rather than taking responsibility for bringing myself into the group." Another member might say, "I realized how many of us struggle with similar conflicts."

Educating Members About Confidentiality

It is a good practice for leaders to remind participants from time to time of the tendency to inadvertently reveal confidences in subtle ways. Educating members about how confidentiality can be unintentionally breached is critical. Group leaders are responsible for educating members about the importance and advantages of keeping information pertaining to the group private (Rapin, 2014). If confidentiality seems to be a matter of concern, the subject should be discussed fully in a group session. For example, a member who discloses personal information such as having an affair may be worried about having shared this information with others. The group leader can remind members about confidentiality as a way of reassuring the member who is disclosing.

A review of the literature on confidentiality in groups showed a lack of clear understanding of the concept of confidentiality and its limits on the part of both group members and leaders. A full discussion of confidentiality is of paramount importance not only because it respects the rights of group members to make autonomous choices, but also because it can influence the overall group experience. Group leaders do well to express the importance of maintaining confidentiality, have members sign contracts agreeing to it, and even impose some form of sanction on those who break it. It is good practice to have a policy statement on confidentiality and to revisit the topic whenever it is appropriate to do so.

Modeling the importance of maintaining confidentiality is crucial in setting norms for members to follow. If group members sense that the leader takes confidentiality seriously, there is a greater likelihood that they will also be concerned about the matter. Even though it is the leader's role to educate members about confidentiality and to monitor safeguarding of disclosures, the members also have a responsibility in respecting and safeguarding what others share in the group. On this topic, the American School Counselor Association (ASCA, 2010) has this standard: "Professional school counselors establish clear expectations in the group setting, and clearly state that confidentiality in group counseling cannot be guaranteed" (A.6.c).

Ethical and Legal Dimensions of Confidentiality

In working with groups, the rights to confidentiality of all the members must be safeguarded. Leaders have a responsibility to discuss any breaches with the group and to take action if a member breaks confidentiality. The American Counseling

Association's *Code of Ethics* (ACA, 2014) makes this statement regarding confidentiality: "In group work, counselors clearly explain the importance and parameters of confidentiality for the specific group" (B.4.a).

Group counselors have an ethical and legal responsibility to inform group members of the potential consequences of breaching confidentiality. The leader should explain that legal privilege (confidentiality) does not apply to group treatment, unless provided by state statute (ASGW, 2008). In groups in institutions, agencies, and schools, where members know and have frequent contact with one another and with one another's associates outside of the group, confidentiality becomes especially critical and also more difficult to maintain. In an adolescent group in a high school, for example, great care must be exerted to ensure that whatever is discussed in the sessions is not taken out of the group. Group leaders must avoid talking to parents and teachers without the appropriate permission of the participants. If some members talk about things that happened in the group, the group process will come to a halt. People are not going to reveal facts about their personal lives unless they feel quite sure they can trust both the leader and the members to respect their confidences.

We expect that members will want to talk about their group experiences with significant people in their lives. We caution them, however, about breaking others' confidences in the process. We tell them to be careful not to mention others who were in the group or to talk about what others said and did. Generally, members do not violate confidentiality when they talk about *what* they learned in group sessions. But they are likely to breach confidentiality when they talk about *how* they acquired insights or how they interacted in a group. For example, Gerd becomes aware in a session that he invites women to take care of him, only to resent them for treating him like a child. He may want to say to his wife, "I realize I often resent you for the very thing I expect you to do." This is acceptable disclosure, but describing the group exercise involving several women in the group that led him to this insight could break confidentiality guidelines.

Leaders may be tested by some members of the group. For instance, a counselor may tell group participants in a juvenile correctional institution that whatever is discussed will remain in the group. The youths may not believe this and may in many subtle ways test the leader to discover whether in fact he or she will keep this promise. Group leaders must not promise to keep within the group material they may be required to disclose.

Limitations to confidentiality should be outlined in the informed consent process, and in mandatory groups counselors should inform members of any reporting procedures required of them. Group practitioners should also mention to members any documentation or record-keeping procedures that they may be required to keep that affect confidentiality. The ACA (2014) guideline with respect to confidentiality is as follows: "Counselors protect the confidential information of prospective and current clients. Counselors disclose information only with appropriate consent or with sound legal or ethical justification" (B.1.c).

In general, licensed psychologists, psychiatrists, licensed clinical social workers, licensed marriage and family therapists and, in many states, licensed professional counselors are legally entitled to privileged communication. The concept of

privileged communication means that these professionals cannot break the confidence of clients unless (1) in their judgment, the clients are likely to do serious harm to themselves, others, and/or physical property; (2) abuse of children or the elderly is suspected; (3) they are ordered by a court to provide information; (4) they are supervisees in a supervisory relationship; or (5) the clients give specific written permission. However, when these professionals are conducting groups, in most states this legal privilege does not apply. The American Group Psychotherapy Association (AGPA, 2002) states: "The group therapist is knowledgeable about the limits of privileged communication as they apply to group therapy and informs group members of those limits" (2.2). Group counselors need to know whether their state protects privileged communication in groups. If privilege is not protected, the group leader needs to explain this special circumstance to group members. The absence of privileged communication does not remove the ethical responsibility to maintain confidentiality (Wheeler & Bertram, 2015). Although group leaders are themselves ethically and legally bound to maintain confidentiality, a group member who violates another member's confidences faces no legal consequences (Lasky & Riva, 2006).

Learning in Action

Google Your Classmate

As counselors we are held to a set of professional standards not only within our professional role but also outside of our role as helpers. Whether fair or not, counselors are often looked upon as role models. How we behave in private arenas can have a direct impact on how we (and our profession) are perceived by others.

Choose the name of a classmate in a random drawing, and conduct a Google search on that person. Look for this person on Facebook, Twitter, and other social media sites. If this person were your counselor, what did you see or read that could influence you positively or negatively? Tell the person what you found, and ask whether he or she would be comfortable having a potential client or group member see this information. Have the same discussion with the person who did a search on you. Do you think you might change your privacy settings or reconsider your postings on social media sites as a result of what you learned from this activity?

Multicultural Dimensions of Confidentiality

Confidentiality must be viewed in a cultural context: "Counselors maintain awareness and sensitivity regarding cultural meanings of confidentiality and privacy. Counselors respect differing views toward disclosure of information. Counselors hold ongoing discussions with clients as to how, when, and with whom information is to be shared" (ACA, 2014, B.1.a). In *Multicultural and Social Justice Competence Principles for Group Workers*, the ASGW (2012) addresses broad areas of race, ethnicity, socioeconomic class, age, gender, sexual orientation, religion, and spirituality. In *Multicultural and Social Justice Counseling Competencies*, the Association for Multicultural Counseling and Development (AMCD, 2015) highlights taking action to promote social justice and emphasizes teaching clients how to advocate for themselves.

Culture may affect a member's views on confidentiality in the following ways:

- Some cultures consider therapy to be shameful and only for mentally ill people. To minimize any risks of breaking confidentiality, avoid leaving phone messages or sending mail to members' home addresses if they live with family members.
- Some group members may not have legal status or residency and may be guarded about providing personal information.
- Members who are seeking asylum or have refugee status may have significant trust issues and may give false personal information to protect themselves and their families.
- Some cultures promote sharing of all personal information with their families, and members could feel pressured to share details with their family members.
- Language barriers or reading difficulties may result in a member not fully understanding the importance of confidentiality and the consequences of breaches. Leaders should be sure that all members have fully comprehended this and other aspects of informed consent.

Confidentiality of Minors in Groups

A particularly delicate problem is safeguarding the confidentiality of minors in groups. Do parents have a right to information that is disclosed by their children in a group? The answer to that question depends on whether we are looking at it from a legal, ethical, or clinical viewpoint. State laws differ regarding counseling minors. It is important for group workers to be aware of the laws related to working with minors in the state in which they are practicing as well as local policies for those working in a school setting. Circumstances in which a minor may seek professional help without parental consent, defining an emancipated minor, or the rights of parents (or legal guardians) to have access to the records regarding the professional help received by their minor child vary according to state statutes.

A recent California statute allows minors who are 12 years or older to receive counseling if the practitioner determines that the minor is mature enough to participate intelligently in outpatient treatment or mental health counseling. The statute does require parental (or guardian) involvement in the treatment of the minor, unless the therapist finds, after consulting with the minor, that this involvement would be inappropriate under the circumstances. Therapists have the responsibility for noting in the client's records whether they attempted to contact the minor's parent or guardian, and whether this attempt was successful or unsuccessful, or why it was deemed inappropriate to make this contact. This law protects the right to seek treatment of certain populations of youth, such as young people from immigrant families, homeless youth, people who are gay, and young people from cultural backgrounds that do not condone receiving mental health services (Leslie, 2010).

Before any minor joins a group, best practice requires school counselors to notify parents or guardians that their children are participating (ASCA, 2010).

Obtaining written permission from parents or guardians, even when this is not a legal requirement, is a good policy, especially for school counselors. Such a statement might include a brief description of the purpose of the group, the importance of confidentiality as a prerequisite to accomplishing these purposes, and the therapist's intention not to violate any confidences. Although it may be useful to give parents/guardians information about their child, this can be done without violating confidences. Parents/guardians may inquire about what their child has discussed in a group, and it is the responsibility of the group leader to inform them in advance of the importance of confidentiality. Parents/guardians can be told about the purpose of the group, and they can be given some feedback concerning their child, but care must be taken not to reveal specific things the child mentioned. One way to provide feedback to parents or guardians is through a session involving one or both parents/guardians, the child, and the group leader. Counselors may provide a general description or purpose for the group session and include suggestions for further discussion questions and topics between parents/guardians and the child. This is particularly useful for social skills groups and other psychoeducational groups with children and adolescents.

Group leaders have a responsibility in groups that involve children and adolescents to take measures to increase the chances that confidentiality will be kept. It is useful to teach minors, using a vocabulary that they are capable of understanding, about the nature, purposes, and limitations of confidentiality. It is helpful to inform and discuss with minors in advance their concerns about confidentiality and how it will be maintained, especially in a school setting. It is critical to teach minors about the limits of confidentiality. Such practices can strengthen the child's trust in the group counselor. It is a good idea for leaders to encourage members to initiate discussions on confidentiality whenever this becomes an issue for them.

It is important to work cooperatively with parents and legal guardians as well as to enlist the trust of the young people. Imagine you are leading a group for teens, and the grandparents of one of your members comes to see you after school and insist on knowing what their grandchild is talking about in group sessions.

- What are your initial concerns when thinking about how you would respond to the grandparents?
- What legal and ethical concerns or obligations do you have?
- What do you need to consider in terms of the relationship you have with the teenager as well as with the grandparents?
- Will the cultural background of the grandparents and the teen influence your response in any way?

A group counselor working with children may be expected to disclose some information to parents if they insist on it, or a leader of a group of parolees may be required to reveal to the members' parole officer any information acquired in the group concerning certain criminal offenses. It is a good policy for leaders to let members know when they may be required to testify against them in court.

Summary Guidelines Regarding Confidentiality

Group leaders would do well to consider certain ramifications of confidentiality. Here are some summary guidelines concerning confidentiality in groups:

- Confidentiality is crucial to the success of a group, but the leader can do little to guarantee that the policy on confidentiality will be respected by all members. Leaders can only ensure confidentiality on their part, not on the part of others in the group.
- Group leaders must become familiar with the local and state laws that will have an effect on their practice. This is especially true in cases involving child molestation, neglect or abuse of older people and children, or incest.
- Group leaders describe at the outset the roles and responsibilities of all parties and the limits of confidentiality (APA, 2010, Standard 10.03).
- Members should be told about the limits of confidentiality so they can determine when, what, and how much personal information they will reveal in group sessions.
- Leaders have the responsibility of helping members, as well as parents or guardians of minors, understand the importance of maintaining confidentiality and for protecting the personal disclosures of other members.
- It is a wise policy to ask participants to sign a contract in which they agree not to discuss or write about what transpires in the sessions or talk about who was present.

It is imperative that the group leader emphasizes at various stages of the group's evolution the importance of maintaining confidentiality. This issue needs to be introduced during the individual screening interview, and it should be clarified at the initial group sessions. At appropriate times during the course of the group, the leader can remind the members not to discuss identities or specific situations. If at any time any member gives indications that confidentiality is not being respected, the leader has the responsibility of exploring this matter with the group as soon as possible.

LO5

The Role of the Leader's Values in the Group

As a group leader, what values of group members would you be inclined to challenge, even if members made it clear that they did not want to modify such values? How would you react if someone questions your values?

We can increase our effectiveness by becoming aware of the values we hold and the subtle and direct ways we might influence group members. We are better able to help clients discover what is right for them if we can appreciate their worldview and work to understand their value system. We may hold a very different set of values, but our ethical obligation is to assist group members in meeting therapeutic goals consistent with *their* worldview and values, not our own. The focus of group process is on the client. Our clients, not us, live with the consequences of the changes they make in a group. If members acknowledge that what they are doing is not enabling them to get what they want from life, then a group context is an ideal place for them to develop new ways of behaving.

Ethical Aspects of Working With Values

The ACA's (2014) *Code of Ethics* reminds us to be aware of our values: "Counselors are aware of—and avoid imposing—their own values, attitudes, beliefs, and behaviors. Counselors respect the diversity of clients, trainees, and research participants and seek training in areas in which they are at risk of imposing their values onto their clients, especially when the counselor's values are inconsistent with the client's goals or are discriminatory in nature" (A.4.b). Members often bring a number of value-laden issues to a group: religion, spirituality, sexual orientation, abortion, divorce, and family problems. The purpose of the group is to help members clarify their beliefs and examine options that are most congruent with their own value system. Group counseling is not a forum in which leaders impose their value perspectives on members, nor is it a forum for any of the members to impose their values on others.

Values are often conveyed in a subtle way, even without conscious awareness. For instance, you may be firmly convinced that the following values are universal and good for us all: autonomy, freedom to make one's own choice, equality in relationships, and independence. But some group members are likely to adhere to a different set of universal values: interdependence, cooperation, loyalty to family, duty and obligation to parents, and putting the welfare of the family above self-interests. If you assume these members would be far better off by changing their values, you are likely to do them a disservice. Although you may not directly impose your values on them, your interventions could be aimed at getting them to do what you think is best for them. For example, assume that you hold a value that women should be primarily responsible for child care. You have a female client who expresses guilt over not being with her children more because of work. You might encourage her to work less or to stay home to alleviate her guilt. Because of your own biases, you might miss having her explore further the origin and meaning of her guilt.

Dealing With Conflicts of Values

When you find yourself struggling with an ethical dilemma over a values conflict, the best course to follow is to seek consultation in working through the situation so the appropriate standard of care is provided (Kocet & Herlihy, 2014). If group leaders disclose their personal values, easily influenced and dependent members may want to please the leader at all costs and hence assume the leader's values automatically. If you are having difficulty maintaining objectivity regarding a certain value, consider this your problem rather than the client's problem. Supervision or personal counseling can help you to understand why your personal values are entering into your professional work in an inappropriate way. At times you may be faced with ethical issues over sharp differences between your own values and certain values of some members of your group. For example, members from some cultural groups may use physical punishment to ensure obedience and conformity of their children to certain cultural values. It may be challenging for you to acknowledge their views of punishment as normative in their culture, or you may want to intervene by encouraging more positive parenting practices.

Leaders must be clear about their own values and remain objective when working with values that are different from their own. We must learn to separate our personal values from the counseling process to the best of our ability. Kocet and Herlihy (2014) describe the process of intentionally setting aside our personal values to provide ethical and appropriate counseling as **ethical bracketing**. We need to take into consideration the ways we may influence our clients, either intentionally or unintentionally. Francis and Dugger (2014) emphasize the need for counselors to monitor the various ways they may communicate their values to clients "and be aware of how the power differential that exists within each counseling relationship may result in the imposition of their values" (p. 132). Take a moment to consider the ethical issues and values that you might find particularly challenging to "bracket" in your work with group members. How might these personal conflicts leak into your professional work, and how might you best safeguard against that happening?

Consider this scenario. A young woman is struggling with deciding whether to stay in college or drop out to get married. She tells the group that her family holds a traditional view of women and that in their culture it is more important for her to be married than to be educated. She feels ambivalent because she is enjoying her education, yet she does not want her family to be disappointed in her. The values you and other group members hold will influence how you relate to and respond to her; however, the group should not be used to persuade her to do what you (or they) think she should do. Your own values might favor staying in college at all costs, or they might favor dropping out to make her family happy. The key point is that it is not your role as leader to make this woman's decision for her, even if she asks you to do so. Your role is to provide a context in which she can examine her feelings, values, and behaviors and eventually arrive at a decision that she will be able to live with. The challenge is to support this client without disrespecting her family or cultural values.

Another factor to consider involves the tendency of some members to give advice and to push their values on other members. Clashes often occur between group members over the matter of values. When this occurs, it is the responsibility of the group leader to intervene so that members cannot impose their values on others in the group.

LO7

The Ethical Imperative of Addressing Diversity in Group Counseling

Debiak (2007) contends that attending to diversity in group psychotherapy is basic to competent group practice: "As the majority of those in the mental health professions have recognized their embeddedness in a heterosexual, White, middle-class worldview, the importance of multicultural competence in clinical work has emerged as an ethical imperative" (p. 10). Attending to and addressing diversity is both an ethical mandate and a route to more effective group work.

Values and Working With Diversity

The values leaders bring to the group process must consciously acknowledge the reality of human diversity in our society. If leaders ignore some basic differences in people, they can hardly be doing what is in the best interests of the group members. ASGW (2008) guidelines require that leaders become aware of the multicultural context in group work, as can be seen in this recommendation regarding group practice:

> Group workers practice with broad sensitivity to client differences including but not limited to ethnic, gender, religious, sexual, psychological maturity, economic class, family history, physical characteristics or limitations, and geographic location. Group workers continuously seek information regarding the cultural issues of the diverse population with whom they are working both by interaction with participants and from using outside resources. (B.8)

Some of the *group norms* generally associated with group participation may not be congruent with the *cultural norms* and values of some clients. One person's sharing may look very different from another's based on his or her cultural upbringing and contextual factors. It is not necessary that everyone participate in the same manner within the same value system. It is essential that leaders provide an environment in which the members believe they are benefiting by participation in the group and that their learning is applicable to their everyday living.

Some group norms that we address in Chapter 6 include staying in the here and now, expressing feelings, asking for what one wants, being direct and honest, sharing personal problems with others, making oneself known to others, being willing to take risks, improving interpersonal communication, giving personal feedback to others, learning to take the initiative in talking, dealing directly with conflict, being willing to challenge others, and making decisions for oneself. Some individuals might have difficulty being direct because their culture values an indirect style of communication. Some members may experience difficulty in asking for time in the group, largely because they have learned from their culture that to do so is rude, insensitive, and self-oriented. Rather than telling these members to speak up or to rely on them to initiate self-disclosure, it may be helpful to ask them to consider sharing at least one reaction they had as they listened to a particular member speak. By providing some structure, you can encourage members to express themselves in a less threatening way. In cultures that place emphasis on respecting power and status, a person is more likely to participate when asked to do so in a specific rather than a general manner.

Some members will not be comfortable making decisions for themselves without considering their extended family. Although some group interventions are designed to assist members in more freely expressing their feelings, certain members could find this offensive. Because of their cultural conditioning, they are likely to be very slow to express emotions openly or to talking freely about problems within their family. They may have been taught that it is good to withhold their feelings and that it is improper to display emotional reactions publicly.

One group member we worked with said that the way of sharing in the group felt unrealistic to her. She remarked that if she were to speak this way in her country of origin, she would be shunned by her own people. Another group member expressed frustration with the pressure from group members and leaders to speak up. She commented to the group that in order for others to understand her words, they must first understand her silence. This was a powerful communication to the group. By respecting her reasons for being silent, members were able to connect with her and to learn more about the value she placed on silence both in her culture and in her participation in the group. Exploration of cultural differences does not always end in resolution of those differences. However, if these subtle and more obvious cultural factors go unnoticed or are ignored by leaders, it can negatively influence the participation of those members. In addition, it means we are not practicing the cultural competencies we are required to have to guide our work.

Cultural diversity affects the issues that members bring to a group and the ways in which they might be either ready or reluctant to explore these issues. As a group counselor, it is of paramount importance that you sensitize yourself to the clues members often give indicating that they would like to talk about some aspect of how their culture is affecting their participation in the group. You need to determine with group members what particular behaviors they are interested in changing. Even if you prize being direct and assertive, it is not your place to insist that members embrace your view of desirable behaviors. Leaders need to work with members to help them identify what they hope to get from the group.

Ethics and Standards of Preparation and Practice

The ethics codes of most of the professional organizations now emphasize the practitioner's responsibility to have a general understanding of the cultural values of his or her clients, so interventions are congruent with their worldviews. The guidelines for competence in diversity issues in group practice have been drawn from a variety of professional associations, including the ACA (2014), the ASGW (2012), and the AMCD (2015). Refer again to the awareness, knowledge, and skills competencies associated with becoming a culturally skilled group counselor that were discussed in Chapter 1. In working with groups characterized by diversity, counselors need to be aware of the assumptions they make about people based on factors such as race, ethnicity, or sexual orientation. It is essential that the goals and processes of the group match the cultural values of the group members. Group workers are challenged to monitor any tendencies to treat people on the basis of stereotypes. To be able to do this, group leaders need to first become aware of their biases based on age, disability, ethnicity, gender, race, religion, social status, and sexual orientation. The best way to examine our own biases is to engage in experiential exercises and other meaningful encounters that require critical thinking and self-examination. For most people, this journey of self-discovery happens most profoundly in relationship with others, especially those who differ from us in a variety of ways. It is difficult to uproot our own biases (and other "isms") if we continue to talk mainly with people who think, feel, and live as we do.

LO8

Social Justice Approach to Group Counseling

The concept of **social justice** "is based on the idea that society gives individuals and groups fair treatment and an equal share of benefits, resources, and opportunities" (Chung & Bemak, 2012, p. 26). As a microcosm of society, groups provide a context for addressing issues of power, privilege, discrimination, and oppression. The *Ethical Standards for School Counselors* (ASCA, 2010) offers the following guideline regarding the social justice mandate: "Professional school counselors monitor and expand personal multicultural and social justice advocacy awareness, knowledge and skills. School counselors strive for exemplary cultural competence by ensuring personal beliefs or values are not imposed on students or other stakeholders" (E.2.a).

As a microcosm of society, groups provide a context for addressing issues of power, privilege, discrimination, and oppression.

Group work often provides the potential to further a social justice agenda. MacNair-Semands (2007) claims that group workers need to search for innovative ways of expanding their competence in addressing social justice issues—such as unfair treatment or inequities that result from racism, sexism, socioeconomics, sexual orientation, ableism, and other forms of "isms" that affect the quality of life—because they emerge regularly in groups. These social inequalities often arise from an intolerance for differences that result in discrimination, oppression, prejudice, and, at times, interpersonal violence. Group leaders have an opportunity to transform the group experience and work toward healing rather than perpetuating these harmful interactions. Leaders can assist group members in expanding their perspectives to understand nuances in the interactions of culturally diverse members.

Many who participate in groups have been discriminated against and oppressed, and because of this they may display healthy suspicions about being involved in a group. By recognizing how these systems may have influenced the psychological health of members, we can ensure that the group experience does not become another force of oppression. Individuals can be encouraged to talk about their pain and the social injustices they have encountered. Power and privilege dynamics operate in a group, and the group is a place where the imbalance of power can be addressed and explored. Those who are in a position of power can perpetuate social injustices, either intentionally or unintentionally. In any group, we may have people with power and those who have been denied power. This can certainly be talked about as these power dynamics emerge in a group.

The main goal is for a group to provide a safe place for members to talk about painful, harmful events and to experience opportunities for healing. Anderson (2007) contends that considerable harm is possible when diversity exists within a group and the leader fails to use a multicultural approach to assessment, diagnosis, and treatment planning. Anderson states, "Multicultural group workers should be keenly aware of differential power, status, and wealth that may result in oppression and victimization or the recapitulation of oppression and victimization" (p. 232).

Anderson (2007) believes multicultural group work may be one of the most powerful therapeutic interventions, and a group can be a force for healing and development. At the same time, a group has the potential to be oppressive: "The ultimate ethical violation of group work is to allow the forces of group process to be an instrument of harm or injury to a client—to be oppressive" (p. 231). Chung and Bemak (2012) underscore the importance of courage: "One cornerstone of doing multicultural social justice work is courage. Courage is the remedy for fear, and fear is ever present in today's world" (p. 266). Singh and Salazar (2010c) believe that group work offers a forum for "courageous conversations" on social justice issues. There are opportunities to address power and privilege dynamics and social injustices as these factors emerge in a group.

Group counselors who base their practice on aspirational ethics will need to involve themselves in opposing all forms of discrimination and oppression and be committed to challenging inherent inequities in social systems. Social justice is "the fair and equitable distribution of power, resources, and obligations in society to all people, regardless of race, gender, ability status, sexual orientation, and religious or spiritual background" (Hage, Mason, & Kim, 2010, p. 103). Social justice issues often surface when people from diverse backgrounds participate in a group. Groups with social justice themes acknowledge and empower people from diverse social identities. These groups also create identity-affirming environments that advocate for the empowerment of marginalized individuals and communities (Hage et al., 2010).

A social justice perspective involves thinking about the therapeutic enterprise and ethics beyond a traditional framework. It calls upon group counselors to recognize and address issues of social privilege and hierarchical power structures both as a part of the group experience and in daily life (Hage et al., 2010). Counseling for social justice requires a paradigm shift. Traditional helping paradigms focus on changing an individual's thoughts, feelings, and behaviors, whereas the social justice model looks beyond the individual to other highly influential factors in the lives of clients (Chung & Bemak, 2012). To be able to translate this paradigm shift into one's practice of group work, it is necessary to acquire a set of social justice and advocacy competencies. The counseling profession "must move beyond the traditional helping paradigm . . . [and be] proactive in advocacy and social change" (p. 42).

Counseling for social justice requires a paradigm shift.

Social justice practice, training, and research are interdependent. Effective training is necessary if group workers hope to understand and address the multiple layers of complexity involved in social justice group work. Hays, Arredondo, Gladding, and Toporek, (2010) discuss ways of integrating social justice in group work. To integrate social justice effectively, it is essential that group workers be mindful about social justice components within a group. Hays and colleagues offer the following recommendations for integrating social justice in group work:

- Group leaders must find new ways of developing groups that will promote equity, access, participation, and harmony.
- Leaders must promote egalitarianism by educating group members about their rights and assisting them in assuming an active role in bringing about social change.

- Leaders have the responsibility to encourage discussion about identity development processes, cultural concerns, and privilege and oppression, and how these factors might affect group process and group members.
- Leaders should focus on how client systems influence group process and outcomes and conduct a cultural assessment of all group members.
- Group leaders can empower the members of their groups by building on the strengths of individual group members and the resources of the group as a whole.

An overarching theme is the centrality of multicultural competence as a basis for doing effective social justice–oriented group work. To deepen the leaders' awareness of social justice as a basic value, it is necessary for supervisors to create a climate that encourages open discussion of social justice topics.

LO9

Special Issues Pertaining to Sexual Orientation

The ethics codes of the ACA, the APA, and the National Association of Social Workers (NASW) clearly state that discrimination on the basis of minority status—be it race, ethnicity, gender, or sexual orientation—is unethical and unacceptable. Included under sexual minority status are people who are lesbian, gay, bisexual, transgender, or are questioning their sexual orientation (Goodrich & Luke, 2015). Working with lesbian, gay, bisexual, transgender, and questioning (LGBTQ) individuals presents a challenge to group counselors who hold more traditional values and must guard against imposing their own values and attitudes on group members. Group leaders have a right to their own values and beliefs, but as counselors it is neither our role nor our right to impose these value judgments or beliefs on our clients. Group members who identify as LGBTQ come to us with a history of victimization and fear of abandonment. As group leaders, we cannot meet them with judgment and possible rejection. We understand that this duty to serve the LGBTQ community and its members may come into direct conflict with some counselors' religious, moral, and ethical standards. As with all cases in which our personal values conflict with our ethical duties, it is essential for clinicians to work with supervisors, colleagues, or through personal counseling, to find ways to separate their personal beliefs from their duty to clients.

Heterosexism can leak out in various ways, ranging from blatantly discriminating to more subtle and covert messages of disapproval. Regardless of the intensity of the offense, the result can be damaging to group members and to your own status as a professional. Some therapists have communicated to clients that they do not approve of their sexual identity and sexual orientation and cannot continue to work with them because of moral or religious beliefs, and countless stories from people who identify as LGBTQ indicate that they have felt judged, ridiculed, embarrassed, and pressured to be less than who they are by mental health practitioners as a result of their sexual identity and sexual orientation. Unless group counselors become conscious of their own biases, heterosexism, and homophobia, they may project their misconceptions and their fears onto those in their groups in subtle and not so subtle ways. It is essential that group practitioners be willing to critically examine their personal prejudices, myths, fears, and stereotypes regarding sexual identity and sexual orientation.

We can understand the difficulty that interns and therapists face with deep value conflicts, but the bottom line is always the same: In therapy it is not about us; a client's needs and welfare come before our own. The relationship is not an equal one, nor is it one in which we as clinicians are required to feel comfortable with our clients' choices. We step into our role as therapist to serve our clients and to help them resolve conflicts, heal, and grow in the ways that are most congruent with their values, not our own. In our opinion, it is not appropriate for group leaders to disclose their values when it comes to topics such as abortion, religion, divorce, and same-sex relationships. We prefer to be invested in the process with our clients rather than being wedded to a specific outcome. In some circumstances it may be appropriate and even facilitative to self-disclose, but we caution leaders to weigh heavily the costs against the possible benefits of making certain disclosures regarding their values. Reflect on the purpose of the disclosure, and ask yourself whether you are more likely to regret making a self-disclosure or not disclosing. If you do not work to keep your values from becoming overt judgments or hidden agendas, you are likely to break the code of ethics and standards guiding our profession. Consultation with a peer or supervisor may help you realize the potential benefits or consequences of self-disclosure.

The American Psychological Association's Division 44 (APA, 2000) has developed a set of guidelines for psychotherapy with lesbian, gay, and bisexual clients. In many respects lesbian, gay, bisexual, and transgender clients share common ground with heterosexual clients in groups, but some ethical concerns increase (Goodrich & Luke, 2015). Group practitioners who work with LGBTQ clients have a responsibility to understand the unique concerns these clients may bring to the group and are expected to develop the knowledge and skills to competently deliver services to them. We need to be willing and able to listen deeply to our clients and to encourage them to help us to understand their unique experience of the world. Being able to do this often involves continuing education, seeking supervision, and being willing to consult.

The Association for Lesbian, Gay, Bisexual and Transgender Issues in Counseling (ALGBTIC, 2008) lists these attributes of effective group counselors:

- Counselors are sensitive to the dynamics that occur when groups are formed that include only one representative of any minority culture.
- Counselors establish group norms and make interventions that facilitate the safety and inclusion of LGBTQ group members.
- Counselors strive to establish group norms and create a climate that allows for voluntary self-identification and self-disclosure on the part of LGBTQ clients.
- Counselors take an active stance when other members express either overt or covert disrespect of LGBTQ group members.

Are there any specific attitudes, beliefs, assumptions, and values you hold that might interfere with your ability to effectively work with lesbian, gay, bisexual, transgender, and questioning clients in your groups? If you do become aware of some personal limitations at this time, what changes would you consider making? How would you challenge certain of your attitudes and assumptions pertaining to any of the aforementioned guidelines? For more information on this topic, we recommend *Group Counseling With LGBTQI Persons* (Goodrich & Luke, 2015), *The Handbook of Counseling and Psychotherapy With Lesbian, Gay, Bisexual, and Transgender Clients* (Bieschke, Perez, & DeBord, 2006), and *Casebook for Counseling Lesbian, Gay, Bisexual, and Transgender Persons and Their Families* (Dworkin & Pope, 2012).

LO10

Ethical Concerns in Using Group Techniques

Group techniques can be used to facilitate the movement of a group and to deepen and intensify certain feelings. Although it is unrealistic to expect that leaders will always know exactly what will result from an intervention, they should know how to cope with unexpected outcomes. It is extremely important for group leaders to have a clear rationale for using each technique. This is an area in which theory can be a useful guide for practice.

Techniques can be abused or used in unethical ways. Here are some ways leaders might employ techniques unethically:

- Using techniques with which they are unfamiliar
- Using techniques to enhance their power
- Using techniques whose sole purpose is to create intensity between members or within the group
- Using techniques to pressure members, even when they have expressed a desire not to participate in an exercise
- Using techniques to alter a group member's personal values or beliefs

Group leaders have a responsibility to exercise caution in using techniques, especially if these methods are likely to result in the release of intense feelings. It is important that the leader has had appropriate training to cope with the powerful feelings that can be triggered by certain role-playing activities. For example, guided fantasies into times of loneliness as a child or physical exercises designed to release anger can lead to intense emotional experiences. If leaders use such techniques, they must be ready to deal with any emotional release. Group leaders need to become aware of the potential for encouraging catharsis to fulfill their own needs. Some leaders push people to express anger, and they develop techniques to bring about this catharsis. Although these are legitimate feelings, expressing anger in the group may satisfy the leader's agenda more than it meets the needs of the members. This question ought to be raised frequently: "Whose needs are primary, and whose needs are being met—the members' or the leader's?" If you push members to express intense emotion, do you know what to do once emotions are released?

Another major ethical issue pertaining to the use of group techniques relates to providing immediate help for any group member who shows extreme distress during or at the end of a group session, especially if techniques were used to elicit intense emotions. Although some unfinished business promotes growth, the client should not feel abandoned at the end of a session that incited strong emotional reactions because time has run out. Leaders must take care to allow enough time to deal adequately with the reactions that were stimulated in a session. It is unwise to introduce techniques in a session when there is not enough time to work through the feelings that might result, or in a setting where there is no privacy or where the physical setup would make it harmful to employ certain techniques. Adequate time needs to be allotted to closing each group session.

Group leaders need to understand the potential adverse effects of certain techniques. One way for group leaders to learn is by taking part in groups themselves. By being a group member and first experiencing a range of techniques, a therapist can develop a healthy respect for using techniques appropriately to meet clients' needs. In our training workshops for group leaders, we encourage spontaneity and inventiveness in the use of techniques, but we also stress the importance of striking a balance between creativity and irresponsibility.

Group techniques are a means to an end, not an end in themselves.

The reputation of group work has suffered from the actions of irresponsible practitioners, mostly those who use techniques randomly without a clear rationale or without any sense of the potential outcome. If the group leader has a strong academic background, has had extensive supervised group experience, has participated in his or her own therapy or personal-growth experience, and has a basic respect for clients, he or she is not likely to abuse techniques. Group techniques are a means to an end, not an end in themselves. For a more in-depth treatment of using group techniques in an ethical and effective manner, see *Group Techniques* (Corey, Corey, Callanan, & Russell, 2015).

Competence and Training of Group Counselors

LO11

Experienced as well as beginning group leaders must provide only those services and use only those techniques for which they are qualified by training and experience. It is our responsibility to market our professional services to accurately represent our competence. Although we encourage you to think of creative ways of reaching diverse populations, we also emphasize the need for adequate training and supervision in leading groups with such members. If we lead groups that are clearly beyond the scope of our preparation, we are practicing unethically and are at risk for malpractice.

Competence as an Ongoing Developmental Process

Different groups require different leader qualifications. Some professionals who are highly qualified to work with college students are not qualified to lead children's groups. For example, professionals who are trained to lead psychoeducational groups may lack either the training or the experience necessary to administer group therapy to an outpatient population. The basic question is: Who is qualified to lead *this type* of group with *this type* of population?

Competence is one of the major ethical issues in group work. Lacking adequate training or experience, some leaders hastily gather a group together without taking the time to screen members or to prepare them for a group. Many interns and even some professionals may be placed in situations in which they are expected to lead groups despite having little or no training to do so. Professional group workers know their limitations. They familiarize themselves with referral resources and do not attempt to work with clients who need special help beyond their level of competence. An ASCA (2010) guideline states "professional school counselors develop professional competencies, and maintain appropriate education, training, and supervision in group facilitation and any topics specific to the group" (A.6.e). Furthermore, responsible group workers are keenly aware of the importance of continuing their education. Even licensed and experienced professionals attend conventions and workshops, take courses, seek consultation and supervision, and get involved in special training programs from time to time.

Professional competence is not arrived at once and for all. Rather, professional growth is an ongoing developmental process for the duration of your career. The "Best Practice Guidelines" (ASGW, 2008, A.8) provide these general suggestions for increasing one's level of competence as a group worker:

- Remain current and increase knowledge and skill competencies through activities such as continuing education, professional supervision, and participation in personal and professional development activities.
- Seek consultation and supervision to ensure effective practice regarding ethical concerns that interfere with effective functioning as a group leader.
- Seek appropriate professional assistance for personal problems or conflicts that are likely to impair professional judgment or work performance.

Competent group workers have reasons for the activities they suggest in a group. They are able to explain to their clients the theory behind their group work and how it influences their practice. They can tell the members in clear language the goals of a group, and they can state the relationship between the way they lead the group and these goals. Effective group leaders are able to conceptualize the group process and to relate what they do in a group to this model. They continually refine their techniques in light of their model.

Professional Training Standards for Group Counselors 

For proficient group leaders to emerge, a training program must make group work a priority. Various professional organizations have identified training standards for group counselors. The "Professional Standards for the Training of Group Workers" (ASGW, 2000) specifies two levels of competencies and related training. A set of core *knowledge* competencies and *skill* competencies provide the foundation on which *specialized* training is built. At a minimum, one group course should be included in a training program, and it should be structured to help students acquire the basic knowledge and skills needed to facilitate a group. These group skills are best mastered through supervised practice, which should include observation and participation in a group experience.

The Council for Accreditation of Counseling and Related Educational Programs (CACREP, 2016) identify the following standards specifically devoted to group work in which students in counseling are to develop a set of competencies:

a. theoretical foundations of group counseling and group work
b. dynamics associated with group process and development
c. therapeutic factors and how they contribute to group effectiveness

d. characteristics and functions of effective group leaders
e. approaches to group formation, including recruiting, screening, and selecting members
f. types of groups and other considerations that affect conducting groups in varied settings
g. ethical and culturally relevant strategies for designing and facilitating groups
h. direct experiences in which students participate as group members in a small group activity, approved by the program, for a minimum of 10 clock hours over the course of one academic term

Adjuncts to a Training Program

We highly recommend three types of experience as adjuncts to a training program: personal (private) psychotherapy, group therapy or a self-exploration group, and participation in group supervision.

Personal Psychotherapy for Group Leaders It is important for trainees to get involved in their own personal counseling, both individual and group. They can explore the biases that might hamper their receptiveness to clients, any unfinished business that might lead to distortions in their perceptions of group members, other needs that might either facilitate or inhibit the group process, current conflicts, and ways they can fully recognize and utilize their strengths. In short, group counselors demonstrate the courage to do for themselves what they expect members in their groups to do.

Self-Exploration Groups for Group Leaders We have discovered that participation in a self-exploration group (or some other type of interactive process-oriented group) is an extremely valuable adjunct to a group leader's internship training experiences. Beginning group leaders typically experience some anxiety regarding their adequacy, and their interactions with group members frequently lead to a surfacing of unresolved past or current problems. A therapeutic group provides an opportunity for trainees to explore these personal issues. In addition to the therapeutic value of this kind of a group, it can be a powerful teaching tool for the trainee.

Group Supervision for Group Leaders Group supervision with group counselors provides trainees with many experiential opportunities to learn about the process and development of a group. Group supervision is of paramount importance in training group leaders as well as in monitoring the quality of care of those who participate (Riva, 2014). Christensen and Kline (2000) emphasize that supervisees have many opportunities to learn through both participation and observation. Their investigation lent support to the numerous benefits of group supervision, a few of which include enhancement of knowledge and skills, ability to practice techniques in a safe and supportive environment, integration of theory and practice, richer understanding of patterns of group dynamics, opportunities to test one's assumptions, personal development through connection with others, and opportunities for self-disclosure and for giving and receiving feedback. By being in a supervision group, trainees learn not only from the supervisors who conduct the group but also from others in the group by the questions they raise and the discussion that follows.

Group supervision lends itself to a variety of role-playing approaches that enable trainees to become aware of potential countertransference issues and to acquire alternative perspectives in working with group members they perceive as being "difficult." A trainee can assume the role of a member of his or her group by role-playing this member while the supervisor demonstrates other ways to deal with a group member who displays problematic behavior. Other trainees in the supervision group can assume various roles for one another, which often generates rich discussion material after a situation is enacted. Role-playing techniques tend to bring concrete situations to life. Instead of merely *talking about problems* with clients, trainees can bring these concerns to life by enacting them in the here and now.

Although a supervision group is not a therapy group, it can lead to insights and awareness. Trainees can learn a great deal about their response to criticism, their competitiveness, their need for approval, their jealousies, their anxieties over being competent, their feelings about certain members of the group they lead, and their power struggles with coleaders or members of their group. Trainees can gain insights into their personal dynamics, such as potential areas of countertransference, which can influence their ability to competently facilitate groups. By identifying areas that can lead to countertransference, trainees are in a position to do further work in their own therapy outside of the group.

Ethical Issues in Training Group Counselors

LO14

One controversial ethical issue in the preparation of group leaders involves combining experiential and didactic methods in training. We consider an experiential component to be essential in teaching group counseling courses. Struggling with trusting a group of strangers, risking vulnerability, receiving genuine support from others, developing good working relationships with peers, and being challenged to examine the impact of one's behavior on others are all vital learning experiences for future group leaders. We think group experience for leaders is indispensable, if for no reason other than that it provides an understanding of what clients face.

Although it is common practice to combine the didactic and experiential aspects of learning in group work courses, doing so requires educators to address a number of ethical considerations, such as learning to work effectively within the context of multiple roles. In experiential training, participants engage in self-exploration and deal with interpersonal issues within the training group as a way of learning how to best facilitate groups. It is our position that the potential risks of experiential methods are offset by the clear benefits to participants who become personally involved in experiential group work as a supplement to didactic approaches to group courses. Many group work educators see a need for an experiential component to assist students in acquiring the skills necessary to become effective group leaders.

Managing Multiple Roles as an Educator Group work educators must manage multiple roles and fulfill many responsibilities to their trainees, some of which include facilitator of a group, teacher, evaluator, and supervisor. Faculty who teach group courses cannot realistically be restricted to a singular role in teaching. At various times educators may teach group process concepts, lead a demonstration group in class, set up an exercise to illustrate an intervention in a group situation, and evaluate students' work.

Although there have been some ethical problems in the attempt to train using experiential approaches, we do not think this warrants the conclusion that experiential approaches are inappropriate or unethical. Overcorrection of a problem of potential abuse does not seem justified to us. Teaching group process by involving students in personal ways is the best way for them to learn how to eventually set up and facilitate groups. We agree with Stockton, Morran, and Chang (2014) who point out that there is a fine line between offering experiential activities and safeguarding against gaining information that could be used in evaluating students. Faculty who use experiential approaches are often involved in performing multiple roles, and they need to exercise caution so that they offer training opportunities that will be ethical and efficacious (Stockton et al., 2014). When experiential activities are used, faculty can preface the activity by discussing the boundaries and limitations of student self-disclosure while promoting the importance of self-reflection throughout the process.

The Benefits of Experiential Group Training The CACREP (2016) standards require students to gain at least 10 hours of experience in a small group as a group member. This requirement is typically met by structuring an experiential group as part of a group counseling course. Students often have an opportunity to be part of a group experience and at times to facilitate the process of this group. In an experiential learning environment that involves extensive self-disclosure and dual relationships between instructors and students, students need to know they can trust their instructor's skill, ethics, and professionalism. Students engaged in experiential training must be willing to engage in self-disclosure, to become active participants in an interpersonal group, and to engage themselves on an emotional as well as a cognitive level.

Research on including experiential groups in a training program has increased over the past decade. St. Pierre's (2014) survey of ACA members found that a key factor contributing to students feeling comfortable in the group experience is the perception that the instructor is competent. McCarthy, Falco, and Villalba (2014) "believe strongly in the ability of students to overcome their initial reluctance to share more openly and trust each other, particularly since this is what they will ask of members when they lead groups" (p. 187). Luke and Kiweewa (2010) found that participation in experiential groups has many benefits in the areas of personal growth and awareness in addition to offering opportunities for learning about group process. In a qualitative study of an experiential group led by doctoral students, Ieva, Ohrt, Swank, and Young (2009) found that the master's students experienced personal growth, professional growth, and a better understanding of the group process, self-awareness, empathy for future clients, and an enhanced ability to give and receive feedback.

In a study of graduate students that addressed group leaders' perceptions of their training and experiences, Ohrt, Frier, Porter, and Young (2014) reported that participants expressed appreciation for opportunities to gain practice and have responsibilities, both in the group class and in the community and schools. Although initially hesitant about being required to be in a group, participants gained valuable knowledge about group dynamics, leadership in action, effectively managing conflicts, and seeing the stages of a group unfold. Participants welcomed the opportunity to colead groups with an experienced leader and learned a good deal by the modeling they observed.

Keeping the Purpose of the Group Course in Perspective It is essential to keep in mind the primary purpose of a group counseling course, which is teaching students leadership skills and providing an understanding of how group process works. Although the main aim of a group course is not to provide personal therapy for students, participating in such a group is inevitably a therapeutic and growth-enhancing learning experience. Encouraging students to make decisions about what personal concerns they are willing to share and to determine the depth of their personal disclosures leads to a more productive group experience that reinforces the importance of empowering their clients and group members to determine the nature and extent of their own self-disclosures.

A group course is not designed to be a substitute for an intensive self-exploration experience, yet learning about how groups function can be enhanced through active and personal participation in the group process. If students take personal risks, they are bound to be uncomfortable at times. Being willing to explore the meaning of their discomfort rather than seeking comfort at all costs can provide insight into how their future clients may be feeling as they begin counseling. If the leader is capable, professional, and well-acquainted with complex experiential group issues such as dual relationships, the leader will provide a safe group space. The facilitator should keep in mind the main purpose and objective of the training group and the best interests of the participants.

The focus of a small group for trainees can be on what is happening in the here and now. There is rich material in what takes place among members in a group. For example, some people find dealing with conflict quite difficult and uncomfortable, perhaps due to the way conflict was handled in their family of origin. By encouraging members to directly address the conflict in the group and work toward its resolution, trainees can see the value of working through conflict (rather than avoiding it) and have a corrective experience. Students can profit, both personally and professionally, by learning how to manage conflicts as a group member. Counselors-in-training need to understand their own reactions to conflict and see the conflict resolution process being modeled in a healthy and constructive manner. If members openly and honestly learn to deal with one another, they will make great strides toward learning how to facilitate a group and how to improve their own interpersonal functioning.

Dealing With Problematic Student Behaviors That Emerge in a Group Educators also have a monitoring (or "gatekeeping") function, especially in intervening when students demonstrate unhealthy, unproductive, or damaging behavior, are unable to give or receive feedback appropriately, or are unable to relate to others effectively. Group work educators have a responsibility to the students, future clients, the profession, the community, and the training institution to take action when students in a group course give evidence that they are not suited personally to working as group facilitators. Goodrich and Luke (2012) have written about the ethical issues in dealing with students who exhibit problematic behavior in an experiential group. Group work is inevitably one setting in which students' unhealthy aspects may be exposed. When this situation arises, the group counselor-educator has multiple responsibilities: (a) to the individual student who displays problematic behavior, (b) to the other students in the experiential group, and (c) to the training program.

A multitude of problematic behaviors can disrupt the cohesion of a group and impede the learning of the other members. Behavior patterns such as these can be identified and explored in an experiential group: (a) members who habitually give others advice, yet remain unknown; (b) members who are hostile and make it difficult for others to feel safe; (c) members who are judgmental and critical; (d) arrogant members who are convinced they can learn little in an experiential group; (e) members who monopolize time in the group; and (f) members who have a difficult time attending to others. The group format provides excellent opportunities for learning to deal with challenging behaviors. One effective intervention is to simply invite other members to provide here-and-now feedback to the member exhibiting the problematic behavior. The instructor or group facilitator must block unproductive interactions while this feedback is being delivered to prevent the group member from being scapegoated or overwhelmed with negative feedback. It is important to remember that the point is for the group member to understand the impact of his or her behavior, not to cause the member to become even more defensive. As difficult and tense as it might be in the moment, everyone in the group may benefit from the experience of successfully working through the conflict.

When a student trainee manifests problematic behaviors in the group setting, the instructor is responsible for giving the student honest and sensitive feedback about his or her behavior, providing suggestions on how to remediate problematic behavior, and explaining the policies and processes established to remediate the situation. For this to be effective, the instructor needs to be reasonably skilled at switching from the group leader role to the counselor-educator gatekeeper role, and back to the group leader role. Some behavior patterns may persist, and the student may not be open to self-reflection and change. Group work instructors have a responsibility to protect the other group members, and this may involve scheduling an individual meeting with the student to discuss how his or her interactions are detrimental to the group process and to provide support to help the student continue to make gains both personally and professionally through the experience.

Informed Consent and Experiential Learning Students have a right to be informed of the specific nature of course and program requirements before they enter a program and to be aware that many aspects of their program will involve their participating in personal ways to learn both about themselves and to learn the art of counseling. Students who apply to a counseling program must be made aware of the fact that counseling involves a personal investment, which goes beyond gaining knowledge and acquiring skills. Prospective students need to be cognizant that they will be affected personally in many of their courses (as well as throughout their careers). Students have a right to be informed about the ramifications of self-disclosing personal information in an academic setting, as well as being told about the rationale for becoming personally involved in their program. Prospective students who harbor negative attitudes about this approach to learning may need to be advised to explore other educational opportunities or career paths that do not require such a personal investment.

Shumaker, Ortiz, and Brenninkmeyer (2011) recommend that experiential groups include a detailed informed consent process and train students in learning what constitutes appropriate self-disclosure in such a group. Clear guidelines must be established so students know their rights and responsibilities. We echo the importance of a thorough informed consent process and recognize that it puts pressure on both the instructor and the students as it requires honesty, maturity, and professionalism. Even with safeguards in place, students may be hesitant to share meaningful personal information if they have an undue fear of the gatekeeping function of the experiential part of the group class. Group leaders should be prepared to understand and process this hesitation in a way that respects students' concerns. In addition, systematic self-reflection on the part of the instructor is a critical component for promoting a positive experiential group experience.

At the first class meeting of a group course we teach, we discuss some of the potential problems, challenges, and benefits inherent in a course that combines academic and personal learning. We tell the students that the experience of leading groups, even under supervision, often touches them in personal ways and brings to the surface their own personal struggles. Students become aware of the rationale for them getting involved in personal ways in learning group counseling. Students learn that they will not be able to encourage their future clients to deal with pain in their lives if they have not become aware of their own unresolved personal issues and dealt with their own personal pain. We encourage students taking the group course to consider seeking some form of personal counseling as a way to deal with the personal concerns that may emerge for them as group trainees.

We take care to combine both the experiential and didactic dimensions in our group counseling courses because we believe this balance is crucial for learning how to lead groups. As emotionally intense as the groups may become, we do not abandon the educational dimension. We operate on the premise that students can be involved in personal self-exploration and still put their learning into a cognitive framework. Students have the opportunity both to be a member and to colead with another student, always with a supervisor in the group. Self-reflection time with the supervisor following the group session is provided so students can process their coleadership experience. Students typically have reservations at the beginning of their small group, but they gain confidence as they challenge these reservations. In talking about their fears, doubts, and concerns, they are fully present in the group and see many of the group process concepts come to life. Once students experience a group, they can talk more meaningfully about how to create trust in a group, how to invite honest interaction among the members, how to challenge reluctant behavior, how to establish helpful group norms, and how to build a cohesive group community.

LO15

Guidelines for Ethical and Legal Practice

Most professional organizations affirm that practitioners should be aware of the prevailing community standards and of the possible impact on their practice of deviation from these standards. Ethical and legal issues are frequently intertwined, which makes it imperative that group practitioners not only follow the code of ethics of their profession but that they also know their state's laws and their legal boundaries and responsibilities.

Those leaders who work with groups of children, adolescents, and certain involuntary populations are especially advised to learn the laws restricting group work. Issues such as confidentiality, parental consent, informed consent, record keeping, protection of member welfare, and civil rights of institutionalized patients are a few areas in which group workers must be knowledgeable. Because most group workers do not possess detailed legal knowledge, it is a good idea to obtain some legal information concerning group procedures and practices. Awareness of legal rights and responsibilities as they pertain to group work protects not only clients but also those who conduct groups from needless lawsuits arising from negligence or ignorance.

Legal Liability and Malpractice

Group counselors who fail to exercise due care and act in good faith are liable to a civil suit. Professionals leading groups are expected to practice within the code of ethics of their particular profession and to abide by legal standards. Practitioners are subject to civil liability for not doing right or for doing wrong to another. If group members can prove that personal injury or psychological harm is due to a group leader's failure to render proper service, either through negligence or ignorance, then this leader is open to a malpractice suit. Negligence consists of departing from the "standard of care"; that is, breaching the therapist's duty in providing what is determined as commonly accepted practices of others in the profession that leads to injury to the client.

Some aspects of this standard of care involve keeping careful records, consulting when necessary, and documenting your consultations. Consult and document all ethical and legal issues as well as the clinical implications that arise during your groups. In most situations it is a good idea to have consulted with three colleagues and to be sure that you cite each of these consultations in your case notes. In terms of documentation and record keeping, be aware of the guidelines and requirements of the setting in which you work. There are a variety of ways to keep group notes. Some leaders keep group process notes, and simply list the names of each group member in attendance. Others write individual notes on each group member and keep these notes in separate files. Knauss (2006) indicates that although notes written about the entire group may capture key themes at different points in a group, these notes can compromise the privacy and confidentiality of individual group members. Knauss recommends that group practitioners keep an individual record for each group member. Regardless of the method of record keeping, it is important to have some form of documentation of group sessions, treatment goals, and outcomes.

Legal Safeguards for Group Practitioners

LO16

The key to avoiding a malpractice suit is to maintain reasonable, ordinary, and prudent practices. The group leader guidelines that follow are useful in translating the terms *reasonable, ordinary*, and *prudent* into concrete actions.

1. Take time and exercise care in screening candidates for a group experience.
2. Give the potential members of your groups enough information to make informed choices about group participation, and do not mystify the group process. Develop written informed consent procedures at the outset of a group, and make sure that you review this information with the members. Doing this will go a long way toward building a trusting climate.
3. Obtain written parental or guardian consent when counseling minors in groups. This is generally a good practice even if not required by state law. However, know that if a parent or guardian denies this consent, the minor will not be able to participate in the counseling group.
4. Keep records of group sessions in compliance with codes of ethics and institutional policies. Keep relevant notes on each group member and each group session, especially if there are any concerns about a particular member.
5. Be aware of those situations in which you legally *must* break confidentiality. Explain to members the limits of confidentiality, such as when it must be breached.
6. Restrict your scope of practice to client populations for which you are prepared by virtue of your education, training, and experience.
7. Be aware of the state laws and the ethical guidelines of various professional organizations that limit your practice, as well as the policies of the agency for which you work. Inform members about these policies, and practice within the boundaries of these laws and policies.
8. Make it a practice to consult with colleagues or clinical supervisors whenever there is a potential ethical, legal, or clinical concern. Clearly document the nature of the consultation.
9. Have a clear standard of care that can be applied to your services, and communicate this standard to the members. The best safeguard against legal liability is to practice good client care.
10. Document reasons for a group member's termination and any referrals or recommendations given.
11. Do not promise the members of your group anything you cannot deliver. Help them realize that their degree of effort and commitment are the key factors in determining the outcomes of the group experience.

12. Do not engage in sexual relationships with either current or former group members.
13. Make it a practice to assess the general progress of a group, and teach members how to evaluate their individual progress toward their own goals.
14. If you work for an agency or institution, have a contract that specifies the employer's legal liability for your professional functioning.
15. Learn how to assess and intervene in cases in which group participants pose a threat to themselves or others, and be sure to document actions taken.
16. Recognize when it is appropriate to refer a group member for another form of treatment.
17. Remain alert to the ways your personal reactions might inhibit the group process, and monitor your countertransference.
18. Be careful of meeting your own needs at the expense of the members of your group.
19. Incorporate established ethical standards in your practice of group work. Following the spirit of the ethics code of your professional organization is important.
20. The best way to protect yourself from a malpractice suit is to take preventive measures, such as not practicing outside the boundaries of your competence and creating collaborative relationships with the members of your groups.
21. Attend risk management workshops periodically with the goal of familiarizing yourself with current standards of practice.
22. Realize that you will never be completely safe from a potential claim or lawsuit, regardless of how competent and ethical you are. However, proactive risk management strategies can lessen the possibility of such claims. Carry malpractice insurance.

This discussion of ethical and legal issues relevant for group work is not intended to increase your anxiety level or make you so careful that you avoid taking any risks. Leading groups can be a risky as well as a professionally rewarding venture. You will make some mistakes, so be willing to acknowledge and learn from them. By making full use of supervision, you not only learn from what may seem like mistakes but you also minimize the chances of harming clients. Being frozen with anxiety over needing to know everything or being afraid to intervene for fear of becoming embroiled in a lawsuit only creates a bigger problem. It is a disservice to treat group members as though they were fragile and, thus, never challenge them. Perhaps the best way to prevent a malpractice action is by having a sincere interest in doing what is going to benefit your client. Be willing to ask yourself these questions throughout your professional career: *What* am I doing, and *why* am I doing it? And *how* would it be if my colleagues observed my professional behavior? For a more detailed discussion of ethical and legal issues, see Corey, Corey, Corey, and Callanan (2015).

Several useful resources for risk management practices that can be applied to group work are Kennedy, Vandehey, Norman, and Diekhoff (2003), Bennett, Bricklin, Harris, Knapp, VandeCreek, and Younggren (2006), and Wheeler and Bertram (2015).

Points to Remember

Ethical and Legal Issues in Group Counseling

You are challenged to take a position on basic professional issues pertaining to your role as a group practitioner. The guidelines presented here provide a quick reference as you read the remainder of this book. Our aim in presenting these guidelines is to stimulate you to think about a framework that will guide you in making sound decisions as a leader.

- Take time to reflect on your personal identity. Think about your needs and behavior styles and about the impact of these factors on group participants. It is essential for you to have a clear idea of what your roles and functions are in the group so you can communicate them to members.
- Codes of ethics have been established by various professional organizations, and those who belong to such organizations are bound by them. Familiarize yourself with these established codes of ethics and with the laws that may affect group practice.
- Have a clear idea of the type of group you are designing and why it is the treatment of choice. Be able to express the purpose of the group and the characteristics of the clients who will be admitted.
- Be aware of the implications of cultural diversity in designing groups and in orienting members to the group process.
- Tell prospective group members what is expected of them, and encourage them to develop a contract that will provide them with the impetus to obtain their personal goals.
- Make prospective participants aware of the techniques that will be employed and of the exercises that they may be asked to participate in. Give them the ground rules that will govern group activities.
- Promote an atmosphere of respect for diversity within the group context.
- Make clear from the outset of a group what the focus will be.
- Avoid undertaking a project that is beyond the scope of your training and experience. Make a written statement of your qualifications available to the participants.
- Point out the risks involved in group participation both before members join and also when it is appropriate throughout the life of the group. It is your responsibility to help members identify and explore their readiness to deal with these potential risks. It is also your job to minimize the risks.
- Protect members' rights to decide what to share with the group and what activities to participate in. Be sensitive to any form of group pressure that violates the self-determination of an individual and to any activity that undermines a person's sense of self, such as scapegoating or stereotyping.
- Develop a rationale for using group exercises and be able to verbalize it. Use only techniques you are competent to employ, preferably those you have experienced as a group member.
- Relate practice to theory and remain open to integrating multiple approaches in your practice. Keep informed about research findings on group process, and use this information to increase the effectiveness of your practice.
- Begin and end group sessions on time. Facilitate group sessions in a safe, private location free from distractions or interruptions.
- Be aware of the power you possess by virtue of your role as a leader, and take steps to share this power to empower group members.
- Emphasize the importance of confidentiality to members before they enter a group, during the group sessions when relevant, and before the group terminates.
- Explain to members that legal privilege (confidentiality) does not apply to group counseling (unless provided by state statute).
- Avoid imposing your values on members. Recognize the role culture and socialization play in the formulation of members' values. Respect your clients'

capacity to think for themselves, and be sure that members give one another the same respect.

- Be alert for symptoms of psychological debilitation in group members, which might indicate that participation in the group should be discontinued. Make referral resources available to people who need or desire further psychological assistance.
- Encourage participants to discuss their experience in the group and help them evaluate the degree to which they are meeting their personal goals. Devote some time at the end of each session for members to express their thoughts and feelings about that session.
- Do not expect the transfer of learning from the group to daily life to occur automatically. Assist members in applying what they are learning. Prepare them for setbacks they are likely to encounter when they try to transfer their group learning to their daily lives.
- Develop some method of evaluation to determine the effectiveness of the procedures you use. Even informal research efforts can help you make informed judgments about how well your leadership style is working.

Exercises

In-Class Activities

1. **Confronting gossiping.** It comes to your attention that certain members have been gossiping about matters that came up in a high school group you are leading. Do you deal with the offenders privately or in the group? What do you say?
2. **Limits of confidentiality.** You are about to begin leading a high school counseling group, and the policy of the school is that any teacher or counselor who becomes aware that a student is using drugs is expected to report the student to the principal. How do you cope with this situation?
3. **Dealing with parents.** You are conducting a self-exploration group with children in a family clinic. The father of one of the children in your group meets with you to find out how his child is doing. What do you tell him? What do you not tell him? Would you be inclined to meet with the father and his child? How might you handle this same situation with a request made by a noncustodial parent where the parents are divorced?
4. **Forming a group.** You are a private practitioner who wants to colead a weekend assertiveness training workshop. How would you announce your workshop? How would you screen potential members? Whom might you exclude from your workshop, and why?
5. **Coping with reluctant group members.** You are employed as a counselor in the adolescent ward of a county mental hospital. As one of your duties you lead a group for the young people, who are required to attend the sessions. You sense an unwillingness on the part of the members to come to group. What are the ethical problems involved? How do you deal with this situation?
6. **Leading an involuntary group.** You are asked to lead a group composed of involuntary clients. Because their participation is mandatory, you want to take steps to clearly and fully inform them of procedures to be used, their rights and responsibilities as members, your expectations of them, and matters such as confidentiality. If you were to write an informed consent document, what would you most want to put in this brief letter?
7. **Confronting an unhappy group member.** A member in a group you are leading comes to you after one of the sessions, saying, "I don't want to come back next week.

It doesn't seem as if we're getting anywhere, because all that ever goes on is people putting each other down. I don't trust anyone in here!" She has not said any of this in the sessions, and the group has been meeting for 5 weeks. What might you say or do? Would you work with her? Why or why not?

8. **Leader's values.** Consider some of the following areas in which your values and those of group members might clash. How would you respond in each of these situations that could arise in your group?
   - **a.** A member discloses how excited she is over a current affair and wonders if she should continue staying with her partner.
   - **b.** A woman whose cultural background is different from yours and that of the other members in the group says she is having difficulty expressing what she wants and in behaving assertively (both in the group and at home). She says she has been taught to think of the interests of others and not to be concerned about what she wants.
   - **c.** An adolescent relates that his life feels bland without drugs.
   - **d.** A pregnant 16-year-old is struggling to decide whether to have an abortion or give up her baby to an adoption agency.
   - **e.** A chronically depressed man says that at times he thinks about suicide as his way out of a hopeless situation.
   - **f.** A man says he is very unhappy in his marriage but is unwilling to get a divorce because he is afraid of being alone.
   - **g.** A member who is from a different culture than the other members says he is having difficulty in the group because he is not used to speaking so freely or openly about family problems.
9. **Diversity and social justice guidelines.** You are on a committee to formulate guidelines to help counseling students learn how to deal effectively with diversity and social justice concerns in their groups. What issues most need to be addressed? What guidelines might you suggest to address these issues? What experiences would help students examine their attitudes and beliefs about diversity? What kind of information do you think students most need, and how might they best acquire this knowledge? What are your recommendations for developing skill in leading culturally diverse groups?
10. **Informed consent.** Create your own informed consent form for a group. What aspects would you want to make sure to include? How would you ascertain whether a member understood the various elements contained in your form?
11. **Experiential work.** In small groups, discuss what you think a university program should inform students about regarding experiential work. Come up with a brief statement about what students can expect regarding experiential aspects of the program. What are your ideas about making sure students have this information prior to enrolling in the program?
12. **Contacting the Association for Specialists in Group Work (ASGW).** Information about the Association for Specialists in Group Work (ASGW) is available from the main website (www.asgw.org).The following standards and guidelines can be downloaded from the website:
    - ASGW (2000) "Professional Standards for the Training of Group Workers"
    - ASGW (2008) "Best Practice Guidelines"
    - ASGW (2012) "Multicultural and Social Justice Competence Principles for Group Workers"

This material can be discussed in class for both Chapter 2 and Chapter 3.

13. **Contacting the Association for Multicultural Counseling and Development (AMCD).** Information about the Association for Multicultural Counseling and Development is available from the main website (www.multiculturalcounseling.org). Endorsed by both the AMCD and the American Counseling Association in 2015, "Multicultural and Social Justice Counseling Competencies" (available online as a pdf) highlights taking action to promote social justice and emphasizes teaching clients how to advocate for themselves.

Questions for Discussion

1. What key points would you stress in educating members of your groups about confidentiality? If members express concerns about honoring confidentiality and wonder if they can trust what they say in a group, how would you respond?
2. What measures would you take to ensure confidentiality in your group? How would you deal with a member who broke confidentiality?
3. Under what circumstances would you feel compelled to breach confidentiality of a member in a counseling group? How would you handle this situation?
4. What are your thoughts about how you can best obtain the informed consent of members of your groups?
5. What special ethical issues may arise when working with a group composed of involuntary members?
6. What psychological risks are associated with group membership? How can these risks be minimized?
7. How are multicultural and social justice issues related to ethical group practice?
8. What guidelines might you use to determine the ethical use of techniques in group work?
9. In what ways might your personal values influence your work with group members? In what ways might you be concerned about your ability to bracket your personal values as you work with group members?
10. If a value conflict emerged between you and a group member, what specific steps would you take in managing this conflict?
11. Do you think students should or should not be required to participate in an experiential group as a part of their training in becoming group workers?
12. What kind of experiences have you had as a student in a group counseling course? What did you learn from these experiences?
13. What benefits and potential disadvantages can you envision in an experiential group as a part of the group course?
14. Which risk management procedures listed in this chapter do you consider to be especially important as legal safeguards for group counselors?
15. What legal liability and malpractice issues most concern you as a group worker?

MindTap for Counseling

Additional resources can be found on CengageBrain.com and by logging into the MindTap course created by your professor. There you will find a variety of study tools and useful resources that include quizzes, videos, interactive exercises, and more.

CHAPTER

4 Theories and Techniques of Group Counseling

CHAPTER LEARNING OBJECTIVES

1. Provide a general framework for theory applied to practice
2. Understand how techniques are associated with each theory of group work
3. Consider ways of viewing a group through a multicultural lens
4. Provide an overview of the theoretical foundations of group counseling and group work (CACREP, 2016, Standard A)
5. Describe the key concepts and techniques of psychoanalytic approaches to group work
6. Describe the key concepts and techniques of experiential and relationship-oriented approaches to group work
7. Describe the key concepts and techniques of cognitive behavioral approaches to group work
8. Describe the key concepts and techniques of postmodern approaches to group work
9. Delineate practical ways to develop an integrative approach to group counseling

It is the first week for you at your internship at a residential treatment center. You were just informed by your supervisor that next week you will be starting a dialectical behavior therapy (DBT) group for six to eight women struggling with borderline personality disorder.

- What are your immediate reactions to leading this type of group?
- How would you approach conducting this group if DBT is (or is not) your theoretical orientation to counseling?
- What theories do you find yourself most drawn to and why?
- How do the theories you use fit with your personality?
- How might your own cultural background, identity, and life experiences influence the theories from which you draw?

Introduction

In this chapter we provide a brief introduction to some of the major theories of counseling that have applicability to group counseling. At the end of each of the theory sections, we list selected readings that we have found particularly useful. To formulate your own perspective on how to apply theory to the practice of group work, you will need to do extensive reading on each of the theories that interest you and the techniques that you might find useful. Our main purpose here is to present a framework for thinking about how to apply techniques in groups and to show the connection between theory and technique.

You may ask why a theory is important and why we devote an entire chapter to this subject. A theory provides you with a structure for designing appropriate interventions and evaluating the outcomes of the group as a whole and of the individual members. This is a way of organizing information you get from the multiple interactions within a group. We think that it is particularly important that you develop a personal stance toward the practice of group counseling that fits the person you are and is flexible enough to meet the unique needs of the members that make up the group.

A theory informs the way you operate in facilitating a group, guiding the way you are with the members and defining both your role and the members' roles in a group. A theory provides a frame of reference for understanding and evaluating the world of the client, especially when it comes to building rapport, making an assessment, defining problems, and selecting appropriate techniques in meeting the goals of the members. Attempting to make interventions and implement techniques as a group leader without having a clear theoretical rationale is much like trying to build a house without a set of blueprints. If you are unable to draw on theory to support your interventions, your groups may not achieve the maximum benefit.

Theory is not a rigid set of structures that prescribes, step by step, what and how you should function as a leader. Rather, theory is a general framework that helps you make sense of the many facets of group process, providing a sense of direction for what you do and say in a group. Theory helps you think about the possible results of your interventions. Being able to articulate your theoretical stance is beneficial for clients as well because it can help to define the roles and expectations of group members.

LO1

Theory as a Roadmap

A theory can guide you, much like a road map or a navigational instrument. A set of directions tells you where you are starting out, where you hope to end, and the steps along the way. If you do not have a navigational instrument, you may get lost and lose time trying to find your way. However, even with a directional guide you will encounter detours and unforeseen circumstances. Although you have a plan, you will need to be flexible in modifying the way you try to reach your goals. In this chapter we describe our own integrative approach, emphasizing the role of thinking, feeling, and acting in human behavior, which is based on selected ideas from most of the theories presented here.

There are many different theoretical approaches to understanding how the group process works and how change occurs. Different group practitioners work in a variety of ways as they deal with the same themes that emerge in a group, largely based on their theoretical orientation. Some leaders focus on feelings, believing that what members need most is to identify and express feelings that have been repressed. Other leaders emphasize gaining insight and increased self-awareness. For some leaders the emphasis is on practicing new behavior in a group and assisting members in developing specific action plans to bring about desired behavior changes. Others encourage group members to examine their beliefs about themselves and about their world; these leaders believe that change will result if the participants can eliminate inaccurate thinking and replace it with constructive thoughts and self-talk. Each of these choices represents a particular theoretical orientation, and the various theoretical approaches can work in concert to enhance your understanding of how groups work.

Group counselors may give primary attention to these time frames: the past, the present, or the future. It is important to consider whether you see the past, present, or future as being the most productive focus for group work. If you believe your members' past is a crucial aspect to explore, many of your interventions may be aimed at assisting them in understanding how their past is connected to their present behavior. If you think your members' goals and strivings are important, your interventions are likely to focus on the future. If you are oriented toward the present, many of your interventions are likely to emphasize what the members are thinking, feeling, and doing in the moment. With this present-centered orientation, you will probably ask members to bring both past events and future concerns into the here and now.

Our Theoretical Orientation

We are sometimes asked to identify what theory we follow. None of us subscribe to any single theory in its totality. Rather, we function within an integrative framework that we continue to develop and modify as we practice. We draw upon concepts and techniques from most of the contemporary therapeutic models and adapt them to our own unique personalities, our therapeutic styles, and to the needs of the members of a particular group. We operate on the assumption that who we are as a person is as important as our knowledge of counseling theory and the level of our skills. Certainly skills and techniques are critical. The techniques we employ can be practiced and refined, and our level of skill development enhances our practice. Although it is essential to use skills and techniques effectively—and to have a theoretical base from which to draw a range of techniques—this ability does not constitute the entire picture. The quality of the therapeutic relationship we establish with members is critical in determining successful outcomes. The methods we use and our theory of choice are important variables, but the relational factors are the foundation of effective group work. We use our skills to enhance our ability to create a sense of connection with the members of our groups. Building upon this relational foundation, our conceptual framework takes into account the *thinking*, *feeling*, and *behaving* dimensions of human experience.

An Integrative Approach to Group Practice We suggest that you study all the contemporary theories to determine what concepts and techniques you most want to incorporate in your leadership style. Developing your counseling theory is a process that will likely take years and will evolve as you gain experience and fine tune your own clinical style. In developing and conceptualizing your integrative approach to counseling, consider your own personality, interpersonal strengths, life experiences, and worldview as you choose the concepts and techniques that work best with a range of clients. To make effective choices, you need to be well grounded in a number of theories. Remain open to the idea that some aspects of these theories can be unified in some ways, and test your hypotheses to determine how well they are working. Getting regular feedback from the members of your groups is one of the best ways to assess how well your interventions are working.

An integrative approach involves the process of selecting concepts and methods from a variety of systems, and there are multiple pathways to achieving this integration. Two of the most common are technical integration and theoretical integration. **Technical integration** tends to focus on differences, uses techniques drawn from many approaches, and is based on a systematic selection of techniques. This path combines techniques from different schools without necessarily subscribing to the theoretical positions that spawned them. In contrast, **theoretical integration** refers to a conceptual or theoretical creation beyond a mere blending of techniques. The underlying assumption of this path is that the synthesis of the best of two or more theoretical approaches offers richer possibilities than restricting practice to a single theory. Integrative counseling is an intentional process of selecting concepts and methods from a variety of therapeutic systems. An integrative perspective is well suited to meeting the diverse needs of members that are typically found in many groups.

Knowing when and how to use a particular therapeutic intervention in a group session is an art as well as the result of applying knowledge to practice. Begin by asking yourself the following questions:

- What is occurring in the group from moment to moment?
- What kind of relationships am I developing with the members of my group?
- What role(s) do I take in the group, and how does this influence group process?

- What techniques am I drawn to, and can I explain why I am using various techniques?
- How do I evaluate my client's strengths and resources, define problems and solutions, and think about desired outcomes?

The answers to these questions will help you begin to formulate a picture of who you are as a group leader.

I (Cindy) draw upon a variety of theories, but I maintain a thread of continuity in who I am, how I make sense of my client's world, and how I intervene with a client's story. I am most influenced by the theories of Gestalt therapy and multicultural counseling and therapy, but I also utilize cognitive behavioral interventions and systemic thinking. I am very focused on the relationship I have with my clients. I believe that their style of relating to me represents what they do in the outside world. I also use myself and my reactions toward my clients as feedback, which is rooted in a Gestalt orientation. For example, I might ask clients to observe specific thoughts or behaviors they want to change. This cognitive behavior technique is grounded in my Gestalt approach, which means that the intervention would not be a predetermined assignment but would come from the spontaneous, here-and-now interactions with my clients.

In addition, I often find myself viewing clients' dilemmas through a multicultural and systemic lens, in which I see them and their presenting problems as embedded within other systems. Drawing from the feminist therapy approach, I place value on attending to how gender and power dynamics operate in a group, and I tend to avoid diagnosis without consideration of systemic, cultural, and dynamic influences. This helps me to stay away from victim blaming, and clients can see that their symptoms are often contextual. I find this helps to empower the individual to make life changes in spite of the challenges and resistance from outside forces.

A Thinking, Feeling, and Behaving Model We (Marianne and Jerry) base our practice on an integrative approach. When leading a group, we pay attention to what group members are thinking, feeling, and doing. This entails attending to the cognitive, affective, and behavioral domains. There is a reciprocal interaction between what people are thinking, and how these thoughts influence what they are feeling and doing. What we are feeling can also affect our thinking and behavior. How we behave has an influence on what we are feeling and thinking. Combining these three domains is the basis for a powerful and comprehensive approach to counseling practice. From our perspective, if any of these dimensions is excluded, the therapeutic approach is incomplete.

Both of us (Marianne and Jerry) draw from approaches in the *cognitive domain,* which focuses on the *thinking* or *thought processes* of group members. We typically challenge members to think about early decisions they have made about themselves. We pay attention to members' self-talk: "How are members' problems actually caused by the assumptions they make about themselves, about others, and about life?" "How do members create their problems by the beliefs they hold?" "How can they begin to be more self-directed by critically evaluating the sentences they repeat to themselves?" Many of our group techniques are designed to tap members' thinking processes, to help them reflect on events in their lives and how they have interpreted these events, and to explore their beliefs so that they can change in the direction they wish. We tend to draw much more from the cognitive behavioral approaches during the initial stage, when we are helping members to identify specific goals that will guide their participation, and then again during the ending stage, when we assist members in consolidating their learning and designing action plans to implement in everyday life.

The *affective domain* focuses on the *feelings* of group members. In the groups we lead, we help members identify and express their feelings. If members are able to experience the range of their feelings and talk about how certain events have affected them, their healing process is facilitated. If members feel listened to, understood, and accepted, they are more likely to express their feelings. Although group members can benefit from expressing repressed feelings, some cognitive work is essential if the maximum benefit is to be gained. Thus we integrate cognitive and affective work in our groups. We invite members to reflect upon their emotional work and to discuss how their emotional experience is connected to some of their beliefs about themselves, others, and life events.

The cognitive and affective domains are essential parts of the therapeutic process, but the *behavioral domain* (*acting* and *doing*) is central to the change process. Gaining insights and expressing pent-up feelings are oftentimes important, yet at some point members need to get involved in an action-oriented program of change. Group leaders can ask members useful questions such as these: "What are you doing?" "Does your present behavior have a reasonable chance of getting you what you want now, and will it take you in the direction you want to go?" If the focus of group work is on what people are doing, chances are greater that members will be able to change their thinking and feeling.

In addition to highlighting the thinking, feeling, and behaving dimensions, we help group members in consolidating what they are learning and encourage them to apply these new behaviors to situations they encounter every day. Some strategies we use are contracts, homework assignments, action programs, self-monitoring techniques, support systems, and self-directed programs of change. These approaches all stress the role of commitment on the members' part to practice new behaviors, to follow through with a realistic plan for change, and to develop practical methods of carrying out this plan in everyday life.

People in a group cannot be understood without considering the various systems that affect them—family, social groups, community, church, and other cultural forces. For a group process to be effective, it is critical to understand how individuals influence and are influenced by their social world. Effective group leaders need to acquire a holistic approach that encompasses all facets of human experience. By observing how members interact in the group, group leaders gain insight into how members may interact with other systems in their lives.

Underlying our integrative emphasis on thinking, feeling, and behaving is our (Marianne and Jerry's) philosophical leaning toward the existential approach, which places primary emphasis on the role of choice and responsibility in the therapeutic process. We invite people to look at the choices they *do* have, however limited they may be, and to accept responsibility for choosing for themselves. Thus we encourage members to identify and clarify what *they* are thinking, feeling, and doing as opposed to trying to change other people in their lives. Most of what we do in our groups is based on the assumption that people have the capacity to take a significant role in changing situations in their lives. We help members discover their inner resources and learn how to use them in resolving their difficulties. We do not provide answers for those in our groups, but we facilitate a process that will lead them to greater awareness of the knowledge and skills they can draw on to solve both their present and future problems.

An effective therapeutic relationship fosters a creative spirit that focuses on developing techniques aimed at increasing awareness, which enables group members to change their thinking, feeling, and behaving. Empirical evidence indicates that both the client–therapist relationship *and* the methods a therapist uses are directly related to treatment outcome. Researchers have repeatedly discovered that a positive alliance and a collaborative therapeutic relationship are the best predictors of therapy outcome (Elkins, 2016; Hubble, Duncan, Miller, & Wampold, 2010). Some neuroscience research suggests that a mutually positive connection based on empathic understanding helps set the stage for the neural integration of the brain, which promotes change in the way clients are able to deal with problematic issues (Badenoch, 2008; D. Siegel, 2010).

Part of the therapeutic relationship involves listening to client feedback about the therapy process. Client feedback can be used to inform, guide, and evaluate the treatment process. The active role members assume in a group, along with their experience of meaningful change in the early stage of a group, are the most potent contributors to positive outcome. One of the best ways to improve the effectiveness of any form of psychotherapy is by taking direction from clients through client-directed, outcome-informed therapy (Duncan, Miller, & Sparks, 2004; Miller et al., 2010).

As we introduce techniques in a group, we take into account an array of factors about the client population. We consider the members' readiness to confront an issue, the members' cultural background and value system, and the members' trust in us as group facilitators. A general goal that guides our practice is helping members identify and experience whatever they are feeling, identifying ways in which their assumptions influence how they feel and behave, and experimenting with alternative modes of behaving. We have a rationale for using the techniques we employ, and our interventions generally flow from some aspects of the theories that we describe in this chapter.

This discussion of our theoretical orientation provides only a brief introduction to this topic. For a more detailed discussion of the various theoretical orientations as they are applied to group counseling, see *Theory and Practice of Group Counseling* (Corey, 2016). For other works on theories of counseling we suggest *Case Approach to Counseling and Psychotherapy* (Corey, 2013b), *Theory and Practice of Counseling and Psychotherapy* (Corey, 2017), *Counseling and Psychotherapy: Theories and Interventions* (Capuzzi & Stauffer, 2016), *Current Psychotherapies* (Wedding & Corsini, 2014), *Contemporary Psychotherapies for a Diverse World* (Frew & Spiegler, 2013), *Counseling Theory and Practice* (Neukrug, 2011), *Systems of Psychotherapy: A Transtheoretical Analysis* (Prochaska & Norcross (2014), and *Theories of Psychotherapy and Counseling: Concepts and Cases* (Sharf, 2016).

Developing Your Own Theory of Group Practice

Your theory needs to be appropriate for your client population, setting, and the type of group you offer. But a theory is not something divorced from you as a person. Ultimately, the most meaningful perspective is one that is an extension of your personality. At best, a theory becomes an integral part of the person you are and an expression of your uniqueness.

Throughout this book we stress that your ability to draw on your life experiences and personal characteristics is a powerful therapeutic tool. Particularly important is your willingness to become aware of and examine how your behavior, personality, cultural background, status, and position of privilege might either enhance or hinder your work as a group leader. A thorough understanding of theories applicable to group work, skill acquisition, and supervised experience provide a basic foundation for becoming an effective group leader. However, you also must be willing to take an honest look at your own life to determine if you are willing to do for yourself what you expect of your group members. If you are currently a student-in-training, developing an integrated, well-defined theoretical model will likely require extensive reading and years of practice leading groups. We suggest you exchange ideas with other group workers and modify old practices to fit new knowledge, making changes over time.

In my teaching, I (Jerry) encourage students to learn as much as they can about the various theories, and then begin to look for ways of drawing from several approaches to develop their own integrative perspective that guides their practice. For a detailed treatment of developing an integrative approach, see *The Art of Integrative Counseling* (Corey, 2013a).

Learning in Action

Identifying Your Personal Theory

To develop your personal theory of counseling, it is essential to examine your worldview, beliefs, and personal history pertaining to how people grow, heal, and change. Many students struggle to find the theories that are most congruent with their beliefs and behaviors. We have a strong sense of our own personal theory of counseling, and this has been useful in our work with beginning helpers. The following examples illustrate some ways in which life experiences leave us with beliefs about the world. You will find that the different counseling theories presented in this chapter are more likely to resonate with particular life experiences and the resulting worldview of that person. Think about what your own life experiences have taught you as you examine these examples.

Example 1

Life Experience: While an undergraduate, Finn recalls being involved in several emotionally and physically abusive relationships. She described feeling traumatized and has found it difficult to heal from these relationships.

Life Lesson: "I was stuck and wanted an apology from the person who hurt me, but I was not going to get what I needed from that person. At some point I realized that I didn't have to heal with the same person who had hurt me. This freed me to move on in my life. Instead of waiting for the person who hurt me to acknowledge wrongdoing or to apologize, I took my power back and healed myself through other relationships."

Application to Counseling Theory: A number of counseling theories focus on the healing that occurs in relationship. People who are wounded in relationship can heal in relationship. As group leaders, we can create a healthy relationship with our clients or between group members to help them heal old wounds. Person-centered therapists place considerable emphasis on the therapeutic relationship based on the assumption that clients can apply what they are experiencing in their therapy to their personal lives. Take a moment to look over the counseling theories in this book and identify those that emphasize the power of relationships in the healing process.

Example 2

Life Experience: Ryan, a 35-year-old professional, was living under chronic stress due to an unhealthy relationship, unresolved resentment and anger, and a demanding yet unrewarding job. He struggled with many physical symptoms, including headaches, chronic respiratory infections, stomach ulcers, digestive problems, sleep problems, weight gain, depression, anxiety, and eventually cancer.

Life Lesson: "My body was sending me warning signals that I did not pay enough attention to. My physical illnesses culminated in cancer, which finally got my attention. It was time to change the way I was living. The lesson I took from this time in my life is, 'If you don't scream, your body will'."

Application to Counseling Theory: Several theoretical orientations focus on a holistic approach to working with clients, paying attention to clients' physical symptoms, mannerisms, and behaviors. A Gestalt therapist might see neck pain in a client as a symptom of something or someone literally being a pain in the neck in that person's life. The Gestalt therapist helps clients listen to their body and engages them in a dialogue with their physical symptoms. Cognitive behavior therapy also works holistically by attending to the integration of thinking, feeling, and behaving dimensions. A practitioner with a cognitive behavior therapy orientation might help clients identify how their beliefs and thinking patterns have influenced what they are doing and how they are feeling.

Directions

Take a few minutes to reflect on significant events or critical incidents that have occurred in your life. It could be your parents' divorce, an abusive relationship, losing a job, having a child, getting sober, or some other event.

Life Experience: Briefly describe the event or incident, when it occurred, what happened, and why it was significant or life-changing for you.

Life Lesson: What was the outcome of this event, and how did it affect you emotionally, cognitively, and behaviorally? How did it influence the way you see the world or others? What belief or worldview did you develop from this experience?

Theoretical Application: With the help of your instructor or with classmates, discuss which counseling theories are most compatible with the belief or worldview you now hold as a result of this life experience. Try this exercise with several life experiences to see if the resulting beliefs and life lessons lead you in the direction of specific counseling theories.

LO2

Using Group Techniques Effectively

Techniques are leader interventions aimed at facilitating movement within a group. Virtually anything a group leader does could be viewed as a technique, including being silent, suggesting a new behavior, inviting members to deal with a conflict, offering feedback to members, presenting interpretations, and suggesting homework assignments to be done between group sessions. A **technique** refers to a leader's explicit and directive request of a member (or members) for the purpose of focusing on material, augmenting or exaggerating affect, practicing behavior, or consolidating insight and new learning. Techniques may include asking a group to clarify the direction it wants to take when the group seems to lose energy, inviting members to share a significant story, asking a member to role-play a specific situation, asking a member to practice a new behavior, asking members to bring past events into the here and now, encouraging a person to repeat certain words or to complete a sentence, helping members summarize what they have learned from a group session, working collaboratively with members in designing homework assignments, challenging a member's belief system, and working with the cognitions that influence a member's behavior.

In facilitating a group, we use a variety of techniques drawn from many theoretical models. Techniques are adapted to the needs of the group participants, and we consider several factors: the purpose and type of group, readiness of members to deal with a personal concern, cultural background, value system, and trust in us as leaders. We also consider the level of cohesion and trust among group members when deciding on appropriate interventions. We encourage group participants to become aware of whatever they are feeling, identify the ways their assumptions influence how they feel and behave, and experiment with alternative modes of behaving.

We also consider as techniques those procedures aimed at helping group leaders get a sense of the direction they might pursue with a group. In many types of groups, the most useful techniques grow out of the work of the participants and are tailored to situations that evolve in a particular session. Techniques are the *tools* and interventions used to facilitate what is going on in a group. For example, if the group members are being silent, the leaders may ask each person to complete the sentence, "Right now one thing I am silent about is . . .".

Rationale for Use of Techniques

Techniques are most useful when they evolve from the work of the group participants and are tailored to the situations that evolve in a particular group meeting. As group leaders, it is imperative that we consider the rationale underlying the use of a particular technique and consider whether the technique is likely to foster the client's self-exploration and self-understanding. If a supervisor or coleader were to ask us about our rationale for using a technique, we should be able to answer these questions:

- Why did we use this particular technique?
- What did we hope to accomplish by using a technique?
- What did we expect the group members would learn from the intervention?
- What theoretical framework guided our choice of a technique?

Consider the following case as a basis for reflecting on the purpose of having a theoretical justification for making interventions in a group.

Rebecca, a trainee leading a small group, was asked by the supervisor, "What was your rationale for introducing the exercise during a group session when the energy seemed low and members were reluctant to participate?" Rebecca was somewhat defensive and said she was following her intuition that what the group needed was a booster shot to get moving again. When the leader explored with Rebecca how her theory might influence the interventions she makes, she replied: "I don't think a theory is really necessary. I have a tool kit of techniques, and I feel confident in drawing from them when they are needed. My preference is to go with the flow of the group rather than imposing my theory on a group."

The supervisor explained to Rebecca that a theory provides a general framework that can help her make sense of what is going on in the group, and that a theory also can provide a sense of direction for what she says and does in a group. Rebecca insists that trying to fit into a theory limits her creativity and is likely to result in mechanical interventions. Rebecca sees little value in having a theory to guide her work. She would rather rely on her clinical hunches and create interventions that "feel right."

What are your reactions to what Rebecca is saying? It is possible to trust your clinical intuitions and at the same time to reflect on the conceptual basis for your interventions. Theory can inform and provide a structure for expressing your clinical impressions and interpretations of what is going on in a group. If a supervisor asked you what your preferred theory was, would you be able to describe it? To what extent do you think the techniques you employ in a group need to have some theoretical basis?

It is important to use techniques you have some knowledge about, preferably those you have experienced personally or have received supervision in using. We use the following guidelines in our practice to increase the effectiveness of techniques or any structured exercises that we might introduce in a group session:

- Techniques used have a therapeutic purpose and are grounded in some theoretical framework.
- Techniques (and exercises) are presented in an invitational manner; members are given the freedom either to participate in or to not participate in a given experiment.
- Techniques are introduced in a timely and sensitive manner and are abandoned if they are not working.
- Techniques are modified so that they are suitable for the client's cultural and ethnic background.
- Participants have an opportunity to share their reactions to the techniques or activities used.
- The client's self-exploration and self-understanding is fostered.

LO3

Viewing a Group Through a Multicultural Lens

All people are comprised of multiple identities, and layers of cultural influences are evident in their behaviors. To work effectively with culturally diverse group members, all dimensions of identity including age, gender, sexual orientation, social status, ability, and religious affiliation must be considered regardless of your theoretical perspective. Leaders need to be aware of the power frequently attributed to them by group members and recognize that they may symbolize various institutions of oppression for some members. When introducing exercises or suggesting experiments, it is essential for leaders to be mindful of being invitational and not abusing the authority and power often given to them by group members.

If experiences with discrimination and oppression are not validated and understood, it is highly unlikely that a leader will be able to develop trust and build rapport with people of color or members of other oppressed groups. The pain that the members encounter must be addressed before challenging them to respond differently. Some theoretical approaches challenge clients to examine the way they are interpreting events in their lives and to assume control over their thoughts and feelings. Other theories place a great deal of emphasis on identifying and expressing emotion.

Members of some cultural groups might find the goal of emotional expression to be incompatible with their cultural upbringing and gender-role norms. For example, if a male group member has been taught not to express his feelings in public, it may be both inappropriate and ineffective to quickly introduce techniques aimed at bringing feelings to the surface. In this case it is important to first find out whether this member is interested in exploring what he has learned from his culture about expressing his feelings. Leaders must respect the cultural values and experiences of members, yet at the same time they may invite members to think about how their values, life experiences, socialization, and upbringing continue to affect their behavior and the choices they are making. If members indicate they want to talk about how their cultural background is affecting them today, then leaders can assist members in examining the pros and cons of making behavioral changes and the cost of doing so.

Western therapeutic models reflect values such as choice, the uniqueness of the individual, assertiveness, personal growth, and a strong ego. Therapeutic outcomes include improving assertive coping skills by changing the environment, changing one's coping behavior, and learning to manage stress. Western therapeutic models—such as the cognitive behavioral therapies and the relationship-oriented approaches—are oriented toward individual change. In contrast, many non-Western cultures focus more on the social framework than on development of the individual and teach the value of interdependence, play down individuality, think of the collective good, and emphasize healing in community. Asians, Latinos/as, and African Americans often come from collectivistic cultures. Many Asian cultures stress self-reliance, and some Asian group members may remain quiet rather than disclose their personal problems or reveal personal details about their family (Chung & Bemak, 2014). The goals, structure, and techniques used in a group need to be modified to make a group culturally appropriate and inclusive of members' various worldviews. In an increasingly pluralistic society, there is an ethical imperative to avoid forcing all clients to fit a mold that may not be appropriate for their cultural background. Even within Western cultures norms may differ. For example, Native American cultures emphasize family and community and place less emphasis on individualism.

As group counselors, we need to be aware of how our assumptions and underlying theoretical orientation influence practice with diverse clients. Just as we as group leaders need to attend to our cultural effectiveness with clients, so too do the theories and techniques we use need to be adjusted and tailored to suit the members' cultural and ethnic backgrounds. Being willing to tailor our methods to the needs of members increases the chances of creating positive outcomes.

LO4

Relationship of Theories to Techniques

Some techniques cut across a variety of theories, and others are linked to particular theoretical approaches. The following sections consider the key concepts and techniques of a number of counseling theories, which we have grouped into four general categories:

1. **Psychodynamic approaches** stress insight in therapy (psychoanalytic and Adlerian therapy).
2. **Experiential and relationship-oriented approaches** stress feelings and subjective experiencing (existential, person-centered, Gestalt therapy, and psychodrama).
3. **Cognitive behavioral approaches** stress the role of thinking and doing and tend to be action-oriented (behavior therapy, cognitive therapy, rational emotive behavior therapy, and reality therapy).
4. **Postmodern approaches** stress understanding the subjective world of the client and tap existing resources for change within the individual (solution-focused brief therapy, narrative therapy, motivational interviewing, and feminist therapy).

Although we have separated the theories into four general clusters, this categorization is somewhat arbitrary. Overlapping concepts and themes make it difficult to neatly compartmentalize these theoretical orientations.

In the *Groups in Action*: *Evolution and Challenges DVD and Workbook*, see Part Three, which consists of a lecture overview of the main theoretical approaches to group work and provides many examples of techniques that can be applied to a wide range of groups. This 1-hour lecture program covers the basic concepts of the four general theories briefly described in this chapter.

LO5

Psychodynamic Approaches

First we consider the psychodynamic approaches to group counseling. **Psychoanalytic therapy** is based largely on insight, unconscious motivation, and reconstruction of the personality. The psychoanalytic model has had a major influence on all of the other formal systems of psychotherapy. Some of the therapeutic models we consider are basically extensions of the psychoanalytic approach, others are modifications of analytic concepts and procedures, and still other theories emerged as a reaction against psychoanalysis. Many theories of counseling and psychotherapy have borrowed and integrated principles and techniques from psychoanalytic approaches.

Adlerian therapy differs from psychoanalytic theory in many respects, but it can broadly be considered from a psychodynamic perspective. Adlerians focus on meaning, goals, purposeful behavior, conscious action, belonging, and social interest. Although Adlerian theory accounts for present behavior by studying childhood experiences, it does not focus on unconscious dynamics.

Psychoanalytic Approach

Key Concepts of Psychoanalytic Therapy The psychoanalytic approach views people as being significantly influenced by unconscious motivation and early childhood experiences. Because the dynamics of behavior are buried in the unconscious, group therapy often consists of a lengthy process of analyzing inner conflicts that are rooted in the past. Longer-term analytic group therapy is largely a process of restructuring the personality, which has broader treatment goals than most approaches. Brief psychodynamic group therapy approaches address more modest goals in a limited time frame.

Psychoanalytic group therapy focuses on the influence of the past on current personality functioning. Experiences during the first 6 years of life are seen as the roots of one's problems in the present. Contemporary analytically oriented group practitioners are interested in their members' past, but they intertwine that understanding with the present and with the future. The past is relevant only as it influences the present and the future, and in this sense all three have an essential place in group therapy (Rutan, Stone, & Shay, 2014).

Therapeutic Goals of Psychoanalytic Therapy A primary goal is to make the unconscious conscious. Rather than solving immediate problems, the goal is the restructuring of personality. Successful outcomes of psychoanalytic therapy result in significant modification of an individual's personality and character structure.

Therapeutic Relationship Leadership styles vary among psychoanalytically oriented group therapists, ranging from leaders characterized by objectivity, warm detachment, and relative anonymity to those who favor a role that is likely to result in a collaborative relationship with group members. A significant development of psychoanalytically oriented group therapy is the growing recognition of the central importance of the therapeutic relationship. In contrast to the classical model of the impersonal and detached analyst, the contemporary formulation emphasizes the therapeutic alliance. Establishing a working relationship in which the therapist communicates caring, interest, and involvement with members is now the preferred model.

Techniques Major techniques include maintaining the analytic framework, free association, interpretation, dream analysis, analysis of resistance, and analysis of transference. These techniques are geared to increasing awareness, acquiring insight, and beginning a working-through process that will lead to a reorganization of the personality. Two key features of psychodynamic group therapy are the ways transference and countertransference play out in the context of the current group situation.

Groups offer many opportunities for the exploration of transference reactions that have roots in prior relationships. The group constellation lends itself to **multiple transferences** that provide for reenacting past unfinished events, especially when other members stimulate such intense feelings in an individual that he or she "sees" in them some significant figure such as a father, mother, sibling, life partner, spouse, ex-lover, or boss. A basic tenet of psychodynamic therapy groups is the idea that group members, through their interactions within the group, re-create their social situation, implying that the group becomes a microcosm of their everyday lives. The leader has the task of helping members discover the degree to which they respond to others in the group as if they were their parents or siblings. A psychoanalytic group provides a safe, neutral environment in which members can express spontaneous thoughts and feelings, and the group is a conducive milieu in which to relive significant past events. For example, if a female group member has an intense reaction to a male member, she may discover that she is projecting some old hurts from a critical father onto this member. If both members are willing to explore her transference, she can gain insight into ways that she brings her past relationship with her father into present relationships with certain males.

Groups can provide a dynamic understanding of how people function in out-of-group situations. By reliving the past through the transference process, members gain increased awareness of the ways in which the past is obstructing present functioning. By interpreting and working through their transferences, participants become increasingly aware of the ways in which past events interfere with their ability to appraise and deal with reality in everyday life.

The other side of members' transferences is the countertransference of the group leader, whose feelings may become entangled in the therapeutic relationship with members, obstructing objectivity. Countertransference can be viewed as the group therapist experiencing feelings from the past that are reactivated by the group member in the present (Rutan et al., 2014). In a broader sense, countertransference involves the group therapist's total emotional response to a member. To the degree that countertransference is present, group therapists react to members as if they were significant figures of their own original family. Group leaders need to be alert to signs of their unresolved conflicts that could interfere with their leadership and create a situation in which members are used to satisfy their own unfulfilled needs. For example, a group leader who feels unappreciated by others in his personal life may experience difficulty working with members who are demanding and communicate that he is failing to meet their needs. The difficulty in recognizing one's own countertransference and the necessity that such reactions be acknowledged and therapeutically dealt with provide a rationale for group leaders to experience their own therapy. Personal therapy is valuable in helping leaders to recognize signs of countertransference and in discovering how their own needs and motivations influence their group work. It is critical that countertransference be managed and used for the benefit of working with the group members. When group therapists study their own internal reactions and use them to understand the members of their groups, countertransference can greatly benefit the therapeutic work.

Multicultural Applications of the Psychoanalytic Approach

With this orientation emphasis is placed on how group members' past experiences have a contemporary influence on their personality. The briefer forms of psychodynamic therapy have particular relevance in taking into consideration clients' cultural context and ways that early experiences can provide a new understanding of current problems. With this briefer form of psychoanalytically oriented therapy, clients can relinquish old patterns and establish new patterns in their present behavior.

To learn more about the psychodynamic approach to group practice, we recommend *Psychodynamic Group Psychotherapy* (Rutan et al., 2014).

The Adlerian Approach

Key Concepts of Adlerian Therapy According to the Adlerian approach, people are primarily social beings, influenced and motivated by societal forces. Human nature is viewed as creative, active, and decisional. The approach focuses on the unity of the person, on understanding the individual's subjective perspective, and on the importance of life goals that give direction to behavior. Adler holds that inherent feelings of inferiority initiate a natural striving toward achieving a higher level of mastery and competence in life. The subjective decisions each person makes regarding the specific direction of this striving form the basis of the individual's lifestyle (or personality style). The style of life consists of our views about others, the world, and ourselves; these views lead to distinctive behaviors that we adopt in pursuit of our life goals. We can influence our own future by actively and courageously taking risks and making decisions in the face of unknown consequences. Individuals are not viewed as being "sick" or suffering from a psychopathological disorder and needing to be "cured."

Both psychoanalytic and Adlerian groups often replicate the original family in many respects, which enables members to reexperience conflicts that originated in their family. Because of the family-like atmosphere, the group provides opportunities to evoke associations to both family-of-origin and present life experiences (Rutan et al., 2014). Adlerians place emphasis on the family constellation as a key factor in influencing one's style of life. The group is viewed as a representation of society, which allows members to better understand their own dynamics by seeing patterns of family dynamics emerge within the group.

In Adlerian groups the members are able to bring their personal history into the present group. Members can gain practice acquiring new behavioral patterns by acting *as if* they had made some of the changes they most desire. For example, Darlene struggles with feeling inferior and is unable to express herself effectively both in her daily life and in the group. Interestingly, most members view Darlene as extremely bright and able to communicate clearly—when she does participate. They encourage her to speak more often because they like what she has to say. The group leader suggests to Darlene that she experiment in one group session by *acting as if* she has all the attributes other members see in her. As a result of doing this experiment, Darlene begins to recognize and appreciate her talents. She is encouraged to continue practicing this new behavior for one week in her outside life and to report to the group what the experience was like for her.

Therapeutic Goals of Adlerian Counseling A key goal of an Adlerian group is fostering **social interest**, or facilitating a sense of connectedness with others. Adlerian leaders want to cultivate in members the desire to contribute to the welfare of others, to enhance a sense of identification and empathy with others, and to enhance a sense of belongingness with a group. To accomplish this goal, an Adlerian leader creates a democratic climate within the group. Adlerians do not screen members for their groups because this is viewed as being inconsistent with the spirit of democracy and equality. Sonstegard and Bitter (2004) contend that the screening and selection process itself fails to provide an opportunity for those who most need a group experience. They believe screening is more often done for the comfort of the group leader than for ensuring that those who can most benefit from a group are included.

Counseling is not simply a matter of an expert therapist making prescriptions for change. It is a collaborative effort, with the group members and the group leader working together on mutually accepted goals. The members recognize that they are responsible for their behavior. Adlerians are mainly concerned with challenging clients' mistaken notions and faulty assumptions. Therapy provides encouragement and assists group members in changing their cognitive perspectives and behavior.

Therapeutic Relationship Adlerians base their therapeutic relationship on cooperation, mutual trust, respect, confidence, collaboration, and alignment of goals. They especially value the group leader's modeling of communication and acting in good faith. From the beginning of a group, the relationship between the leader and the members is collaborative and is characterized by working toward specific, agreed-upon goals. Adlerian group therapists strive to establish and maintain an egalitarian therapeutic alliance and a person-to-person relationship with the members of their groups.

Techniques Adlerians have developed a variety of techniques and therapeutic styles. Adlerians are not bound to follow a specific set of procedures; rather, they can tap their creativity by applying those techniques that they think are most appropriate for each client. Some of the specific techniques they often employ are attending, providing both confrontation and support, summarizing, gathering life-history data, lifestyle analysis, interpretation of experiences within the family and early recollections, suggestion, offering encouragement, homework assignments, and assisting group members in searching for new possibilities. Adlerian therapy has a psychoeducational focus, a present and future orientation, and is a brief or time-limited approach.

Interpretation is a key technique of Adlerian group counselors and involves the leader addressing members' underlying motives for behaving the way they do in the here and now. Interpretations are never forced on group members but are presented tentatively in the form of hypotheses, as shown in these examples: "Could it be that your frequent reaction of feeling ignored in this group has something to do with being unnoticed by your family when you were a child?" "I have a hunch that I'd like to share with you." "It seems to me that you are more willing to help others in this group than you are to attend to yourself." "Perhaps you could entertain the idea that waiting to the end of a session to bring up your concerns results in you sabotaging yourself." "I get the impression that no matter how many times people tell you that they like to hear from you, you continue to convince yourself that you have nothing to say."

Interpretations are open-ended presentations of clinical hunches that can be explored in group sessions. Interpretations are best achieved collaboratively within groups with group members offering hunches about possible meanings of their own behavior. The ultimate goal of this process is that participants will come to a deeper psychological understanding of themselves. The aim is for members to acquire deeper awareness of their own role in creating a problem, the ways in which they are maintaining the problem, and what they can do to improve their life situation.

During the advanced stage of an Adlerian group (the reorientation stage), the members are encouraged to take action based on what they have learned from their group participation. The group becomes an agent of change because of the improved interpersonal relations among members. The group process enables members to see themselves as others do and to recognize faulty self-concepts or mistaken goals that they are pursuing. Change is facilitated by the emergence of hope.

During the action stage of an Adlerian group, members make new decisions and their goals are modified. To challenge self-limiting assumptions, members are encouraged to **act as if** they were already the person they would like to be. Adlerians often use this action-oriented technique as a way to facilitate shifting one's view of a situation, enabling members to reflect on how they could be different.

Group members may be asked to "catch themselves" in the process of repeating old patterns that have led to ineffective or self-defeating behavior, such as having many reactions in a session, yet not expressing them verbally. The technique of **catching oneself** involves helping individuals identify signals associated with their problematic behavior or emotions. If participants hope to change, they need to set tasks for themselves and do something specific about their problems. Furthermore, commitment is needed to translate new insights into concrete action.

Adlerian brief group counseling applies a range of techniques within a time-limited framework. Characteristics of this brief approach include initial establishment of a therapeutic alliance, identifying target problems and goal alignment, rapid assessment, active and directive interventions, a focus on strengths and resources of the members, and an emphasis on both the present and the future. Adlerians are flexible in adapting their interventions to each group member's unique life situation.

Multicultural Applications of the Adlerian Approach This approach offers a range of cognitive and action-oriented techniques to help people explore their concerns in a cultural context. Adlerians' interest in helping others, in social interest, in pursuing meaning in life, in belonging, and in the collective spirit fits well with the group process. This approach respects the role of the family as influential in personality development and stresses social connectedness and establishing meaningful relationships in a community. Adlerian therapists tend to focus on cooperation and socially oriented values as opposed to competitive and individualistic values. Adlerian practitioners are flexible in adapting their interventions to each client's unique life situation. The approach has a psychoeducational focus, a present and future orientation, and is a brief, time-limited approach. All of these characteristics make the Adlerian approach to group counseling suitable for working with a wide range of client problems.

An excellent resource for learning more about the Adlerian approach to group work is *Adlerian Group Counseling and Therapy: Step-by-Step* (Sonstegard & Bitter, 2004).

LO6

Experiential and Relationship-Oriented Approaches

Therapy is often viewed as a journey taken by counselor and client, a journey that delves deeply into the world as perceived and experienced by the client. This journey is influenced by the quality of the person-to-person encounter in the therapeutic situation. The value of the therapeutic relationship is a common denominator among all therapeutic orientations, yet some approaches place more emphasis than others do on the role of the relationship as a healing factor. Both existential therapy and person-centered therapy place central prominence on the person-to-person relationship. Emphasizing the human quality of the therapeutic relationship lessens the chances of making group counseling a mechanical process. It is not the techniques we use that make a therapeutic difference; rather, it is the quality of the relationships with group members that heals. If the members of our groups are able to sense our presence and our intention to make a real connection, then a solid foundation is being created for the hard work that follows.

The relationship-oriented approaches (sometimes known as experiential approaches) are all based on the premise that the quality of the therapeutic relationship is primary, with techniques being secondary. Under this general umbrella are *existential therapy, person-centered therapy, Gestalt therapy,* and *psychodrama.* With the experiential and relationship-oriented approaches, group leaders are not bound by a specific set of techniques. They use techniques in the service of broadening the ways in which group members live in their world. Techniques are tools to help the members become aware of their choices and their potential for action.

The experiential approaches are grounded on the premise that the therapeutic relationship fosters a creative spirit of inventing techniques aimed at increasing awareness, which allows individuals to change some of their patterns of thinking, feeling, and behaving.

Some of the key concepts common to all experiential approaches include the following:

- The quality of the leader-to-member encounter in the therapeutic situation is the catalyst for positive change.
- Emphasis is placed on the leader's ability to establish a climate that fosters authentic interchanges among the members.

- The I/Thou relationship (a genuine person-to-person connection) enables members to experience the safety necessary for risk-taking behavior.
- Awareness emerges within the context of a genuine meeting between the leader and the members, or within the context of authentic relating.
- The group leader's main role is to be present with members during the group time. One way to increase this presence is through appropriate self-disclosure by the leader.
- Members can best be invited to behave authentically by a group leader modeling authentic behavior.
- A therapist's attitudes and values are at least as critical as are his or her knowledge, theory, or techniques.
- A group leader who is not sensitively tuned in to his or her own reactions to the members may become more a technician than a skilled facilitator.
- The basic work in a group is done by the members. A leader's job is to create a climate in which members are likely to try out new ways of being.
- Attending to feelings is a useful route to changing one's thinking and behaving.

Counselors who operate in the framework of the relationship-oriented therapies are much less anxious about using the "right technique." Their techniques are most likely designed to enhance some aspect of the client's experiencing, rather than being used to stimulate clients to think, feel, or act in a certain manner.

The Existential Approach

Key Concepts of Existential Therapy The **existential perspective** holds that we define ourselves by our choices. Although outside factors restrict the range of our choices, we are ultimately the authors of our lives. Because we have the capacity for awareness, we are basically free. Along with our freedom, however, comes responsibility for the choices we make. Our task is to create a meaningful existence. Existential group practitioners contend that clients often lead a "restricted existence," seeing few if any alternatives for dealing with life situations and tending to feel trapped or helpless. A group experience can help members recognize outmoded patterns of living and accept responsibility for changing their future. For instance, if you have suffered great rejection in your childhood, you may cling to a view of yourself as being unacceptable, in spite of the fact that many group members are accepting of you and claim they admire you.

There are six key propositions of existential therapy: (1) We have the capacity for self-awareness. (2) Because we are basically free beings, we must accept the responsibility that accompanies our freedom. (3) We have a concern to preserve our uniqueness and identity; we come to know ourselves in relation to knowing and interacting with others. (4) The significance of our existence and the meaning of our life are never fixed once and for all; instead, we re-create ourselves through our projects. (5) Anxiety is part of the human condition. (6) Death is also a basic human condition, and the reality of our mortality heightens our sense of ultimate aloneness. The reality of death can lead to increased awareness that we do not have forever to actualize our being. Death awareness can give significance to living.

Therapeutic Goals of Existential Therapy The principal goal of an existential group is to assist the participants in recognizing and accepting the freedom they have to become the authors of their own lives. Group leaders encourage members to examine the ways in which they are avoiding their freedom and the responsibility that accompanies it.

The existential group represents a microcosm of the world in which participants live and function. It is assumed that over time the interpersonal and existential problems of the participants become manifest in the here-and-now interactions within the group. The central purpose of this kind of group is to enable members to discover themselves as they are by sharing their existential concerns.

Therapeutic Relationship The existential approach places primary emphasis on understanding members' current experience, not on using therapeutic techniques. The therapeutic relationship is of paramount importance, for the quality of the I/Thou encounter (interpersonal relationships in the group) offers a context for change. Existential group therapists value being fully present and strive to create caring relationships with the members of their groups. Therapy is a collaborative relationship in which both members and the leader are involved in a journey of self-discovery.

Techniques Existential therapy reacts against the tendency to view therapy as a system of well-defined techniques; it affirms looking at those unique characteristics that make us human and building therapy on them. Existential group therapists are free to adapt their interventions to their own personality and style, as well as paying attention to what each group member requires. Existential group leaders are *not* bound by any prescribed procedures and can use techniques from other therapy schools; however, their interventions are guided by a philosophical framework about what it means to be human.

Multicultural Applications of the Existential Approach Because the existential approach is based on universal human themes, and because it does not dictate a particular way of viewing reality, it is highly applicable when working in a multicultural context. Themes such as relationships, finding meaning, anxiety, suffering, and death are concerns that transcend the boundaries that separate cultures. Clients in existential group therapy are encouraged to examine the ways their present existence is being influenced by social and cultural factors. The existential approach is particularly relevant for multicultural situations because it does not impose particular values and meanings; rather, it investigates the values and meanings of group members. Existential group counselors respect the different elements that make up a member's philosophy of life. They respect the uniqueness of the particular situation of each client and do not impose their cultural values on the person. With this understanding of different worldviews, group practitioners are in a position to establish mutually agreed-upon goals with individuals that will provide a direction for change.

If you are interested in learning more about the existential approach to group work, we recommend *Existential-Humanistic Therapy* (Schneider & Krug, 2010), *Existential Psychotherapy* (Yalom, 1980), and *The Schopenhauer Cure: A Novel* (Yalom, 2005a).

The Person-Centered Approach

Key Concepts of Person-Centered Therapy The **person-centered approach** rests on the assumption that we have the capacity to understand our problems and that we have the resources within us to resolve them. The group facilitator focuses on the constructive side of human nature and on what is right with people. Group members are able to change without a high degree of structure and direction from the facilitator. Group facilitators provide understanding, genuineness, support, acceptance, caring, and positive regard. This approach emphasizes fully experiencing the present moment, learning to accept oneself, and deciding on ways to change. The person-centered approach stresses the active role and responsibility of the group member. It is a positive and optimistic view and calls attention to the need to account for a person's inner and subjective experiences.

Therapeutic Goals of Person-Centered Therapy A major goal is to provide a climate of safety and trust in the therapeutic setting so that the client, by using the therapeutic relationship for self-exploration, can become aware of blocks to growth. Because this approach stresses the client–therapist relationship as a *necessary and sufficient condition* leading to change, it minimizes directive techniques, interpretation, questioning, probing, diagnosis, and collecting history. Group members are trusted to identify personally meaningful goals and to find their own way without active and directive structuring from the group leader.

Therapeutic Relationship Emphasizing the crucial role of the therapist's attitudes and personal characteristics, this approach makes the therapeutic process relationship-centered rather than technique-centered. The qualities of the facilitator that determine the relationship include the attitudes of genuineness, nonpossessive warmth, accurate empathy, unconditional acceptance of and respect for the client, caring, and the communication of those attitudes to the client.

The primary function of the facilitator is to create an accepting and healing climate in the group. Person-centered therapy is best considered as a "way of being" rather than a "way of doing." The group leader is called a *facilitator,* which reflects the importance of interactions between group members and the leader's ability to assist members in expressing themselves. Person-centered group facilitators use themselves as instruments of change in a group. Their central function is to establish a therapeutic climate in which group members will interact in increasingly authentic ways.

Person-centered therapy is best considered as a "way of being" rather than a "way of doing."

The person-centered group approach emphasizes certain attitudes and skills as a necessary part of the facilitator's style: listening in an active and sensitive way, accepting, understanding, reflecting, clarifying, summarizing, sharing personal experiences, responding, encountering and engaging others in the group, going with the flow of the group rather than trying to direct the way the group is going, and affirming a member's capacity for self-determination. Other relational qualities and attitudes embraced by person-centered therapists include receptivity to experience, contact and engagement, a therapeutic alliance, authentic dialogue, understanding the client's experience, and hopefulness regarding the client's capacity for the relationship (Cain, 2010).

Techniques Person-centered therapy has evolved through diversity, inventiveness, creativity, and individualization in practice. In newer versions of the person-centered approaches, group facilitators have increased freedom to participate in the relationship, to share their reactions, to confront clients in a caring way, and to be active in the therapeutic process (Cain, 2010; Kirschenbaum, 2009). Current formulations of the approach assign more importance to therapists' bringing in their own here-and-now reactions to what is occurring with a group. Doing so can motivate members to explore themselves at a deeper level. These changes from Carl Rogers's original view of the counselor have encouraged the use of a wider variety of methods and a considerable diversity of therapeutic styles. Therapists need to evolve as people rather than being intent on expanding their repertoire of techniques. However, it is important to remember that effective group facilitators need to be therapeutic people, *and* they also must have the knowledge and skills required to assist members in reaching their personal goals in a group.

Group practitioners can adapt the person-centered approach to their personal convictions and therapeutic style, integrating their own life experiences and ideas into their work with groups. Integrative personal-centered therapists subscribe to a fundamental philosophy, yet they may blend concepts and methods from existential, Gestalt, and experiential approaches in facilitating their groups.

Natalie Rogers (2011) has made a significant contribution to the application of the person-centered approach by incorporating the expressive arts as a medium to facilitate personal exploration in a group context. *Person-centered expressive arts therapy* uses various artistic forms—movement, drawing, painting, sculpting, music, writing, and improvisation—toward the end of growth, healing, and self-discovery. This is a multimodal group approach integrating mind, body, emotions, and spiritual inner resources. Individuals who have difficulty expressing themselves verbally can find new possibilities for self-expression through the various nonverbal forms of expression available to them.

Multicultural Applications of Person-Centered Therapy The emphasis on universal, core conditions provides the person-centered approach with a framework for understanding diverse worldviews. Empathy, being present, and respecting the values of group participants are particularly important attitudes and skills in groups with culturally diverse individuals. These attitudes are not limited to any one cultural group but transcend culture. Person-centered counselors convey a deep respect for all forms of diversity and value understanding the client's subjective world in an accepting and open way. One potential limitation of this approach is the fact that some clients come to a group to find solutions for pressing problems. Individuals from certain cultures may expect a directive leader who functions in an expert role as an authority, who offers advice and recommends a specific course of action, and they may experience difficulty with a leader who does not provide the structure they want.

For more information on the person-centered approach, we recommend *The Creative Connection for Groups: Person-Centered Expressive Arts for Healing and Social Change* (N. Rogers, 2011), *Person-Centered Psychotherapies* (Cain, 2010), and *Humanistic Psychotherapies: Handbook of Research and Practice* (Cain, Keenan, & Rubin, 2016).

Gestalt Therapy

Key Concepts of Gestalt Therapy The **Gestalt approach** is an existential and phenomenological approach based on the assumption that individuals and their behavior must be understood in the context of their ongoing relationship with the present environment. The group therapist's task is to support the members as they explore their perceptions of reality. The fundamental method to assist in this exploration is awareness of the internal (intrapersonal) world and contact with the external environment. Change occurs naturally as awareness of "what is" increases. Heightened awareness can lead to a more thorough integration of parts of the group member's reality that were fragmented or unknown.

This approach focuses on the here and now, direct experiencing, awareness, bringing unfinished business from the past into the present, and dealing with unfinished business. Other concepts include energy and blocks to energy, contact, and paying attention to nonverbal cues. Group members identify their own unfinished business from the past that is interfering with their present functioning by reexperiencing past situations as though events were happening in the present moment.

Therapeutic Goals of Gestalt Therapy The primary goal of Gestalt therapy is attaining awareness and greater choice. Awareness includes knowing the environment and knowing oneself, accepting oneself, and being able to make contact. Group members are helped to pay attention to their own awareness process so that they can be responsible and can selectively and discriminatingly make choices.

Therapeutic Relationship As is true for the other experiential approaches, the focus is not on the techniques employed by the therapist but on who the therapist is as a person and the quality of the relationship. Factors that are emphasized include the therapist's presence, authentic dialogue, gentleness, direct self-expression by the therapist, and a greater trust in the client's experiencing. There are many different styles of practicing Gestalt therapy in a group, but all styles share common elements: direct experiencing and experimenting and attention to *what* and *how* and *here* and *now*.

Techniques Gestalt group leaders think more in terms of experiments than techniques. Although the therapist functions as a guide and a catalyst, presents experiments, and shares observations, the basic work of therapy is done by the group members. Group leaders do not force change on the members; rather, leaders create experiments within a here-and-now framework of what is going on in the group. These experiments are the cornerstone of experiential learning. Gestalt therapy utilizes the experiment to move group members from talk to action and experience. For example, assume a member is talking about a problematic relationship with a friend. The leader is likely to invite this member to bring the friend symbolically into the room, either by talking to an empty chair or talking directly to another group member as though he or she were the friend. With the emphasis given to the relationship between client and therapist, there is a creative spirit of suggesting, inventing, and carrying out experiments aimed at increasing awareness.

Although the group leader suggests the experiments, this is a collaborative process with full participation by the group members. Gestalt experiments take many forms: setting up a dialogue between a group member and a significant person in his or her life; assuming the identity of a key figure through role playing; reliving a painful event; exaggerating a gesture, posture, or some nonverbal mannerism; or carrying on a dialogue between two conflicting aspects within an individual. For effective application of Gestalt procedures, it is essential that clients be prepared for such experiments.

Sensitively staying in contact with a group member's flow of experiencing involves paying attention to the person and not on being concerned with the mechanical use of techniques to bring about a certain effect. Gestalt practitioners who have truly integrated their approach are able to apply their skills in a flexible way by adapting their methods to each individual. They have solid training in Gestalt theory and practice, which allows them to design experiments that will deepen the work of members. They strive to help members experience themselves as fully as possible in the present.

Gestalt therapy is truly an integrative orientation in that it focuses on whatever is in the individual's awareness. From the Gestalt perspective, feelings, thoughts, body sensations, and actions are all used as pathways to understand what is central for the client in each moment. The centrality of whatever is in the group member's awareness is an ideal way to understand his or her world. By paying attention to the verbal and nonverbal cues provided, a group leader has a starting point for exploring the member's world.

Multicultural Applications of Gestalt Therapy There are many opportunities to apply Gestalt experiments in creative ways with diverse client populations. Gestalt experiments can be tailored to fit the unique way in which an individual perceives and interprets his or her culture. Gestalt leaders approach each client in an open way without preconceptions. They do this by checking out their views in dialogue with the group member. This is particularly important in working with individuals from diverse cultural backgrounds. They are concerned about how and which aspects of this background become central, or figural, for them and what meaning clients place on these figures.

Because Gestalt therapy is practiced with a phenomenological attitude, therapists are less likely to impose their own values and cultural standards on their clients. Gestalt therapy can be used creatively and sensitively with culturally diverse populations if interventions are used flexibly and in a timely manner. One of the advantages of drawing on Gestalt experiments is that they can be tailored to fit the unique way in which an individual member perceives and interprets his or her culture. Before Gestalt procedures are introduced, it is crucial that the group members have been adequately prepared. Gestalt group practitioners focus on understanding the person and not on the use of techniques. Experiments are done with the collaboration of the group member and with the attempt to understand the background of the member's culture.

For further information on the Gestalt approach to group counseling, we recommend *Beyond the Hot Seat Revisited: Gestalt Approaches to Groups* (Feder & Frew, 2008) and *Gestalt Group Therapy: A Practical Guide* (Feder, 2006).

Psychodrama

Key Concepts of Psychodrama **Psychodrama** is primarily an action approach to group counseling in which clients explore their problems through role playing, enacting situations using various dramatic devices to gain insight, discover their own creativity, and develop behavioral skills. The scenes are played as if they were occurring in the here and now, even though they might have their origins in a past event or an anticipated situation. Using psychodrama, the client acts out or dramatizes past, present, or anticipated life situations and roles to gain deeper understanding, to explore feelings and achieve emotional release, and to develop new ways of coping with problems. Significant events are enacted to help the members of the group get in contact with unrecognized and unexpressed feelings, to provide a channel for the full expression of these feelings and attitudes, and to broaden their role repertoire.

A main concept of psychodrama involves encouraging members to work in the present moment, as is also true of Gestalt therapy. At times group members will *talk about* situations in the past or the future to distance and defend themselves against experiencing their feelings. By re-creating those difficult situations as if they were happening in the present moment, the actual encounter is brought into consciousness. When the protagonist (group member who is the focus of the work) slips into narrating, or begins to *talk about* a problem, the psychodrama leader steers the protagonist into action by saying, "Don't tell me *about* it, show me what happened, as if it's happening now." By bringing a problem into the here and now, the participants move away from abstract and intellectual discussions. A key concept of psychodrama is that reliving and reexperiencing a scene from the past gives the participants both the opportunity to examine how that event affected them at the time it occurred and a chance to deal differently with the event *now.* By replaying a past event "as if" it were happening in the present, the individual is able to assign new meaning to it. Through this process, the person can work through unfinished business and reframe that earlier situation.

Therapeutic Goals of Psychodrama Psychodrama aims at fostering creativity in the individual, the group, and ultimately in the culture as a whole. Key goals of psychodrama are to facilitate the release of pent-up feelings, to provide insight, and to help group members develop new and more effective behaviors. In a group situation emotions tend to be released, which is the **catharsis** that often accompanies the experiential aspect of therapy. Catharsis is a natural part of the psychodramatic process, but it is not in itself a goal. Simply rediscovering buried emotions will not bring about healing; these feelings must be worked through for integration to occur. For those who have lost awareness of the roots of their feelings, emotional release may lead to insight, or to an increased awareness of a problem situation. Other goals of psychodrama include encouraging participants to live in the present and to behave in more spontaneous ways. A main aim is to open up unexplored possibilities for solving conflicts and for living more creatively.

Therapeutic Relationship The underlying philosophy of psychodrama is consistent with many of the premises of existential therapy, person-centered therapy, and Gestalt therapy, all of which emphasize understanding and respecting the group member's experience and the importance of the therapeutic relationship as a healing factor. Although practitioners who employ psychodramatic methods assume an active and directive role, these techniques are most effective when the group counselor adopts a person-centered spirit. Practitioners who are authentic, able to make connections with members, able to be psychologically present, demonstrate empathy, and exhibit a high level of respect and positive regard for the members of their groups are most effectively able to implement a range of psychodrama techniques.

Techniques The active techniques, such as role playing, are useful for many different kinds of groups. These methods enable group members to directly experience their conflicts to a much greater degree than is the case when members *talk about* themselves in a storytelling manner. This direct experiencing tends to bring emotions to the surface. Oftentimes one member's deeply emotional work will trigger emotional reactions in other members. The work of members can be linked to common themes emerging in a session. Participants in a psychodrama can be encouraged to reflect on how their beliefs and early decisions may be contributing to some of the emotional reactions they reexperienced in the psychodrama. The techniques of psychodrama encourage people to express themselves more fully, explore both intrapsychic conflicts and interpersonal problems, get constructive feedback on how they come across to others, reduce feelings of isolation, and experiment with novel ways of approaching significant others in their lives.

Psychodrama uses a number of specific techniques designed to intensify feelings, clarify implicit beliefs, increase self-awareness, and practice new behaviors. One of the most powerful tools of psychodrama is **role reversal**, which involves the group member taking on the part of another person. Through role reversal, people are able to get outside of their own frame of reference and enact a side of themselves they would rarely show to others. In addition, by reversing roles with a significant person, the person is able to formulate significant emotional and cognitive insights into his or her part in a relationship. This technique also creates empathy for the position of the other person.

A technique that has many applications for various kinds of groups is the technique of **future projection**, which is designed to help group members express and clarify concerns they have about the future. In future projection, an anticipated event is brought into the present moment and acted out. These concerns may include wishes and hopes, dreaded fears of tomorrow, and goals that provide some direction to life. Members create a future time and place with selected people, bring this event into the present, and get a new perspective on a problem.

Members may act out either a version of the way they hope a given situation will ideally unfold or their version of the most horrible outcome. When participants in psychodrama enact anticipated events as though they were taking place in the here and now, they achieve an increased awareness of their available options. Rehearsals for future encounters, coupled with constructive and specific feedback, can be of real value to those members who want to develop more effective ways of relating to significant people in their lives.

Caution should be used when employing psychodrama techniques. Competent practitioners who use a psychodrama framework for practice devote a great deal of time to developing their skills, and they will have undergone a training program under the supervision of an experienced clinician. Psychodrama works best with clinicians who are well grounded in professional judgment and open to drawing methods from various approaches. It is important to remember that practitioners can use certain aspects or techniques of psychodrama without employing a complete enactment.

Multicultural Applications of Psychodrama If group members are uncomfortable in talking about deeply personal matters, let alone displaying their emotions in front of others, some psychodrama techniques are most likely not appropriate. Many of these techniques can be adapted to a problem-solving approach that makes use of cognitive and behavioral principles. It is possible to combine both didactic and experiential methods in structured groups with members who are culturally diverse. Role-playing techniques can be productively adapted to structured situations dealing with trying on a new set of specific behaviors. This makes for a possible integration of certain psychodrama techniques with many of the cognitive behavioral approaches.

An easy-to-read treatment of psychodrama is *Acting-In: Practical Applications of Psychodramatic Methods* (Blatner, 1996); we also recommend *Foundations of Psychodrama: History, Theory, and Practice* (Blatner, 2000).

LO7

Cognitive Behavioral Approaches

Some of the main cognitive behavioral group approaches include behavior therapy, cognitive therapy, rational emotive behavior therapy, and reality therapy. Although the cognitive behavioral approaches are quite diverse, they do share these attributes:

1. A collaborative relationship between the group member and the therapist
2. The premise that psychological distress is largely a function of disturbances in cognitive processes
3. A focus on changing cognitions to produce desired changes in affect and behavior
4. A present-focused model
5. A generally time-limited and educational treatment focusing on specific and structured target problems
6. A model that relies on empirical validation of its concepts and techniques

The cognitive behavioral approaches are based on a structured, psychoeducational model, and they tend to emphasize the role of homework, place responsibility on the group member to assume an active role both during and outside of the group sessions, and draw from a variety of cognitive and behavioral techniques to bring about change.

A basic assumption underlying the cognitive behavioral approaches is that most problematic behaviors, cognitions, and emotions have been learned and can be modified by new learning. Members of a group are involved in a teaching and learning process and are taught how to develop a new perspective on ways of learning. They are encouraged to try out more effective behaviors, cognitions, and emotions. Problems may arise due to a skills deficit—adaptive behaviors or cognitive strategies that have not been learned—and group members can acquire coping skills by participating in this educational experience. An example would be providing social effectiveness skills to people with social phobias who are interested in confronting their fears.

A strength of the cognitive behavioral approaches is the wide range of techniques that participants can use to specify their goals and to develop the skills needed to achieve these goals. The specificity of the cognitive behavioral approaches helps group members translate fuzzy goals into concrete plans of action, which enable the members to keep these plans clearly in focus.

Cognitive behavioral therapy (CBT) has many applications to a variety of counseling groups in many different settings. Cognitive behavioral group therapy is effective for treating a wide range of emotional and behavioral problems. CBT in groups has been demonstrated to have beneficial results for specific problems such as anxiety, depression, phobia, obesity, eating disorders, dual diagnoses, and dissociative disorders. Some factors that make CBT effective in working with diverse clients include tailoring treatment to each individual, addressing the role of the external environment, the active and directive role of the therapist, the emphasis on education, relying on empirical evidence, the focus on present behavior, and the brevity of the approach.

Behavior Therapy

Key Concepts of Behavior Therapy The cornerstone of **behavior therapy** is the identification of specific goals at the outset of the therapeutic process, which serves as a way to monitor and measure the progress of group members. Because therapy begins with an assessment of baseline data, the degree of progress can be evaluated by comparing group members' behavior on a given dimension at any point in a group with the baseline data. Participants in a group are frequently challenged to answer the question, "Is what we are doing in here helping you make the changes you desire?" With this information, members are in the best position to determine the degree to which their personal goals are being achieved.

Behavior therapy as applied to group work is a systematic approach that begins with a comprehensive assessment of the individual to determine the present level of functioning as a prelude to setting therapeutic goals. After the group member establishes clear and specific behavioral goals, the therapist typically suggests strategies that are most appropriate for meeting these stated goals. Evaluation is used to determine how well the procedures and techniques are working. Empirically supported techniques are selected to deal with specific problems because this approach is grounded in evidence-based practice. **Evidence-based practice** is best conceived of in a broad way and includes clinician expertise, the best available research, and evaluating the client's characteristics, culture, and preferences. Even in behavior therapy, the therapeutic relationship is of central importance and critical to outcome.

Therapeutic Goals of Behavior Therapy The general goals of behavior therapy are to increase personal choice and to create new conditions for learning. An aim is to eliminate maladaptive behaviors and to replace them with more constructive patterns. The client and therapist collaboratively specify treatment goals in concrete, measurable, and objective terms. Goals must be clear, concrete, understood, and agreed on by the members and the group leader. Behavior therapists and group members alter goals throughout the therapeutic process as needed.

Therapeutic Relationship A good working relationship is an essential precondition for effective group therapy to occur. The skilled group counselor can conceptualize problems behaviorally, use a range of specific behavioral techniques, and make use of the therapeutic relationship in bringing about change. The group counselor's role is to teach concrete skills through the provision of instructions, modeling, and performance feedback. Leaders tend to be active and directive and to function as consultants and problem solvers. Group members must be actively involved in the therapeutic process from beginning to end, and they are expected to cooperate in carrying out therapeutic activities, both in the sessions and outside of therapy.

Techniques Assessment is done at the outset of group treatment to determine a treatment plan. The leader follows the progress of group members through the ongoing collection of data before, during, and after all interventions. Such an approach provides both the group leader and the members with continuous feedback about therapeutic progress. Behavioral interventions are individually tailored to specific problems experienced by different group members.

Any technique that can be demonstrated to change behavior may be incorporated in a treatment plan. Techniques such as relaxation methods, role playing, behavioral rehearsal, coaching, guided practice, modeling, giving feedback, mindfulness skills, cognitive restructuring, systematic desensitization, in vivo desensitization, flooding, problem solving, and homework assignments can be included in any group counselor's practice, regardless of theoretical orientation. Some of these techniques can be demonstrated by both group leaders and other members in the group. For example, both the leader and members can provide modeling, such as dealing with others respectfully, taking risks by moving outside their comfort zone, and expressing empathy for others. During role-playing situations, both members and the leader can function as coaches by suggesting alternative and more productive dialogue. Both the leader and members offer beneficial feedback to others.

Behavioral treatment interventions are individually tailored to specific problems experienced by different group members. The behavioral group practitioner uses strategies that have research support for use with a particular kind of problem.

These evidence-based strategies are used to promote generalization and maintenance of behavior change. Many of these research-based behavioral interventions can be fruitfully integrated into other therapeutic approaches.

Multicultural Applications of Behavior Therapy Behavioral approaches can be appropriately integrated into counseling with culturally diverse client populations when culture-specific procedures are developed. In designing a change program for clients from diverse cultures, effective practitioners conduct a functional analysis of the problem situation. This assessment includes the cultural context in which the problem behavior occurs, the consequences both to the client and to the client's sociocultural environment, the resources within the environment that can facilitate change, and the impact that change may have on others in the client's surroundings. The approach emphasizes teaching group members about the therapeutic process and stresses changing specific behaviors. By developing their problem-solving skills, clients learn concrete methods for dealing with practical problems within their cultural framework. Behavioral group practitioners typically spend time preparing members to participate in a group experience. The group process is demystified and norms are made clear. This approach is likely to appeal to clients who have doubts about the value of a group experience but are interested in learning practical ways of coping with immediate problems.

For further discussion of behavioral group therapy, we recommend *Cognitive-Behavioral Therapy in Groups* (Bieling, McCabe, & Antony, 2006), which has ideas on how to structure and lead cognitive behavioral groups and describes a wide variety of cognitive and behavioral strategies useful in groups.

Cognitive Therapy

Key Concepts of Cognitive Therapy According to **cognitive therapy (CT)**, psychological problems stem from commonplace processes such as faulty thinking, making incorrect inferences on the basis of inadequate or incorrect information, and failing to distinguish between fantasy and reality. Cognitive therapy assumes that people are prone to learning erroneous, self-defeating thoughts but that they are capable of unlearning them. People perpetuate their difficulties through the beliefs they hold and their self-talk. By pinpointing these cognitive errors and correcting them, individuals can create a more fulfilling life.

Automatic thoughts are personalized notions that are triggered by particular stimuli that lead to emotional responses. For example, a group member's automatic thought might be: "I am stupid because I can't follow what others are saying in this group." These negative automatic thoughts come up quite spontaneously, and when this happens the group member feels anxious and embarrassed. The cognitive group therapist is interested in helping members identify their automatic thoughts and teaching them how to evaluate their thoughts in a structured way. The techniques are designed to identify and test members' misconceptions and faulty assumptions. Cognitive therapists are continuously active and deliberately interactive with the members of their groups. The leader strives to engage members' active participation and collaboration throughout all phases of the group experience.

A cognitive behavioral orientation places emphasis on the group leader functioning as a teacher who encourages group members to learn skills to deal with the problems of living. The emphasis is on changing specific behaviors and developing problem-solving skills rather than expressing feelings. The cognitive therapist teaches group members how to identify inaccurate and dysfunctional cognitions through a process of evaluation. The group leader assists members in forming hypotheses and testing their assumptions, which is known as **collaborative empiricism**. The group leader rarely directly challenges the beliefs of members, but instead works collaboratively with members to examine the evidence for certain beliefs, test the validity of these beliefs, and look for more adaptive ways of thinking. Thus a group member might say, "Once people get know me, they will reject me." The validity of this assumption can be questioned and explored in the group context. Through a process of feedback, this member might discover that several people in the group are drawn to him and express a liking for him. This feedback can help him to evaluate the merits of his assumptions.

Through a collaborative effort, group members learn to discriminate between their own thoughts and events that occur in reality. Members learn the influence that cognition has on their feelings and behaviors and even on environmental events, particularly the distortions that they have acquired.

Cognitive restructuring plays a central role in the cognitive therapies. Group members sometimes engage in catastrophic thinking by dwelling on the most extreme negative aspects of a situation. The leader can assist members in detecting those times when members get stuck imagining the worst possible outcome of a situation by asking these questions: "What is the worst thing that could occur?" and "If this happens, what would make this such a negative outcome?" Group participants are able to make changes by listening to their self-talk, by learning a new internal dialogue, and by learning coping skills needed for behavioral changes. In the group context, members are taught to recognize, observe, and monitor their own thoughts and assumptions, especially their negative automatic thoughts. Once members discover certain beliefs that are not accurate, they are encouraged to try out a different set of beliefs and behaviors, both in the group and in daily life.

Therapeutic Goals of Cognitive Therapy The goal of cognitive behavior therapy is to change the way clients think by identifying their automatic thoughts and begin to introduce the idea of cognitive restructuring. Changes in beliefs and thought processes tend to result in changes in the way people feel and how they behave. Members learn practical ways to identify their underlying faulty beliefs, to critically evaluate these beliefs, and to replace them with constructive beliefs.

Therapeutic Relationship Group leaders combine empathy and sensitivity with technical competence in establishing their relationship with members. A therapeutic alliance is a necessary first step in cognitive group therapy, especially in counseling difficult-to-reach group members. Group leaders must have a cognitive conceptualization of cases, be creative and active, be able to engage clients through a process of Socratic questioning, and be knowledgeable and skilled in the use of cognitive and behavioral strategies. Cognitive practitioners are continuously active and deliberately interactive with group members, helping them frame their conclusions in the form of testable hypotheses.

Techniques Cognitive therapy is present-centered, psychoeducational, and time-limited. Cognitive therapy in groups emphasizes a **Socratic dialogue** and helping group members discover their misconceptions for themselves. After group members have gained insight into how their unrealistically negative thoughts are affecting them, they are trained to test these inaccurate thoughts against reality by examining and weighing the evidence for and against them. This process involves empirically testing their beliefs by actively participating in a variety of methods, such as engaging in a process of guided discovery (or a Socratic dialogue) with the therapist, critically evaluating the bases for their beliefs, carrying out homework assignments, gathering data on assumptions they make, keeping a record of activities, and forming alternative interpretations. Through this process of **guided discovery**, the group leader functions as a catalyst and guide who helps the members understand the connection between their thinking and the ways they feel and act. Through the use of questioning the members acquire new information and different ways of thinking, acting, and feeling. The cognitive strategies of Socratic questioning and guided discovery are central to cognitive therapy, and they are frequently employed in a cognitively oriented groups.

The leader teaches group members how to be their own therapist. This includes educating participants in a group about the nature and course of their problems, about how cognitive therapy works, and how their thinking influences their emotions and behaviors. Cognitive behavioral practitioners function as teachers; group members acquire a wide range of skills to use in dealing with the problems of living. This educational focus appeals to many clients who are interested in learning practical and effective methods of bringing about change. Homework is often used in cognitive therapy, which is tailored to the member's specific problems and arises out of the collaborative therapeutic relationship. Homework is generally presented as an experiment, and group members are encouraged to create their own self-help assignments as a way to keep working on issues addressed in their group sessions. The educative process includes providing clients with information about their presenting problems and about **relapse prevention**, which consists of procedures for dealing with the inevitable setbacks clients are likely to experience as they apply what they are learning to daily life.

Multicultural Applications of Cognitive Therapy Cognitive therapy tends to be culturally sensitive because it uses the individual's belief system, or worldview, as part of the method of self-change. The therapist's attention is on the degree to which these beliefs are adaptive for the client. Cognitive therapists do not impose their beliefs on group members; rather, they help members assess whether a given belief fosters emotional well-being. The collaborative nature of CT offers members of a group the structure many people want, yet the group counselor still strives to enlist clients' active participation in the therapeutic process.

Some useful resources for learning more about cognitive therapy include *Cognitive Behavior Therapy: Beyond the Basics* (Beck, 2011) and *Cognitive Therapy for Challenging Problems: What to Do When the Basics Don't Work* (Beck, 2005).

Rational Emotive Behavior Therapy

Key Concepts of Rational Emotive Behavior Therapy From the perspective of **rational emotive behavior therapy (REBT)**, our problems are caused by our perceptions of life situations and our thoughts, not by the situations themselves, not by others, and not by past events. It is our responsibility to recognize and change self-defeating thinking that leads to emotional and behavioral disorders. REBT also holds that people tend to incorporate these dysfunctional beliefs from external sources and then continue to indoctrinate themselves with this faulty thinking. To overcome irrational thinking, therapists use active and directive therapy procedures, including teaching, suggestion, and giving homework. REBT in groups emphasizes education, with the group leader functioning as a teacher and the group members as learners. Although REBT is didactic and directive, its goal is to get people to think, feel, and act for themselves. In a REBT group, members are consistently encouraged to do what is necessary to make long-lasting and substantive changes.

REBT group practitioners employ a directive role in encouraging members to commit themselves to practicing in everyday situations what they are learning in the group sessions. They view what goes on during the group as important, but they realize that the hard work between sessions and after therapy is terminated is even more crucial.

Therapeutic Goals of Rational Emotive Behavior Therapy The goals of REBT are to eliminate a self-defeating outlook on life, to reduce unhealthy emotional responses, and to acquire a more rational and tolerant philosophy. REBT offers group members practical ways to identify their underlying faulty beliefs, to critically evaluate these beliefs, and to replace them with constructive beliefs. Participants in a group learn how to substitute preferences for demands.

Therapeutic Relationship REBT practitioners strive to unconditionally accept the members of their groups and to teach them to unconditionally accept others and themselves. Group leaders do not blame or condemn members; rather, they teach members how to avoid rating and condemning themselves. REBT practitioners accept their clients as imperfect beings who can be helped using a variety of techniques.

Techniques REBT utilizes a wide range of cognitive, emotive, and behavioral methods with most group members. This approach blends techniques to change members' patterns of thinking, feeling, and acting. Techniques are designed to induce clients to critically examine their present beliefs and behavior. REBT focuses on specific techniques for changing a group member's self-defeating thoughts in concrete situations. In addition to modifying beliefs, REBT helps clients see how their beliefs influence what they feel and what they do.

One cognitive technique used in REBT groups is teaching members **coping self-statements**. Group members are taught how faulty beliefs can be countered by rational, coping self-statements. They are expected to monitor their manner of speaking by writing down and analyzing the quality of their language. For example, a member might tell herself: "I *must* perform well, which means being perfect.

People will give me approval only when I'm perfect, and I very much need this approval from others to feel worthwhile." By becoming aware of the demanding quality of her internal and external speech, she can learn how what she tells herself is setting her up for failure. She can replace these self-defeating statements with coping statements: "I can still accept myself even though I am imperfect."

In REBT groups, **faulty thinking** is confronted. For example, when Jeffrey says, "I am a failure as a father, and I am sure that my children will never forgive me for the mistakes I have made," Jeffrey could be invited to go to each person and list one of the ways he has failed his children. The leader can ask Jeffrey to tell a few members in the group how he came to the conclusion that he is a failure and then acknowledge that he has made mistakes. Jeffrey might then critically evaluate the conclusion that he believes he is a total failure because he has made mistakes. Without knowing some of Jeffrey's history, it is difficult to assess the accuracy of his conclusion that he failed his children and that they would never forgive him. Exploring some of the details regarding the ways Jeffrey believes he has failed his children could help him move toward being more self-accepting in spite of his imperfections.

Multicultural Applications of Rational Emotive Behavior Therapy Some factors that make REBT effective in working with diverse client populations include tailoring treatment to each individual, the focus on present behavior, and the brevity of the approach. REBT group practitioners function as teachers, and this educational focus appeals to many group members who are interested in learning practical and effective methods of bringing about change. REBT stresses the relationship of individuals to the family, community, and other systems. This orientation is consistent with valuing diversity and the interdependence of being an individual and a productive member of the community.

For a comprehensive coverage of group REBT in different contexts and with different client populations, see *Rational Emotive Behavior Therapy* (Ellis & Ellis, 2011).

Choice Theory/Reality Therapy

Key Concepts of Choice Theory/Reality Therapy Choice theory rests on the assumption that humans are internally motivated and behave to control the world around them according to some purpose within them. **Choice theory**, which is the underlying philosophy of the practice of reality therapy, provides a framework that explains the why and how of human behavior. **Reality therapy** is based on the assumption that human beings are motivated to change (1) when they determine that their current behavior is not getting them what they want and (2) when they believe they can choose other behaviors that will get them closer to what they want.

Reality therapy group leaders expect group members to make an assessment of their current behavior to determine if what they are doing and thinking is getting them what they want from life. Group members are encouraged to explore their perceptions, share their wants, and make a commitment to counseling. Because clients can directly control their acting and thinking functions more than they can control what they are feeling, their actions become the focus of work in the group. The group members explore the direction in which their behavior is taking them and evaluate what they are doing. They then create a plan of action to make the changes they want. A key concept of reality therapy and choice theory is that no matter how dire our circumstances may be, we always have a choice. An emphasis of reality therapy is on assuming personal responsibility and on dealing with the present.

Therapeutic Goals of Reality Therapy The overall goal of this approach is to help people find better ways to meet their needs for survival, love and belonging, power, freedom, and fun. Changes in behavior tend to result in the satisfaction of basic needs. Much of the work in a group centers around members exploring the degree to which they are meeting their needs and determining better ways of meeting their needs and the needs of others in their lives.

Therapeutic Relationship Group members need to know that the leader cares enough about them to accept them and to help them fulfill their needs in the real world. Both *involvement with* and *concern for* group members are demonstrated by the leader throughout the life of a group. Once this therapeutic relationship has been established, the leader challenges members with the reality and consequences of their actions. The group leader avoids criticism, refuses to accept members' excuses for not following through with agreed-upon plans, and does not easily give up on members. The leader assists members in the continual process of evaluating the effectiveness and appropriateness of their current behavior.

Techniques The practice of a reality therapy group can best be conceptualized as the cycle of counseling, which consists of two major components: (1) the counseling environment and (2) specific procedures that lead to change in behavior. Reality therapy is active, directive, and didactic. The group leader assists members in making plans to change those behaviors that they determine are not working for them. Skillful questioning and various techniques are employed to help members make this self-evaluation.

Reality therapy is active, directive, and didactic.

Some of the specific procedures in the practice of reality therapy have been developed by Robert Wubbolding (2011). These procedures are summarized in the **WDEP model**, which refers to the following clusters of strategies:

W = wants: exploring wants, needs, and perceptions.
D = direction and doing: focusing on what clients are doing and the direction this is taking them.
E = evaluation: challenging clients to make an evaluation of their total behavior.
P = planning and commitment: assisting clients in formulating realistic plans and making a commitment to carry them out.

In a group, members explore what they want, what they have, and what they are not getting. The cornerstone of a reality therapy group is assisting members in making a self-evaluation of their current behavior. This self-assessment provides a basis for making specific changes that will enable the members to reduce their frustrations. Useful questions can help them pinpoint what they want: "What kind of person do you wish you were?" "What would you be doing if you were living the way you wished?" "Is this choice to your best short-term and long-term advantage, and is it consistent with your values?" The purpose of such questions is to help clients move from a sense of external control to a sense of internal control. This line of questioning sets the stage for the application of other procedures in reality therapy.

Creating an **action plan** is an essential part of the process of a reality therapy group. Carrying out plans enables people to gain effective control over their lives. Therapy is best directed toward providing members with new information and helping them discover more effective ways of getting what they want. A large portion of the therapy time consists of making plans and then checking to determine how these plans are working. In a group context, members learn how to plan realistically and responsibly through contact with both the other members and the leader. The members are encouraged to experiment with new behaviors, to try out different ways of attaining their goals, and to carry out an action program. Effective plans are modest in the beginning and specify what is to be done, when it will be done, and how often. In short, plans are meant to encourage group members to translate their talk and intentions into actions.

Multicultural Applications of Reality Therapy Reality therapy assumes that the basic needs (survival, belonging, power, freedom, and fun) are universal, yet the ways in which these needs are expressed depend largely on the cultural context. When working with culturally diverse clients, it is essential that group leaders allow latitude for a diverse range of acceptable behaviors to satisfy these needs. Reality therapists demonstrate their respect for the cultural values of their clients by helping them explore how satisfying their current behavior is, both to themselves and to others. After group members make a self-assessment, they identify those areas of living that are *not* working for them. Members are then in a position to formulate specific and realistic plans that are consistent with their cultural values.

For more on reality therapy, we recommend *Reality Therapy: Theories of Psychotherapy Series* (Wubbolding, 2011).

LO8

Postmodern Approaches

The postmodern approaches (solution-focused brief therapy, narrative therapy, motivational interviewing, and feminist therapy) challenge many of the assumptions of traditional therapies. Postmodernism is based on the premise that there is no single truth. Postmodern perspectives are marked by acceptance of plurality and the notion that individuals create their own reality. The basic premise is that people are resourceful, competent, healthy, resilient, and have the capacity to discover solutions that can change the direction of their lives. Individuals are the experts on their own lives. The postmodern approaches have in common the basic assumption that we generate stories to make sense of ourselves and our world.

Both solution-focused brief therapy and narrative therapy cast the role of a therapist in a different light from traditionally oriented therapists who view themselves as experts in assessment and treatment. Solution-focused therapists and narrative therapists adopt a "not-knowing" position and believe the members of their groups are the true experts on their own lives. Solution-focused brief therapy moves quickly from "problem-talk" to "solution-talk" and focuses on keeping therapy simple and brief. By talking about the exceptions to a problem, group members are able to conquer what seem to be major problems. In narrative therapy, people are empowered by learning how to separate themselves from their problems. By emphasizing positive dimensions of human experience, clients become actively involved in resolving their problems. Instead of aiming to make change happen, the practitioners who operate from these two approaches attempt to create an atmosphere of understanding and acceptance that enables individuals to utilize their own resources to make constructive changes.

Motivational interviewing is a humanistic, client-centered, psychosocial, and modestly directive counseling approach that was developed by William R. Miller and Stephen Rollnick in the early 1980s. Motivational interviewing was initially designed as a brief intervention for problem drinking, but it has been effectively applied to a wide range of problems. Practitioners stress client self-responsibility and promote working cooperatively with the client to generate alternative solutions to behavioral problems.

From the beginning, feminist therapy groups actively worked to establish shelters for battered women, rape crisis centers, and women's health and reproductive health centers. Building community, providing authentic mutual empathic relationships, creating a sense of social awareness, and emphasizing social change are all significant strengths of this approach to group work. Feminist theory encompasses a broader perspective than do most theories that value the marginalized voices of both men and women. Members in a group that is structured by feminist principles can expect more than simple problem-solving strategies. They need to be prepared for major shifts in their way of viewing the world around them, changes in the way in which they perceive themselves, and transformed interpersonal relationships.

Solution-Focused Brief Therapy

Key Concepts of Solution-Focused Brief Therapy A central concept of a **solution-focused brief therapy (SFBT)** group includes a movement from talking about problems to talking about and creating solutions. Members learn to pay attention to what is working, and then do more of this. Change is constant and inevitable, and small changes pave the way for larger changes. Little attention is paid to pathology or to giving people a diagnostic label. There are exceptions to every problem, and by talking about these exceptions, group participants are able to conquer what seem to be major problems in a brief period of time.

Therapeutic Goals of Solution-Focused Brief Therapy The solution-focused model emphasizes the role of participants establishing their own goals and preferences. Much of what the group process is about involves members thinking about their future and what they want to be different in their lives. Leaders concentrate on clear, specific, observable, small, realistic, achievable changes that may lead to additional positive outcomes. Because success tends to build upon itself, modest goals are viewed as the beginning of change.

Therapeutic Relationship SFBT is a collaborative venture; the group therapist strives to carry out therapy *with* an individual, rather than doing therapy *on* an individual. Empathy and the collaborative partnership in the therapeutic process are seen as more important than assessment or technique. Instead of aiming to *make* change happen, the leader attempts to create an atmosphere of understanding and acceptance that allows individuals to tap their resources for making constructive changes. Group members are the primary interpreters of their own experiences. Together the group members and the leader establish clear, specific, realistic, and personally meaningful goals that will guide the process of a group. This spirit of collaboration opens up a range of possibilities for present and future change.

Solution-focused group counselors believe that the way problems and solutions are talked about makes a difference. The language used signals how problems are conceptualized. The concepts of care, interest, respectful curiosity, openness, empathy, contact, and even fascination are seen as relational necessities. Group leaders create a climate of mutual respect, dialogue, inquiry, and affirmation in which the members are free to create and coauthor their evolving stories. Because solution-focused counseling is designed to be brief, the leader has the task of keeping group members on a *solution track* rather than a *problem track*. If members concentrate on talking about their problems, it is difficult for them to move in a positive direction.

Techniques Solution-focused therapists use a range of techniques including pretherapy change, exception questions, the miracle question, scaling questions, homework, and summary feedback. Some group practitioners ask the member to externalize the problem and focus on strengths or unused resources. Others challenge group members to discover solutions that might work. Techniques focus on the future and how best to solve problems rather than on understanding the cause of problems.

Solution-focused brief therapists often ask clients at the first session, "What have you done since you called for an appointment that has made a difference in your problem?" Asking about **pretherapy change** tends to encourage clients to rely less on the therapist and more on their own resources to reach their goals.

Questioning is a main intervention. Solution-focused group leaders use questions as a way to better understand a group member's experience rather than simply to gather information. Group leaders do not raise questions to which they think they know the answer. Questions are asked from a position of respect, genuine curiosity, sincere interest, and openness. Instead of presenting members with a barrage of closed, interrogation-style questions, open-ended questions can enhance solutions by providing space for members to be heard and to reflect on future possibilities. Asking questions enables members to describe things in their own words: "Tell me more about your concerns."; "What do you think needs to happen to make things a little better at work?"; "Who will be the first to notice when things get better, and how might they react?"

Exception questions direct group members to those times in their lives when their problems did not exist. Exploring exceptions offers group members opportunities for discovering resources, engaging strengths, and creating possible solutions. Solution-focused group counselors listen attentively for signs of previous solutions, exceptions, and goals. For example, Randy says: "I feel tired and *depressed* most of the time; I get angry at my kids over something they didn't do *almost* every night." Exception-finding questions include "When is this problem absent or less noticeable?"; "Has anything changed for the better since the last group session?" Once an exception is discovered, the leader can explore exception-related conditions and encourage a member to replicate these conditions: "What was different about yesterday when you felt less depressed?" "What will it take to keep depression at bay more often?" The intent of this solution-focused intervention is to guide Randy in a self-chosen direction based on what has worked previously. Randy can be asked what has to happen for these exceptions to his problems to occur more often.

A related intervention to exception questions involves changing what one is doing. For example, the leader might ask Chuck if he is willing to do something different the next time he feels worried and anxious. After hearing Chuck say that he worries most of the time and has tried many methods to stop without success, the leader might invite Chuck to schedule an intensive 10-minute worry session in the morning to give his concerns the undivided attention these worries deserve. If Chuck carries out this experiment, he is likely to discover that he has some control over his feelings by changing what he is doing in certain situations.

The **miracle question** allows members of a group to describe life without the problem. The miracle question is often presented as follows: " If a miracle happened and the problem you have disappeared overnight, how would you know it was solved, *and what would be different*?" Group members are then encouraged to enact "what would be different" in spite of perceived problems. This question involves a future focus that encourages group members to consider a different kind of life than one dominated by a particular problem. The miracle question focuses clients on searching for solutions and recognizing small improvements toward their goals.

Scaling questions require group members to specify improvement on a particular dimension on a scale of zero to 10. This technique enables clients to see progress being made in specific step and degrees. Solution-focused therapists use scaling questions when changes in human experiences are not easily observed, such as feelings, moods, or communication. For example, a group member reporting feelings of anxiety in social situations might be asked, "On a scale of zero to 10, with zero being how you felt when you first came to this group and 10 being how you feel the day after your miracle occurs and your problem is gone, how would you rate your anxiety right now?" Even if the group member has only moved away from zero to 1, she has improved. How did she do that? What does she need to do to move another number up the scale? Scaling questions enable clients to pay closer attention to what they are doing and how they can take steps that will lead to the changes they desire.

Therapists may provide **summary feedback** in the form of genuine affirmations or pointing out particular strengths that clients have demonstrated. Solution-focused practitioners typically allow time in each group session for sharing feedback with one another. The leader gives members credit for the changes they are making through statements such as these: "How did you manage to make these improvements?" "How does your family treat you differently now compared to before?" "What have these improvements taught you about yourself?" "What is the biggest difference between the old you and the new you?" These questions provide encouragement for members to search within themselves for the credit they deserve for making changes. This kind of questioning and feedback assists members in carrying their learning outside of the group sessions into daily living.

Multicultural Applications of Solution-Focused Brief Therapy Solution-focused brief therapists learn from their clients about their experiential world rather than approaching clients with a preconceived notion about their worldview. The nonpathologizing stance taken by solution-focused practitioners moves away from dwelling on what is wrong with a person to emphasizing creative possibilities. Instead of aiming to make change happen, the SFBT practitioner attempts to create an atmosphere of understanding and acceptance that allows a diverse range of individuals to utilize their resources for making constructive changes. Murphy (2015) claims that the emphasis on strengths and resources in solution-focused counseling supports culturally competent services to individuals regardless of ethnicity and cultural background. Some specific aspects of solution-focused counseling that lend themselves to culturally competent practice include (a) treating each client as a unique individual, (b) collaborating on the goals of counseling, (c) tailoring services to each client, and (d) obtaining ongoing feedback from clients on the usefulness of interventions and adjusting them accordingly.

For a more comprehensive account of SFBT, we highly recommend *Solution-Focused Counseling in Schools* (Murphy, 2015) and *Solution-Focused Group Therapy: Ideas for Groups in Private Practice, Schools, Agencies and Treatment Programs* (Metcalf, 1998).

Narrative Therapy

Key Concepts of Narrative Therapy **Narrative therapy** is based partly on examining the stories that people tell and understanding the meaning of their stories. Each of these stories is true for the individual who is telling the story; there is no absolute reality. Some key concepts of narrative therapy include a discussion of how a problem has been disrupting, dominating, or discouraging the person. The therapist attempts to separate clients from their problems so that they do not adopt a fixed view of their identity. Group members are invited to view their stories from different perspectives and eventually to co-create an alternative life story. They are asked to find evidence to support a new view of themselves as being competent enough to escape the dominance of a problem and are encouraged to consider what kind of future they could expect if they were competent. In essence, group members reauthor their stories about themselves and their relationships.

Therapeutic Goals of Narrative Therapy Narrative therapists invite group members to describe their experience in fresh language, which tends to open new vistas of what is possible. The heart of the therapeutic process from the perspective of narrative therapy involves identifying how societal standards and expectations are internalized by people in ways that constrain and narrow the kind of life they are capable of living. Narrative therapists collaborate with the members of their groups to help them experience a heightened sense of personal agency to act in the world. The member is asked to find evidence to support a new view of being competent enough to escape the dominance of a problem and is encouraged to consider what kind of future could be expected from the competent person who is emerging.

Therapeutic Relationship Therapy is a collaborative venture aimed at assisting group members to construct meaningful goals that will lead to a better future. Narrative therapists do not assume that they have special knowledge about the lives of clients. The members of a group are the primary interpreters of their own experiences. In the narrative approach, the therapist seeks to understand the lived experience of each of the group participants. Through a systematic process of careful listening, coupled with curious, persistent, and respectful questioning, the group leader works collaboratively with members to explore the impact of the problem and what they are doing to reduce its effects. Members then work with the therapist to co-construct enlivening alternative stories. For example, the group leader may explore with Leilani her lived experiences about her courage, her ability to be decisive, her willingness to take risks in the face of uncertainty, and her ability to deal directly with her fears. In this discussion, occasions when Leilani has demonstrated courage in the face of her fears are identified. These include making a decision to pursue a master's degree program in counseling, taking risks by leaving a job that was stifling to her, and her ability to pursue social action projects that are meaningful to her. The group experience provides opportunities for Leilani to create a changing identity and to recruit an audience who will provide support for her as she moves more fully into her preferred story.

Techniques Narrative therapy emphasizes the quality of the therapeutic relationship and the creative use of techniques within this relationship. Narrative therapy's most distinctive feature is captured by the statement, "The person is not the problem, the problem is the problem." Narrative therapists engage clients in **externalizing conversations** that are aimed at separating the problem from the person's identity. Members learn that they are not cemented to their problem-saturated stories and can develop alternative and more constructive stories.

"The person is not the problem, the problem is the problem."

Narrative therapists use questions as a way to generate experience rather than to gather information. The aim of questioning is to progressively discover or construct the client's experience so that the client has a sense of a preferred direction. Therapists ask questions from a not-knowing position, meaning that they do not pose questions to which they already know the answers. Through the process of asking questions, therapists provide clients with an opportunity to explore various dimensions of their life situations.

As narrative therapists listen to clients' stories, they pay attention to details that give evidence of clients' competence in taking a stand against an oppressive problem. Problems are not viewed as pathological manifestations but as ordinary difficulties and challenges of life. In the practice of narrative therapy, there is no recipe, no set agenda, and no formula to follow that will ensure a desired outcome.

Multicultural Applications of Narrative Therapy Narrative therapists operate on the premise that problems are identified within social, cultural, political, and relational contexts rather than existing within individuals, which makes this approach especially relevant for counseling culturally diverse clients. Narrative practitioners are concerned with considering the specifications of gender, ethnicity, race, disability, sexual orientation, social class, and spirituality and religion as therapeutic issues. The sociopolitical conceptualization of problems offers understanding of cultural notions and practices that produce dominant and oppressive narratives. Practitioners deconstruct, or take apart, the cultural assumptions that are a part of a client's problem situation. As a part of the group experience, members come to understand how oppressive social practices affect them, which allows for the possibility of creating alternative stories.

For a further treatment of narrative therapy, see *Narrative Counseling in Schools: Powerful and Brief* (Winslade & Monk, 2007).

Motivational Interviewing

Key Concepts of Motivational Interviewing **Motivational interviewing (MI)** is rooted in the philosophy of person-centered therapy, but with a "twist." Unlike the nondirective and unstructured person-centered approach, MI is deliberately directive, yet it stays within the client's frame of reference. Group counselors can integrate the principles of motivational interviewing with a number of approaches, especially person-centered therapy, cognitive behavior therapy, choice theory/reality therapy, and solution-focused brief therapy. MI practitioners believe in the client's abilities, strengths, resources, and competencies. MI has been effective in working with a wide range of behavioral issues, including substance abuse, compulsive gambling, eating disorders, anxiety disorders, depression, suicidality, chronic disease management, and health-related practices.

Therapeutic Goals of Motivational Interviewing The major goals of motivational interviewing are to explore an individual's ambivalence, to minimize this ambivalence, and to build intrinsic motivation. MI is built on the premise that people who seek therapy are often ambivalent about change and that motivation tends to ebb and flow during the course of therapy. By understanding both sides of a member's ambivalence regarding change, group counselors begin to work with this ambivalence rather than working against the client's struggles. MI can be a significant factor in helping clients commit to the therapy process, which improves client involvement, adherence, and retention in cognitive behavioral and other action-oriented therapies.

Techniques MI emphasizes being purposeful and getting to the point to guide group members toward positive change. MI group leaders encourage members to decide whether they want to make certain changes. If members decide to change, group leaders ask what kinds of changes will occur and when they will occur. The attitudes and interventions in MI are based on a person-centered philosophy and include using open-ended questions, employing reflective listening, creating a safe climate, affirming and supporting the client, expressing empathy, responding to resistance in a nonconfrontational manner, guiding a discussion of ambivalence, summarizing and linking at the end of sessions, and eliciting and reinforcing *change talk*.

Therapeutic Relationship Practitioners emphasize the relational context of therapy, known as the "MI spirit." When this MI spirit is applied to group counseling, the group leader establishes collaborative partnerships with members and draws on their ideas and resources rather than assuming a role as the expert. All choices ultimately rest with the members, not the leader. MI is a collaborative, conversational style of working that strengthens an individual's own motivation to change. As group members begin to show signs of readiness to change, they increasingly talk about change, express a desire to change, experiment with possible change actions between sessions, and envision a future for themselves after the desired changes have been made.

Multicultural Applications of Motivational Interviewing MI is a phenomenological approach in which the counselor attempts to see life from the client's perspective. This perspective makes this approach suitable for working with clients from diverse cultural backgrounds. In MI groups, members are not persuaded to adopt the counselor's advice, nor are they expected to operate within the framework of the leader's values. Instead, members are encouraged to consider a menu of alternative interventions or options that fit well in their own lives.

For a further treatment of motivational interviewing, see *Motivational Interviewing: Helping People Change* (Miller & Rollnick, 2013) and *Motivational Interviewing in Groups* (Wagner & Ingersoll, 2013).

Feminist Therapy

Key Concepts of Feminist Therapy **Feminist therapy** focuses on issues of diversity, the complexity of sexism, and the centrality of social context in understanding gender issues. Feminist therapists have challenged the male-oriented assumptions regarding what constitutes a mentally healthy individual. Practitioners with a feminist orientation emphasize that gender-role expectations profoundly influence our identity from birth onward. Thus group counseling has the task of bringing to one's awareness how gender-role socialization is deeply ingrained in adult personality.

A key concept of feminist therapy is the notion that societal gender-role messages influence how individuals view themselves and behave. Throughout therapy the impact of these socialization patterns are identified so that clients can critically evaluate and modify early messages pertaining to appropriate gender-role behavior. The practice of contemporary feminist therapy is based on the assumption that gender cannot be considered apart from other identity areas such as race, ethnicity, class, and sexual orientation. A key concept pertaining to understanding symptoms is that problematic symptoms can be viewed as coping or survival strategies rather than as evidence of pathology. Although individuals are not to blame for personal problems largely caused by dysfunctional social environments, they are responsible for working toward change.

The first step toward change is becoming aware of how society has influenced our beliefs and behaviors, especially with respect to views pertaining to gender roles. Group members have an opportunity to identify their biases pertaining to gender-role identity. This can be a subtle learning, but it can lead to significant changes in how we relate to one another. For example, in one of our groups a man consistently referred to "the girls" that worked for him in the office. Several women in the group let him know they thought his remarks were inappropriate because his employees were mature women. He replied that he did not see it as a "big deal" that he called the women "girls," but eventually he was able to understand the implications of his references.

In my (Cindy) private practice, I have worked with numerous women struggling with symptoms of postpartum depression and have found a feminist perspective to be extremely helpful in understanding this complex issue. Many of the women I worked with were trying to balance work and being a new mother with little or no support from their male partners. Even though they had loving husbands and partners, the inequities in the responsibilities of child care and housework were startling. These women were doing it all and wondering why they were feeling inadequate, unfulfilled, isolated, and depressed. When viewed from a feminist perspective, postpartum depression is identified as a systemic issue rather than an individual illness. Rather than medicating these women for depression, feminist therapists would look toward a reexamination of role expectations and the distribution of work in relation to child care and other household duties. The symptoms these female clients were experiencing made sense in the context of their relationships. Their duties had been drastically increased without a corresponding increase in the amount of support provided by their partners.

Therapeutic Goals of Feminist Therapy The major goal of feminist therapy is empowerment; members of a group strive for a sense of self-acceptance, self-confidence, self-esteem, joy, and self-actualization. Other therapy goals include enhancing the quality of interpersonal relationships, assisting both women and men to make decisions regarding role performances, and helping group members to come to an understanding of the influence of cultural, social, and political systems on their current situation. Emphasis is on balancing independence and interdependence, social change, and valuing and affirming diversity. Feminist therapists do not see the therapeutic relationship alone as being sufficient to produce change. Insight, introspection, and self-awareness are springboards to action. Both individual change and social transformation are basic goals of therapy. At the individual level, therapists work to help women

Both individual change and social transformation are basic goals of therapy.

and men recognize, claim, and embrace their personal power. As a consciously political enterprise, another goal is social transformation.

Therapeutic Relationship Feminist therapists work in an egalitarian manner and use empowerment strategies that are tailored to each client (Brown, 2010; Evans, Kincade, & Seem, 2011). They aim to empower clients to live according to their own values and to rely on an internal (rather than external or societal) locus of control in determining what is right for them. Group leaders with a feminist orientation are concerned about power relations in the world in general. The group leader and members take active and equal roles, working together to determine goals that members will pursue in a group.

The group practitioner works to demystify the therapeutic process and to include each member as an active partner in the treatment process. Collaboration with the members of the group leads to a genuine partnership with the members. When members are not informed about the nature of the therapeutic process, they are denied the opportunity to actively participate in the group experience. When practitioners make decisions about a client *for* the client rather than *with* the client, they rob the client of power in the therapeutic relationship.

Feminist therapists share common ground with Adlerian therapists in their emphasis on social equality and social interest. Also in line with Adlerians, feminist therapists believe the therapeutic relationship should be a nonhierarchical, person-to-person relationship. Like person-centered therapists, feminist therapists convey their genuineness and strive for mutual empathy between client and therapist. A common denominator of both feminist and other postmodern approaches is the assumption that each member is an expert on his or her own life.

Techniques Feminist therapy does not prescribe any particular set of interventions; rather, feminist group therapists tailor interventions to members' strengths. Feminist practitioners have borrowed techniques from traditional approaches including the use of therapeutic contracts, homework, bibliotherapy, therapist self-disclosure, empowerment, role playing, cognitive restructuring, reframing, relabeling, and assertiveness training. They typically draw techniques from the cognitive behavioral approaches in a group. In addition, Enns (2004) describes several unique techniques that feminist therapists have developed such as gender-role analysis and intervention, power analysis and intervention, and social action. **Gender-role analysis** explores the impact of gender-role expectations on the individual's psychological well-being and draws upon this information to make decisions about modifying gender-role behaviors. **Power analysis** refers to methods aimed at helping individuals understand how unequal access to power and resources can influence personal realities. Together the group leader and members explore how inequities or institutional barriers often limit self-definition and well-being. **Social action** is a defining feature of feminist therapy. As clients become more grounded in their understanding of feminism, therapists may suggest that clients become involved in activities such as volunteering at a community mental health center, lobbying lawmakers, or providing community education about gender issues. Participating in such activities can empower clients and help them see the link between their personal experiences and the sociopolitical context in which they live.

Multicultural Applications of Feminist Therapy Feminist therapy and multicultural perspectives have a great deal in common. The feminist perspective on power in relationships has application for understanding power inequities due to racial and cultural factors. The "personal is political" principle can be applied both to counseling women and counseling culturally diverse client groups. Neither feminist therapy nor multicultural perspectives focus exclusively on individual change. Instead, both approaches emphasize direct action for social change as a part of the role of therapists. Many of the social action and political strategies that call attention to oppressed groups have equal relevance for women and for other marginalized groups. Both feminist therapists and multicultural therapists have worked to establish policies that lessen the opportunities for discrimination of all types—gender, race, culture, sexual orientation, ability, religion, and age.

For a further treatment of feminist therapy, see *Introduction to Feminist Therapy: Strategies for Social and Individual Change* (Evans et al., 2011) and *Feminist Therapy* (Brown, 2010).

LO9

An Integrative Approach

An **integrative approach** to the practice of group counseling is based on concepts and techniques drawn from various theoretical approaches. One reason for the current trend toward an integrative approach to the helping process is the recognition that no single theory is comprehensive enough to account for the complexities of human behavior when the full range of client types and their specific problems are taken into consideration.

Most clinicians now acknowledge the limitations of basing their practice on a single theoretical system and are open to the value of integrating various therapeutic approaches. Those clinicians who are open to an integrative perspective may find that several theories play crucial roles in their personal approach. Each theory has its unique contributions and its own domain of expertise. By accepting that each theory has strengths and weaknesses and is, by definition, different from the others, practitioners have some basis to begin developing a counseling model that fits them.

We encourage you to remain open to the value inherent in each of the theories of counseling. All the theories have some unique contributions as well as some limitations. Study all the contemporary theories to determine which concepts and techniques you can incorporate into your approach to the practice of group work. You will need to have a basic knowledge of various theoretical systems and counseling techniques to work effectively with diverse client populations in various settings. Functioning exclusively within the parameters of one theory may not provide you with the therapeutic flexibility that you need to deal creatively with the complexities associated with the diversity found in many groups.

Each theory represents a different vantage point from which to look at human behavior, but no one theory has the total truth. Because there is no "correct" theoretical approach, it is well for you to search for an approach that fits who you are and to think in terms of working toward an integrated approach that addresses thinking, feeling, and behaving. To develop this kind of integration, you need to be thoroughly grounded in a number of theories, be open to the idea that these theories can be unified in some ways, and be willing to continually test your hypotheses to determine how well they are working.

For those of you who are beginning your counseling career, it is probably wise to select the primary theory closest to your basic beliefs. Learn that theory as thoroughly as you can, and at the same time be open to examining what other theories can offer. If you begin by working within the parameters of a particular theory, you will have an anchor point from which to construct your own counseling perspective. But do not think that simply because you adhere to one theory you can use the same techniques with all of your clients. Even if you adhere to a single theory, you will need to be flexible in the manner in which you apply the techniques that flow from this theory as you work with diverse members in your groups.

If you are currently a student-in-training, it is unrealistic to expect that you will already have an integrated and well-defined theoretical model. An integrative perspective is the product of a great deal of reading, study, supervision, clinical practice, research, and theorizing. With time and reflective study, you can develop a consistent conceptual framework to use as a basis for selecting from the multiple techniques available to you. Take time to think about your therapeutic style and its influence on the process and outcomes of your group, then answer these questions: Can you describe the key features of your style in clear terms? To what degree are you able to conceptualize what you are attempting to accomplish through the group process? Developing your personalized approach that guides your practice is a lifelong endeavor that will be refined with experience.

Points to Remember

Theories and Techniques of Group Counseling

Here are some key points to remember; many of the following chapters are built on these basic concepts.

- It is important to have a theoretical rationale to help you make sense of what occurs in a group. Take the time to understand several theoretical orientations, and then select concepts from each to form your own personal style of working.
- A general theoretical framework helps you make sense of the many facets of group process, provides you with a map that allows you to intervene in a creative and effective manner, and provides a basis for evaluating the results of your interventions.
- The psychodynamic models of group counseling include psychoanalytic and Adlerian approaches.
- The experiential and relationship-oriented approaches to group counseling include existential, person-centered, Gestalt therapy, and psychodrama.
- The cognitive behavioral models include behavior therapy, cognitive therapy, rational emotive behavior therapy, and reality therapy.
- The postmodern perspectives include solution-focused brief therapy, narrative therapy, motivational interviewing, and feminist therapy.
- An integrative approach incorporates the thinking, feeling, and doing dimensions of human behavior and offers a number of advantages over subscribing to a single theoretical framework.

Exercises

Questions for Discussion

1. In a small group, explore ways that you might have a primary theory and also draw from a couple of other theories to broaden your approach. At this point, what would be your primary theory, and what are your reasons for selecting it? What aspects from other models would you want to incorporate into your approach as a group counselor?
2. What are the advantages of practicing within a single theoretical perspective? What are some disadvantages? Do you see value in developing an integrative stance that draws on concepts and techniques from diverse theoretical perspectives? What are the potential difficulties when integrating elements from different theoretical models?
3. In a small group, discuss some aspects of your personal approach to counseling practice. The questions below may help you clarify your theoretical stance.
   a. What is your worldview, and how does it influence the way you make sense of your world, the people in it, and the interactions you have with others?
   b. In what ways are you willing to modify your approach to better serve diverse populations?
   c. What are your thoughts about how change happens?
   d. What do you believe about how people heal? In what context do people heal? What must be present in order for people to heal? What methods work to help people heal?
   e. What was your own counseling experience like for you? What was helpful or not helpful for you?
   f. What role or importance do you place on the relationship between client and counselor?
   g. What are the roles of the group member and the group counselor from your perspective?
   h. How do you define problems, problem situations, and problem behaviors?
   i. How do you decide what techniques to use in a group?

Guide to Groups in Action: Evolution and Challenges DVD and Workbook

If you are not seeing the DVD (*Groups in Action*) in class or working with this program, you can skip the exercises pertaining to this group program. If you are viewing the DVD, here are some suggestions for making the best use of this chapter along with Part One of the program, "Theories and Techniques of Group Counseling." This third and final part of the DVD program is based on a brief lecture by Gerald Corey that complements Chapter 4 of this textbook. In addition, the main points for each of the general theory areas discussed in this chapter are summarized in the workbook, along with questions for discussion that can provide the basis for small group activities in the classroom.

MindTap for Counseling

Additional resources can be found on CengageBrain.com and by logging into the MindTap course created by your professor. There you will find a variety of study tools and useful resources that include quizzes, videos, interactive exercises, and more.

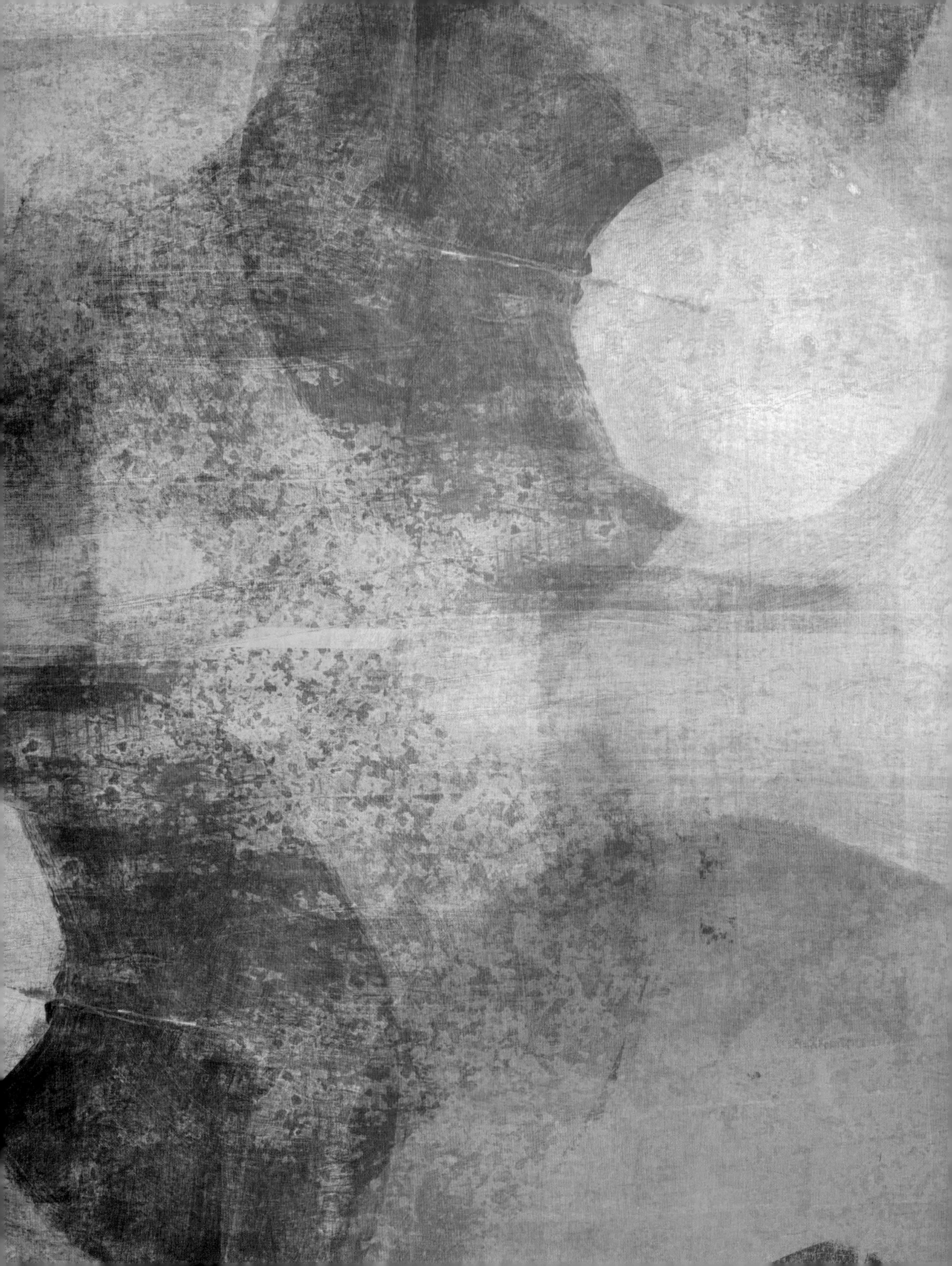

PART TWO

Group Process: Stages of Development

The stages of a group do not generally flow neatly and predictably in the order described in the following chapters. In actuality there is considerable overlap between the stages, and once a group moves to an advanced stage, it is not uncommon for it to stay at a plateau for a time or to temporarily regress to an earlier stage. Similarly, the fact that certain tasks have been accomplished in a group does not mean that new conflicts will not erupt. Groups are dynamic and ever-changing, and both members and leaders need to pay attention to the factors that affect the direction a group takes. In addition, not all participants within the group will progress at a similar pace. It requires practice and skill to facilitate individual processes and group process simultaneously.

Understanding the typical patterns during different stages of a group will give you a valuable perspective and help you predict problems and intervene in appropriate and timely ways. Knowledge of the critical turning points in a group serves as a guide in helping participants mobilize their resources to successfully meet the tasks facing them at each stage. Although we discuss these stages as taking place over the lifetime of the group, it is important to remember that members may work through many of these stages in a single session as well, moving from initial comments to a brief transition, followed by productive work, and ending with reflection on what has been accomplished. Each stage of group life—pregroup, initial, transition, working, and final—is described in a separate chapter.

The **pregroup stage** consists of all the factors involved in the formation of a group. Careful thought and planning are necessary to lay a solid foundation for any group, including designing a proposal for a group, attracting members, screening and selecting members, and the orientation process. All these practical considerations take a great deal of time, yet attending to this preliminary phase will increase the chances of having a productive group.

The **initial stage** of a group is a time of orientation and exploration, and members tend to present the dimensions of themselves they consider to be socially acceptable. This phase is generally characterized by a certain degree of anxiety and insecurity about the structure of the group. Members are tentative because they are discovering and testing limits, and some may wonder whether they will be accepted. Typically, members bring to the group certain expectations, concerns, and anxieties, and it is vital that they be allowed to express them openly. As members get to know one another and learn how the group functions, they develop the norms that will govern the group, explore fears and expectations pertaining to the group, identify personal goals, clarify personal themes they want to explore, and determine if this group is a safe place. The manner in which the leader deals with the reactions of members largely determines the degree of trust that develops.

Before group members can interact at the depths they are capable of, the group generally goes through a somewhat challenging **transition stage.** During this stage, the leader's task is to help members learn how to begin working on the concerns that brought them to the group. It is the members' task to monitor their thoughts, feelings, reactions, and actions and to learn to express them verbally. Leaders can help members come to recognize and accept their fears and defensiveness and can assist members in working through their anxieties and any reluctance they may be experiencing. Members decide whether to take risks and speak of the things they may be holding back because of what others might think of them.

Productive work takes place during all stages of a group, but the quality and depth of the work takes different forms during each developmental phase. The **working stage** is characterized by a deeper level of exploration, which builds on the significant work done in the initial and transition stages. Mutuality and self-exploration increase, and the group is focused on making behavioral changes. In actual practice, the transition stage and the working stage merge with each other. During the working stage, the group may return to earlier themes of trust, conflict, and reluctance to participate. As the group takes on new challenges, deeper levels of trust can be achieved. New conflicts may emerge as the group evolves, and commitment is necessary to do the difficult work of moving forward. All members may not be able to function at the same level of intensity, and some may remain on the periphery, holding back and being more afraid to take risks. Indeed, there are individual differences among members at all stages of a group. Some groups may never reach a working stage, but significant learning often occurs anyway and individuals still benefit from their group experience.

The **final stage** is a time to further identify what was learned and to decide how this new learning can become part of daily living. Group activities include terminating, summarizing, pulling together loose ends, and integrating and interpreting the group experience. As the group is ending, the focus is on conceptualization and bringing closure to the group experience. During the termination process, the group will deal with feelings of separation, identify unfinished business, review the group experience, practice for behavioral change, design action plans, identify strategies for coping with relapse, and build a supportive network.

CHAPTER 5

Forming a Group

- Introduction
- Developing a Proposal for a Group
- Attracting and Screening Members
- Practical Considerations in Forming a Group
- The Uses of a Pregroup Meeting
- Building Evaluation Into Group Work
- Coleader Issues on Forming a Group
- Points to Remember
- Exercises
- Guide to Groups in Action: Evolution and Challenges DVD and Workbook

CHAPTER LEARNING OBJECTIVES

1. List and discuss the main tasks required in forming a group
2. Address approaches to group formation, including recruiting, screening, and selecting members (CACREP, 2016, Standard E)
3. Understand the practical considerations in forming a group
4. Describe the purpose and uses of pregroup meetings
5. Identify some key coleadership issues in forming a group

Imagine that you are a middle school counselor assigned the task of starting a group for children from divorced homes. You will need to recruit members, conduct pregroup screenings, and plan for each group meeting. In addition, you will need to be sure that you obtain permission from the children's guardians or parents. Use these questions as guidelines for thinking about factors to consider in the formation of your group.

- How will you go about forming this group?
- What support or consultation will you need?
- What personal and/or professional experience have you had working with this population, and how do you anticipate you will join with group members?
- What issues of credibility might you face with group members, and how will you address them?
- What possible clinical and ethical issues do you anticipate being of importance in forming your group?
- How might you go about educating yourself in the areas necessary for you to effectively lead this group?

Introduction

Group practitioners are creating an increasing variety of groups to fit the special needs of a diverse clientele in many different settings. The types of groups that can be imagined are limited only by your own creativity and the needs of your clients. For example, Joan VanderSchaaf (2013) created a unique group that combined yoga classes with group psychotherapy. The participants reported an increased sense of well-being and self-awareness along with increased strength and a sense of empowerment. Practitioners continue to find creative ways to design groups that blend various themes and modalities in new ways.

Groups have become increasingly popular and have been designed to meet both the needs of clients and the demands of agency settings. Group members have opportunities to gain insight and to practice new skills, both within the group and in their everyday interactions outside of the group. Feedback from other group members and the counselor help members gain new perspectives. Groups offer many opportunities for modeling, and members often learn how to cope with their problems by observing the work of others with similar concerns.

We cannot overemphasize the importance of giving careful attention to the preparation of the members for a successful group experience. It is useful to think about what kind of group you will lead and to prepare yourself for your leadership role and functions for that group. The more clearly you can state your expectations as early as possible, the better you will be able to plan and the more meaningful the experience is likely to be for participants. Some situations for forming groups are less than ideal and may limit your ability to adequately prepare and plan ahead. Even in such circumstances, it is helpful for you to consider the information in this chapter on how to set up your group experience for success.

LO1

Developing a Proposal for a Group

Many excellent ideas for developing and implementing groups never reach fruition, sometimes due to a lack of resources or training, and at other times due to a lack of adequate preparation on the part of the group leaders. These five general areas can serve as guidelines for forming a proposal:

1. **Rationale.** Do you have a clear and convincing rationale for your group, and can you present data to support your rationale? Are you able to answer questions that might be raised about the need for this group?
2. **Objectives.** Can you clearly state what you most want to attain and how you will go about doing so? Are your objectives specific, measurable, and attainable within the specified time?
3. **Practical considerations.** Is the membership defined? Are meeting times, frequency of meetings, and duration of the group reasonable? Is the physical location of the group easily accessible to all members?
4. **Procedures.** Have you selected specific procedures to meet the stated objectives? Are these procedures appropriate and realistic for the given population?
5. **Evaluation.** Does your proposal contain strategies for evaluating how well the stated objectives were met? Are your evaluation methods objective, practical, and relevant?

The following questions can be considered by both you and your coleader and by the participants of the group. Discussion of group rules and guidelines may be better suited for initial group sessions with all members present to increase members' sense of ownership in the group process. We suggest that you bring these questions for discussion to your supervisor and your colleagues.

- What type of group are you forming? Will it be long term or short term?
- For whom is the group intended? Identify the specific population. What do you know about the developmental needs of this population?
- What is your motivation for forming this type of a group? Have you conducted a needs assessment, and if so, how can this be a help in designing your group?
- How will members be recruited for participation in your group? Are there any people that you would want to exclude from this particular group? What is your rationale for your exclusion criteria?
- What is the cultural mix of the group, and what are the implications of the cultural mix for forming the group?
- Are you skilled in both group process and the content of the group you are proposing? If not, what supervision or support is available to help you in facilitating the group?
- Is the group composed of voluntary or involuntary members? If it is a mandatory group, what special considerations will you address?
- What are the general goals and purposes of this group? What will members gain from participating in it?
- What screening and selection procedures will be used? What is your rationale for these particular procedures?

- How many members will be in the group? Where will the group meet? How often will it meet? How long will each meeting last? Will new people be allowed to join the group once it has started, or will this be a closed group?
- How will the members be prepared for the group experience? What ground rules will you establish at the outset?
- What structure will the group have? What techniques will be used? Why are these techniques appropriate? In what ways can you employ your techniques in a flexible manner to meet the needs of culturally diverse client populations?
- How will you handle the fact that people may be taking some risks by participating in the group? What will you do to safeguard members from unnecessary risks? Will you take any special precautions if some of the participants are minors?
- How will you handle situations such as a member arriving at a group session while under the influence of alcohol or drugs?
- How will you deal with a group member who wants to leave the group before it is over?
- What evaluation procedures will you implement? What follow-up procedures are planned?
- What topics will be explored in this group?

Regardless of the type of group you expect to form, having a compelling written proposal is key when translating ideas into action. Twelve sample proposals for groups in schools and community settings are presented in Chapter 10 and Chapter 11. These proposals will give you good ideas for designing a group, even if you are dealing with a different population and different topics. As you review these proposals, consider how you can draw from each of them to fit your interests and to meet the needs of the clients you serve.

Working Within the System

If you hope to have your proposal accepted both by your supervisors in a community agency and by the potential members, you will need to develop the skills necessary to work within a system. To get a group started, you need to negotiate sensitively with the staff of the institution involved. In all clinics, community agencies, schools, and hospitals, power issues and political realities play a role. You may become excited about organizing groups only to encounter resistance from your coworkers or your administrators. Sometimes colleagues or the system can sabotage your efforts without you fully understanding why your efforts are being undermined.

In some cases, the representatives of institutions need to be educated about the potential value, as well as the realistic limitations, of groups for their clients. It is helpful to be able to predict some of the major concerns that administrators and agency directors are likely to have about the proposal you submit. For example, if you are attempting to organize a group in a public high school, the administrators may be anxious about parental complaints and potential lawsuits. If you are able to appreciate their concerns and speak directly to the ethical and legal issues, you stand a better chance of having your proposal accepted. If it is not clear in your own mind what you hope to accomplish through group work or how you will conduct the meetings, the chances are slim that a responsible administrator will endorse your program. By attending to the suggestions described in this chapter for designing a group, you stand a better chance that your proposal will be met with success.

LO2

Attracting and Screening Members

Once you have been successful in getting a proposal accepted, the next step is to find a practical way to announce your group to prospective participants. How a group is announced influences both the way it will be received by potential members and the kind of people who will join. Although professional standards should prevail over a commercialized approach, we have found that making personal contact with potential members is one of the best methods of recruiting.

Guidelines for Announcing a Group and Recruiting Group Members

Professional issues are involved in publicizing a group and recruiting members. The "Best Practice Guidelines" (ASGW, 2008) state that prospective members should have access to relevant information about the group (preferably in writing), such as the following:

- A professional disclosure statement
- A statement of the goals and purposes of the group
- Policies related to entering and exiting the group
- Expectations for group participation, including voluntary and involuntary membership
- Policies and procedures governing mandated groups (where relevant)
- Confidentiality and exceptions to confidentiality
- Leader's theoretical orientation that includes possible interventions
- The qualifications of the leader to lead a particular group
- Role expectations of members and leader(s)
- The rights and responsibilities of both group members and the group leader
- Documentation procedures and disclosure of information to others
- Implications of out-of-group contact or involvement among members
- Procedures for consultation between group leader(s) and group member(s)
- Education, training, and qualifications of the group leader
- The logistics of a group including fees, cancellation policies, and methods of communication with the leaders outside of group
- A realistic statement of what services can and cannot be provided within a particular group structure
- Potential impact of group participation
- The potential risks and benefits of participating in a group

These guidelines can assist you in creating an informed consent document for your group. Give an accurate picture of the group, and avoid making promises about the outcomes of the group that may raise unrealistic expectations. As we have indicated, making direct contact with the population most likely to benefit from the group is an excellent way to follow up printed announcements. These personal contacts, which can include distributing printed information to those interested, lessen the chance that people will misunderstand the purposes and functioning of the group.

It is also important in announcing and recruiting for a group to inform your agency colleagues. They can then refer clients to you who are appropriate for your particular group. In addition, they may do the preliminary screening, including giving written information on the group to potential members with whom they have contact. Involve your coworkers as much as possible in every phase of organizing your group.

Screening and Selection Procedures

After announcing a group and recruiting members, the next crucial step is arranging for screening and selecting the members who will make up the group. The ASGW (2008) "Best Practice Guidelines" state: "Group Workers screen prospective group members if appropriate to the type of group being offered. When selection of group members is appropriate, Group Workers identify group members whose needs and goals are compatible with the goals of the group" (A.7.a). This guideline raises several questions: Should screening be used? If so, what screening method suits the group? How can you determine who would be best suited for the group, who might have a negative impact on the group process, or who might be hurt by the experience? How can you best inform those candidates who, for whatever reason, are not selected for your group?

Sometimes leaders screen out individuals due to their own personal dislike or countertransference issues even though these individuals might be appropriate clients for the group. Whether the group leader likes or dislikes a potential member is not an appropriate basis for selecting members of a group. The goal of screening is to prevent potential harm to clients, not to make the leader's job easier by setting up a group of homogeneous members. For some types of groups, screening is based on whether potential members have a specific problem area that is in alignment with the general objectives of the group. For example, in Chapter 10 Teresa Christensen describes a group for children who have been abused. In selecting children for her group, she finds it essential that these children be ready to participate in the various interactive activities that are involved in the group. In addition, all the children she selects have completed or are concurrently involved in individual or family counseling. She believes screening is essential to determine when children would benefit from her particular group. In a women's support group for survivors of incest described in Chapter 11, Lupe Alle-Corliss seeks clients who display a readiness to deal openly with the trauma of incest. In both of these sample groups, screening is done to determine the readiness and the appropriateness of group treatment for potential members.

When selecting members of your group, it may be appropriate to consider diversity issues. You may want to put together a group of individuals who share common experiences but also are different in a number of respects. Through interaction in a diverse group, members often have an opportunity to dispel stereotypes and misconceptions about one another. If member composition is carefully considered and balanced, members have opportunities both to connect with and to learn from each other.

Ultimately, the type of group should determine the kind of members accepted. A person who can work well in a structured, short-term group designed to teach social skills or to cope with stress might not be ready for an intensive therapy group. Individuals with severe emotional trauma would probably be excluded from a counseling group, but they might benefit from a weekly group for outpatients at a mental health center. Carefully evaluate your screening and selection process to confirm that your criteria are appropriate for your particular group. The question that needs to be considered is: Should *this* particular person be included in *this* particular group at *this* time with *this* group leader?

Ultimately, the type of group should determine the kind of members accepted.

Preliminary Screening Sessions We support screening procedures that include a private session between the candidate and the leader. In the event there are coleaders, ideally they would interview each of the potential group members together. There are some clear benefits when potential members are interviewed by both coleaders, including seeing how the individual reacts to both of them. This practice will give the coleaders a sense of how this member might be in the group situation. During the individual session, the leader or coleaders might look for evidence that the group will be beneficial to the candidate. How motivated is this person to change? Is this a choice of the individual or of someone else? Why this particular type of group? Does this person understand what the purposes of the group are? Are there any indications that group counseling is contraindicated for this person at this time?

Group applicants are to be encouraged, at their private sessions, to interview the group leader or coleaders. They can be invited to ask questions concerning the procedures, basic purposes, and any other aspect of the group. This questioning is important as a means not only of getting information but also of developing a feeling of confidence in the group leader or coleaders, which is necessary if productive work is to take place. Questions the applicants ask can help to establish their readiness for the group, their curiosity about the group process, and their interpersonal style. We believe screening is best viewed as a two-way process and that potential members should be encouraged to form their own judgment about the group and the leaders. Given enough information about the group, a member can make a more informed decision about whether to join.

From our perspective, screening and selection procedures are subjective and the intuition and judgment of the leader are crucial. We are concerned that those who are considering a group benefit from a group, but we are even more concerned that they might be psychologically hurt by it or might drain the group's energies excessively. Certain members can remain unaffected by a group yet sap its energy for productive work. This is particularly true of hostile people, people who monopolize, extremely aggressive people, people in a state of crisis, and people who act out. The potential gains of including certain of these members must be weighed against the probable losses to the group as a whole. Group counseling is contraindicated for individuals who are suicidal, extremely fragmented or acutely psychotic, sociopathic, facing extreme crises, highly paranoid, or extremely self-centered (Yalom, 2005b).

A leader needs to develop a system for assessing the likelihood that a candidate will benefit from a group experience. Factors that must be taken into consideration are the level of training of the leader, the proposed makeup of the group, the setting, and the basic nature of the group. For example, it might be best not to accept a highly defensive individual into an ongoing adolescent group, for several reasons. A group may be too threatening for a person so vulnerable and may lead to increased defensiveness and rigidity, or such a person may have a counterproductive effect on group members by impeding their attempts to work.

In some cases it may not be possible to conduct individual interviews, and alternatives will have to be used. If you work in a county facility or a state hospital, you may simply be assigned a group and have no opportunity to screen members. The basis for assigning members could be their diagnosis or the unit in a residential facility where they are placed. Even if you are not able to select members for your group, you can make at least brief individual contact to prepare them. You will also have to devote part of the initial sessions to preparation because many of the members may not have the faintest idea why they are in the group or how the group might be of any value to them. In "open groups," whose membership changes when some individuals leave and new ones are added, it is a good practice to meet individually with incoming members so you can orient them.

If you cannot screen members for your group, you could still have a successful group. However, you will need to provide some form of orientation so members understand what the group is about and how to best participate in it. The more you can assist members in being informed about group process, the better are the chances that the group will be effective.

Assessing and Choosing Members We are often asked these questions: "How do you decide who will best fit into the group, who will most benefit from it, and who is likely to be harmed by the experience?" "If you decide to exclude a person from the group, how do you handle this in a respectful and therapeutic manner?" As a group leader, you are expected to make the ultimate decision to include or exclude certain clients. Because the groups we typically offer are voluntary, one factor we look for during the interview is the degree to which a candidate wants to make changes and is willing to expend the necessary effort. We consider whether a group seems the appropriate method of intervention to accomplish the desired changes. We also weigh heavily how much the candidate seems to want to become a member of this group, especially after he or she is given information about it.

There have been times when we were reluctant to let certain people into a group in spite of their desire to join. As we've mentioned, we do pay attention to our clinical hunches concerning a person, so in the last analysis our screening and selection process is a subjective one. A variety of clinical reasons might lead us to exclude a person, but whatever our reservations are, we discuss them with the prospective member. At times, after we've discussed our concerns, we see matters differently. At other times, we simply cannot with a clear conscience admit a person. In making decisions about selecting members for a group, the leader needs to think of what is best for all the members, not just what one member may want.

If we do not accept people, we tell them how the group might not be appropriate for them. We strive to break the news in a manner that is honest, direct, respectful, and sensitive, and when possible we suggest other options. Ethical practice involves offering those candidates who are not accepted into the group the support they need in dealing with their reactions to not be included in the group, and as well, suggesting alternatives to group participation. For example, we might determine that a highly defensive and extremely anxious person who is very frightened in interpersonal relationships is likely to benefit from a series of individual counseling sessions before being placed in a group situation. We would explain our rationale and encourage the person to consider accepting a referral for an appropriate type of intervention. In other words, we do not close the door on people we exclude from a group with no explanation, nor do we convey that there is something intrinsically wrong with them because they were not included in this particular group.

When we do in-service training workshops for group leaders in various agencies and institutions, many leaders tell us they do not screen people for their groups. They cite any number of reasons: they do not have the time; they do not have much voice in choosing group members because people are simply assigned to a group; they do not really know how to determine who will or will not benefit or will be negatively influenced by a group experience; they are not convinced that screening is important; or they do not want to make a mistake by turning away people who might gain from a group. When individual screening is not practical, we encourage practitioners to devise alternative strategies. For example, instead of screening people individually, screening and orientation can be done with several potential group members at once. If this is not possible, it is a good idea to at least briefly meet the members of your group prior to the first session. Another alternative is to make the first session of a group the time for orientation and getting a commitment from the members.

LO3

Practical Considerations in Forming a Group

Group Composition

Whether a group should have a homogeneous membership or a heterogeneous one depends on the group's purpose and goals. In general, for a specific target population with given needs, a group composed entirely of members of that population is more appropriate than a heterogeneous group. Consider a group composed entirely of older people. It can focus exclusively on the specific problems that characterize their developmental period, such as loneliness, isolation, lack of meaning, rejection, and financial pressures. This similarity of the members can lead to a great degree of cohesion, which in turn allows for an open and intense exploration of their life crises. Members can express feelings that they typically withhold, and their life circumstances can give them a bond with one another. Even though members may share a common problem, their life experiences will differ, which brings another level of diversity into these homogenous groups. Several group proposals for groups for older people are described in Chapter 11: "A Successful Aging Group," "An Older Adult Bereavement Group," and "A Group Treatment Program for Institutionalized Older Adults." Each of these groups has a different purpose and focus, and the general goal of the group will guide member selection.

Sometimes a microcosm of the outside social structure is desired, and in that case diverse membership should be sought. Personal-growth groups, process groups, interpersonal groups, and certain therapy groups are often heterogeneous. Members can experiment with new behavior and develop interpersonal skills with the help of feedback from a rich variety of people in an environment that represents everyday reality. Many groups offered at college counseling centers are process oriented or have an interpersonal focus. Other groups may have a particular theme, and some psychoeducational groups have both an educative and a therapeutic slant. Some of these groups are briefly described in Chapter 10.

Group Size

What is a desirable size for a group? The answer depends on several factors: age of clients, experience of the leader, type of group, and problems to be explored. For instance, a group composed of elementary school children might be kept to 3 or 4, whereas a group of adolescents might be made up of 6 to 8 people. There may be as many as 20 to 30 children in developmental group guidance classes. For a weekly ongoing group of adults, about 8 people may be ideal. A group of this size is big enough to give ample opportunity for interaction and small enough for everyone to be involved and to feel a sense of the "group."

Frequency and Duration of Meetings

How often should a group meet? For how long? Should a group meet twice weekly for 1-hour sessions? Or is 1½ to 2 hours once a week preferable? With children and adolescents, it may be better to meet more frequently and for a shorter period to suit their attention span. If the group is taking place in a school setting, the meeting times can correspond to regularly scheduled class periods. For groups of relatively well-functioning adults, a 2-hour weekly session might be preferable. This 2-hour period is long enough to allow some intensive work yet not so long that fatigue sets in. You can choose any frequency and duration that suit your style of leadership and the type of people in your group. For an inpatient group composed of lower functioning members, it is desirable to meet on a daily basis for 45 minutes. Because of the members' psychological impairment, it may not be possible to hold their attention for a longer period. Even for higher-functioning inpatient groups, it is a good practice to meet several times a week, but these groups might be scheduled for 90 minutes.

Length of a Group

What should the duration of a group be? For most groups a termination date can be announced at the outset, so members will have a clear idea of the time limits under which they are working. Our college groups typically run about 15 weeks—the length of a semester. With high school students, the same length seems ideal. It is long enough for trust to develop and for work toward behavioral changes to take place. Elementary and middle school groups typically run for 6 to 8 weeks, depending on administrator and teacher support for allowing students to miss class for the group sessions.

One of our colleagues has several closed therapeutic groups in his private practice that last 16 weeks. The advantages of time-limited groups are that the time span allows for cohesion and productive work and that members can then continue practicing newly acquired interpersonal skills with a new group of people. Members are often motivated to work because they realize that they do not have forever to attain their personal goals. At different points in this 16-week group, members are challenged to review their progress, both individually and as a group. If they are dissatisfied with their own participation or with the direction the group is taking, they have the responsibility to do something to change the situation.

Of course, some groups composed of the same members meet for years. Such a time structure allows them to work through issues in some depth and to offer support and challenge in making life changes. These ongoing groups do have the potential for fostering dependency, and it is important that both the leader and the members are aware of that.

Place for Group Meetings

Where might the group hold its meetings? Many places will do, but privacy is essential. Members must be assured that they will not be overheard by people in adjoining rooms. Groups often fail because of their physical setting. If they are held in a day hall or ward full of distractions, productive group work is not likely to occur. We like a group room that is not cluttered and that allows for a comfortable seating arrangement. We prefer a setting that enables the group to sit in a circle. This arrangement lets all the participants see one another and allows enough freedom of movement that members can spontaneously make physical contact. It is a good idea for coleaders to sit across from each other. In this way the nonverbal language of all members can be observed by one leader or the other and a "we-versus-them" atmosphere can be avoided. This also allows the coleaders to read each other more easily.

Open Versus Closed Groups

Open groups are characterized by changing membership. As certain members leave, new members are admitted, and the group continues. **Closed groups** typically have some time limitation, with the group meeting for a predetermined number of sessions. Generally, members are expected to remain in the group until it ends, and new members are not added. The question of whether a group should be open or closed depends on a number of variables.

There are some advantages to open groups that incorporate new members as others leave, one of which is an increased opportunity for members to interact with a greater variety of people. This also more accurately reflects people's everyday lives wherein different people enter or exit our relationships. A potential disadvantage of open groups is that rapid changing of members can result in a lack of cohesion, particularly if too many clients leave or too many new ones are introduced at once. Therefore, it may be better to bring in new members one at a time as openings occur. It is a challenge to provide new members of open groups with the orientation they need to learn how to best participate in a group. One way to educate incoming members about group process is by providing a videotape explaining group rules, which can be followed by a face-to-face contact with the group leader. One colleague who coleads open groups in an agency stresses reviewing the ground rules with each incoming member. Rather than taking group time whenever a new person is included, he covers the rules with the new member as part of the intake interview. He also asks other members to teach the new member about a few of the guidelines in an attempt to have them take more responsibility for their own group. If members are dropped and added sensitively, these changes do not necessarily interfere with the cohesiveness of the group and can even enhance cohesion.

In some settings, such as a mental health facility in a state hospital or some day-treatment centers, group leaders do not have a choice between an open and a closed group. Because the membership of the group changes almost from week to week, continuity between sessions and cohesion within the group are difficult to achieve. Cohesion is possible, even in cases where members attend only a few times, but a high level of activity is demanded of inpatient group therapists. These leaders must structure and activate the group. They need to call on certain members, they must actively support members, and they need to interact personally with the participants (Yalom, 1983).

If you are forming an open group, you want to have some idea about the rate of turnover of the members. How long a given member can participate in the group may be unpredictable. Therefore, your interventions need to be designed with the idea in mind that many members may attend for only one or two sessions. In conducting an open group, it is good to remind all the members that this may be the only time they have with one another. The interventions that you make need to be tailored to that end. For example, you would not want to facilitate a member's exploration of a painful concern that could not be addressed in that session. You also have a responsibility to facilitate member interactions that can lead to some form of resolution within a given session. This involves leaving enough time to explore with members what they have learned in a session and how they feel about leaving each session.

One of our colleagues regularly conducts several open groups in a community mental health agency. Even though the membership does change somewhat over a period of time, he finds that trust and cohesion do develop in most of these groups because there is a stable core of members. When new members join, they agree to attend for at least six sessions. Also, members who miss two consecutive meetings without a valid excuse are not allowed to continue. These practices increase the chances for continuity and for trust to be developed.

LO4

The Uses of a Pregroup Meeting

Research on the Value of Pregroup Preparation

A good deal of research has examined the value of pretherapy preparation for both individual and group psychotherapy. The overwhelming consensus is that preparation positively affects both early therapeutic processes and later client improvement (Burlingame, Fuhriman, & Johnson, 2004b; Fuhriman & Burlingame, 1990). Pregroup preparation (setting expectations, establishing group rules and procedures, role preparation, skill building) is positively associated with group cohesion and members' satisfaction with their experience (Burlingame et al., 2004b); preparing members for a group experience is a key aspect of informed consent (Rapin, 2014).

Pregroup orientation is a standard practice for members of short-term therapy groups. A number of factors make such orientation sessions necessary for these clients: the diversity of members in a typical group, the range of personal concerns, the different settings, the time-limited framework, and the unfamiliarity of the group format. The content of this pregroup orientation reflects the perspective of leaders who conduct short-term group therapy. A thorough orientation sets the stage for later development of leader–member and member–member therapeutic relationships (Burlingame & Fuhriman, 1990).

Members who understand what behaviors are expected of them tend to be more successful. When goals, role requirements, and behavior expectations are understood by members from the outset, therapeutic work proceeds more effectively. Unproductive anxiety can be reduced by informing members about group norms in advance. Available research shows that preparatory training increases the chances of successful outcomes because it reduces the anxiety participants often experience during the initial sessions, provides a framework for understanding group process, and increases self-disclosure (Yalom, 2005b).

Orientation and Preparation of Members at a Pregroup Meeting

We suggested earlier that a preliminary meeting of all those who were thinking of joining the group was a useful device when individual interviews were impractical. Such a pregroup session provides an excellent way to prepare members and to get them acquainted with one another. This session also provides the members with more information to help them decide whether they are willing to commit themselves to what would be expected of them. If an individual interview or a pregroup session with all members is impractical, the first group meeting can be used to cover the issues we are discussing in this chapter. Our preference is for a separate individual screening and orientation session followed by a pregroup meeting for all participants.

At this initial session, or at the pregroup meeting, the leader explores the members' expectations, clarifies the goals and objectives of the group, imparts some information about group process, and answers members' questions. This is an ideal time to focus on the clients' perceptions, expectations, and concerns. This process does not have to consist of a lecture to the members; it can involve the members and encourage them to interact with one another and the leader. This interactive model of preparation can reveal interesting information about both the dynamics of the individuals and the "personality of the group." Patterns begin to take shape from the moment a group convenes. Structuring the group, including the specification of procedures and norms, will likely be accomplished early in the group's history. Some of this structuring can be done during the individual intake sessions, but a continuation of it can be the focus of the first group session. Group counselors may either establish ground rules or ask the group to do so. Ideally, group rules are cooperatively developed by the leader and the members as part of the group process.

Patterns begin to take shape from the moment a group convenes.

In conducting pregroup preparation, we caution against providing too much information at the preliminary meeting. Many of the topics that relate to participation in the group can be handed out in written form to the members, and members can be encouraged to raise any questions or concerns they have after they have read this material. Throughout the life of a group, there are critical times when structuring and teaching can assist members in becoming actively involved in the group process.

Many groups that get stuck at an early developmental stage do so because the foundations were poorly laid. What is labeled "resistance" could be the result of a failure on the leader's part to adequately explain what groups are about, how they function, and how members can become actively involved. If extensive preparation is not possible, even brief preparation is better than none at all. In addition to preparing members for a group, it is a good practice to periodically review with the members some of the guidelines on how they can make the best use of group time. This will increase the chances that the group will become a cohesive autonomous unit that encourages individuals to engage in productive work.

Clarifying Leader and Member Expectations

The pregroup session is the appropriate time to encourage members to express the expectations they are bringing with them to the group. We typically begin by asking these questions:

- What are your expectations for this group?
- What did you have in mind when you signed up?

Their replies give us a frame of reference for how the members are approaching the group, what they want from it, and what they are willing to give to the group to make it a success.

We also share *our* expectations by giving members an idea of why we designed the group, what we hope will be accomplished, and what we expect of ourselves as leaders and them as members. This is a good time to reemphasize and clarify what you see as your responsibilities to the group and to further discuss the members' rights and responsibilities.

Goals of Pregroup Preparation

In his system of pregroup preparation, Yalom (2005b) emphasizes the collaborative nature of group therapy. He not only describes how a therapy group helps members enhance their interpersonal relationships but assists members in anticipating disappointments, including predicting stumbling blocks participants are likely to encounter. Demystifying the therapeutic process is central in preparing members for a group.

Demystifying the therapeutic process is central in preparing members for a group.

As a leader, during the screening and pregroup meetings it is important to clarify what needs can or cannot be met within the group. For instance, if you do not view your role as being the expert who provides answers, potential members have a right to know this so that they can determine if this group is what they are seeking. For some groups, it may be both appropriate and useful for you to engage in teaching members the purposes and functions of the group. It is important to invite the members of your groups to verbally state *their* reasons for joining a group, and it is critical that you be willing to explore these expectations during the initial session. It is also useful to encourage members to raise questions about the purpose and goals of the group, as well as to identify and talk about what they most want from the group and to begin formulating personal goals. You will want to strive for congruence between members' purposes in attending the group and the overall purpose you had in mind when you designed the group. A great deal can be done to prevent unnecessary anxiety by allowing members to talk about their reactions to coming to the group and by considering ways the group can lead to their empowerment.

Establishing Basic Ground Rules

The pregroup session is the appropriate place to establish some procedures that will facilitate group process. Some leaders prefer to present their own policies and procedures in a nonauthoritarian manner. Other leaders place the major responsibility on the group members to establish procedures that will assist them in attaining their goals. Whatever approach is taken, some discussion of ground rules is necessary. Some group leaders also choose to review these rules at the beginning of each group session, especially for open groups.

In formulating procedures that govern a group, it is important for leaders to protect members by defining clearly what confidentiality means, why it is important, and the difficulties involved in enforcing it. Ideally, confidentiality will be discussed during the individual interview, but it is so important to the functioning of a group that you need to restate it periodically during the life of a group. At the pregroup session, it is a good idea to state that confidentiality is not an absolute and to outline the restrictions. Members have a right to know of the circumstances when leaders must break confidentiality for ethical or legal reasons. In cases of incest and child abuse, elder or dependent adult abuse, and in cases of clients who pose a danger to themselves, others, and/or physical property, confidentiality must be breached. Limitations to confidentiality apply especially to groups with children and adolescents, groups with parolees, groups composed of involuntary populations such as prisoners, and groups of psychiatric patients in a hospital or clinic. Members in these groups should be told that certain things they say in the group may be recorded in their chart, which might be available for other staff members to read. Furthermore, these individuals need to be informed that if they attend a group session and do not participate, that also will be recorded. The members then have a basis for deciding what and how much they will disclose. This kind of honesty about confidentiality will go a long way toward establishing the trust that is essential for a working group. Review Chapter 3 for a further discussion of confidentiality.

Leaders must be aware of and discuss with members any additional ground rules and policies particular to the setting in which they are working. You will not be able to fully discuss all the policies and procedures you deem essential to the smooth functioning of your group in one or two sessions, but having an established position on these matters will be an asset when particular issues arise at some point in the development of the group.

Critical Incident

On the Outside, Looking In

1. Description of Incident

This situation occurred in a pregroup session for an interpersonal-growth group for master's degree students in counseling, which is a required component of an introduction to counseling class. The second half of the class is devoted to participating in the small group, which was facilitated by Anahi, a doctoral student under the supervision of her professor. The goals for this first session included members getting to know one another, identifying any concerns members had about participating in the group, discussing their expectations, and formulating personal goals to assist them in being active participants in the small group.

As the session began, Anahi invited all of the members to form a circle and to begin introducing themselves. Milena took a chair but placed it outside the circle near the corner of the room. When it was Milena's turn to introduce herself, she briefly commented in a vague and disinterested tone. Milena remained quiet for the remainder of the session.

Anahi found herself very distracted by Milena and decided to ask if there was something Milena would like the group to know about why she chose to sit outside of the circle. Milena responded, "I just don't like to be close to other people. Whenever I go into a room, I always find a place in the corner to sit." Anahi asked the other group members how they were affected by Milena choosing to sit outside the circle during the session. The members reported (1) being curious as to why Milena chose to sit in the corner, (2) being distracted by her behavior, (3) feeling uncomfortable with her sitting outside the circle, and (4) wondering if she was judging them.

After the preliminary group session, the group leader met with Milena privately to discuss her involvement in the group. Anahi inquired about her feelings of safety and about her participation in the group. Anahi also asked Milena about her expectations, what she thought about the group being a part of a required course, and what she imagined it would be like for her to be in this group, especially if she kept herself apart from others. Milena indicated that she was planning to remain in the group because she did not have other options, but she did not want to receive any pressure to be a part of the group circle, nor did she want to feel pressured to talk about her personal problems with others in her cohort.

2. Process Questions for Group Leaders

- What could the group leader have done during this first session to address Milena's behavior?
- Should Milena be allowed to remain in this group if she has no intention of participating?

- If Milena stays in the group, how might Anahi address her ongoing decision to remain seated outside of the group and engage minimally?
- If you are facilitating this group, how might you address this situation?
- If you were the group leader, what agenda would you prepare for this pregroup meeting? What would you most want to say to the members about being in this group?

3. Clinical Reflections

Milena's behavior and minimal participation in the preliminary session could not be ignored. This situation illustrates how crucial it is to engage members in a thorough informed consent process as a vital part of orienting members to their rights and responsibilities as participants in the group. We would be interested in knowing what kind of informed consent process took place. Students give informed consent when they enter a master's program, but we don't know how the instructor of this introduction to counseling course introduced the interpersonal-growth group that would take place each week during the second half of the class session.

Anahi could have asked members to say something about their thoughts and feelings about being expected to be in such a group. This discussion is central to clarifying expectations and taking some steps toward creating a trusting climate that would allow the members to participate in a way each of them found meaningful. If members are not oriented to the purpose of the group and of what is expected of them, a hidden agenda is likely to operate that makes meaningful interaction extremely difficult. Preliminary preparation is necessary for this kind of group to be successful.

4. Possible Interventions

- Anahi could explore Milena's feelings of "not wanting to be close to people."
- Anahi could ask all members to share how their cultural backgrounds might influence their comfort level with sitting in a circle or sharing openly with others.
- Anahi could let Milena know that she is puzzled by her behavior and decide to verbalize her internal dialogue, which might go something like this: "As Milena remained silent in the corner, I felt distracted by her behavior. As much as I tried to focus on the other group members, my thoughts were on why she does not want to be part of the group. Could it be that Milena is fearful of group interaction? Is she not trusting others in the group, and if so, what can any of us do to make the group a safe place for her? Is she concerned that any disclosures she makes can be used against her in her evaluation in the program?"
- Anahi could invite Milena to comment on hearing the leader's self-talk.
- The leader can assure all members that they will not be pressured to disclose personal problems or experiences. However, members are expected to find some way to participate, even if they restrict their participation to here-and-now reactions to what is taking place in the group and how they are affected by being in the group.

Building Evaluation Into Group Work

If you do group work in a community agency or an institution, you may be required to demonstrate the efficacy of your treatment approach. Federal and state grants typically stipulate measures for accountability. In most settings you will be expected to devise procedures to assess the degree to which clients benefit from the group experience. We suggest that you include in your proposals for groups the procedures you intend to use to evaluate both the individual member outcomes and the outcomes of the group as a unit. (Developing a research orientation to practice is addressed in detail in Chapter 2.)

There is no need to be intimidated by the idea of incorporating a research spirit in your practice. Nor do you have to think exclusively in terms of rigorous empirical research. Various qualitative methods are appropriate for assessing a group's movement, and these methods may be less intimidating than relying exclusively on quantitative research techniques. One alternative to the traditional scientific method is evaluation research, which provides data that can be useful when making improvements within the structure of a group. The practice of building evaluation into your group programs is a useful procedure for accountability purposes, but it can also help you sharpen your leadership skills, enabling you to see more clearly changes you might want to make in the format for future groups. We have been greatly influenced by feedback we have received from member evaluations.

LO5

Coleader Issues on Forming a Group

We have emphasized the value of preparing members for a group experience, but coleaders also must prepare themselves for a group. When coleaders meet prior to the formation of a group, they can explore their philosophy and leadership styles and enhance their relationship, which will have a beneficial impact on the group. According to Luke and Hackney (2007), the relationship between coleaders can either enhance or complicate the group process. Luke and Hackney's review of the literature suggests that the coleader model offers different and perhaps better leadership dynamics than can be offered by the single-leader model. However, effective coleadership requires coleaders to have a good working relationship, which entails a willingness to address any relevant aspects of their work together.

If group leaders are prepared, they are more likely to be able to effectively prepare members for a meaningful group experience. If you are coleading a group, it is useful for you and your coleader to have equal responsibility in forming the group and getting it going. Both of you need to be clear about the purpose of the group, what you hope to accomplish with the time you have, and how you will meet your objectives. Cooperation and basic agreement between you and your coleader are needed to get your group off to a good start.

This cooperative effort might well start with you both meeting to develop a proposal, and ideally both of you will present it to the appropriate authority. This practice ensures that designing and originating the group are not solely one leader's responsibility. This shared responsibility for organizing the group continues throughout the various tasks outlined in this chapter. You and your coleader will be a team when it comes to matters such as announcing and recruiting for membership; conducting screening interviews and agreeing on whom to include and exclude; agreeing on basic ground rules, policies, and procedures and presenting them to members; preparing members and orienting them to the group process; and sharing in the practical matters that must be handled to form a group.

It may not always be possible to share equally in all of the responsibilities. Although it is *ideal* that both leaders interview the applicants, time constraints often make this impractical. Tasks may have to be divided, but both leaders need to be involved as much as possible in making the group a reality. If one leader does a disproportionate share of the work, the other can easily develop a passive role in the leadership of the group once it begins.

Time spent planning and getting to know one another as coleaders can greatly influence the success of your work together and start you off in a positive direction. Here are a few questions you and your coleader could discuss before the initial session:

- What kind of group work has each of you experienced? In what ways will your theory and leadership styles influence the direction the group takes?
- Will your cultural and ethnic background influence your way of being in the group and with each other? How might your differences be strengths in your working relationship? How might your differences be a challenge?
- Do you have reservations about coleading with each other, and if so, are you willing to talk about them?
- What are your strengths and weaknesses, and how might they affect your leading together?
- What ethical issues related to group work do you and your coleader consider most important?
- What types of members or situations might arise in a group that could pose a challenge for you personally and professionally?
- Are you willing to identify and manage conflict and disagreements as a coleader team?

These questions do not represent all the possible areas coleaders may explore in getting to know each other, but they provide a basis for focusing on significant topics.

Learning in Action

Leader/Listener

This activity can be done with two group members, classmates, or group coleaders to gain insight into how you lead, follow, and communicate with others. Each dyad will need a pen and two pieces of paper.

Instructions

Leader: Draw a simple image on your paper, but do not allow your partner to see it. When you have completed the drawing, tell your partner how to re-create the image on his or her paper without showing your paper to your partner. As the leader, your job is to help your partner re-create the image you drew without ever seeing it.

Listener: Your job is to follow the leader's instructions as best as you can. You may ask questions.

Discussion Questions

After you and your partner have each had a chance to be Leader and Listener, discuss the following questions with each other.

As the Leader

- How did you feel in the role of the Leader? Was there anything about it that you particularly liked or disliked?
- Which role did you find easiest or most challenging? Describe.
- How would you describe your style as a Leader? How would you describe the Listener's style?
- How well did you feel the Listener did in following your instructions?
- Did you ever feel frustrated with the Listener, yourself, or the process in general?
- What challenges might you and your partner have in working together as coleaders?
- In what ways might your and your partner's style complement each other as coleaders?

As the Listener

- How did you feel in the role of the Listener? Was there anything about it that you particularly liked or disliked?
- Which role did you find easiest or most challenging? Describe.
- How would you describe your style as a Listener? How would you describe the Leader's style?
- Did you ever feel frustrated with the Leader, yourself, or the process in general?
- What challenges might you and your partner have in working together as coleaders?
- In what ways might your and your partner's style complement each other as coleaders?

Points to Remember

Forming a Group

Member Functions

Group members need to be active in the process of deciding whether a group is right for them. To do this, potential members need to possess the knowledge necessary to make an informed decision concerning their participation. Here are some issues that pertain to the role of members at this stage:

- Members can expect to have adequate knowledge about the nature of the group and understand the impact the group may have on them.
- Members can be encouraged to explore their expectations and concerns with the group leader to determine if *this* group with *this* particular leader is appropriate for them at *this* time.
- Members need to be involved in the decision of whether or not they will join the group; members should not be coerced into joining a group. In mandatory groups, leaders do their best to show involuntary members how a group can be personally beneficial, which can result in a shift of members' attitudes.
- Members need to understand their purpose in joining the group. They can prepare themselves for the upcoming group by thinking about what they want from the experience and how they might attain their goals.

Leader Functions

Here are the main tasks of group leaders during the formation of a group:

- Develop a clearly written proposal for the formation of a group.
- Present the proposal to your supervisor or administrator and get the idea accepted.

- Announce and market the group in such a way as to inform prospective participants.
- Conduct pregroup interviews for screening and orientation purposes.
- Provide potential members with relevant information necessary for them to make an informed choice about participation.
- Make decisions concerning selection of members and composition of the group.
- Organize the practical details necessary to launch a successful group.
- Get parental permission, if necessary.
- Prepare psychologically for leadership tasks, and meet with the coleader, if any.
- Arrange a preliminary group session for the purposes of getting acquainted, orientation to ground rules, and preparation of members for a successful group experience.
- Make provisions for evaluating the outcomes of the group in a community agency.
- Meet with the coleader prior to beginning a group to get to know one another and to plan the general structure of the group.

Exercises

Group Planning

Discussion Questions

Take time to review the proposals for groups in school or community settings presented in Chapter 10 and Chapter 11. Select a proposal that captures your interest, and imagine forming a group similar to that group. Describe your group (psychoeducational, counseling, or other) and the target population and setting. Then answer the following questions for the group you are planning to design and lead.

1. What do you most want to occur in your group? State your purposes simply and concretely.
2. What is the main emphasis of your group?
3. What kind of screening methods would you use in forming your group?
4. What characteristics would people need to have to be included? What is the rationale?
5. What importance would you place on preparation and orientation of the members of the group? What would you most want to convey in this orientation process?
6. What procedures and techniques would you use in your group? Are your procedures practical? Are they related to the goals and the population of the group?
7. What evaluation methods might you use to determine the effectiveness of your approaches? Are your evaluation procedures appropriate to the purposes of your group?

Interviewing

1. **Screening Interview.** Ask one person in the class to play the role of a group leader conducting a screening interview for members for a particular type of group. The group leader conducts a 10-minute interview with a potential member, played by another student. The prospective member then tells the group leader how he or she felt and what impact the group leader made. The group leader shares his or her observations about the prospective group member and tells whether the person would have been accepted in the group, and why or why not. Repeat this exercise

with another student-member so the group leader can benefit from the feedback and try some new ideas. Then give other students a chance to experience the roles of interviewer and interviewee. The rest of the class can offer feedback and suggestions for improvement after each interview. This feedback is essential if students are to improve their skills in conducting screening interviews.

2. **Group Member Interview.** We have recommended that prospective group members examine the leader somewhat critically before joining a group. This exercise is just like the preceding one, except that the group member asks questions of the leader, trying to learn things about the leader and the group that will enable the member to make a wise decision about whether to join. After 10 minutes the leader shares observations and reactions, and then the member tells whether he or she would join this leader's group and explains any reservations. Again, the class is invited to make observations.
3. **Group Proposal.** Think of a population or clinical issue that you would like to develop a group for, and select three questions from the six discussion questions listed in the Group Planning exercise. Take 10 to 15 minutes to answer the questions on your own and make notes, then form small groups and discuss your answers with your classmates or colleagues. Ask for feedback on how compelling your proposal would be if you were to submit it as an actual proposal.

Group Class

If the group class that you are presently in contains an experiential group component, or if you are required to be in some kind of process group as a part of your group course, observe the parallel processes between what you are learning in the book and what is happening in your experiential group. Your group class is likely to go through the same stages of group formation as those you are studying. For example, the class may begin slowly, with students being anxious and apprehensive. As students begin to develop trust, they will identify and explore some personal issues, work toward specific goals, and finally evaluate the group experience and say good-bye. For each of the chapters that deal with the stages of group development (Chapters 5 through 9), you will be asked to reflect on these parallel processes. Reflect on your experiences in this group and write about this in your journal.

Guide to Groups in Action: Evolution and Challenges DVD and Workbook

We have developed the *Groups in Action: Evolution and Challenges DVD and Workbook* (Corey, Corey, & Haynes, 2014) to enhance your study of *Groups: Process and Practice.* At the end of each chapter in Part Two of the text, we refer you to specific segments in the DVD as examples for each of the stages of a group. Also refer to the corresponding lessons in the workbook, which require you to become an active learner as you study the group process in action.

Before beginning the DVD and workbook program, read the first few pages of the workbook, which contains a synopsis of the DVD program, learning objectives, and how to make the best use of the DVD and workbook. Consider the following questions regarding the group in the video presentation:

1. If you were a prospective member of this group, what kind of information would you want before you made a decision to participate?
2. How important would you consider informed consent to be for this kind of group?
3. How might being a member of this video group for educational purposes affect your participation?
4. How would you deal with issues of confidentiality?
5. What kind of ground rules or policies would be essential in this video group?

MindTap for Counseling

Additional resources can be found on CengageBrain.com and by logging into the MindTap course created by your professor. There you will find a variety of study tools and useful resources that include quizzes, videos, interactive exercises, and more.

6

CHAPTER

Initial Stage of a Group

CHAPTER LEARNING OBJECTIVES

1. Identify and define the key characteristics of a group during the initial stage
2. Explore ways to deal with conflict early in a group
3. Examine a framework for effective ways to establish trust in a group
4. Explain ways to assist members in defining personal goals for group participation
5. Discuss the specific therapeutic factors and how they contribute to group effectiveness (CACREP, 2016, Standard C)
6. Understand research findings on effective therapeutic relationships
7. Delineate guidelines for getting the most from a group experience
8. Examine some of the major issues facing coleaders during the initial stage
9. Explore guidelines for opening and closing group sessions

You have just completed your first session with a group of sexual abuse survivors. Several of the members were very quiet throughout the meeting, and others expressed a high degree of anxiety. One member tended to dominate the session. She interrupted others while they were speaking and often moved the discussion away from other members back onto herself by saying how she could "relate" to what they were saying.

Issues of trust and anxiety are common in initial sessions. Consider interventions you can make that will help create trust. How can you assist members in exploring any fears they may have over participating in a group? Reflect on these questions:

- How might you address the issues of trust and anxiety that seem to permeate this group? What do you think will help the silent members feel safe enough to share?
- How might you invite members to identify and explore any sources of their anxiety?
- What ideas do you have for addressing the member who dominated the discussion?
- What possible "function" does a talkative member's behavior serve in the group dynamics?
- Which members (quiet, anxious, or dominant) would be most challenging for you as the group leader?

Introduction

This chapter contains many examples of teaching members about how groups function. We describe the characteristics of a group in its early stages, discuss the importance of creating trust as the foundation for a group, explore the topic of establishing goals early in the life of a group, discuss formation of group norms and the beginnings of group cohesion, explain research findings on effective therapeutic relationships, and provide guidelines for helping members get the most from a group. We also suggest some leadership guidelines for opening and closing group meetings.

Group Characteristics at the Initial Stage

LO1

The central process during the initial stage of a group is orientation and exploration. Members are getting acquainted, learning how the group functions, developing spoken and unspoken norms that will govern group behavior, exploring their fears and hopes pertaining to the group, clarifying their expectations, identifying personal goals, and determining whether this group is safe. This stage is characterized by members expressing fears and hesitations as well as hopes and expectations. The degree of trust that can be established in the group will be determined by how the leader deals with these reactions.

Some Early Concerns

It is common during the initial phase of a group that members may appear rather hesitant to get involved. Caution on the part of members is to be expected, and it makes sense. Participants are often tentative and vague about what they hope to get from a group experience. Most members are uncertain about group norms and expected behavior, and there may be moments of silence and awkwardness. Some members may be impatient and ready to work, whereas others may appear hesitant or uninvolved. Still others may be looking for quick solutions to their problems. If your leadership style involves very little structure, the level of anxiety is likely to be high because of the ambiguity of the situation, and there will probably be hesitation and requests from members for direction. Members may ask "What are we supposed to be doing?" or state "I really don't know what we should be talking about." When someone does volunteer a problem for discussion, other members are likely to offer suggestions and give what they consider to be helpful advice. Although this may seem like progress because there is the appearance of group interaction, giving advice bypasses the necessity for members to explore their problems and discover their own solutions.

During the first few group sessions, members watch the leader's behavior and think about safety in the group. Trust can be lost or gained by how the leader handles conflict or the initial expression of any negative reactions. The group leader's task is to be aware of the tentative nature of explorations during these early sessions and to treat critical comments nondefensively and with acceptance.

Initial Hesitation and Cultural Considerations

Many group members hold attitudes and expectations that make it difficult for them to participate fully in a group experience. In some cultures, individuals are discouraged from expressing their feelings openly, talking about their personal problems with people they do not know well, or telling others how they perceive or react to them. Group practitioners need to be aware that hesitation to participate in a group may be more the result of cultural background than of an uncooperative attitude. For example, Latinos/as may approach people cautiously because of their experiences with oppression, discrimination, and marginalization (Torres-Rivera, Torres Fernandez, & Hendricks, 2014). Some African American clients may experience difficulty in a group, especially if they are expected to make deeply personal disclosures too quickly. In general, group counselors need to be aware of the heritage, values, and background of African American clients and incorporate them into group work (Steen, Shi, & Hockersmith, 2014). Group leaders can encourage members to say something about what makes their participation difficult. Rather than ignoring members, the leader can invite members to explore how they can best benefit from the group experience.

In a group situation, individuals may seem to be reserved or "holding back" when they are only being true to their cultural values or gender-role norms. It is a mistake to assume that behaving cautiously is a sign of an uncooperative attitude. Some members may believe it is distasteful to talk publicly about private matters. Others may feel it is a sign of weakness to disclose personal problems or to express feelings. Those members who have cultural injunctions against talking about their family in a group may be reluctant to engage in role playing involving symbolically talking to their parents. They may not want to reveal certain struggles out of fear that their disclosures would entrench already existing stereotypes and prejudices. Members from certain racial, cultural, and ethnic populations have learned a healthy paranoia about self-disclosing too quickly in a group with members from a dominant population. Their experience of oppression and their reservations in making themselves known to others and determining who is safe in the group needs to be viewed in this context.

One of the groups I (Cindy) led was a woman's HIV prevention/education group that consisted of Caucasian, Latina, and African American women. Getting the women to discuss personal issues pertaining to sexual values and behaviors was a challenge. I designed the first meeting to address the differences among the members and to help draw out a discussion about the ways in which the women were both similar and different. Putting the topic of difference on the table enabled these women to share the concerns and fears they had about sitting in a diverse group of women. It also brought to their attention the many overlapping experiences and issues they shared with one another. This discussion set a tone for the rest of the group meetings, and group members talked openly about the ways their lives and sexual behaviors were influenced by their cultural identities.

In your role as a group leader you can minimize reluctance on the part of members by inviting a discussion of how they could participate in the group in a way that does not violate their cultural norms and values. If you are aware of the cultural context of the members of your group, it is possible to both appreciate their cultural values and respectfully encourage them to deal with the concerns that brought them to the group. An important leadership function is assisting members in understanding how their initial hesitation to reveal themselves may relate to their cultural conditioning. It is important to understand the role society has played with some members by oppressing them into silence or caution. These social factors shed a different light on the reluctance of some group members to engage in self-disclosure.

Regardless of the type of group, some hesitation is to be expected in the initial stage, even if people are eager to join the group. This reluctance can be manifested in many different ways. What members do talk about is likely to be less important than what they keep hidden—their real fears about being in this group at this moment. Because cautious behavior often arises from fearful expectations, identifying and discussing these fears now will benefit the whole group. It is not helpful to say to an anxious member: "You don't need to be afraid in here. Nobody will hurt you." You cannot honestly make such promises. Some members may feel hurt by another's response to them. It is helpful to let members know that you want them to express when they feel hurt and that you will not abandon them. Although members may make mistakes and step on each other's toes, it can be reassuring for members to know that this provides an opportunity to learn how to recover and to experiment with new behaviors in a supportive atmosphere.

Learning in Action

Testing the Waters

By opening a dialogue about members' fears and hesitations, group members can learn to deal with these feelings in an honest and productive way. Discuss these questions as a group during an initial stage of group:

1. When faced with a task that is scary for you, how do you typically respond? Do you retreat or run away from the fear? Do you face the fear head on? Do you pretend that you are not afraid? Do you ask for support from others or work it out independently?
2. How do you predict you will behave in this group if you feel afraid?
3. Is your way of responding to fear the way you would like to behave, or is there anything about how you react that you would like to change?
4. If you felt afraid to participate in the group or to share a part of yourself, what could you do or say that would help you to move through your fear? How might the leaders or group members support you?

Identifying and Exploring Common Fears of Group Members

Members test the waters at the early sessions to see if their concerns will be taken seriously and if the group is a safe place to express what they think and feel. If their reactions, positive or negative, are listened to with respect and acceptance, they have a basis to begin dealing with deeper aspects of themselves. A good way for you to start dealing with members' fears is by listening to them and encouraging full expression of their concerns. Here are some common fears participants identify:

- Will I be accepted or rejected?
- Will others be able to understand me?
- How will this group be any different from other groups in which I have experienced discrimination, oppression, and prejudice?
- I'm afraid of being judged by others, especially if I am different from them.
- Will I feel pressured to disclose deeply personal matters?
- What if my friends or family members ask me about what I share in my group?
- I fear being hurt.
- What if the group attacks me?
- What if I feel like my cultural values are not being respected or understood?
- What if I find out things about myself that I can't cope with?
- I'm afraid I'll change and that those I'm close to won't like my changes.
- I'm afraid that I might break down and cry.

In the initial stage, we begin by asking group members to identify their fears and begin to explore them. It sometimes helps in building a trusting atmosphere to ask people to split up into pairs and then to join to make groups of four. In this way members can choose others with whom to share their expectations, get acquainted, and talk about their fears or reservations. Talking with one other person, and then merging with others, is far less threatening to most participants than talking to the entire group. This subgroup approach is an excellent icebreaker, and when the entire group gets together again, there is generally a greater willingness to interact.

Usually group members are reserved in the beginning, but some group members may jump in full force without much testing of the waters. This is another way in which anxiety can manifest itself, and sometimes these members need the leader's help in slowing down and not sharing too much too quickly.

Learning in Action

Wall of Fears

Before the group session, the group leader writes each of the following fears and concerns on separate pieces of paper and posts them on the wall in different places around the room:

"I'm afraid/concerned I won't fit in."

"I'm afraid/concerned I won't be understood."

"I'm afraid/concerned about being judged."

"I'm afraid/concerned about people knowing my secrets."

"I'm afraid/concerned I won't get anything out of this group."

"I'm afraid/concerned that I will be too much for people."

"I'm afraid/concerned that the leaders won't know how to help me."

"My fear/concern is . . ."

Ask members to stand by the "fear" that most resonates with them. Once all members have chosen their spot, ask them to stay there and silently look around the room at where others are standing. Then ask members the following discussion questions.

Discussion Questions

- Will you share with the group the fear you chose and why?
- Were you surprised by some of the places other members stood? Did it match your initial impression of them?
- In what ways do you need to challenge yourself in this group if you choose to move through your fear or concern?
- How can the group and the leader help you to move through your fear or concern?

Hidden Agendas

A common form of resistance in groups relates to the presence of an unidentified or **hidden agenda**—an issue that is not openly acknowledged and discussed and may not even be in the members' conscious awareness. If encouragement to face these issues is lacking, the group process gets bogged down because the norm of being closed, cautious, and defensive replaces the norm of being open. When there are unspoken reactions (by one member, several members, or the entire group), a common set of features emerges: trust is low, interpersonal tensions emerge, people are guarded and unwilling to take risks, the leader seems to be working harder than the members, and there is a vague feeling that something just does not make sense.

Consider these scenarios. In one group a member said, "There's someone in this room I don't like." The entire group was affected by this comment, and several members later disclosed that they had wondered if they were the disliked person. It was not until the member was willing to deal directly with the conflict he was having with another participant that the atmosphere in the room cleared up. In another group, composed of adolescents, many members displayed a great unwillingness to talk. The hidden agenda was the concern over rumors that some gossiping was taking place. Members who were concerned about confidentiality were reluctant to express their feelings because of the fear of repercussions.

A group made up mostly of members from a fundamentalist religious background also suffered from a hidden agenda. Some of the members eventually disclosed that their hesitation to get involved in the group was out of fear that they, as well as their religion, would be unfavorably judged if they revealed any struggles regarding their faith. They were anxious about the reactions of both those members who shared their faith as well as those who did not. Only after addressing their fears of being judged was the group able to move forward.

In another group, one member (Roger) had expressed considerable emotion during a session, which inhibited the trust level in the group in the following session. Although many members seemed involved in this member's work, at the next session there was a mood of quietness in the group. With the prodding of the group leader, members eventually revealed what was behind their hesitation to speak up. Some had been frightened by the intensity of Roger's feelings and were not sure what they should do about the reactions they had. Others who had been deeply touched wanted to get involved by discussing their own problems, but they didn't want to interrupt Roger's continued work. Some who were moved personally were afraid to acknowledge this for fear that they might "lose control" as Roger had. Other members were angry because they felt Roger had been "left hanging"; they couldn't see what good it had done for him to get so worked up and then not get an answer to his problem. Still others eventually confessed that they were burdening themselves with "performance anxiety." They thought they would have to display a great deal of emotional intensity to be accepted in the group. If they did not cry, they were afraid others might perceive them as being superficial.

In our training and supervision workshops, we have sometimes made an erroneous assumption that all the participants are there voluntarily. In several cases in various agencies, reluctant behavior was initially high because some members were pressured by their superiors to attend. Workshop participants often wondered how information they revealed about themselves would be used outside of the group. This was a critical part of the informed consent process. We encouraged them to raise any questions they had about the workshop and also to express any of their concerns or grievances. Even though we were not able to remove the pressure they felt over having to attend, our willingness to listen to and respect what they had to say did help them overcome their reluctance to participate.

All of these reactions are material for possible productive interaction if group members are willing to bring them up. By fully expressing and exploring such reactions, members genuinely develop the basis of trust. On the other hand, if members stifle their reactions, the group loses its vitality. Group issues that do not get talked about almost always develop into a hidden agenda that immobilizes the individuals and shatters trust in the group.

It is generally a good idea to begin working with the reluctant behavior in a group. Reluctance to speak out may function as a healthy boundary rather than being an expression of resistance. For example, a person who has been abused may not be so quick to trust. If leaders go where the energy is and facilitate its direct expression, they are less likely to get stuck. The screening processes we do prior to beginning a group helps us learn the history of group members, which enables us to better understand some of their reactions during the group process.

As a group leader, you cannot burden yourself with knowing all of the potential hidden agendas present in a group, but you can anticipate possible hidden agendas that may operate given the nature of a specific group. Reflect on the existence of such agendas and find ways to assist members to identify and articulate their concerns. Once group members recognize that some dynamics are affecting the group process, the hidden agenda is less likely to sabotage the group process. The members can then be challenged to decide how they will deal with their concerns.

Groups do not progress unless hidden agendas are uncovered and discussed. This process often requires patience from the leader and a willingness to continually check with members to find out if they are saying what they need to say. What bogs down groups is not so much what people *are* saying but what they *are not* saying. Although it is generally not comfortable for leaders to deal with these undercurrents, respectfully yet firmly challenging members to express persistent thoughts and feelings about what is emerging in the group is extremely valuable.

Groups do not progress unless hidden agendas are uncovered and discussed.

One of the best ways to facilitate the exploration of a potential hidden agenda in a group is for you to reflect on your own experience as a member of a group. Have you been in a group where a hidden agenda was present? If so, how did this affect you? Were you inclined to talk about how you were being affected by the presence of a hidden agenda? What may have inhibited you or helped you to feel empowered to talk about this in your group? How can you apply your experience as a group member to groups you will be facilitating?

Address Conflict Early

Conflict can emerge in any stage of group work, although it is most common later during the transition stage. Conflict that arises early in a group must be adequately dealt with, or it is likely to inhibit the cohesion of the group. When conflict first occurs, members are keenly aware of and observe a leader's actions. The leader must respond to and, whenever possible, facilitate a resolution of the conflict so the group can progress.

Let's examine a conflict that might surface during the first group session:

Leader: What are you aware of as you look around the room?

Elijah: I need to be in a group with strong men, and I don't think this is the right group for me.

Travis: That's the most homophobic remark! Just because I'm gay you think I'm not a strong man.

Elijah: That's not what I mean. You're taking it the wrong way.

Travis: I know exactly what you meant.

Leader: Travis, please say more about your reactions to Elijah and how his comment affected you.

This interaction immediately raised the tension in the room. Such comments can trigger old wounds, as well as open fresh wounds, in some members. It introduces a conflict as well as a cultural issue that needs to be worked through and attended to so the group will be safe for everyone. The leader could work with this in a variety of ways. One is to have Elijah talk more about what it means for him to be with "strong men." How is this significant in his life, and what is its significance right now? How does he see himself on the strong–weak continuum? The leader could ask Travis, as well as other members, if and how they were affected by Elijah's remark. The male members of the group are likely to have some reactions, and Elijah and other group members need to hear this. A goal of the leader might be to explore the transference reactions that were triggered as a result of Elijah's comment. The other goal is to help Elijah see how his comment may have been offensive to some and triggered some vulnerabilities in certain members who have been subjected to homophobic remarks.

Because this conflict arose during the early stage of the group, it is critical that the leader teach the norm of appropriate and effective confrontation. If the matter is bypassed, ignored, or smoothed over by the leader's lack of intervention, members are likely to feel unsafe and to behave cautiously. This unaddressed conflict can easily negatively affect the energy in the room and impede the group's progress.

Self-Focus Versus Focus on Others

A characteristic of many members in beginning groups is the tendency to talk about others and to focus on people and situations outside of the group. Individuals who talk excessively may do so for any of the following reasons:

- They are disconnected from their feelings, and staying on an intellectual level helps them to avoid feelings.
- They may have difficulty connecting with others or getting support from them, and talking makes them less anxious.
- They may be testing the leader and the members to assess how they will respond to them.
- They may come from a culture in which "small talk" is a way to connect and gain trust.

Some participants may engage in storytelling, believing they are really working, when in fact they are avoiding addressing and dealing with their own feelings. They may talk about life situations, but they have a tendency to focus on what other people do to cause them difficulties. Skilled group leaders help such members examine their own reactions to others.

During the initial phase of a group, the leader's primary task is to get group members to focus on themselves. Of course, trust is a prerequisite for this openness. When members focus on others as a way to avoid self-exploration, our leadership task is to enable them to focus on their own reactions. We might say, "I'm aware that you're talking a lot about several important people in your life. They're not here, and we won't be able to work with them. But we are able to work with your feelings and reactions toward them and how their behavior affects you." An awareness of proper timing is essential. The readiness of a client to accept certain interpretations or observations must be considered. We must be skilled not only in helping people recognize that their focus on others can be defensive, but also in encouraging them to express their feelings. Not all such behavior is defensive; it may be culturally appropriate for some members to avoid focusing on themselves. Only by exploring the members' behavior can you get a sense of the meaning underlying the focus on others.

Here-and-Now Focus Versus There-and-Then Focus

Some groups have a primary focus on what is occurring right now in the room. The predominant theme these groups explore is present member–member interactions, and the material for discussion emerges from these encounters. Other groups focus largely on outside problems that members bring to the session or deal with specified topics for exploration. The practitioner's theoretical orientation influences whether the focus is on what is presently happening within the group or on past events outside of the group. As you saw in Chapter 4, the experiential and relationship-oriented approaches emphasize the here and now, the cognitive behavioral approaches are mainly concerned with a present-centered focus, and the psychodynamic approaches consider a there-and-then focus. Our groups combine both a here-and-now and a there-and-then focus. Members are often not ready to deal with significant issues pertaining to their lives away from the group until they first deal with their reactions to one another in the room. To meaningfully explore personal problems, members must first feel safe and trusting.

During the initial sessions, we ask members to make connections between personal problems they are facing in their world and their experience in the group. If a member discloses that she feels isolated in her life, for instance, we ask her to be aware of how she may be isolating herself in the group setting. If another member shares how he overextends himself in his life and rarely attends to himself because of his concern for others, we would ask him how this might become an issue for him in this group. If a member states that she feels like an outsider, we tend to ask if she often feels this way in her daily life. These members may isolate, overextend themselves, and feel like outsiders in the group sessions, and dealing with these here-and-now occurrences can serve as a springboard for exploring deeper personal concerns. Staying focused with what is presently happening within the group can help members identify specific aspects of their behavior they want to change.

Paying attention to here-and-now interactions is of the utmost value, for the way members behave in the present context of the group is reflective of how they interact with others outside the group. The opportunities for interpersonal learning that groups provide are unique. One of the best ways to learn more about members' interpersonal style is by paying attention to their behavior in the group setting. Members learn a great deal about how they function interpersonally in their world by becoming aware of their patterns in the group sessions.

Interventions that direct members to gain awareness of what they are experiencing in the here and now tend to intensify the emotional quality of interactions. Rather than having members talk about their problems in a reporting fashion, we consistently encourage members to note what it is that they are experiencing presently. If members have a problem in daily life that they want to explore, we typically intervene by helping them bring this concern into the present group context. Although group participants often have a self-protective tendency to avoid the here and now, one of the main tasks of the group facilitator is to consistently assist members in directing their attention to what they are thinking, feeling, and doing in the moment. The more members are able to immerse themselves in the here and now, the greater chance they have to enhance the quality of their interpersonal relationships in everyday life.

There are both strengths and limitations in working from a here-and-now perspective. By focusing on what is happening in the room, we are able to help members work through their personal concerns. Here-and-now communication also helps to move the group process along and gives members a chance to express what they are experiencing. However, if someone is talking about an important personal matter such as past spousal abuse or another trauma and we try to direct the member toward the here and now too quickly, we may be interfering with important grief work that needs to be done. In addition, if we raise questions or make interventions in an untimely way, we may risk insulting or invalidating the member's experience. This is especially true with racial issues. If, for example, we are too quick to confront a person of color who is talking about not trusting White people because of past experiences, we may risk devaluing this member's past life experiences in an effort to help her gain a new perspective. In general, it is most helpful to validate a member's experience and to have the person discuss the impact of those experiences before making interventions that might leave the member feeling discounted or misunderstood. Sometimes our efforts to be culturally responsive can leave us feeling paralyzed. We cannot fully anticipate the impact of our interventions, so it is important to check in with members and ask how they are doing with us and with the interventions we make. When we ask members questions, we must be open to hearing their answers. Respond respectfully and integrate their feedback into your practice.

Trust Versus Mistrust

If a basic sense of trust is not established at the outset of a group, problems are likely to arise later. Signs of developing trust include members expressing feelings without fear of censure; members being willing to decide for themselves specific goals and personal areas to explore; members focusing on themselves, not on others; and members being willing to risk disclosing personal aspects of themselves. Trust entails a sense of safety, but it does not necessarily entail being comfortable. Members often say that they are uncomfortable in a group session.

It is important to teach members that they are not apt to feel comfortable when they are talking about matters of significance. We hope they will be willing to endure the anxiety and discomfort associated with taking risks.

Trust entails a sense of safety, but it does not necessarily entail being comfortable.

In contrast, a lack of trust is indicated by an undercurrent of anger and suspicion in the group and members being unwilling to talk about these feelings. Other manifestations of lack of trust are participants' taking refuge in being abstract or overly intellectual and being vague about what they expect from the therapeutic group. Before a climate of trust is established, people tend to wait for the leader to decide for them what they need to examine. Any disclosures made tend to be superficial and rehearsed, and risk-taking is at a low level. Members are more likely to push themselves when they perceive the group as being a safe place to challenge themselves. It is through taking risks that safety is created.

LO3

Creating Trust: Leader and Member Roles

The Importance of Modeling

Our success in creating a climate of trust within a group has much to do with how well we have prepared both the members and ourselves. As described in Chapter 4, presence on the part of the leader is the cornerstone of most of the experiential and relationship-oriented approaches to group counseling. To be an effective leader, we must be psychologically present in the group and be genuine. In behavior therapy, leader modeling is viewed as basic to establishing trust within a group. We can facilitate the group process by sharing our own expectations for the group during the initial sessions and by modeling interpersonal honesty, respect, and spontaneity.

If we have given careful thought to why we are organizing the group, what we hope to accomplish, and how we will go about meeting our objectives, the chances are greatly increased that we will inspire confidence. The members will see our willingness to think about the group as a sign that we care about them. Furthermore, if we have done an adequate job with the pregroup issues—informing members of their rights and responsibilities, giving some time to teaching the group process, exploring the congruence between the cultural values of members and what they are expected to do, and preparing the members for a successful experience—the members will realize that we are taking our work seriously and that we are interested in their welfare.

Regardless of a leader's theoretical orientation, establishing trust is a central task for the initial stage of a group. It is not possible to overemphasize the significance of the leader's modeling and the attitudes expressed through the leader's behavior in these early sessions. Reflecting on your role as a leader, ask yourself:

- How competent do I feel in leading or coleading this particular group?
- How confident am I that I can establish trust with the group and between group members?

The person you are and, especially, how you behave in the sessions are crucial factors in building a trusting community. (Refer to our discussion of the personal characteristics of the effective leader in Chapter 2. Also see the discussion of the leader as a person in the experiential and relationship-oriented approaches in Chapter 4.)

If we trust in the group process and have faith in the members' capacity to make significant changes in themselves, they are likely to see value in their group as a pathway to personal growth. If we listen nondefensively and respectfully and convey that we value members' subjective experience, they are likely to see the power in active listening. If we are genuinely willing to engage in appropriate self-disclosure, we will foster honesty and disclosure among the members. If we are truly able to accept others for who they are and avoid imposing our values on them, our members will learn valuable lessons about accepting people's rights to differ and to be themselves. In short, what you model through what you do in the group is one of the most powerful ways of teaching members how to relate to one another constructively and deeply.

Students in my (Cindy's) classes tell me that they value the personal experiences I share and that my doing so helps them to relate to me, which encourages them to become more open. Although my self-disclosures are often spontaneous, they are purposeful and meant to help facilitate the work of group members. For example, I might talk about a relationship difficulty I have had to help a member who is feeling shame about a similar issue. Sometimes my aim in disclosing is to normalize a member's experience and to promote disclosure among the members, which is likely to happen if they feel less alone in their experience. Leaders need to be careful in self-disclosing so that they do not interfere with the work of group members. However, appropriate self-disclosure can enhance group trust and promote universality.

If you are coleading a group, you and your colleague have ample opportunities to model a behavioral style that will promote trust. If the two of you function harmoniously with a spontaneous give and take, for example, members will feel more trusting in your presence. If your relationship with your coleader is characterized by respect, authenticity, sensitivity, and directness, the members will learn about the value of such attitudes and behaviors. Furthermore, the way the two of you interact with the members contributes to or detracts from the level of trust. If one coleader's typical manner of speaking with members is sharp, short, and sarcastic, for example, members are likely to quickly pick up this leader's lack of respect for them and tend to become closed or defensive. Therefore, it is wise for coleaders to examine each other's style of interacting and to talk about this when they meet privately outside of the group.

It is a mistake to assume that as a leader or a coleader you have sole responsibility for the development and maintenance of trust. The level of trust is engendered by your attitudes and actions, yet it also depends to a large degree on the level of investment of the members. If members want very little for themselves, if they are unwilling to share enough of themselves so that they can be known, if they simply wait passively for you to "make trust happen," and if they are unwilling to take risks in the sessions, trust will be slow to develop. The tone set by your leadership will influence members' willingness to disclose themselves and to begin taking those steps necessary to establish trust.

For a good example of how a group practitioner lays a foundation of trust-building during the initial phase of a group, see the women's support group for survivors of incest in a community agency in Chapter 11. The therapist believes that what takes place during the early stage of a group is crucial to what will occur later in the group. At the first group meeting, she emphasizes the importance of regular attendance, being prompt, confidentiality, the limitations of time, and bringing any unresolved issues back to the group rather than dealing with them outside of the group. Bonding begins quickly as members express empathy with one another over the difficulty of sharing the incest issue. As members realize that they have a common experience, they share at a deeper level and find the support available in the group to be very meaningful. By sharing the incest experience, members free themselves to deal with the effects the incest continues to have on their lives.

The issue of trust is never settled once and for all; it will continue to manifest itself in different forms throughout the life of the group. Ongoing attention to trust issues is necessary for members to continue to trust one another. Members need to learn that the more threatening the material explored becomes, the more the issue of trust becomes central. It is essential that the members demonstrate a willingness to acknowledge their lack of trust, and a good place to begin is by talking about what makes it difficult for them to trust. Certainly the delicate nature of trust is a focal point for the early stage of any group.

Learning in Action

Developing Trust

If you were to think of building trust as occurring in stages, how might you describe your own process for cultivating trust in a group? Think of your willingness to trust others as well as your ability to be a trustworthy member or participant.

Stage 1: Checking Out the Scene

- How do you go about observing others? Do you process internally? Are you quiet or talkative? Do you form opinions of others quickly? Are you open-minded, guarded, or judgmental?
- What do your behaviors and interactions look like when you are "checking out the scene"?

Stage 2: Experimenting With Trust

- How do you test others to see if they are trustworthy? Do you let others risk first, or do you take the first step? Do you expect others to be trustworthy or not? How do you show others that you can be trusted?
- What do your behaviors and interactions look like when you are experimenting with trust?

Stage 3: Trusting and Being Trustworthy

- Once you have decided that trust has been established, do you still proceed with caution or open up easily? Do you find it easier to be trusted or to trust others?
- What do your behaviors and interactions look like when you are trusting others and being trustworthy?

Stage 4: Surviving Breaches in Trust

- If someone breaks your trust, what impact does this have on you? Are you able to easily forgive? Does it permanently damage the relationship? How does a person go about rebuilding trust with you once it has been broken?
- What feelings are evoked within you when trust is broken? What do your behaviors and interactions look like when trust has been breached in a relationship?

Attitudes and Actions Leading to Trust

Certain attitudes and actions of leaders enhance the level of trust in a group. Some of these factors include attending and listening, understanding both verbal and nonverbal behavior, empathy, genuineness, self-disclosure, respect, and caring confrontation. These attitudes on the part of the group leader are given prominence in the person-centered approach to group counseling (see Chapter 4).

Attending and Listening Careful attending to the verbal and nonverbal messages of others is necessary for trust to occur. If genuine listening and understanding are absent, there is no basis for connection between members. If members feel that they are being heard and deeply understood, they are more likely to trust that others care about them too.

If genuine listening and understanding are absent, there is no basis for connection between members.

Both leaders and members may demonstrate a lack of attending in different ways. Here are some of the most common ones: (1) not listening to the speaker because you are thinking of what to say next, (2) asking many closed questions that probe for irrelevant and detailed information, (3) doing too much talking and not enough listening, (4) giving advice too quickly instead of encouraging the speaker to explore a struggle, (5) paying attention only to what people say explicitly and thus missing what they express nonverbally, (6) engaging in selective listening (hearing only what you want to hear), and (7) failing to ask people to give voice to what their body is experiencing.

Group members do not always possess good listening skills, nor do they always respond effectively to what they perceive. Therefore, teaching basic listening and responding skills is a major part of the trust process. If members do not feel listened to, they are not likely to get very deep or personal.

Understanding Nonverbal Behavior Inexperienced group workers frequently make the error of focusing exclusively on what members are saying and miss the more subtle nonverbal messages. People often express themselves more honestly nonverbally than they do verbally. Detecting discrepancies between verbal and nonverbal behavior is an art to be learned. Examples of clients displaying these discrepancies include a member who is talking about a painful experience while smiling; a member who speaks very softly and proclaims that nobody listens to him; a client who is verbally expressing positive feelings yet is very constricted physically; a person who says that she really wants to work and to have group time but consistently waits until the end of a session before bringing up her concerns; a participant who claims that she feels comfortable in the group and really likes the members yet sits with her arms crossed tightly and looks at the floor; and a member who displays facial expressions and gestures but denies having any reactions.

Although these gestures may seem fairly easy to interpret, leaders should not too quickly offer an interpretation. For example, in a group we were coleading, a male group member would often clear his throat before speaking about emotional topics. We wondered if this was a way for him to distance himself emotionally from what he was about to express. When we brought the mannerism to his attention, his initial response was to dismiss it as "just a bad habit." We continued to draw his attention to the times when he would clear his throat, and he eventually connected this mannerism to his own discomfort with feeling and showing emotion. This led him to other realizations about how he held back his feelings. If we had been too quick to make an interpretation or to back off from his initial defensiveness, he may not have acquired these insights. Coincidentally, when this member was able to more openly share his feelings, this habit seemed to disappear.

Although you may think you have a clear idea of what a nonverbal behavior means, it is a good idea to file away some of your impressions and draw on them as the group unfolds and as a pattern of behavior becomes manifest. When you do explore nonverbal behavior with a member, it is best to describe the behavior. For example, "I notice that you're smiling, yet you're talking about painful memories, and there are tears in your eyes. Are you aware of that?" When you describe behavior, you are less likely to analyze. After describing what you are seeing, invite the participant to offer the meaning of the nonverbal behavior. At times you may misunderstand nonverbal information and even label it as resistance. The nonverbal behavior may well be a manifestation of a cultural injunction. For example, a leader is role playing Javier's father and asks Javier to make eye contact with him as he is talking. In spite of many invitations, Javier continues to look at the floor as he talks to his symbolic father. The leader is unaware that Javier would have felt disrespectful if he looked directly at his father or another authority figure. This is something that can be explored if the leader respectfully listens to Javier and strives to understand the meaning of his behavior.

Another avenue for helping clients to give full expression to their feelings is by asking clients to pay attention to what they are experiencing physically. For example, if you have a client who is talking a lot, but seems emotionally detached from the content, you could ask her what she is most aware of in her body at that moment. She may respond by saying, "I feel heat in my chest area." This might open up an entirely new way for you to help her connect to her feelings and to express feelings in a more integrated and holistic manner.

In summary, it is essential that we avoid making assumptions and interpretations about what members are experiencing and, instead, assist members to recognize and explore the possible meanings of their nonverbal behavior and their bodily experience. If we misread or ignore nonverbal messages or insensitively confront certain behavior, the level of trust in the group will suffer. When we point out what we are observing, we do so respectfully, giving members the opportunity to explore what they are experiencing.

Empathy Empathy is the ability to tune in to what others are subjectively experiencing and to see the world through their eyes. Empathy is not the same thing as sympathy, which entails providing comfort to others. When people experience empathic understanding without critical judgment, they are more likely to reveal their deeper concerns because they believe others understand and accept them as they are. This kind of nonjudgmental understanding is vital to establishing trust.

One of our leadership functions is to help members develop greater empathy by pointing out behaviors that block this understanding. Examples of these counterproductive behaviors include responding to others with pat statements, not responding to others at all, questioning inappropriately, telling others how they should be, responding with critical judgments, or being defensive.

Empathy is an avenue of demonstrating support. For example, Judy benefits when others are able to understand her. If she talks about going through an extremely painful divorce, Clyde can let her know the ways in which he identifies with and understands her pain. Though their circumstances are different, he empathizes with her pain and is willing to share with her his feelings of rejection and abandonment when his wife left him. What helps Judy is Clyde's willingness to tell her about his struggles rather than providing her with quick answers. Instead of telling her what he did or offering her reassurance, he helps her most by sharing his struggles and pain with her.

Genuineness Genuineness implies congruence between a person's inner experience and what he or she projects externally. Applied to our role as a leader, genuineness means that we do not pretend to be accepting when internally we are not feeling accepting, we do not rely on behaviors that are aimed at winning approval, and we avoid hiding behind our professional role. Through our own authenticity, we offer a model that inspires members to be real in their interactions.

Consider a couple of examples in which you might be challenged to provide authentic responses rather than expected ones. A member who is new to your group might spontaneously ask you, "What do you think of me?" You could politely respond with, "I think you're a very nice person." Here is a more honest response: "I don't know you well enough to have strong reactions to you. As I get to know you better, I'll share my perceptions with you." You might want to ask this person what prompted her question and discover that she is intimidated by your position in the group and needs quick reassurance. By helping her identify the reason for her question, you can help her be more authentic with you. In another case, in the middle of a conflict a member says to you, "Oh, give me a hug; I don't like this tension between us." Chances are that you don't really feel like hugging him at this moment. It is nevertheless important that you give an honest reply to his request. You could say, "I'm struggling with you right now, and I want to continue working this through. If I were to hug you right now, it would not feel consistent with what I'm experiencing with you. However, that doesn't mean that I won't want to hug you later."

Self-Disclosure Our authenticity can sometimes be expressed in appropriate self-disclosure. We can invite members to make themselves known by revealing our own thoughts and feelings related to what is going on within the group. If we avoid hiding, we will encourage the rest of the group to be open about their concerns. Sometimes group participants will challenge us by saying, "We tell you all of our problems, but we don't know any of yours." We could surrender to this pressure to prove that we are "genuine" and disclose a personal problem, but this forced disclosure may not be in the best interests of the group. A more appropriate response might be: "Yes, in this group, due to my role, I'm likely to learn more about the nature of your problems than you will learn about my personal concerns, but this doesn't mean that I don't have difficulties in my life. If you and I were members in another group, I expect that you'd learn more about me. While I'm not likely to bring my outside problems into this group, I'm very willing to let you know how I'm being affected in these sessions and also to reveal my reactions to you."

Decisions about self-disclosure are culture-bound and value laden. In some cases, the willingness of a leader to engage in self-disclosure is both culturally appropriate and a way to create trust. For some members it would seem unnatural not to know anything personal about the leader, whereas other members may be extremely uncomfortable knowing personal information about the leader. It is important to discuss the difference in needs that the group members may have and how culture might be a large part of the members' expectations of the leader. The goal is to understand what the member wants from the leader and to decide how this might be accomplished. For example, when I (Cindy) was working with refugees from Sudan, I was struck by how important it was to share some information about my family. In Sudanese culture it was unheard of to discuss personal topics with someone if they did not know something about the family and where he or she came from. Sharing this information is not typical, but I felt it was necessary and appropriate to do so with the young men from Sudan so they could open up about their experiences in the civil war and as refugees. If I had maintained a stance of "no personal self-disclosure," I doubt that a trusting bond would have developed between us.

Group members may ask personal questions of leaders for a variety of reasons. Clinicians need to be aware of the limits of their sharing both for their own and their members' benefit. Many therapists will answer personal questions (about their age, significant relationships, past experiences) and then question the member about what it was like to hear the response. Self-disclosure can be useful when it is intentional and keeps the focus of attention on the group members rather than on the leader.

Respect Respect is shown by what the leader and the members actually do, not simply by what they say. Attitudes and actions that demonstrate respect include avoiding critical judgments, avoiding labeling, looking beyond self-imposed or other-imposed labels, expressing warmth and support that is honestly felt, being genuine and risking, and recognizing the rights of others to be different. For example, if a member discloses his strong sense of filial piety (an accepted norm in his culture), others in the group demonstrate respect when they strive to understand rather than judge his loyalty and need to please his parents. If people receive this type of respect, they are supported in their attempts to talk about themselves in open and meaningful ways.

Nina may express her fear of being judged by others and talk about how she is reluctant to speak because of this fear of criticism. Members are not offering her respect if they too quickly reassure her that they like her just as she is and that they would not judge her. By encouraging Nina to explore where in her life she feels judged by others, she may discover that her feelings of being judged reside within her and that she projects them onto others. Although group members could reassure Nina, as soon as she is away from the group her internal judge would take over again. It would be more helpful to encourage her to explore her fear of being judged, both in past situations and in the group.

Caring Confrontation The way in which confrontations are handled can either build or inhibit the development of trust in a group. A confrontation can be an act of caring that takes the form of an invitation for members to examine some discrepancy between what they are saying and what they are doing or between what they are saying and some nonverbal cues they are manifesting. We can teach members directness coupled with sensitivity, which results in their seeing that confrontation can be done in a caring yet honest manner. Some members may have difficulty with even the most caring confrontation and may interpret it as a personal attack, although that is far from what was intended. We make it a practice to check in with members to see how they are receiving the confrontation and how they are doing with us after we have made the intervention. We do not assume that because a member looks fine on the outside he or she is feeling fine.

When confrontations are made in an abrasive, "hit-and-run" fashion, or if the leader allows verbal abuse, trust is greatly inhibited. Attacking comments or aggressive confrontations close people up by making them defensive. Caring confrontations help members learn to express even negative reactions in a way that respects those they are confronting. For example, Claire is very willing to speak on everything and constantly brings herself in on others' work. An ineffective confrontation by a group leader is this: "I want you to be quiet and let others in here talk." An effective leader confrontation is this: "Claire, I appreciate your willingness to participate and talk about yourself. However, I'm concerned that I have heard very little from several others in the group, and I want to hear from them too."

Maintaining Trust The attitudes and behaviors described in these sections have an important bearing on the level of trust established within a group. Although trust is the major task to be accomplished at the initial stage of a group's development, it is a mistake to assume that once trust has been established it is ensured for the duration of that group. Trust ebbs and flows, and new levels of trust must be established as the group progresses toward a deeper level of intimacy. A basic sense of safety is essential for the movement of a group beyond the initial stage, but this trust will be tested time and again and take on new facets in later stages.

LO4

Identifying and Clarifying Goals

A major task during the initial stage is for leaders to assist members in identifying and clarifying specific goals that will influence their participation. In the absence of a clear understanding about the purpose of a group and the meaningful goals of members, much needless floundering can occur. Members may have difficulty making progress until they know *why* they are in the group and *how* they can make full use of the group to achieve their goals.

The process of setting goals is important both at the beginning of a new group and at intervals as the group evolves and goals are met. Both group goals and individual goals must be established. Examples of general group goals include creating a climate of trust and acceptance, promoting self-disclosure in significant ways, and encouraging the taking of risks. If these goals (and norms, which we discuss later) are not explicitly stated, understood, and accepted by the members early in the group, considerable confusion is likely to occur at a later stage. Some general goals common to most therapeutic groups and some examples of goals for specialized groups are discussed in the following sections.

General Goals for Group Members

Although the members must decide for themselves the specific aims of their group experience, here are some broad goals common to many different types of groups:

- Become aware of one's interpersonal style
- Increase awareness of what prevents intimacy
- Learn how to trust oneself and others
- Become aware of how one's culture affects personal decisions
- Increase self-awareness and thereby increase the possibilities for choice and action
- Discover one's strengths and resources
- Challenge and explore certain early decisions (most likely made during childhood) that may no longer be functional
- Recognize that others have similar problems and feelings
- Clarify values and decide whether and how to modify them
- Become both independent and interdependent
- Find better ways to resolve problems
- Become more open and honest with selected others
- Become sensitive to the needs and feelings of others
- Provide others with helpful feedback

Once members have narrowed down their list of general goals, group leaders have a responsibility to monitor the group's progress toward attainment of these group goals (ASGW, 2008). Our colleague Gerald Monk, a professor at San Diego State University, suggests the following questions to assist clients in identifying their goals for counseling (personal communication, August 20, 2002):

- In what ways might I feel and behave differently if my life were as I want it to be?
- What steps can I take to help bring about these desired changes in my emotions and in my behaviors?
- What internal and external barriers exist that interfere with reaching my goals?
- What support systems can I use in reaching my goals?

Helping Members Define Personal Goals

Forming clear goals is important regardless of the theory a leader operates from, but this is given particular emphasis in the cognitive behavioral approaches. For instance, in cognitive therapy the leader strives to create a collaborative partnership with group members. In behavioral group therapy, the definition of specific goals is central to both assessment and treatment. (For more discussion of how a leader's theory affects the process of establishing goals, see Chapter 4.)

Regardless of the type of therapeutic group, leaders have the task of helping participants develop concrete goals that will give them direction. Participants are typically able to state only in broad terms what they expect to get from a group. It is critical that members learn how to translate general goals into measurable ones. For example, one member's broad goal may be, "I want to love myself more." The member's concrete goal might be, "I will do the things that bring me joy such as exercise, listening to music, spending time with friends, and journaling." Another member, Ebony, may want to learn to "relate to others better." The leader's questions should help her become more specific about relationship goals. With whom is she having difficulties? If the answer is her parents, then what specifically is causing her problems with them? How is she affected by these problems? How does she want to be different with her parents? With all this information, the leader has a clearer idea of how to proceed with this member.

Here are some examples of how leaders can intervene to help different members make a vague goal more specific:

Member A: I want to get in touch with my feelings.

Leader: What kind of feelings are you having difficulty with?

Member B: I want to work on my anger.

Leader: With whom in your life are you angry? What is it about the way you express your anger that you dislike? What do you most want to say to these people you are angry with?

Member C: I have very low self-esteem.

Leader: List some of the ways in which you devalue yourself.

Member D: I have trouble with intimacy.

Leader: Who in your life are you having trouble getting close to, and what might you be doing to prevent the intimacy you want?

Member E: I don't want to feel marginalized.

Leader: How do you experience being marginalized, and with whom? Is feeling marginalized an issue for you in this group?

Defining personal goals is an ongoing process, not something that is done once and for all. Throughout the course of a group, it is important to help members assess the degree to which their personal goals are being met and, if appropriate, to help them revise their goals. As members gain more experience, they are in a better position to know what they want from a group, and they also come to recognize additional goals that can guide their participation. Their involvement in the work of other members can act as a catalyst in getting them to think about ways in which they can profit from the group experience.

Establishing a contract is one excellent way for members to clarify and attain their personal goals. Basically, a contract is a statement by participants of what problems they want to explore and what behaviors they are willing to change. In the contract method, group members assume an active and responsible stance. Contracts can be open-ended so that they can be modified or replaced as appropriate. Contracts can be useful for most of the groups discussed in this book, but they are most often used by cognitive behavioral group practitioners.

Contracts and homework assignments can be combined fruitfully. In Ebony's case, a beginning contract could commit her to observe and write down each time she experiences difficulties with her parents. If she discovers that she usually walks away in times of conflict with them, she might pledge in a follow-up contract to stay in one of these situations rather than avoid the conflict.

LO5

Group Process Concepts at the Initial Stage

The group process, as we have said, involves the stages groups tend to go through, each characterized by certain feelings and behaviors. Initially, as the members get to know one another, there is a feeling of anxiety. Each typically waits for someone else to begin. Tension and conflict may build up. If things go well, however, the members learn to trust one another and the leader, and they begin to openly express feelings, thoughts, and reactions. Thus, included under the rubric **group process** are activities such as establishing norms and group cohesion, learning to work cooperatively, establishing ways of solving problems, and learning to express conflict openly. Two group process concepts especially important during the initial stage are group norms and group cohesion.

Group Norms

Group norms are the shared beliefs about expected behaviors aimed at making groups function effectively. It is helpful to have clearly-stated and well-defined expectations for group members. Norms and procedures that will help the group attain its goals can be developed during the early stage. Norms can be explicitly stated, but many groups also have implicit (or unspoken) norms.

Implicit norms may develop because of preconceived ideas about what takes place in a group. Members may assume, for example, that a group is a place where everything must be said, with no regard for privacy. Unless the leader calls attention to the possibility that members can be self-disclosing and still retain a measure of privacy, members may misinterpret the norm of openness and honesty as a policy of complete candor, with no privacy. Another example of an implicit norm is pressure to experience catharsis and crying. In most of our intensive therapeutic groups, there is a fair amount of crying and expression of pent-up feelings. We need to be careful to avoid reinforcing emotional expression that suggests that "real work" consists of catharsis. Many individuals engage in significant self-exploration with little, if any, emotional catharsis. Members can learn from cognitive and behavioral exploration as well as from emotional expression and exploration.

Implicit norms may develop because of modeling by the leader. If a leader uses hostile and abrasive language, members are more likely to adopt this pattern of speech in their group interactions, even though the leader has never encouraged people to talk in such a manner. Implicit norms do affect the group, either positively or negatively. Norms are less likely to have a negative impact if they are made explicit.

Here are some **explicit norms**, or standards of behavior, that are common in many groups:

- Members are expected to attend regularly and to show up on time. When they attend sessions only sporadically, the entire group suffers. Members who regularly attend may have reactions to the lack of commitment of those who miss sessions.
- Members are encouraged to be personal and share meaningful aspects of themselves, communicating directly with others in the group and, in general, being active participants.
- Members are expected to give feedback to one another. They can evaluate the effects of their behavior on others only if the others are willing to say how they have been affected. It is important for members not to withhold their perceptions and reactions but, rather, to let others know what they perceive.
- Members are encouraged to focus on here-and-now interactions within the group. Members focus on being immediate by expressing and exploring conflicts within the group. Immediacy is called for when there are unexpressed thoughts and feelings about what is happening in a session, particularly if these reactions will have a detrimental effect on the group process. Thus, one of your leadership functions is to ask questions such as these: "What is it like to be in this group now?" "With whom do you identify in here?" "What are some of the things that you might be rehearsing to yourself silently?" "Who are you most aware of in this room?" You can also guide members into the here and now by asking them to share what they think and feel about what is going on in the group moment by moment.
- Members are expected to bring into the group sessions personal problems and concerns that they are willing to discuss. They can be expected to spend some time before the sessions thinking about the matters they want to work on. This is an area in which unspoken norms frequently function. In some groups, for example, participants may get the idea that they are not good group members unless they bring personal issues from everyday life to work on during the sessions. Members may get the impression that it is not acceptable to talk about here-and-now matters within the group itself and that they should work on outside problems exclusively.
- Members are encouraged to provide therapeutic support. Ideally, this support facilitates both an individual's work and the group process rather than distracting members from self-exploration. But some leaders can implicitly "teach" being overly supportive or, by their modeling, can demonstrate a type of support that has the effect of short-circuiting painful experiences that a member is attempting to work through. Leaders who are uncomfortable with intense emotions (such as anger or the pain associated with past memories) can collude with members by fostering a pseudosupportive climate that

prevents members from fully experiencing and expressing intense feelings of any kind. Some groups are so supportive that challenge and confrontation are ruled out. An implicit norm in this kind of group results in expressing only positive and favorable reactions.

- The other side of the norm of support is providing members with encouragement to look at themselves. Members need to learn how to confront others without arousing defensiveness. Early in our groups, for example, we establish a norm that it is not acceptable to dismiss another in a judgmental and labeling way, such as by saying, "You are too judgmental." Instead, we teach members to directly and sensitively express the anger they are feeling, avoid name-calling, and avoid pronouncing judgments. Members are asked to express the source of their anger, including what led up to their feelings. For example, if Ann says to Rudy, "You're self-centered and uncaring," the leader can ask Ann to let Rudy know how she has been affected by him and by what she perceives as his uncaring behavior. Ann can also be encouraged to express the stored-up reactions that led her to judge him. In contrast, if leaders model harsh confrontations, members soon pick up the unexpressed norm that the appropriate way to relate to others in this group is by attacking them.
- Groups can operate under either a norm of exploring personal problems or a norm of problem solving. In some groups, for example, as soon as members bring up situations they would like to understand better, they may quickly be given suggestions about how to "solve" these problems. The fact of the matter is that solutions are often not possible, and what members most need is an opportunity to talk. Of course, problem-solving strategies are of use in teaching members new ways of coping with their difficulties. But it is important that clients have an opportunity to explore their concerns before suggested solutions are presented. Ideally, this exploration will enable members to begin to see a range of possibilities open to them and a direction they might pursue in finding their own answers. It is generally more useful for clients to arrive at their own solutions than to follow the advice of others.
- Members can be taught the norm of listening without thinking of a quick rebuttal and without becoming overly defensive. Although we do not expect people to merely accept all the feedback they receive, we do ask them to really hear what others are saying to them and to seriously consider these messages—particularly ones that are repeated consistently.

Group norms need to be followed throughout the life of a group. Many groups become bogged down because members are unsure of what is expected of them or of the norms of the group. For instance, a member may want to intervene and share her perceptions while a leader is working with another client, but she may be inhibited because she is not sure whether she should interrupt the group leader at work. Another member may feel an inclination to support a fellow group member at the time when that member is experiencing some pain or sadness but may refrain because he is uncertain whether his support will detract from the other's experience. A member who rarely participates may keep her feelings, thoughts, and reactions to herself because she is not sure of the appropriateness of revealing them. Perhaps if she were told that it is useful to express her reactions, she might be more open with her group and, consequently, be able to participate in personal ways more frequently.

If group norms are clearly presented and members see the value of them and cooperatively decide to work with them, norms can be potent forces in shaping the group. Ideally, group norms will be developed in a collaborative way as much as possible rather than being handed down by the leader. Part of the orientation process consists of identifying and discussing norms that are aimed at developing a cohesive and productive group.

If members are struggling to abide by group norms, it may be useful to discuss this as a group and to evaluate how those norms were established and modeled. Members' unwillingness to adhere to group norms may be due to a lack of collaboration or an absence of role modeling and teaching by group leaders. It is important to establish norms that are developmentally appropriate for the group members in terms of age, emotional and social intelligence, and the readiness of members to change.

In the university graduate program in which I (Cindy) taught, we had a policy and an explicit norm pertaining to consensus decision making. The student group makes decisions collaboratively with leaders (faculty). We collapse the hierarchy as much as possible so the "community" can find ways to reach decisions that serve the whole community. This collaborative model results in enhanced group cohesion, but the process often poses challenges for students who come from backgrounds that are more hierarchical or individualistic. Students often struggle to adapt to a method that is not based on a simple "majority rules" concept. The complexity within this process often leads to the greatest learning on the part of group members, and in our experience it leads students to become more powerful change agents and community leaders. For many students, having a voice in what they learn and how they learn it increases ownership of their education and empowers them in ways they had not experienced in more traditionally organized educational settings.

Group Cohesion

During the early stage of a group, members do not know one another well enough for a true sense of community to be formed. There is usually some awkwardness as members become acquainted. Though participants talk about themselves, it is likely that they are presenting more of their public selves rather than deeper aspects of their private selves. **Group cohesion** is a sense of togetherness, or community, within a group, and it begins to take shape during the initial stage. Genuine cohesion typically comes after groups have struggled with conflict, have shared pain, and have committed themselves to taking significant risks. Members have incentives for remaining in the group and share a feeling of belongingness and relatedness. Members have committed to actively participating and to establishing a safe and accepting climate. Cohesion is a vital aspect of a group from the initial to final stages. We introduce cohesion here as a norm for the initial stage, and we return to this topic in more depth when we address the therapeutic factors operating during the working stage in Chapter 8.

Some indicators of this initial degree of cohesion are cooperation among members; a willingness to show up for the meetings and be punctual; an effort to make the group a safe place, including talking about any feelings of lack of trust or fears of trusting; support and caring, as evidenced by being willing to listen to others and accept them for who they are; and a willingness to express reactions to and perceptions of others in the here-and-now context of group interactions. Genuine cohesion is an ongoing process of solidarity that members earn through the risks they take with one another throughout the life of the group. Group cohesion can be developed, maintained, and increased in a number of ways. Here are some suggestions for enhancing group cohesion.

- Leaders can model meaningful sharing by sharing their own reactions to what is occurring within the group and encouraging members to take similar risks. When group members do take risks, they can be reinforced with sincere recognition and support, which will increase their sense of closeness to the others.
- Members can be encouraged to disclose their ideas, feelings, and reactions to what occurs within their group. The expression of both positive and negative reactions should be encouraged. If this is done, an honest exchange can take place, which is essential if a sense of group belongingness is to develop.
- Group goals and individual goals can be jointly determined by the group members and the leader. If a group is without clearly stated goals, animosity can build up that will lead to fragmentation of the group.
- Cohesion can be increased by inviting all members to become active participants. Members who are silent or withdrawn can be encouraged to express their reactions toward the group. These members may be observing and not verbally contributing for a number of reasons, and these reasons can be productively examined in the group.
- Group leaders can promote member-to-member interactions by asking the members to respond to one another, by encouraging feedback and sharing, and by searching for ways to involve as many members as possible in group interactions.
- Group leaders can increase the value of a group to its members by dealing with matters that interest group members, by showing respect for members, and by providing a supportive atmosphere.

Conflict frequently emerges in groups. It is desirable for group members to recognize sources of conflict and to deal openly with them when they arise. A group can be strengthened by acceptance of conflict and by the honest working through of interpersonal tensions. Members can be asked to predict how they are likely to handle conflict in the group when it arises and talk about their typical ways of dealing with conflict. Leaders can ask if members are willing to commit to working on more effective ways of dealing with conflict within the group. In a group we (Marianne and Jerry) led, we asked members about their style of managing conflict. One member said that if she got angry she would get up and leave the group. Another member said he would get quiet and stop talking. By giving voice to their typical patterns of behavior in conflict situations, we were able to contract with them to work on doing something different the next time conflict arose in the group. When group participants communicate their feelings out loud, leaders have an opportunity to intervene and work with members to come up with new ways of managing conflict that will enable them to move through a situation rather than staying stuck in it.

Critical Incident

Should He Stay or Should He Go?

1. Description of Incident

During the first session of a personal-growth group, a heated interchange broke out between two members: Mr. Soto, an HIV-positive, Latino, gay man, and Mr. Ortiz, a Latino minister in a small Latino community. When Mr. Soto shared information about his sexual identity and HIV status, Mr. Ortiz expressed homophobic remarks such as that Mr. Soto was a "sinner" and was "being punished by God." Mr. Ortiz was direct and open with his anger at "gays" and expressed further disdain because Mr. Soto was a Latino and should be more of a "real man." This outburst had a strong effect on everyone in the room. Mr. Soto was extremely angry and hurt and began yelling back at Mr. Ortiz. Everyone in the room seemed stunned by the interchange, including the group leaders.

During a scheduled break in the group, the coleaders talked privately about whether it was appropriate for Mr. Ortiz to remain in the group and whether his homophobic attitudes might harm other group members. Because Mr. Ortiz would be counseling people in his congregation, the coleaders felt the minister needed the help that group participation might offer. The coleaders decided to meet with Mr. Ortiz at a later date and continued to process the conflict that occurred when they returned to the group.

2. Process Questions for Group Leaders

1. What feelings would Mr. Ortiz's comments evoke in you?
2. How would your reactions to Mr. Ortiz affect how you would work with him?
3. If you had a negative reaction to Mr. Ortiz, how would you address this, if at all?
4. If your personal values were similar to those of Mr. Ortiz, would you voice that? Why or why not?
5. If you held the same beliefs as Mr. Ortiz, how would this affect how you saw his actions and how you might intervene?
6. How would you intervene with Mr. Soto or other members of the group?
7. What concerns might you have about keeping Mr. Ortiz in the group?
8. If you decided to ask Mr. Ortiz to leave the group, how would you facilitate the process of removing him?
9. What ethical concerns do you have regarding this incident?
10. Does any part of you feel protective of Mr. Ortiz? If so, in what ways?
11. Would you meet with Mr. Ortiz privately to address your concerns, or would you do this in the group? Explain your reasons.

3. Clinical Reflections

Group leaders have a duty to create an environment in which all members feel safe and free from direct discrimination, and the leaders were extremely concerned about Mr. Ortiz's remarks and how his actions may have affected other group members. A group is in many ways a microcosm of society, and the leaders recognized that many of the beliefs Mr. Ortiz held were prevalent outside of the group (and perhaps held by some group members). The leaders wanted to minimize further harm to Mr. Soto and others who may have been on the receiving end of heterosexism and discrimination, but they also wanted to provide a space where members could work through conflict.

As the leaders processed their feelings in supervision, they realized that their first instinct was to remove Mr. Ortiz from the group. As they spoke further, they wondered aloud what it would be like to help Mr. Ortiz explore his homophobia without being verbally abusive. For example, what function did this belief serve in his life? How was he taught to believe as he did, and how might his own identity as a Latino minister be threatened if he did not object so directly? They also wondered if Mr. Ortiz may have used this outburst as a way to protect himself in the group and to avoid making himself vulnerable. Could the leaders use this situation to enhance assertive communication skills among group members and to model appropriate conflict resolution while enhancing safety within the group? The leaders wanted

continued

to balance the opposing needs in the group, giving space to those who felt hurt or angry by what Mr. Ortiz said without shutting down the minister or shaming him into silence. How powerful might it be for the leaders to discuss this in the group session, modeling all of the issues and concerns with which they were wrestling?

4. Possible Interventions

1. Check in with Mr. Soto to see how he is feeling after hearing Mr. Ortiz's remarks. Create an opportunity for Mr. Soto to talk about the way homophobia has affected him in the past and present.
2. Invite other group members to share their reactions to the interchange.
3. Explore with Mr. Ortiz his own experience with discrimination.
4. Ask Mr. Ortiz to talk about how he learned what it meant to be a man.
5. Ask Mr. Ortiz what it would mean to his own identity as a Latino man and minister if he did not openly object to Mr. Soto. (Would he feel that his own sexual identity was threatened? Would he see himself as less masculine? Would his congregation judge him?)
6. Share your concerns with Mr. Ortiz about the harm his comments and attitudes can cause in the group and your ambivalent feelings about the pros and cons of his participation.

LO6

Effective Therapeutic Relationships: Research Findings

Research has yielded considerable evidence of the importance of a positive therapist–client relationship as a contributing factor to positive change in clients (Burlingame & Fuhriman, 1990). Three key constructs capture the essence of the therapeutic relationship in group treatment: group climate, cohesion, and alliances (Burlingame, Fuhriman, & Johnson 2002). Group leaders play a key role in creating a therapeutic group climate that encourages member-to-member feedback and participation as key group norms.

Support Versus Confrontation

Forging an effective group requires achieving an appropriate balance between support and confrontation. Groups that stress confrontation as a requisite for peeling away the defensive behaviors of members lead to increasingly defensive interactions. The reviews of research that describe negative outcomes in groups consistently cite aggressive confrontation as the leadership style with the highest risks (Yalom, 2005b). As group leaders become overly confrontational and actively negative, the odds are that members will be dissatisfied and potentially harmed by the group experience. Leaders should avoid confrontational interventions until they have earned that right by building a trusting relationship with the members. Once the foundation of interpersonal trust is established, group members tend to be more open to challenge (Dies, 1994).

When confrontations are rooted in compassion, members will often be receptive to such interventions.

How leaders challenge members does much to set the tone of the group. Members have a tendency to follow the leader's manner of confronting. When confrontations are rooted in compassion, members will often be receptive to such interventions. In addition, leaders should be clear about what role confrontation occupies in their theoretical orientation. There is no single right way to confront members. What works for some may not work for others. We need to be secure in our role as leaders and trust that confrontations are a part of counseling as well as be willing to adapt when our style of challenging others seems ineffective.

Guidelines for Creating Therapeutic Relationships With Members

In this section we present further guidelines for group leadership practice based on research summaries done by Burlingame, Fuhriman, and Johnson (2002, 2004b) and Morran, Stockton, and Whittingham (2004).

- Strive for positive involvement in the group through genuine, empathic, and caring interactions with members. Impersonal, detached, and judgmental leadership styles can thwart the development of trust and cohesion.
- Develop a reasonably open therapeutic style characterized by appropriate and facilitative self-disclosure. Be willing to share your own reactions and emotional experiences, especially as they relate to events and relationships within the group.
- Keep in mind that leader self-disclosure can have either a constructive or a detrimental effect on the group process and outcome, depending on specific factors such as the type of group, the stage of its development, and the content and manner of the disclosure.
- Help members make maximum use of effective role models, especially those members who demonstrate desirable behavior. Members can be encouraged to learn from one another. If you have a coleader, model openness with your partner.
- Provide an adequate amount of structuring, especially during the early phase of a group, but avoid a controlling style of leadership.
- Provide opportunities for all members to make maximum use of the group's resources by teaching members skills of active participation in the group process.
- Demonstrate your caring by being willing to confront members when that is called for, but do so in a manner that provides members with good modeling of ways to confront sensitively.
- Set and reinforce clear norms as one way to establish cohesion within the group.
- When necessary, protect group members and strive to promote a feeling of safety.
- Intervene when a member is preventing others from using the group's resources by engaging in nonconstructive confrontations, sarcasm, and indirect exchanges. Help members deal with one another in direct, respectful, and constructive ways.

We want to underscore our belief that you can do much to encourage members to give up some of their defensiveness by reacting to them in respectful ways. Members are more likely to develop a stance of openness in a group that they perceive as being safe for them, and your modeling has a lot to do with creating this therapeutic atmosphere.

Group leaders often have to balance care, confrontation, modeling, and cultural competence simultaneously. For example, a group member (Kim) frequently expressed a sense of being trapped and suffocated by strict gender roles within her culture. She described her situation as hopeless and said there was nothing she could do to change her life. As a group leader, I (Cindy) felt stuck with how to challenge her yet remain culturally sensitive to her personal dilemma. In challenging Kim, I needed to be as transparent as possible, letting her know that I cared very much for her, and that I recognized the possible ramifications of any changes she might make in her cultural environment. Working with Kim took time and patience, yet I was able to challenge her because she felt that I cared both about her and about her culture. Other group members who had diverse cultural backgrounds observed my work with Kim and had a chance to decide for themselves whether they could trust me. It is important to be authentic and to allow trust to unfold rather than attempt to "prove" ourselves trustworthy. By doing this, we further model our belief and trust in the group process.

LO7

Helping Members Get the Most From a Group Experience

Some behaviors and attitudes promote a cohesive and productive group—that is, a group in which meaningful self-exploration takes place and in which honest and appropriate feedback is given and received. We begin orienting and preparing members during the preliminary session, but we typically find that time allows only an introduction to the ways in which clients can get the most from their group experience. Consequently, during the initial phase of the group's evolution, we devote some time to teaching members the basics of group process, especially how they can involve themselves as active participants. We emphasize that they will benefit from the experience in direct proportion to how much they invest of themselves, both in the group and in practicing on the outside what they are learning in the sessions.

We do not present group guidelines as a lecture in one sitting, and we do not overwhelm members with more information than can be assimilated at one time. We begin by giving members written information about their participation in the group. We also allocate time to discuss these topics as they occur naturally within the sessions, which increases the likelihood that members will be receptive to thinking about how they can best participate. We continue to provide information in a timely manner at various points in a group. We encourage you to use these guidelines as a catalyst for thinking about your own approach to preparing members. Reflecting on this material may help you develop an approach that suits your own personality and leadership style and that is appropriate for the groups you lead. The following suggestions are written from the leader's point of view and directed to the members.

Leader Guidelines for Members

Building Trust We are convinced that confidentiality is essential if members are to feel a sense of safety in a group. Even if nobody raises questions about the nature and limitations of confidentiality, we still emphasize the importance of respecting the confidential character of the interactions within the group and caution members about how it can be broken. We explain how easy it might be to breach confidentiality without intending to do so. We emphasize to members that it is their responsibility to continually make the room safe by addressing their concerns regarding how their disclosures will be treated. If members feel that others may talk outside the sessions, this uncertainty is bound to hamper their ability to fully participate.

In our groups the members frequently hear from us that it does not make sense to open up quickly without a foundation of safety. One way to create this safe and trusting environment is for the group members to be willing to verbalize their fears, concerns, and here-and-now reactions during the early sessions. It is up to each member to decide what to bring into group and how far to pursue these personal topics. Participants often wait for some other person to take the first risk or to make some gesture of trust. They can challenge this, paradoxically, by revealing their fear of trust. Members can gain from initiating a discussion that will allow genuine trust to develop.

EXAMPLE: Harold was older than most of the other group members, and he was afraid that they would not be able to empathize with him, that they would exclude him from activities, and that they would view him as an outsider—a parent figure. After he disclosed these fears, many members let Harold know how much they appreciated his willingness to reveal his fears. His disclosure, and the response to it, stimulated others to express some of their concerns. This sharing stimulated trust in the entire group by making it clear that it was appropriate to express fears. Instead of being rejected, Harold felt accepted and appreciated because he had been willing to make a significant part of himself known to the rest of the group.

Expressing Persistent Feelings Sometimes members keep their feelings of disinterest, anger, or disappointment a secret from the rest of the group. It is most important that persistent feelings related to the group process be aired. We often make statements to members such as "If you are feeling detached and withdrawn, let it be known" or "If you are experiencing chronic anger or irritation toward others in this group, don't keep these feelings to yourself."

EXAMPLE: In a group of adolescents that met once a week for 10 weeks, Luella waited until the third session to disclose that she did not trust either the members or the leader, that she was angry because she felt pressured to participate, and that she really did not know what was expected of her as a group member. She had experienced reluctance since the initial session but had not verbalized her reactions. The leader let Luella know how important it was for her to reveal these persistent feelings of distrust so they could be explored and resolved.

Self-Disclosure Group members are sometimes led to believe that the more they disclose about themselves, the better. Though self-disclosure is an important tool in the group process, it is up to each participant to decide what aspects of his or her life to reveal. This principle cannot be stressed too much, for the idea that members will have to "tell everything" contributes to the reservations of many people to becoming participants in a group.

The most useful kind of disclosure expresses a present concern and may entail some vulnerability and risk. As participants open up to a group, they have fears about how other people will receive what they reveal. If a member shares that he is shy, often quiet, and afraid to speak up in the group, the other members will have a frame of reference for more accurately interpreting and reacting to his lack of participation. Had he not spoken up, both the leader and other members would have been more likely to misinterpret his behavior.

Self-disclosure is not a process of making oneself psychologically naked. Members need to understand that they are responsible for deciding *what, how much,* and *when* they will share personal conflicts pertaining to their everyday life.

EXAMPLE: In a weekly group, Luis earlier disclosed that he was gay. At work he had not been willing to talk openly about his sexual orientation. Although Luis was willing to share with his group many of his struggles in being a gay Latino, he said he was not ready to talk about the difficulties he was experiencing in his relationship. At this time in his life, Luis felt shame about his sexual orientation, especially with respect to his extended family. Although it was difficult for him to talk about his feelings about being gay in the group, Luis challenged himself to trust others with some of his deepest concerns. One of the cultural values he grew up with was to keep personal concerns private. Although he did not feel comfortable discussing his relationship with his partner, Luis was willing to share with the group many of his doubts, fears, and anxieties over not being accepted for who he was. Luis did not want to go through life living a lie. Other group members respected Luis for his willingness to explore his struggles about being gay, especially his fear of judgment and rejection. Because of this understanding that he felt from other members, Luis was able to share more of his life in the group than he could do with anyone outside of the group.

Participating Fully A participant might say, "I'm not the talkative type. It's hard for me to formulate my thoughts, and I'm afraid I don't express myself well. So I usually don't say anything in the group. But I listen to what others are saying, and I learn by observing. I really don't think I have to be talking all the time to get something out of these sessions." Although it is true that members can learn by observing interactions and reacting nonverbally, their learning tends to be limited. If members assume the stance of not contributing, others will never come to know them, and they can easily feel cheated and angry at being the object of others' perhaps flawed observations.

Some members keep themselves on the fringe of group activity by continually saying, "I have no real problems in my life at this time, so I don't have much to contribute to the group." Other members remain passive by stating that they see no need to repeat what other members have already expressed because they feel the same way. We attempt to teach these members to share their reactions to their experience in the group as well as to let others know how they are being affected. Members who choose to share little about events outside of the group can actively participate by keeping themselves open to being affected by other members. Leaders can contribute to group cohesion by helping those members who feel that they have nothing to contribute recognize that they can at least share how they are reacting personally to what others are saying.

EXAMPLE: When Thelma was asked what she wanted from the group, she replied, "I haven't really given it that much thought. I figured I'd just be spontaneous and wait to see what happens." The leader let Thelma know that sometimes other people's work might indeed evoke some of her own issues and that she might spontaneously react. However, the leader pointed out to her that it was important for her to think about and to bring up the concerns that initially brought her to the group. As the sessions progressed, Thelma did learn to let the other members know what she wanted from them, and she began to take the initiative. She showed that she wanted to talk about how lonely she was, how desperate and inadequate she frequently felt, how fearful she was of being vulnerable with men, and how she dreaded facing her world every morning. As she moved from observer to active participant, Thelma found that she could benefit from her weekly sessions.

Embracing Change Participants in therapeutic groups should be given the warning that their involvement may complicate their outside lives for a time. As a result of group experiences, members tend to assume that the people in their lives will be both ready and willing to make significant changes. It can be shocking for members to discover that others thought they were "just fine" the way they were, and the friction that results may make it more difficult than ever to modify familiar patterns. Therefore, it is important for members to be prepared for the fact that not everyone will like or accept some of the changes they want to make.

EXAMPLE: Ricardo came away from his group with the awareness that he was frightened of his wife, that he consistently refrained from expressing his wants to her, and that he related to her as he would to a protective mother. If he asserted himself with her, he feared that she would leave. In the group he not only became tired of his dependent style but also decided that he would treat his wife as an equal and give up his hope of having her become his mother. Ricardo's wife did not cooperate with his valiant efforts to change the nature of their relationship. The more assertive he became, the more disharmony there was in his home. While he was trying to become independent, his wife was struggling to keep their relationship the way it was; she was not willing to respond differently to him.

Discovering New Dimensions of Yourself Oftentimes people in groups begin to realize that they can control more aspects of their lives than they previously thought possible. When members explore intense feelings of pain in a group, they may come to realize that this unrecognized and unexpressed pain is blocking them from living a truly joyous life. By working through these painful experiences, they begin to reclaim a joyful dimension of themselves. For instance, many participants experience an inner strength, discover a real wit and sense of humor, create moving poetry or songs, or dare for the first time to show a creative side of themselves that they have kept hidden from others and from themselves.

EXAMPLE: Finn expressed the positive side of group experience when he remarked, "I used to think that what I had to say didn't matter and that I had little to offer. Through my interactions with people here, I have come to realize that what I feel and say makes a difference to others and is even highly valued at times."

Listening Group members can be taught to listen carefully to what the other members say about them, neither accepting it entirely nor rejecting it outright. Members are advised to be as open as possible, yet to also listen discriminatingly, deciding for themselves what does and what does not apply to them. Before they respond, they can be asked to listen and to let what is being said to them sink in, and to take note of how it is affecting them. Members cannot fully comprehend what is being communicated to them if they are not totally engaged in listening.

EXAMPLE: In an adolescent group, members told Brendan that it was hard for them to listen to his many stories. Although some of his stories were interesting, they gave no clue to the nature of his struggles, which were the reason he was in the group. Other members told him that it was easier to hear what he was saying when he talked about himself. Brendan became defensive and angry and denied that he had been acting that way. The leader asked Brendan to observe himself, both in the group and in everyday life, and to think about how he was affected by the feedback and to consider what had been said to him before he so rigorously rejected the feedback.

Taking in Feedback Members will learn that feedback is a valuable source of information that they can use in assessing what they are doing in the group and how their behavior is affecting others. Members do well to listen carefully to consistent feedback they receive. A person may get similar feedback from many people in different groups yet may still dismiss it as invalid. Although it is important to discriminate, it is also important to realize that a message that has been received from a variety of people is likely to have some degree of validity.

EXAMPLE: In several groups Liam heard people tell him that he did not seem interested in what they had to say and that he appeared distant and detached. Although Liam was physically in the room, he often looked at the ceiling and sighed, moved his chair away from the circle, and yawned a lot. Members wondered out loud if he was interested in them and said that it was difficult for them to get close to him. Liam was surprised by this feedback and insisted that his behavior in the group was very different from his behavior in his outside life—that on the outside he felt close to people and was interested and involved. It seems unlikely that someone could be so different in the two areas, however, and the leader intervened in this way: "You may be different in here than you are on the outside. But would you be willing to notice how people respond to you away from here and be open to noticing if any of the feedback given to you might be similar?" The leader's response eliminated unnecessary argumentation and debates over who was right.

Other Suggestions for Group Members Some additional guidelines for group members that we bring up early in a group, as they seem appropriate, are briefly listed here:

- Be willing to do work both before and after a group. Consider keeping a journal as a supplement to the group experience. Create homework assignments as a way of putting your group learning into practice in everyday living.
- Develop self-evaluation skills as a way of assessing your progress in the group. Ask yourself these questions: "Am I contributing to the group?" "Am I satisfied with what is occurring in the sessions? If not, what am I doing about it?" "Am I using in my life what I'm learning in my group?"
- Spend time clarifying your own goals by reviewing specific issues and themes you want to explore during the sessions. This can best be done by thinking about specific changes you want to make in your life and by deciding what you are willing to do both in and out of the group to bring about these changes.
- Concentrate on making personal and direct statements to others in your group, as opposed to giving advice, making interpretations, and asking impersonal questions. Instead of telling others how they are, let them know how they are affecting you.
- Realize that the real work consists of what you actually do outside of your group. Consider the group as a means to an end, and give some time to thinking about what you will do with what you are learning. Expect some setbacks, and be aware that change may be slow and subtle.

Avoid Too Much Structuring and Teaching

Even though we have stressed the value of preparing members for how groups function, be aware that too much emphasis on providing information about the group process can have a negative influence. All the spontaneous learning can be taken out of the group experience if members have been told too much of what to expect and have not been allowed to learn for themselves. Moreover, it is possible to foster a dependency on the structure and direction provided by the leader.

We hope that members will increasingly be able to function with less intervention from the leader as the group progresses. There is a delicate balance between providing too much structure and failing to give enough structure and information. Especially important, perhaps, is that the leader be aware of factors such as group cohesion, group norms, and group interactions at any given point. With this awareness the leader can decide when it is timely and useful to suggest a discussion of certain behavior that is occurring in the here and now.

As we stated earlier, the stages in the life of a group are not rigidly defined but are fluid and somewhat overlapping. How we teach members about the group process can have a lot to do with the level to which the group may evolve. Yalom (2005b) has identified particular therapeutic characteristics that are primarily linked to the various stages of a group. During the beginning phase, the crucial factors are identification, universality, hope, and cohesion. During the middle phase, catharsis, cohesion, interpersonal learning, and insight are essential. As termination approaches, existential factors surface. Understanding these group characteristics will aid you in deciding how much to teach—and when.

Journal Writing as an Adjunct to Group Sessions

Group members can add to the group experience by participating in journal writing exercises outside of the group. One way is to ask members to spend even a few minutes each day recording in a journal certain feelings, situations, behaviors, and ideas for courses of action. Alternatively, members can be asked to review certain periods of time in their lives and write about them. For example, they can get out pictures of their childhood years and other reminders of this period and then freely write in a journal whatever comes to mind. Writing in a free-flowing style without censoring can be of great help in getting a focus on feelings.

Members can bring the journals to the group and share a particular experience they had that resulted in problems for them. They can then explore with the group how they might have handled the situation differently. In general, however, these journals help members improve their personal focus for a session, and as such, members can decide what to do with the material they write.

Another way to use journals is as a preparation for encountering others in everyday life. For instance, Jenny is having a great deal of difficulty talking with her husband. She is angry with him much of the time over many of the things he does and does not do. But she sits on this anger, and she feels sad that they do not take time for each other. Jenny typically does not express her sadness to him, nor does she let him know of her resentment toward him for not being involved in their children's lives. To deal with this problem, she can write her husband a detailed and uncensored letter pointing out all the ways she feels angry, hurt, sad, and disappointed and expressing how she would like their life to be different. It is not recommended that she show this letter to her husband. The letter writing is a way for her to clarify what she feels and to prepare herself to work in the group. This work can then help her to be clear about what she wants to say to her husband as well as how she wants to say it. This process works in the following way: In the group Jenny can talk to another member by relating the essence of what she wrote in her letter. This member can role play Jenny's husband. Others can then express how they experience Jenny and the impact on the way she spoke. Aided by such feedback, she may be able to find a constructive way to express her feelings to her husband.

Still another technique is for members to spontaneously enter in their journals their reactions to themselves in the group, especially during the first few meetings, and to review these thoughts as the group is coming to an end. Answering these questions can help members understand their group experience:

- How do I see myself in this group?
- How do I feel about being in the group?
- What reactions do I notice myself having to people in this group?
- What are my initial fears or concerns about being in the group?
- How do I most want to use the time in the group sessions?
- What would I like to leave this group having learned or experienced?

If participants write down their reactions, they are more likely to verbalize them during group sessions. If members are afraid to open up in a group because they think others may judge them in a negative way, writing about this in a journal can prepare members for expressing these fears verbally during group sessions.

In our groups we strongly encourage members to engage in regular journal writing as a part of their homework. Depending on the needs of a group, we might suggest some incomplete sentences for members to spontaneously complete either at the end of a group meeting or as material for journaling at home.

Here are some incomplete sentence assignments that work well in the initial stage of a group:

- What I most want from this group is . . .
- The one thing I most want to be able to say about the changes I am making at our final meeting is . . .
- When I think about being in this group for the next 12 weeks, I . . .
- A fear I have about being a group member is . . .
- One personal concern or problem I would hope to bring up is . . .
- My most dominant reaction to being in the group so far is . . .
- The one aspect I'd most like to change about myself is . . .

The incomplete sentence technique helps members focus on specific aspects of their experience during the early sessions, and several of these questions pertain to member goals. The practice of reflecting on personal goals, and writing about them, is an excellent means of clarifying what it is members want and how they can best obtain what they want.

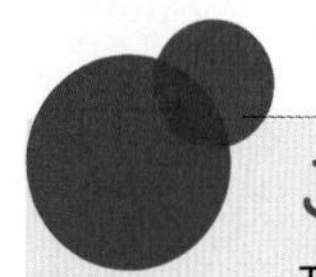

Journal Prompts

The following questions are meant to serve as prompts for members of a group during the initial stages. If you are leading groups, you might find it useful for group members to either discuss these questions in group or journal about them between sessions. In addition, we encourage you to think about your responses to these questions as either a real or imagined group member.

1. In what ways did you test the group, the leaders, or individuals?
2. How willing were you to take risks in the group?
3. How close or distant did you feel to the group, the leaders, or to individuals?
4. In what ways did you feel included or excluded, and how did you or others contribute to this dynamic?
5. What contributed to your ability or inability to trust group members or leaders?
6. What negative or positive reactions did you have to group members, leaders, or individuals?

Homework During the Initial Stage

Perhaps one of the best ways to maximize the value of any group experience is to design homework assignments that members can carry out both in and out of the group. Group leaders can model active participation and collaboration by their involvement with members in creating an agenda, designing homework, and teaching skills and new behaviors.

Homework can be a valuable instrument to ensure behavioral change. The more time group members are willing to commit to working on their problems outside of the therapeutic context, the more likely it is that they will make positive gains (Ledley, Marx, & Heimberg, 2010). In Chapter 4 we discussed homework as a cognitive behavioral strategy, but homework can be incorporated into any group, regardless of the leader's theoretical foundation. Homework assignments provide a valuable opportunity to reinforce and extend the benefits of the work done during therapy sessions. It is important for leaders to review homework and the outcomes of the assignment. Members can be asked what difficulties they encountered in trying to complete their homework.

LO8

Leader Issues at the Initial Stage

Early in the history of a group it is especially important to think about the balance of responsibility between members and the leader (or coleaders) as well as the degree of structuring that is optimal for the group. If you are working with a coleader, discussing these issues is essential because divergent views are bound to hurt the group. If you assume the majority of the responsibility for keeping the group moving, for example, and your coleader assumes almost no responsibility on the ground that the members must decide for themselves what to do with group time, the members will sense this division and are bound to be confused by it. Similarly, if you function best with a high degree of structure in groups and your coleader believes any structuring should come from the members, this difference of opinion will have a detrimental effect on the group. It is wise to select a coleader who has a philosophy of leadership that is compatible with yours, although this does not mean that both of you need to have the same *style* of leading. Effective coleaders often have differences that complement each other.

When differences between leaders result in conflict between them, it can be a source of anxiety for both members and leaders. If handled skillfully, leaders can model healthy confrontation and conflict resolution for group members. Modeling nondefensiveness and a willingness to challenge and be challenged by one another can prove to be a valuable learning opportunity. It is likely that some group members come from families in which the "parental" or "authority" figures fought in destructive or abusive ways. It can be a healing experience for group members to see the group leaders manage a conflict well. On the other hand, a badly handled conflict or confrontation places an unfair burden on the members and in extreme cases can be harmful to the group process and outcome. It is up to the leaders to determine whether the issue is best addressed in the moment with the group members or in private between the leaders. There are pros and cons to both of these approaches. If the members witnessed the conflict, we prefer to address it in the group.

Division of Responsibility

A basic issue you will have to consider is responsibility for the direction and outcome of the group. If a group proves to be nonproductive, will this failure stem from your lack of leadership skills, or does the responsibility rest with the group members?

We tend to be highly active during the initial period in the evolution of a group. In our view, it is our responsibility to intervene in very directive ways to establish certain norms within the group. Our intention is not to promote leader dependency but to teach members how they can best attain what they want to accomplish by being a part of this group. We encourage members to take an active role in the process of monitoring what they are thinking, feeling, and doing and to pay attention to the times when they may be engaging in behavior that is not going to help them in this group.

We strive to balance responsibility between leaders and members. We encourage group leaders to make use of journal writing to clarify how much responsibility they are assuming for the overall functioning of the group. When training group leaders, we ask them to write about themselves and the reactions that are evoked in them as they lead or colead their groups. Rather than describing the dynamics of their members, we suggest that they focus on how specific members affect them personally. Here are some questions we recommend that group leaders address and write about in their journals:

- How did I feel about myself as I was leading or coleading my group?
- How much responsibility did I assume for the outcome of this particular session?

- What did I like best about the group today?
- What most stood out for me during this session?
- How am I being affected personally by each of the members?
- How involved am I in this group? If I am not as involved as I would like to be, what specific steps am I willing to take to change this situation?
- Are any factors getting in the way of me effectively leading this group?

This journal technique for group leaders provides an excellent record of patterns that are shaping up in a group. The practice of writing can also be a useful catalyst for focusing leaders on areas in their own lives that need continued attention. These questions can be useful when discussing your group experience with your coleader or supervisors. Spending time thinking about and expressing your experiences can help tremendously in refining your effectiveness and development as a leader.

Degree of Structuring

The issue is not *whether* a group leader should provide structure but *what degree* of structure should be provided. Like responsibility, structuring exists on a continuum. The leader's theoretical orientation, the type of group, the membership population, and the stage of the group are some of the factors that determine the amount and type of structuring employed. Person-centered groups have a limited degree of leader structuring because counselors have faith in the members of the group and in the group process itself. Leader-imposed structuring is likely to undermine this trust in the group to move in a constructive direction. In contrast, most cognitive behavior group counselors rely on a clear structure for each session. The group leader would have a clear plan for each session even though the leader would seek participation of the group members in deciding how to use the session.

Research indicates the positive value of an initial structure that builds supportive group norms and highlights positive interactions among members. Leaders must carefully monitor this therapeutic structure throughout the life of a group. Structuring that offers a coherent framework for understanding the experiences of individuals and the group process is of the most value. Yalom (1983, 2005b) sees the basic task of the group leader as providing enough structure to give a general direction to the members while avoiding the pitfalls of fostering dependency. Yalom's (2005b) message for leaders is to structure the group in a fashion that facilitates each member's autonomous functioning. An example of fostering dependency on the leader would be encouraging members to speak only when they are invited to do so. Instead, the leader can encourage members to bring themselves into the interactions without being called on.

Our style of structuring is aimed at reducing unnecessary floundering and maximizing full participation. We do this by teaching participants a number of ways to derive the maximum benefit from a group. By providing some structure, we give group members the opportunity to experiment with new levels of awareness and to build new forms of behavior from this awareness. During the initial stage, our structure is aimed at helping members identify and express their fears, expectations, and personal goals. We often use dyads, go-arounds, and open-ended questions to make it easier for members to talk to one another about current issues in their lives. After talking to several people on a one-to-one basis, members find it easier to talk openly in the entire group. The leadership activity we provide is designed to help members focus on themselves and the issues they most want to explore in the group.

Many short-term psychoeducational groups are structured around a series of topics. In a group for learning effective parenting skills, for example, the sessions are guided by topics such as listening well, setting limits, learning to convey respect, and providing discipline without punishment. Group leaders sometimes strictly adhere to a structured exercise or a discussion of a topic when another pressing matter demands attention. If there is conflict in the group, it is more important to suspend the topic or exercise until the conflict has been attended to. If the conflict is brushed aside, there is a greater likelihood that discussion of the topic will be superficial. At other times members may spontaneously bring up unrelated concerns, and leaders have difficulty keeping the group focused on the topic in a meaningful way. The leader and members of the group need to explore whether the shift in the topic is due to their discomfort with the issue or to the fact that a more relevant subject has surfaced. If the shift is an avoidance tactic, the facilitator might point out the dynamics of what is occurring. The art consists in learning how to help members relate topics to themselves in significant ways so that group interaction and group learning can occur. The effective leader provides just enough guidance so that group members can take responsibility for defining their own structure.

Opening and Closing Group Sessions

LO9

We discuss opening and closing group sessions here because it is an essential aspect of group leadership from the very beginning. These skills are important throughout the group process, and we suggest that you return to this discussion as you read about subsequent stages. The interventions we describe here are not the only "right" ones. There are many effective ways to intervene, depending on your theoretical orientation or leadership style and also on the kind of group you are leading. We have found the following guidelines useful.

Guidelines for Opening Each Group Session Sometimes group leaders focus on the person who speaks first and may stay with that member for an undue length of time. Other common oversights include neglecting to link a present session with the previous session or failing to check in to determine how members want to use the time for a particular session. Starting a session with a brief check-in can set the group up to involve as many members as possible in productive work for that session. In our training workshops, we (Marianne and Jerry) are sometimes asked if we participate in this check-in process. If we have something on our minds pertaining to the group, we are likely to remark on this during the check-in. However, more often than not we do not participate, especially if we are asking members to state what they want to talk about or explore in this session.

For groups that meet on a regular basis, such as once a week, we suggest some of the following procedures to open each session in an effective way:

- Ask all members to participate in a check-in process by briefly stating what they want from the session. During the check-in time, our aim is to hear what the members remember from the last session and what they want to say. A quick go-around is all that is needed for members to identify issues they are interested in pursuing; in this way an agenda can be developed that is based on some common concerns. We generally do not stay with one member before we have completed the check-in process because we want all the participants to have a chance to express what they are bringing to this session. If you stay with the first member who speaks, a norm is developed that the first person to speak will be the focus of work for much of a session. The check-in procedure provides a basis for identifying emerging themes present at the beginning of a meeting. If you do not find out what issues the members have brought to a particular session, much important material will be lost.
- Give members a brief opportunity to share what they have done in the way of practice outside of the group since the previous session. If members are making use of journal writing and carrying out homework assignments, the beginning of a session is a good time for members to briefly state some of the outcomes of their reflections, writing, and homework. Some may want to talk about problems they are experiencing in transferring their learning from the group into everyday situations. This difficulty can then be the basis for work in that session.
- Ask members if they have any thoughts or unresolved feelings about the previous session. If members do not have a chance to mention these concerns, hidden agendas will probably develop and block effective work. However, we avoid working on it during the check-in. It is important to get a commitment from members to address their concerns once the check-in has been completed.
- Have members form dyads to discuss how they would like to use the time in this session. After about 5 minutes, each person can state what was shared in the dyad. This exercise helps members take an active part in the session and is a good way to formulate an agenda.
- We begin some sessions by asking members to briefly state what they have been thinking regarding how the group is progressing. This practice is especially appropriate when we see certain problems emerging or when we sense the group is getting stuck. Our self-disclosure can lead the way for members to be open with their reactions to what is or is not going on in the sessions, especially if we state our reactions in a nonblaming way.
- In an open group (in which the membership changes somewhat from week to week), it is a good practice to introduce any new members. Rather than putting the spotlight on the incoming member, we favor asking the continuing members to briefly reflect on what they have been learning about themselves in the group. We recognize that some members may be attending for only a few sessions, thus we tend to ask them how they expect to get the most from their brief time in the group. We sometimes ask this question: "If this were the only session you had, what would you most want to accomplish?"

- Introduce a session with a mindfulness exercise to bring members into the present moment. **Mindfulness** can be thought of as "awareness of present experience with acceptance" (R. Siegel, 2010, p. 27). In mindfulness practice, group members train themselves to intentionally focus on their present experience in a nonjudgmental way. The mindfulness skills learned in the group can be practiced in all of their daily activities, including being mindful when standing, walking, eating, and doing chores. For a good introduction to mindfulness practice, we recommend Ron Siegel's (2010) book, *The Mindfulness Solution: Everyday Practices for Everyday Problems.*

Although we do not suggest that you memorize certain lines to open a session, the following questions may be useful prompts for you in opening a session.

- What were you thinking and feeling before coming to the group?
- Before we begin today's session, I'd like to ask each of you to take a few minutes to silently review your week and think about anything you want to tell us.
- Who in the group were you most aware of as you were coming here today?
- Did anyone have any afterthoughts about last week's session?
- Who are you most aware of in this room right now, and why?
- What would you most like to be able to say by the end of this session?
- What is one thing you can do differently in this group to help you reach your goals?
- To what degree are you applying what you are learning in this group to your daily life?

Guidelines for Closing Each Group Session Just as important as how you open a session is the way in which you bring each meeting to a close. Too often a leader will simply announce that "time is up for today," with no attempt to summarize and integrate and with no encouragement for members to practice certain skills. Our preference for closing each group meeting is to establish a norm of expecting each member to participate in a brief checkout process. Some time, if even only 10 minutes, should be set aside to give participants an opportunity to reflect on what they liked or did not like about the session, to mention what they hope to do outside of the group during the week, and to give some indication of how they experienced the session. Attention to closing ensures that consolidation of learning will take place.

For groups that meet weekly, summarize what occurred in that session. At times, it is useful to stop the group halfway through the session and say, "I notice that we have about an hour left today, and I'd like to ask how each of you feels about what you've done so far today. Have you been as involved as you want to be? Are there some things you'd like to raise before this session ends?" This does not need to be done routinely, but sometimes such an assessment during the session can help members focus their attention on problem areas, especially if we notice that they are not talking about what they stated they needed to address.

In closing a weekly group meeting, consider these guidelines:

- Not everyone will feel comfortable or think that every concern raised has been dealt with adequately. Group members can reflect on what they experienced during a session and can bring their concerns back to the following session.
- If participants report feeling uninvolved, we tend to ask them what they are willing to do to increase their investment in the group: "Is your lack of involvement all right, or is this something that you want to change?"
- Members can be asked to tell the group briefly what they are learning about themselves through their relationships with other members. The participants can briefly indicate some ways they have changed their behavior in response to these insights. If participants find that they would like to change their behavior even more, they can be encouraged to develop specific plans or homework assignments to complete before the next session.
- If members suggest homework that seems unrealistic, the leader can help members refine their ideas into more manageable homework assignments.
- Members can be asked if there are any topics, questions, or problems they would like to put on the agenda for the next session. This request creates a link between one session and the next.
- Members can give one another feedback. Especially helpful are members' positive reactions concerning what they have actually observed. For instance, if Doug's voice is a lot more secure, others may let him know that they perceive this change.
- If your group is one with changing membership, remind members a week before certain participants will be leaving the group. Not only do the terminating members need to talk about what they have learned from the group, but other members may want to share their reactions as well.
- Identify any unfinished business, even if it cannot be explored before the group session ends.

As we did for opening sessions, we offer some comments to consider in ending a particular session. Of course, not all of them need be asked at any one time:

- What was it like for you to be in this group today?
- What affected you the most, and what did you learn?
- What would each of you be willing to do outside of the group this week to practice some of the new skills you are acquiring?
- I'd like a quick go-around to have everyone say a few words on how this group has been so far.
- What are you getting or not getting from this group?
- If you are not satisfied with what is happening in this group, what can you do to change things?
- Before we close, I'd like to share with you some of my reactions and observations of this session.
- Before ending today, I'd like everyone to share the color that best represents you after experiencing group today. How did it change from the beginning of group?

By developing skills in opening and closing sessions, you increase the possibility of continuity from meeting to meeting. Such continuity can help members transfer insights and new behaviors from the group into daily life and, along with encouragement and direction from your leadership, can facilitate the participants' ongoing assessment of their level of investment for each session.

If you work with a coleader, the matter of how the sessions are opened and closed should be a topic for discussion. Here are a few questions for exploration:

- Who typically opens the sessions?
- Do the two of you agree on when and how to bring a session to a close?
- With 5 minutes left in the sessions, does one leader want to continue working, whereas the other wants to attempt some summary of the meeting?
- Do both of you pay attention to unfinished business that might be left toward the end of a session?

Although we are not suggesting a mechanical division of time and functions when you begin and end sessions, it is worth noting who tends to assume this responsibility. If one leader typically opens the session, members may be likely to direct their talk to this person. In our groups one of us may open the session while the other elaborates and makes additional remarks. In this way spontaneous give-and-take between coleaders can replace an approach characterized by "Now it's your turn to make a remark."

Points to Remember

Initial Stages of a Group

Initial Stage Characteristics

The early phase of a group is a time for orientation and determining the structure of the group. At this stage:

- Participants test the atmosphere and get acquainted.
- Members learn what is expected, how the group functions, and how to participate in a group.
- Risk-taking is relatively low, and exploration is tentative.
- Group cohesion and trust are gradually established if members are willing to express what they are thinking and feeling as it pertains to being in the group.
- Members are concerned with whether they are included or excluded, and they are beginning to define their place in the group.
- Negative reactions may surface as members test to determine whether all feelings are acceptable.
- Trust versus mistrust is a central issue.
- Periods of silence and awkwardness may occur; members may look for direction and wonder what the group is about.
- Members are deciding whom they can trust, how much they will disclose, how safe the group is, whom they like and dislike, and how much to get involved.
- Members are learning the basic attitudes of respect, empathy, acceptance, caring, and responding—all attitudes that facilitate building trust.

Member Functions

Early in the course of the group some specific member roles and tasks are critical to shaping the group:

- Take active steps to create a trusting climate; distrust and fear will increase members' reluctance to participate.
- Learn to express your feelings and thoughts, especially as they pertain to interactions in the group.

- Be willing to express fears, hopes, concerns, reservations, and expectations concerning the group.
- Be willing to make yourself known to the others in the group; members who remain hidden will not have meaningful interactions with the group.
- As much as possible, be involved in the creation of group norms.
- Establish personal and specific goals that will govern group participation.
- Learn the basics of group process, especially how to be involved in group interactions; problem solving and advice giving interrupt positive group interactions among members.

Leader Functions

The major tasks of group leaders during the orientation and exploration phase of a group are these:

- Teach participants some general guidelines and ways to participate actively that will increase their chances of having a productive group.
- Develop ground rules and set norms.
- Teach and reinforce the basics of group process.
- Assist members in expressing their fears and expectations, and work toward the development of trust.
- Model the facilitative dimensions of therapeutic behavior.
- Be open with the members and be psychologically present for them.
- Clarify the division of responsibility.
- Help members establish concrete personal goals.
- Deal openly with members' concerns and questions.
- Provide a degree of structuring that will neither increase members' dependence nor result in floundering.
- Assist members in sharing what they are thinking and feeling about what is occurring within the group.
- Teach members basic interpersonal skills such as active listening and responding.
- Assess the needs of the group and lead in such a way that these needs are met.

Exercises

Facilitation of Initial Stage of a Group

1. **Initial Session.** For this exercise six students volunteer to assume the roles of group members at an initial group session, and two volunteer to take on the roles of coleaders. Have the coleaders begin by giving a brief orientation explaining the group's purpose, the role of the leader, the rights and responsibilities of the members, the ground rules, group process procedures, and any other pertinent information they might give in the first session of a group. The members then express their expectations and fears, and the leaders try to deal with them. This lasts for approximately half an hour, and the class members then describe what they saw occurring in the group. The group members describe how they felt during the session and offer suggestions for the coleaders. The coleaders can discuss with each other the nature of their experience and how well they feel they did, either before any of the feedback or afterward.
2. **The Beginning Stage of a Group.** This exercise can be used to get group members acquainted with one another, but you can practice it in class to see how it works. The class breaks into dyads and selects new partners every 10 minutes. Each time you change partners, consider a new question or issue. The main purpose of the exercise is to get members to contact all the other members of the group and to begin to reveal themselves to others. We encourage you to add your own questions or statements to this list of issues:
    - Discuss your reservations about the value of groups.
    - What do you fear about groups?

- What do you most want from a group experience?
- Discuss how much trust you have in your group. Do you feel like getting involved? What are some things that contribute to your trust or mistrust?
- Decide which of the two of you is dominant. Does each of you feel satisfied with his or her position?
- Tell your partner how you imagine you would feel if you were to colead a group with him or her.

3. **Meeting With Your Coleader.** Select a person in your class with whom you might like to colead a group. Explore with your partner some of the following dimensions of a group during the initial stage:
   - How would both of you assist the members in getting the most from this group? Would you be inclined to discuss any guidelines that would help them be active members?
   - How would the two of you attempt to build trust during the initial phase of this group?
   - How much structuring would each of you be inclined to do early in a group? Do both of you agree on the degree of structure that would help a group function effectively?
   - Whose responsibility is it if the group flounders? What might you do if the group seemed to be lost at the first session?
   - What are some specific procedures each of you might use to help members define their personal goals regarding what they want to explore in a group?
4. **Brainstorming About Ways of Creating Trust.** In small groups explore as many ideas and ways you can think of that might facilitate the establishment of trust in your group. What factors do you think are likely to lead to trust? What would it take for *you* to feel a sense of trust in a group? What do you see as the major barriers to the development of trust?
5. **Assessing Your Group.** If there is an experiential group associated with your group class, assess the degree to which the characteristics of your group are similar to the initial stage described in this chapter. What is the atmosphere like in your group? What kind of group participant are you? What is your degree of satisfaction with your group? Are there steps you can take to bring about any changes you may want to see in your group? To what degree is trust being established, and what is the safety level in the group? What kinds of norms are being formed at this early stage?

Guide to Groups in Action: Evolution and Challenges DVD and Workbook

Here are some suggestions for making the best use of this chapter along with the initial stage segment of the first program, *Evolution of a Group*. If you are not viewing the DVD (*Groups in Action*) in class or working with this program, skip the following exercises.

1. **Group Characteristics of the Initial Stage.** Think about how the characteristics described in this chapter are evident in the initial stage of the group depicted in the DVD. What are the members anxious about, and how safe did most of them feel

from the very beginning? What early concerns did the members voice? Are there any potential hidden agendas? If so, what might they be? What process is being employed to help the members get acquainted?

2. **Creating Trust: Leader and Member Roles.** Trust issues are never settled once and for all. As you view the first section of the DVD, how would you describe the level of trust during the initial stage in this group? Think about ideas for facilitating trust in groups you will lead. What factors do you think are likely to lead to trust? What would it take for you to feel a sense of trust in a group? What are the major barriers to the development of trust? What are some specific fears members raised, and how were these fears dealt with during this initial session? What did you learn about some ways to create trust in a group by viewing the early phase of this group?
3. **Identifying and Clarifying Goals.** If you were leading this group, would you have a clear sense of what the members wanted to get from the group experience?
4. **Group Process Concepts at the Initial Stage.** Structuring is an important process during the early phase of a group. What kind of structuring did you observe us providing? How might you provide a different kind of structuring if you were leading or cofacilitating this group? How did we deal with the issue of cultural diversity that emerged early in the life of the group? What specific norms are we actively attempting to shape early in this group?
5. **Opening and Closing Group Sessions.** Notice the use of the check-in and the check-out procedures in the DVD. What techniques would you use to open a session in a group you are leading? What did you learn about leader interventions in getting members to check in and state how they would like to use time for a session? What specific techniques for ending a session did you read about and also observe in the DVD? What are some lessons you are learning about the importance of bringing a group session to a close?
6. **Using the Workbook With the DVD.** If you are using the DVD and workbook, refer to Part 2: Initial Stage of the workbook and complete all the exercises. Reading this section and addressing the questions will help you conceptualize group process by integrating the text with the DVD and the workbook.

MindTap for Counseling

Additional resources can be found on CengageBrain.com and by logging into the MindTap course created by your professor. There you will find a variety of study tools and useful resources that include quizzes, videos, interactive exercises, and more.

7 CHAPTER

Transition Stage of a Group

CHAPTER LEARNING OBJECTIVES

1 Describe the dynamics associated with group process and development (CACREP, 2016, Standard B)

2 Identify and understand key characteristics of a group during the transition stage

3 Explore ways of effectively dealing with defensiveness and reluctant behaviors

4 Critically evaluate the notion of resistance

5 Understand common fears and anxiety of members

6 Gain a deeper appreciation for ways to explore conflict in a group

7 Differentiate between effective and ineffective styles of confrontation

8 Explore ways to therapeutically address problematic behaviors

9 Understand the dynamics of members' problematic behavior

10 Describe behaviors indicating avoidance by the whole group

11 Understand the dynamics of transference and countertransference in a group

12 Identify coleadership issues during the transition stage

You are coleading a weekly therapy group in a community agency and find you are having increasing difficulties working with one of the members. You realize that it is difficult for you to like him because he reminds you of someone from your past. In addition to your own countertransference, several members seem very defensive with you and your coleader. They often collude with each other when you attempt to challenge them. In your last group meeting, one of the members openly confronted you and asked, "How can you help me if you have never walked in my shoes?" After the session, you and your coleader process the group.

- In what ways are these issues normative or common to the transition stage of a group? How will you work with your countertransference issues?
- What strategies will you and your coleader use to address the "defensiveness" of group members?
- How did you react to the member's direct challenge to you?
- In what ways can you therapeutically respond to his question?
- What feelings do you think underlie his question to you?

LO1

Introduction

Before groups progress to a level of deeper work, which we refer to as the working stage, they typically experience a transitional phase. If group members are not willing to disclose the ways in which they are struggling with both themselves and one another, they are not able to move forward and develop the trust necessary for deeper work. What the members and leaders do during this transitional period often will determine whether or not a group develops a cohesive community that allows members to engage in meaningful interpersonal exploration. A group's ability to move forward is dependent on the ability and willingness of both members and leaders to work with whatever emerges in the here and now.

The transition stage of a group is particularly challenging for group leaders, and it is a difficult time for members as well. During this phase, groups are often characterized by anxiety, defensiveness, guardedness, ambivalence, resistance, a range of control issues, intermember conflicts, challenges to the leader, and various patterns of problematic behaviors. These difficulties are a normal part of the unfolding process of a group, and remaining curious about members' defensive behavior will serve you better than reacting critically. To avoid entrenching what appears to be uncooperative behavior, it can be useful to shift your attitude and acknowledge that certain behaviors may be the result of members' fear, confusion, and cautiousness. For instance, if you can understand a reluctant member's behavior as symptomatic of being scared or another member's silence as indicative of his lack of knowledge regarding how to best participate in a group, you will have a more positive attitude toward these behaviors. By changing the label "resistant" to more descriptive and nonjudgmental terminology, it is likely that you will change your attitude toward members who represent a challenge for you.

As you change the lens by which you perceive members' behaviors, it will be easier to adopt an understanding attitude and to encourage members to explore ways they are reluctant and self-protective. It is essential to remain nondefensive and help members express their legitimate feelings about not wanting to trust you or other members. By viewing members' behavior in this manner, you are also more likely to access the cultural dimensions associated with certain signs of reluctant behaviors. For example, a member who is silent, one who defers to authority, or one who gives a lot of advice may be doing so due to cultural norms rather than purposefully exhibiting difficult behaviors. Assist these members in giving voice to their past and present experiences and acknowledge their feelings before interpreting their behavior as based on a lack of trust in you as a leader or of other members. When people feel heard and acknowledged, they may be more open to change.

Some of the most productive work in the life of a group takes place during this time of transition. This is a time in the group in which both members and leaders are learning about each other's capacity and style for change. Members may learn new ways of dealing with challenges, such as staying with a conflict situation rather than avoiding it. As members continue talking, they may eventually reach a resolution and a deepening of the relationship. The manner in which members display their defensive behavior is also a window into their ego strength. It is useful for leaders to observe and file away this information, which later may be brought to bear on interventions during the working stage.

In assisting a group to meet the tasks of the transition stage, you need to have a clear understanding of the characteristics and dynamics of a group during this phase of development. Be particularly mindful of your own reactions, especially the tendency to assume total responsibility for whatever is happening in the group—or of putting full responsibility on the members. In this chapter we deal with the typical characteristics of a group during the transition stage and suggest interventions for dealing with problems that may occur at this stage.

LO2

Characteristics of the Transition Stage

Anxiety and defensiveness underlies much of members' behavior in the transitional phase. To get beyond this phase, members must be able to deal effectively with defensiveness. A leader's task is to help members identify and confront their fears and to work through possible conflict and control issues. The goal of this stage is to create a safe and trusting climate that encourages members to take risks. Some members may lack understanding or experience in participating in groups, and their struggle to learn new behavior patterns should not be labeled as defensive. People bring their typical ways of communicating to a group, and they are often open to learning more effective ways of expressing themselves.

Establishing Trust

Establishing trust is a central task of the initial phase in the evolution of a group, but members may still be wondering if the group is a safe place for them during the transition phase. Considerable hesitation and observing both the other members and the leader are common. As a climate of trust is gradually created, members can express their reactions without fear of censure or of being judged. Often one member's willingness to take the risk to disclose a concern or fear will lead others to do the same. These disclosures are a turning point in establishing a greater degree of trust.

When trust is high, members are actively involved in the activities in the group: making themselves known to others in personal ways, taking risks both in the group and out of group, focusing on themselves and not on others, actively working in the group on meaningful personal issues, disclosing persistent feelings such as lack of trust, and supporting and challenging others in the group.

By contrast, here are some clear signs that trust is lacking:

- Members will not initiate work.
- Members frequently show up late, leave early, or miss sessions.
- Members are reluctant to participate due to their fear of being confronted.
- Members keep their reactions to themselves or express them in indirect ways.
- Members take refuge in storytelling.
- Members are excessively quiet.
- Members put more energy into helping others or giving others advice than into sharing their own personal concerns.
- Members demand that group leaders take charge; they may say "Tell us what to do."
- Some members may say they have problems too big for the group; others may say they have no problems.
- Members avoid dealing openly with conflict and may not even acknowledge it.
- Members may have split into subgroups.
- Members may keep their agenda hidden from leaders or other members.

When trust is lacking, members are still checking out what is happening in the room, yet they may be doing so quietly, which makes it difficult to explore what is occurring within the group. Some members may be testing the leader, especially those who have had negative experiences with authority figures. This is not uncommon for individuals who have experienced oppression and who are checking to see whether the leader, or other members, may be prejudiced in some way. It may be helpful to encourage members to make this testing process explicit by putting words to what they are seeing and concluding. Other members may make judgmental statements, which have the effect of inhibiting open participation. We find over and over that many of the problems arising in a group are not due to the feelings and thoughts people *do* express but to those reactions they *do not* express. Our central leadership task at the transition stage is to encourage members to say aloud what they are thinking and feeling about what is happening within the group. We often provide prompts, asking members to complete sentences like these: "One thing I am afraid to say in this group is . . ." "If you really knew me, you would . . ." "It is difficult for me to trust people because . . .".

Mistrust is normal in the beginning stages of a group. If leaders are able to acknowledge that members have different styles of building trust and can normalize this, it may encourage members to begin talking about their past and current experiences with building and maintaining trust in relationships. Each member must actively work to open him- or herself to trusting others and to addressing the issues that get in the way of doing so.

In rare instances, a scripted exercise may be useful to get members to begin to open up and take some risks with one another. In a group I (Cindy) led, members were well aware of the silence and lack of participation in the room. Using an exercise I adapted from my colleague Denny Ollerman, I asked if they were willing to try something that involved a significant amount of risk. I participated in the activity myself as a way of modeling my own willingness to be vulnerable and to take a risk within the group. By going first I set a tone for the members. Each person was asked to stand in front of three different members and complete the following sentence: "Something I don't want you to know about me is . . ." For example, one member might say, "Something I don't want you to know about me is, I hate my body," and then she may say to another member, "Something I don't want you to know about me is, I don't trust men." After everyone had taken turns completing the sentence three times, an abundance of topics were ready to be discussed and reactions to be shared. This type of exercise should be done with care, and leaders need to be skilled at helping members process their feelings as a result of participating in such vulnerable and powerful ways.

Using dyads is another way of infusing untapped energy into a quiet or reserved group. A small group I (Cindy) coled was characterized by low energy, and I wanted to shift the energy in the room. I decided to have the members break into dyads and take turns answering two prompts: "How are you experiencing me?" and "Something that keeps me from feeling close to you is . . ." This exercise led to some very honest and insightful conversations, and the energy level of the whole group was heightened. At the next session, members seemed more willing to share on deeper levels and to take risks with one another that they previously had not been willing to take.

Defensiveness and Reluctant Behavior

Participants are often torn between wanting to be safe and wanting to risk. It makes sense for members to proceed with caution. Members will not begin intensive work unless there is a climate of safety. Both the leader and members must understand the meaning of defensive or cautious behavior. It is essential that leaders be respectful and patient of members' processes and defenses.

> Members will not begin intensive work unless there is a climate of safety.

From a psychoanalytic perspective, resistance is defined as the individual's reluctance to bring into conscious awareness threatening material that has been previously repressed or denied. It also can be viewed as anything that prevents members from dealing with unconscious material. From a broader perspective, resistance can be viewed as behavior that keeps us from exploring personal conflicts or painful feelings. Resistance is one way we attempt to protect ourselves from anxiety.

Respecting a member's defensiveness means the leader does not chastise a reluctant person but explores the source of his or her hesitation. Members often have realistic reasons for their reluctance. For example, one woman was typically quiet during group and would speak only when others addressed her. When the group leader pointed this out, she said that she felt embarrassed to speak because of her accent. She was convinced that she did not speak English well enough to be understood; this kept her silent. Although she wanted to bring up this subject, the thought of being the center of attention was so anxiety-provoking for her that she said as little as possible. To dismiss this client as *resistant* would show a lack of respect for her genuine reluctance and could serve to discount her very real and painful experiences with discrimination as a bilingual person.

As a bilingual person, I (Marianne) was very self-conscious speaking English and worried about using correct grammar. I was even more self-conscious around fellow Germans who had a better command of English than I did. When conducting a group in Korea with Korean nationals, I found that this feeling is widespread. Inquiring about their hesitation to speak up in group during several sessions, some members said they were rehearsing in their head how to express themselves in English without making grammatical mistakes. Some shared that they would reflect on how they expressed themselves in English when outside the group and that they practiced what they wanted to say for an upcoming session. Being in an all-Korean group with members who had varying degrees of command of the English language increased their anxiety about speaking "correctly." Exploring their reasons for not speaking up gave new meaning to their lack of participation.

Clients' reluctance to express themselves sometimes represents a coping strategy that at one time served an adaptive function but that no longer serves a useful purpose. Leaders can assist members in reframing their resistance. If you are able to understand their hesitation, members may come to realize and appreciate that a particular coping strategy was the best possible response to a difficult situation earlier in life but that it is no longer effective. Resistance is a natural part of the therapeutic process and can lead to productive exploration in the group; it needs to be acknowledged, talked about, and understood.

The most therapeutic way to deal with difficult behaviors is for leaders to simply describe to members what they are observing and let members know how they are affected by what they see and hear. This approach is an invitation for members to determine if what they are doing is working for them. If leaders do not respect members' defenses against anxiety, they are not respecting the members themselves. For example, Melody reveals some painful material and then suddenly stops and says that she doesn't want to go on. In respecting Melody's reluctance, the leader asks her what is stopping her rather than pushing her to continue dealing with her pain. Melody indicates that she is afraid of losing people's respect. The issue now becomes her lack of trust in the group rather than a painful personal problem. If the leader proceeds in this manner, Melody is more likely to eventually talk openly about personal matters. If the leader ignores Melody's initial hesitation by pushing her to open up, she is more likely to close up and not talk. However, if the leader does not inquire about the meaning of her reluctance, she might close off useful avenues of self-exploration.

Sometimes members' hesitations are the result of factors such as an unqualified leader, an aggressive and uncaring leadership style, or a failure to prepare members for participation in the group. One of the key tasks of leadership is to accurately appraise whether the source of difficulty is the members' fears or ineffective leadership. If you show a willingness to understand the context of the members' behavior, the likelihood of cooperation and risk-taking is increased.

Members of an involuntary group may exhibit a lack of cooperation through sarcasm and silence. This gives members some power in a situation in which they feel powerless. If you respond in a negative way to this behavior, you are likely to entrench this pattern. It is important not to respond with defensiveness when dealing with a client who does not want to participate.

Dwight: I don't want to be here! This group won't do me any good.

Leader [*in a nondefensive tone*]: So you don't want to be here. Do you know why you are here? From your perspective, why do you think you were asked to be here?

Dwight: They sent me, and I don't need this group. [*shrugs shoulders*] I don't have a choice.

Leader: It's difficult to do something you don't want to do. Tell me about other times when people tell you what to do. What is that like for you?

Dwight: I don't know what it's like. I just know I really don't have any choices.

Leader: I guess I could argue that everyone ultimately has a choice, but that won't get us anywhere. I know that other members have felt the same way you do about this group. Can we talk about how we dealt with it as a group?

It is important to follow the member's lead and *go with* his negative reaction rather than fighting it or taking it personally. Dwight's reluctance can be responded to in a variety of ways. Here are some intervention statements that may increase the odds that an involuntary member will become a voluntary participant:

- Many group members have felt the same way you do now. Maybe they could tell you what it was like for them.
- What do you know about counseling? Have you ever participated in a group?
- Why do you think you were sent here?
- What would the person who sent you here tell me about why you're here?
- How do you cope with having to do something you don't want to do?
- How would you like it to be? What can you do to get there?

If you understand the dynamics of a group member's negative reactions and do not respond defensively, the intensity of the problematic behavior is likely to diminish. As the recipient of this uncooperative behavior, you may feel personally rejected, but you cannot afford the luxury of feeling vulnerable to rejection. Process your reactions at a later time through self-reflection, supervision, or consultation.

A Critique of the Notion of Resistance

LO4

A number of writers in the psychotherapy field have challenged the traditional view of resistance and have reconceptualized the role of resistance in therapy. Erving Polster and Miriam Polster (1973), leading figures in Gestalt therapy, suggest that what often passes for resistance is not simply a barrier to therapy but is a "creative force for managing a difficult world" (p. 52). They assert that the idea of resistance is unnecessary and incompatible with Gestalt therapy (Polster & Polster, 1976). The problem associated with labeling a behavior as resistance is the implication that the behavior or trait is "alien" to the person and needs to be eliminated if the person is to function in healthy ways. By avoiding the use of the term *resistance*, the therapist avoids the assumption that the client is behaving inappropriately. Instead of trying to change a client's behavior or make something happen, the Polsters focus on what is actually happening in the present and explore this with the client.

Steve de Shazer (1984), one of the pioneers of solution-focused brief therapy, wrote about "The Death of Resistance." He believes the notion of client resistance attributes most of the blame for lack of progress to the client while allowing the practitioner to avoid responsibility for what is happening in therapy. De Shazer assumes that clients are competent in figuring out what they want and need. It is the practitioner's responsibility to assist clients in identifying their competencies and using them to create satisfying lives. If the notion of client competence is accepted, then *client resistance* is better viewed as *practitioner resistance*. According to de Shazer, therapeutic impasses result from the therapist's failure to listen to and understand clients.

Like de Shazer, Bill O'Hanlon (2003) attributes client resistance to misunderstanding and inflexibility on the therapist's part. From O'Hanlon's perspective, what therapists call resistance often reflects genuine concerns on the part of clients. O'Hanlon's solution-oriented therapy challenges the basic belief of many therapists who assume that clients do not really want to change and are thus resistant to therapy. O'Hanlon and Weiner-Davis (2003) invite therapists to question their basic assumptions about clients and monitor the ways they use language in therapy. They also caution therapists not to focus on finding resistance, lest this becomes a self-fulfilling prophecy.

In writing about resistance in therapy from the perspective of narrative therapy, Winslade, Crocket, and Monk (1997) emphasize the therapeutic relationship. When therapy becomes difficult, they avoid placing the responsibility on the client, for doing so results in blaming the client for what is happening in the therapeutic relationship. Instead, Winslade and colleagues pay close attention to the conversations with their clients to discover possible reasons for the difficulty in therapy.

Motivational interviewing reframes resistance as a healthy response and emphasizes reflective listening, which is a way for practitioners to better understand the subjective world of clients (Miller & Rollnick, 2013). Reluctance to change is viewed as a normal and expected part of the therapeutic process. Although individuals may see advantages to making life changes, they also have many concerns and fears about changing. People who seek therapy are often ambivalent about change, and their motivation may ebb and flow during the course of therapy. A key goal of motivational interviewing is to increase internal motivation to change based on the values of the client. Those who practice motivational interviewing assume a respectful view of resistance and work therapeutically with any reluctance or ambivalence on the part of clients. When clients are slow to change, it may be assumed that they have both compelling reasons to remain as they are as well as having reasons to change.

Group practitioners with a cognitive behavioral orientation tend to reframe the concept of resistance so that group members are not blamed. Attention is given to assessment and then designing a treatment plan that is customized to the needs of the members (Beck, 2005, 2011). These group counselors emphasize a therapeutic partnership with group members so that goals are agreed upon by both the members and the leader. Through this collaborative style, cooperation is more likely to increase.

In summary, Gestalt therapy, solution-focused therapy, narrative therapy, motivational interviewing, and cognitive behavior therapy, are therapeutic approaches that question the validity and usefulness of the way resistance is typically used. Each of these therapeutic models reconceptualizes the phenomenon of resistance by encouraging therapists to pay attention to what is transpiring in the present context of the therapeutic relationship and in the group itself. We try to think of ways to describe to members what we are observing rather than suggesting they are resisting, and we ask members to consider whether the ways they are behaving are helping or hindering them in getting what they want. By approaching member resistance with respect, interest, and understanding, defensive behavior is likely to decrease.

Learning in Action

Reflection on Intention

The way we interpret a person's action directly affects the way we respond. If someone lies to you, you have a right to feel hurt or angry. However, if you want to move past those feelings, look for the reasons the person may have lied. Was the person afraid to disappoint you? Was the person worried about being rejected? Would you respond differently to someone who lied to you versus someone who was afraid? How might your interventions differ if you look at the interaction from a different perspective?

We judge our own behaviors with more understanding than we do the behaviors of others. For example, if you are changing lanes on the freeway and don't see the car next to you, you know that your actions were unintentional. But the person whose car you cut off on the road may assume you did so intentionally and be angry. Think of an action by someone close to you that bothered you. What did you feel when this occurred? What was your initial reaction to that person? How did you judge this individual's behavior? Now look at the same action but describe it in a less defensive way. This is often difficult to do in our personal lives, but it is a helpful skill when working with clients who exhibit problematic behavior in a group.

Common Fears and Anxieties Experienced by Members LO5

When group members keep their fears to themselves, they may be expressed through a variety of avoidant behaviors. Although members cannot be forced to discuss their fears, you can invite them to recognize that they may be experiencing something that is common to many members. It is almost always helpful to acknowledge the members' feelings first, before pushing them to move through their fears or too hastily reassuring members that their fears will not be realized in this group experience. Leaders cannot promise members that their willingness to take risks in a group will end positively, but a therapeutic group is one of the best places for members to have new experiences in relating to others. It can result in healing old wounds and fears from past or present relationships. As members use the group as a safe place to explore their fears, they learn new ways to address their concerns both in the group and in their everyday lives with others.

During the transition stage, anxiety is high within individuals and within the group as a whole. If members are willing to voice their anxious thoughts, these feelings can be explored and more fully understood. For example, Christie expresses internal concerns: "I'm really afraid to go further for fear of what I'll find out." Sunny is more anxious about what others are thinking: "I'm afraid to speak up in here because some people seem judgmental." These concerns may be projections on the part of Christie and Sunny, but their willingness to express their feelings is pivotal in moving from a transition to a working stage in the group. As participants come to more fully trust one another and the leader, they are increasingly able to share their concerns. This openness lessens the anxiety group members have about letting others see them as they are.

Members may fear exposing their pain, sounding trite, being overcome by intense emotions, being misunderstood, being rejected, or not knowing what is expected. Brief descriptions of common fears and anxieties manifested during the transition stage are presented next along with possible interventions that might be helpful to members. It can be useful to share some of the common fears and concerns with group members in an effort to normalize what they may be feeling and to help establish a safe environment in which they can express their own fears with the group.

The Fear of Self-Disclosure Members often fear self-disclosure, thinking that they will be pressured to open up before they are ready. It helps to reinforce emphatically to members that they can make themselves known to others and at the same time retain their privacy. Consider this example: "I can't imagine myself talking about my parents in the negative ways that others are doing in here," Nicole said. "If I were to talk this way about my parents, I would be overcome with shame and disloyalty." Because the leader is aware of certain cultural values that Nicole holds, he lets her know that he respects her decision. He did not push her to do something that she would later regret. But he did encourage her to think of ways she could participate in the group that would be meaningful to her. There is a delicate balance between reluctance because of cultural injunctions and cautiousness in moving into frightening territory. As we explained in Chapter 5, it is the choice of members to determine *what* and *how* much they share. When they recognize that they control what they choose to tell others about themselves, participants tend to be less fearful of self-disclosure.

The Fear of Being Exposed and Vulnerable Some members may hesitate to participate fully out of a desire to avoid feeling vulnerable. Having been shamed, attacked, blamed, or ridiculed for expressing themselves to others in their everyday relationships, these members may feel it is too risky to share themselves in personal ways. It is important for the leader to help members express their past experiences while also inviting them to have a new and perhaps healthier experience with being vulnerable in the group. For example, Marisa had a prior negative experience in attempting to express her feelings in her family. She was asked what she needed from the leader and other group members in order to feel safe. Others then responded to her disclosure. The leader asked Marisa to talk about how safe it felt for her to listen to the responses of both the leader and group members. In the group, she learned that once her feelings were recognized and accepted her sense of safety increased. In this case, the group leader helped Marisa to overcome her fear by allowing her to base her current level of exposure on what was happening in the room rather what had happened to her in her family.

The Fear of Rejection We sometimes hear participants say that they are reluctant to get involved with others in the group because of the fear of rejection. Stephen repeatedly spoke of his fears that people would not want anything to do with him. He had erected walls to protect himself from the pain of rejection, and he made the assumption that the group would turn against him if he did reveal himself. The leader asked, "Are you willing to look around the room and see if you feel that every person in this room would reject you?" Stephen took some time to look around the room at the 10 group members: he was convinced that 4 of them would reject him, and he was not sure of 2 of them. Stephen agreed to continue working and was asked if he was willing to "own" his projections by addressing the following sentence to those he thought might reject him: "I'm afraid that you will reject me because. . . ." He also talked to the people he felt were more accepting and explained why he thought differently about them. When Stephen was finished, others reacted to him in a sensitive way and explained why they were afraid of him or found it difficult to get close to him. Through this exploration, Stephen learned about his part in creating a sense of rejection. With exercises like these, leaders must intervene if members become defensive and want to respond, thus interrupting the flow of Stephen's work. It is important that members learn that what Stephen is saying is more about him than about them. The work is about dealing with Stephen's projections and his perception of being rejected rather than establishing, at this moment, whether members are rejecting him or not.

The Fear of Being Misunderstood or Judged For some people, the fear of being judged or misunderstood is a very real barrier to letting themselves be known in a group. This can be especially difficult for members who have experienced oppression or discrimination in various forms. It is common in our work to hear members from various cultural groups share painful experiences of being labeled or judged for who they are and feeling as if they have to defend themselves and others from their cultural group. Some members have early memories of being in groups (typically in school settings) in which they were ridiculed and discriminated against both overtly and covertly for being "different." For these people, it is crucial that the leader understands and respects the members' history and does not move too quickly to reassure them that this group will be different. By helping members express their previous pain around being misunderstood and judged, the leader can provide tools for exploring new ways of taking risks that will result in more positive outcomes.

The Fear of Being Challenged or Singled Out Some members may stay silent or hidden in group as a way of avoiding the fear of being challenged by group leaders or other members. Some people have extreme difficulty with conflict and may be fearful of having attention given to them in the group. They may be engaging in *all or nothing* thinking, believing that if "called upon" it would be negative. Whether this fear is due to temperament, cultural factors, or life experiences, leaders can help reluctant members find ways of participating in the group and engaging with others that do not paralyze them with fear. By helping these members see that they are cheating themselves and others of potentially rich encounters by remaining invisible, leaders may help fearful members begin to take steps toward making themselves seen.

The Fear of Losing Control Marin expressed her fear that she might open up some potentially painful areas and be left even more vulnerable. She was anxious about "going too deep" as she put it. She wondered, "Will I be able to stand the pain? Maybe it would be best if things were just left as they are. If I started crying, I might never stop! Even though I might get support in the group, what will I do when group is over?" The leader responded, "I'm sure you've been alone and have found it painful. What do you normally do when this happens?" Marin replied, "I lock myself in the room, I don't talk to anyone, and I just cry by myself and then get depressed." The leader asked Marin to pick two or three people in the room that she thought would be most able to understand her pain and tell them, while looking at them, about some of the distress in her life. As she did this, she would be likely to discover the difference between isolating herself in pain and sharing it with others and experiencing their support. She could also come to the realization that she did not have to deal with her pain alone, unless she chose to do so. She could be challenged to identify a few people in the group and in her outside life whom she could reach out to in time of need.

Some Other Fears A variety of other fears are often expressed by members:

- I'm concerned about seeing these people out of group and what they will think of me.
- I'm afraid I will be talked about outside of group.
- I'm afraid I'll get too dependent on the group and rely too much on others to solve my problems.
- If I get angry, I'm afraid I'll lose control and hurt somebody.
- I worry that once I am open I might not be able to close up again.
- I'm uncomfortable with physical contact, and I'm afraid that I'll be expected to hug others when I don't want to.
- I'm worried that I'll take too much group time by talking about my problems, that I'll bore people.
- I'm afraid I'll get close to people here and then never see them again when the group ends.

Though it is not realistic to expect that all these fears can be eliminated, we do think members can be encouraged to face these fears by talking about them. Through what you model as a leader, you can help create a trusting climate in which members will feel free enough to test their fears and discriminate between realistic and unrealistic fears. If members decide to talk about their fears and if this decision is made relatively early in a group, a good foundation of trust is created that will enable them to deal constructively with other personal concerns as the group evolves.

Journal Prompts

It can be helpful to reflect on your own fears as a way of reminding yourself of how vulnerable members can sometimes feel. It is easy to hide behind the safety of a leadership role and forget to connect to the parts of yourself that may be uncomfortable to look at but that increase your compassion and empathy.

1. What is an example of one fear that you have experienced in a group?
2. How has this fear affected your participation in a group?
3. How could you challenge this fear?

Struggles With Control

Maintaining a sense of control is a common theme at the transition stage. Some characteristic group behaviors include discussions about the division of responsibility and decision-making procedures. Participants' main anxieties in the transition phase relate to having too much or too little responsibility. To deal constructively with these issues, members must bring them to the surface and talk about them. If the here-and-now problems are ignored, the group will be inhibited by the hidden agenda.

The leader's task is to help members understand that their struggle to maintain control may be a way of protecting themselves from doing more in-depth work. For example, Heather may say, "No matter what I say or do, it never seems to be the right thing. Why can't I just do it my way?" The leader might respond, "I'm not looking at what you're doing in terms of right or wrong. I'm more concerned that what you do will help you achieve the goals you set for yourself. I've noticed that you seem to avoid talking about difficult areas in your life." Another intervention would be to ask Heather, "How would you like to use your time in this group?" Or the leader might say, "Tell me more about what has been helpful to you in this group and what has not."

Conflict

Conflict is a difficult subject for some people to deal with, both in groups and in daily living. There is an assumption that conflict is a sign of something intrinsically wrong and that it should be avoided at all costs. Within a group, the leader and the members sometimes want to avoid conflict rather than spending the time and effort necessary to work through it, but this may interfere with the work of the group. Conflict can be expected in all relationships; it is frequently the avoidance of conflict that is problematic. Unexplored conflict is typically expressed in defensive behavior, indirectness, and a general lack of trust. Groups offer an ideal environment for learning to deal with conflict effectively. During any stage of a group's development, but especially during the early phase, it is crucial that conflict be acknowledged and managed effectively so that the level of trust will increase. A primary task of leaders is to teach members the value of working through conflicts in a constructive way.

Jennifer expressed a conflict within one group: "Some people in here never say anything." Houston immediately replied, defensively, "Not everybody has to be as talkative as you." Leticia joined in, sarcastically, "Well, Jennifer, you talk so much you don't give me a chance to participate!" Alejandro's contribution was, "I wish you would stop this arguing. This isn't getting us anywhere." Ineffective interventions by the leader are: "I agree with you, Alejandro. Why don't we just try to get along? Or "Jennifer, you're right. There are people in here who say very little. I wish they would take as many risks as you do!" Such remarks increase members' defensiveness.

The emerging conflict was dealt with constructively when the leader took the approach of exploring the underlying dynamics of what had been said and what was *not* being said: "I agree with you, Alejandro, that right now we are struggling, but I don't want people to stop talking because we need to know what all this means." Turning to Jennifer, the leader asked: "How are you affected by all these reactions? Is there anyone in particular you want to hear from? How does it affect you when people don't say much? How would it be helpful if people talked more?"

Jennifer's original statement was a defensive and chastising remark to the group in general. The group reacted with understandable defensiveness. The leader addressed Jennifer's difficulty with the group and tried to get her to be more specific about how she was affected by people whom she saw as being silent. The conflict found resolution when she let people know that she was afraid that they were judging her when they said very little and that she was interested in how they perceived her. Chances are that this conflict would not have come about if Jennifer had said something like this to Leticia: "I notice that you're quiet, and I often wonder what you think of me. I'd like to hear from you." Such a statement would have reflected more accurately what was going on with Jennifer than did her punitive remark. It is important for the leader not to cut off the expression of conflict but to facilitate more direct and personal expression of feeling and thinking among the members.

Conflict may be created by not attending to the diversity issues that exist within a group. Some of the areas of diversity in a group that are potential sources of conflict and distrust include differences in age, gender, language, sexual orientation, socioeconomic status, power, privilege, disability, race, ethnicity, and educational attainment. Leaders need to be aware that people from different cultures may address conflict in different ways. What looks like conflict in one culture may be a normative interaction in another culture.

Regardless of their cultural background, members can have a difficult time dealing with conflict because of learned patterns in their family of origin. Some people come from families in which conflict meant that someone was hurt or there was a winner and a loser. These members may not have learned to deal with conflict as a part of healthy relationships. Individuals from privileged groups may find it difficult to understand the experience of those who are not privileged. For example, George, a White male, contends that he does not see himself as privileged in any way and that his life is completely the result of his hard work. George adamantly denies any privileges associated with his race or gender. Members of color and women often express frustration and sometimes anger at assertions like these, claiming that George (and others like him) shows either a lack of awareness or an unwillingness to examine his own privileged status. As in many of these cultural conflicts, the key is to be able to facilitate exploration of the topic and the emotions around it without judging or condemning members. This type of facilitation requires an understanding of complex multicultural issues and experience in group process.

As another example, consider a bicultural group member (Maria) who speaks with an accent. If Maria talks about her anxiety over people's reactions to her accent, and if others in the group who have not struggled with discrimination are unable to empathize with her concerns, she may be wounded in the group just as she has been so often in her everyday life. Maria is then unlikely to disclose other significant issues because she does not feel understood or safe. Any conflict that results from failing to understand and appreciate member differences must be openly addressed and worked through if a trusting climate is to be established. If this conflict is ignored, mistrust is bound to appear and the group's progress can be stalled.

Leaders need to balance what can feel like opposing sides with great care and attention, challenging members to hear the experience of other members while not shutting them down by the interaction. This does not mean that the interaction has to be polite or even comfortable. On the contrary, meaningful and authentic discussions of diversity often are carried out with some level of intensity and heightened emotion. Our task is to facilitate in a way that the emotions do not immobilize people from moving forward but motivate members to struggle through the interchange to gain greater self-awareness and a better understanding of the perspectives of others in relation to their diverse cultural contexts and lives.

Cohesion within a group typically increases after conflict is recognized and expressed in a healthy way. Stating what is keeping you cautious is one way of testing the freedom and trustworthiness of the group. During the transition stage participants continue to test whether this group is a safe place in which to disagree openly and whether they will be accepted in spite of the intensity of their feelings. When conflict is constructively discussed, members learn that their relationships are strong enough to withstand an honest level of challenge, which is what many people want to achieve in their outside relationships.

Reflect on your concerns about managing conflict when it emerges in a group you are leading:

- How confident are you that you can address conflict when it is aimed at you?
- Do you have the skills you need to deal effectively with conflict between or among group members?
- What steps can you take to improve your ability to assist members in dealing effectively with conflict that arises in a group?

Confrontation

If people want to take a deeper and more honest look at themselves, it is necessary that they be willing to risk expressing what is on their minds, even though doing so may be difficult both to say and to hear. If confrontations are examined in a caring and respectful manner, these interventions often promote change. It is essential that group members see that confrontation is a basic part of the group process, as it is of most every healthy relationship.

Leaders have a responsibility to teach members what confrontation *is* and what it *is not* and how to interact in constructive ways. Confrontation is not (1) tearing others down, (2) hitting others with negative feedback and then retreating, (3) being hostile with the aim of hurting others, (4) telling others what is basically wrong with them, or (5) assaulting others' integrity. Caring confrontation is designed to help members make an honest assessment of themselves or to speak more about their own reactions. Ideally, we see confrontation as a form of constructive feedback—an invitation for participants to look at some aspect of their interpersonal style or their lives to determine if they want to make changes.

There are variations in how people from different cultures confront others and in how they react to confrontations. In working with culturally diverse clients, it is important to remember that being "indirect" may be a cultural value for some group members. If confronted on their indirectness, or if they are expected to change, these group members may perceive such confrontations as signs of rudeness. They may even feel a sense of embarrassment, which could result in their deciding not to return to the group. Timing and sensitivity to members' cultural backgrounds are key factors in determining whether confrontations will be effective. A confrontation between people who share a similar culture may be addressed less defensively than one between members from different cultural or racial groups because they share some common understandings already. For example, comments between two African American males may be received less defensively than comments from a White male to a Black male.

In our work with groups, we provide members with these guidelines for appropriate and responsible confrontation:

- Members or leaders know why they are confronting.
- Confrontations are not dogmatic statements concerning who or what a person is.
- The person being confronted is told what effect he or she has on others rather than being labeled or judged or analyzed.
- Confrontations are more effective when they focus on specific, observable behaviors.
- One of the purposes of confrontation is to develop a closer and more genuine relationship with others.
- Sensitivity is an important element of effective confrontation; it is helpful for the person doing the confronting to imagine being the recipient of what is said.
- Those confronting might ask themselves if they are willing to do what they are asking others to do.
- Confrontation gives others the opportunity to reflect on the feedback they receive before they are expected to respond or to act on this feedback.
- Confrontation is a means to get a client to consider an alternative perspective.

The quality of the confrontations that occur in a group is a measure of how effective the group is. The more cohesive a group, the more challenging the members and leaders can be.

To make the issue of confrontation more concrete, let's look at some examples. The first statement in each set illustrates an ineffective confrontation; this is followed by an effective confrontation statement. These examples show some of the ways group members might speak with one another. It is our role as leaders to model and to teach members to utilize the more *effective* ways of confronting. As you read each of these statements, imagine that you are the recipient of both the effective and ineffective confrontations. Take note of what it might be like to hear each of these statements. How would you be inclined to respond in each situation?

Ineffective: You're always giving everyone advice. I wish you would just focus on yourself for once.

Effective: It's difficult for me to listen to you when you give me advice. I would be more receptive if you told me more about your experiences.

Ineffective: You aren't getting anything from this group. You never talk, you just observe. We're just interesting cases for you.

Effective: I'd like to get to know you better. It's hard for me to feel close to you because you seem more interested in hearing from us than in sharing yourself.

Ineffective: You sound really homophobic.

Effective: You have made many generalizations about the LGBTQ community, and I feel hurt by what you have said. I would like for you to know me better, but I don't feel safe being more open and making myself vulnerable with you.

Ineffective: You're always so judgmental.

Effective: I feel uncomfortable with you because I'm afraid of what you think of me. Your opinion is important to me.

Ineffective: You are dishonest. You're always smiling, and that's not real.

Effective: I find it difficult to trust you. When you say you're angry, you're often smiling. That makes it hard for me to know what to believe.

Ineffective: I'm tired of your games.

Effective: I have trouble believing what you say. It bothers me that I feel this way with you, and I would like to talk to you about it.

In each of the ineffective statements, the people being confronted are being told how they are, and in some way they are being discounted. In the effective statements, the member doing the confronting is revealing his or her own perceptions and feelings about the other member: "When I am affected by you, what I say to you is about me too, not just about you." By not blaming others for their struggle, members can confront one another with respect and understanding.

Challenges to the Group Leader

Although leaders may be challenged throughout a group, they are more often confronted both personally and professionally during the transition stage. For example, several members may complain about not getting the "right" type of leadership, thereby challenging the leader's competence. It is a mistake for leaders to assume that every confrontation is an attack on their skills or integrity. Instead, they need to examine what is being said so they can differentiate between a *challenge* and an *attack*. How leaders respond to members' confrontations has a bearing on how trustingly the participants will approach confrontation in the future.

Oscar says to the leader, "I'm bored in here, and I wish you'd do something to make this a better group." A therapeutic response might include: "Tell me more about what you'd like from me or what you'd like from the group." "Say more about what's missing for you in this group." "What could you continue to do to make this a more meaningful group for you?" (By speaking up, Oscar has already taken the first step in changing the situation for himself.) It is not necessary that the leader quickly comply with Oscar's demand to conduct the group differently, but the leader should listen and promote a full expression of Oscar's dissatisfaction. The leader does not assume total responsibility for his boredom. However, she explores with Oscar their mutual responsibility to make this a meaningful and productive group, and she invites others to express their reactions to what is being said.

Though challenges may never be comfortable for the leader, it is important to recognize that these confrontations are often members' significant first steps toward testing the leader and thus becoming less dependent on the leader's approval. How a leader handles a confrontation to his or her leadership, at any stage, has a profound impact on the trust level in the group. Leaders can be good role models if they respond openly and avoid becoming defensive. If leaders are overly sensitive to criticism and have fragile egos, they are more likely to take such interchanges personally, which limits their effectiveness as well as the groups' ability to establish trust and openness with each other.

Many of the challenges described in this section may seem negative, pessimistic, difficult, and uncomfortable for both members and leaders. However, only when group members are ready to express their difficulties can there be a positive and productive outcome. Many of the topics in this chapter, if dealt with effectively, result in deepening interpersonal relationships, increasing cohesion, and increasing trust in the group.

The Leader's Reactions to Defensive Behaviors

Many forms of defensive behaviors emerge during the transition stage. It is important that you learn to recognize and deal with members' defenses, and that you become aware of your own reactions to the defensive behaviors exhibited by members. Some leaders have a tendency to focus on "problem members" or difficult situations rather than on their own dynamics and how they are affected personally when they encounter a difficult period in a group. Typically, leaders have a range of feelings: feeling threatened by what they perceive as a challenge to their leadership role; anger over the members' lack of cooperation and enthusiasm; feelings of inadequacy to the point of wondering if they are qualified to lead groups; resentment toward several of the members, whom they label as some type of problem; and anxiety over the slow pace of the group.

Leaders who work with involuntary groups are likely to encounter uncooperative behaviors by members. A group proposal in Chapter 11 by Paul Jacobson, who designed a domestic violence group, provides a good example of a therapist working therapeutically with mandated groups. Paul Jacobson describes specific strategies he uses to minimize a lack of member cooperation and demonstrates how to maximize positive therapeutic outcomes. Even though individuals may be mandated to participate in group therapy, a therapist has many options for effectively dealing with a range of problematic behaviors.

One of the most powerful ways to intervene when you are experiencing intense feelings over what you perceive as defensiveness is to deal with your own feelings and possible defensive reactions to the situation. If you ignore your reactions, you are leaving yourself out of the interactions that occur in the group. Furthermore, by giving the members your reactions, you are modeling a direct style of dealing with conflict and problematic situations rather than bypassing them or putting up with them. Your own thoughts, feelings, and observations can be the most powerful resource you have in dealing with defensive behavior. When you share what you are feeling and thinking about what is going on in the group—without blaming or criticizing the members for deficiencies—you are letting the members experience an honest and constructive interaction with you. Doing this builds trust, which is often being tested during this stage. For many members, honesty from the leader is crucial to creating a working climate.

We hope you will keep these thoughts in mind as you read the next section, which deals with problem behaviors and difficult group members. Although it is understandable that you will want to learn how to handle "problem members" and the disruption they can cause, your emphasis should be on actual *behaviors* rather than on labeling members. It is helpful to consider problematic behaviors as manifestations of protecting the self that most participants display at one time or another during the course of a group.

LO9

Group Members Who Pose a Challenge for Leaders

Sometimes members become difficult because of problematic behaviors on the part of group leaders. But even in groups with the most effective group leader interventions, members have the potential to display problematic behaviors that are a source of difficulty to themselves, other members, and the leader. In establishing norms that minimize problematic behaviors, leaders do well to provide the members with a rationale for not engaging in particular nonproductive behaviors. For example, when members ask why they are discouraged from asking questions, from giving advice, or from telling detailed stories, members deserve a full response. It is the leader's task to educate members to involve themselves in productive group behaviors that will maximize the benefits of their group experience. Leaders can assist members in communicating more effectively. Leaders need to be mindful of how their interventions can either decrease or escalate members' problematic behaviors.

The basic purpose of a therapeutic group is to provide people with opportunities to see themselves in a new light and get a more accurate picture of how others perceive them. To facilitate insight and change, the leader should not rush in too quickly in an attempt to eradicate difficult behaviors. Initially, the leader should observe the group to ascertain whether members see themselves as causing problems for themselves or others and to discover what members might be attempting to communicate through their behavior. Both other members and the leader must be patient and nonjudgmental if defensive behaviors are to give way to more constructive expressions. A productive group experience can teach members that they do not have to persist in behavioral patterns that are no longer working for them. With the security afforded in a group, members can begin to take risks and discover more effective ways of being.

We have found some of these interventions helpful when interacting with group members who posed a difficulty for us:

- Express your difficulty with a member without denigrating the character of the person.
- Avoid responding to sarcasm with sarcasm.
- Educate the members about how the group works.
- Encourage members to explore their defensiveness rather than too quickly expecting them to give up their ways of protecting themselves.
- Avoid labeling a member and instead describe the behavior of the member.
- Do your best to state observations and hunches in a tentative way as opposed to being dogmatic.
- Demonstrate sensitivity to a member's culture and avoid stereotyping the individual.
- Monitor your own countertransference reactions.
- Challenge and encourage members in a caring and respectful way to do things that may be painful and difficult.
- Find ways to explore the conflict rather than retreating from it.
- Avoid personalizing members' reactions, and do not respond in overly defensive ways.
- Strive to facilitate an exploration of a problem rather than offering simple or quick solutions.
- Pay attention and be honest about instances when you are meeting your own needs at the expense of your clients.
- Invite group members to state how they are personally affected by problematic behaviors of other members while blocking judgments, evaluations, and criticisms.
- If members evoke reactions in you, share this in a way that is therapeutic or process it with your coleader or your supervisor.

Leaders need to be mindful of how their interventions can either decrease or escalate members' problematic behaviors.

Be aware of your power as the group leader, and recognize the impact of the power differential between members and leaders. Take a look at your own behavior and examine whether your personal reactions might be creating some of the client's defensive behaviors. Answer these questions:

- What am I thinking and feeling as I work with this client?
- What am I doing to create or exacerbate the problems?
- Does the client remind me of anyone in my personal life?
- What is it about this individual that presents difficulty for me?

When working with behaviors that are counterproductive to group functioning, it is useful to understand the meaning these behaviors have for the individual member. People in a group are likely doing the best they know how, even if they become aware that what they are doing is not working well for them. We must remind ourselves that the very reason people seek a group is to assist them in finding more effective ways of expressing themselves and dealing with others. When group leaders understand the dynamics of various problematic behaviors, they can find ways to therapeutically manage and explore these behaviors in a group. If you find yourself frequently questioning your ability to lead a group, seek supervision or the support of a colleague. Use these opportunities to grow both personally and professionally, and recognize that you are learning and that it is normal to have some doubts.

Silence and Lack of Participation

Silence and lack of participation are two forms of behavior that most group leaders encounter. Even though the verbally silent member may not seem to interfere with a group's functioning, this behavior may constitute a problem for both the member and the group. If quiet members go unnoticed, their pattern of silence could hide a problem that may need to be addressed in the group. Typically members are affected by people who are silent in a group.

Some silent group members may argue that their lack of verbal participation is not due to lack of their involvement. They may maintain that they are learning by listening and by identifying with others' problems. These members may say, "I feel like what others are saying is more important then what I have to say." Or "I don't want to interrupt people when they are talking, so I wait and then what I have to say doesn't seem relevant anymore." Group leaders need to explore the meaning of silence with the members. When members say that they are uncomfortable verbally participating, we have no way of knowing how they are affected by what is going on during the sessions. They may be triggered by other members' explorations, and if they do not talk about this, then being in the group can be counterproductive for them and the group.

Group leaders need to avoid consistently calling on a silent person, for in this way the member is relieved of the responsibility of initiating interactions. This can lead to resentment on the part of both the member who is silent and the rest of the group, as well as frustration on the part of the leader. However, leaders may need to increase their efforts to include members of some cultural groups so that they become comfortable enough to participate in the group. There are many potential reasons for nonparticipating behavior:

- Showing respect and waiting to be called on by the leader.
- Feeling that one does not have anything worthwhile to say.
- Feeling that one should not talk about oneself or that one should be seen and not heard.

- Uncertainty about how the group process works, such as the fear of not knowing what is appropriate and when to make comments.
- A fear of certain members in the group or of the authority of the group leader.
- A protection against oppression from the leader or other members.
- Fear of being rejected.
- Lack of trust in the group.
- Unexpressed feelings of anger with group members or leaders.
- Fears about confidentiality.
- Feeling that one doesn't measure up when compared with other group members.

It is important that members not feel chastised for their silence but instead be invited to participate. Approach such members by expressing concerns rather than judgments about their silence. Leaders can work to help quiet members share themselves in a number of creative ways. It may be helpful to explore whether the member has other avenues of self-expression, such as art, poetry, or music. Thinking outside the box can open creative ways to participate not only for quiet members but for all members.

Another way of encouraging quiet members to participate is to watch for their nonverbal reactions to what others are saying. You can comment on what you are observing and use this as a way to bring them in. For example, if Nora is talking about her experience with her abusive mother and you notice a "quiet" member tearing up or listening intently, you might say, "You seemed to be touched emotionally by what Nora was saying. Would you be willing to tell Nora what she is bringing up in you?"

At times leaders and members may focus so much on active verbal participation that they miss the richness of the nonverbal communication clients from various cultural backgrounds may exhibit. All members will not participate equally, and some members may need more time to establish trust. Understanding members' cultural norms can shed light on their lack of verbal participation. When leading groups with a diverse population, counselors must recognize and appreciate the various ways in which people make themselves known, both verbally and nonverbally.

It is often useful to invite members to explore what their silence means. For example, are they this way outside of the group as well? How does it feel for them to be in this group? Have they any desire to be more verbally active participants? The rest of the group can participate in this discussion, for group members generally do have reactions to silent members. They may feel cheated that they know so little of that person, or they may fear that the person is observing them as they risk and reveal themselves. If there are several participants who rarely talk in a group, the verbally active members may become less revealing because of trust issues.

The checkout process at the end of a group session is often used to prompt minimal participation from quiet members. This is a less threatening way for members who tend to be quiet to share how they are experiencing the group. It is also important to teach nonparticipating members that others in the group are more likely to project onto them if they say very little during the sessions. The leader may ask members to make a contract to participate at every session, sharing with the group at some point how they responded to the session that day. They can also be asked toward the end of a meeting what it was like for them to be in the group. A leader might ask them if they are getting from the group what they had wanted. If they indicate that there were moments when they wanted to participate, but that time ran out before they got a chance, they can be invited to make a contract to be first on the agenda at the next group meeting.

Monopolistic Behavior

At the other end of the participation continuum is the person who exhibits a high degree of self-centeredness by monopolizing the activities of the group. The member who monopolizes often claims to identify with others but takes others' statements as openings for detailed stories about his or her own life. This person prevents others from getting their share of group time. People sometimes operate under the assumption that a good group member is one who talks a lot. Leaders need to help these members explore the possible dynamics of their behavior. They may be talking excessively out of anxiety, they may be accustomed to being ignored, they may be attempting to keep control of the group, or they may be members of privileged status who are accustomed to having others listen to them and take advantage of any opportunity to speak. These monopolizing members may talk a lot, but the end result is similar to that of silent members: they reveal very little about themselves.

During the beginning stage of a group, members as well as some leaders may be relieved that someone else is going first, and no one will intervene to stop the person from taking center stage. As time goes on, however, both leaders and members will become increasingly frustrated. As meetings continue, the group generally becomes less tolerant of the person who monopolizes, and unless these feelings of annoyance are dealt with early, they may be released in an explosive way.

For both ethical and practical reasons, it is essential that the monopolizing person be respectfully challenged to look at the effects of such behavior on the group. Ethical practice dictates that group leaders acquire intervention skills necessary to block rambling. It is desirable that the leader intervene before the members react out of frustration and become hostile. Here are some possible leader interventions:

- "Tanya, you seem to participate a lot, and I notice that you identify with most of the problems that are raised. I am not sure I know what you are trying to tell us. In one sentence, what do you most want us to hear?"
- "Tanya, you say a lot. I wonder if you're willing to go around the room to different members and finish the following sentence: 'What I most want you to hear about me is . . . '." Other possible incomplete sentences that could lead to fruitful exploration include "If I didn't talk . . ." "If I let others talk . . ." "I have a lot to say because . . ." "When people don't listen to me I feel . . ." "I want you to listen to me because . . ."

Tanya can be asked to make the rounds by addressing each person in the group through the process of completing any one of these sentences. It is important for her not to elaborate or explain but to say the first thing that comes to her mind.

It is best to instruct members not to respond during the go-around. Through such exercises we usually discover crucial information that helps everyone get a better sense of the function served by the monopolizing behavior.

Assume that another member, Vance, confronts Tanya in a hostile manner before the leader has said anything about her behavior. Vance asks Tanya: "Why don't you stop talking for a change? Do you think you're the only one who has something to say?" An appropriate leader intervention could be, "Vance, I hear your frustration with Tanya. Could you say a bit more to Tanya about how she is affecting you without judging her? It might also help to share with her what you were feeling and thinking before you spoke up."

We can dismiss Tanya's behavior as simply a nuisance, or we can see it as a defense and encourage her to explore her defenses, as we would any other defense mechanism. Consider that she initially appeared to be a motivated member, yet she seemed to try too hard to fit into the group. She revealed personal aspects of herself, she readily made suggestions to others, she could identify with most who spoke, and she told detailed stories of her past. Although Tanya might not express this, her behavior could be conveying the message "Please notice me and like me." In her own mind she may have felt that she was doing what was expected of her and viewed herself as an eager participant. One of the issues that she had initially presented to look at was her difficulty in getting close to people. She acknowledged that she had few friends and that people were typically annoyed with her, which she found perplexing. By confronting Tanya in an honest and sensitive manner, the leader can help her learn what she is doing that prevents her from getting close to people. She may discover that during her childhood she was often ignored and no one listened to her. She may have decided that if she didn't talk a lot, she would be ignored, or if she tried a little harder, people would respond to her. The fact is that her familiar behavior is not getting her what she wants, either inside or outside the group. The group experience offers her the possibility of finding ways that can satisfy her wants.

A leader can approach difficult members like Tanya with a sense of interest. The leader's *internal* dialogue might go something like this: "How is it that Tanya is working so hard at getting me to pay attention to her, yet I have no sense of her? How is it that she can get a whole group of people to be angry with her? How is she replicating, in this group, behavior that is problematic on the outside?" You cannot be effective with Tanya if all you feel toward her is annoyance. Instead, explore the context of how her behavior might make sense in her life. Alternatively, ask yourself, "Is there something I am doing that is making it difficult for her to be different in this group?"

Many times our most challenging members have become the people we most treasure.

At times student leaders comment that they would not want a particular member (such as Tanya) in their group because the person is problematic. We do our best to help them shift this attitude toward a more accepting stance because some members will go out of their way to make themselves unlovable. Oftentimes the members who do the most damage have also been the most damaged. As group leaders, we need to find a way to help members who affect us negatively to profit from the group despite our initial reaction to them. If we are able to see the difficult behavior as symptomatic of pain rather than as a sign of the person's character, we are more likely to develop patience and intervene effectively with this member. Many times our most challenging members have become the people we most treasure.

Storytelling

Self-disclosure is frequently misunderstood by some group members to imply a lengthy recitation of their lives, both past and present. If they are confronted about the excessive details of their history, they may express resentment, maintaining that they are risking disclosing themselves. In teaching group process, leaders need to differentiate between storytelling, which is merely talking about oneself or about others in great detail, and disclosure, which is talking about what a person is thinking and feeling now. Questions the leader should consider include the following: "Does the story help me to understand the member better, or does it distract me from hearing and understanding her problem?" "Does the story give me information to better assist the member in reaching his goal?"

During the beginning stages of a group, some members may express themselves through telling stories. People who are new to groups frequently need to hear facts about others or to share some of their own past to become comfortable in the group. However, if storytelling behavior becomes the norm (either for the whole group or for one member), the leader should recognize this problem and deal with it. For example, if Vincent presents a detailed story about how he is treated by his boss, we would be inclined to focus on how he is feeling rather than on the details of his story. We might intervene in this way: "How does this situation affect you? What is it like for you to have such a strained relationship with her? You seem to be talking more about your boss right now than about yourself. Tell us about *you*, Vincent." The group leader's task is to help members move beyond simply telling irrelevant stories and teach them to express themselves in personal and concrete ways. This requires active intervention on the leader's part. The group leader might say, "If I allowed you only one sentence to express what you have just said, what would it be?" Vincent's detailed story could be simply stated as "I resent my boss for the way she treats me!"

Leaders need to be able to distinguish between storytelling that is healing and meaningful to members and counterproductive storytelling. We can assist members in sharing the essence of their concern without getting lost in their story. For example, Angelica typically told every detail of her earlier experiences, but even though the group knew a lot about the events in her past, they knew very little about what she thought about or how she felt about what she had experienced. She believed she was being open in sharing her private life with the group, yet her group wanted to know more about how she was affected by her life situations. The group leader let her know that he was indeed interested in knowing her but that the information she was offering was not helping him do so.

Used as a defense, storytelling can be any form of talking about out-of-group life that is done in a detached manner. Although the member telling the story is giving many details, he or she is unknown. Feedback from the group given directly, without judgment, can assist the person to speak in personal terms and keep the focus on feelings, thoughts, and reactions. However, all storytelling should not be thought of as negative or as a sign of avoidance. Leaders can assist members in telling their stories in a way that is likely to keep the interest of others. Ultimately, members need to reveal their stories in ways that enable them to reach their personal goals. One way to enliven members' presentations of self is to ask them to write their stories as a homework assignment and then only share in the group what it was like to have done this assignment.

Questioning

Another counterproductive form of behavior in the group is questioning that resembles interrogation. Some members develop a style of relating that involves questioning others, and they intervene at inappropriate times in unhelpful ways. Leaders can teach people who habitually ask questions to see that this behavior generally is not helpful for them or for others. Asking questions of others may be a way of hiding, of remaining safe and unknown in a group. It also directs them toward others, not themselves. It is helpful to teach members that questions tend to direct people toward thinking and away from feelings they may be experiencing at the moment.

Rather than repeatedly saying "Don't ask questions; make statements," leaders can educate members about the function of questions and how asking questions often interferes with an individual's process. Questions can be very intrusive and put others on the spot while the questioner doesn't reveal anything about him- or herself. We usually invite the person asking the question to state what prompted him or her to ask the question. For example, if Miriam asked another member why he was so quiet, the leader could encourage her to say what had been going on in her mind before she asked the question. Miriam may tell the leader, "I noticed that Joel hardly says anything, and I'm interested in him and would like to get to know him." With such a statement Miriam discloses her investment in her question without putting Joel on the spot. Questions often arouse defensiveness, whereas personal statements are less likely to do so.

Because questions do not tell the entire story, we typically ask members who raise them to fill in the details. We might say: "What prompted you to ask . . . ?" "How come you want to know . . . ?" "What are you aware of right now that makes you want to ask that question?" Or "Tell [the person] what led up to your question." Here are some examples of questions and the possible hidden messages they contain:

- "How old are you?" ("I'm much older than you, and I wonder if I'll be able to identify with you.")
- "Why did you make Shirley cry?" ("I don't trust what you did, and I would never open myself up to you the way she did.")
- "Why do you push people so hard?" ("I'm scared, and I don't know how far I want to go.")
- "Why are you laughing?" ("I don't think you take seriously what goes on in this group.")
- "What do you think of me?" ("I like and respect you, and your view of me matters a lot.")

- "Why don't you leave your husband?" ("I care about you and the way you struggle, and I wonder what influences your decision to stay.")
- "Why do you always criticize your parents?" ("I'm a parent, and I wonder if my kids criticize me.")

Teaching members how to share themselves through statements rather than questioning is most effective when done in a timely, appropriate, and sensitive manner as these behaviors or interactions occur in the session.

Giving Advice

A problem behavior related to questioning is giving advice. It is one thing to offer a perception or an opinion to other members and quite another to tell people what they should feel or what they should or should not do. We often ask members to share the way in which they struggle with a particular problem rather than give others their suggested solutions to a problem. Giving advice is not always done directly, such as "I think what you ought to do is . . . ." The advice giving may be subtle: "You shouldn't feel guilty that your parents divorced because that was their decision and not something you made them do." Although this is true, the point is that the young woman does feel guilty and believes her parents might still be married if it had not been for her. It does not serve the best interest of the woman to advise her not to feel guilty. She has to resolve this feeling herself. The man who had a need to tell her that she shouldn't feel guilty could profit from examining his own motives for wanting to remove the guilt. What does it say about him? At this point the focus might be shifted to the person giving advice, and the meaning of his giving such advice can be explored.

Sometimes advice giving is less subtle. Nisha has been considering not only leaving her husband but also leaving her two teenage daughters with him. She thinks she wants to live alone, but she feels somewhat guilty. Robin intervenes: "Nisha, you owe it to yourself to do what you want to do. You have been the main caregiver for 9 years. Why not let him have major time with them?" This type of behavior raises a lot of questions about Robin. What are her values and possible unresolved problems? Why does she feel a need to so direct Nisha? Could Robin talk about herself instead of deciding what is best for Nisha? The group might now focus on Robin's need to provide others with solutions. Robin might learn about what she is getting from giving advice, and she may need to learn that what works for her might not work for others.

Advice giving has the tendency to interrupt the expression of thoughts and feelings and to increase dependency. If Nisha is given enough time to explore her conflict more fully, she will be better able to make her own decision. In essence, an abundance of advice tells her that she is not capable of finding her own way, and it conditions her to become more dependent on others for direction. Even if the advice given is helpful and sound, in the long run it does not teach Nisha the process of finding her own solutions to new problems as they occur. It is more helpful for members to share their own struggles than to provide ready-made solutions.

It is more helpful for members to share their own struggles than to provide ready-made solutions.

Both members and leaders need to acquire the skill of assisting others in arriving at their own insights about actions they need to take to bring about the changes they desire. Certainly leaders can provide information and ideas to members for coping with difficulties. However, it is more powerful and creates less dependency if members are first asked about their own thoughts about resolving challenging situations. By paying attention to the process rather than being wedded to a specific outcome, leaders can assist members in examining the consequences of their decisions and what outcomes they can best live with. For example, if a group member is contemplating whether to disclose that he is gay in his work environment, it is not our job to push him in a certain direction, nor is dispensing advice generally helpful. It is the client who must live with the decision he makes, not the leader. To help members learn how to solve problems, the leader may ask: "What have you done that has worked or not worked well for you?" "What advice might you give to yourself?" This may be especially relevant in working with members from cultures in which advice giving is seen as a positive way to connect with others.

As a group leader, you must be clear about the goals and purposes of the groups you design and facilitate. Furthermore, it is essential that you inform potential members about the purpose of the group during the screening and orientation meetings. Some psychoeducational groups are designed specifically to provide information and guidance and to teach specific skills. At times, people will join a group with the particular intention of getting advice on solving their problems. These group members may view you as an expert whose job it is to provide them with suggestions and specialized knowledge. Discuss the expectations of members who are seeking advice, and inform them if this is indeed something you will be offering.

Dependency

Group members who are excessively dependent typically look either to the group leader or to the other members to direct them and take care of them. Leaders sometimes foster member dependency. Some leaders have a great desire to be wanted and needed, and they feel a sense of importance when participants rely on them. This is an example of the leader's unmet psychological needs interfering with the therapeutic outcome of a group. Leaders may collude with members to form a dependent alliance for many reasons:

- The leader may need the economic rewards from the members' attendance.
- The group may be filling the leader's unmet needs for a social life.
- Some leaders have a need to be parental in the sense of directing others' lives.
- Leaders may rely on their groups as the primary source of feeling appreciated and recognized.
- Leaders may attempt to work through their own unresolved conflicts by using the group.

These examples show how the personality of the leader cannot be separated from what sometimes appears as problem behavior within the group. The behaviors of the leader and the members have a reciprocal effect on each other.

Dependent behavior is not always problematic. Such behavior needs to be viewed through a cultural lens to determine its function. What may be viewed in one culture as a manifestation of overly dependent behavior might well be viewed by another culture as an appropriate behavioral norm. As is true of seeking and giving advice, the member's cultural background must be considered along with their stated behavioral change goals.

Offering Pseudosupport

Like questioning and giving advice, providing inappropriate support needs to be examined for the meaning it holds for the person who offers it. People who have little tolerance for feeling their own pain may find it difficult to sit with the pain of others. These supportive individuals may attempt to distract a member who is expressing pain, not realizing the healing power of being able to share a painful experience. For example, Ernesto was finally able to feel his sadness over the distance between his sons and himself, and he cried as he talked about how much he wanted to be a better father. Before Ernesto could express what he was feeling, Randy put his hands on Ernesto's shoulders and tried to reassure him that he wasn't such a bad father because at least he lived with his kids. Randy might have wanted to make Ernesto feel better so that he himself would feel more comfortable. Members who want to bypass experiencing painful emotions often do so because of their own discomfort with these emotions. However, in the process of doing so, Ernesto was cut off from finally being able to express some of the sadness locked up inside of him.

There is a real difference between offering pseudosupport and behavior that is a genuine expression of care, concern, and empathy. When there is real caring, the interests of the members who are experiencing the pain are given paramount importance. Sometimes it is best to allow them to experience the depths of their pain; ultimately, they may be better off for having done so. The release of pain is often the necessary first step toward healing. This is a lesson that may need to be explicitly stated by the leader.

> The release of pain is often the necessary first step toward healing.

Touching can be a genuine expression of caring that comforts a member who is experiencing pain, but sometimes it can get in the member's way. It is useful to talk with members about the pros and cons of touch and of the ways in which it can support or interrupt a member's process. The motivation behind the touch is crucial. Does the person offering touch want to communicate "I can't tolerate seeing you in pain, and I want you to stop"? Or is the person saying "I know how hard this is for you, and I want you to know that I support you"? It is surprising to us how often people who are in pain accurately pick up the message of the touch.

Hostile Behavior

Hostility is difficult to deal with in a group because it is often indirect. Hostility can take the form of caustic remarks, jokes, sarcasm, and other passive-aggressive tactics. Members can express their resentment by missing group sessions, coming late, acting obviously detached, leaving the group, being overly polite, or rolling their eyes to express boredom or annoyance. Extremely hostile people are not good candidates for a group because they can have a devastating effect on the group climate. People are not going to make themselves vulnerable if there is a good chance that they will be ridiculed or in some other way devalued. If hostile behavior is not confronted in a group, it can hold the group members and the group process hostage. We have witnessed some situations in which the hostile member was so powerful that the other members did not want to confront the individual, thus giving him or her even more control over the group.

One way to deal with the person who behaves in a hostile way is to request that he or she listen without responding while the group members tell how they are being affected by that individual. The techniques for caring confrontation described earlier should be modeled in this discussion. Members can describe how they feel in the group with the hostile person and what they would like the person to do differently. Then it should be ascertained what the hostile individual wants from the group. Hostile behavior may be a manifestation of fear of getting intimate or of a limited capacity for vulnerability. If the fears underneath the hostility can be brought to the surface and dealt with, the hostility may decrease.

For example, Karl, who has a good relationship in the group with Sana, suddenly calls her a "control freak." Before she has a chance to express her surprise, hurt, and anger, he tells her that he sees his wife in her and that it is not really her he is upset with. Karl has attempted to take back what he said, yet Sana is still stuck with her hurt feelings. On an intellectual level Sana may understand that Karl is transferring his reactions to her, but on an emotional level she is hurt and has become distrustful of him. Sana needs some time to recover emotionally. Eventually, Karl acknowledges that he indeed had some negative feelings toward her personally, not just as his symbolic wife. But he wanted to quickly retreat when he saw that she had responded strongly.

Individuals who grew up in families in which they received attention primarily for negative behaviors often repeat these dynamics within the group by activating a negative response from both leaders and members. One member we worked with lashed out with criticism, hostility, and sarcasm whenever she felt a tinge of vulnerability. Kara's sarcasm was a mask she wore that externally communicated to others, "I don't care about you." Her more honest message might have been, "I care too much, and I'm afraid you'll hurt me." This type of behavior can be exhausting to deal with, and it is tempting for leaders to respond to this hostility with frustration and anger. By working with members to find the functions served by their hostility within the group as well as within their family history, "hostile" members can become less defensive. As with most of our defenses, hostility provides a barrier that protects us. If we first examine the way in which these behaviors serve us, it is easier to choose alternate and healthier methods of self-protection.

Acting Superior

Some group members take on an attitude of superiority. They may be moralistic and find ways to judge or criticize others for their behavior. They are unable to identify any pressing problems in their lives. Their attitude and behavior tend to have the same effect on a group as hostility. Participants freeze up, for they are more hesitant to expose their weaknesses to someone who projects an image of being perfect. Take the example of Arron, who says, "My problems are nothing compared to yours. I feel sorry that so many of you had such terrible childhoods, and I feel fortunate that my parents really loved me." Arron is likely to respond to someone who is sharing a problem with "I used to have your problem, but I don't anymore." He will antagonize others with comments such as "I can identify with you, because at one time I was where you are."

You can challenge Arron's comments by asking him what he wants from the group. Here is one possible intervention: "You're comparing your problems with those of others in here. What is it that you'd like to get from this group? How is it for you to be here? How are you being affected personally by what you're hearing? How does it feel that people are annoyed with you?" This intervention lessens the chances of pressuring Arron to come up with problems that he is likely to deny having. Instead, it gives him some room to talk about how he is being affected in the group. Taking an argumentative stance generally leads to a fruitless and frustrating debate. It is more constructive to explore the reasons Arron continues to come to the group.

Another option is to ask group members to respond to Arron by letting him know how his behavior is affecting them. It is important, however, that members speak about themselves and not judge Arron. Ask Arron if he is open to hearing feedback about how his behavior is affecting others, and be careful to moderate the amount of feedback given. If it appears that Arron is getting more feedback than he can assimilate at one time, the leader may intervene by saying, "Perhaps Arron has enough to think about right now. Let's focus more on what is going on with each of us." It is also crucial to block a tendency to use Arron as a scapegoat and to insist that he needs to have a problem.

Socializing

In certain groups, member socialization within the group, and even outside the group, is encouraged. When members meet outside of group sessions, group cohesion can be increased. They can extend what they are learning in their group to the informal gatherings. Such meetings can also be useful in challenging members to follow through with their plans and commitments. For some populations, such as an inpatient group for older adults, this may be their only network of support. Group leaders should have an open discussion with members about the ways in which these out-of-group relationships can be an asset and the types of problems that can arise when social relationships are formed and not managed well within a group dynamic.

Some types of out-of-group relationships can be problematic and impede group cohesion. This is especially true when participants form subgroups and talk about group matters but are unwilling to share what they talked about in the group sessions. Other signs that indicate counterproductive socializing include forming cliques and excluding certain members from such gatherings, forming romantic involvements without a willingness to share them in the group, refusing to challenge one another in the group for fear of jeopardizing friendships, and relying on the group exclusively as the source of social life.

When meetings outside of the sessions hamper group progress, it is crucial that this situation be openly examined by the group. You can ask the members if they are genuinely committed to developing the kind of group that will function effectively. You can help them see that forming cliques and making pacts to keep information out of the regular sessions is counterproductive and impedes group development.

Intellectualizing

Most of us rely on thinking, and nothing is amiss in using our intellectual faculties. When intellectualizing is used as a defense against experiencing feelings, however, it may become problematic in a person's life and in his or her functioning in a group. When group members discuss emotionally laden topics in a very detached way as though out of intellectual interest, they can be said to be intellectualizing. For maximum effect, it is best that cognitive and affective work be integrated.

People who intellectualize need to be made aware of what they are doing. A question you might raise with members who rely heavily on their intellect is this: "Does what you are doing most of the time get you what you want? Is this something you want to change?" Some experiential techniques (borrowed from Gestalt therapy and psychodrama) can be useful in helping these group members more directly experience the emotions associated with the events they talk about. Clients can be directed to reexperience events in the here and now through role playing.

Group leaders do well to avoid making quick judgments about members who do not readily display intense emotions and labeling them as "removed from their feelings" or "detached" or pathologizing in their interpersonal style. For many people, operating from a cognitive perspective may be more culturally appropriate than displaying feelings publicly. It is more beneficial to help members identify when this style of communication works for them, and the times when it works against them. It is easier to help members make adjustments to their defenses than to have them eradicate these coping mechanisms entirely.

It is important to avoid communicating that intellectualization is undesirable; the strengths of this type of communication should be acknowledged. Although it may not serve the person well relationally, this style of communication may be related to one's gender or vocation. Male clients are more apt to utilize intellectualization in their communication style as a result of gender socialization. For example, Miguel learned to use his intellect to get him through difficulties in his life. He admits that he would like to add an emotional dimension in addition to relying on his intellect. It is important to help Miguel see the use of intellectualization on a continuum, and to help him explore the ways in which it works for him and how it might not. If you approach Miguel with the goal of fine tuning his communication style as opposed to giving up his style, he is much more likely to be open to working on his learned patterns and consider augmenting his behaviors.

Members Becoming Assistant Leaders

Another way that group members may distance themselves is by aligning themselves with the leaders. These members protect themselves from vulnerability by developing an interpersonal style of taking on the role of assistant leaders, asking questions, probing for information, attempting to give advice, and paying attention to the dynamics of individuals and the group. Instead of paying attention to how they may be affected in the group, they shift the focus to others by making interventions and assuming a counselor's role. Members who take refuge in adopting such a role are deprived of the opportunity to work on the problems that brought them to the group in the first place. They can be challenged to evaluate whether what they are doing will get them what they ultimately want. It is necessary to deal with this problematic behavior because it is likely to be resented by other members, and it often impedes the progress of a group.

Recognizing this behavior as a possible defense, the leader can sensitively block it by pointing out to such members that they are depriving themselves of the maximum benefit from the group by paying more attention to others than to themselves. They joined the group to explore their own concerns, and they can lose sight of this goal if they leave themselves out of the process by constantly assuming leadership functions. These members should not be chastised or dismissed for their way of interacting; rather, they can be asked to look at the possible motivations for their behavior. They need to determine if they are pursuing their goals for this group experience.

LO9

Dealing With Defensive Behavior Therapeutically

Many interventions can facilitate working *with* challenging group members rather than fighting them. The statements that follow may help members get beyond their reluctance to fully participate. First we give examples of comments that illustrate a particular hesitation or difficulty. These are followed by several responses leaders may employ that often help clients move forward. Of course, not all these responses are made simultaneously to each member comment.

Randy: I don't know.

Leader: Pretend you know. And if you did know, what might you say?

What do you know?

What are you aware of as you look at me or others in the room?

Say the first thing that comes to your mind.

Henry [*during a role play*]: I don't know what to say to my father.

Leader: That's a good place to start. Tell him that.

If this is the last chance you have to speak to him, what do you want to tell him?

If you were your father, what would you want to say? If you were your father, what do you fear you would say?

Tell your father what stops you from talking to him.

Sylvana: I try so hard to say things the right way.

Leader: Say the first thing that comes to your mind right now.

Rehearse out loud.

What do you fear will happen if you say things the wrong way?

Kate: I don't want to be here.

Leader: Where would you rather be?

What makes it difficult for you to be here?

Who or what made you come here?

What made you come if you didn't want to be here today?

Valerie [*after an intense piece of work*]: I don't want the spotlight on me any longer.

Leader: What or whom do you want to get away from?

Go to a few people and finish the sentence: "I want to get away from you because . . ."

Say more about your feeling.

Sophia: I'm afraid to talk more about this.

Leader: Can you talk about what's stopping you?

What do you fear would happen if you said more?

What do you imagine will happen if you don't talk about it?

What would it take for you to feel safer in here?

I hope you'll say more about your fears of talking.

Several Members: It's far easier to talk in the coffee shop to other group members than it is to express ourselves here.

Leader: Form an inner circle. Imagine you're out having coffee. What are you saying to each other?

Say at least two things to several members about your difficulty in being here. (Some possibilities for incomplete sentences to be completed by a client are: "I find it hard to talk in here because . . . ," "I'm afraid to talk because . . . ," and "When I stop myself from talking, I'm most aware of. . . .")

Joel: I'm very uncomfortable with the anger in the group.

Leader: Tell those whom you see as angry how you're affected by them.

What happens [happened] when people express [expressed] their anger in your life? (Some possibilities for incomplete sentences to be completed by the client are: "I'm afraid to get angry like this because . . . ," "When you're angry with me, I . . . ," "I'm afraid of my anger because . . . ," and "When I witness anger, I want to. . . .")

Chelsea [*who typically engages in storytelling*]: But you don't understand. I need to tell you all the details so that you'll understand me.

Leader: Bear with me. I have a hard time following you when you give so many details. In one sentence, what do you most want me to hear?

What is it like not to feel understood in this group?

What is it like to discover that people don't want to hear your stories?

How does this story relate to the way you are struggling now in your life?

What makes it important that I listen to your story?

Erica: I feel that my problems are insignificant.

Leader: Whose problems in here are more important?

If you didn't compare your problems with those of others, what could you tell us about yourself?

How are you affected by hearing all these problems?

Tell us about one of your insignificant problems.

Skylar [*who has been feeling close to others in the group*]: I'm afraid of this closeness, because I'm sure it won't last.

Leader: What did you do to get close to people?

Tell a few people what scares you about remaining close to them.

Tell us how you can get close in here but not in your life.

What would it be like for you if you had people close to you? What is one thing that might keep you from maintaining the closeness you felt?

If nothing changed for you, how might this be? Tell us the advantages of isolating yourself.

Kyle [*who is typically silent*]: I don't think I need to be talking all the time. I learn a lot by observing.

Leader: Tell us some things you have been observing.

Are you satisfied with being silent, or would you like to change?

What are some of the things that make it difficult to speak out more?

Would you be willing to select two people you've been observing and tell them how they have affected you?

I'm interested in knowing what you have to say, and I'd like to hear from you.

When you observe me and quietly make assumptions about me, I feel uncomfortable. I'd like to be included in the conclusions you're drawing about me. I hope you are open to that.

When you don't talk about yourself, people are likely to project onto you, and there's a good chance you'll be misunderstood.

Perry [*who tends to give people advice*]: I think you should stop criticizing yourself because you're a wonderful person.

Leader: For several weeks now you've observed people in this room. Give each person an important piece of advice.

When you give advice, does it remind you of anyone you know?

How is it for you when your advice is rejected?

What triggers the advice you give to others?

Would you be willing to share what you are feeling when you give advice?

Are you able to receive advice from others? Is it always helpful?

Most of these suggestions for responses by the leader provide encouragement for members to say more rather than stopping at the point of initial resistance. The questions are open ended and are presented in an invitational manner. The interventions all grow out of clues provided by members, and they are designed to offer directions clients might pursue in becoming unstuck.

LO10

Dealing With Avoidance by the Whole Group

We have focused on how to deal therapeutically with the defensive behaviors of individuals, but sometimes an entire group exhibits behavior that makes it almost impossible to achieve a productive level of work. In this section we (Marianne and Jerry) describe one of our experiences when this was the case. This illustrates what might happen if an entire group makes the choice of not working and demonstrates an unwillingness to deal with several hidden agendas. We also describe some ways these hidden agendas affect the members as individuals as well as the group as a whole.

At one of our training workshops for group counselors, it was not possible to individually screen candidates. In lieu of screening, we provided all who were interested with a detailed letter describing the workshop and outlining our expectations of participants. We repeated this information at the first session, and participants had an opportunity to raise questions. It was especially crucial to us that they understood that they were to become personally involved and would function both as members and as coleaders during different sessions. The group was divided into two groups of eight. As supervisors, we changed groups after each 2-hour session. This change presented problems for some of the trainees, who said they were inhibited because the same supervisor was not continually in their group.

Group 1 was formed by people who got up and actively chose to be with one another. By contrast, Group 2 was largely formed by one member who remained seated and said: "I'm staying here. Anyone who wants to join my group can come over here." As the week progressed, some interesting differences arose between the two groups. Group 2 was characterized by an unwillingness to meaningfully interact with one another. Many of them complained that they had not understood that they were to become personally invested in the group process. They said they had expected to learn about groups by observing us do the work rather than by getting actively involved. Although a few of the members disclosed readily, others refused to share and did very little interacting, which eventually led to an increased sense of withholding on the part of all members.

The participants in Group 2 were apparently feeling many things that they had not disclosed. Some of them said that they were enjoying the group time, yet most of them were reticent to participate and appeared disinterested. During the breaks, members talked about difficulties they were experiencing in the sessions, but they did not bring this information back to their group. Two members ended a session with an unresolved conflict and decided to clear the air during the break, but they did not inform the group of the outcome. Only after some exploration by the supervisor did the members eventually acknowledge that they were preoccupied and concerned about the two people who had had the conflict. The supervisor attempted to teach again how subgrouping can be deleterious to a group's level of trust.

Several women in Group 2 confronted one of the male members in a harsh manner. When a supervisor asked how he was affected by the confrontations, he quickly insisted that he was fine. After several sessions, however, he unloaded on everyone in the group (including the supervisor) and let them know how angry he was. He declared that he was ready to leave. The group mood was again one of hesitancy, and members interacted very tentatively.

Group 2 members tended to compare themselves unfavorably to those in Group 1. During a combined session, people in Group 2 revealed the jealousy they had felt over the intensity and closeness that seemed to characterize Group 1.

On the next to last day, Group 2's level of trust remained minimal. The members showed great reluctance to be personal and to interact with one another. One of the supervisors (Jerry) again asked them to reflect on their level of trust and to assess the degree to which they were meeting their goals. He said to them: "This workshop is almost over. If today were the end, how would that be for you? If you aren't satisfied, what do you see that you can do to change the situation?" The members of Group 2 decided to have lunch together for the first time. The group sessions were scheduled to resume at 1 o'clock. When the group finally returned at 1:30, they were laughing and joking, obviously in a happy mood. They let the supervisor know what a wonderful time they had had at lunch and said they felt more comfortable and cohesive at lunch than they ever had in the group.

As a group we explored the dynamics of what was occurring. I (Marianne) confronted them by saying: "You say that talking at lunch was very easy and that you felt close to one another. You also say that when you come into this room, you feel stifled. What do you think is different?" Of course, the most obvious variable was the presence of the supervisor. As they began to open up, they initially lashed out at both supervisors. They perceived us as demanding too much, expecting them to be personal and academic at the same time, wanting them to perform, and demanding that they have problems (even if they didn't). They insisted that we had been unclear with them about our expectations. I listened to their grievances, attempting not to be defensive, which was not easy with the degree of hostility that was directed toward me. I did acknowledge that it was a difficult workshop and that indeed much was demanded of them, but I was not apologetic about my standards.

Finally, as a group, they admitted their envy over the intimacy the other group seemed to have, and they said they had tried to replicate this closeness at lunch. It was then that I challenged them again, as had Jerry before lunch, to reflect and begin to verbalize what they were rehearsing internally and what they were keeping from one another.

At the last session the members finally risked being more honest. They had taken our challenges seriously and had given thought to their behavior during the workshop. They were willing to take personal responsibility for their actions in the group, and there was no blaming. They accomplished more work in this final session because of their willingness to say what was on their minds. They learned in an experiential way that what they had not expressed during much of the week had kept them from having a productive group. Yet neither they nor we thought that their group had been a failure. They realized how their behavior had thwarted their progress as a group, and most were able to identify some of the ways in which their low level of risking had inhibited the trust level in their group. Because they were finally willing to talk in honest ways about their involvement in the group, they learned some important lessons about themselves as individuals as well as about the group process.

In the required follow-up papers, members of Group 2 wrote about their reactions during the week that they had never mentioned in the sessions. Had they chosen to express them at the time, we are quite certain their experience as a group and their individual experiences would have been very different. As supervisors, we experienced how draining it can be to work with a group that has a number of hidden agendas. Our experience has taught us the importance of making a commitment to face whatever may be going on, to bring hidden agendas to the surface, and, most of all, not to give up. As leaders we need to be careful not to indulge in our feelings of frustration and annoyance. It is not about us, but about how we can continue facilitating a group to a more productive level of work. Even though this group did not become cohesive, the members' willingness to process the group with us resulted in them learning important lessons about what had held them back as individuals and how this impasse at the transition stage had stalled their efforts to become a cohesive and working group.

Learning in Action

Barriers to Change

Contemplation is often the first stage of change. Even the thought of change is sometimes overwhelming and can stop a person before he or she has begun. Think of something you would like to change in yourself. For example, would you like to speak up more, or be less reactive when you feel angry? Once you have a specific goal in mind, create a collage. Using either a paper bag or a shoe box, decorate the outside of the bag or box with all of the images or words that symbolize the external barriers that you feel exist when you contemplate making this change. *External barriers* might be things such as a lack of support from others, limited resources, oppressive circumstances, or threat of negative reactions from others. Next, place images or words inside of the box or bag that symbolize the internal barriers that you engage in that keep you from reaching your desired change. *Internal barriers* to change are the beliefs we have about ourselves and the things we say that sabotage our successes along the way. They may also be behaviors that we engage in that stop us from moving in the direction of our desired change. Look through old magazines or newspapers to find images and words to use on your collage project, or draw or write your own images. Once you have completed the project, we encourage you to share it in your class or group.

Process Questions for Sharing

As you share your collage, consider discussing these ideas:

- What is the change you want to make, and how can you use the group to make this change?
- As you created your collage, what was the process of making it like for you? Did you struggle with it? What feelings came up for you, and what was your internal dialogue as you selected images and words and placed them on your collage?

- What external barriers did you identify?
- What internal barriers did you identify?
- What parts of your collage are you drawn to most?

Tips for Listening and Giving Feedback

- Refrain from making too many comments or asking questions of the person who is sharing the collage. As an observer, your role is to listen without making interpretations about what you see.
- If you do relate to what the person is sharing, be cautious in your comments so you do not take the spotlight away from the person who is sharing.

LO11

Dealing With Transference and Countertransference

As we have emphasized, when you are leading groups, strive to recognize how your own unresolved personal issues can feed into problematic behaviors in members. This interplay involves transference and countertransference. **Transference** consists of the feelings clients project onto the counselor. These feelings usually have to do with relationships the clients have experienced in the past. When such feelings are attributed to the group counselor, the intensity of the feelings may have more to do with unfinished elements in a member's life than with the current situation. Transference originating from the client's conflicts is considered a healthy and normal part of therapy, and the therapist's job is to remain neutral. **Countertransference** occurs when counselors project their own unresolved conflicts onto the client. If countertransference is not properly managed by the leaders, it can be damaging to members. Rather than attempting to eliminate countertransference, the leaders should use their reactions in productive and therapeutic ways. Group practitioners who are psychodynamically oriented recognize the value of understanding the dynamics of both transference and countertransference. These key concepts are fundamental to furthering the work that occurs in a group.

A group context has the potential for multiple transferences. Members may project not only onto the leaders but also onto other members in the group. Depending on the kind of group being conducted, members may identify people who elicit feelings in them that are reminiscent of feelings they have for significant people in their lives, past or present. Again, depending on the purpose of the group, these feelings can be productively explored so members become aware of how they are keeping these old patterns functional in present relationships. The group itself provides an ideal place to become aware of certain patterns of psychological vulnerability. Members can gain insight into the ways their unresolved conflicts create certain patterns of dysfunctional behavior. By focusing on what is going on within a group session, the group provides a dynamic understanding of how people function in out-of-group situations.

Group members bring their life history and previous experiences with them to the group. Some members may hold beliefs about individuals from different cultural groups that interfere with their ability to connect with or to trust other group members or the group leader. For example, a man who identifies himself as gay may have experienced numerous judgments and rejections from the heterosexual community and therefore may have made an early decision that the heterosexual members are not going to accept him. One of the benefits of a therapeutic group is that members can explore how their past experiences are playing out in present interactions.

When group members appear to work very hard at getting the facilitator to reject them, it can be therapeutically useful to explore what potential gains they may be deriving from this self-defeating behavior. The transference reactions members develop toward the group leader and other members can bring out intense feelings in those who are the target of this transference. Handled properly in the therapeutic setting, members can experience and express feelings and reactions toward others in the group and discover how they are projecting outside situations onto the group. When these feelings are productively explored in the group, members often are better able to express their reactions appropriately.

Group leaders would do well to consider their countertransference as a possible cause of difficulties that develop in a group. Leaders can project their own problems and unfinished business onto "difficult members." Furthermore, some leaders have not recognized their own power and privilege and feel powerless when they are confronted by members who challenge their authority or competence. If leaders are not willing to deal with their own issues, how can they expect members to take the risks necessary for them to change? As you reflect on ways you may be emotionally triggered in groups you lead, examine your response to members that you perceive as being difficult. Remember, it is generally not useful to assume that your clients merely want to annoy you. Ask yourself these questions:

It is generally not useful to assume that your clients merely want to annoy you.

- How do I respond to the different forms of transference exhibited by members?
- What kind of transference tends to elicit my countertransference?
- Do I take the defensiveness of members in a personal way?
- Do I blame myself for not being skillful enough?
- Do I become combative with clients I view as problematic?
- Does the way in which I respond to problematic behaviors tend to increase or decrease defensiveness on the part of members?

As a group leader, you are faced with the task of dealing with the transference reactions members develop toward you, but the solution is often complex and depends on the circumstances under which the relationship develops. Do not quickly discount members' reactions to you as mere transference. Be willing to explore the possibility that members have genuine reactions to the way you have dealt with them. Do not believe uncritically whatever group members tell you, particularly initially. Be careful about quickly accepting some unrealistic attributions of group members. On the other hand, avoid being overly critical and discounting genuine positive feedback. All members who see a leader as helpful or wise do not have "transference disorders." Members can feel genuine affection and respect for group leaders. By the same token, just because participants become angry with you does not mean that they are transferring anger toward their parents onto you. They might well feel genuine anger and have negative reactions toward you personally largely because of certain behaviors you display. It takes courage on your part to acknowledge that you may have been insensitive to a client and are now receiving warranted reactions. However, members will frequently treat you as if you were a significant figure in their lives, and you get more reactions than you deserve. This is especially likely to be true if members exhibit intense feelings toward you when they have had very little contact with you. In short, all feelings that members direct toward the group leader should not be "analyzed" as transference to be "worked through" for the client's good. A useful guideline that we apply to ourselves is that if we hear a consistent pattern of feedback, then we seriously examine what is being told to us. When we see the validity of this feedback, we are likely to make some changes in our behavior.

The well-known Gestalt therapist Erving Polster (1995) avoids thinking in terms of transference phenomenon because he believes the concept of transference can have depersonalizing effects. Instead, Polster emphasizes the experience of real contact between client and therapist: "the contact experience is composed of telling, responding, suggesting, laughing, experimenting—everything that is actually going on. Adding to the power of this contactful engagement, however, is the symbolic component, which is represented by transference" (p. 190). For Polster, focusing on transference takes the therapist out of the here-and-now relationship by discounting what is actually going on in the therapeutic encounter. In addition, when therapists make interpretations of certain events, they may mistakenly discredit a client's own experience of those events. Thus the conceptualization of transference may result in diminished connectedness.

It is important to consider both members' reactions based on reality and those representing the symbolic component of transference. Even if you strongly suspect transference feelings, you would be discounting the person if you said, "I think you are projecting. This isn't about me." A less defensive response is, "Tell me more about how I affect you." This intervention elicits additional information about how the group member developed a set of reactions to you. The timing of making such a statement is crucial, and it is important to explore the member's reactions prior to suggesting any interpretation of the member's behavior.

When group members identify you as an object of transference, there is the potential for good therapeutic work. You can take on a symbolic role and allow the person to talk to you and work through unfinished business. Additionally, you and the person can engage in role reversal as a way to explore feelings and to gain insight. Assume that a member (Paul) becomes aware that he is behaving around you much as he does with his father. During a role play in which he is talking to you as his father, he says, "I don't feel important in your life. You're too busy and never have time for me. No matter what I do, it's never enough for you. I just don't know how to go about getting your approval." Because you do not know how Paul's father relates to him, you could ask Paul to take on the role of his father by responding as he imagines that his father would respond. After Paul has several interchanges in which he is both himself and his father, you will have a clearer sense of how he struggles with his father. With this information, you can help him work through his unresolved issues with both his father and with you. Through the process of his therapeutic work, Paul may be able to see you as the person you are rather than as the father with whom he is struggling. He might also gain awareness of the ways he talks to his father and how he transfers his feelings toward him to others in everyday life.

These are but a few illustrations of how transference problems can be worked through. The important elements are that these feelings first (1) be recognized and expressed and then (2) be interpreted and explored in a therapeutic way. Interpreting transference is a route to elucidating the group member's intrapsychic life (Wolitzky, 2011b). Interpretations can be offered in a collaborative manner to help group members make sense of their lives and to expand their consciousness. The group leader needs to use the member's reactions as a gauge in determining a member's readiness to make an interpretation. It is important that interpretations be appropriately timed because the group member will reject poorly timed interpretations given by leaders.

A more delicate issue is how the leader can best deal with feelings toward a group member. Even in the psychoanalytic tradition, which dictates that therapists spend years in analysis to understand and resolve blocked areas, countertransference is a potential problem. It can be a big problem for the beginning group leader. Some people are attracted to this profession because, on some level, they imagine that as a helper they will be respected, needed, admired, looked to as an expert, and even loved. Perhaps they have never experienced the acceptance and self-confidence in their ordinary lives that they feel while helping others. Such leaders may be using groups to fulfill needs that would otherwise go unmet.

The leader's countertransference reactions are inevitable because we all have unresolved conflicts, personal vulnerabilities, and unconscious "soft spots" that are activated through our professional work (Curtis & Hirsch, 2011; Hayes, Gelso, & Hummel, 2011; Wolitkzy, 2011a). Self-knowledge and supervision are central factors in learning to deal effectively with both members' transference and your own countertransference reactions. Your blind spots can easily hamper your ability to deal with various difficult behaviors displayed by members or with your old wounds that surface as you work with the members' pain. Ongoing supervision will enable you to accept responsibility for your reactions and at the same time prevent you from taking full responsibility for directions that specific members take. Meeting with your coleader to talk about how you are affected by certain members is an excellent way to get another's perspective on difficult situations.

Recognize that not all of your feelings toward members can be classified as countertransference. You may be operating under the misconception that you should remain objective and care for all members equally. Countertransference is indicated by exaggerated and persistent feelings that tend to recur with various clients in various groups. You can expect to enjoy some members more than others, yet all the members of your group deserve a chance to be respected and liked by you. It is important that you recognize your own feelings for what they are and that you avoid emotional entanglements that are not therapeutic.

The issue of power is relevant to understanding countertransference. As group members elevate the leader to the level of expert, perfect person, or demanding parent, members give away most of their power. A self-aware therapist who is interested primarily in clients' welfare will not encourage members to remain in an inferior position. The insecure leader who depends on clients' subordinate position for a sense of adequacy and power will tend to keep the group members powerless.

We do not want to convey the impression that it is inappropriate for you to meet some of your needs through your work. Nor are we suggesting that you should not feel powerful. In fact, if you are not meeting your needs through your work, we think you are in danger of losing your enthusiasm. But it is crucial that you do not exploit the members as a way of fulfilling yourself. The problem occurs when you put your own needs first or when you fail to be sensitive to the needs of group members.

Countertransference feelings are likely to develop in the romantic or sexual realm, particularly when a group member indicates a romantic interest in a group leader. Group leaders may never have felt desirable before assuming their professional role. Now that they do, there is the danger that they will depend on group members for this feedback. Through your training, you may have the opportunity to explore with a supervisor your feelings of attraction or repulsion toward certain members. If you are conducting groups independently and become aware of a pattern that indicates possible countertransference problems, seek consultation with another therapist to work through these problems.

Critical Incident

Overcorrecting for Fear of Overidentifying

1. Description of Incident

During the fifth session of an inpatient eating disorder group, Reem, the only Persian member in the group, shared her experiences as a minority woman in her master's program. Initially Reem spoke about feeling that she did not fit in with her classmates because of her ethnicity. She shared that she often felt she had to prove herself to her classmates and professors. The rest of the group began asking questions about her experiences, to which Reem responded, "None of you will every fully understand me because you are not Persian and don't know what it's like to be a minority." Another group member, Chelsea, became defensive and said that her best friend was Persian. Chelsea went on to share that her friend often talked about the cultural differences between them and that she felt as if her friend was overemphasizing their differences and sometimes saw her as "complaining too much." The discussion between Reem and Chelsea grew in intensity as the group members sat silent and anxiously watched the interchange.

The group leader felt caught off guard and didn't know how to best address the situation in the moment. The leader, who was also a Persian woman, was struggling to sort through her own internal conflict about how to intervene. The leader felt that Chelsea was invalidating Reem's experiences and shifting the focus onto herself. If the leader intervened on behalf of Reem, however, she feared it would appear that she was being "biased and fostering an unfair alliance with Reem." The leader was also worried that it might look as if she were "rescuing" Reem if she were to say anything to Chelsea.

2. Process Questions for Group Leaders

1. Have you ever felt immobilized as a group leader because you were concerned about how your intervention would be perceived?
2. Do you think it would have been appropriate for the leader to share some of her internal struggle about responding to Reem and Chelsea with the group? Why or why not?

continued

3. What potential harm could have come from the leader sharing her own experience as a Persian woman or confirming what Reem was sharing?
4. What potential benefits might there have been for the leader identifying with Reem?
5. Could the leader have helped Chelsea see the impact of her comments without speaking for Reem or coming to her "rescue," as the leader feared it might appear?
6. What differences exist, if any, when a Caucasian leader or a leader of color intervenes using his or her cultural identity and experiences?

3. Clinical Reflections

The leader in this incident was so fearful of overidentifying with Reem that she temporarily missed seeing the potential benefits of having a group member and leader with cultural commonalities. Her internal struggle inhibited her from intervening therapeutically with the group. As a person of color, she has likely experienced some of the judgments and the need to seek the approval of others about which Reem had spoken. Ironically, the leader was holding her self back in ways similar to those of the member. What would it have been like for the leader to feel free enough to share her own struggle in the moment with the group members? Sharing her own process of not wanting to appear to be unfairly aligning with Reem or coming to her rescue may have freed the leader to make an intervention. She also could have given the group members more insight into what it feels like to be different from everyone else, validating Reem's experiences of feeling like "no one in the group would ever understand her." Most interventions leaders make will have an impact on members, and we often cannot predict the outcome of what we share in group. One potential downside of the leader not intervening in this incident is that Reem may have felt abandoned and even more misunderstood then before sharing her story. In an effort to keep the entire group comfortable, the leader missed an opportunity for a teachable moment.

4. Possible Interventions

1. The leader could model to the group members the benefits of editing aloud by sharing with them some of her own internal struggle. For example, she might say, "I want to talk about the ways in which I identify with Reem as a fellow Persian woman, but I find myself aware of how others might perceive this as me taking sides." Saying this potentially frees the leader to share her feelings while inviting members to comment and react to what she is saying. It then becomes a group conversation that is relevant to the cultural issues already shared by Reem and Chelsea. By sharing her own thoughts and feelings, the leader could help create trust and authenticity within the group.
2. The leader could share her internal struggle and ask all the members if they see any similarities to what the leader is feeling in the group and the experiences Reem shared about graduate school. Again this uses the leader's reactions but places the work on the group rather than on the leader.
3. The leader could use her personal experiences without stating directly that they are her own. The leader may have some understanding of what Reem is saying, and the leader can share some of that knowledge with the group without necessarily disclosing her own story. Depending on the theoretical orientation of the leader as well as her personal comfort level, this gives her options for using her identity and intervening.
4. The leader might ask group members to share a time when they felt left out of a group.
5. Ask Reem and Chelsea if they will participate in a role play. Reem could be asked to look at Chelsea and complete a few unfinished sentences: "One way I feel different from you is . . ." "A way I perceive you don't understand me is . . ." Reem could also make the rounds of all the members and complete the sentence, "One way I feel different from you is . . ."

   During this role-play exercise, group members could be asked to avoid responding and to simply take in what they hear Reem saying. If Reem stays focused on the theme of her difference, members gain information about how she sees herself as being different. It may also give Chelsea some insight about her friend outside of the group.
6. The leader may say, "I am having a reaction to Reem and Chelsea's discussion, and I am willing to share my reaction, but I want to invite other group members to share how they are experiencing Reem and Chelsea's discussion first." Inviting group members to share their thoughts first may facilitate the group's process of moving into the working stage.

LO12

Coleader Issues at the Transition Stage

As you can see, the transition stage is a critical period in the history of the group. Depending on how conflict and resistance are handled, the group can take a turn for the better or for the worse. If you are working with a coleader, you can efficiently use the time you have for meeting before and after sessions to focus on your own reactions to what is occurring in the group. Here are a few problems that can develop between leaders at this time.

Negative Reactions Toward One Leader If members direct a challenge or express negative reactions toward a coleader, it is important to avoid either taking sides with your colleague in attacking clients or siding with the members in ganging up against the coleader. Instead, nondefensively (and as objectively as possible) continue your leadership by facilitating a constructive exploration of the situation. You might do this by asking the member who has a reaction to your coleader to speak directly to him or her. You could also invite your coleader to say *what* he or she is hearing and *how* he or she is being affected.

Challenges to Both Leaders Several members may direct criticism to both you and your coleader, saying, "You leaders expect us to be personal in here, but we don't know anything about you that's personal. You should be willing to talk about your problems if that's what you expect us to do." In such a case, difficulties can develop if one of you responds defensively while the other is willing to deal with this confrontation from the members. Ideally, both leaders should talk about the confrontation objectively. If not, this disagreement would surely be a vital topic to discuss in the coleaders' meeting outside of the group or during a supervision session. All such difficulties should not be reserved for a private discussion between coleaders. As much as possible, matters that pertain to what is happening during sessions should be discussed with the entire group.

Dealing With Problem Behaviors We have discussed a variety of difficult member behaviors that you and your coleader may have to confront. We want to caution against the tendency of coleaders to chronically discuss what such members are doing or not doing and never to explore how such behavior affects them as leaders. It is a mistake to dwell almost exclusively on strategies for "curing" problem members while ignoring your own personal reactions to such problematic behaviors.

Dealing With Countertransference It is not realistic to expect a leader to work equally effectively with every member. At times ineffectiveness results from countertransference reactions on the part of one of the leaders. For example, a male leader could have strong and irrational negative reactions to one of the women in the group. It may be that he is seeing his ex-wife in this member and responding to her in nontherapeutic ways because of his own unresolved issues over the divorce. When this situation occurs, the coleader can be therapeutic for both the member and the leader who is not being helpful. The colleague can intervene during the session itself as well as exploring these countertransference reactions with the other leader outside the session. Coleaders who are willing to be objective and honest with each other can have a positive impact through this process of mutual confrontation.

Journal Prompts

The following questions are meant to serve as prompts for members of a group during the transition stage. If you are conducting groups, you might find these useful for your group members to either discuss in group or journal about between sessions. In addition, think about your responses to these questions as either a real or imagined group member.

1. In what ways were you concerned or aware of being accepted or rejected by the group or individual members?
2. How did you test leaders or other members in the group to see if the group was safe for you?
3. In what ways did you play it safe or take risks in the group?
4. How did you express or navigate issues of control and power in the group?
5. What did you observe in leaders to determine whether they were trustworthy or not?

Points to Remember

Transition Stage of a Group

Transition Stage Characteristics

The transition phase of a group's development is marked by feelings of anxiety and defenses in the form of various behavior patterns.

- Members are concerned about what they will think of themselves if they increase their self-awareness and about others' acceptance or rejection of them.
- Members test the leader and other members to determine how safe the environment is.
- Members struggle between wanting to play it safe and wanting to risk getting involved.
- Control and power issues may emerge, or some members may experience conflict with others in the group.
- Members observe coleaders to determine whether they are trustworthy.
- Members learn how to express themselves so that others will listen to them.

Member Functions

A central role of members at this time is to recognize and deal with the many forms of resistance.

- Members recognize and express any persistent reactions; unexpressed feelings may contribute to a climate of distrust.
- Members respect their own defenses but work with them.

- Members move from dependence to independence.
- Members learn how to confront others in a constructive manner so that they do not retreat into defensive postures.
- Members face and deal with reactions toward what is occurring in the group.
- Members work through conflicts rather than remaining silent or forming subgroups outside of the sessions.

Leader Functions

The major challenge facing leaders during the transition period is to provide a safe environment with clear boundaries. Another challenge is to intervene in the group in a sensitive and timely manner. The major task is to provide the encouragement and the challenge necessary for members to face and resolve conflicts and negative reactions that exist within the group and certain behaviors that stem from their defenses against anxiety. To meet this challenge, leaders have the following tasks:

- Teach members the value of recognizing and dealing fully with conflict situations.
- Assist members in recognizing their own patterns of defensiveness.
- Teach members to respect anxiety and defensive behavior and to work constructively with attempts at self-protection.
- Provide a model for members by dealing directly and tactfully with any challenges, either personal or professional.
- Avoid labeling members, but learn how to understand certain problematic behaviors.
- Assist members to become interdependent and independent.
- Encourage members to express reactions that pertain to here-and-now happenings in the sessions.

Exercises

Self-Assessment Scale for Group Members

This self-assessment is primarily aimed at helping group members evaluate their behavior in a group, but it also can be used by group leaders. Use this self-assessment scale to determine your strengths and weaknesses. Rate yourself as you see yourself at this time. If you have not had some type of group experience, rate yourself in terms of your behavior in the class you are in now. This exercise can help you determine the degree to which you may be a productive group member. If you identify specific problem areas, you can decide to work on them in your group.

After everyone has completed the inventory, the class should break into small groups, each person trying to join the people he or she knows best. Members of the groups should then assess one another's self-ratings.

Rate yourself from 1 to 5 on each of the following self-descriptions using this scale:

5 = This is almost always true of me.
4 = This is frequently true of me.
3 = This is sometimes true of me.
2 = This is rarely true of me.
1 = This is never true of me.

_____ **1.** I am readily able to trust others in a group.
_____ **2.** Others tend to trust me in a group situation.
_____ **3.** I disclose personal and meaningful material.
_____ **4.** I am willing to formulate specific goals and contracts.
_____ **5.** I am generally an active participant as opposed to an observer.

_____ **6.** I am willing to openly express my feelings about and reactions to what is occurring within a group.

_____ **7.** I listen attentively to what others are saying, and I am able to discern more than the mere content of what is said.

_____ **8.** I do not give in to group pressure by doing or saying things that do not seem right to me.

_____ **9.** I am able to give direct and honest feedback to others, and I am open to receiving feedback about my behavior from others.

_____ **10.** I prepare myself for a given group by thinking of what I want from that experience and what I am willing to do to achieve my goals.

_____ **11.** I avoid monopolizing the group time.

_____ **12.** I avoid storytelling by describing what I am experiencing now.

_____ **13.** I avoid questioning others; instead I make direct statements to them.

_____ **14.** I am able to be supportive of others when it is appropriate without giving pseudosupport.

_____ **15.** I am able to confront others in a direct and caring manner by letting them know how I am affected by them.

Scenarios for Exploration

Many of the following exercises are ideally suited for small group interaction and discussion. Explore these questions from the vantage point of a group leader.

1. **Working With Members' Fears**. Assume that various members make these statements:
   - "I'm afraid of looking like a fool in the group."
   - "My greatest fear is that the other members will reject me."
   - "I'm afraid to look at myself because, if I do, I might discover that I'm empty."
   - "I'm reluctant to let others know who I really am because I've never done it before."

With each of these statements, what might you say or do? Can you think of ways to work with members who express these fears?

2. **Moving Beyond Playing It Safe**. Imagine that you are leading a group that does not seem to want to get beyond the stage of "playing it safe." Members' disclosures are superficial, their risk-taking is minimal, and they display a variety of resistances. What might you do in such a situation? How do you imagine you would feel if you were leading such a group?
3. **Confronting Conflicts**. Assume that there is a good deal of conflict in a group you are leading. When you point this discord out to members and encourage them to deal with it, most of them tell you that they do not see any point in talking about the conflicts because "things won't change." What might be your response? How would you deal with a group that seemed to want to avoid facing and working with conflicts?
4. **Intervening With a Silent Member**. Betty is a group member who rarely speaks, even if encouraged to do so. What are your reactions to the following leader interventions?
   - Ignore her.
   - Ask others in the group how they react to her silence.
   - Remind her of her contract detailing her responsibility to participate.
   - Ask her what is keeping her from contributing.
   - Frequently attempt to draw her out.

What interventions would you be likely to make?

5. **Redirecting a Questioner**. Larry has a style of asking many questions of fellow group members. You notice that his questioning has the effect of distracting members and interfering with their expression of feelings. What are some things you might say to him?
6. **Confronting a Member Who Is Storytelling**. Jessica has a habit of going into great detail in telling stories when she speaks. She typically focuses on details about others in her life, saying little about how she is affected by them. Eventually, another member says to her, "I'm really having trouble staying with you. I get bored and impatient with you when you go into such detail about others. I want to hear more about you and less about others." Jessica responds, "That really upsets me. I feel I've been risking a lot by telling you about problems in my life. Now I feel like not saying any more!" What interventions would you make at this point?
7. **Addressing Hostility of Group Members**. Imagine that you have been meeting with a group of middle school children whose parents are incarcerated. The members have begun to develop strong connections to you and to one another. Several of the members have opened up about some painful memories they have endured. One member of the group begins to lash out and "pick fights" with other members. He also uses racial slurs and makes homophobic comments when certain members speak up. Another member remarks, "This is stupid, I'm not coming to group anymore." Form small groups to consider these questions:
    - What are some of the dynamics you see occurring in the group?
    - What motivations might be behind these problem behaviors?
    - How would you respond to the racial slurs and homophobic comments made by one member, and what strategies would you use with the member who doesn't want to return?
    - How would you go about processing all of this within the group?
8. **Assessing Your Experiential Group**. If you are involved in an experiential group as part of your group class, this is a good time to assess any characteristics in your group that are typical of the transition stage. Assess your own level of participation in the group. What changes, if any, would you like to make as a member of your group? As a group, spend some time exploring these questions:
    - How is resistance being dealt with in the group?
    - How trusting is the climate?
    - If conflict is present, how is it being dealt with and how does this influence the group process?
    - Are any hidden agendas present?
    - What are you learning about what makes groups function effectively or what gets in the way of effective group interaction?

Questions for Discussion

Select one or more of these questions for exploration in a small group in the classroom:

- How do you understand the concept of resistance? What alternative concepts can you think of to explain what is often viewed as resistance?
- What member behavior would you find most difficult or challenging to deal with as a leader? Why? How do you think this member's behavior is likely to affect the way you lead the group?

- How would you intervene if a member remained silent? What factors might explain the lack of participation by a group member?
- What would you say or do if a group member reminds you of someone in your life? How would you deal with this potential countertransference?
- How can you challenge members in a caring way without increasing their defensiveness?
- What cultural dimensions will you need to consider before confronting a member?

Guide to Groups in Action: Evolution and Challenges DVD and Workbook

Evolution of a Group

Here are some suggestions for making effective use of this chapter along with the transition stage segment of *Evolution of a Group*, the first program in *Groups in Action*.

1. **Characteristics of the Transition Stage**. In this chapter we identify some key characteristic of groups in transition. As you view the DVD, what characteristics do you observe unfolding in the group during the transition stage?
2. **Common Fears of Members**. Some common fears are typical during the transition stage. On the DVD members articulate some of their fears. What kind of fears might you have if you were in this type of group?
3. **Dealing With Conflict and Confrontation**. Although conflict often occurs during the transition stage, it can surface during the initial group session. On the DVD conflict occurs during both the initial and the ending stages. Did you learn anything about how to deal with conflict, regardless of when it occurs, from viewing the sessions? What are the possible consequences of ignoring conflict or dealing with it ineffectively? What guidelines would you want to teach members of your group about how to confront effectively?
4. **Using the Workbook**. If you are using the DVD and workbook, refer to Segment 3: Transition Stage of the workbook and complete all the exercises. Take the self-inventory and review the Coreys' commentary.

Challenges Facing Group Leaders

Here are some suggestions for making effective use of this chapter along with the first segment of *Challenges Facing Group Leaders*, the second program in *Groups in Action*.

1. **Characteristics of the Transition Stage**. As you view this second program, what characteristics do you observe in this group that are typical of the transition stage?
2. **Challenges During the Transition Stage**. As coleaders, we see our task as intervening in a way that makes the room safe and provides a climate whereby members can talk about their hesitations. What is the importance of carefully working with whatever members bring to a group regarding their fears, concerns, or

reservations? How is this transitional work essential if you hope to help a group move to a deeper level of interpersonal interaction? From reading this chapter and viewing the DVD, what are you learning about the leader's task during the transition stage in a group?

3. **Problem Behaviors and Difficult Group Members**. As you watch and study Segment 1, notice signs of problematic behaviors on the part of members. Also notice signs of defensiveness and reluctance and how members express and work with their resistance. The themes that are enacted in segment one of the DVD are illustrative of challenges that group leaders typically encounter in many different groups. These themes include the following:

   - Checking in: What was it like to return to group?
   - The leaders let me down.
   - I'm not feeling safe in here.
   - I didn't want to come back to group.
   - I'm in this group against my will.
   - Emotions make me uncomfortable.
   - I'm self-conscious about my accent.
   - I want the leaders to disclose more.
   - I learn a lot by being quiet.
   - Silence serves a function.
   - I feel pressured to disclose.
   - What's wrong with helping others?
   - Can't we stop all this conflict?
   - I feel weak when I show feelings.
   - Checking out: What are each of you taking from this session?

   In small groups, explore these questions: What kind of difficult group member would present the greatest challenge to you? Do you have any ideas about why a certain problematic member might "trigger" you more than others? What do you see the coleaders doing when members display behaviors that could be seen as problematic? What lessons are you learning about how to work therapeutically with resistance of group members? How can you apply the discussion of reframing resistance in this chapter to better understand what is going on in the DVD?

4. **Challenging Members and Creating Linkages**. Establishing trust is especially important as members identify some of the ways they typically protect themselves and express how they are holding back. What are you learning about the critical balance between support and confrontation? As you watch the first segment, how are members being challenged? How do they respond? As coleaders, we are consistently asking members to say more about what they are thinking and feeling as it pertains to being in the group. We also look for opportunities for members to establish linkages with one another and to talk to each other directly in the group. What are you learning about how to encourage members to express themselves more fully?

5. **Using the Workbook**. If you are using the DVD and workbook, refer to Segment 1: Challenges of Dealing With Difficult Behaviors in Group of the workbook and write your comments in the "Reflection and Responses" section. Review the Coreys' reflections on the session and their commentary.

MindTap for Counseling

Additional resources can be found on CengageBrain.com and by logging into the MindTap course created by your professor. There you will find a variety of study tools and useful resources that include quizzes, videos, interactive exercises, and more.

8

CHAPTER

Working Stage of a Group

CHAPTER LEARNING OBJECTIVES

1 Describe the dynamics associated with group process and development (CACREP, 2016, Standard B)

2 Demonstrate various leader interventions for exploring a member's fears at various stages of a group

3 Identify and define the key characteristics of a group during the working stage

4 Highlight the differences between a working group and a nonworking group

5 Identify ethical and culturally relevant strategies for designing and facilitating groups (CACREP, 2016, Standard G)

6 Become familiar with choices to be made during the working stage

7 Discuss the specific therapeutic factors and how they contribute to group effectiveness (CACREP, 2016, Standard C)

8 Present guidelines for member self-disclosure

9 Present guidelines for leader self-disclosure

10 Describe guidelines for giving and receiving feedback

11 Identify coleader issues at the working stage

You have been conducting a domestic violence group for male offenders for the past several months. In your last meeting, one of the members began to talk about his experiences of being raised in a home with violence and severe domestic abuse. The member went into painful details about an incident in which his father was drunk and almost killed his mother. As the member shared his story, other group members seemed visibly affected. Some were fighting back tears, and others were agitated. One member who rarely participated remarked, "Your story is so disturbing. I can hardly stand listening to it." The member who shared his experiences replied, "I've never talked about this stuff to anyone before. It feels like a weight is off of me to finally say it out loud." Another member responded by telling him that he was brave to tell his story and then revealed his own history of having been abused as a child.

- What would you say to the members who disclosed their stories of abuse?
- Would you address the reactions of the other members?
- How would you decide which member to attend to when several had observable emotional reactions?
- Are there any ethical or legal implications related to these disclosures?
- How might you link the members' acts of domestic violence to their own victimization as children?
- If a member were to ask, "Why do we need to talk about all these painful experiences?" how would you reply?
- How would you handle the situation if your own painful childhood memories were evoked?

Introduction

The working stage is characterized by the commitment of members to explore significant problems they bring to the sessions and by their attention to the dynamics within the group. At this time in a group's evolution, we find that less structuring and intervention is required than during the initial and transition stages. By the working stage, participants have learned how to involve themselves in group interactions without waiting to be invited into an interaction. As members assume greater responsibility for the work that occurs, they play a key role in the direction a group takes. This does not mean that the members become coleaders, but members do initiate work more readily.

There are no arbitrary dividing lines between the phases of a group. In practice there is considerable overlapping of stages, and this is especially true of movement from the transition stage to the working stage. For example, assume that Vance says, "There is something I want to talk about, but I'm afraid that some people might make fun of me." If Vance stops with this comment and declines an invitation to say more, his behavior would be transitional. However, if he decides to go further, he may discover that the very people he feared would make fun of him support him. With that decision and Vance's willingness to express what is on his mind, he may be able to accomplish deeper work.

Groups do not all evolve to a true working level, but significant work takes place at every stage of a group. Even when groups are stuck, embroiled in conflict, or when members are extremely anxious and hesitant, many lessons can be learned. Some groups may not reach the working stage because members do not develop sufficient trust, cohesion, and continuity. As we described earlier, group participants who are unwilling to deal with hidden agendas, refuse to work with conflicts that are obvious, lack the motivation to participate in a group, or are stopped by their anxieties and fears are unable to create the climate and cohesion within the group that allows for deeper exploration. Factors such as time limits and shifting membership from session to session also may contribute to a group not reaching a working stage.

Being in a working stage as a group does not imply that all members function optimally. All members are not at the same level of readiness. Indeed, some members may be on the fringe, some may not yet be ready for in-depth exploration, and some may not feel they are an integral part of the group. Conversely, a difficult group might well have one or more members who are willing to engage in productive work. Some may be more motivated than others, and some may be less willing to take risks. Individual differences among members are characteristic of all group stages.

Here are some of the questions we examine in this chapter:

- How does a leader facilitate a group's movement from the transition stage to the working stage?
- Once a member identifies a fear, how might you work differently with this fear depending on the stage of a group's development?
- What are some of the factors that influence change within an individual and a group, and how do these changes come about?
- How does cohesion foster a spirit of productivity among group members?
- How are leader and member self-disclosures particularly important during the working stage?
- What kind of feedback is especially valuable to members during a working stage? What are some guidelines for giving and receiving feedback?
- What are some potential coleader issues to consider at this stage?

LO1

Progressing to the Working Stage

For a group to reach the working stage, it is essential that members make a commitment to face and work through barriers that interfere with the group's progress. Meaningful work and learning occur at every stage of a group; however, deeper exploration and an increased level of group cohesion are typical of the working stage of a group. The following examples illustrate how a leader's interventions can assist a group in transition to move deeper into a working phase.

EXAMPLE: Frank and Judy complain that the group is stagnant and that they are getting tired of it. They are likely to back off if the leader responds defensively. Therapeutic interventions could be any of the following:

- What would you like to see happening?
- What can you do to make this group more productive for you?

- Is there anything you can do to be more the type of member you want others to be?
- You might have some reactions to the way I'm leading. Is there anything you need to say to me?

These interventions can help Frank and Judy go beyond complaining, explore the source of their dissatisfaction, and express what they would like to see happen.

When Ryan, another member, makes a sarcastic remark ("If you don't like it, leave the group."), the leader asks Ryan to make some direct statements to Frank and Judy instead of dismissing them. As Ryan talks about his own reactions to Judy and Frank, he might well identify and get involved in his own issues in a deeply personal way, bringing into the group some unresolved business he has with others in his life. If the leader does not address Ryan's sarcastic remarks, they most likely will have a negative impact on the group.

EXAMPLE: Sunny says that she is afraid of talking about herself in the group. A good place to begin is with her admission that she feels judged. The leader can further Sunny's work by intervening in any of these ways:

- Would you be willing to talk to one person in here who you think might judge you? Tell that person all the things you imagine he or she would think about you?
- Go around to each member and finish this sentence: 'If I let you know me, I'm afraid you would judge me by..."
- Would you be willing to close your eyes and imagine all the judgments people in here could possibly make about you? Don't verbalize what you imagine, but do let yourself feel what it is like to be judged by everyone in the group.

Each of these interventions has the potential for leading to greater exploration, which can assist Sunny in learning how she allows herself to be inhibited by her fear of others' judgments. If she follows any of these leader suggestions, she has a basis for working through her fears. She will probably discover that she makes many unfounded assumptions about people.

EXAMPLE: Jennifer says to the group leader: "I never get any attention in the group, and you seem more attentive to other members." The leader does not rush to convey that she is indeed a valued member, instead he asks Jennifer to talk directly to the members she believes get more of his attention. She talks about her feelings about being pushed aside. At some point the leader intervenes, saying "I wonder if the feelings you are having in this group are familiar to you in your life outside of group?" This intervention can encourage Jennifer to work in greater depth on connecting her past and present outside life with reactions she is having in the here-and-now context of her group.

If Jennifer acknowledges that she often feels ignored and pushed aside in her family of origin, especially by her father, the leader can give her an opportunity to continue her work by helping her explore some of the ways she might be identifying the leader with her father. Once Jennifer recognizes that she is mixing feelings toward the leader with feelings she has toward her father, she is freer to work on her issues with her father. She may discover that she is often overly sensitive to the ways older male authority figures interact with her. She has read into these interactions much more than is warranted.

Jennifer's declaration that she does not get proper attention in the group is a typical reaction during the transition stage. As the leader works with this feeling, Jennifer ends up having new insight regarding how she is making the group leader (and others) into her father. Jennifer's insights and behavior changes are indicative of significant interaction in the working stage. The leader's intervention did not entrench her feelings of being ignored further but resulted in some significant work on her part. In addition, she might well experience intense emotions over her feelings about her father, and she is likely to express and explore such painful feelings in the group. As a result of her work in the group, Jennifer now pays attention to how she feels when she is with her father and tries out new ways of responding to him. Because she is aware of her tendency to attribute certain qualities to men in authority, she is now in a position to react differently toward them.

LO2

Leader Interventions in Working With a Member's Fear

Members may become more aware of their apprehensions as they experience the group process. As the group (and individuals) moves through the stages, the leader's relationship with individual members will become deeper, and the leader's interventions will likely be different. To illustrate this progression, let's examine how one member's fear would be addressed at each group stage. Grace, a member of an ongoing group, says, "I'm afraid people in here will be critical. I rehearse endlessly before I speak because I want to express myself clearly so others won't think I'm incoherent." Grace is aware that she wants to appear intelligent. She states that her fears get in the way of freely participating in the group. We find that group members often express a range of apprehensions similar to those disclosed by Grace, fearing that others will see them as stupid, incoherent, weird, selfish, and the like. The techniques we describe in working with Grace's particular fear of being judged can easily be applied to these other fears. The way we work with her differs according to the depth of the relationship we have established with her.

Interventions at the Initial Stage

During the initial stage, our interventions are aimed at providing encouragement for Grace to say more about her fear of being judged and to talk about how this fear is affecting what she is doing in the group. We facilitate a deeper exploration of her concern in any of the following ways:

- We encourage other members to talk about any fears they have, especially their concerns over how others perceive them. If Susan also says that she fears others' reactions, we can ask her to talk directly to Grace about her fears. (Here we are teaching member-to-member interaction.)
- After the exchange between Susan and Grace, we ask, "Do any of the rest of you have similar feelings?" (Our aim is to involve others in this interaction by stating ways in which they identify with Susan and Grace.)
- Members who have fears that they would like to explore are invited to share their fears with Grace. We leave the structure open ended, so they can talk about whatever fears they are experiencing. (In a nonthreatening way we link Grace's work with that of others, and both trust and cohesion are being established.)

Interventions at the Transition Stage

If during the transition stage Grace makes the statement, "I'm afraid people in here will be critical," we are likely to encourage her to identify ways in which she has already inhibited herself because of her fear of judgment. She can be asked to say *how* she experiences her particular fear in this group. Such an intervention demands more of her than our interventions at the initial stage. We ask her questions such as these:

- When you have that fear, who are you most aware of in this room?
- What are your fears about?
- How have your fears stopped you in this group?
- What are some of the things you have been thinking and feeling but have not expressed?

Grace eventually indicates she is concerned about how three group members in particular will think about her and about how they might judge her. We suggest to Grace that she speak to the people she feels would most likely judge her and tell them what she imagines they are thinking and feeling about her. In this way we get Grace to acknowledge her possible projections and to learn how to check out her assumptions. We are also gathering data that can be useful for exploration later in the group.

We can bring group members into this interaction by inviting them to give their reactions to what Grace has just said. The interchange between her and other members can lead to further exploration. Grace has probably created some distance between herself and others in the group by avoiding them out of fear of their negative reactions. By talking about her reactions to others, she is taking responsibility for the distance she has partially created. She can work out a new stance with those she has been avoiding.

The work that we have just described could be done during any stage. What makes this scenario characteristic of the transition stage is the fact that members are beginning to express reactions and perceptions that they have been aware of but have kept to themselves.

Interventions at the Working Stage

If Grace discloses her fear during the working stage, we look for ways to involve the entire group in her work. Members may acknowledge how they feel put off by her, how they feel judged by her, or how they really do not know her. Of course, these members' reactions need to be dealt with in an effective way. By expressing feelings that they have kept to themselves, members are moving out of the transition stage and into the working stage. They acknowledge reactions and perceptions, clear up projections and misunderstandings, and work through any possible conflict. The group can get stuck in the transition stage if people do not go further and express reactions that have undermined their level of trust. A group moves into the working stage as members commit to working through an impasse, particularly their own end of it.

We can use other techniques to help Grace attain a deeper level of self-exploration. One is to ask her to identify people in her life who she feels have judged her, enabling her to connect her past struggles to her present ones. We may then ask her to tell some members how she has felt toward significant people in her life. She may even let others in the group "become" these significant figures and may say things to them that she has kept to herself. Of course, doing this may well serve as a catalyst for getting others to talk about their unfinished business with important figures in their lives.

Here are some other strategies we might use:

- Grace can be invited to simply talk more about what it is like for her to be in this group with these fears: "What have you wanted to say or do that you were afraid to say or do?" "If you didn't have the fear of being judged, how might you be different in this group?"
- Grace can role-play with a member who reminds her of her mother, who often cautioned her about thinking before she speaks.
- Grace can write an uncensored letter to her mother, which she does not mail.
- By using role reversal, Grace can "become" her mother and go around to each person in the room, telling them how they should behave.
- Grace can monitor her own behavior between group sessions, taking special note of those situations in daily life in which she stops herself because of her fear of being judged.
- Using cognitive procedures, Grace can pay more attention to her self-talk and eventually learn to give herself new messages. Instead of accepting self-defeating messages, she can begin to say constructive things to herself. She can change her negative beliefs and expectancies to positive ones.
- Grace can decide to try new behaviors during the group such as thinking out loud instead of rehearsing silently as she typically does.
- Both in the group and in daily life, Grace can make a contract to forge ahead with what she wants to say or do despite her fears.

As can be seen, our interventions in working with Grace's fear are geared to the level of trust that has been established in the group, the quality of our relationship with her, and the stage of the group's development. We hope Grace has learned the value of checking out her assumptions about others. We challenge her to continue acting in new ways, even if this means putting herself in places where she runs the risk of being judged for some of her thoughts, feelings, and actions. By now Grace may have developed the personal strength to challenge her fears rather than allowing herself to be controlled by them. She realizes that it is not necessary for her to think through everything she wants to say. Instead, she can be spontaneous in expressing her thoughts and feelings without expecting judgment.

Interventions in the Final Stage

We ask Grace to reflect on how the changes she has practiced in the group might affect significant people in her life. She considers the possible consequences of relating in this new way and whether her new behaviors will help her to be heard. Although Grace's work may be effective in her group, we caution her that these new behaviors may not work as well in her everyday life. In the final stage of the group, we emphasize the importance for Grace to review what she has learned, to understand how she acquired these insights, and to continue to translate her insights into behavioral changes outside of the group.

LO3

Tasks of the Working Stage

Even if the group reaches a high level of intensity during the working stage, the group may not remain at that level. The group may stay on a plateau for a time and then return to an earlier developmental phase characterized by issues faced during the initial and transition stages. Periods of stagnation are normal and can be expected; if they are recognized, they can be challenged and resolved. Because groups are not static entities, both the leader and the members have the task of accurately assessing a group's ever-changing character, as well as its effectiveness.

Group Norms and Behavior

During the working stage, group norms that were formed in earlier stages are further developed and solidified. Members are more aware of facilitative behaviors, and unspoken norms become more explicit. At this time the following group behaviors tend to be manifested:

- Members are provided with both support and challenge; they are reinforced for making behavioral changes both inside and outside of the sessions.
- The leader employs a variety of therapeutic interventions designed for further self-exploration and that lead to experimentation with new behavior.
- Members increasingly interact with one another in more direct ways; there is less dependence on the leader for direction and less eye contact directed toward the leader as members talk.
- If interpersonal conflicts emerge within the group, they become the basis of discussion and tend to be worked through. Members discover how they deal with conflict in everyday situations by paying attention to how they interact with one another in the group.

- A healing capacity develops within the group as members increasingly experience acceptance of who they are. There is less need to put up facades as members learn that they are respected for showing deeper facets of themselves.

In the next section we discuss the factors that differentiate a working group from a nonworking one.

Contrasts Between a Working Group and a Nonworking Group

Growth and progress look different depending on the type of group and the members in it. For example, progress in a group of court ordered sex offenders may look very different from progress in a group of graduate students in the counseling profession. The table describes typical member behaviors that you may experience as the leader during the working stage of a group. Which member behaviors would act as a trigger for you as a leader? How would you respond? Would you tend to take on all the responsibility for what is occurring in the group? Would you blame yourself, your coleader, or the members for what is happening in the group? Would you share your reactions with the group? Why or why not? Refer to the table as a guideline and a catalyst to get you thinking about what progress will like look in your members and in the group.

In the working group list, the behavioral descriptions represent the ideal; even in the best groups, not everyone will function at this level. Consider, also, that groups displaying nonworking group behaviors may be working but in less overt or easily recognizable ways. Change does not happen at the same pace or in the same manner for members or for groups. Some members may be ready and willing to dive in during the working stage, whereas other members may need to continue to work to build trust. It is important for leaders to recognize that members are moving in the direction of the change they want for themselves. Sometimes working hard to resist the change is a necessary step in a member's process. An effective leader will use all of the "working" and "nonworking" behaviors in a group as grist for the mill.

Working Group	Nonworking Group
Members trust other members and the leaders, or at least they openly express any lack of trust. There is a willingness to take risks by sharing meaningful here-and-now reactions.	Mistrust is evidenced by an undercurrent of unexpressed hostility. Members withhold themselves, refusing to express feelings and thoughts.
Goals are clear and specific and are determined jointly by the members and the leader. There is a willingness to direct group behavior toward realizing these goals.	Goals are fuzzy, abstract, and general. Members have unclear personal goals or no goals at all.

(continued)

Working Group	Nonworking Group *(continued)*
Most members feel a sense of inclusion, and excluded members are invited to become more active. Communication among most members is open and involves accurate expression of what is being experienced.	Many members feel excluded or cannot identify with other members. Cliques are formed that tend to lead to fragmentation. There is fear of expressing feelings of being left out. There is a tendency to form subgroups and alliances.
There is a focus on the here and now, and participants talk directly to one another about what they are experiencing.	People tend to focus on others and not on themselves, and storytelling is typical. Members are unwilling to deal with their reactions to one another.
People feel free to bring themselves into the work of others. They do not wait for permission from the leader.	Members lean on the leaders for all direction. There are power conflicts among members as well as between members and the leader.
There is a willingness to risk disclosing threatening material; people become known.	Participants hold back, and disclosure is at a minimum.
Cohesion is high; there is a close emotional bond among members based on sharing universal human experiences. Members identify with one another and are willing to risk new and experimental behavior because of the closeness and support for new ways of being.	Fragmentation exists; members feel distant from one another. There is a lack of caring or empathy. Members do not encourage one another to engage in new and risky behavior, so familiar ways of being are rigidly maintained.
Conflict among members or with the leader is recognized, discussed, and most often resolved.	Conflicts or negative reactions are ignored, denied, or avoided.
Members accept responsibility for deciding what action they will take to solve their problems.	Members blame others for their personal difficulties and are not willing to take action to change.
Feedback is given freely and accepted without defensiveness. There is a willingness to seriously reflect on the accuracy of the feedback.	What little feedback is given is rejected defensively. Feedback is given without care or compassion.
Members feel hopeful; they feel that constructive change is possible—that people can become what they want to become.	Members feel despairing, helpless, trapped, and victimized.
Confrontation occurs in such a way that the confronter shares his or her reactions to the person being confronted. Confrontation is accepted as a challenge to examine one's behavior and not as an uncaring attack.	Confrontation is done in a hostile, attacking way; the confronted one feels judged and rejected. At times the members gang up on a member, using this person as a scapegoat.

(continued)

Working Group	Nonworking Group (continued)
Communication is clear and direct. There is a minimum of judgments and a maximum of respectful discourse.	Communication is unclear and indirect.
Group members use one another as resources and show interest in one another.	Members are interested mostly in themselves.
Members feel good about themselves and others. They feel a sense of power with one another.	Members do not appreciate themselves or others.
There is an awareness of group process, and members know what makes the group function effectively.	Indifference or lack of awareness of what is going on within the group is common, and group dynamics are rarely discussed.
Issues of diversity, power, and privilege are addressed; there is a respect for individual and cultural differences.	Conformity is prized, and individual and cultural differences are devalued. Members are disrespectful to those who are different from themselves and defensive when discussing issues of power and privilege.
Group norms are developed cooperatively by the members and the leader. Norms are clear and are designed to help the members attain their goals.	Norms are imposed by the leader without the input of members. These norms may not be clear.
There is an emphasis on combining the feeling and thinking functions. Catharsis and expression of feeling occur, but so does thinking about the meaning of various emotional experiences.	The group reinforces the expression of feelings, but with little emphasis on integrating insights with emotional expression.
Group members use out-of-group time to work on problems raised in the group.	Group members think about group activity very little when they are outside the group.

Deepening Trust During the Working Stage

Safety within a group can become an issue even at a later stage of its development, and trust may need to be reestablished. Some members may close off and withdraw because intensive work threatens them, they have doubts about the validity of what they have experienced, they have second thoughts about how involved they want to remain, they are frightened by the display of conflict between members or the expression of painful experiences, or they are anticipating the eventual ending of the group and are prematurely winding down.

The reality of the changing character of trust within a group is illustrated in this example of an adolescent group. Members had done some productive work, both with individuals outside of the group and with one another during the sessions. At one previous meeting, several members experienced intense emotional catharsis. Felix, who had initially identified his worst fear as "breaking down and crying in front of everyone," did cry and released some repressed pain over being denied his father's acceptance. In role playing with his "father," Felix became angry and told him how hurt he felt because of his seeming indifference. Later in this scenario, he cried and told his "father" that he really loved him. Before he left the session, Felix said that he felt relieved.

The session just described was characterized by a high level of trust, risk-taking, caring, and cohesion. At the next session, however, the group leader was surprised at how difficult it was to draw people out. Members were hesitant to speak. Felix said very little. The leader described what she saw in the room and asked the members what made it so hard to talk, especially in light of the fact that the previous session had gone so well. Several members expressed annoyance, making comments such as these: "Do we always have to bring up problems?" "Do we need to cry to show that we're good members?" "I think you're pushing people too hard." Felix finally admitted that he had felt very embarrassed over "breaking down" and that during the week he had convinced himself that the other group members saw him as weak and foolish. He added that in his culture men never show their tears in public. Some others admitted that although they saw value in what Felix had done they would not want to go through what he had out of fear of what others might think of them. Again, the task of this group was to deal with the lack of trust that members had in one another ("I'm afraid of what others will think of me"). Several of the members' statements implied a lack of trust in the leader, which made it imperative that she encourage the members to discuss this dynamic.

In retrospect, what could the leader have done differently? It is possible that Felix might have felt less embarrassed had the leader remembered his original fear and dealt with it, and also checked out some possible cultural injunctions against public display of emotions. She might have said: "Felix, I remember that one of your fears was crying in the presence of others. You just did. How was it for you to have done this?" She could also have invited others to tell him how they had been affected by his work. Assume that Felix had said: "I feel good, and I got a lot from what I did." Then the leader might have replied: "Imagine two days from now, when you think about what you did this morning. What do you imagine you might think, feel, or say to yourself?" Felix might say: "I am likely to be critical of what I did here." The leader could then suggest that if he catches himself discounting his work it would be helpful to remember the support he felt from everyone in the room and how they had acknowledged his courage.

On the other hand, assume that Felix had responded to the leader's inquiry by saying "I feel embarrassed" while looking down at the floor. She might have replied: "I know how hard it was for you to express yourself in this way. I really hope you won't run away. Would you be willing to look at different people in this room, especially the ones whom you feel most embarrassed with? What do you imagine they're saying about you right now?" After Felix told others what he imagined they were thinking of him, they could be invited to give their honest reactions. Typically, members do not make disparaging remarks after someone has done significant work. As this example shows, it is not uncommon for the issue of trust to resurface in an intense and productive session. After times like this, members may be frightened and may have a tendency to retreat. Leaders who are aware of this tendency can take some preventive measures, as we have described. When a group does appear to regress, the most critical intervention is for the leader to describe what is happening and to get members to put to words what they are observing, thinking, and feeling.

Critical Incident

Conflict With a Cultural Twist

1. Description of Incident

Nadine, a female White leader, facilitated a racially and ethnically diverse adult therapy group of 10 people. The group was to meet for 12 weeks, and this was their 8th meeting. The group was highly cohesive, trusting, willing to give and receive feedback, and highly motivated. Not only did they work well together in the group, but they also applied what they were learning in the group to their outside life. Nadine was surprised when she noticed tension between two group members. Nicole, an African American woman, talked about her conflict with her partner. Beth, a White woman, said under her breath, "Not that again." Nicole overheard the comment and told Beth that this comment really upset her. In a dismissive manner, Beth told Nicole that she was being "too sensitive." In a slightly raised voice, Nicole continued to let Beth know how upsetting her comments were to her. Beth told Nicole to stop shouting and to calm down, which resulted in Nicole becoming even more frustrated. With a look of pain in her eyes, Nicole asked Beth, "Why is it that if I raise my voice a little, you accuse me of shouting?" Beth became very quiet, teared up, got out of her seat, and made a move to leave the room. The other members fell silent. The group leader strongly encouraged both Nicole and Beth to continue to explore their conflict within the group.

2. Process Questions for Group Leaders

1. What are the key issues in this scenario that initially stand out for you? (Think about the clinical issues and the cultural issues.)
2. What cultural factors are at play in how Nicole's raised voice is perceived by Beth? How would you facilitate the discussion around these issues?
3. As the leader, where would you focus your attention? On yourself and your discomfort with this conflict? Concern for the other group members? Concern for Beth and Nicole?
4. What interventions would you make with Nicole and why?
5. What interventions would you make with Beth and why?
6. What are your thoughts about the shift in the level of group cohesion illustrated by this conflict?
7. As the group leader, what feelings might this scenario trigger for you?
8. How might you intervene with Beth as she attempted to leave the room?
9. How would you address the silence in the group?
10. How would you address group members who may intervene and side with or rescue Beth or Nicole?

continued

3. Clinical Reflections

We need to recognize that conflicts can emerge even in a cohesive and trusting group. Nadine was aware that Beth and Nicole had done some significant work in the group and that they were friends outside of the group. Nadine had a hunch that Beth's dismissive comment to Nicole was even more hurtful because they had an outside friendship. Nadine's primary goals were to facilitate their interaction so neither of them shut down and to assess the impact of the conflict on the other group members. Although the situation was uncomfortable, Nadine wanted to help the group deal with this conflict.

The leader was surprised by the sudden intensity of this situation and realized that Beth had triggered a cultural stereotype in Nicole. In a conflict between members, the goal of the leader is to take the side of the relationship, not the side of one person over the other. For the group to trust the leader, Nadine needs to show a willingness to address the conflict rather than trying to smooth it over too quickly. The members also need to make a commitment to talk about their reactions to the conflict and how they are affected by it. Trust is unlikely to be reestablished if members avoid dealing with uncomfortable situations such as this one. There were several layers of conflict in this scenario, but this was also a teachable moment. Nadine could help to bring about an honest discussion involving culture and styles of communication. If she avoids the topic, some members may feel misunderstood and marginalized.

4. Possible Interventions

1. The leader can ask both Nicole and Beth how they were affected by each other's reactions and comments.
2. The leader might want to facilitate a process in which Nicole is able to express her frustrations as an African American in communicating with White people.
3. The leader could check in with all of the members so they can express how they felt as they witnessed the conflict between Nicole and Beth.
4. Because Nadine is White, she could ask Nicole if she has reactions to her as a leader.
5. The leader can model cultural responsiveness by talking out loud about what she observes occurring between Nicole and Beth and how cultural stereotypes may be at play.
6. With tears in her eyes, Beth was set to leave the room. The leader could ask Beth to talk to Nicole about what was evoked in her and what prompted her to want to leave.
7. The leader could ask the group to explore the various ways their culture influences their expression of pain. For example, in one group tears may be common and in another anger may feel like a safer way to show vulnerability.
8. The leader could explore possible transference reactions after facilitating the here-and-now conflict. Assume that the leader knew from prior sessions that Beth had an angry and abusive father and that Nicole had been taught it is best to avoid challenging White people. The leader could explore deeper issues with both Nicole and Beth that could account for their reactions to each other.

Choices to Be Made During the Working Stage

In discussing the initial stages of a group's evolution, we described several critical issues, such as trust versus mistrust, the struggle for power, and self-focus versus focus on others. During the more intense working period of a group, key issues at stake include disclosure versus anonymity, authenticity versus guardedness, spontaneity versus control, acceptance versus rejection, and unity versus fragmentation. A group's identity is shaped by the way its members resolve these critical issues.

Disclosure Versus Anonymity Members can decide to disclose themselves in a significant and appropriate way, or they can choose to remain hidden out of fear. People may protect themselves through anonymity, yet the very reason many become involved in a therapeutic group is because they want to make themselves known to others and to come to know others and themselves in a deeper way. If the group process is to work effectively, members need to share meaningful dimensions of themselves, for it is through self-disclosure that others come to know them.

Authenticity Versus Guardedness It is fundamental to the success of a therapeutic group that authenticity prevail and that members do not feel they have to disguise or hide their true selves to be accepted. Genuine intimacy is not possible when people remain unknown or when they feel compelled to guard their true feelings. Members may present themselves in less then genuine ways for a variety of reasons. Sometimes people hide parts of themselves out of a fear of rejection; others may wear masks in certain settings because of their experience with racism and other forms of discrimination.

Genuine intimacy is not possible when people remain unknown or when they feel compelled to guard their true feelings.

Spontaneity Versus Control We expect group participants to make the choice to relinquish some of their controlled and rehearsed ways and allow themselves to respond more spontaneously to events of the moment. We encourage members to "rehearse out loud" so that both they and others get a glimpse of their internal processing. Spontaneity can be fostered indirectly by helping clients feel that it is all right to say and do many of the things they have been preventing themselves from saying or doing. This does not mean that members "do their own thing" at the expense of others. Members sometimes stifle themselves by endlessly rehearsing everything they say. As a result, they often sit quietly and rehearse internally. We generally make contracts with clients like this, asking them to agree to rehearse out loud and to speak more freely, even at the risk of not making sense. We encourage them to try out unrehearsed behavior in the group setting, and then they can decide which aspects of their behavior they may want to change away from the group.

Acceptance Versus Rejection Throughout the course of a group, the members frequently deal with the acceptance–rejection polarity. We sometimes hear a member say, "I'd like to be myself, yet I'm afraid that if I'm me, I'll not be accepted. I worry about this because I often feel that I really don't fit into the group." The basis of this fear can be explored, which most often results in challenging fears without foundation. Members are likely to find that they reject themselves more often than others reject them. These members may also discover that they are frightened about the prospects of being accepted as well as of being rejected. Although they do not enjoy rejection, it has become a familiar feeling, and feelings of acceptance can be unsettling: "If you accept me or love me or care for me, I won't know how to respond."

The group setting provides opportunities for members to learn some of the ways in which they are setting themselves up to be rejected by behaving in a certain manner. As group members begin to recognize their own role and responsibility in the creation of an accepting or rejecting climate, they come to understand that their own behavior helps to determine whether they as individuals will be accepted or rejected.

Lara struggled with whether to disclose her eating disorder to the group. No other members have raised this topic, and Lara is fearful that if others know they will judge her or be disgusted by her eating disorder behaviors. When she shared her struggles with someone outside the group, that person told Lara that she needed to exert more willpower over food and her urge to binge and purge. Lara has convinced herself that it is best not to share her problems with anyone.

As the leaders work with Lara on how she is holding herself back in the group, she begins to express her fear of exposing herself more intimately to the group. The leaders encourage Lara to talk more about the response she expects to get from members without telling the group what the specific issue is. Lara's willingness to be honest led her to have a different experience than she had anticipated, which helped her to begin to build trust with the other group members.

Unity Versus Fragmentation Unity is largely the result of the group's choice to work actively at developing a sense of community and establishing bonds with each other. Members achieve this sense of community mainly by choosing to make themselves known to others, by sharing their pain, by allowing caring to develop, by initiating meaningful conversation, and by giving honest feedback to others. A unified group comes from working with members' meaningful, painful realities as well as from intimately sharing humorous and joyous moments.

If a group makes a decision to remain comfortable or to stay with superficial interactions, there will be little group togetherness. There are times when members choose not to express their fears, suspicions, disappointments, and doubts. When members conceal their reactions, fragmentation and lack of trust typically result. When some members meet outside the group or form cliques and gossip about the leader or other members, the level of trust within a group can be eroded. This kind of subgrouping can represent a powerful hidden agenda that will continue to block meaningful interchanges. The behavior of this subgroup needs to be recognized and discussed with the entire group for this fragmentation to be repaired.

Not all meetings outside of the group are necessarily damaging to a unified group. Certain kinds of subgroupings can be beneficial. For example, in a residential facility, inpatient group members may meet outside of the group to participate in a range of activities to gain practice in working together on projects or participating in recreational activities. These kinds of subgroups are not meant to exclude others but to give members further opportunities to interact with others in the treatment facility. Another example of potentially beneficial meetings in subgroups can be found in the weeklong residential personal-growth groups that we (Marianne and Jerry) organized for 25 years each summer. These groups consisted of 16 members and 4 group leaders. We met with the entire group each day, yet each day we also met in small groups (of 8 members and 2 leaders). In addition, free time each day provided members with the opportunity to participate in various activities with different people. These informal get-togethers often stimulated therapeutic work that the members brought back to the group.

Homework During the Working Stage

The group is not an end in itself. Members may learn new behaviors and acquire a range of skills in living during group sessions, but members need to practice these skills and behaviors outside of the group. Members can be encouraged to devise their own homework assignments, ideally at each of the group sessions. Homework maximizes what is learned in the group and translates this learning to many different situations in daily life. If members are willing to create homework and follow through with it, their motivation and the overall level of cohesion in the group will increase.

Although we often suggest an activity for members to consider doing outside of the group, we avoid being prescriptive and telling members what they should do for homework. We encourage group members to keep a journal, and these writings can be a catalyst for them to engage in new behavior within the group. Our suggestions for homework are presented in the spirit of assisting members in increasing their chances to get what they say they want from the group experience. Homework is especially useful at this stage of a group because it provides encouragement and direction for members to practice actual skills they are learning in the group. Homework often helps members translate their insights into action plans aimed at change. As much as possible, homework is best designed collaboratively with group members. Homework is a basic part of all of the cognitive behavioral approaches, but it is an appropriate technique for use in groups that are structured with other theoretical frameworks as well. See Chapter 4 for specific theories that make use of homework.

Oftentimes members do intense exploration of their significant relationships in group sessions. Although talking about a relationship can be therapeutic and members may gain insights into the dynamics of the relationship, this is only the beginning of change. Members then can decide whether they are interested in talking differently to this person in their life. For example, Rosa decides on the following homework. She wants to approach her mother in a different manner than she typically does—without arguing and getting defensive. First in the group she practices what she wants to express to her mother. She receives feedback and support from other members regarding her symbolic interaction with her mother in this way. When Rosa clearly understands what she wants with her mother based on her behavioral rehearsal in the group, she will be better prepared to behave differently with her mother. Group practice and homework can often be combined in this way to help members make important changes in their everyday lives.

LO7

Therapeutic Factors That Operate in a Group

A variety of forces within groups can be healing, or therapeutic, and these forces play a key role in producing constructive changes. The **therapeutic factors** discussed in this section operate to differing degrees in all stages of a group, but they are most often manifested during the working stage. The therapeutic factors discussed here reflect our experiences in leading groups and the reports of the many people who have participated in our groups. (In many of our groups, we ask participants to write follow-up reaction papers describing what factors facilitated their changes in attitudes and behavior.) We are particularly indebted to Irvin Yalom (2005b) for his pioneering work in identifying therapeutic factors in therapy groups.

Self-Disclosure and the Group Member

LO8

The willingness to make oneself known to others is part of each stage of a group, but at the working stage self-disclosure is more frequent and more personal. Members are expected to self-disclose in a group, and the leader needs to teach and to facilitate member self-disclosure. Although a norm of member self-disclosure is desirable, clinical findings do not support the idea that more disclosure is always better. Too much or too little disclosure can be counterproductive, and leaders should monitor such disclosures so a single member does not lead the others by too great a gap in terms of frequency and depth of disclosure (Yalom, 2005b). Although disclosure is not an end in itself, it is the means by which open communication occurs within the group.

Group members are able to deepen their self-knowledge through disclosing themselves to others. Members develop a richer and more integrated picture of who they are, and they are better able to recognize the impact they have on others. Through this process, the participants experience a healing force and gain new insights that often lead to desired life changes. If disclosures are limited to safe topics, the group does not progress beyond a superficial level.

We tell our group members that it is essential to let others know about them, especially as it pertains to their experience of being in the group. Otherwise, they are likely to be misunderstood because people tend to project their own feelings onto members who keep themselves unknown. For example, Andrea thinks that Walter is very critical of her. When Walter finally talks, he discloses that he is both attracted to and fearful of Andrea. Walter can be asked to share what it was like for him to admit this to Andrea. Self-disclosure entails revealing current struggles with unresolved personal issues; goals and aspirations; fears and expectations; hopes, pains, and joys; strengths and weaknesses; and personal experiences. If members keep themselves anonymous and say little about themselves that is personal, it is difficult for others to care for them. Genuine concern comes from knowledge of the person. As you can see, this disclosure is not limited simply to revealing personal concerns; it is equally important to disclose ongoing persistent reactions toward other members and the leader.

In leading groups, you cannot apply the same criteria in assessing the value of self-disclosure for all members equally. Differences exist among people due to variables such as cultural background, sexual orientation, and age. For example, an older woman who has never publicly talked about some personal aspects of her marriage may be taking large steps in even approaching this subject. Respect the risks she is taking, and avoid comparing her with members who self-disclose freely. A woman who discloses for the first time that she is lesbian may experience self-doubts due to internalized homophobia. The leader needs to be attentive to any possible afterthoughts or regrets the member may have for sharing, as well as any negative reactions the group may have toward the member who disclosed her sexual identity. Even if this is not the first time she has disclosed that she is lesbian, the leader will most likely want to ask what it was like for her to make this disclosure in this new group of people.

The cultural context also needs to be considered in what you might expect in terms of self-disclosure from some members. For example, it may be overwhelming and frightening if you were to ask a recent immigrant to participate in an exercise in which members are exploring conflicts with their parents. He may consider any discussion pertaining to his family as shaming or betraying them. In all of these examples, it is important to explore how the members can meaningfully participate in a way that enables them to reach their goals in this group.

What Disclosure Is Not Group participants frequently misunderstand what it means to self-disclose, equating disclosure with keeping nothing private and saying too much. By displaying hidden secrets to the group, members may feel that they are disclosing useful information, which is often not the case. Those who participate in a group need to learn the difference between appropriate and inappropriate self-disclosure. Here are some observations on what self-disclosure is *not*:

- Self-disclosure is not merely telling stories about one's past in a rehearsed and mechanical manner. It is not a mere reporting of there-and-then events. A client needs to ask the question, "How is what I reveal related to my present conflicts?"
- In the name of being open and honest and as a result of the pressure of other group members, people often say more than is necessary for others to understand them. They confuse being self-disclosing with being open to the extent that nothing remains private. As a result, they may feel overly exposed in front of others.
- Expressing every fleeting feeling or reaction to others is not to be confused with self-disclosure. Judgment is needed in deciding how appropriate it is to share certain reactions. Persistent reactions are generally best shared, but people can be honest without being tactless and insensitive.

Guidelines for Appropriate Member Self-Disclosure In our groups we suggest the following guidelines as a way of assisting participants in determining *what* to disclose and *when* self-disclosure is both appropriate and facilitative:

- The degree of self-disclosure should be related to the purposes, goals, and type of the group.
- If members have persistent reactions to certain people in the group, members are encouraged to bring them out into the open without blaming, especially when these reactions are inhibiting their level of participation.
- Members must determine *what* and *how much* they want others to know about them. They also have to decide what they are willing to risk and how far they are willing to go.

- Reasonable risks can be expected to accompany self-disclosure. If groups are restricted to overly safe disclosures, the interactions can become fairly meaningless.
- The stage of group development has some bearing on the appropriateness of self-disclosure. Certain disclosures may be too deep for an initial session but quite appropriate during the working stage.

Related to the issue of member self-disclosure is the role of leader self-disclosure. We now turn to some guidelines designed to assist leaders in thinking about how their disclosures can have a facilitative effect on a group.

Self-Disclosure and the Group Leader

Leaders who self-disclose do so for a variety of reasons. The key question is not whether leaders should disclose themselves to the group but, rather, *how much, when,* and *for what purpose.* Appropriate leader self-disclosure can be used to model risk-taking and may be a key element in joining and building trust. Leader self-disclosures pose some risks, but skilled clinicians can use even a disclosure gone awry to facilitate a useful discussion with group members. Sometimes the decision to disclose is thought out by the leader ahead of time; other times it is a more spontaneous contribution either because it feels right for the moment or because a member has asked the leader a direct question of a personal nature.

Some group leaders are careful not to make themselves personally known to the group, striving to keep their personal involvement in the group to a minimum. Some do this because of a theoretical preference, such as psychoanalytically oriented group therapists who view their role as that of a "transference figure" on whom group members can project feelings they have experienced toward parents and other significant people in their lives. By remaining anonymous, the leader encourages members' projections from an earlier relationship. When these unresolved conflicts are exposed, they can be worked through within the group. Group counselors with an experiential and relationship orientation are likely to make therapeutic use of self-disclosure as a way to involve themselves more fully in a group. Person-centered group facilitators, existential therapists, and Gestalt therapists tend to employ self-disclosure to deepen the trust between members and leader and to provide modeling.

Some members come from cultural backgrounds in which trust requires some personal knowledge of the other person. Sharing life experiences and identity issues has helped us to join with members who are very different from us, and members have said that this sharing helped them to feel more trusting toward us. On occasion we share a reaction or feelings we are having because not doing so will keep us distant from the group and therefore interrupt their process. When a member asks for specific personal information, the leader should try to understand why this is important to the member. By responding too quickly to a request for self-disclosure, the leader may miss an opportunity to learn more about what is truly important to that member. Disclosures are best used to promote members' self-understanding.

Group leaders sometimes engage in too much self-disclosure, blurring the boundaries and becoming personally involved in the group they are responsible for facilitating. Avoid submitting to group pressure to cease being a leader and becoming more of a group member. Even though group leaders can participate in personal ways at times, their primary role in the group is to initiate, facilitate, direct, and evaluate the process of interaction among members. Leader self-disclosures should be appropriate, timely, helpful, purposeful, and done for the good of the group members. As a group leader, ask yourself, "How will what I'm about to say be therapeutic or useful to the group members?" Group leaders should be able to support their self-disclosure on theoretical grounds. Group leaders need to accurately assess their own motivations for engaging in self-disclosure and the impact such disclosures will have on individual group members and the group as a whole.

Leader self-disclosures should be appropriate, timely, helpful, purposeful, and done for the good of the group members.

Beginning counselors tend to misjudge the use of leader self-disclosure. Sometimes the desire to self-disclose stems from a need to be liked by group members rather than being a tool for facilitating the process of the group. Self-disclosing too readily can blur boundaries and, in some cases, undermine the leader's perceived competence. Yalom (2005b) stresses that leader self-disclosure must be instrumental in helping the *members* attain their goals. He calls for selective therapist disclosure that provides members with acceptance, support, and encouragement. Group leaders who disclose here-and-now reactions rather than detailed personal events from their past tend to facilitate the movement of the group.

There have been times when I (Marianne) have disclosed something personal that was preventing me from being fully present with the group. I find that trying to hide my distractions or my inability to listen results in a disconnection, which group members may personalize. On one occasion, this resulted in some members' hesitation to work with their problems because they wanted to take care of me and did not want to burden me with their pain. When I noticed this, I let the group know that simply sharing my present experience was what I needed to make myself available to them. My guideline for self-disclosure can be summed up as follows: When something is so much in the foreground that it distracts me from being present and available to the members, I am likely to acknowledge this in a brief way without burdening the group with details.

There is no steadfast rule as to when a leader should or should not self-disclose. In general, the more experience we gain with facilitating groups, the better we are at determining the moments when self-disclosure may be beneficial for members. Although disclosure may be appropriate in the advanced stages of a group, sharing it initially may burden the participants with the feeling that they should help you or should take your pain away. In leading a group for incest survivors, most members were relieved that the leaders did not disclose whether they had or had not been incest survivors themselves. Most members felt they would have been protective of the leaders if they knew the leaders were incest survivors, and this would have limited members' ability to lean on the leaders for support. One member felt that knowing more about the leaders would have helped her to feel more trusting of them.

Timing and considering the population of your group are crucial in doing what is compatible with your personal therapeutic style. It is important to realize that some group members may respond with embarrassment and discomfort over a leader's self-disclosure, especially if they view the leader as an expert. Certain leader self-disclosures, such as sharing performance anxiety, could diminish members' perceptions about a leader's competence and thus impede establishing trust.

The decision to self-disclose should be based on your theoretical orientation, your clinical intuition, and the potential benefit to the member(s). A question we might ask is, "Whom does this disclosure serve?" Consider the following four guidelines in determining your own position on the issue of leader self-disclosure:

1. If you determine that you have problems you wish to explore, consider finding your own therapeutic group. This would allow you to be a participating member without the concern of how your personal work would affect the group. You have a demanding job and should not make it even more difficult by confusing your role with that of the participants.
2. Ask yourself why you are disclosing certain personal material. Is it to be seen as a "regular person," no different from the members? Is it to model disclosing behavior for others? Is it because you genuinely want to show private dimensions to the members? It may be therapeutic for group members to know you and your struggles, but they do not need to know them in elaborate detail. For instance, if a member is exploring her fear of not being loved unless she is perfect, you might reveal in a few words that you also wrestle with this fear, if indeed you do. Your sharing makes it possible for your client to feel a sense of identification with you. At another time it may be appropriate for you to talk a bit more.
3. Disclosure that is related to what is going on in the group is the most productive. For instance, any persistent feelings you have about a member or about what is happening (or not happening) are generally best revealed. If you are being affected by a member's behavior, it is usually advisable to let the member know your reaction. If you sense a general reluctance in the group, it is best to talk openly about the cautiousness and about how it feels to experience it. Disclosure related to how you feel in the group is generally more appropriate than disclosure of personal material that is not relevant to the ongoing interaction of the group.
4. Ask yourself how much you want to reveal about your private life to the many people with whom you will come into contact. In our workshops, other groups, and classes we want to feel the freedom to function openly as people, but at the same time we want to preserve a measure of our privacy. Moreover, if we always gave detailed accounts about ourselves, we would lose spontaneity. It is impossible to maintain a fresh and unrehearsed style with such repetition.

Discussing the role and purpose of leader self-disclosure with members can be useful whether the leader discloses or does not. Take time to reflect on your guidelines for determining when self-disclosure is appropriate and furthers interaction within the group. Address these questions as a way to formulate your views of leader self-disclosure:

- How willing are you to share aspects of your personal life if members ask you questions?

- How can you decide if revealing aspects of yourself would be helpful to members?
- Do you consider it important to disclose what you are experiencing if you are being triggered by the work of certain members?
- How open would you want to be in letting members know of your ongoing reactions to what is happening within the group?
- If you are having difficulty with a group member, are you willing to let this member know how you are being affected?

Feedback

One of the most important ways learning takes place in a group is through a combination of member self-disclosure and group feedback. This often leads to deeper levels of intimacy in the group. Interpersonal feedback influences the development of many therapeutic factors. **Feedback** occurs when group members or leaders share their observations and personal reactions regarding the behavior of another. Feedback has been associated with increased motivation for change, greater insight into how one's behavior affects others, increased willingness to take risks, and group members evaluating their group experience more positively. When feedback is given honestly and with sensitivity, members are able to understand the impact they have on others and decide what, if anything, they want to change about their interpersonal style. Through a process of feedback exchange, members have opportunities to view their interpersonal style from new perspectives and are able to make meaningful changes in their behavior (Stockton, Morran, & Chang, 2014). The process of interpersonal feedback encourages members to accept responsibility for the outcomes of a group and for changing the style in which they relate to others.

Like self-disclosure, group leaders need to teach participants how to give and receive feedback. Leaders do well to model effective delivery of feedback and to encourage members to engage in thoughtful feedback exchange (Stockton et al., 2014). In cognitive behavioral groups, members are given specific instructions about what kind of feedback is helpful and how to best receive feedback from others. For members (or leaders) to benefit from feedback, it is critical that they be willing to listen to the reactions and comments others offer. Members are more likely to consider feedback that may be difficult to hear when there is a balance between positive or supportive feedback and corrective or challenging feedback (sometimes referred to as "negative" feedback), and when a level of trust has been established. Members can gain from feedback that is given in a clear, caring, genuine, and personal manner.

Members can gain from feedback that is given in a clear, caring, genuine, and personal manner.

Feedback as a process in groups is given further consideration in Chapter 9, but effective feedback is an important component of the working stage. Here are some guidelines we use for teaching members about effective feedback during the working stage:

- Clear and concise feedback is more helpful than statements with qualifiers. For instance, Lilia is being quite clear and direct with Brad when she tells him:

"I feel uncomfortable when I'm sharing very personal things about myself and I see you smiling. It makes me wonder if you're taking me seriously."

- In offering feedback to other group members, share with them how they affect you rather than giving them advice or judging them. In the preceding example, Lilia is speaking about her own discomfort and how she is affected by Brad's smiling, rather than calling Brad insensitive. This is what makes this feedback challenging, rather than negative.
- Specific here-and-now feedback that pertains to behavior in the group is especially useful. Lilia's comments to Brad addressed how his behavior was affecting her. If Lilia does not speak up now, her discomfort may continue to increase until she reacts at a time when her statements are out of context.
- Feedback that is given in a timely and nonjudgmental way increases the chances that the person receiving it will reflect on this information. In Lilia's case, her feedback to Brad is focused on her personal reactions and how she is affected, and it represents a risky self-disclosure.
- Feedback that pertains to the interpersonal relationship can be powerful. For instance, in giving feedback to Brad, Lilia might add: "I want to feel closer to you. But I'm careful of what I say when I'm around you because I don't know what you are thinking. When you look away and either smile or frown when I talk, I'm left wondering how what I'm saying affects you. I do want to be able to trust you more." With this kind of statement, Lilia is talking about her feelings of fear and uncertainty, but she is also letting Brad know that she would like a different kind of relationship with him.
- Addressing a person's strengths rather than concentrating exclusively on the difficulties you are experiencing with this person can improve reactions to that feedback. For example, a leader might say to a member who is getting lost in the details of her story: "I'm glad you spoke up. I did have some difficulty following your story and staying focused because you were talking more about others than about yourself. However, I do have a better understanding of your struggle now, and I hope you strive to keep focused on your own experience."

Members sometimes make a sweeping declaration, spontaneously asking the group for feedback and putting other members on the spot. Here is an example that typifies this approach:

EXAMPLE: Fernando says, "I'd like to know what you think of me, and I'd like some feedback!" If we were to hear this, we would probably say to the group, "Before anyone gives you feedback Fernando, we'd like you to say more about what prompted you to ask for these reactions." This intervention requires that Fernando make significant disclosures about himself before insisting that others disclose themselves to him. Members are more likely to respond to him when they know more about his need for their feedback. Behind his question may well be any of these statements: "I'm afraid, and I don't know if I'm liked." "I'm afraid people are judging me." "I don't have many friends in my life, and it's important that these people like me."

If Fernando has said very little about himself, it is difficult to give him many reactions. To find out how others perceive him, it is necessary that he let himself be known. After he has explored his need for feedback, the group leader can ask members if they want to react to him. However, the leader should not pressure everyone in the group to give him their comments. When people do offer their reactions, the leader can ask Fernando to listen attentively, to hear what others have to say to him, and to consider what, if anything, he may want to do with this information.

As the group progresses to a working stage, we typically see a willingness of members to freely give one another their reactions. The norm of asking for, receiving, and giving feedback needs to be established early in a group. Furthermore, it is the leader's task to teach members how to give useful feedback. Feedback is at its best when members spontaneously let others know how they are affected by them and their work. For example, a member might say, "I was very affected by the way you role-played talking to your mother; it reminds me of the difficulty I have in feeling understood by my mother." This kind of feedback connects members to each other through similar struggles. Here is another example of how useful feedback can benefit a member:

EXAMPLE: Chan joined a group because he found himself isolated from people. Soon he found that he felt isolated in the group also. He was sarcastic in his group, a trait that quickly alienated others. Because the members were willing to tell him in a caring way that they felt put off and distanced by his sarcastic style, he was able to examine and eventually assume responsibility for creating the distance and lack of intimacy he typically experienced. With the encouragement of his group, he sought out his son, from whom he felt disconnected. When he gave up his sarcasm and talked honestly with his son, he found that his son was willing to listen.

Confrontation

As was discussed in Chapters 6 and 7, constructive confrontation is a form of feedback that is a basic part of a productive group, and also of any healthy relationship. It is through acts of caring and respectful confrontation that members are invited to examine discrepancies between what they say and do, to become aware of potentials that are dormant, and to find ways of putting their insights into action. Sensitive confrontation by others helps members develop the capacity for self-confrontation, a skill they will need in applying what they have learned to the problems they face in their daily lives. This kind of feedback can result in sustained behavior change.

EXAMPLE: Alexander complained of feeling tired and drained. He asserted that everyone in his life was demanding. In the group his style of interacting involved being a helper. He was attentive to what others needed, yet he rarely asked anything for himself. In one session he finally admitted that he was not getting what he wanted from the group and that he did not feel like returning again. The leader confronted Alexander: "I have seen you do many times in this group what you say you typically do with people in your life. I see you as being very helpful, yet you rarely ask for anything for yourself. I'm not surprised about your reluctance over coming back to the group. You've created the same environment in here as the one at home. I'm glad you're seeing this. Is this something you are willing to change?"

Cohesion and Universality

Group cohesion is a norm for the early phase of a group (see Chapter 6), and we return to this topic now because group cohesion is also a therapeutic factor in an effective working group, providing a climate in which members feel free to do meaningful work. Characteristics of a cohesive group include a climate of support, bonding, sharing of experiences, mutuality within the group, a sense of belonging, warmth and closeness, and caring and acceptance. Members' willingness to let others know them in meaningful ways deepens the level of trust, which allows for increased cohesion.

Group cohesion fosters action-oriented behaviors such as self-disclosure, giving and receiving feedback, discussion of here-and-now interactions, the constructive expression of conflicts in the group, a willingness to take risks, and translating insight into action. Cohesion is necessary for effective group work, but it is not a sufficient condition. Some groups choose to stop at the level of comfort and security and do not push ahead to new levels. Other groups reach an impasse because members are unwilling to have meaningful interactions with one another.

Yalom (2005b) maintains that cohesion is related to many positive characteristics within a group. Highly cohesive groups tend to be characterized by better attendance and less turnover. Members of a cohesive group show greater acceptance, intimacy, and understanding; cohesion also helps members recognize and work through conflicts. Members feel free to express anger and deal with conflict if they feel a sense of commitment to the group and if they perceive the group as a safe place. Our experience in facilitating groups has convinced us that cohesion is a valuable concept and that it can be a unifying force for group members. Cohesion operates as a therapeutic factor at first by enhancing group support and acceptance, and later by playing a crucial role in interpersonal learning.

At the working stage, members are able to see commonalities, and they are often struck by the universality of their life issues. For example, our therapeutic groups are composed of a very wide mixture of people. The members come from all walks of life, and they differ in many respects: age, sexual orientation, social and cultural backgrounds, career paths, and level of education. Although in the earlier stages members are likely to be aware of their differences and at times feel separated, as the group achieves increased cohesion, these differences recede into the background. Members comment more on how they are alike than on how they are different. A woman in her early 50s discovers that she is still striving for parental approval, just as is a man in his early 20s. A man learns that his struggles with masculinity are not that different from a woman's concern about her femininity. A woman in a heterosexual relationship discovers that she can relate to a lesbian's fear of intimacy in her relationship. Both women are able to connect with each other as they explore their fear of rejection in their relationships.

The circumstances leading to hurt and disappointment may be very different from person to person or from culture to culture, but the resulting emotions have a universal quality. Although we may not speak the same language or come from the same society, we are connected through our feelings of joy and pain. It is when group members no longer get lost in the details of daily experiences and instead share their deeper struggles with these universal human themes that a group is most cohesive. The leader can help the group achieve this level of cohesion by focusing on the underlying issues, feelings, and needs that the members seem to share.

This bonding provides the group with the impetus to move forward, for participants gain courage by discovering that they are not alone in their feelings. A woman experiences a great sense of relief when she discovers, through statements by other women, that she is not alone in feeling resentment over the many demands her family makes on her. Men find that they can share their tears and affection with other men without being robbed of their masculinity. In the proposal for a men's group in a community agency (see Chapter 11), the group provided a place for men to discover universal themes, and by exploring deeply personal concerns the bond among the members was strengthened.

The leader can foster the development of cohesion by pointing out the common themes that unite members of the group. Universal themes include remembering painful experiences of childhood and adolescence, experiencing loneliness and abandonment, becoming aware of the need for and fear of love, learning to express feelings that have been blocked from awareness, searching for meaning in life, recognizing universal themes that link us together as humans, recognizing unfinished business with parents, and seeking meaningful connections with significant people. This list is not exhaustive but merely a sample of the universal human issues that participants recognize and explore with one another as the group progresses, regardless of their sometimes obvious differences. The cohesion that is characteristic of the working stage is a deeper intimacy that develops with sharing by members, time, and commitment. This bonding is a form of affection and genuine caring that often results from sharing the expression of painful experiences.

EXAMPLE: A couple of women, both of whom immigrated to this country, express the pain they feel over having left their own countries. Until this time, they had felt rather isolated from other group members. Sharing their struggle touched just about everyone in the group. Members could identify with their pain and loss even though they did not share the same experiences. The work of these two women was productive for them, but it also stimulated other members to talk about times in their lives when they felt deep loss. During closure of the session, as members made comments about how they were affected by the meeting, they talked about how close they felt and the bond of trust that had developed. Despite having different backgrounds, these group members were brought together by a deeply personal sharing of common themes and feelings.

Hope

Hope is the belief that change is possible. Some people approach a group convinced that they have absolutely no control of external circumstances. Members who are mandated to attend group may feel extremely hopeless and be convinced that nothing will really change. In the group, however, they may encounter others who have struggled and found ways to assume effective control over their lives. Seeing and being associated with such people can inspire a new sense of optimism that their lives can be different. Hope is therapeutic in itself because it gives members confidence that they have the power to choose to be different, or to change their life circumstances.

People are sometimes so discouraged that they are unable to see any way to change a life situation. Group leaders must guard against being drawn into the hopelessness of such members and continue to approach their groups with a conviction that change and a better outcome are possible. For example, a client of mine (Marianne) worked hard at convincing me that there was no hope for change in her life. One day she exclaimed, "You don't understand. I am *really* hopeless." I let her know that if I felt as hopeless about her as she did, I would not be of much help to her. I empathized with her sense of despair while encouraging her not to give up. A hopeful sign that I saw and she did not was the fact that she was seeking help. A lack of hope may spring from a series of disappointments, injuries, or even abuses, but it serves to keep people stuck. It is helpful to understand and support members but at the same time challenge them to examine the situation surrounding their hopelessness and despair. We need to understand the function of their lack of hope before we can help them move past it.

EXAMPLE: Travis, a veteran, was left paralyzed as a result of an injury suffered during a war. He spent most of his energy thinking about all that he could no longer do. With the encouragement of his physician, Travis joined a rehabilitation group where he met several other wounded veterans who had at one time felt as he was feeling now. By listening to their struggles and how they had effectively coped with their disabilities, Travis found hope that he, too, could discover more effective ways of living his life.

Willingness to Risk and to Trust

Risking involves opening oneself to others, being vulnerable, and actively doing in a group what is necessary for change. Taking risks requires moving past what is known and secure toward more uncertain terrain. If members are primarily motivated to remain comfortable, or if they are unwilling to risk challenging themselves and others, they stand to gain very little from the group. Members' willingness to reveal themselves is largely a function of how much they trust the other group members and the leader. The higher the level of trust in a group, the more likely members are to push themselves beyond their comfort level. From the outset, members can be invited to risk by talking about their feelings of being in the group. As a few members engage in even minor risk-taking, others will follow suit. By taking risks in disclosing here-and-now observations and reactions, members are actively creating trust and making it possible to engage in deeper self-exploration. Trust is a healing agent; it enables people to show the many facets of themselves, encourages experimental behavior, and allows people to look at themselves in new ways.

EXAMPLE: Carmen expressed considerable resentment to the men in her group. Eventually, she took a risk and disclosed that as a child she had been sexually abused by her stepfather. As she explored ways in which she had generalized her distrust of men in everyday life and in her group, she began to see how she was keeping men at a distance so they would never again have the chance to hurt her. This led to a new decision that all men would not necessarily want to hurt her and if they did she could take care of herself. Had she been unwilling to risk making the disclosure in her group, it is unlikely that she would have made this attitudinal and behavioral change.

Caring and Acceptance

Caring is demonstrated by listening and by involvement. It can be expressed by tenderness, compassion, support, and even confrontation. One way caring is demonstrated is by staying present with someone who has received some feedback that was difficult to hear. If members sense a lack of genuine caring, either from other members or from the leader, their willingness to make themselves vulnerable will be limited. Members are able to risk being vulnerable if they sense that their concerns are important to others and that they are valued as people.

Caring implies acceptance, a genuine support from others that says, in effect: "We will accept all of your feelings. You matter to us. It is acceptable to be yourself—you do not have to strive to please everyone." Acceptance involves affirming each person's right to have and express feelings and values.

Caring and acceptance develop into empathy, a deep understanding of another's struggles. Commonalities emerge in groups that unite the members. The realization that certain problems are universal—loneliness, the need for acceptance, the fear of rejection, the fear of intimacy, hurt over past experiences—lessens the feelings that we are alone. Moreover, through identification with others we are able to see ourselves more clearly.

EXAMPLE: In a group for children, Bobby finally began to talk tearfully about his sadness over the loss of his father due to a fatal accident. Other children were very attentive. When Bobby said that he was embarrassed by his crying, two other boys told him that they also cried. This sharing of loneliness and hurt bonded the children. It assured them that what they were feeling was normal.

Power

A feeling of power emerges from the recognition that one has untapped internal reserves of spontaneity, creativity, courage, and strength. This strength is not a power over others; rather, it is the sense that one has the resources necessary to direct one's own life. In groups personal power is experienced in ways that were formerly denied. Some people enter groups feeling that they are powerless. They become empowered when they realize they can take certain steps in their current situation to make life more rewarding. However, it is crucial for leaders to understand and appreciate the context surrounding the lack of power that some members may experience. This is particularly important for members from marginalized groups who have often been disempowered by various social systems. It is not safe for some individuals to assert newly founded power in every life situation. For example, Alfonso's father may never speak to him again if Alfonso asserts himself by confronting his father. Leaders need to assist members in assessing the potential consequences, as well as when and where it may not be safe to express themselves fully. Here is an example of a member reclaiming a sense of power.

EXAMPLE: As a child, Edith was often hit by her parents if she made herself visible. She made an early decision to keep a low profile to avoid being abused physically and psychologically. Through her participation in a group, she discovered that she was still behaving as if everyone was out to get her, and that her defensive ways were no longer warranted. Because she chose not to make her presence known in her group, people saw her as distant, cold, and aloof. Edith gradually discovered that she was no longer a helpless child who could not protect herself in a cruel adult world. By challenging her assumptions and by taking risks with people in her group, Edith also assumed more power over how she felt about herself and how she allowed herself to be treated by others.

Catharsis

Energy is tied up in withholding threatening feelings. Unexpressed feelings often result in physical symptoms such as chronic headaches, stomach pains, muscle tension, and high blood pressure. At times group members say that they do not want to remember painful feelings, not understanding that the body can be carrying the pain and giving expression to it with various physical symptoms. When people finally do express their stored-up pain and other unexpressed feelings, they typically report a tremendous physical and emotional release, known as catharsis. For instance, a group member reported that all of her chronic neck pains were gone after she expressed some very painful feelings. Catharsis is frequently associated with the experiential approaches, especially Gestalt therapy and psychodrama.

Emotional release plays an important part in many kinds of groups, and the expression of feelings facilitates trust and cohesion. But it is not true that the only real work is done by catharsis. Members who do not have an emotional release may become convinced that they are not really "working." Leaders may become seduced by the intensity that comes with catharsis and press for such releases without having a clear direction or the confidence and skill to work with the material that is uncovered. Sometimes beginning leaders feel that only the cathartic expressions are meaningful, and they may underestimate the power of other work done by members. Group leaders do well to ask: "What am I doing, why am I doing it, and how capable am I and the members of handling such work?"

Although it is often healing, catharsis by itself is limited in terms of producing long-lasting changes. Members need to learn how to make sense of their catharsis, and one way of doing so is by putting words to those intense emotions and attempting to understand how they influence and control their everyday behavior. Often the best route to assisting members in examining their thought patterns and behaviors is by encouraging them to identify, express, and deal with what they are feeling. It can be tempting to emphasize catharsis and view the release of emotions as an end in itself, but this is not the final goal of the group experience.

After the release of feeling, it is essential to work with a member's insights associated with the emotional situation and the cognitions underlying these emotional patterns. Ideally, group leaders will help members link their emotional exploration to cognitive and behavioral work. Group leaders can help members face intense feelings and at the same time encourage them to translate insights into positive action within the group setting. Emotional work can be furthered by drawing on concepts and techniques from the cognitive behavioral orientations illustrated in Chapter 4.

EXAMPLE: Selene learned that she could experience both love and anger toward her mother. For years she had buried her resentment over what she saw as her mother's continual attempts to control her life. In one session Selene allowed herself to feel and to fully express her resentment to her mother in a symbolic way. Through a role play the group leader assisted Selene in telling her mother many of the things that had contributed to her feelings of resentment. She felt a great sense of relief after having expressed these pent-up emotions. The leader cautioned her about the dangers of repeating in real life everything that she had just said in the therapy session. It would not be necessary to harshly confront her mother and to expose the full range of her pain and anger. Instead, Selene learned that it was important to understand how her resentment toward her mother was continuing to affect her now, both in her present dealings with her mother and in her relationship to others. The issue of control was a problem to Selene in all her relationships. By releasing her feelings she became more aware that everyone does not control her. It was essential that Selene clarify what she really wanted with her mother and what was still keeping her from getting closer to her and to others. Selene can choose what she wants to tell her mother, and she can also deal with her in more direct and honest ways than she has in the past.

The Cognitive Component

Members who *experience* feelings often have difficulty integrating what they learn from these experiences. Some conceptualization of the meaning of the intense feelings associated with certain experiences is essential to further deeper exploration of one's struggles. The cognitive component includes explaining, clarifying, interpreting, formulating ideas, and providing the cognitive framework for creating a new perspective on problems.

The cognitive behavioral approaches stress the thinking and doing aspects of behavior, and this emphasis can be productively integrated into experientially oriented groups (see Chapter 4). Yalom (2005b) cites substantial research demonstrating that to profit from a group experience the members require a cognitive framework that will enable them to put their here-and-now experiencing into perspective. When asking members to cognitively process an emotional experience, timing is crucial. If members are asked to make sense of an intense emotional experience too quickly, they may feel that the leader is insensitive. However, at some point members can be asked to put into words what expressing their emotions meant to them and what insights they may have gained.

EXAMPLE: Felix, the adolescent who expressed pent-up hurt, initially felt better after an outburst of crying, but he soon discounted the experience. Felix needed to put into words the meaning of his emotional interchange. He may have learned any of the following: that he was storing up feelings of anger toward his father, that he had a mixture of resentment and love for his father, that he had made a decision that his father would never change, that there were many things he could say to his father, or that there were numerous ways that he could act differently with his father. It was therapeutically important for him to release his bottled-up emotions. It was also essential that he clarify his insights and discover ways to use them to improve his relationship with his father.

Commitment to Change

The commitment to change involves members' being willing to make use of the tools offered by group process to explore ways of modifying their behavior. Participants need to remind themselves why they are in the group, and they need to formulate action plans and strategies to employ in their day-to-day existence to implement change. The group affords them the opportunity to plan realistically and responsibly and offers members the opportunity to evaluate the effectiveness of their actions. It is crucial for members to commit themselves to following through on their plans, and the group itself can help members develop the motivation to follow through with their commitments. If members find that carrying out some of their plans is difficult or if they do not do what they had planned, it is essential that they talk about these difficulties in the group sessions.

EXAMPLE: Pearl discovered her tendency to wait until the session was almost over to bring up her concerns. She described many situations in her life when she did not get what she wanted. She insisted that she wanted to make some changes and behave differently. The leader issued the following challenge:

"Pearl, would you be willing to be the first to speak at the next group session? I'd like you to also think of at least one situation this week in which your needs are not being met because you are holding yourself back. What could you do to bring about a more positive outcome for yourself?" Thus the leader provided Pearl with alternatives for taking the initiative to try new ways of acting, both in real life and in the group sessions. If she continued to sabotage meeting her needs by not doing what she said she would do, the leader and members might confront her by sharing their observations.

Freedom to Experiment

The group situation provides a safe place for experimentation with new behavior. Members are able to show facets of themselves that they often keep hidden in everyday situations. In the accepting environment of a group, a shy member can exhibit spontaneous behavior and be outgoing. A person who typically is very quiet may experiment with being more verbal. After trying new behaviors, members can gauge how much they want to change their existing behavior.

EXAMPLE: Yesenia said she was tired of being so shy all the time and would like to let people know her better. The leader responded, "Yesenia, would you be willing to pick out a person in this group who seems the opposite of you?" Yesenia identified Mayra. After getting Mayra's approval, the leader suggested to Yesenia: "Go around to each person in the room, and act in a way that you have seen Mayra behave. Assume her body posture, her gestures, and her tone of voice. Then, tell each person something that you would want them to know about you." What Yesenia gained from this experiment was the recognition that she did possess the capacity to be outgoing and that she could practice giving expression to this dimension of herself.

As a variation, Yesenia could have been asked to share with all of the members her observations and reactions to them. Yet another variation would have included asking Mayra to be Yesenia's coach and assist her in carrying out this task. It can be surprising how outgoing members are when they pretend to be in someone else's skin.

Humor

Humor can help group members get insight or a new perspective on their problems, and it can be a source of healing. But humor should never be used to embarrass a group member. Effective feedback can sometimes be given in a humorous way. Laughing at oneself and *with* others can be extremely therapeutic. As a matter of fact, much has been written about the healing effects of humor, and some workshops focus on the therapeutic aspects of humor.

Humor requires seeing one's problems in a new perspective. Laughter and humor can draw everyone in the group closer. Humor often puts problems in a new light, and it sets a tone in a group indicating that work can occur in a context of fun. The power of humor as a therapeutic tool is often underrated. Humor often balances the relationship between members and leaders, it can empower members, and it establishes an environment that is maximally therapeutic to members. Humor is a coping strategy that enables group members to find the absurd or ironic aspects in their situations. It also has a transformational character in that it enables members to gain a sense of perspective and control over situations not under their direct control. Like self-disclosure, humor can be overused or misused. Is the leader uncomfortable with a situation and using humor to lighten the mood of the group or to decrease the leader's own anxieties? Does people laughing satisfy the leader's need to be liked by group members? Group leaders should be aware of the purpose for which humor is used and monitor how members perceive it.

Spontaneity seems to be the key to using humor effectively, for "planned humor" can certainly fall flat. A level of trust must be established before taking too many liberties with humor. This brand of humor is not laughing *at* people but laughing *with* them out of a sense of affection and caring.

EXAMPLE: Samuel was a serious person who tended to sit back quietly and observe others in the group. When the leader challenged Samuel on his observational stance, he said that he could write a comedy about this group. The leader knew that he was a creative writer and, hoping to get him involved in verbal ways, asked him to write in his journal a comical account of what he saw taking place in the group. When he later read parts of what he had written in his journal about this group, just about everyone in the group laughed. In the process Samuel also shared many of his own reactions to others in the group through his humor. Clearly he was not laughing at them, yet he was able to capture some of the humorous dimensions of what was taking place. By getting active through humor he was able to give a number of members some very insightful feedback, which they would have been denied had he continued sitting silently and observing others. In his account he was able to capture some very funny sides of his own behavior, which gave others a completely different picture of him.

LO11

Coleader Issues During the Working Stage

When we colead groups or intensive workshops, we become energized if the group is motivated to work. In effective groups, the members do the bulk of the work, for they bring up subjects they want to talk about and demonstrate a willingness to be known. Between group sessions we devote time to discussing our reactions to group members, to thinking of ways of involving the various members in transactions with one another, and to exploring possible ways of helping participants understand their behavior in the group and resolve some of their conflicts. We also look critically at what we are doing as leaders, examine the impact of our behavior on the group, and analyze how the group is affecting us. Toward this end we reflect on the patterns of feedback we have received from the members about how our behavior has affected them. We also talk about the process and dynamics of the group. If we find that we have differing perceptions of the group process, we discuss our differences.

Topics for Coleader Meetings

We cannot overemphasize the importance of meeting with your coleader throughout the duration of the group. Many suggestions in earlier chapters for issues for discussion at these meetings also apply to the working stage. Here are a few other topics that are particularly relevant to the working stage.

Ongoing Evaluation of the Group Coleaders can make it a practice to devote some time to appraising the direction the group is taking and its level of productivity. In a closed group, one with a predetermined termination date (such as 16 weeks), coleaders would do well to evaluate the group's progress around the 8th week. This evaluation can be a topic of discussion both privately and in the group itself. If both leaders agree that the group seems to be bogging down and that members are losing interest, for example, leaders should bring these perceptions into the group so that the members can look at their degree of satisfaction with their direction and progress.

Discussion of Techniques It is useful to discuss techniques and leadership styles with a coleader. One of the leaders might be hesitant to try any technique because of a fear of making a mistake, because of not knowing where to go next, or because of passively waiting for permission from the coleader to introduce techniques. Such issues, along with any stylistic differences between leaders, are topics for exploration.

Theoretical Orientations As we mentioned earlier, it is not essential that coleaders share the same theory of group work, for sometimes differing theoretical preferences can blend nicely. You can learn a lot from discussing theory as it applies to practice. Therefore, we encourage you to read, attend workshops and special seminars, and discuss what you are learning with your coleader. Doing so can result in bringing to the group sessions some new and interesting variations.

Self-Disclosure Issues Coleaders should explore their sense of appropriate and therapeutic self-disclosure. For example, if you are willing to share with members your reactions that pertain to group issues yet are reserved in disclosing personal outside issues, whereas your coleader freely and fully talks about her marital situation, members may perceive you as holding back. This issue, too, can be discussed both in the group and privately with your coleader.

Confrontation Issues What we have just said about self-disclosure also applies to confrontation. You can imagine the problems that could ensue from your coleader's practice of harsh and unrelenting confrontations to get members to open up if you believe in providing support to the exclusion of any confrontation. You might easily be labeled as the "good leader" and your coleader as the "bad leader." If such differences in style exist, the two of you need to talk about this at length if the group is not to suffer.

Journal Prompts

The following questions are meant to serve as prompts for members of a group during the working stage. If you are leading groups, you might find these to be useful for your group members to discuss in group or to journal about between sessions. In addition, we encourage you to think about your responses to these questions as either a real or an imagined group member.

1. What have you observed that demonstrates that a high level of trust or cohesion between group members has developed?
2. What patterns of communication do you see happening in this stage of the group?
3. How satisfied are you with your level of participation? Explain.
4. In what ways are you willing to take risks or not in the group?
5. How are members and the leaders handling conflicts that occur in the group?
6. How are you dealing with feedback and confrontation from group members or from the leaders?
7. In what ways do you feel supported or not by the group members or the leaders?
8. What changes do you feel hopeful about making as a result of being in this group?
9. How willing are you to take action to bring about change outside of the group?

Points to Remember

Working Stage of a Group

Working Stage Characteristics

When a group reaches the working stage, its central characteristics include the following:

- The level of trust and cohesion is high.
- Communication within the group is open and involves an accurate expression of what is being experienced.
- Members interact with one another freely and directly.
- There is a willingness to take risks and to make oneself known to others; members bring to the group personal topics they want to explore and understand better.
- Conflict among members, if it exists, is recognized and dealt with directly and effectively.
- Feedback is given freely and accepted and considered nondefensively.
- Confrontation is caring and respectful and is accepted as a challenge to examine one's behavior.
- Members are willing to work outside the group to achieve behavioral changes.

- Participants feel supported in their attempts to change and are willing to risk new behavior.
- Members feel hopeful that they can change if they are willing to take action; they do not feel helpless.

Member Tasks and Functions

The working stage is characterized by the exploration of personally meaningful material. To reach this stage, members will have to fulfill these tasks and roles:

- Bring into group sessions personal concerns they are willing to discuss.
- Offer feedback and remain open to feedback from others even though this may increase anxiety for some members.
- Be willing to practice new skills and behaviors in daily life and bring the results to the sessions; insight alone will not produce change.
- Be willing to take risks; the work of the group will stop if members become too relaxed and comfortable.
- Continually assess their level of satisfaction with the group and actively take steps to change their level of involvement in the sessions if necessary.

Leader Functions

Leaders address these central leadership functions at the working stage:

- Continue to model appropriate behavior, especially caring confrontation, and disclose ongoing reactions to the group.
- Support the members' willingness to take risks and assist them in carrying this into their daily living.
- Interpret the meaning of behavior patterns at appropriate times so that members will be able to engage in a deeper level of self-exploration and consider alternative behaviors.
- Explore common themes that provide for some universality, and link one or more members' work with that of others in the group.
- Emphasize the importance of translating insight into action; encourage members to practice new skills.
- Promote those behaviors that will increase the level of cohesion.

Exercises

Assessment of the Working Stage

1. **Key Indicators.** What signs do you look for to determine whether a group has attained the working stage? Identify specific characteristics you see as especially related to this stage. To what degree has your group class evolved to the working stage? To what degree are you accomplishing your personal goals in the group?
2. **Changing Membership in Open Groups.** Assume that you are leading a group with a changing membership. Although there is a core of members who attend consistently, clients eventually terminate, and new members join the group. What obstacles will the members have to deal with if this group is to reach a working stage? How would you work to increase cohesion in this type of group? How would you handle the reality of members' terminating and new members' assimilating into the group?
3. **Personal and Appropriate Self-Disclosure.** What guidelines would you offer to members on appropriate self-disclosure? Can you explain to members the value of being personal and sharing who they are? How might you respond to this statement made by a member? "I don't see why there is so much emphasis on telling others what I think and feel. I've always been a private person, and all this personal talk makes me feel uncomfortable." How might you deal with this member in a voluntary group? In an involuntary group?

4. **Effective Confrontation.** There are important differences between effective and ineffective confrontation. How would you explain this difference to group members? Think about how you might respond to a person who had been in your group for some time and who said, "I don't see why we focus so much on problems and on confronting people with negative feelings. All this makes me want to retreat. I'm afraid to say much because I'd rather hear positive feedback."

Questions for Discussion

In small groups, explore the following questions:

1. What are the major differences between a working and a nonworking group? Between a working and a nonworking member?
2. What three therapeutic factors do you consider to be most important in bringing about change during the working stage?
3. What specific guidelines would you follow to determine whether self-disclosure would be appropriate and facilitative for you as a leader?
4. What would you want to teach members during the working stage about giving and receiving feedback?
5. Although productive work can occur at all the stages of a group, not all groups reach what are described in this chapter as being characteristic of a working stage. What prevents a group from reaching a working stage?

Member's Weekly Evaluation of a Group

Directions: This evaluation exercise can be given to members at the end of each group session you may be leading to give you a quick index of the level of satisfaction of the members. You can summarize the results and begin a session with the trends you are noticing from the evaluation sheets. Have the members circle the appropriate number for each item, using the following scale:

1 or 2 = very weak
3 or 4 = moderately weak
5 or 6 = adequate
7 or 8 = moderately strong
9 or 10 = very strong

1. What degree of preparation (reacting, thinking about the topic, reading, and writing) did you do for this week?

   1 2 3 4 5 6 7 8 9 10

2. How would you rate your involvement in the group today?

   1 2 3 4 5 6 7 8 9 10

3. How would you rate the group's level of involvement?

   1 2 3 4 5 6 7 8 9 10

4. Rate yourself on the degree to which you saw yourself today as willing to take risks, to share with other members what you thought and felt, and to be an active participant.

   1 2 3 4 5 6 7 8 9 10

5. To what degree do you feel satisfied with your experience in the group?

   1 2 3 4 5 6 7 8 9 10

6. To what degree do you feel that the group dealt with issues in a personal and meaningful way (sharing feelings as opposed to intellectual discussion)?

   1 2 3 4 5 6 7 8 9 10

7. To what degree do you experience trust within the group?

   1 2 3 4 5 6 7 8 9 10

8. How would you rate the group leader's level of involvement and investment in today's session?

   1 2 3 4 5 6 7 8 9 10

9. Rate your leader on the dimensions of his or her ability today to create a good working climate as characterized by warmth, respect, support, empathy, and trust.

   1 2 3 4 5 6 7 8 9 10

Guide to Groups in Action: Evolution and Challenges DVD and Workbook

Here are some suggestions for making use of this chapter along with the working stage segment of *Evolution of a Group*, the first program in *Groups in Action*.

1. **Characteristics of the Working Stage.** In a concise way, identify the key characteristics of a group in a working stage. On the DVD, how does the group seem different during the working stage than it did during the initial and transition stages? Review the section in this chapter on the contrasts between a working group and a nonworking group. How do these points apply to this group?
2. **Therapeutic Factors That Operate in Groups.** As you view the DVD, look for specific illustrations of members' work unfolding in that group. See the workbook for a few of the scenarios that are played out during the working stage by various members, and list examples of the work of different members and the therapeutic factors that are operating. What can you learn about the value of role playing, encouraging the group members to work in the here and now, and sharing reactions to one another? What is the value of members expressing their feelings over painful issues? What is the value of linking members together with common themes and pursuing work with several members at the same time? How does role playing influence the process of the group?

On the DVD can you identify one member's work that acted as a catalyst to bring others into the interactions? Both the text and the DVD illustrate examples of symbolically speaking to a parent in one's primary language through role playing. What are you learning about techniques to facilitate self-exploration through symbolically dealing with a parent in a group? How does staying in the here and now enhance the depth of self-exploration?

3. **Working With Metaphors.** The DVD demonstrates ways we, as coleaders, can follow a client's lead by paying attention to his or her metaphors. What metaphors did you hear, and how would you work with them?
4. **Applying the DVD Group to Yourself.** As you view the working segment, answer these questions: Which member (or members) most stands out for you in this segment, and why? What leader functions do you see being illustrated?
5. **Using the Workbook.** Refer to Segment 4: Working Stage in the workbook and complete the inventories and exercises.

MindTap for Counseling

Additional resources can be found on CengageBrain.com and by logging into the MindTap course created by your professor. There you will find a variety of study tools and useful resources that include quizzes, videos, interactive exercises, and more.

CHAPTER

9 Final Stage of a Group

CHAPTER LEARNING OBJECTIVES

1. Describe the dynamics associated with group process and development (CACREP, 2016, Standard B)
2. Discuss the main leader and member tasks of the final stage of a group
3. Identify issues in effectively terminating a group experience
4. Explain the importance of dealing with feelings of separation
5. Suggest guidelines for dealing with good-byes in an effective manner
6. Explain some methods for reviewing the group experience
7. Understand how practice outside of the group is necessary for behavioral change to occur
8. Clarify the kind of feedback that is useful during the final stage of a group
9. Describe how contracts and homework help members consolidate their learning
10. Understand how to deal with setbacks and explain relapse prevention strategies
11. Explore guidelines for applying what is learned in a group to daily life
12. Identify methods for evaluation of a group experience
13. Explore coleader issues at the end of a group
14. Describe methods of follow-up after a group ends

Your internship is coming to an end, and you will need to close the group you have been leading for 10 months. You have been working with inpatient, single mothers dealing with drug rehabilitation and childhood abuse issues. Many of the women have issues of abandonment and loss in their history. During your final meeting, one of the members is absent and you don't know why. Another member brings up a serious problem that cannot be adequately attended to at this late stage. The group had achieved a high degree of cohesion, and you are surprised by a hostile confrontation between two of the members.

- How will you address these issues with the members during the termination phase?
- Could you have done anything to prevent these occurrences?
- What would you be inclined to do about the member who was not present?
- How would you address the member's absence in the group?
- What issues around loss do you have, and how do you typically handle good-byes in your own life?
- What key clinical issues will members be dealing with at this stage?
- What ethical considerations are pressing?
- How might your theoretical orientation influence how you make sense of these client behaviors and intervene with group members?

Introduction

The initial phase of a group's development is crucial—participants are getting acquainted, basic trust is being established, norms are being determined that will affect later intensive work, and a unique group identity is taking shape. The final stages of the evolution of a group are equally vital—members have an opportunity to clarify and integrate the meaning of their experiences in the group, consolidate the gains they have made, and decide what newly acquired behaviors and changes they are committed to bringing to their everyday lives.

In this chapter we discuss ways of bringing the group experience to an end and describe how you can help members evaluate their experience in the group. The group leader's theoretical orientation will influence the way termination issues are approached. Important topics we address for the final stage of a group include the following:

- Tasks members need to accomplish in the termination process
- Techniques to help members consolidate learning and deal with unfinished business
- Importance of exploring members' thoughts and feelings about the ending of the group
- How to prepare members for leaving the group and applying their new behaviors in daily life
- How to evaluate the effectiveness of the group and gain feedback from the group members

Endings in a therapeutic group are frequently emotionally charged and complex events. Several tasks need to be accomplished in the final stage of a group's history, but it is difficult to offer one general guideline that covers all kinds of groups. Many variables must be considered in deciding how much time to allow for ending. For example, the number of sessions devoted to reviewing and integrating the group experience is dependent on how long the group has been in existence and whether the group is an open or closed group. Whatever the type of group, adequate time should be set aside for integrating and evaluating the experience. There is a danger of attempting to cover too much in one final meeting, which can have the effect of fragmenting the group instead of leading to transferable learning. The most important thing about the group experience is what the members take with them by way of new learning to enhance the quality of their lives.

Endings in a therapeutic group are frequently emotionally charged and complex events.

LO2

Tasks of the Final Stage of a Group: Consolidation of Learning

The final phase in the life of a group is the time for members to consolidate their learning and develop strategies for transferring what they learned in the group to daily life. At this time members need to be able to express what the group experience has meant to them and to state where they intend to go from here. This is a time for members to process their feelings and thoughts about their experience in the group. For many group members, endings are difficult. Members need to face the reality of termination and learn how to say good-bye. If the group has been truly therapeutic, members will be able to extend their learning outside, even though they may experience a sense of sadness and loss.

As a leader, your task is to assist members in learning to put what has occurred in the group into a meaningful perspective. One of the purposes of a group is to implement in-group learning in the daily life of members. The potential for learning permanent lessons is likely to be lost if the leader does not provide a structure that helps members review and integrate what they have learned.

In a *closed* group that has had the same members for all sessions, the task of leaders is to help members review their individual work and the evolving patterns from the first to the final session. In these groups it is particularly valuable for members to give one another feedback on specific changes they have made.

An *open* group has different challenges because members leave the group and new members are incorporated into the group at various times. The termination process is most meaningful when members have ample time to explore their thoughts and feelings both when a member is leaving and when a new member enters the group. Here are some tasks to be accomplished with a person who is terminating membership in an *open* group:

- Educate members to give adequate notice when they decide it is time to terminate. This will ensure that members have time to address any unfinished business with themselves or others in the group.
- Allow time for the person who will be leaving to prepare emotionally for termination.

- Give an opportunity to others to say good-bye, to share their own reactions, and to give feedback. Remaining group members often have reactions about the loss of a member, and it is essential that they have an opportunity to express their thoughts and feelings.
- Explore cultural influences on members' perceptions and understandings of endings. For cultures that emphasize continuity of relationships, endings may be viewed as an interruption rather than a permanent reality. Other cultures may view an ending as a permanent severing. These different understandings and reactions to endings need to be processed within the group (Mangione, Forti, & Iacuzzi, 2007).
- Help members who are leaving the group identify how they can incorporate what was meaningful in the group into their daily life. Their experiences and lessons learned can help them face future challenges throughout their lifetime.
- Assist the member who is leaving to review what has been learned in the group and, specifically, what to do with this learning. Review and reinforce changes made by each of the members of the group.
- Make referrals, when appropriate.

Sometimes members will terminate without any prior notice. If it is at all possible, group leaders can encourage such members to explore their motivations for terminating and to remain in the group long enough to address possible reasons for termination. How would you deal with a member who stated that she has to leave the group due to unforeseen circumstances? If this member wanted to remain in the group, but would be absent for a considerable time, how would you address this request?

Termination of the Group Experience

LO3

The issues that arise during the termination stage are as varied as the members, however, several themes are common to many groups. Some members will engage in behavior that makes it easier for them to leave the group. They might present themselves as distant, problematic, and argumentative. In some cases, they diminish the work that they themselves or other members have accomplished. Just like members' behaviors throughout the group, their style of leaving reveals a great deal about how they handle pain, unresolved loss, and grief. Many people have experienced negative or unhealthy good-byes in their life, and group leaders can teach members how to process endings and have a sense of closure both in the group and in relationships outside of the group.

Some group counselors believe that termination begins on the first day of group and that leaders should prepare members throughout for the eventual ending of a group. This is a task that the leader in the opening vignette may not have adequately attended to, such as stressing the importance of bringing up unfinished business before the last session to allow time to address these concerns. The key is to raise issues of termination at the right time. The way group leaders talk about the upcoming ending will differ based on a variety of factors:

whether the group is an open or closed one, the loss or abandonment concerns that members have experienced, the length of time the group has been together, the age of the group members, the psychological functioning of the group, and the level of cohesion within the group. Group members may experience and express closure differently due to their cultural background, and leaders should be aware of these cultural differences in the termination process. These are just a few of the factors to consider when determining *when* and *how* to address termination.

Critical Incident

An Uneventful Termination Session

1. Description of Incident

In the final session of a personal-growth group, the group leader noticed that group members appeared disengaged and were unwilling to interact with one another. The leader was concerned that this termination session was an anticlimactic end to the group. When the group facilitator shared his observations with the group, one group member stated, "I guess we just feel like our work in the group is done, so we don't really know what to talk about." Another member commented that he was angry with several group members but didn't want to talk about it because the group was ending. A third member said, "I don't like good-byes. Can't we just keep meeting as a group?"

2. Process Questions for Group Leaders

1. Why might group members seem silent during a termination session?
2. What feelings might group members be having at a closing session?
3. How could you prepare group members for the termination session?
4. What types of closing activities might you present to the members?
5. At what stage would you talk about termination issues with group members?
6. How might a group member's style of exiting the group be indicative of his or her past or present relationships outside of the group?
7. How would you describe what an effective good-bye looks like?
8. How do you typically handle endings or good-byes in your own life?

3. Clinical Reflections

The group leader interpreted the members' behaviors as being "low energy" and "uninvolved." In fact, members were experiencing a wide array of feelings and thoughts about the ending of the group. The sense of flatness may have been a way for some members to minimize the importance of the group. Some members may have stirred up conflict or disengaged emotionally to avoid painful good-byes. Sometimes it is easier for members to leave one another if they are angry or tell themselves they don't really care. Acknowledging positive feelings and leaving others on good terms is a foreign experience for many people.

Leaders need to prepare members early for termination. Deciding when to talk about termination depends on many factors. For some members, two or three sessions before the end of group will be enough, and for others it may need to be talked about at each stage of the group. How the group members end with one another often is as important as what they learned throughout the group. We find that many group members have regrets about good-byes they have had in their lives and are not sure how to end in effective ways. Termination can be a bittersweet stage of a group, providing

continued

members with new ways of experiencing loss, having closure, and acknowledging the impact that they have had on one another. Leaders' feelings about dealing with endings in their own lives can have a significant impact on how they address termination issues in their groups.

4. Possible Interventions

1. Instead of being too quick to interpret the silence as members checking out, share what you are noticing with the group: "I notice that there is a great deal of silence in the group today."
2. Leaders can use incomplete sentences as a way of introducing the unspoken reactions in the room. Facilitate a "go-around" and ask members to finish one of these incomplete sentences: "As this group is coming to an end, I am aware of. . ." "One regret I have about this being our last session is. . ." "I don't like good-byes because. . ." "I want others to remember me as. . ." "Something I hope I will remember about this group experience is. . ." The leader can use this activity to help bring to the surface unfinished business that is present but not being verbalized by the group.
3. Create a "group metaphor," in which the facilitator prompts, "If this group were a movie, what would be the plot? The title? The characters' roles?"
4. Conduct a group art activity in which members co-create a piece of art, allowing each member to take a piece of the creation home.
5. Several sessions before the termination session, ask members how they would like to bring their group to closure. This intervention will likely raise numerous reactions to the reality that they will need to say good-bye, which prevents the good-bye from happening without any forethought or intention.
6. Provide group members with a memento to take home, such as a quote that resonates for each member or a small totem to represent the individual, so members can remember the group and what they learned.

Group Proposals Illustrate Ending of a Group

In Chapters 10 and 11 various group proposals illustrate how to prepare members for the ending of a group and how to structure the final session. In a group for children who have been abused in Chapter 10, the last session is devoted to a celebration of the group experience. The main purpose is to provide a context for members to reflect on what they have learned about themselves and others. Because Teresa Christensen gives the children in her group an opportunity to participate in structuring the closing sessions, the structure for this termination often varies. However, she requests that the members share this kind of information: (a) what they have learned about their individual strengths and talents, (b) how they plan to continue making positive choices and building healthy relationships outside of group, and (c) their individual plans about how to take care of themselves.

In Chapter 11 participants in an older adult bereavement group are provided with a further opportunity to learn how to deal with loss in a healthy manner as this group ends. Alan Forrest encourages members in his bereavement group to address any unfinished business toward the deceased or toward other group members or the facilitators. Group participants also are encouraged to provide each other with feedback on their experience in the group and to say good-bye. The members can talk about what it will be like for them to no longer have this group, to explore what the group experience has meant to them, and to examine their plans for continued support. Rituals, such as having each participant light a candle that represents the deceased and share their reactions about the deceased, helps members consolidate what they have learned and provides further emotional healing. In this final shared experience, light is used as a metaphor for insight and illumination, and the candle provides each participant with something concrete to take home. As you look at the other group proposals in Chapters 10 and 11, you will notice that all of the group counselors take the matter of termination seriously and prepare members to deal with their thoughts and feelings about the ending of their group.

Dealing With Feelings of Separation 

In discussing the initial phase of a group, we commented on the importance of encouraging members to express their fears and expectations so that trust would not be inhibited. As members approach the ending of a group or are leaving an ongoing group, it is equally essential that they be encouraged to express their reactions. They may have fears or concerns about separating. For some, leaving the group may be as anxiety producing as entering it. Certain members are likely to be convinced that the trust they now feel in the group will not be replicated outside. A central task of the leader at this time is to remind members that the cohesion they now have is the result of active steps they took. Members need to be reminded that close relationships do not happen by accident; rather, they are the product of considerable struggle and commitment to work through interpersonal conflicts.

Even if the participants realize that they can create meaningful relationships and build a support system outside the group, they still may experience a sense of loss and sadness over the ending of this particular community. Termination often evokes emotional reactions pertaining to death and mortality, separation and abandonment, and hopes for a new beginning (Rutan et al., 2014). To facilitate members' expressions of their feelings over separation, it is important for leaders to examine their own experiences or difficulties with saying good-bye. Psychoanalytically oriented group practitioners focus on identifying and managing their countertransference, which could interfere with their ability to assist members in exploring their reactions about the termination of the group. Mangione and colleagues (2007) stress that group leaders must be aware of their personal limitations pertaining to endings or loss if they expect to act ethically and effectively in assisting members in dealing with termination. Sixty-two percent of the group therapists who participated in their survey indicated they had experienced difficulties in endings in a group because of events in their personal lives.

Although leaders can take partial credit for group outcomes, they need to assist members in identifying what they did to create a successful group. In our experience, when members want to give us more credit than we think we deserve, we may reply with: "The group was successful because all of us worked hard. If you can remember what you specifically did in here that resulted in desired changes, then you are more likely to be able to create a context for similar changes in your everyday life once this group ends."

Learning in Action

Good-Bye Letter

As you reflect on your time in a group that is coming to a close, write a good-bye letter to the experience. You may want to include the answers to some of these questions in your letter and reflection:

- What has your experience in this group been like for you?
- Describe your journey from the beginning to now?
- How did you enter the group?
- How are you leaving the group?
- What did you learn about yourself that you want to remember?
- What did you learn about others that will help you in your relationships?
- What are you taking from other members that you want them to know about?
- Who would you like to thank in the group and for what?
- As you look back on how you participated in the group, is there anything you wish you had done differently?
- In general, how do you handle good-byes?
- What feelings and thoughts are coming up for you as your time in this group is coming to a close?
- Is there a part of you that you want to say good-bye to or leave in the group?
- Do you have any hopes or wishes for others in the group that you would like to share?
- How does your cultural background influence the way you say good-bye?

We encourage you to share the letter you have written with your group members. Make a note to yourself to reread the letter 6 months from now as a reminder of what you worked toward and want to continue learning.

NOTE: This activity can be completed as a member of a class, as a graduating cohort, or as a group member. You also may want to use this exercise at the closing of a group that you are leading.

Comparing Early and Later Perceptions in the Group

In many of the groups we have led, we typically ask members at the first session to spend a few minutes looking around the room quietly. We say: "As you are looking at different people, be aware of your reactions. Are you already drawn to certain people more than others? Are there some in here whom you already feel intimidated by? Are you catching yourself making judgments about people?" After a few minutes of this silent scanning of the room, we ask members to refrain from sharing anything that they have just thought or felt. Generally, we let the members know that we will ask them to repeat this exercise at the final group session. When this time arrives, we tell them: "Check out the room again, being aware of each person here. Do you remember the reactions you had at that first meeting? How have your reactions changed, if at all? How does it feel to be in here now compared with what it was like for you when the group began?" A main task for members during the final session is to put into words what has transpired from the first to the final session and what they have learned about others and themselves. If the group appears different at this final meeting, we ask members to reflect on what they did, both individually and as a group, to bring about these changes.

Dealing With Unfinished Business

During the final phase of a group, allow time for expressing and working through any unfinished business relating to transactions between members or to the group process and goals. Leaders cannot prevent unresolved conflicts from surfacing at the time of termination, and there are many possible reasons for such an outburst. A member may be trying to lessen the pain of leaving by "devaluing" others, or the member may have a pattern of leaving relationships in anger. A member may have been sitting on unresolved feelings toward another member for some time. Despite how much we prepare members not to wait until the last session of a group to address lingering reactions, at times these issues come up at the end. Although there may be little time to "resolve" the conflict or unfinished business at the last session, it is still useful to discuss the relevance and impact of the member's choice to withhold reactions until the end of a group. The member could learn from this experience and assess whether or not it is worth it to express his or her thoughts and feelings in similar situations in the future.

It is not realistic to assume that all of the issues that were explored will have been worked through. As mentioned earlier, if members are given this reminder a few sessions before the final meeting, they can be motivated to use the remaining time to complete their own agenda. We often ask this question: "If this were the last session of this group, how would you feel about what you have done, and what would you wish you had done differently?" In addition, the group may point out many areas on which people could productively focus once they leave the group.

Personal Gestures in Expressing the Meaning of a Group Experience

During closing sessions it is not uncommon for members to want to offer gifts or tokens of appreciation to the leaders and perhaps even to one another. Your counseling theory and personal style will likely influence how you view this practice. In our experience it can be a meaningful part of the work that was accomplished as well as lead to a fruitful discussion about being open to both giving and receiving gifts. Whatever your policy on gift giving may be, it can be beneficial to explore the members' intentions within the group. For example, is it a sign of appreciation, or is it out of a desire to have a personal relationship with you once counseling has ended? Is it common in the member's culture to give gifts to mentors or teachers? Exploring the member's intentions in a curious and interested manner can lead to a rich discussion.

Another common occurrence during termination is that clients may ask to give you a hug, or you may be moved to want to hug them. In general it is safest to wait for a client to ask for a hug rather than initiating one yourself. It is useful to think about how you would respond to this ahead of time. For some counselors the idea of touching a client feels off limits, and for others it is a natural expression of the connections that can be made throughout counseling. There is not one way to handle this that fits all situations.

Reviewing the Group Experience

At the final stage of a group, we review *what* members have learned throughout the sessions and *how* they learned these lessons. For example, Adam learned that denying his anger had contributed to his feelings of depression and to many psychosomatic ailments. In the sessions he practiced expressing his anger more constructively instead of smiling and denying those feelings, and as a result he acquired important skills. It is helpful for Adam to recall what he actually did to get others to listen to him, for he could easily forget these hard-learned lessons.

Part of our practice for ending groups involves setting aside time for all the participants to discuss matters such as what they have learned in the group, turning points for them, what was helpful and what was difficult about the group, ways that the sessions could have had a greater impact, and the entire history of the group as seen in some perspective. To make this evaluation meaningful, we encourage participants to be concrete. When members make global statements such as "This group has been fantastic, and I grew a lot from it" or "I don't think I'll ever forget all the things I learned in here," we assist them in being more specific. We might ask some of these questions:

- In what ways has the group been meaningful to you?
- When you say that you have grown a lot, what are some of the specific changes you have made?
- What are a few of the things you've learned that you'd most want to remember?

By asking members to pinpoint what they learned about themselves in the group, they are in a better position to determine what they are willing to do with this increased knowledge. We frequently emphasize to members the importance of putting what they have learned into specific language and stating the ways in which they have translated their insights into action.

Learning in Action

Reviewing the Class and Group Experience

Form small groups and discuss what you have learned about yourself up to this point that you think would either contribute to or detract from your effectiveness as a group leader. Explore the following questions:

- How willing have you been to take risks in this class?
- What have you learned about how groups best function (or what gets in the way of an effective group) through your experience in your class and your group experience?
- To what degree did you accomplish your personal goals in your group?
- How did your group deal with the tasks of termination?
- What were significant turning points in your group?
- As a group, how would you evaluate the level of interaction and the cohesion attained?

Practice for Behavioral Change

In groups that meet weekly there are many opportunities for practicing new behaviors during each group session. It is good to encourage members to think of how they can continue such work between sessions. Members can carry out homework assignments and give a report in the next session on how well they succeeded with trying new ways of behaving in various situations. In this way the transfer of learning is maximized. Members practice new behaviors in the group sessions as well as putting into practice these more effective coping skills when dealing with emerging concerns.

During the final stage of a group, we draw from many concepts and techniques that are a part of cognitive behavioral approaches in solidifying members' learning. We reemphasize the value of practice (both in group situations and in outside life) as a way of solidifying and consolidating their learning. We rely heavily on role-playing situations and behavioral rehearsals for anticipated interactions, teaching members specific skills that will help them make their desired behavioral changes. We encourage members to continue to take action and to try out new behavioral patterns with selected others outside the group.

We ask members to look at themselves and how they want to continue changing rather than considering how they can change others. If Damien would like his wife to show more interest in the family and be more accepting of his changes, we encourage him to tell his wife about *his* changes and about himself. We caution him about the temptation of demanding that his wife be different. In rehearsals and role-playing situations, we typically ask members to state briefly the essence of what they want to say to the significant people in their lives so that they do not lose the message they most want to convey.

Carrying Learning Further

One of the tasks of the final phase of a group is to develop a specific plan of action for ways to continue applying changes to situations outside of the group. Assisting members in carrying their learning into action is a key function of leaders. It is our practice to routinely discuss with participants various ways in which they can use what they have learned in the group in other situations. For many members a group is merely the beginning of personal change. Some members use the group to do their work, but for others the group is a place of "preparing to change." Sometimes group members spend their time resisting growth or only contemplating change. Then, when the time seems to have run out, they may find motivation for beginning the process of doing things differently in their lives. It is critical to assist these members in defining the steps they will take to translate their new awareness into action. It's never too late to change, and group members can use both their insights gained during the group and their ambivalence to learn new ways of being in their lives.

Assisting members in carrying their learning into action is a key function of leaders.

If a group has been successful, members now have some new directions to follow in dealing with problems as they arise. Furthermore, members acquire some needed tools and resources for continuing the process of personal growth. For this reason, discussing available programs and making referrals is especially timely as a group is ending.

One strategy for assisting members in conceptualizing some long-term directions is asking them to project themselves into the future either by writing a letter to themselves or expressing their thoughts in the group. The leader can ask members to think of the changes they would most like to have made by the end of 6 months or 1 year from now. Members can then imagine that the entire group is meeting at one of these designated times and say what they'd most want to tell each other at that time. They can also describe what they will have to do to accomplish these long-term goals.

The technique of **future projection**, often used in psychodrama, is designed to help group members express and clarify concerns they have about their future. Rather than merely talking about what they would like in their lives at some future time, members are invited to create this future time in the here and now. For example, they might role-play with another group member a conversation they hope to have with a loved one. By enacting this future time and place with selected people and by bringing this event into the present, they are able get a new perspective on how best to get what they want. More information on the rationale for using the future projection technique is included in Chapter 4.

Giving and Receiving Feedback

Feedback from others in the group is especially helpful to members who identify and discuss changes they expect to make in their everyday lives. This preparation for dealing with others outside the group is essential if members are to maximize the effects of what they have learned. Members benefit by practicing new interpersonal skills, by getting feedback, by discussing this feedback, and by modifying certain behaviors so that they are more likely to bring about desired changes once they leave the group.

Throughout the history of a group the members have been giving and receiving feedback, which has helped them assess the impact they are having on others. During the closing sessions, however, we like to emphasize a more focused type of feedback for each person. We generally begin by asking members for a brief report on how they have perceived themselves in the group, how the group has affected them, what conflicts have become clearer, and what (if any) decisions they have contemplated. Then the rest of the members give feedback concerning how they have perceived and been affected by that person.

A potential problem as a group is ending is that members have a tendency to give global feedback, which will not be remembered nor be very helpful. We caution against expressing global sentiments such as "I really like you." "I feel close to you." "You are a super person." or "I will always remember you." Being influenced by the cognitive behavioral approaches, we provide guidelines on how to give meaningful feedback, suggesting that members begin with one of these ideas:

- My hope for you is . . .
- If I could give you one thing, it would be . . .
- Some of the things I've learned from you are . . .

Feedback at this point has a focus on integration and synthesis of learning. As the group nears termination, constructive feedback is stated in such a manner that the individual is given an opportunity for closure. This is not a time to "hit and run." We do not want people to leave one another with negative or critical feedback, and we ask members to refrain from saying to others what they have never said in prior sessions. This is not the time for members to unload stored-up negative reactions, for the member being confronted does not have a real opportunity to work through this feedback. During this feedback session, we emphasize that participants can make some specific contracts to explore further areas after the group ends. In our practice, we have found that some type of group follow-up session at a later date is useful. This can give the members added incentive to think about ways to keep their new decisions operative.

Journal Prompts

The following questions are meant to serve as prompts for members during the final stage of a group. If you are running groups, you might find these to be useful for your group members to discuss in group or to journal about between sessions. Consider your responses to these questions as either a real or imagined group member.

1. How are you feeling about the ending of the group and the reality of separation between you and group members? What are you doing to cope with these feelings in the group? (Are you pulling back, picking fights, disengaging, expressing grief?)
2. In what ways are you sharing your reactions toward ending with other group members?
3. How are you planning to translate what you have been learning in the group into other areas of your life?
4. What issues of loss or abandonment are being triggered for you, if any?
5. How would you like to say good-bye to the group members and leaders and to your group experience?

Use of a Contract and Homework

A useful way to assist members in continuing the new beginnings established during the group is to devote time during one of the final sessions to writing contracts. These contracts outline steps the members agree to take to increase their chances of successfully meeting their goals when the group ends. It is important that members develop their own homework and that the plan is not so ambitious that they are setting themselves up for failure. Many of the cognitive behavioral approaches draw heavily from homework interventions during the final stage of a group. For example, reality therapists spend considerable time teaching members specific ways to create successful action plans. If your theoretical orientation is experiential and relationship oriented, your members also may benefit from the planning procedures that are central in a reality therapy group.

If the participants choose to, they can read their contracts aloud so others can give specific helpful feedback. It is also of value to ask members to select at least one person in the group to whom they can report on their progress toward their goals, especially now when they are about to lose the support of their weekly group. This arrangement is useful not only for encouraging accountability but also for teaching people the value of establishing a support system as a way to help them bring about desired changes. Here are a few illustrations of contracts members have made during final group sessions:

- Amanda has worked on speaking up more frequently in her classes. She contracts to continue her verbal participation in class and to call at least two of her friends at the end of the semester to let them know about her progress.
- Roland has explored his tendency to isolate himself from people and has made some gains in reaching out to others, both in and out of group. He says that he feels better about himself, and he contracts with several people outside of the group to call, email, or text them once a month.
- Jason became aware of his bias against people who think and act differently from him. In his group he has challenged himself to approach members that he might typically shy away from because of such differences, which resulted in favorable outcomes. Jason wants to continue this new behavior when he leaves the group. With the permission of members, he agrees to email, text, or phone several people whom he initially backed away from to inform them of his progress.

We have recommended using homework during all the stages of a group. As a group is approaching its ending phase, however, homework of a different nature must be crafted. Homework can be included in the contracts members formulate, and measures can be discussed that will help members when the assignments they have given themselves do not materialize as they had expected.

Dealing With Setbacks

Even with hard work and commitment, members will not always get what they expected from their encounters. During the final stages of a group, it is helpful to reinforce members so that they can cope with realistic setbacks and avoid getting discouraged and giving up. Assisting members in creating a support system is a good way to help them deal with setbacks and keep focused on what they need to do to accomplish their goals. It is important for them to realize that even a small change is the first step in a new direction.

Relapse prevention is a basic part of many cognitive behavioral groups. Whatever your theoretical orientation may be, it is important to have a discussion about relapses and how to cope with unexpected outcomes. The chances of disappointing outcomes are lessened if members have given themselves homework that is manageable. Homework needs to be tailored to each member's contract, and members need to be careful about overambitious plans. If there is a follow-up meeting after the group terminates, this is an excellent time to reevaluate contracts and evaluate the degree to which members' homework is effective. (We consider follow-up meetings later in this chapter.) We stress to members how important it is that they attend the follow-up meeting, especially if they have not done all that they had agreed to do after the termination of the group. The follow-up session is another opportunity to evaluate each member's plan for future action.

Guidelines for Applying Group Learning to Life 

Certain behaviors and attitudes increase the chances that meaningful self-exploration will occur in a group. At this time we suggest that you refer to the section in Chapter 6 on "Helping Members Get the Most From a Group Experience." As members enter a group during the early phase, we teach them how to actively involve themselves. This teaching continues throughout the life of the group. At the final phase we reinforce some teaching points to help members consolidate what they have learned and to apply their learning to daily life. Toward the end of a group, the participants are likely to be receptive to considering how they can implement what they have learned.

Realize That the Group Is a Means to an End We do not consider a group experience an end in itself. Although feeling close to others may be pleasant, the purpose of a group is to enable participants to make decisions about how they will change their lives, including being able to be close to the important people in their lives. Groups that are therapeutic encourage people to look at themselves, to decide whether they like what they see, and if they so desire, to make plans for change.

As a group approaches termination, your task is to help members reflect on *what* they have learned, *how* they have learned it, and *what* they intend to do with their insights. Members are now in a position to decide what they are willing to do about what they have learned.

Change May Be Slow and Subtle People sometimes expect change to come about automatically, and once they do make changes, they may expect them to be permanent. This expectation can lead to discouragement when temporary setbacks occur. Ideally, members will bring these setbacks back to their group. This realization that the process of change can be slow makes useful material for exploration in a group.

One Group Alone May Not Permanently Change Your Life Those who seek a therapeutic group sometimes hold unrealistic expectations of rapid and dramatic change. Members need to be reminded that a single therapeutic experience, as potent as it may be in itself as a catalyst for significant change, is rarely sufficient to sustain these decisions. People spend many years creating a unique personality with its masks and defenses. It takes time to establish constructive alternatives. People do not easily relinquish familiar defenses, for even though the defenses may entail some pain, they do work. In some ways, the change process is just that—a process, not a final state. Once people make decisions regarding how they want to change and develop a realistic action plan for daily life, implementation of that plan requires ongoing attention and reflection.

What Will You Do With What You Have Learned? At its best, a group will provide moments of truth during which clients can see who they are and how they present themselves to others. It is up to the members to do something with the glimpses of truth they gain. Members may exercise caution in translating what they have learned in a group to their everyday lives. Many people seek therapy

It is up to the members to do something with the glimpses of truth they gain.

because they have lost the ability to live life meaningfully and have become dependent on others to direct their lives and take responsibility for their decisions. They expect the group to decide for them, or they are sensitively attuned to being what the group expects them to be. If groups are truly useful, members will have gained greater awareness and are likely to make decisions about how they want to be different in everyday life.

Reminding Members About Confidentiality

At the final session we again comment on the importance of keeping confidentiality, even after the group has ended. We caution that confidences are often divulged unintentionally by members enthusiastically wanting to share with others the details of their group experience. We provide examples of how they can talk about the group without breaking confidences. A suggestion we offer is that members can tell others *what* they learned but should be careful about describing the details of *how* they learned something. It is when members discuss the "how" of their experience that they are inclined to inappropriately refer to other members. Also, we encourage participants to talk about themselves and not about the problems of other participants.

Evaluation of the Group Experience

Evaluation is a basic aspect of any group experience, and it can benefit both members and the leader. Evaluation is an ongoing process throughout the life of a group—or at least at important turning points in the group—that tracks the progress of individual members and the group as a whole. Some type of rating scale can be devised to give the leader a good sense of how each member experienced and evaluated the group. Standardized instruments can also tap individual changes in attitudes and values. Such practical evaluation instruments can help members make a personal assessment of the group and can help the leader know what interventions were more, or less, helpful. A willingness to build evaluation into the structure of the group is bound to result in leaders improving the design of future groups.

After a group ends, we have at times sent a questionnaire to the members. It is quite possible for members to have different perceptions about the group once they have had some distance from it. Asking members to address some of our questions in writing encourages them to again reflect and one more time put into words the meaning of their experience in the group. By writing about their perceptions of the group experience, they are able to evaluate again how effective the group has been for them. Here is a sample questionnaire:

1. What general effect has your group experience had on your life?
2. What were some specific things you became aware of about your lifestyle, attitudes, and relationships with others? What are some changes you have made in your life that you can attribute at least partially to your group experience?

3. What problems did you encounter on leaving the group and following up on your decisions to change?
4. What effects do you think your participation in the group had on the significant people in your life?
5. Have there been any crises in your life since the termination of the group? How did you handle them?
6. How might your life be different now if you had not experienced the group?
7. Do you have anything to add about yourself and your experience either during or since the group ended?

We use the following measures to evaluate the effectiveness of our groups:

- We conduct individual follow-up interviews with members or keep in contact with members; letters and telephone conversations have been substituted when person-to-person interviews were not feasible.
- We hold one or more postgroup meetings, which is described in a later section.
- We ask members to complete brief questionnaires, such as the one included here, to assess what they found most and least valuable in their group experience.
- We strongly suggest (depending on the type of group) that members keep process notes in a journal. On the basis of their journal notes, which are private, members write several reaction papers describing their subjective experience in the group as well as what they are doing outside the group. These reaction papers are given to us both during the life of the group and after the group has terminated.

Members have continued to report to us that they found the writing they did both during and after the group extremely valuable to them in maintaining their commitment to change. Through the process of writing in a journal, members are able to focus on relevant trends and the key things they are discovering about themselves. They have a chance to privately clarify what they are experiencing and to rehearse what they want to say to significant people. Through their writing, members can recall turning points in the group, evaluate the impact of the group, and put the group experience into a meaningful perspective.

LO13

Coleader Issues as the Group Ends

It is helpful if coleaders are in agreement with each other about not bringing up new material that cannot be dealt with adequately before the end of the group. Members sometimes save up topics until the very end, almost hoping that there will be no time to explore them. It could be tempting to one of the coleaders to initiate new work with such a member, whereas the other coleader may be ready to bring the group to an end.

Here are some specific topics that you can discuss with your coleader during the final stage to ensure that you are working together:

- Are either of you concerned about any member? Are there any things you might want to say to certain members?
- Do you or your coleader have perceptions and reactions about the group that would be useful to share with the members before the final session?

- Are both of you able to deal with your own feelings of separation and ending? If not, you may collude with the members by avoiding talking about feelings pertaining to the termination of the group.
- Have both of you given thought to how you can best help members review what they have learned from the group and translate this learning to everyday situations?
- Do you have some plan to help members evaluate the group experience before the end of the group or at a follow-up session?

Once the group ends, we encourage coleaders to meet to discuss their experience in leading with each other and to put the entire history of the group in perspective. This practice is consistent with the ASGW (2008) "Best Practice Guidelines," which encourage leaders to process the workings of the group with themselves, group members, supervisors, or other colleagues. Here are some ideas that you might want to process with your coleader as a way to integrate your experiences and learning:

- Discuss the balance of responsibility between the coleaders. Did one coleader assume primary responsibility for directing while the other followed?
- Did a coleader overfunction or underfunction in any area?
- How did your styles of leadership blend, and what effect did this have on the group?
- Did you agree on basic matters such as evaluation of the group's direction and what was needed to keep the group progressing?
- Talk about what you liked and what was challenging about leading with each other. You can benefit by a frank discussion of what each of you learned from the other personally and professionally, including weaknesses and strengths, skills, and styles of leading.
- Evaluate each other in addition to evaluating yourself. Comparing your self-evaluation as a leader with your coleader's evaluation of you can be of great value. Look for areas needing further work; in this way each of you can grow in your capacity to lead effectively.
- You both can learn much from reviewing the turning points in the group. How did the group begin? How did it end? What happened in the group to account for its success or failure? This type of overall assessment helps in understanding the group process, which can be essential information in leading future groups.

It is a good policy for group leaders to write an assessment of the group as a whole and to also make summary comments about individual members, if appropriate. Keeping good notes, especially about the progress of a group, is particularly helpful in terms of making changes in future groups.

LO14

Follow-Up

Postgroup Sessions

In our practice we typically build follow-up group sessions into the scheduled meetings. Such follow-up is recommended by the ASGW (2008) "Best Practice Guidelines": "Group Workers conduct follow-up contact with group members, as appropriate, to assess outcomes or when requested by a group member(s)" (C.3).

Because members know that they will come together to evaluate their progress toward their stated goals, they are likely to be motivated to take steps to make changes. Participants can develop contracts at the final sessions that involve action between the termination and the follow-up session. Members often use one another as a support system. If they experience difficulties in following through on their commitments after the group, they can discuss these difficulties. It is a matter not so much of relying on one another for advice as of using the resources of the group for support.

At follow-up sessions, the participants can share difficulties they have encountered since leaving the group, talk about specific steps they have taken to keep themselves open for change, and remember some of the most positive experiences during the group itself. Follow-ups also give members a chance to express and possibly work through any afterthoughts or feelings connected with the group experience. As members gain distance from a group experience, they may identify certain regrets or afterthoughts. A follow-up meeting provides an avenue to express such thoughts and feelings about their group experience after the passage of some time.

The group proposal for a women's support group for survivors of incest described in Chapter 11 provides an example of a group that has follow-up procedures built into the treatment program. The group therapist, Lupe Alle-Corliss, schedules several follow-up meetings (6 to 12 weeks after the end of the group) to help the members make the transition from the weekly sessions to being on their own and relying on their support networks outside of the group. Also in Chapter 11 is a group proposal for a men's group in a community agency. As a way to evaluate the group outcomes, the group leader (Randy Alle-Corliss) schedules a follow-up group meeting called the "reunion group." The reunion group gives members a chance to take another look at what the group meant to them and how they have been applying their learning in their everyday lives. The men also have an opportunity to discuss any problems they have encountered in implementing a new style of behavior.

In our groups, we make sure that group members know about the goals for a follow-up session. It is not geared to doing new work; rather, this session is for finding out what people did with their experience in the group in their daily living. The members are asked to report on whether and how they are using their expanded self-awareness in their relationships in the outside world. The follow-up group session is a means of accountability for both the leader and the members. We ask members at the follow-up session whether they are continuing to reach out for what they want. What changes are they making, if any? Are they taking more risks? If they are trying out new behavior, what results are they getting? These are but a few of the topics we explore at a follow-up group session. For additional topics and questions, refer to the questionnaire presented earlier that we use as a basis for evaluation.

A follow-up session offers us one more opportunity to remind people that they are responsible for what they become and the necessity of putting forth the effort required for significant change. This session provides a timely opportunity to encourage and to discuss once more other avenues for continuing the work they did in a group.

If you administered any pretests to assess beliefs, values, attitudes, and levels of personal adjustment, the postgroup meeting is an ideal time to administer some of these same instruments for comparison purposes. We support the practice of developing an assessment instrument that can be given before members join a group (or at the initial session), again at one of the last sessions, and finally at some time after termination. If you meet with the members on an individual basis to review how well they have accomplished their personal goals, these assessment devices can be of value in discussing specific changes in attitudes and behaviors.

Of course, follow-up group sessions with the entire group are not always practical or possible, but alternative methods are available. Group leaders can send a brief questionnaire to assess members' perceptions about the group and its impact on their lives. Another option is to contact the members of the group via a secure online live video chat program. It is important to have advanced informed consent about how to contact members to avoid potential invasion of privacy or breach of confidentiality.

Points to Remember

Final Stage of a Group

Final Stage Characteristics

During the final phase of a group these characteristics are typically evident:

- There may be some sadness and anxiety over the reality of separation.
- Members are likely to pull back and participate in less intense ways in anticipation of the ending of the group.
- Members are deciding what courses of action they are likely to take.
- There may be some fears of separation as well as fears about being able to carry over into daily life some of what was experienced in the group.
- Members may express their fears, hopes, and concerns for one another.
- Group sessions may be devoted partly to preparing members to meet significant others in everyday life. Role playing and behavioral rehearsal for relating to others more effectively are common.
- Members will be involved in evaluation of the group experience.
- There may be some talk about follow-up meetings or some plan for accountability so that members will be encouraged to carry out their plans for change.

Member Functions

The major task facing members during the final stage of a group is consolidating their learning and transferring it to the outside environment. This is the time for members to review and put into some cognitive framework the meaning of the group experience. Here are some tasks for members at this time:

- Deal with feelings about separation and termination so members do not distance themselves from the group.
- Prepare to generalize learning to everyday life so members do not get discouraged and discount the value of the group work.

- Complete any unfinished business, either issues brought into the group or issues that pertain to people in the group.
- Evaluate the impact of the group and remember that change takes time, effort, and practice.
- Make decisions and plans concerning changes members want to make and how they will go about making them.

After their group ends, the members' main functions are applying in-group learning to an action program in their daily lives, evaluating the group, and attending some type of follow-up session (if practical). Here are some key tasks for members:

- Find ways to reinforce themselves without the support of the group.
- Find ways to continue new behaviors through some kind of self-directed program for change without the supportive environment of the group.

Leader Functions

The group leader's central goals in the consolidation phase are to provide a structure that enables participants to clarify the meaning of their experiences in the group and to assist members in generalizing their learning from the group to everyday life. Here are some group leader tasks at this stage:

- Assist members in dealing with any feelings they might have about termination.
- Provide members with an opportunity to express and deal with any unfinished business within the group.
- Reinforce changes members have made and ensure that members have information about resources to enable them to make further progress.
- Assist members in determining how they will apply specific skills in a variety of situations in daily life.
- Help members to summarize changes they made and to see commonalities with other members.
- Work with members to develop specific contracts and homework assignments as practical ways of making changes.
- Assist participants in developing a conceptual framework that will help them understand, integrate, consolidate, and remember what they have learned in the group.
- Provide opportunities for members to give one another constructive feedback.
- Reemphasize the importance of maintaining confidentiality after the group is over.

After the termination of a group, leaders have these tasks:

- Offer private consultations if any member should need this service, at least on a limited basis, to discuss members' reactions to the group experience.
- If applicable, provide for a follow-up group session or follow-up individual interviews to assess the impact of the group.
- Provide specific referral resources for members who want or need further consultation.
- Encourage members to find some avenues of continued support so that the ending of the group can lead to new directions.
- If applicable, meet with the coleader to assess the overall effectiveness of the group.
- Administer some type of end-of-group assessment instrument to evaluate the nature of individual changes and the strengths and weaknesses of the group.
- Document a summary report of the group and file your records in a confidential location.

Exercises

Final Stage of a Group

Here are a few exercises appropriate to the final stage of a group. Again, most of the exercises we suggest are suitable both for a classroom and for a counseling group.

1. **Discounting.** When Sophia left her group, she felt close to many people and decided that it was worth it to risk getting close. She tried this at work, was rebuffed, and began telling herself that what she had experienced in the group was not real. Discounting

the group experience or allowing old patterns to block establishment of new behaviors are common reactions after a group ends. For this exercise, imagine all the things you might say to yourself to sabotage your plans for change. The idea is to openly acknowledge tendencies you have that will interfere with establishing new behavior.

2. **Group Termination.** Students take turns pretending that they are leaders and that the class is a group about to terminate. Consider how to prepare members for leaving a group.
3. **Termination Interview.** A person in the class volunteers to become a group leader and to conduct an interview with a group member (also a volunteer) as though they had just completed a group experience together. For about 10 minutes the group leader interviews the client regarding the nature of his or her group experience. After the exercise the client reacts to the interview.
4. **Future Projection.** During the last session, members can be asked to imagine that it is 1 year (or 5 years or 10 years) in the future, and the group is meeting for a reunion. What would they most hope to be able to say to the group about their lives, the changes they have made, and the influence the group had on them? What fears might they have concerning this reunion?
5. **Remembering.** It is helpful to simply share memories and turning points during the group's history. Members could be given the task of recalling events and happenings that most stand out for them.
6. **Working on Specific Contracts.** During the final sessions, members might formulate contracts that state specific actions they are willing to take to enhance the changes they have begun. These contracts can be written down and then read to the group. Others can give each member feedback and alternative ways of completing the contract.

Questions for Discussion

Here are a few questions for exploration in a discussion group in class:

1. What are the leader's responsibilities when bringing a group to an end?
2. How might you handle an individual's leaving in an open group? How would you introduce a new member into the group?
3. What personal characteristics of yours could get in the way of helping members in your groups deal with separation and termination issues?
4. What guidelines can you develop to help members think about what they learned in a group and identify ways they can apply these lessons to daily life?
5. What are key characteristics of an effective action plan, and how would you encourage members to formulate a plan?
6. What assessment techniques might you use at both the beginning and the end of a group?
7. How can you build evaluation research into your group design? Do you see any value in combining research and practice in group work?
8. What issues would you think of exploring with your coleader after a group terminates?

Guide to Groups in Action: Evolution and Challenges DVD and Workbook

Here are some suggestions for making use of this chapter along with the final stage segment of *Evolution of a Group*.

1. **Tasks of the Final Stage.** Review the tasks that need to be accomplished during the final stage of the group that are presented in this chapter. As you study the ending stage of the DVD group, how do you see these tasks being accomplished?
2. **Termination of the Group Experience.** How are the group members prepared for the termination of a group? How do the members conceptualize their learning? How does the group seem different at this stage than during the early phases of its development?
3. **Using the Workbook.** Refer to Segment 3: Ending Stage in the workbook and complete all the exercises. Reading this section and addressing the questions will help you conceptualize group process by integrating the text with the DVD and the workbook.

MindTap for Counseling

Additional resources can be found on CengageBrain.com and by logging into the MindTap course created by your professor. There you will find a variety of study tools and useful resources that include quizzes, videos, interactive exercises, and more.

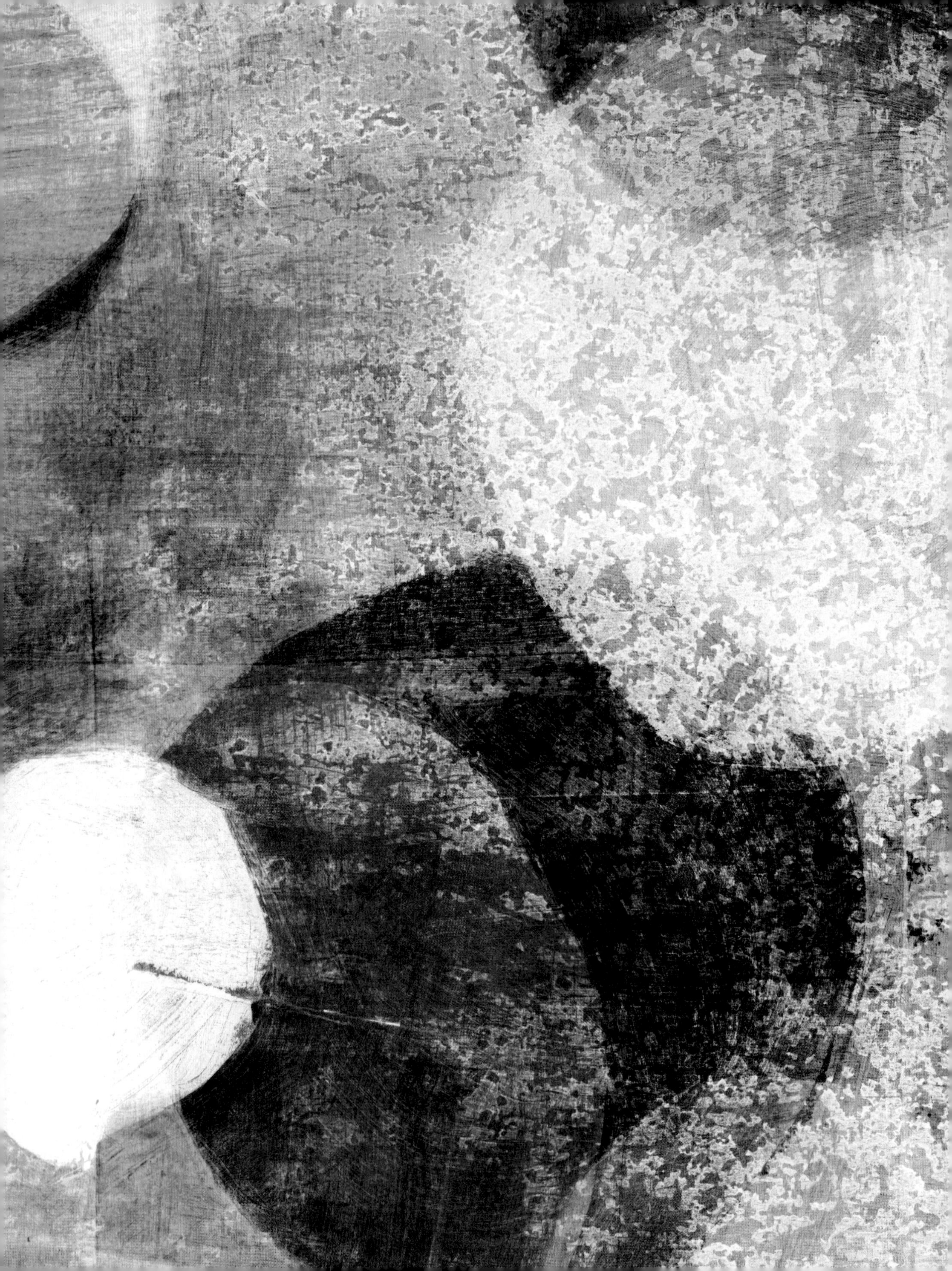

Application of Group Process to Schools and Community Agency Settings

Part Three illustrates how group process concepts and practices are used in groups geared to the needs of particular client populations. Group leaders who work with children, adolescents, adults, and older adults each have special responsibilities. Guest contributors help us describe how to set up these specialized groups and share approaches that may be useful as you design your own groups. In planning and leading any of these special types of groups, leaders must have the necessary competence to facilitate them. In addition to the skills and knowledge about group process discussed in Chapter 2, group leaders must be familiar with the particular needs of the target population for a group.

Students in counseling and related programs are often required to complete an internship involving work with a variety of people: children or adolescents, college students, older adults, clients with substance use disorders, hospitalized patients, or outpatients in a community agency. As a mental health worker, you may be asked to set up and lead a variety of groups. Of course, not all of these specialized groups can be described in this book, but a sample of programs can give you ideas to apply in creating a group that is suitable for your personal style, your clients, and the setting in which you work. Most of the group proposals described have the following components: organizing the group, group goals, group format, and group outcomes. After you have read the various group proposals, look for common denominators among these groups that may help you structure your own groups.

Regardless of the kind of group you design, you will be concerned with factors such as securing informed consent, creating trust, dealing with possible hidden agendas, and facilitating members through the various stages of a group, to mention a few. You are also responsible for documenting the process and outcomes of your groups. The kind of group you are leading, the setting in which you work, and your client population will influence your decisions about the kind of notes you may need to keep.

Group practitioners in school settings and in various community agency settings developed the proposals presented in Part 3. These practitioners followed their interests and the clients' needs of their work setting. These sample proposals provide practical examples of how group counselors are applying many of the concepts discussed in the previous chapters to their own groups. We encourage you to investigate ways to implement a group that interests you while meeting the needs that arise with the client population you serve.

CHAPTER 10

Groups in School Settings

CHAPTER LEARNING OBJECTIVES

1. Describe the types of groups and other considerations that affect conducting groups in school settings (CACREP, 2016, Standard F)
2. Describe approaches to group formation, including recruiting, screening, and selecting members (CACREP, 2016, Standard E)
3. Identify guidelines for group work with children and adolescents
4. Identify therapeutic factors associated with play therapy in groups with children and adolescents
5. Describe key developmental themes of adolescence
6. Discuss challenges in leading adolescent groups
7. List guidelines in helping adolescents deal with anger and conflict
8. Describe topics used to structure groups in college counseling centers

LO1

Introduction

In this chapter we describe groups for children and adolescents that are appropriate for school settings. The general group format described here can be applied in various other settings, including college and university counseling centers, private practice, and public and private clinics. Many of the ideas in this chapter also are useful for designing groups dealing with a variety of special needs of children, adolescents, and college students. This chapter alone will not provide you with enough information to conduct your own groups in a school setting. You will need to acquire and practice group facilitation skills and apply your knowledge of group process to any group you are planning. We encourage you to do further reading, attend specialized workshops, look for ways to cofacilitate groups with more experienced practitioners, and arrange for supervised field experience in facilitating groups.

Although the groups described here are in school settings, similar groups often are offered in community mental health agencies and in other settings. The roles and functions of school counselors differ from those of community mental health counselors, and the groups often have a different focus. Laws, regulations, policies, and the mission of the school or agency also may differ. Group practitioners need to be knowledgeable of these differences. There are no clear lines of demarcation for the many groups that are available in both school and community settings.

LO2

Group Counseling in the School Setting

Counseling groups in school settings cover a wide array of topics and formats. The group counseling services provided for children and adolescents in schools occupy a major place because of their efficacy in delivering information and treatment. Small groups have the potential to reach many students before they need remedial treatment for more serious mental health problems. School-based groups emphasize prevention and intervention strategies to support healthy student development and more effective ways of dealing with the tasks of daily living (Sink, Edwards, & Eppler, 2012). School-based counseling research confirms that small groups are of value for both the student participants and the school counselors; these programs influence the personal and social functioning of students and have been shown to improve academic performance (Sink et al., 2012; Steen, Bauman, & Smith, 2007). Groups play a key role in a comprehensive developmental school counseling program for children and adolescents because of their efficacy in delivering information and treatment (Steen, Henfield, & Booker, 2014).

Many school counseling groups focus on enhancing personal and social development and, at the same time, have a psychoeducational purpose (such as teaching study skills). Steen and colleagues (2014) describe a group counseling model designed to help K–12 school counselors integrate students' academic and personal-social development into their group work. Villalba (2007) examined the use of psychoeducational groups to address the social and academic concerns of children in K–12 school settings. Group work with children and adolescents was effective in decreasing bullying behaviors, increasing self-esteem for children of alcoholics, decreasing trauma-related anxiety in young survivors of natural disasters, and decreasing levels of anxiety and increasing academic performance for children from divorced parents. Villalba believes that wellness, like prevention, is an ideal conceptual approach for small and large group work in school settings.

DeLucia-Waack, Segrist, and Horne's (2007) DVD illustrates the value of a structured psychoeducational group for high school students. The leaders show flexibility and encourage members to interact with each other, and the structured exercises facilitate interaction. The value of preparation in forming a group, ways of developing group ground rules, icebreaker activities, how to encourage members to make connections, and how to assist members in identifying what they learned are also illustrated. The purpose of a psychoeducational group is different from the purpose of a therapy group, yet a similar process unfolds in both types of groups.

Groups in the schools are generally brief, structured, problem focused, homogeneous in membership, and may have a cognitive behavioral orientation. Both counseling and psychoeducational groups that focus on wellness and prevention are well suited for school settings. Teaching basic skills to all students in classroom guidance lessons and providing further services in small groups to children and adolescents who are at risk helps young people develop coping and communication skills. Treatment of more severe problems is generally not within the scope of counseling services offered in a school setting, although developmental groups with remedial aims may be offered. Because not all children or adolescents are ready for group participation, it is important to know how to suggest alternative helping approaches. School counselors need to make it a practice to know about referral resources and be willing to make use of these resources when it is in the child's or adolescent's best interest.

Typically, school counselors have an unrealistically large caseload. Regardless of how talented the counselor might be, there are limitations on what can be done to bring about significant behavior change. The counselor's time is often spent reacting to the immediate needs of children rather than on developing prevention programs. Given adequate resources and increased numbers of competent counselors, we would like to see school guidance programs include group counseling on the elementary, middle, and secondary levels. Group counseling aimed at cultivating caring and compassionate individuals can be an ideal forum for creating what Adlerians term "social interest." In the context of a group, priority could be given to helping children and adolescents deal with feelings of rejection, anger, alienation, and isolation. The group is also a place where young people can learn the meaning of belonging and contributing to society.

For a more detailed discussion of group counseling in the school setting, see Falco and Bauman (2014), Sink, Edwards, and Eppler (2012), Sklare (2005), Steen (2009), Steen, Bauman, and Smith (2007, 2008), Steen and Bemak (2008), Steen, Griffin, and Shi (2011), Steen, Henfield, and Booker (2014), Murphy (2015), and Winslade and Monk (2007).

LO3

Guidelines for Group Work With Children and Adolescents

This section contains practical guidelines for school counselors who are considering setting up groups for both children and adolescents.

Developing a Sound Proposal

Designing group proposals is discussed in detail in Chapter 5, and the same principles apply here to planning groups for children and adolescents in school settings. As you develop your group proposal, keep these steps in mind:

- Describe your goals and purposes clearly.
- Develop a clearly stated rationale for your proposed group, including the reason a group approach has merit.
- Provide evidence to school administrators demonstrating that group counseling is an integral part of the school counseling program and that it is effective in changing student behavior and enhancing the educational experience (Sink et al., 2012).
- Clearly articulate to administrators, teachers, and parents the benefits children or adolescents derive from participating in a therapeutic group experience and identify how this group complements the mission of the school and will help students achieve not only academically but personally and socially as well (DeLucia-Waack, 2006c; Steen, Bauman, & Smith, 2007).
- State your aims, the procedures to be used, the questions for processing, the evaluation/assessment process, and the form of documentation you will use.
- Develop an attendance policy.
- Provide an orientation to the group for the parents of the children.

Legal Considerations

Be aware of your state's laws regarding group work with minors. Know the policies and procedures of the school district or agency where you work as they apply to your school, as well as the ethical principles specific to counseling children and adolescents. Do not tell children that you can keep everything they discuss confidential because you may be required to disclose information about them to your agency or school administrator. Be clear about what you can and cannot promise in the way of privacy. Be aware of your legal responsibility to report abuse or suspected abuse of minors. When a minor discloses information that creates even a suspicion of abuse or neglect, a school counselor has a duty to report this matter to Child Protective Services. In this situation confidentiality *must* be broken; the law requires you to take action by notifying the appropriate authorities. Bertram (2011) provides a concise overview of ethical and legal issues in group counseling, including the standard of care, member screening, informed consent, confidentiality and privilege, situations requiring breach of confidentiality, and danger to self or others. For other ethical considerations in setting up groups for minors, review the discussion of such standards in Chapters 3 and 5.

Practical Considerations

The size and duration of a group depend on the age of the members. As a general rule, younger children should be in smaller groups with shorter sessions. Take into account the fact that the attention span of children ages 4 to 6 is quite different from that of children who are 10 or 12. Another consideration in forming a group is the severity of the children's problems. For example, a group of acting-out 12-year-olds might have to be as small as a group of preschoolers. It might also be important to find out whether a child in your group is currently taking any medications or experiencing other health issues. A child who has been diagnosed with ADHD might be taking medications that have behavioral side effects. This could provide a context for understanding some of the behaviors and symptoms you observe in the group. You must also consider your own tolerance for dealing with children who may be challenging for you. As is the case with adult clients, children can evoke your own countertransference. If you are aware of this, there is less chance that your feelings and reactions will interfere with your ability to work with children.

The Setting Consider the meeting place in terms of its effectiveness for the work you want to do with your young clients. Will they be able to roam around freely and not have to be continually asked to talk softly so as not to disturb others in an adjacent room? Will the site for group meetings provide privacy and freedom from interruptions? Is there anything in the room that could easily be damaged by the children or that is obviously unsafe for them? Will the furniture in the room comfortably accommodate active children?

Communicate Your Expectations Be able to tell the children or adolescents in their language about the purpose of your group, what you expect of them, and what they can expect from you. Make sure that they understand the basic, nonnegotiable ground rules, and attempt to involve them in establishing and reinforcing the rules that will govern their group.

Children and adolescents often test their limits as a way to ensure that you will keep them safe. This testing is typically a phase and will likely decrease as safety is established in the group. However, it can be expected to arise from time to time. Be intentionally patient within each session to avoid becoming more of a disciplinarian than a counselor.

Preparation Prepare adequately for each session, yet be flexible enough to adjust your format and topics for a given session to respond to spontaneous situations. Avoid insisting on "covering your agenda" no matter what; be creative, but not careless. Remember the broad goals of your group and use incidents in the group as teachable moments to help the members work on new skills. Be open to processing the interactions occurring within the group in the here and now as the power of peers' influence is very effective.

Involve Parents For some groups written parental permission may not be a legal requirement, but we think it is a good policy to secure the written consent of parents or guardians of any person under 18 who wishes to participate in group counseling as a school-related program. Doing so also tends to enhance the working relationship and gain the cooperation of legal guardians. Include some questions on the consent form to help you assess their perspective regarding how their child is currently functioning. Even if you have a meeting with the parents or guardians, ask them to sign a form; this reinforces their commitment to cooperate with their child's treatment. You can include group policy, meeting times and dates, and confidentiality policies on this form. As well, you can solicit suggestions on ways to contact them to follow up on the progress of the group or other important information.

Parents (or legal guardians) and counselors are partners with a common goal, which is helping the child or adolescent. As with the young people, explain to their parents your expectations and purposes in such a way that they can understand and not become suspicious. Approach them with an attitude of "How can you help me in my work with your child or adolescent, and how can we work as a team for a common purpose?" Doing so reduces the chances of encountering defensiveness on the part of parents. Spend an evening presenting your program in a group meeting of parents, or send them a letter briefly describing your groups. Providing parents with an outline of the goals of the groups and the topics, even sample activities, helps them to understand what is happening in the group without asking the group leader to break confidentiality. If you have the staff resources, organize a parent group at the same time that their children are participating in their own counseling group. As their children develop new or additional skills, the parents and families are able to benefit from similar opportunities.

Steen, Bauman, and Smith (2007) suggest that school counselors give presentations to parents, teachers, and administrators about the therapeutic factors involved in small group work as a way to increase their understanding of how groups work and the value of small groups in the overall mission of the academic program. Getting input from parents and teachers about their concerns can be an important step in gaining needed support for doing groups in the school.

Strategies in the Group

Self-Disclosure Consider the purposes and goals of your group in deciding how much to encourage self-disclosure, especially in matters relating to family life or personal trauma. Some personal topics may be beyond the scope of the group's purpose and more appropriate for individual therapy. Use judgment as to the appropriateness of letting a child go into detail about personal matters in a group. Anticipate some personal material they may disclose and how you might address this. For example, in a group in an elementary school, you may not want to let a child go into detail about an apparent physical abuse situation. If this occurs, encourage the child to express how he or she was affected by the incident. After the session ends, follow the procedures outlined by your school or agency to report suspected child abuse.

Emphasize Confidentiality It is more difficult to maintain confidentiality in a school setting than in private practice. In school settings children and adolescents spend much time together outside of the group, where confidentiality leaks are more possible. As with adults, it is helpful to teach students how to talk about the group experience in a way that does not betray confidentiality. Help students understand that the information they share within a group belongs to them but that the information they hear or learn in a group belongs to the group. The counselor needs to communicate the importance of confidentiality by using language that is developmentally tailored for the age level. It is helpful to teach and to practice with the children how to talk about the group in appropriate ways and to give specific guidelines on what to say if someone probes them for information. Parental and teacher support can be solicited by encouraging parents to ask questions about their child's participation in the group. Remind parents, families, and teachers to avoid probing for specifics about other children, which could result in their child breaching confidentiality.

Special attention should be paid to orienting children to their responsibilities to one another. In group work with adults it is relatively simple to have a discussion about honoring the personal nature of the material that other group members reveal. Both adults and adolescents can clearly understand the ramifications associated with failing to honor the confidentiality of their peers. However, children need this clearly explained, and this matter deserves discussion in the group. A leader working with children might ask, "How would you feel if you found out a group member had told someone in class or on the playground something you said or did?" or "What if someone in this group shared with the teacher something another student said or did in this group?" Children need to know that the group counselor may talk with parents and teachers, and they have a right to know what kind of information will and will not be shared with adults. Children are more thoughtful than they are typically given credit for and are capable of understanding feelings and being sensitive to others.

Maintain Neutrality Avoid siding with children or adolescents against their parents or a particular institution. Young people may like and admire you for your patience and understanding and complain about missing these traits in parents or teachers. It is enough to acknowledge that their experience with you as their group leader is different from other adults.

Use Appropriate Exercises and Techniques During the beginning stage of the group it is appropriate to use interactive exercises that do not require deeply personal self-disclosure. As children and adolescents become more acquainted with the group process, the activities or exercises can become more challenging. Explain the purpose of the activity in a general way without diminishing its impact. Young people should not be pressured into participating in certain activities if they are uncomfortable doing so. Although their unwillingness to take part in exercises often stems from a lack of understanding, children or adolescents will sometimes be reluctant to participate because they may wonder about the purpose of such exercises or they may worry about being embarrassed and appearing silly.

Through patience and by observing others in the group it is possible that reluctant members will eventually decide to participate more fully.

An excellent resource with appropriate exercises and activities for group work with children and adolescents is Foss, Green, Wolfe-Stiltner, and DeLucia-Waack (2008). For group activities for various types of multicultural groups and diversity-related groups, see Salazar (2009). Bauman and Steen's (2009) six-session DVD for a counseling group with a diverse group of fifth-grade students helps students achieve increased self-understanding and appreciate cultural diversity, demonstrates choosing activities appropriate for the developmental level of children, and shows how to process exercises in a group. Bauman and Steen (2012) also have a DVD for a diverse group with eighth-grade students titled *Celebrating Diversity: Leading Multicultural Groups for Middle School Students*.

Listen and Remain Open A skillful group counselor will listen to behavior as well as words. Leaders can provide children and adolescents with some reflective communication to help group members find words for their experiences. The use of creative arts activities—especially music, dance, movement, art, drama, play, and humor—are valuable ways to facilitate communication in groups (Gladding, 2016; Veach & Gladding, 2007).

Let children and adolescents lead the way, and follow their clues. Encourage young people to express themselves in their own words. Listen to their words, but pay attention to the possible meanings of their behavior as well. For example, if a child is acting out, is she telling you "Please stop me, because I can't stop myself"? If a child is continually calling out, he might be saying "Notice me! Nobody else does." Remaining open to what children are trying to tell us about themselves is essential if we are going to help them. Be aware of preconceived labels and diagnoses that may subtly influence your interactions. The children you work with are often categorized and labeled. Be careful not to limit the ability of children to change by responding to them as if they are their labels. You may be one of only a few people with the training to advocate on their behalf. Continue to explore other factors that may be hindering them from reaching their fullest potential.

Prepare for Termination Children and adolescents are quick to form attachments with adults who display a concerned and caring attitude toward them. Well before your group ends—for example, three sessions before the end of a 12-session group and as soon as possible for shorter groups—you should let those who participate in a group know that the termination point is not far off. This notice enables the children to express their reactions, and it enables you to share your reactions with them. Avoid promising them that you will keep in contact with them, if that is not possible. If you do not deal with these issues, they may see you as running out on them and consider you as one more adult they cannot trust. Help children identify support networks outside of the group throughout the duration of the group. To provide children or adolescents with a sense of closure, choose activities that help them identify what they have learned from the group and how they have been affected by others (DeLucia-Waack, 2006a, 2006b).

Children and adolescents who will not be continuing with another cycle of group counseling could benefit from experiencing some kind of graduation. For example, a certificate of completion can provide group members with a sense of accomplishment. Offer students the opportunity to meet together again if new information, struggles, or successes arise. These meetings are often referred to as reunions, and it is reassuring for students to know that such reunions are possible. Take a moment to review the guidelines for the final stage of a group described in Chapter 9 for more information on termination.

Personal and Professional Qualifications

You need to recognize the impact that conducting a group with children or adolescents can have on you personally. For example, in working with youngsters who are abused and neglected, you might find it difficult to separate yourself from their life situations. If you are consistently preoccupied with their problems, you may discover that this is affecting your life and your relationships negatively. It is a personal matter for you to discover how much you are capable of giving, as well as how much and what you need to do to replenish yourself to stay excited and creative in your work.

Some of the *personal characteristics* that are important when working with children are patience, caring, authenticity, playfulness, a good sense of humor, the ability to tune in to and remember one's own childhood and adolescent experiences, firmness without punitiveness, flexibility, the ability to express anger without sarcasm, great concern for and interest in children, optimism that children can be active participants in their healing processes, and the other characteristics of group leaders that were described in Chapter 2.

We believe the following *professional qualifications* are especially important for those leading groups with children or adolescents:

- A thorough understanding of the developmental tasks and stages of the particular age group
- A good understanding of group process as it applies to working with children and adolescents
- Awareness, knowledge, and skills necessary to work effectively with children and adolescents from culturally diverse populations
- Supervised training in working with children and adolescents in groups before leading a group alone
- Knowledge of the literature and significant research pertaining to counseling children and adolescents within a group setting
- A clear understanding of the expectations of the school or agency where the groups are conducted

It is easy to overextend yourself when working with children and adolescents whose problems are pressing and severe. Be realistic and realize that you cannot work effectively with every student or provide all the needed services. Becoming knowledgeable about resources in your community can enable you to assist clients in finding services that meet their needs. Know the boundaries of your competence and the scope of your job description. Know how to differentiate between therapy groups and groups with a developmental, preventive, or educational focus. Groups in school settings typically focus on preventive and developmental issues, and they are linked to educational goals.

Getting Support for School Counseling Groups

The support of administrators and teachers in schools and agencies is especially important in setting up groups (Sink et al., 2012; Steen et al., 2007). If your design for a group is well organized, you will probably receive support and constructive suggestions from them. Remember that the school principal—not you—will probably be the target of criticism if your counseling group is ineffectively run or compromises the integrity of the school. If you have overlooked the need to get parental permission (where required), it is the principal who will field the calls from upset family members. The proposals described in this chapter have been carefully considered and have met with success; many of these ideas can be applied in designing your own groups.

One practitioner reported that she had encountered resistance from her school principal when she suggested forming a "divorce group" for children. She then renamed it the "loss group," which she thought would be more descriptive, and as a result gained support for the group. However, this new title confused the children. They reported to the office saying, "We're the *lost* group; we're here to be found." A group name should accurately describe the purpose of the group but not raise confusion or concerns for participants, parents, or the principal.

If you are interested in learning more about group counseling with children in the school setting, we recommend Ashby, Kottman, and DeGraaf (2008); DeLucia-Waack, Bridbord, Kleiner, and Nitza (2006); Falco and Bauman (2014); Foss, Green, Wolfe-Stiltner, and DeLucia-Waack (2008); Halstead, Pehrsson, and Mullen (2011); Murphy (2015); Salazar (2009); and Sink, Edwards, and Eppler (2012).

LO4

Play Therapy in Group Work With Children and Adolescents

Play therapy is increasing in popularity in groups for children and adolescents. The University of North Texas and some others offer a degree program in play therapy, and many books are now available on this subject. Play therapy has a long history in the treatment of children. Garry Landreth (2002), the founder and former director of the Center for Play Therapy at the University of North Texas, built on the philosophy of client-centered therapy in developing his child-centered approach to play therapy. Landreth views play therapy as an interpersonal relationship between child and therapist. The therapist provides selected play materials and creates a safe place in which the child can express and explore his or her feelings, thoughts, experiences, and behaviors through play. Play is the natural language that children most readily speak. Play therapy allows for self-expression in a less threatening way than direct verbal communication. Play supports the development of cognitive skills, language skills, coping skills, and other developmental tasks in childhood. Group play therapy in schools can focus on exploring interpersonal issues that help or hinder academic progress. Connecting the interventions of play therapy with academic success helps to justify this approach in school settings. Group play therapy can be instrumental in helping children feel safe, in creating positive school relationships, and in providing a space for learning with few internal distractions (Sweeney, Baggerly, & Ray, 2014).

Regardless of the type of group you are leading, play-based activities can help children process the material generated in the group. Play therapy is most commonly used for children under the age of 12, but it is sometimes practiced with adolescents as well. Children respond very warmly to these activities because of their developmental appropriateness. Playing provides some psychological distance from material that might be too difficult or painful for a child to talk about. Children often leave a play therapy experience in a happy state, and they look forward to coming with great enthusiasm. In group play therapy, children tend to feel like they are coming in to play for an hour with friends.

Any existing group format can be altered to integrate some play therapy elements. There are many different theoretical orientations to play therapy, including Adlerian play therapy, psychoanalytic play therapy, child-centered play therapy, cognitive behavioral play therapy, ecosystemic play therapy, Gestalt play therapy, Jungian play therapy, and thematic play therapy, (Sweeney et al., 2014). The Adlerian approach lends itself especially well to group work with children (see Kottman & Meany-Walen, 2016). Sandtray therapy, which can be applied as a way of exploring developmentally appropriate treatment options for preadolescents with behavioral difficulties, has been proved to be effective with preadolescents (Flahive & Ray, 2007). Concept and methods from the various theoretical orientations can be incorporated into a variety of groups for children, as you will see in the group proposals detailed later in this chapter.

If you expect to employ group play therapy with children or adolescents, it is important to obtain formal training and supervised clinical experience from a play therapy practitioner. Many graduate programs are now offering courses in play therapy, and organizations such as the Association for Play Therapy and its chapters offer training all over the country. The Association for Play Therapy (2008) provides guidelines for registered play therapists and supervisors. Conferences, training, networking, research, and other resources are available through this organization. For more information on play therapy, see *Play Therapy: Basics and Beyond* (Kottman, 2011), *Partners in Play: An Adlerian Approach to Play Therapy* (Kottman & Meany-Walen, 2016), *Group Play Therapy: A Dynamic Approach* (Sweeney, Baggerly, & Ray, 2014), and *The Handbook of Jungian Play Therapy With Children and Adolescents* (Green, 2014).

A School Counseling Group for 6- to 11-Year-Olds

This section is written from the perspective of Marianne Schneider Corey.

I designed a group for children ranging in age from 6 to 11 at an elementary school. My caseload included 10 to 15 children, and I was to see each child once a week for about an hour for a total of 24 visits. The principal, the teacher, or the school nurse referred the children to me; almost without exception, these children were identified as having learning problems. Often these learning disabilities were a reflection of their emotional conflicts. It was up to me to design a group that would improve the children's behavior in school.

Organizing the Group

Contact With School Personnel

Being aware that outsiders are sometimes mistrusted in schools, my first goal was to earn the trust of the teachers and administrators. I met with them to determine what they hoped the project would accomplish. I told them that I wanted to work closely with them, providing feedback about the children, making specific recommendations, and getting their suggestions. I let them know that I intended to work with the children individually and in groups and to involve the parents in the treatment process as much as possible.

Accordingly, I developed a program in which I was in continuous contact with the children's teachers, principal, and parents. The teachers and the principal were very cooperative about meeting with me. I also spoke frequently with the school psychologist and the school secretaries about particular children, gathering as much information as I could. This information turned out to be most helpful.

The Setting

The setting for my work with the children was not ideal. The school was short on space (a new school was being built), and I was continually looking for a place to meet with the children.

When the weather allowed, we often met on the school lawn. I needed a place where the children could explore, touch, talk loudly, shout if they were angry, or give vent to any other emotions they were experiencing. If I took them off campus or did anything special with them, I first obtained written permission from the parents and the school authorities. Although I never had an ideal place to work, this did not keep me from working effectively with the children, as we often improvised together. The children were very adaptive, and I too had to learn to adapt to less than ideal situations.

Due to the setting, I had to pick up the children from their classrooms, which concerned me. How would the children react to being singled out? Would my special attention to them amid their peers affect them negatively? Fortunately, I found the contrary to be true. The children responded very positively to my coming to pick them up and were always ready to come with me, even during recess time.

Initial Contact With the Parents

After meeting with the school staff, who identified which children I would be working with, I contacted the parents of each child and attempted to arrange for an individual meeting with the parents. They knew before I visited them about my intended involvement with their child because I had asked the principal and the child's teacher to contact them. During my initial contact, I explained that the teacher had become concerned about the student's behavior in class and had referred the child to me. This interview gave the parents a chance to get to know me and to ask questions, and it gave me the chance to get the parents' permission to work with their child. At this time I gathered information regarding any difficulties the parents were having with the child and collected the data I needed to complete numerous forms. If parents became anxious over my probing or over the fact that *their* child had been singled out for counseling, I explained to them that because teachers have to deal with so many children they cannot always provide all the attention a child needs. It would be my job, I said, to provide this extra attention.

Although the school's policy stipulated obtaining parental permission for children to become participants in a group, this is not a required policy in all school districts. State laws regarding parental permission to counsel minors also vary. As a general rule, I think it is best to get the parents' permission and to work with them as allies rather than risk their disapproval by counseling their children without their knowledge and consent. There are exceptions, however. When counselors are not legally required to secure the consent of parents and when notifying them could be detrimental to the minor client, the welfare of these children always takes priority.

For the most part parents were willing to cooperate and gave their consent. In response to my question about any difficulties they might be experiencing with their child at home, which I asked to get clues to the child's behavior in school, the parents were guarded at first. They became much more open with time and frequent contacts. My aim was not to communicate in any way that they were "bad" parents, as this would certainly have aroused their defensiveness. Their children were experiencing difficulties, and I wanted to solicit their help in assisting the students to work through these problems. By going into the child's home, I was able to get information relating to the problems the child was exhibiting that would otherwise have been difficult, if not impossible, to obtain.

I told the parents that their children would be discussing with me problems related to school, home, and peers. I explained that I wished to keep as confidential as possible what the child and I would be exploring in our sessions. Therefore, I explained, I would let them know in a general way how I was proceeding with the child but would not reveal any of the specifics, unless I was required to do so by law.

I also told them that I hoped to see them sometimes together with their children. It was difficult to see some parents again after my initial contact, however, because every one of them was employed. I was able to make at least some additional contact with most parents, and I spoke with others on the telephone.

Special Problems Requiring Out-of-Group Attention

Like the parents, the teachers provided me with ongoing information regarding the children's progress. I was able to use this information in deciding how long to see a particular child or what problem area to focus on. In addition, the teachers prepared written evaluations for the program director, and they shared these evaluations with me. I kept documentation of my work with each child in the group, my observation of the child, my recommendations for teachers, and as well, I kept notes regarding my contacts with teachers and parents.

In doing these groups I learned that children have a multitude of developmental issues with which they must cope. There are many avenues of help for these problems. In working effectively with children, counselors do well to involve as many resources and people as possible. There is room for creativity in developing groups to meet the diverse needs and the diverse cultural backgrounds of children. It is important to let the parents or legal guardians know about these programs and resources so that they, too, are involved in the helping process.

Because I was unable to provide the necessary tutorial assistance, I contacted a nearby university and recruited five graduate students to tutor the children for credit in their child psychology course. In addition to providing tutorial services, they gave the children additional positive individual attention. This tutoring proved very successful for both the children and the university students.

When I detected health problems, I referred the child to the school nurse. When I suspected neglect or abuse, I took the appropriate action. As counselors who work with minors, we need to be aware of the reporting laws for suspected abuse in our state as well as our work setting. We must know the specific steps to be taken in making the required reports. In a school setting the first step may be to report a situation to the principal. It is always helpful to communicate with Child Protective Services (or the Department of Social Services) to obtain information on assessing and reporting suspected child abuse.

Many children are undernourished, inappropriately clothed, and in need of medical assistance, recreational opportunities, or supervision after school. Counseling is more likely to have an effect if the child's basic needs are being met. I found it necessary to do much of the legwork required to obtain food, clothing, money, or special services for the children and their families. Essentially, I had a lot of case management responsibilities. Some families resisted turning to outside agencies because of pride or fear that strings would be attached or simply out of ignorance about where to go for help. When a family did want help with emotional, economic, or medical problems, I referred them to one of the appropriate agencies, but I often also made the contacts with the agencies and did the paperwork they required. More often than not counselors do not have time to make the contacts I have described, but they can be creative in finding ways to delegate these tasks to others.

Group Format

Initial Contact With the Children

The children were reluctant to initiate a conversation, being accustomed only to answering questions. They needed some structure and some guidelines for expressing themselves and an acknowledgment that it was difficult for them. I introduced myself to them, saying that I was a special type of teacher called a counselor. I explained that their teacher was concerned about their behavior in class and that they would be talking with me several times a week—individually, as a group, and in their homes. I told them that we would be discussing problems they had in school, at home, or with fellow students.

Because of my belief that children's rights to privacy are often ignored and violated, I let them know that I would be talking about them with their parents and teachers. I explained that I would tell them when I made such contacts. Although I said I did consider much of what we would talk about in the group to be confidential, I told them I would discuss with their parents and teachers anything that would be important in helping them work through any of their difficulties. At this time I also let them know that they were not to talk to others about what fellow group members revealed. This was one of the rules we discussed again in the group sessions. I told them that they could talk about matters that concerned them, including their fears and their hurts. Additionally, I let them know that I could not keep everything confidential, especially if it concerned their safety. In language that they could understand, I explained the purpose of confidentiality and its limitations. They were also informed that they would not be allowed to hurt other children, either physically or verbally, or to destroy any property. Other rules were established, and I made the children aware of their responsibility. To be part of the group, they had to agree to follow these rules.

Working With the Children in a Group

My goal was to pinpoint some of the children's maladaptive behaviors, teach them how to express emotions without hurting themselves or others, and provide a climate in which they would feel free to express a range of feelings. I wanted to convey to the youngsters that feelings such as anger did not get them into trouble; rather, it is certain ways of acting on these feelings that can lead to problems. In an effort to teach them ways of safely expressing the full gambit of their feelings, I involved them in a variety of activities, including role playing, play therapy, acting out special situations, painting, finishing stories that I began, putting on puppet shows, playing music, movement, and dancing.

The groups that were easiest to work with and most productive were composed of 3 to 5 children of the same age and gender. In larger groups I found myself (1) unable to relate intensely to individuals, (2) slipping into the role of disciplinarian to counteract the increased distractions, (3) feeling frustrated at the number of children competing for my attention, and (4) not having enough time left over to pay attention to the underlying dynamics. In addition, children between the ages of 6 and 11 tend to become impatient if they have to wait very long for their turn to speak.

I took care to combine withdrawn children with more outgoing ones, but I also felt that it was important for the children to be with others who were experiencing similar conflicts. For example, I put in the same group two boys who felt much anger, hurt, grief, and frustration over their parents' divorces and subsequent remarriages. They slowly learned how to express their feelings about not having much contact with the parent they didn't live with. At first the boys could only express their feelings symbolically, through play; later they learned to put words to their emotions and to talk about their feelings.

As I had planned, I provided some time for each child during which he or she could have my attention alone. I noticed that in the group all the children became less jealous of one another about me and trusted me more once I had begun to provide this individual time.

Alone, the children were more cooperative and less competitive. They felt less need to seek attention in undesirable ways. Having an adult spend time with them individually gave them a sense of importance. With the teacher's consent I frequently visited the children who were in my group in their classrooms and on the playground, sometimes just observing and sometimes making a brief contact through touch or words. Although this was time consuming, it proved to be productive in the long run.

Our scheduled group and individual sessions took place twice a week and lasted from half an hour to an hour. It would have been a mistake for me to insist that sessions always last a certain length of time because the children's patience varied from session to session.

When they wanted to leave a group session, I would say in a friendly manner that they were free to leave, but I wished they would stay until the session was over. They usually elected to stay. If they chose to leave, I would not have them come back to that session. Most of the time the children enjoyed the sessions. It was a good practice to let them know in advance that a session was coming to an end and then to be firm about having them leave and not give in to their demands that the group continue.

My groups were open, in that new members could join. The children already in the group handled this situation very well. They knew the newcomer from school and did not meet the child with any negative reactions. During the sessions, I let the children lead the way and listened to what they had to say, directly or through various symbolic means. Playing with puppets turned out to be an excellent means of revealing a variety of emotions and dramatizing situations that produce conflict. I made puppets available to the first- and second-grade children but found that even the fourth- and fifth-grade students were able to use them to vent their pent-up emotions.

The groups offered the children the opportunity to act out situations that aroused conflicting feelings. Sometimes I would suggest a problem situation, and at other times the children would select a problem to act out. The children would take the role of teacher, friend, principal, parent, brother, sister, or whoever else was involved. In this way they were able to release their emotions without hurting others.

Several sessions might pass before a child would speak freely. I sat on the floor close to the children during the sessions, often maintaining physical contact, which seemed to have a calming effect by itself. I listened to them attentively and often reflected for them what they were saying. More important, however, I communicated to them, usually nonverbally, that I was with them, that what they were saying was important, and that I cared about what they had to say. I insisted that other members in the group listen, and I reassured all of them that each would have a time to speak. This is a very difficult concept to get across, especially to a 6- or 7-year-old who is still learning to share.

After a session that I thought had been unproductive, I was sometimes surprised to hear a teacher comment on a child's changed behavior. After one such session, a boy who had previously been very destructive and disobedient became cooperative and able to relate to his peers. Pounding a lump of clay, which could be interpreted as nonproductive, turned out to have been very important to him. It had relieved much of his anger and so reduced his need to strike out at others.

At times I questioned whether my work with the children was doing any good. Changes in their behavior were slow in coming and sometimes temporary.

Some children gave the appearance of improving one week, yet the next week their behavior would again be very negative. My firm belief that a child can change if afforded the opportunity to change was challenged again and again. However, most children did make definite changes, as observed by the teacher, the principal, the parents, and me. Children who were truant began to come to school more regularly. A boy who was in the habit of stealing and giving his loot to other children so they would like him learned that his behavior was one of the reasons others disliked him in the first place, and he began to get their attention through more positive actions. A girl who had been conditioned not to trust learned to make friends and to reach out first, doing what at one time she had most feared.

These changes, though encouraging, needed to be reinforced at home. Although most parents welcomed many of their child's new behaviors, some found the new behavior threatening. For instance, one girl caused her mother some anxiety by beginning to ask probing questions about her absent father. I encouraged this mother—and other parents facing similar problems—to try to listen to the child nondefensively.

It was disconcerting to know that some of the children frequently faced difficult circumstances at home, and yet I realized that I did not have control over that domain. Rather than allowing myself to get too discouraged over the fact that I could not change their situation at home, I had to remind myself that I could provide them with a positive experience at school that would have a constructive impact on them. As counselors, we need to remind ourselves to focus on what we can do and not become overwhelmed by all that we cannot do.

Termination of the Group

When I began to work with the children, I told them that the sessions would go on for only a limited time during the school year. Several sessions before termination, I reminded them that the group and individual sessions would be ending soon, and we discussed the coming end of our meetings.

Although I had been affectionate with the children during our time together, I had not deceived them by becoming a substitute mother or by establishing myself as a permanent fixture who would totally satisfy all their needs. I was aware of establishing appropriate boundaries in carrying out the primary purpose of the group experience. By being realistic about the limits of my job from the beginning, I was able to prevent termination from being a negative experience for the children.

Teacher Evaluation of the Counseling Program

Like the parents, the teachers provided me with ongoing information regarding the children's progress. I was able to use this information in deciding how long to see a particular child or what problem area to focus on. In addition, the teachers completed written evaluations for the program director, and they shared these evaluations with me.

A Group for Elementary School Children of Divorce and Changing Families

This section is written from the perspective of Karen Kram Laudenslager, a school counselor. (For more information on these groups, contact Karen at Allentown School District, 31 S. Penn Street, Box 328, Allentown, PA 18105; telephone: 484-765-4055; email: Klaudenslager@aol.com.)

It is not uncommon for many children in any elementary school to come from divorced homes. These pupils face a number of personal and social problems, which include being lonely, feeling responsible for the divorce, experiencing divided loyalties, not knowing how to deal with parental conflicts, and facing the loss of family stability. Researchers have demonstrated the effectiveness of groups in addressing the psychological, social, and academic problems associated with children of divorce

(DeLucia-Waack, 2011). Schools and community agencies are offering groups for children structured around these themes. This proposal describes counseling groups designed for children from divorced and changing families.

Organizing the Group

Before actually getting a group going, a great deal of careful preliminary work needs to be done. This preparation includes conducting a needs survey, announcing the group to children and teachers, obtaining parental permission, orienting the children to the rules for participating in a group, and presenting my goals in a clear way to the children, parents, teachers, and administrators. If adequate attention is not given to these preliminary details, the group may never materialize.

Survey the Children's Needs

It is helpful to assess the needs of children before deciding on a program. I do this by making an initial classroom visit to discuss with both the teachers and the children how small group counseling can be beneficial. I explain the topical focus of these groups or, as I later refer to them, "clubs." The family club is geared for grades 2 through 5. I explain that a specific day and time have been scheduled for club meetings at each grade level and that all clubs run for 30 minutes once a week for six sessions.

The needs survey is then handed out, and I ask all students to think about the issues and react truthfully. I explain that these surveys are private and will be read only by the classroom teacher and me. The selection of students is based on comments by both students and teachers. For a sample survey form, see DeLucia-Waack (2001).

Obtain Parental Permission

A letter is sent home with every child who has agreed to participate in the group. The letter outlines the issues and topics to be discussed, requests parental permission, and encourages parental support and involvement. I am convinced of the value of involving both parents whenever possible. I encourage each child to discuss the group with his or her parents. For a sample consent form, see DeLucia-Waack (2001).

Group Rules

All students voluntarily agree to be members of the club. I encourage children who are shy or slightly reluctant to give it a try. Anyone who wishes to leave the group is free to do so.

Children always have the right to remain silent. I reinforce the importance of listening and learning from one another. Some students feel more comfortable knowing that they will never be forced to share or discuss any issue that they feel is private. Other rules include (1) anyone who wants to may have a turn, (2) everyone is listened to, (3) no laughing or making fun of what anyone says, (4) honesty is required, and (5) confidentiality is respected.

The students, with my guidance, make up the rules during the first session. They usually come up with all of the rules mentioned earlier on their own. If the group does not identify some critical norms, I will add them to our list of rules. I explain the reasons for the rules, which increases the chances that the children will abide by them. Finally, we all sign our names, making a commitment and agreeing to follow the rules. These rules are posted and reviewed before each session.

Group Goals

What Children Need to Know

Through my research, reading, and direct contact with children, I have discovered some important messages children need to hear. I continually discuss, explain, and reinforce these statements throughout the six weekly sessions:

- You are special.
- You can get through this difficult time.
- You have people who care about you.
- It (the divorce or separation) is not your fault.
- You are not to blame.
- It is not your divorce, and no one is divorcing you. Your parents are divorcing each other.

- You did not cause the problems between your parents, and you cannot fix them.
- You can help each other.

What I Hope to Accomplish

Some objectives of the groups are:

- Give support when needed
- Let children know they are not alone
- Teach coping skills
- Reinforce students' need to talk and deal with feelings
- Help children deal with emotional and behavioral concerns so they can concentrate on learning and work to reach their potential
- Offer resources to students and parents such as bibliotherapy and outside private counseling when needed
- Help children open lines of communication with other students, teachers, and parents

Counseling groups, support groups, and psychoeducational groups for children of divorce focus on coping with the reality of the divorce situation and the feelings associated with this reality. Falco and Bauman (2014) capture the essence of a support group for children of divorce when they state: "Group counseling can be a practical, efficient, and effective treatment because it provides a mechanism for students to talk aloud about feelings and experiences that may assist in reducing some of the negative emotions associated with divorce" (p. 321).

DeLucia-Waack (2001) has identified seven specific goals for children of divorce groups, all of which are goals for my group as well: (a) help children acquire an accurate picture of the divorce process through discussion and information, (b) normalize common feelings around divorce, (c) create a safe and supportive place for children to talk about their concerns related to the divorce situation, (d) identify, express, and understand feelings about the divorce, (e) acquire new coping skills to deal with feelings and situations experienced as a result of divorce; (f) help children test reality, and (g) make plans for the future.

Group Format

The focus of these clubs is developmental and preventive. The groups are designed to provide support, teach coping skills, and help children of changing families explore ways to express and deal with their feelings. When more involved counseling is needed, the parents are always contacted and an outside referral is made.

Any counselor who works in an elementary school can testify to the importance of getting feedback and support from teachers and parents. I have found that it is critical to involve parents, teachers, and administrators in these group programs so that they become allies of the children and the counselor. Their support of the program goes a long way toward ensuring its success; their resistance can thwart its progress.

Teachers' feedback is critical because they see the student daily and can monitor changes in behavior. I make an effort to talk with each classroom teacher as often as possible. Teachers can tell counselors about pupils' self-esteem, self-confidence, interaction with their peers, and homework completion. They can also share comments and reactions that students make in class, both orally and in their written work. All of this information helps me monitor the students' emotional and social progress.

Sessions of 30 minutes each, once a week for 6 weeks, work well. This schedule gives me time to run more groups and see more children. With so many students experiencing family changes, I try to help as many as possible. This time structure interferes only minimally with classroom learning. I try to be sensitive to the reactions of both students and teachers to interrupting the learning process. Too much time out of class for extended periods can cause additional stress, and we are all concerned with supporting and enhancing the learning process, not disrupting it.

The Initial Meeting

The first session is clearly structured by focusing on a discussion of the purpose of the club, on my role as a group facilitator, and on helping the children identify why they are in the group. We play a "name game" in which the children introduce themselves by selecting an adjective describing them that starts with the first letter of their first name (such as Wonderful Wanda or Nice Nick). The only guideline is that the adjective must be a positive one. We define *family,* and each child introduces him- or herself by answering the question "Who am I, and who lives at my house?" I ask younger children to draw pictures of who lives in different houses. We discuss how many different places we live and with whom. I encourage them to describe how it is for them to be in their family. At this session the ground rules are established and written on chart paper for use as a reminder at all subsequent sessions. My goal for this first meeting is to help the children find out that they are not alone in their situation. If time allows, I encourage them to see similarities and differences in their family situations. I may ask "Who would like to share how your family is the same as or different from others in this group?"

The Next Four Sessions

I have found that my groups differ somewhat depending on the themes brought out at the initial session. I use selected exercises as a focus for interaction. The middle four sessions are structured in accordance with the needs of those who are in the group. Here are a few of the activities that are often part of these sessions:

- We play the "feeling game." Students brainstorm feelings, and we write them down. The children then select three feelings that describe how they feel about their family situation, and we discuss them.
- The children identify three wishes they have for their family. One overwhelming wish that generally emerges is that their mother and father will get back together. They also wish to spend more time with the noncustodial parent. These children often express how difficult it is for them to be placed in the middle of a struggle, and they wish for peace. They would like this harmony at any cost, and they are willing to do anything to bring it about.
- We go around the table taking turns to "check in," sharing on a scale from 1 to 10 how we are feeling and why.
- The children decide "what I want each of my parents to know." (Stepparents and stepbrothers and stepsisters may also be included, if appropriate.) I often find that children are hesitant to reveal some differences they might have with their new stepmother or stepfather. They frequently want their parents to understand their feelings about being in a new family. Sometimes children feel forced to make an adjustment before they are ready, and they often have uncomfortable feelings that have not been discussed.
- We discuss what children can control and what they cannot. For example, they can control their own behavior. We also talk about ways they can control certain feelings. However, they cannot control the decisions that their parents make about the divorce or current living situations. I also talk with the children about the fact that this is not *their* divorce. In other words, Mom and Dad are divorcing each other, not the children. What I hope to get across to the group members is that they did not cause the divorce and cannot "fix" the situation. Much of the group time is devoted to exploring and brainstorming alternatives for the children to change themselves in their situations at home.
- We discuss how change comes about. The children identify what they consider to be positive and negative changes in their lives as a result of the new family situation.
- A question box is available during all sessions. Students can anonymously write questions or concerns that they might not feel comfortable sharing in group and drop them in the question box. These issues are discussed at the next session.

The Last Session

As is true of the initial session, the final meeting is also fairly structured, this time around involving the tasks of termination. The children typically discuss feelings about the club ending and identify what they have learned from these sessions. There is also some time for a special celebration with cupcake or popcorn treats. Each student receives a recognition certificate, which says: *The Counselor Said I Am Special!*

Group Outcomes

Student Perceptions

Students report feeling more comfortable with themselves and with their family situations when they belong to the club and realize that they are not alone. They need to identify with other children who are experiencing similar concerns and feelings. Together, group members can begin to understand the stages that everyone goes through and can learn skills to help themselves feel better. Through the group process, they help one another let go of what they cannot control and take responsibility for what they can control.

Parent Perceptions

Parents report that their children enjoy the club meetings and often come home and share what was discussed. Their children gain a better understanding of divorce by learning how others adjust. Parents are often in so much pain and conflict themselves during the separation or divorce that they are relieved and happy that someone else is there supporting their children.

Parents show an interest in what their children are doing in the group, and parents often read some of the recommended books with their children. Many parents have expressed a need for more information on how they can help their children. I have offered evening workshops and parenting classes. I would like to develop an ongoing parent support group to meet the needs of adults. I have also thought it might be helpful to facilitate one or two sessions with both parents and children together.

Follow-Up

My follow-up consists of checking with teachers on the students' progress and checking with the students themselves by classroom visits, by seeing them individually, and by encouraging self-referrals. I also hold club "reunions" the following year to see how things have been going.

Personal Sources of Frustration

The biggest frustration for me is ending the clubs. The children always resist terminating and bargain or plead to continue with more sessions. I find it extremely difficult to end when I know how much these children need to talk and learn. I am unable to directly solve some of the children's problems, and that adds to my level of frustration. Here are some of the complex problems these children face:

- Infrequent visitations with a parent as a result of the parent's emotional problems
- Dislocations because a child is "interfering" with a parent's relationships
- Frequent court testimony in sexual abuse cases
- Violence in the family
- Parental neglect
- Conflicts over being asked by parents to choose sides
- Parents' extramarital affairs
- Alcohol and drug abuse
- Spousal abuse
- Physical or emotional abuse
- Custody battles
- Financial concerns

Another source of frustration is time. There never seems to be enough time to see all the students who need help. Nor is there enough time to meet with all the parents to discuss the progress of each child. I do, however, refer families for outside counseling if during the club sessions I see a need for more in-depth therapy.

Concluding Comments

I have found the group experience to be very effective and instrumental in supporting students with changes and family issues. Students are able to connect with each other and offer support, encouragement, suggestions, and hope. In the group they can help each other to understand feelings and learn how to handle difficult situations in a safe place. It has been my experience that this small group structure is extremely beneficial. I strongly recommend that counselors provide this kind of counseling service for students.

For those interested in designing a children of divorce group, a useful resource is Janice DeLucia-Waack's (2001) book, *Using Music in Children of Divorce Groups: A Session-by-Session Manual for Counselors*. This manual shows how exercises and music can help children express emotions and apply what they learn in a group to their daily lives.

A Group for Children Who Have Been Abused

This section is written from the perspective of Teresa M. Christensen, PhD. (For further information, contact Teresa at Regis University, CPS, Department of Education and Counseling; telephone: 303-964-5727, ext. 5727; email: tchriste@regis.edu.)

Introduction

The effects of child abuse are pervasive and often multifaceted. Aside from the obvious physical injury sustained by any number of abusive violations, children who are abused often experience a range of feelings and thoughts related to anger and hostility, fear and anxiety, vulnerability and powerlessness, sadness and loss, shame, and guilt. The detrimental outcome of child abuse often presents itself in children who struggle with trust issues, self-blame, depression, isolation, poor self-image, and many other interpersonal relationship issues (Gil, 2006). The literature and research have called for an increase in literature that illuminates mental health services specific to children affected by abuse and trauma. Experts in the field have responded to such needs (Gil, 2010; Terr, 2009), but counselors continually yearn for new ideas about how to work with children affected by abuse. Many experts contend that effective interventions focus on the appropriate expression of emotions, a positive self-image, interpersonal relationship skills, and rebuilding trust in a variety of social situations (Gil, 2010). Therefore, interventions that explore interpersonal and social relationships can be highly effective with those who suffer from abuse. In particular, group counseling provides a nonjudgmental and safe climate in which children are encouraged to address a multitude of issues and in which they have the opportunity to establish relationships with their peers who have similar experiences. After several years of experience, I have found group counseling to be very helpful for children affected by abuse. The model that follows has emerged from my experiences as an individual, group, and family counselor with children affected by varying forms of abuse.

Group Goals

The main goal of this group is to foster a therapeutic relationship in which children who have been abused feel safe enough to risk trusting other children and another adult. The group is designed to establish a safe environment, empower children, and enhance their sense of self. This group is also structured to assist children in discovering that they are not alone in their experiences and feelings, thus providing an environment in which children have an opportunity to express difficult and complex emotions and act out the intrusive and abusive experiences. By assisting children to express the full range of mixed and confusing emotions felt toward the perpetrator, children experience a sense of control and mastery (Gil, 2010), which is another goal of this group. By the end of the group, it is hoped that all children will have learned to express their feelings appropriately and acknowledged their personal strengths, and will have developed the skills they need for healthy interpersonal interactions and relationships.

Setting Up the Group

Screening

Screening is crucial when counseling children who have been abused, and timing is essential when determining when children are ready for group. Most of all, children must be ready and willing to interact with other children in a therapeutic setting as evidenced by their desire to play games, talk, and generally spend time with peers. All children in my groups have completed or are concurrently involved in individual and family counseling, and I utilize case notes and clinical impressions to assist in the screening process. When I believe children are ready, I invite them to participate in group counseling. I emphasize that they can decline, thus empowering them to make choices.

Group counseling is contraindicated if (a) the abuse happened recently, (b) the abuse is still highly traumatizing to the child, (c) the child has experienced serious psychological disturbances such as suicidal behavior, self-mutilation, severe mood swings, or thought disturbances (hallucinations or delusions), or (d) the child was abused by more than one person at a time. However, it is my belief that all children can benefit from group counseling when they are ready.

The functioning and climate of the group are dependent on the behavioral patterns of prospective members. Accordingly, it is essential to balance the group with members similar in age, physical size, and gender. Likewise, the type and severity of the abuse must be considered when composing the group so that children are not retraumatized by other children's stories. Once children are deemed appropriate for group counseling, consent from the legal guardian must be obtained.

Parent/Legal Guardian Consent

In most cases, I converse with parents/legal guardians in person, but sometimes I send a letter of consent. The letter outlines issues of confidentiality, therapeutic factors, topics to be discussed in the group, and a description of the process, which provides a rational for group counseling with children affected by abuse (see letter). I emphasize that group does not take the place of individual or family counseling, but that it is a supplement to the current treatment plan.

Written consent is obtained from legal guardians prior to informing the child about the group. (It is important to attain proof of legal guardianship, particularly when children don't reside with their biological parents.) Legal guardians may include foster or adoptive parents, grandparents, or other members of the extended family.

Group Composition and Characteristics

This type of group works most efficiently with children of similar ages (only 1 to 3 years apart) who have suffered the same type of abuse. Adolescents can also benefit from such a group, but the activities described here pertain to a group for children ages 7 to 12 who have been sexually abused. Because developmental and gender issues need to be considered, each group is structured a bit differently depending on the specific needs of the members. Due to factors such as trust, power and control, group cohesion, and boundary issues, this is a closed group. The group consists of five to seven members who meet for 45 to 60 minutes once a week for 10 consecutive sessions.

Setting

The ideal setting to facilitate groups with children ages 4 to 12 is a playroom or similarly structured space that is large enough to accommodate the number of members. This space should enable a variety of activities that incorporate both nondirective and directive play, including a variety of expressive arts activities. Necessary materials include therapeutic toys and games, art supplies, puppets, blowing bubbles, sand and miniatures, and other creative materials.

Group Format

I incorporate directive and nondirective techniques throughout the entire group process. Development and process issues are addressed by dividing each group session into three segments: warm-up, work, and wrap-up. All sessions begin with 5 to 10 minutes for warm-up,

Dear Parent/Legal Guardian:

As you are well aware, the detrimental outcome of child abuse often presents itself in children who struggle with trust issues, self-blame, depression, anxiety, isolation, poor self-image, and many other interpersonal relationship issues. While such problems are currently or have been addressed with your children in individual and/or family counseling, I believe that group counseling is yet another opportunity that can be highly therapeutic and beneficial to your child's mental well-being.

Throughout my experience as a counselor and play therapist, I have found that many children affected by abuse struggle with relationships, namely peer relationships. Research has indicated and I firmly believe that group counseling can assist many children in (a) learning how to trust others, (b) understanding that they aren't alone in their experiences, (c) developing healthy interpersonal relationship skills, and (d) increasing their sense of control and mastery when in social situations. By interacting with others who have similar feelings, experiences, and concerns, children learn how to accept and cope with their emotions and thoughts more effectively.

Based on clinical observations and my professional judgment, I believe that your child is ready and prepared for a group counseling experience. Accordingly, I am requesting that you grant permission for ________________________(child's name) to take part in a 10-week group that will be made up of approximately five to seven other children who have similar concerns and are compatible in terms of age, size, and gender.

Group sessions will include an array of structured and non-structured conversations and activities related to abuse and other mental health issues. All children and parents will be informed about confidentiality, but I cannot control what children say or do outside of the session. However, I will make every effort to enforce confidentiality and ensure the physical and emotional safety of your child. Should you have any questions or concerns about the group, please contact me at ___________.

By signing this form, you acknowledge and support your child's participation in this group counseling experience and hereby provide written consent.

______________________________ ________________

Parent's/Guardian's Signature Date

______________________________ ________________

Witness's Signature Date

______________________________ ________________

Teresa M. Christensen, PhD Date

which includes (a) a check-in with each member about how he or she is feeling today, (b) time to reflect on and talk about what happened in the last session, and (c) discussion about what the group session will be like. The next 25 to 35 minutes is the work phase, which includes either a structured activity or free play. The final 10 to 15 minutes is reserved for wrap-up, also known as T&T (Treat and Talk Time). During T&T group members are offered a healthy snack and encouraged to take turns sharing their reactions to the session. Discussions focus on what members learned in the session and on how these experiences might be generalized to their life outside of the group.

The structure and topic for each session varies depending on the issues and needs of the individual members and the group as a whole. Therefore, aside from the initial session (Orientation) and the last session (Celebration), weekly sessions alternate between structured and nonstructured activities. Sessions 1–4, 6, 8, and 10 are highly structured through one or more activities focused on topics related to abuse. I use a variety of expressive arts, activities, role plays, and games in the structured sessions that are derived from my clinical experience and other resources. Sessions 5, 7, and 9 are process oriented and begin with nonstructured time in a playroom or a space with a variety of games, toys, art supplies, and activities from which group members are free to choose. The following outline includes examples of topics and activities for each of the sessions.

Session 1: Orientation

The initial session includes discussions about confidentiality, the purpose and structure of the group, and some basic ground rules (policies) such as no hitting, one person talks at a time, and confidentiality. I usually begin by thanking members for choosing to be a part of this group. I also state that everyone in the group has been abused but that this is not the only reason members were selected for this experience. I indicate that this group is about getting to know others, learning how to express feelings appropriately, and learning how to make positive choices. To assist children in getting acquainted with one another, I facilitate an icebreaker in which children take turns stating their name and something about themselves (favorite color, animal, or time of day). This type of go-around continues for approximately 15 to 20 minutes.

During the last half of the session, I use the term "group policies" to discuss rules and enlist the help of group members in making a list of rules for this group. This sets the tone by empowering children to co-construct the group experience. I record this information on a poster titled our "Group Declaration Banner" and provide a variety of art materials and encourage children to sign their names and decorate the Group Banner, which will be displayed during each group session and referred to whenever necessary to set limits. I closely monitor what policies members choose to adopt and make certain that we include rules to protect physical and emotional safety. I make certain that our declaration gives children the freedom to remain silent or pass on go-around activities, and I also emphasize boundary issues such as self-disclosure, confidentiality, and physical touch. In most cases, group members come up with policies that far surpass the rules or limits that I would enforce. Accordingly, I monitor the group to make certain that they don't make too many policies, or that the policies aren't too rigid. This group session ends with a final wrap-up T&T go-around.

Session 2: Awareness Activity

The relationship-building activity assists members in gaining insight and promotes healthy member interactions. Each member of the group creates an "identity collage," choosing four or five magazine images, phrases, or words that describe how the member sees her- or himself. Therapists are encouraged to select a wide range of magazines that support diversity and are developmentally appropriate. Once members have had the opportunity to share their collages, they are encouraged to reflect on how they have changed since the abuse. Group members are then encouraged to select at least one more item, word, or phrase that represents how they believe they have changed as a result of the abuse and how they feel about this change. These items are used to alter the existing collage, and group members are again given the opportunity to share their revised collages.

This activity gives group members an opportunity to self-reflect and engage in self-exploration regarding how the abuse has affected them. When processing this activity, it is important to discuss the multitude of intense feelings children associate with the abuse as well as the changes they have encountered. For example, the following remarks were shared in groups I facilitated with children who had been molested: "I am sad that I don't live with my mom and dad anymore." "I hate being a boy! My body does strange and dirty things." "I don't know if I will ever find a husband, because no boy will want me after they learn about what happened with my dad."

Session 3: Secrets and Touches

This session includes an activity specific to inappropriate and appropriate touching and safe and unsafe secrets. Because this activity is intended to help children learn how to both establish and adhere to appropriate physical boundaries and distinguish between safe and unsafe secrets, it is important to first define these concepts in developmentally appropriate terms to children. For example, I would explain: "A safe secret is not telling about something that won't harm anyone else, like keeping a surprise birthday party a secret. Whereas an unsafe secret is when something hurtful or dangerous is happening to you or someone else and you keep it a secret by not telling anyone." As a group activity, members are then encouraged to come up with lists of appropriate and inappropriate forms of touching and safe and unsafe secrets. This activity ends with members developing a plan about how to handle touching and secrets in a healthy manner in the future.

Session 4: Trust Activity

After the initial check-in, this session focuses on activities pertaining to trust. In the "trust walk," group members partner with one another; one member is blindfolded, and the other serves as a guide. The goal is to trust and communicate with one another as they move through a maze or a series of directions provided by the leader. The blindfolded member confronts issues of vulnerability, powerlessness, risk-taking, anxiety, and having to rely on others for support. The member who isn't blindfolded experiences an opportunity for leadership and mastery. Once members have processed their reactions to the trust walk experience, they are instructed to draw a picture or to create a list of people in their lives whom they can trust and to say why. Members are given the option of sharing their list with the rest of the group. At the end of this session, members are reminded that the next session will involve nondirective play, and they are ask to begin thinking about what they will choose and how they will spend their time together.

Session 5: Process Oriented

After the check-in, members are encouraged to make their own choices about what they would like to do during this session. I may offer a few general ideas about how members might play with one another. For example, I might say, "You can choose to play together (games, activities, role plays), or you may choose to play alone." I may point out some of the materials that are available, but for the most Part 1 remain nondirective. My role as leader in this session is to be a keen observer of group members' interactions and to see whether and how the children choose to engage with other members. I offer verbal and nonverbal encouragers and reflections as members make collective choices or individual ones about what to do in the session. The children often choose to play games or build sandtrays together, but some children use the time to explore the playroom or to create a drawing or painting on their own. The session ends with the traditional T&T time, and the children are offered an opportunity to reflect on their experiences in the group.

Session 6: Interpersonal Interaction Activity

By this point in the process, group cohesion usually is developed, and I focus on helping members address relationship dynamics and potential issues. We cover a variety of topics related to communication: using "I" messages, how to show respect for emotional and physical boundaries, how to ask for what one needs, and ways to appropriately express feelings. Games and structured activities specifically designed to address these topics include (a) the "talking, feeling, doing" game, (b) role plays, (c) puppet shows, (d) family drawings, and (e) the telephone game. We also might read from books, listen to music, and watch movies that address issues related to specific abuse and trauma.

Children who have been abused and traumatized often struggle with transitions (Gil, 2010; Terr, 2009), so I pay particular attention to the termination phase of the group. At the end of this sixth session, I remind members that we only have three more sessions until group ends and ask members to begin to think about how other groups in their lives have ended. I give examples of endings by talking about what it might be like when clubs or teams don't meet anymore or the end of the school year. In particular, we discuss how members have learned to say good-bye to others. We also talk about "good-bye rituals" that members have experienced in their families and communities, and I explain that we can decide how we want to say good-bye to each other and end this important experience. This session marks the beginning of the end of the group.

Session 7: Process Oriented

During this session children are offered another nondirective play experience. They typically read books, play with puppets, or utilize the art materials to create a picture or journal for themselves.

Session 8: Resilience Activity

The goal of this session is to assist members in developing a positive self-image. The focus is on helping children identify personal strengths and learn how to use their strengths to make healthy choices in the future. At the beginning of the session, I clarify what strengths are and encourage members to take a few moments to construct a list of at least four strengths they recognize in themselves. Examples have included: "I am a good listener." "I am a good friend." "I have learned how to show my anger without hitting someone or something." "I know how to say NO." Because self-esteem can be damaged by child abuse, the group counselor's assistance is especially important here. As a group we decide what we can do to creatively exhibit our strengths. Any number of activities and games can be used to accomplish this task, and I encourage members to create something. Sometimes they use art and construction materials to build kites, personal or family shields, personalized license plates, or T-shirts. Then members list their wants and needs in life, and we brainstorm ideas about how they can use their strengths to get their needs met and satisfy their desires in a healthy manner. I emphasize that they still have a choice about many aspects of their lives regardless of what people have said or done to them in the past. We talk about how their strengths can help them make healthy choices, about how to get their needs met in the future, and how to express their feelings and thoughts.

At the end of this session, we discuss the upcoming celebration session. We brainstorm ideas about what they want to do (activities, games, art, talk, sing, or dance). I inform group members that I will provide some sort of drink (usually juice) and at least one treat (usually fruit or popcorn).

Session 9: Process Oriented

Due to the power of group development and enhanced trust, members typically choose activities in which they verbally interact more during Session 9. For example, children often play board games and draw and share their pictures.

Session 10: Celebration

The last session is a celebration and a time to reminisce about the group experience, which includes members talking about what they have learned about themselves and others. The intent of this session is to achieve some sense of closure, and because group members have a hand in planning this session, the structure often varies. Final sessions have included, but are not limited to, the following. Younger children may want to create good-bye pictures that everyone in the group signs, create and act out a skit or role play, or play a game together. Older children and adolescents are more likely to appreciate a nondirective session in which group members have free time to reminisce about previous sessions and talk about their experiences in the group. On many occasions, older children and adolescents have brought refreshments to the last session and created personal journals out of art materials, which were then autographed or decorated by every member in the group as a memory of this experience. Regardless of the format, I request that all members share the following information: (a) what they have learned about their individual strengths and talents, (b) how they plan to continue making positive choices and building healthy relationships outside of group, and (c) their individual plans about how to take care of themselves.

Expected Group Outcomes

Children who have been abused deserve opportunities to express their thoughts, feelings, and overall reactions with others in a safe and constructive environment. After more than 20 years of experience facilitating groups with children who have been affected by abuse, I have come to believe that group counseling provides an ideal environment for these children to learn that they are not alone, to begin a healing process, and to learn how to establish a trusting and healthy relationship with other children, as well as with adults. In the group, children can break down the barriers of isolation, express their inner-most struggles, clarify misplaced blame, and feel more comfortable about interacting with others. In my view, the group atmosphere provides a deeper level of healing for children who have been affected by abuse. Enhanced interpersonal relationship skills, increased confidence and independence, and self-assurance are but a few of the outcomes exhibited by children who participate in these groups. Although assisting children in healing from abusive experiences can be complex and challenging, I encourage group counselors to pursue unique and creative ways to incorporate the therapeutic factors of group work in their interventions with children affected by abuse.

Recommended Resources

Resources that I found useful in designing this group include Gil (1991, 2006, 2010), Hindman (1993), Kleven (1997), Lowenstein (1999), Spinal-Robinson and Wickham (1992a, 1992b, 1993), Sweeney, Baggerly, and Ray (2014), and Terr (1990, 1991, 2008, 2009). For useful resources on the use of creative arts in groups and play therapy, see Gladding (2016), Kottman (2011), and Kottman and Meany-Walen (2016).

LO5

Developmental Themes of Adolescence

A detailed description of the unique needs of adolescents is beyond the scope of this book. For group leaders who work with adolescents, courses in the psychology of adolescents are essential. Reflecting on one's own adolescent experiences and perhaps reliving some of these experiences are also valuable means of preparing to counsel adolescents.

The adolescent period of life is characterized by searching for an identity and clarifying a system of values that will influence the course of one's life. Although adolescence presents stresses and conflicts, it is also a time of significant growth fueled by major cognitive advances, an increased orientation toward the social world, and physiological changes. Adolescents are increasingly interested in understanding how their experiences have shaped their current feelings and behaviors. One of the most important needs of this period is to experience successes that will lead to a sense of individuality and connectedness, which in turn lead to self-confidence and self-respect regarding their uniqueness and their sameness. Adolescents need opportunities to explore and understand the wide range of their feelings and to learn how to communicate with significant others in such a way that they can make their wants, feelings, thoughts, and beliefs known.

During the adolescent years, social relationships are of primary importance. Adolescents utilize these relationships to learn about self, the world, and others. This orientation toward the social world enhances their need for independence. However, adolescents and their parents sometimes mistakenly believe that this equates with a decreased need for parental time and attention. The most resilient adolescents have strong social skills and open, healthy relationships with their parents. This connection to family is crucial for long-term success.

Sources of Stress During Adolescence

Many adolescents experience tension between their lives at home and at school. They may feel stuck between these two worlds because the rules or expectations for these two systems do not match or are in disharmony, which can be a key source of stress. Adolescents from certain racial and cultural groups may experience additional stressors related to the challenges of racism, poverty, and other sociopolitical and social and environmental factors. In seeking their sense of self, adolescents often have difficulty relating to their parents, guardians, or grandparents. Other adolescents face family pressures that require that they work to help support the family. During this period, learning to use freedom and the dependence–independence struggle are central.

Adolescents are pressured to succeed and are expected to perform, frequently up to others' standards. They often feel a need for universal approval yet must learn to distinguish between living for others' approval and earning their own. Whether adolescents are trusted and given the freedom to make significant decisions is often based on cultural expectations. In Western cultures adolescents are encouraged to make decisions with the faith and support of caring adults, but they need guidelines and limits. Cultural conflicts between American-reared adolescents and their immigrant parents are often a significant source of stress. These adolescents may be functioning at a different level of assimilation or integration than their parents. Values, beliefs, and cultural practices can become the source of parent–child conflict.

Developmental Group Counseling With Adolescents

This brief sketch of the main currents of adolescent life highlights the need for developmentally appropriate counseling in this population. Generally, adolescents are more concerned with peer relationships than are younger children, and adolescents struggle with separation from parents and the development of self-identity. Peers become an important source of support, which makes groups a treatment of choice for adolescents (Shechtman, 2014). Group leaders need to understand the developmental needs of adolescents and have a cultural awareness of the community that they serve. In light of our society's rapidly changing demographics, group leaders need to make a concerted effort to address issues of diversity.

The opportunity to relate to peers who are experiencing very similar processes can be a healing experience. Akos, Hamm, Mack, and Dunaway (2007) illustrate the developmental importance of peer relationships during the early adolescent years and how group work provides a useful resource for members to explore their concerns with their peers. Young adolescents naturally look to their peers for affirmation and companionship, which makes group counseling particularly viable for this age group. Middle school counselors have the task of designing groups that can assist young adolescents in dealing with a variety of developmental tasks, providing an appropriate forum for promoting their personal and social development.

Group counseling is an ideal venue for engaging all of the strengths and struggles of adolescents. In addition, group leaders have an opportunity to combine personal themes with educational goals when developing the group structure. Through a positive group experience young people can learn about themselves, what they value, their beliefs, their relationships, and their choices. The group should have clearly defined goals, relevant themes, and a structure that will enable members to develop trust in the group. Their increasing orientation toward the social world blends beautifully with the group process. Isolation is decreased, social skills are gained, and the opportunity to understand psychological factors is provided.

LO6

Issues and Challenges in Leading Adolescent Groups

Motivating the adolescent to become an active group participant can be challenging. Group leaders need to clearly state the guidelines for conduct during sessions and gain members' acceptance. Creativity may be required to keep meetings moving in a meaningful direction. Gladding (2016) describes how creative group techniques such as music, movement, visual art, drama, play, and humor can be used as catalysts for interaction in high school groups. Creative techniques assist adolescents in expressing their emotions appropriately, behaving in different and healthier ways, and gaining insight into themselves and others. Coupling group work with creative techniques is a relatively attractive and familiar format for adolescents. However, regardless of how creative we are, there are definite challenges in facilitating adolescent groups. Some common challenges—developing trust and setting limits to self-disclosure—are discussed in the following sections.

Establishing Trust

The first task for an adolescent group facilitator is building rapport, which hinges on being yourself and avoiding pretense. To develop trusting relationships and to effectively work with young people, group leaders need to possess cultural sensitivity, understand current trends, and demonstrate respect for young people.

Familiarize yourself with the members' subcultures, including their slang, style of speaking to one another, the types of music and entertainment media they enjoy, and their current modes of communication, including the many forms of social media now part of their lives. Group leaders would do well to have a general sense of the various ways adolescents are communicating with each other. However, you may find that adolescents will enjoy teaching you what you don't know. Having an opportunity to share their knowledge can provide a foundation for building trust.

A way to get some insight into the culture dimensions in a group is to begin a group session by asking members to bring in a song that describes their life theme or philosophy or by asking members to identify their favorite movie and then identify themes for discussion. This discussion can help group leaders understand the members' culture, and it creates some metaphors for a common language in a group. It is not necessary for you to talk like your adolescent clients by imitating their slang and manner of speaking, but it can be helpful in joining and understanding their world if you have some sense of their "culture." Understanding the world of young people does not mean that you become one of them. By trying too hard to be accepted, you may lose adolescents' trust and respect.

Deal directly, candidly, and openly with group members. They will know it if you are intimidated by them. If you don't have a clear sense of what you are doing, yet you pretend to be on their wave length, adolescents will detect this. However, being friendly, expressive, and warm goes a long way toward developing rapport with adolescents. In being personable and friendly you are not discounting therapeutic objectivity, but you are conveying acceptance, which tends to put young people at ease.

In an initial session, the discussion should include issues of confidentiality, group norms, ground rules, establishing boundaries to clarify appropriate and facilitative ways of interacting within the group, giving and receiving feedback, and suggestions for applications outside of the group. (For other topics that we typically explore during the early phase of a group as a way of generating trust, refer to the discussion in Chapter 6 on the initial stage.)

Know Your Comfort Zone With Self-Disclosure

Adolescents will ask you direct and personal questions. Sometimes this is a way of testing whether you subscribe to the ideas you are attempting to communicate to them. Adolescents often test group leaders to determine whether they mean what they have told them about the group. For example, adolescents will frequently ask the group leader questions such as "Have you ever experimented with drugs?" "Are your parents divorced?" " Are you married?" "Do you have a boyfriend or girlfriend?" "Do you have kids?" or "What are your thoughts about premarital sex?" Dealing with adolescents in an authentic manner requires some candor in responding, but this must be thoughtful. For example, a possible response to the question of drug use is: "That's a lose–lose question for me. If I say yes, then you can say, 'well, you turned out OK, so it's OK for me to do it.' If I say no, then you'll say 'well, you don't understand' and you'll discount what I say." How leaders respond to confrontational questions tells the members how much they can trust the group leaders. If this testing by adolescents is accepted in a nonjudgmental and nondefensive way, trust is enhanced and reluctance to participate in the group is reduced. Adolescents tend to respond well to leaders who appropriately share themselves with the group, displaying a caring attitude, enthusiasm and vitality, openness, and directness. If you genuinely respect and enjoy adolescents, you will typically be rewarded with a reciprocal respect.

Adolescents are quick to detect any traces of inauthenticity. A key leader task is to model congruence between what is said and what is actually done. However, this does not mean that a leader needs to disclose aspects of his or her private life on demand. A leader can model appropriate choices to resist pressure to disclose, just as he or she would do with adult groups. Many adolescents, especially those in the "system" or those living in difficult family situations, are in need of positive role models, and group leaders can provide this to their adolescent group members.

The group proposal "Teens Making a Change" describes strategies for setting up a group for young people that can be applied to both community and school settings. This is an excellent example of what can be accomplished when the purposes of a group are carefully considered. This group proposal also demonstrates the importance of understanding how to work in a system, whether in a school, a neighborhood, or the community.

GROUP PROPOSAL

Teens Making a Change (T-MAC): A Group for Preventing Teen Delinquency

This section is written from the perspective of Sheila D. Morris, PsyD. (For further information, contact Sheila at 1672 W. Avenue J., Suite 207, Lancaster, CA 93534; telephone: 661-951-4662; email: drsheila_2000@yahoo.com. A more comprehensive look at T-MAC is provided in the guidebook *Combating Teen Delinquency in an Apartment Setting Through Village Building* [Carter, 1998]).

Grassroots community-based groups for troubled youth can be considered the wave of the future. Based on a community psychology perspective, this group is designed as a preventive and intervention measure to help youth that live in an apartment complex. This setting is primarily composed of low socioeconomic status working-class African American and Latino families. The group serves as an additional support to families raising adolescents who may be susceptible to delinquent behaviors due to social, economic, and environmental factors. The group addresses traditional delinquent behaviors as well as teen dating, gangs, and racial differences and similarities. This is accomplished by incorporating several different components to increase awareness, promote dialogue, and instill pride and a sense of belonging. The original group design is community apartment-based, but it has been incorporated in juvenile detention and can be adapted and generalized to school settings and group homes.

Organizing the Group

The group is housed in an apartment complex where the youth live with their families, and it involves neighbors as well as community leaders, business professionals, and politicians. Group members range in ages from 12 to 19 and are self-referred. The group is composed of several different components to help youth become more productive in their community, school, and family. The group has adopted the motto "Hood life isn't the only life," and the group focuses on outings to areas outside their immediate living environment. The group meets weekly for 60 minutes with a group facilitator and parent/neighbor volunteer. Typically, the group is open-ended and ongoing, but this structure is flexible and is based on the needs of the community.

To adapt T-MAC to a school setting, contact the school administration to explore the proposal and to determine what benefit the group would have for the student members, the school, and the community at large. T-MAC members could be referred by teachers, guidance counselors, or parents, or be self-referred. The group could be composed of an entire classroom with participation of a teacher, counselor, or school psychologist or from various classes across grades. The group would be time-limited, with fieldtrips to expose students to locations outside their immediate community being one of the group's activities, thereby reinforcing the motto "Hood life isn't the only life."

The group agrees on rules for group behavior, consequences, and leadership. Confidentiality and safety issues are also discussed and honored. The facilitator explains the importance of parental involvement and the limits of confidentiality when it concerns serious threats of harm to self or others. The group addresses delinquent behaviors through open discussions. The structure includes viewing videotapes and other social media, interacting with guest speakers, and role plays. Several components have proved beneficial to the success of the group:

- *Discussion Groups.* Even in today's technological era, most teens are still searching for a caring ear and a way to express themselves in a healthy way. They are mostly concerned with and interested in subjects such as dating, sex, peer and family relations, careers, gangs, music, and fashion. Many inner-city youth do not have a forum in which to openly express their concerns in these areas, especially with a concerned and caring adult. Group members should be encouraged to present topics of interest.
- *Application to School Settings.* Peer interactions and relationships are important topics, especially among high school teens. The school is often the meeting ground for the beginnings of teen interpersonal relationships including gang activities. Youth exhibiting poor peer relationships, anger, and estrangement at home are all susceptible to gang involvement. T-MAC is a group designed for delinquency prevention and intervention, and in a school setting counselors would select the teens most at risk for delinquent behaviors.
- *Activities and Outings.* Outings play an important part for this group in that they help actualize opportunity. Teens from the neighborhood already know how to survive the social and environmental ills surrounding them. For many this way of life is all they know. Showing youth that the world is large and filled with great opportunities enhances their confidence and gives them a chance to explore new avenues. T-MAC outings have included a trip to the state capitol in Sacramento, hiking, going to museums and amusement parks, taking a trip to the snow in the mountains, going to stage plays, and a host of other outings and activities. Members also have participated in cleaning up graffiti and marching with political figures to protest crime and violence in the neighborhood. In more restrictive settings, T-MAC outings are virtual tours, as well as utilizing social media and the Internet. In school settings, fieldtrips could be prearranged and financially supported by business members and community leaders.
- *Fund-Raising.* T-MAC is a grassroots group. To fund outings and group activities, fund-raising events are employed. Group members present fund-raising ideas, which include bake sales, car washes, Internet raffles, and socials, to help realize the group's mission and motto. In addition, donations and sponsorships are sought from various sources.

- *Guest Speakers.* Guest speakers on topics of gangs, building self-esteem, teen dating, violence, college, and career choices have played an important role in providing members with alternative perspectives and motivation, and they serve as role models and mentors. Speakers from the community, law enforcement, and business and entertainment sector can help to bridge the gap between the community, the school, and the individual.
- *Parental Involvement.* This is the most challenging aspect of the group. Often parents are not available to participate, and group members may not fully engage in the group process when their parents are present. Some parents have contributed by providing transportation, food preparation, and chaperoning.
- *Community Involvement.* Local business owners, community leaders, and politicians have contributed by providing donations, supplies, sponsorships, and other resources. T-MAC serves as a catalyst to bridge neighborhood and community leaders with school officials for the common cause of combating teen delinquency. This bridge helps transition teens from their neighborhood to the school and provides a more secure and stable sense of unity. Community leaders, business owners, and parent advocates could provide presentations and lead discussions in the group, further linking the school and the community.

Group Goals

The primary goal of the group is to end delinquent behaviors by providing alternative ways of dealing with urban stressors such as gangs, drugs, teen pregnancy, peer pressure, crime and violence, and poverty. In addition, it is expected that through group participation the worldview of the members can be expanded and they can find opportunities for success. To that end, this program focuses on these goals:

- Learning positive behaviors
- Linking school and community experiences
- Increasing social skills
- Increasing positive attitudes about self and others
- Increasing school functioning and learning
- Increasing community productiveness
- Alleviating neighborhood vandalism
- Building a sense of community belongingness
- Including as many influential and caring adults as possible to provide positive role modeling
- Providing community resources to aid families

Group Format

T-MAC was designed to meet the needs of a particular population. In keeping with the community psychology perspective, group members and the apartment complex community at large are directly involved in determining the topics and components of the group. T-MAC in school settings or detention facilities can be structured using the topics in this proposal. The 15 weekly sessions outlined here address gangs and gang involvement in the community setting. T-MAC topics in the classroom setting would likely address issues related to peer and relationship interactions, careers, skill building, and broadening members' global awareness through virtual travel. Each session begins by introducing the particular topic and ends by reviewing and incorporating new knowledge. These sessions can be adapted to fit a variety of groups or populations.

Session 1: Group Introduction

- The facilitator describes the purpose and focus of the group and reviews safety and confidentiality.
- Members introduce themselves, create group rules (such as one person talks at a time, respect toward other members, no use of profanity), and develop topics for group discussion.

Sessions 2 and 3: History of Gangs

- The facilitator provides a history of gangs from assorted readings.
- Members discuss the readings and relate this information to their own knowledge about gangs.
- Members pair up in dyads and discuss the readings.
- Dyads discuss their perceptions with the group.

Sessions 4, 5, and 6: Personal Experience With Gangs

- Members discuss which identifiable gangs are in their neighborhood and what colors are not safe to wear.
- Members discuss personal experiences with gang involvement or near involvement.
- Members discuss their worries and fears.
- Members discuss how gangs affect the neighborhood, the schools, and the apartment complex.
- Members discuss personal affiliations with family members or friends.
- One member gives a presentation to the larger group about his or her experiences with gang members.
- Members answer questions from the larger group.

Sessions 7 and 8: Videotape Presentation

- Members view and discuss contents of an episode of *Beyond Scared Straight* or *Gangland.* News stories and Internet clips are also good resources to use in this segment.
- Facilitator summarizes the episode.
- Facilitator identifies alternatives to gang involvement.

Session 9: Making Connections

- Facilitator engages group members in discussing how the episode relates to what is happening in the neighborhood, school, or in their own lives.
- Members discuss alternatives and write different endings for selected characters.
- Members share and discuss the new characters with the group. For instance, they may be asked, "How is the new character's behavior different and how does this difference influence the story?"

Sessions 10 and 11: Making Changes

- Facilitator engages group members in discussing how their neighborhood or apartment complex would change if there were no gang members.
- Members answer questions such as "What positive alternatives for youth could replace gangs?" and "How could gangs change to promote a positive image?"
- Members map out and visualize their neighborhood without gangs.

Session 12: Using Role Plays

- Facilitator provides scenarios for role plays.
- Members create role plays for what they can do if they are approached by gang members or if they are having a bad experience with a peer.
- Members alternate between providing scenarios and participating in role plays.
- Members pair up to write about their experiences and share them with group members.

Sessions 13, 14, and 15: Alternatives

- Guest speaker presents personal experience with gangs and how he or she overcame gang life.
- Facilitator engages group in discussing and summarizing topics about gangs.
- Facilitator helps to identify new knowledge and ways to implement alternative coping strategies to deal with gangs.
- Members discuss new knowledge and alternatives to gang involvement.
- Members discuss their learning and where to go from here.
- Members continue implementing plans for change.

Group Outcomes

Although there are no formal outcome measures for this group, anecdotal reports indicate that group members gained a sense of self-improvement from having a safe place to share normal adolescent developmental issues. They also acquired adaptive coping skills to deal with social and environmental ills plaguing their neighborhood.

As part of the group process, members are encouraged to describe what they are learning and how the group is affecting them. As termination of the group approaches, the members are asked to write about the personal benefits of the experience. One 12-year-old African American boy writes, "The benefits of being in the T-MAC club is having fun, solving problems, and doing lots of activities." According to a 16-year-old Latina, "The benefit of being in T-MAC is that we have experiences that make us think about what we are seeing and doing. It helps me see where I want to go. I also enjoy being in the club because of the activities. Instead of drugs and violence, we go places." These subjective accounts indicate generally positive experiences by group members. Positive benefits to the apartment complex include a lower incidence of vandalism and loitering and a reduction in intentional property destruction. The benefit for schools may include fewer disciplinary actions against T-MAC members and more days present.

Developing and facilitating T-MAC has proved to be challenging as well as rewarding. Designing and generalizing the group concepts to extend to other systems such as schools and detention facilities is an ongoing process. Over a period of years, I have sustained a sense of excitement and satisfaction by helping teens through this transitional developmental time. Providing youth with opportunities for discovering new experiences and helping them face and work through difficult personal issues are among the benefits of designing this group. I have learned many valuable lessons regarding the adolescent world, intervention strategies for preventing delinquency, how to access community resources, and how to interact effectively with business, political, school, and community leaders. Moreover, the ideology of apartment-based prevention and intervention to combat teen delinquency remains an innovative concept. A future study measuring the effectiveness of such a group would be beneficial to the advancement of apartment-based prevention and community psychology.

LO7

Helping Adolescents Deal With Anger and Conflict

As counselors, we know that metal detectors and increased law enforcement presence will not solve the dilemma schools face in light of the increase in the frequency and intensity of violence. Helping young people learn to be aware of and manage anger and conflict can help prevent violent actions. Conflict management groups and groups designed to teach adolescents appropriate ways to express and deal with their anger are excellent means of prevention, and these groups can be most useful in the school environment. These groups are aimed at learning effective ways to deal with anger through interpersonal skills development, problem solving, and learning adaptive self-talk.

A High School Anger Management Group

This section is written from the perspective of Jason Sonnier, who set up and facilitated an anger management group for adolescents at Hamilton High School in Anza, California. (For further information, contact Jason by email: jsonnier@hemetusd.k12.ca.us.)

As a high school counselor, I am in a position to do one-on-one counseling as well as run groups for adolescents on anger management and violence prevention, alcohol and drug awareness and intervention, and other topics as needed. High school counselors will all agree that there never seems to be enough time in the day to get to all of the various responsibilities of the job. In my first year as a school counselor I found that group counseling can be an excellent way to provide services to many students and save valuable time.

Facilitating a group for adolescents for the first time was an intimidating, yet rewarding, experience. I was asked by a student if we could start an anger management group because she was court-ordered to attend counseling and there were no alternatives for her in our small, rural community. Although inexperienced and nervous, I agreed and set up the group. This was my first attempt at implementing a high school anger management group.

Organizing the Group

The student assisted me in recruiting participants for the group. Other students were referred based on administrative action for incidents of violent behavior. In all there were seven students, four males and three females. Four group members were voluntary participants, and three (all males) were referred by the administration. The group was designed to last eight sessions running 1 hour twice a week for 4 weeks. Days chosen were Mondays and Thursdays, with alternating times to limit time missed in each class.

Group Goals

The goals for participants in this anger management group were as follows:

- Become aware of and challenge their own beliefs regarding conflict and violence
- Be able to identify situations and behaviors that lead to violence and conflict
- Understand and identify personal triggers that lead to conflict
- Become conscious of their nonproductive approaches to conflict and the alternatives they have in dealing with certain situations
- Learn skills in communication, negotiation, mediation, violence avoidance, and stress management
- Be able to identify and avoid certain people, places, and situations that will likely lead to conflict

Group Format

Session 1: Group Introduction

- Explain purpose of the group.
- Facilitator and members are introduced to each other.
- Discuss rules of groups with emphasis on confidentiality.
- Explore group members' attitudes toward aggression and violence.

Session 2: Personal Triggers

- Participants tell of how they or their family have been affected by violence.
- Discuss situations that make them angry and how they react.
- Reflect on why they react the way they do and how they learned this.
- Begin to learn to focus on themselves first and identify in advance what gets them angry.

Session 3: Avoiding Conflict and Violence

- Discuss situations likely to lead to conflict and ways to avoid them.
- Students share what strategies have worked for them or others.
- Learn techniques to avoid and to get out of unhealthy situations.
- Students practice techniques with each other in role-play activity.

Session 4: Personal Values and Goals

- Consider family values and personal goals in relation to values, goals, and beliefs of others around them.
- Discuss what values and goals are most important in their lives and how they plan to meet those goals.
- Discuss how anger, violence, and avoidable conflict will prevent them from reaching certain goals in their lives.

Session 5: Improving Communication Skills

- Reflect on how communication problems can lead to conflicts.
- Students identify which communication problems they need to work on.
- Discuss how listening and speaking more carefully can help to avoid conflict.
- Participants learn and practice effective communication techniques.

Session 6: Peer Relationships

- Consider how peer pressure contributes to unhealthy behaviors.
- Review goals discussed in Session 4 and determine whether current peers and friends are interfering with reaching those goals.
- Challenge students to choose friends and groups that will support them in their effort to avoid violence and conflict.
- Identify ways to make good decisions about whom to associate with.

Session 7: Negotiation and Mediation

- Learn and practice basic steps in negotiation.
- Understand when and how to seek out and use mediation.
- Students share how negotiation or mediation worked for them or others.

Session 8: Final Group Session

- Identify areas in their lives that cause the most stress.
- Discuss stress management techniques and coping strategies.
- Students talk about their feelings for the group and what they will work on to reduce conflict and violence in their lives.

Group Outcomes

Although this particular group started out a bit rocky, it ended smoothly. In the beginning I struggled to get two of the members to talk at all, and many of the others were preoccupied with bragging about their violent incidents and asserting their toughness. By the fourth session one of the disruptive students was removed from the group by the administration, and the rest of the members then settled down. As I got past my initial fears and anxiety and began to disclose my own experiences, I found that the students really started to open up. From the first session of just trying to keep order to the last few sessions of good deep philosophical discussions, I certainly learned a great deal about my students and myself. Specifically, I learned that, as the group facilitator, I will not have all of the answers, and that this is acceptable. The group may take an unintended path, which can be of benefit to the members. More important, I learned that it is really the students that help each other, as they will often listen to and trust their peers more than an adult.

The biggest problem I encountered was the tendency of my students to get off track. Even though there were only seven adolescent participants, I had to struggle to keep them on topic, several times each session. So if only one person is facilitating the group, I recommend keeping it small, at least four but no more than eight students. For next time I will try to bring in more exercises and real world examples that will keep the students focused and interested on the day's topic. Of course, it would help if all participants were voluntary or self-referred, but this is not likely in a high school setting. Although it was often tough having students who did not really want to be in the group, I believe they did learn from the other members and left with a new insight into themselves. Some students opened up more readily than others, which helped the rest of the group feel comfortable to eventually share their stories. Many members gave each other feedback regarding ways of dealing with certain situations differently in the future. This group gave students a chance to look at themselves and question their actions and how they may want to change certain behaviors. For some, just knowing that other students have dealt with the same kinds of anger issues within their families was a bonding experience. With the feedback from fellow group members, students have a starting point toward change and a network of support.

Reflections and Afterthoughts

Looking back with a few more years of experience, I can see how I have grown in my ability and approach to facilitate a productive and meaningful group counseling experience. I have learned to be more flexible and responsive to what the students want to discuss. I try not to forcefully lead in one rigid direction, and I avoid the irrational belief that I must cover a certain topic in depth or the time was wasted. I have come to realize that no groups will unfold in the same manner. Some are more successful than others, and some seem to meander aimlessly. In my first few groups, I was more likely to provide the "answers" members were looking for. Now I enjoy watching the students self-reflect and find ways to support each other and come up with their own solutions. They have the responsibility of making choices, accepting the consequences of their decisions, and generating a plan to change. As they help each other through this process, strong ties are built among the students, and they have a feeling of empowerment and self-control, the lack of which brought them to the group in the first place.

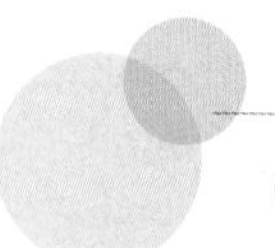

Groups in College Counseling Centers

A common complaint we hear is that it is easy to feel isolated on a university campus. With the emphasis on intellectual development, students often feel that relatively little attention is paid to their personal development. For many students, the college experience is stressful not only academically but in their personal lives as well. A diversity of special needs on the college campus can be explored through a group experience. In a group setting students can formulate goals, discuss common concerns, explore factors that are causing them difficulties in interpersonal relating, and identify the internal blocks impeding the full utilization of their capabilities. By dealing with their personal problems, students are able to free themselves of certain emotional blocks to learning and can become far better students, approaching their studies with a sense of enthusiasm and commitment.

College and university counseling centers often have limited resources with which to address a multitude of issues. Although the value of group work is evident to practitioners in college counseling centers, Parcover, Dunton, Gehlert, and Mitchell (2006) find it is often difficult to recruit members due to client reluctance to participating in a group, staff reluctance to promote groups as a treatment of choice, and ineffective group formats and poor marketing of these groups.

Common Topics in College Groups

Time-limited groups with structured topics or themes are most commonly offered in university counseling centers. College counselors frequently experience difficulty promoting open-ended process groups, personal-growth groups, and groups without a specific theme. Instead, groups are most often designed to address an emerging need or assist clients with specific concerns. On any college campus a number of students are likely to be victims of violence, rape, sexual abuse, sexual harassment, racism, or discrimination. The themes that emerge from a group often reflect the unique composition of that group. A good place to begin designing a group is to conduct a needs survey on the college campus.

A variety of psychoeducational, theme-oriented, and counseling groups are frequently offered at college and university counseling centers. Effective theme groups are time-limited and involve specific change strategies that guide group participants through a learning process. A few examples include career development and career planning groups, anxiety-management groups, stress-management groups, grief groups, cultural identity groups, nontraditional age student groups, groups for those with relationship concerns, groups dealing with body image, group addressing trauma, self-esteem groups, groups for survivors of childhood sexual abuse, and personal identity groups.

These groups typically last from 6 to 16 weeks and are aimed at meeting a variety of special needs by combining both therapeutic and educational components. The scope of the topics for structured groups and for theme groups is limited only by the needs of the population, the creativity of the counselor, and the effort it takes to promote the group. Theme groups, psychoeducational groups, and structured groups in college counseling centers are a cost-effective approach to meeting the needs of a diverse range of college students.

Some Groups for College Students

A wide range of groups can be found at college and university counseling centers. As an internship placement, you might facilitate or colead a group through the college counseling center. In *Group Work and Outreach Plans for College Counselors*, Finch and Marshall (2011) review a variety of psychoeducational and counseling groups structured around specific concerns of college and university students. Following are three examples of these groups:

- *Interpersonal Process Groups in College and University Settings* (Reese, 2011). There is a clear need for college and university groups that focus on relationships and interpersonal processes. College students are at a unique developmental stage, and interpersonal groups can be most useful in assisting them in clarifying their identity and broadening the scope of their relationships. This 10-week group is described in terms of the stages of the group's development.
- *Supporting Students of Color on Campus* (Steen, Griffin, & Shi, 2011). Many students of color and students from low-income families do not remain in college beyond the first year because of limited academic and personal supports. Steen and colleagues describe a group counseling program for students of color, first-generation college students, and students from impoverished backgrounds that helps them develop strategies for coping with the personal and academic challenges of the college experience.
- *Support Groups for Gay and Lesbian Students* (Thomas & Hard, 2011). Gay and lesbian college students can benefit from participating in a support group that

provides participants with opportunities to share their problems in coping with discrimination. Group work can be a powerful vehicle contributing to positive identity development and reduced alienation. The affirmation that members receive in the group helps to counteract family, community, and spiritual difficulties members face outside of the group. This 13-week group includes psychoeducational aspects, but it is primarily designed as a developmental and counseling group.

Group work offers promise for a broad spectrum of college and university students. These groups can assist students who are coping with academic difficulties, but they also provide a supportive climate in which students can acquire insights and skills in managing the personal and social dimensions of their lives. Groups enable people to deal with life transitions and challenges such as forming new relationships, coping with struggles pertaining to self-identity, and dealing with oppression. Group counseling is an effective and efficient route to meeting the developmental needs of college students (Whittingham, 2014).

Points to Remember

Groups in School Settings

Groups Designed for School Settings

Here are some key points in designing and conducting groups for children, adolescents, and college students in school settings:

- As a prerequisite to the effective facilitation of groups for children or adolescents, it is essential to acquire a working knowledge of the developmental needs of those who will be in your group.
- In designing a group in schools or agencies, strive to develop collaborative relationships with agency directors, principals, teachers, and colleagues.
- It is essential to understand the laws of your state regarding minors and the policies of the agency where you work.
- It is a good practice to obtain written permission of parents or guardians for group members who are under the age of 18.
- Confidentiality is particularly important in groups with children and adolescents. Communicate with young people about the importance of keeping confidences.
- Not all students are ready for group participation in a school setting. You need to have clear criteria regarding who can benefit from involvement in a group.
- Having some structure is particularly important in groups with children or adolescents.
- Give thought to helpful methods of evaluating the outcomes of your groups with children or adolescents.
- Groups in the schools can combine personal themes with psychoeducational goals.
- It is wise to conduct a needs assessment in a school setting to identify particular kinds of groups that will be most useful.
- Authenticity and warmth on the part of the group leaders are crucial to group success.
- Role-playing techniques can be used creatively in groups for both children and adolescents.

- A group experience can provide ways for college students to establish connections with other students and to increase their sense of belongingness.
- Theme-oriented groups are especially appropriate for college and university students because they have a clearly defined purpose and are structured with time-limited change strategies.
- College students in a group can explore factors that are causing them difficulties in interpersonal relating. By addressing their personal problems, students are often able to resolve emotional blocks to learning and can improve their academic performance.

Exercises

In-Class Activities

1. **Design a Group for Children or Adolescents.** Break up into small groups in the classroom and work collaboratively to design different kinds of groups for children or adolescents. Each of the subgroups can work on a different kind of group. Identify the specific type of group you would be interested in forming, and brainstorm possible steps for establishing this group. In developing your proposal, consider factors such as type of group, goals and purposes, strategies for recruiting members, format and structure of the group, and methods for evaluating outcomes.
2. **Guest Speaker.** Invite a therapist who conducts groups with children (or adolescents) to your class to discuss how he or she sets up such a group. The speaker could share both the challenges in doing group work with children or adolescents and the unique benefits of group participation.
3. **Review the T-MAC Group Concept.** Review the teens making a change group (T-MAC). If you were the director of an agency, or a school principal, what kind of response would you have toward funding and launching this group in your own setting?
4. **Evaluate the Group Proposals.** In small groups critique the group proposals presented in this chapter. As you review these proposals, pay particular attention to the multicultural dimensions of each proposal. What aspects of each proposal would you want to incorporate in one of your group proposals? What are some of the advantages of using a group format for the kinds of problems explored in each group? Of all the proposals presented in this chapter, which proposal did you find to be the most unusual and why?
5. **Groups Offered at Your University Counseling Center.** Visit the counseling center at your university or college and inquire about specific kinds of groups that are available. Might you be interested in becoming a member of any of these groups?
6. **Community Programs.** Some class members can visit a school or a community agency where groups are available for children or adolescents. Find out what types of groups are offered, the structure of these groups, and the reactions of the members. Present what you find to your class.

MindTap for Counseling

Additional resources can be found on CengageBrain.com and by logging into the MindTap course created by your professor. There you will find a variety of study tools and useful resources that include quizzes, videos, interactive exercises, and more.

CHAPTER 11

Groups in Community Settings

CHAPTER LEARNING OBJECTIVES

1. Describe approaches to group formation, including recruiting, screening, and selecting members (CACREP, 2016, Standard E)
2. Explain the value of group work with women
3. Explain the value of group work with men
4. Describe key aspects of group treatment associated with domestic violence
5. Understand the rationale for group treatment of people with substance use disorders
6. Identify attitudes and skills needed in working effectively with older adults in groups
7. Explore practical and professional considerations in group work with older adults
8. Explore the therapeutic value of grief work in groups

LO1

Introduction

This chapter deals with adult groups designed by various practitioners to meet specific needs in the community agency settings in which they work, oftentimes providing affordable group services to underserved client populations. The group proposals illustrate ways practitioners have applied the concepts discussed in this book to various client populations in a community. We hope these group proposals will help you to think creatively about how to design groups to effectively meet the needs of your diverse client populations.

Among the group proposals are a women's support group for survivors of incest, a men's group in a community agency setting, a domestic violence group, and a group for people with substance use disorders. In addition, the value of group work with older adults in various community settings is highlighted in three proposals: a group on successful aging, an older adult bereavement group, and a group treatment program for institutionalized older people.

Group treatment is the preferred approach in many community agencies devoted to providing services for diverse client populations with a wide range of problems. Group work practitioners also must have an understanding of the functioning of agency systems, including how the agency is structured, policies and procedures that affect clients and treatment staff, political issues, and the existing needs of both the clients and the agency. Group work enables community agencies to offer cost-effective and clinically appropriate therapeutic services typically serving a critical need that otherwise would not be addressed due to limitations on funding in many mental health agencies. Counselors must understand the many types of client populations seen within agency settings to design effective group treatment programs tailored to meet the specific needs of these clients.

LO2

Group Work With Women

Although groups for women are as diverse as the women who comprise them, they share a common theme in their support for the experience of women. Members learn that they are not alone, and they share and begin to critically explore the messages they have internalized about their self-worth and their place in society. A group can provide women with a social network, decrease feelings of isolation, foster a sense of universality, and create an environment that encourages sharing of experiences. Kees and Leech (2014) state that groups help women to understand the systemic origins of many of their concerns and can be instrumental in changing oppressive environments in which they work and live. They believe that group members come to realize their worth and their ability to give back to each other through shared experiences, wisdom, and courage. "Groups provide women with support, hope, and empowerment to overcome adversity and they provide knowledge and education to help improve women's individual situations in life" (p. 518).

Among the many advantages for women who choose to be in a women's group are discovering their personal strengths and resources, working on interpersonal relationships in the group context, eliminating patriarchal oppression, practicing and modeling new behaviors in a safe environment, and finding their "voice." In the group environment the members often find their voice to express their concerns, fears, secrets, and dreams. The dominant voice in a patriarchal society is based on independence, autonomy, and aloneness, and women learn early on that connection is undervalued. They may believe that what they have to contribute is not valued. In a group, women do not risk being taken for granted, for all voices are valued and encouraged.

Another advantage of women's groups is the opportunity to construct a gender analysis of what it means to be female in a patriarchal society. The gender analysis aids women in becoming aware of the external causes of their pain and struggles. It helps women differentiate between the external and the internal causes of the concerns they bring to a group. The power of the group suggests to its members that both personal change and societal change are possible.

GROUP PROPOSAL

A Women's Support Group for Survivors of Incest

The following section is written from the perspective of Lupe Alle-Corliss, LCSW. (For further information about this group, contact Lupe at her private practice; telephone: 909-920-1850; email: LupeLCSW1@aol.com.)

Sexual abuse of children by family members continues to come to the attention of mental health professionals. A sexual encounter with a trusted family member not only typically results in a major psychological trauma itself but also frequently leads to emotional problems for the survivor later in life. Some of the common problems include impaired self-esteem, negative identity formation, difficulty in intimate relationships, sexual dysfunction, and repeated victimization (Gerrity, 2014; Herman, 1992).

Various types of groups are being used in treating survivors of childhood sexual abuse including support groups, psychoeducational groups, time-limited groups, long-term or open-ended groups, and retreats (Courtois, 2010). This group proposal describes a time-limited therapy group designed to enable women to begin the process of working through unresolved issues related to their incestuous past. Today, with the rapidly changing state of mental health care, being able to conduct time-limited groups is even more advantageous because it is cost-effective, efficient, and fits the demands for short-term treatment.

Organizing the Group

The literature reveals that group therapy for survivors of childhood sexual abuse is effective and cost-effective (see Gerrity, 2014). For survivors of childhood sexual abuse, a combination of group and individual therapy may be more effective than either treatment alone (Lubin, 2007). Briere (1996) recommends concurrent group and individual therapy due to the stress resulting from clients' own memories and from hearing the stories of other group members. Structure is an important dimension in group treatment because it provides safety and allows the group members to observe consistent and clear boundaries in the therapeutic process (Gerrity, 2014). In providing a safe and therapeutic environment for incest survivors, the main goal is to empower these women by helping them get past the molestation and the "victimization" role. Victims can become not only survivors but thrivers if they are able to successfully work through their past experience with incest. Other objectives are to help women share their secret and recognize that they are not alone, understand the current impact of this experience, begin to work through and resolve feelings associated with their trauma, and make changes. In a group situation many women find a commonality and a basis for identification, and a new type of family can emerge, one that is different from the client's original family, which may have been dysfunctional.

I recruit potential members by publicizing my groups within my own agency by way of memos, announcements, and personal contact with colleagues. In considering membership, I seek clients who display a readiness to deal openly with the trauma of incest. Typically, these women are in individual therapy. For women who are involved with another therapist, I ask for a release form so I can consult and coordinate with the individual therapist.

Although both nonfamilial rape and incest are very traumatic, women who have experienced incest from a family member have an additional layer of trauma to work through because of the betrayal of trust. I meet regularly with potential members to assess their readiness and the appropriateness of a group experience for them and to orient them to the group process and goals. Through screening I also determine how well they are likely to fit with other potential group members. Some prospective members verbalize their eagerness to be part of the group, yet they may not actually be ready. They might be extremely uncomfortable with certain questions regarding the incest that are sure to come up in the group. Others may have been referred, and it is important to assess their true motivation because they may not be completely ready to involve themselves in this type of intense group. They may be acting on the basis of pressure or the need to please others. Also, based on the emerging composition of the group, it might become clear that a particular client may not be a compatible member in a specific group.

Clients are asked about their interest in such a group, and an attempt is made to determine how ready the individual is to talk in a group setting about the incest and its impact. Other screening questions include the following: "If you have had any previous group experience, what was this like for you?" "Were you, or are you now, involved in individual therapy, and what was this experience like?" "What are your personal goals for the group?" "What are your expectations, hopes, and fears about participating in the group?" Applicants are also encouraged to ask me questions about the group and my therapeutic style.

It is critical that members possess the ego strength to deal with the material that will be explored during the sessions. Members need to have adequate interpersonal skills to deal with others in a group situation. People with suicidal and extremely self-destructive tendencies and people who do not have adequate contact with reality are screened out. Also, clients with recent drug addictions may be at a vulnerable place in their recovery process and therefore may not be ready to enter into such an emotionally demanding group. Care is taken not to include family members or friends in the same group. Also excluded are those who are not ready or willing to talk openly about their experiences.

Group Format

The group is closed and meets weekly for 75 minutes during a 12-week period. This time limitation is designed to facilitate bonding and to produce a reasonable degree of pressure necessary to work through the members' resistances. Although each group has its own process, these groups generally go through the phases described here.

Initial Phase

The initial phase involves getting to know one another, establishing ground rules, and identifying personal goals. This stage is crucial in the development of trust and rapport and in giving members permission for catharsis and ventilation. A signed contract is used to encourage commitment and to help the clients feel that their participation is valued and important.

At the first group meeting I emphasize the importance of regular attendance, being prompt, confidentiality, the limitations of time, and bringing any unresolved issues back to the group rather than dealing with them outside of the group. A date for the postgroup meeting, which is typically about 3 months after termination, is established at the first session. In the early phase of the group, members express empathy with one another over the difficulty of sharing the incest issue. The following guideline questions are provided to help them deal directly with the impact of incest on them: "How did the molestation happen?" "Who molested you?" "How old were you?" "How long did it go on?" "How did you deal with it?" "How did you feel toward the people who were in a position to protect you from the molestation but failed to do so?" "What impact does this experience have on you today?"

Much of the initial phase is focused on identifying and discussing personal goals, which enables all in the group to know of each person's goals and provides a direction for the sessions. Members generally feel much anxiety and apprehension at first. A member often feels that she is the only one with such a terrible burden, and she may feel that she would be an outcast if others knew about her secret. As members realize that they have a common experience, they begin to open up and find the support available in the group useful. By sharing the incest experience, members free themselves to look at how it continues to have an impact on them. The focus of the sessions is not merely on reporting the details of the specific acts but also on exploring their feelings, beliefs, and perceptions about what happened. Although it is important for these women to share their past history, the focus in this group is on helping them deal with the effects the incest continues to have on their lives. They need to acquire present coping skills that will empower them and enable them to move forward.

Middle Phase

During the middle phase, the focus is on accomplishing the goals of individual members. Connections are made between a woman's past behavior and her present behavior. In this way she begins to see patterns and to understand her own dynamics. For instance, a woman might have chosen men who dominated her, abused her, or in some way took advantage of her. She sees with greater clarity her own part in allowing this type of treatment to continue. A group is a good way to help such a woman become aware of and challenge her faulty belief systems. Through the group process, these women can rid themselves of destructive beliefs and can learn to create functional self-statements.

As well as gaining insight into her own dynamics, a woman learns that she can be of help to others through her disclosures. By expressing intense emotions and personal sharing, a safe climate is created that facilitates further explorations of common themes such as isolation, secrecy, shame, powerlessness, hurt, and anger. This mutual sharing tends to increase cohesion within the group.

As the group evolves, other themes in an individual's life are typically identified. A number of therapeutic strategies can promote change in feelings, attitudes, and behaviors. Some specific techniques include providing reassurance for women that they behaved normally in an abnormal situation; reading books in a personal way; keeping a diary or journal that includes thoughts, feelings, and behaviors in certain situations; writing letters that are not sent; talking to other family members; and recording and sharing dreams.

A useful way for helping these women express their emotions is through artwork. By asking them to draw the abused child within, insights unfold surrounding their ordeal. Participating in the expressive arts often enables members to face the total impact of their molestation and to come to an emotional understanding of their past experiences. The therapeutic value of expressive arts for healing and social change is being increasingly recognized (Rogers, 2011).

Members are encouraged to continue to work on recovering memories and dealing with flashbacks, which may seem very real and are a common occurrence for the incest survivor. It is important to remind these women that they are no longer little children and that these flashbacks are only a memory of the past. Much needed support and validation is provided, and clients are assisted in recognizing maladaptive defense patterns and in developing healthier coping styles. Cognitive behavioral techniques and visual exercises also facilitate positive change.

Final Phase

Toward the end of the group the women are reminded of the upcoming termination. I assist members in reviewing what happened in the group as a whole as well as what they individually learned and how they can now continue to apply their insights and newly acquired behaviors to situations outside of the group. Role playing helps in this consolidation process. I give a structured questionnaire to help members pull together and assess their learning. The members evaluate their progress and determine future plans, including what work they still need to do. They give feedback to one another, and they identify certain people in the group who can serve as a support system. Although the women cognitively know that the group will be ending, it is a common reaction for them to not want to terminate.

Members celebrate the ending of the group by sharing food as well as participating in a "Personal Poster" in which each member can give individual support and constructive feedback to every group member. The rationale for this exercise is that each member is able to take with her some constructive feedback or supportive comments and can use this experience for support and encouragement. The poster serves as a reminder of their gains through the group experience. The personal poster exercise tends to be affirming, and group leaders can benefit from participating because doing this kind of work can be emotionally taxing. I also encourage the women in my groups to remain open to further therapeutic work if they are not already concurrently in individual or group therapy.

Group Outcomes

Building follow-up procedures into the group design provides a basis for understanding the longer-term value of the group experience as well as improving the design for future groups. In the short-term groups reported on by Herman and Schatzow (1984), the results of a 6-month follow-up survey of 28 women supported their assumption that this therapeutic approach was particularly effective in resolving the issues of shame, secrecy, and stigmatization associated with incest. Outcomes included improved self-esteem, increased safety, and decreased shame, guilt, and isolation. The single most helpful factor was the contact with other survivors.

I schedule several follow-up meetings to help group members make the transition from the weekly groups to being on their own and relying on the support networks they have developed. Part of the purpose of this follow-up is to reinforce what was learned and to provide renewed support. Follow-up sessions are scheduled 6 to 12 weeks after the end of the group. During these sessions, clients are asked these questions:

- What did you like best about the group?
- What did you like least about the group?
- How do you feel that you have changed as a result of being in this group?

Group members are also asked to rate themselves as "better," "worse," or "the same" in regard to the following areas: work, friendships, relationships with family members, intimate relationships, feelings about sex, feelings about oneself, and the ability to protect and take care of oneself.

Based on many follow-up group meetings with the members of my groups, it is clear that a well-developed group format with proper screening can result in a therapeutic group experience. Overall, I continue to find that carefully planned groups greatly enhance the treatment of incest survivors because they can be seen on a regular basis and can be provided with continuity and the support they need for healing. The women in these groups are able to develop a strong support network that provides them with the strength and courage to begin to resolve past issues, overcome negative patterns, and set healthy goals for their future. Perhaps the greatest message they receive is that they "deserve" to feel good about themselves and lead more productive lives. Through the years, group members have felt safe to return for brief treatment if they feel a need for further consultation.

LO3

Group Work With Men

An increasing number of men are giving expression to both masculine and feminine dimensions of their personalities. However, many men in our society still live according to a traditional masculine model of what it is to be a man. Some men are caught in rigid roles, and they may be sanctioned if they deviate from those roles or display characteristics that are not associated with their gender. Men may be so involved in their roles that they become alienated from themselves. They no longer know what they are like within because they put so much energy into maintaining an acceptable image. There is usually a price to pay for being restricted by and living by traditional male roles, especially for those men who are not in agreement with what is now considered to be truly "masculine" in our society. Men may pay a steeper price than their female counterparts for engaging in gender-atypical behaviors, which encourages men to remain deeply entrenched in masculine roles. Some men become so involved in their roles that they become alienated from themselves and no longer feel connected with their inner selves. Regardless of cultural background, gender roles that men have incorporated from cultural conditioning need to be understood and challenged if men are to make choices about aspects of their masculine identity. The challenge for men is to define who they want to be for themselves, whether that involves conforming to or rejecting traditional gender roles.

An emerging counseling emphasis on *positive masculinity* presents a more optimistic picture of changes taking place in gender roles. Kiselica and Englar-Carlson (2010) contend that positive masculinity should be given center-stage status in counseling boys and men and in conducting psychological research. Working from a framework of positive masculinity, Englar-Carlson and Kiselica (2013) transcend stereotypes and emphasize men's existing strengths; focus on men's capacities and resources; identify the qualities that empower men; view men for who they are and who they can become rather than who they are not; recognize what is right with men rather than dwelling on what it wrong with them; and shift attention to the parts of men that are good, kind, creative, successful, and capable.

Traditional forms of individual therapy may not be the best way to reach male clients. Groups for men offer some unique advantages in assisting men in clarifying their gender roles, helping them cope with life's struggles, and in developing a sense of positive masculinity. Rabinowitz and Cochran (2002) describe how men's groups are able to deepen a man's experiences. In such a group, men are given the opportunity to face and express their disappointments and losses. Rather than denying their psychic pain and wounding, men are provided with a context where they can bring all of their feelings into the open and where they can be healed by the support of others in the group. Themes and issues that often emerge in group work with men include trust, vulnerability, fear, shame, strength, weakness, male–male relationships, competition, family-of-origin issues, sexuality, friendship, dominance, submissiveness, love, hatred, dreams, grief, obsessions, work, and death. In a men's group, members learn a great deal about themselves by sharing their experiences. One powerful intervention is the leader modeling appropriate self-disclosure by sharing some of his own life experiences.

All-male groups provide men with the support they need to become aware of the restrictive rules and roles they may have lived by and provide them with the strength to question the mandate of the masculine role. Men's groups provide a place for connecting with other men, a place to be heard, and a place to talk about being a father, having a father, relationships, divorce, aging, and transitions (Englar-Carlson, 2014). Rabinowitz (2014) states that a major benefit of participating in a men's group is the acceptance, validation, and support that each man receives. For some men, it may be the first time they have been able to reveal past experiences and traumas with the support of other men. The men's group provides the intimate connection that many men desire but often do not receive in their lives.

Most men's groups contain both a psychoeducational component and an interpersonal, process-oriented dimension. The following proposal describes such a group that one of our colleagues has facilitated for about 25 years in a large health maintenance organization in a community agency.

GROUP PROPOSAL

A Men's Group in a Community Agency

The following section is written from the perspective of Randy Alle-Corliss, LCSW, who works in a large health maintenance organization (HMO). (For further information about this men's group, contact Randy via email at RandyLCSW@aol.com.)

This proposal describes a group aimed at helping men explore ways they experience and express their gender roles. It contains both a psychoeducational component and an interpersonal, process-oriented dimension. The purpose of this group is to provide men coming to a psychiatric counseling center with an opportunity to work together on common issues such as depression, stress, marital and relationship difficulties, parenting concerns, work-related issues, loneliness, and isolation.

Organizing the Group

Although no men's groups were being offered in our area, my coleader and I believed that men could profit from talking about life struggles in a safe and supportive group. We assumed that exploring deeply personal concerns would lead to a reduction of isolation and increase the bonding among men. Many of our male clients did not have significant male friendships; if they had friends, they were often distant from them.

Because we were working for a large HMO, we knew the number of group sessions would be limited. The group format, whereby more clients could be seen in a shorter amount of time, at a greater frequency, could serve the needs of the clients and at the same time serve the needs of the organization. We were convinced that the group would have other therapeutic benefits in addition to the cost-effectiveness factor. We assumed that the group would offer a place for men to discover universal themes, to ventilate feelings they had stored up, and to practice skills they could carry outside of the group and apply in various settings in everyday life.

We began by writing a proposal and presenting it to the administration. We developed a memorandum describing the purpose of the group and sent it to other clinicians, asking them to recommend appropriate candidates for this type of group. We excluded from the group candidates who were psychotic or suicidal, in extreme crisis, and those who lacked the psychological strength required for sustained group interaction.

Group Format

The group meets for 90 minutes each week for a total of 16 weeks. In addition, the coleaders meet regularly for 15 minutes before each session and 15 minutes afterward. The group is topically oriented, educationally and therapeutically focused, and combines a variety of techniques. At times it takes longer than one session to cover a particular topic.

The Initial Session

We start the group with general introductions from each member and ourselves. We also cover the basic ground rules in the first meeting, including confidentiality, attendance, and basic HMO policies. During this first meeting, we explore gender-related issues such as what it means to be a man, the messages the men received growing up, and how these messages affect them today. We typically discuss a number of norms pertaining to being a man. The members are invited to share their reactions to adhering to or breaking these norms and how these norms influence their daily behavior. Typical topics discussed at other sessions are described next.

Relationships With Father and Mother

We examine relationships with parents, particularly with fathers, because this seems to be a central influence in the lives of most men. Many of the men are disappointed by their father's absence or are angry about the excessive force and aggression their fathers used to discipline them. We also explore their relationships with their mothers, especially as it relates to how they handled their feelings around them. We typically invite members to write letters to their parents, which they share in the group.

Relationships With Significant Others

It is clear to us that the men in our groups often experience difficulty simply recognizing, let alone expressing, their feelings. One reason some men join the group is because they have trouble expressing feelings and behaving assertively. Members have opportunities to talk about their relationships with significant others, especially with women. Some of them may be going through a divorce or having marital difficulties. We broadened our description of relationships to include gay relationships. Our experience in working with some gay men in these groups has taught us the importance of using language that is free of bias with respect to sexual orientation. Regardless of one's sexual orientation, the men in our groups discover that they have a great deal in common.

Developing and Maintaining Friendships

We include discussion about friendships with other men and women, for we continue to find that men receive conflicting messages about appropriate gender roles. We also find that men have difficulty initiating friendships and maintaining intimacy. They tend to be quite isolated from other men, and one purpose of the group is to provide them with rich sources of support. We encourage the men in the group to get together outside of the group and to develop other sources of support, especially with other men. However, we caution the members about subgrouping in a way that could detract from group cohesion.

Relationships With Children

We typically examine relationships with children, as many of the men enter the group with concerns about being an effective parent. We discuss the importance of men's relationships with their children. We teach assertiveness skills to assist the men in setting limits and following through on consequences with their children. We often have the men write letters to their children, which they read in group, to help them express and explore unrecognized feelings.

Relationship to Work

Those members who have lost a job often struggle with feeling devastated over not working. The members talk about how work affects their lives at home, especially with their partners and children. Men often struggle with working too much, setting limits, and frustration on the job. Many men report feeling overly responsible and stressed when assuming the role of provider. By talking about the importance of work, many of the men learn that there is more to life than simply providing and working and come to realize the importance of a balance between work and play.

Sexuality

Most of the men have a host of concerns regarding sexuality, but they tend to be reluctant to discuss such concerns openly. We have small handouts to spur the men's thinking on particular topics, such as sexual performance, feelings of attraction to other people, erectile dysfunction, differences in sexual appetites, and aging. We have been surprised to find that men in the group felt safe enough to discuss matters pertaining to sexual abuse experiences at early ages. Due to the commonalities among the members, men can explore fears regarding their sexuality and sexual practices in ways that enable them to gain a deeper understanding of their sexuality.

Closing the Group

We end the group with good-byes and reminiscing among members and leaders. Valuable feedback is given, and the members evaluate their experience. We reinforce any gains the members have made and give them tangible items to take with them to remind them of their participation in the group. We have given out certificates of attendance with the statement: "It is okay to be a man." We encourage the members to continue their new behaviors. We also point out to them potential pitfalls they are likely to encounter in applying what they learned in the group to everyday living.

Group Outcomes

It is critical to assist the members in evaluating the impact of the group experience. Toward this end, we arrange for a postsession group, which we call the "reunion group." Between the ending of a 16-week group and the beginning of a new group, we have the members from the previous group meet again. Reminders are sent to all the members urging them to attend. The reunion group gives members a chance to take another look at what the group meant to them. We place special emphasis on how they have been applying their learning in their everyday lives. The men have an opportunity to discuss any problems they have encountered in implementing a new style of behavior. In addition to providing support, we also challenge the members to take further risks where it seems appropriate. The follow-up group gives these men a way to establish a plan for putting their new goals into action now that the group has ended.

The members' evaluations of their experience at the follow-up session are typically positive and constructive. Many of the men say they had been looking for this kind of group for years. They often report that they greatly valued the opportunity to discuss personally significant topics in a group setting. They report feeling less depressed, less isolated, and being more able to recognize and communicate their feelings. Some men return to the group later when their benefits allow them the opportunity for continuing their treatment.

Men report that the group has helped them to manage their anger more effectively, to develop more male friends, and to become more assertive. Many of the men are able to use the feedback they receive in immediate ways by becoming more aware of their feelings and more communicative in their relationships. They begin to think of themselves and other men more positively. In general, they say that they feel more content with themselves, they feel a wider range of emotions, and they are able to laugh and have more fun.

LO4

Group Treatment of Domestic Violence Offenders

Group work is well suited for treating male offenders because of the therapeutic factors operating in a group. These therapeutic factors, discussed in detail in Chapter 8, can be helpful in addressing abusive behavior patterns. Specifically, increased universality, cohesion, and interpersonal learning are potent factors in the reduction of group members' domestic violence recidivism (Waldo, Kerne, & Kerne, 2007). The efficacy of a group approach in treating domestic violence offenders is supported by research for some groups (Lee, Sebold, & Uken, 2003).

In *Solution-Focused Treatment of Domestic Violence Offenders: Accountability for Change,* Lee and colleagues (2003) describe a treatment program that created effective, positive change in domestic violence offenders. This approach has a recidivism rate of 16.7% and a completion rate of 92.9%. More traditional approaches typically generate recidivism rates between 40% and 60% and completion rates of less than 50% (Lee et al., 2003). The approach focuses on holding offenders accountable and responsible for building solutions rather than emphasizing their problems and deficits, which is dramatically different from the traditional approach to this problem. This approach is time limited and is brief when measured against traditional program standards, consisting of only eight sessions over a 10- to 12-week period.

The solution-focused approach strongly emphasizes formation of concrete, achievable, behavior-specific goals that each participant must establish by the third session and must continue to consistently work on throughout the treatment process. The group facilitators use changes associated with each group member's goal to assist him in redefining who he is as an individual, a family member, and a community member.

For more information on this topic, useful resources are Edleson and Tolman (1994), Lee, Sebold, and Uken (2003), Schwartz and Waldo (2004), and Wexler (2000, 2004, 2005, 2006). Wexler's 2000 book describes a well-researched program for domestic violence treatment that contains worksheets, exercises, and theoretical background for group leaders. The following group proposal describes another treatment approach with domestic violence offenders.

GROUP PROPOSAL

An Involuntary Domestic Violence Group

This section is written from the perspective of Paul Jacobson, a licensed marriage and family therapist. (For further information on this group, contact Paul at P. O. Box 1931, Willits, CA 95490; telephone: 707-513-5313; email: 4paulj@gmail.com.)

Organizing the Group

Most group counseling is aimed toward people seeking help, but the domestic violence group I describe here is for a specialized involuntary population. The men who come to this group are ordered into treatment by court judges or probation officers. Most of these group members typically arrive with attitudes of resentment, blaming others, and being convinced that they do not need counseling. The techniques and strategies for working with this type of resistance differ somewhat from those used with a voluntary population.

Resistance to Group Work

An individual assessment interview is conducted for all members prior to attending any group meetings. This often reduces their potential for disruptive hostility and can ease them into the more stressful group situation. During this time, an attempt is made to support the individual, explore the circumstances of the abusive behavior and his arrest, challenge his defenses in a moderate manner, and gain his cooperation through suggestions of therapeutic need.

The assessment interview contributes to developing a therapeutic relationship. Without establishing an honest relationship between the members and facilitator, self-disclosure in a group of guarded strangers is very unlikely. The design of this group is based on the assumption that, when given the opportunity, participants will apply personal information to themselves, even without initially accepting responsibility for their actions.

Men who batter often begin group counseling in a state of denial. They typically externalize the source of their problems, and they rarely attribute their problems to their violent behavior. For change to occur, these men need to understand their own dynamics and take responsibility for their behavior. If they do not eventually recognize and accept their own problematic behavior, it is unlikely they will change. Nor will they understand the impact of their behavior on their partners, their relationships, and themselves.

A Case Illustration

To give a concrete idea of how this resistance influences a member's participation in a group, let's consider Jerome's case. Jerome arrived for this meeting 20 minutes late, complaining that he had totally forgotten the appointment he made 2 days earlier. Jerome, like all the group members, had been ordered into the program following plea bargaining in which he agreed to attend counseling rather than spend 45 days in jail. His charges had been reduced from felony spousal abuse to a misdemeanor.

Although Jerome had chosen the group alternative, he insisted that he did not need counseling and preferred the quicker remedy of jail. He blamed the public defender for getting him into this program rather than pursuing his choice. As we talked, his initial agitation diminished somewhat. But when he described the situation of abuse with his wife, he again become loud, animated, and emotional. Jerome told about coming home late one night after having a few beers and getting angry because his wife had not made him dinner. When he ordered her to do so, she responded with "Make it yourself." With this he apparently lost control and claimed he was not aware of what he was doing, but he insisted he never hit her with a closed fist. Jerome was adamant that if she had only made dinner none of this would have happened. Thus, it was her fault.

In exploring other anger experiences, Jerome admitted that it bothered him a little when he became violent, and he wanted to control himself better. This statement was one of the first signs of a more personal stake for participating in the group. Further questioning found Jerome glad to be working again after several months of unemployment, and he admitted that his drinking had increased a little while he was unemployed. Jerome was clearly removed from his emotions, unaware of his own stress level, and unaware of his dependency on alcohol. Furthermore, he did not take responsibility for his actions or his feelings.

Suggestions for Leading a Domestic Violence Group

- Know your motivation for organizing and facilitating a domestic violence group.
- Be aware of your own stress level and reactions; take steps to prevent burnout.
- Try to maintain equanimity and respond rationally.
- Learn to verbalize theoretical ideas in common everyday language.
- Remember that commonly accepted therapeutic concepts are not universally understood or accepted.
- Discover your own similar issues with group members.
- Expect resistance and avoid taking it personally. Respect resistance and work with it therapeutically by encouraging clients to explore any hesitation or cautions about participating in the group.
- Use any medium at your disposal to teach and intervene (such as art, video, and handouts).
- Learn to recognize small incremental changes as progress toward discrete, obtainable therapeutic goals.
- Develop a good support system for yourself.

Group Goals

Some goals are agreed on during the assessment interview, but most are selected by the leader for individual treatment plans. Here is a list of some group goals:

- Develop behavioral alternatives to physical violence.
- Learn cognitive techniques for anger management.
- Discuss abusive events and behavioral alternatives.
- Gain an overview of relationship dynamics, expectations, and the development of physical abuse.
- Learn about physiological reactions as correlates of stress and stress reduction methods.
- Develop a recognition of feelings and emotional processing.
- Increase self-disclosures, personal discussion, and assertive communications.
- Increase personal responsibility.
- Increase empathy and understanding of significant others.
- Stop or decrease alcohol/drug use and recognize use patterns.

Group Format

Each group session begins with a didactic presentation. The group is designed to address both educational and therapeutic goals. Following the didactic segment of the initial session, members are given a written multiple-choice questionnaire. This allows individual responses without the pressures inherent with group verbalization. Then a go-around is used to stimulate discussion. Verbal participation is one of the facilitator's main goals for each group member.

The 15-week program is conducted using an open group format, and participants are added intermittently throughout the group's duration. The major advantage of an open group is to maintain an adequate number of members in the face of high dropout rates. The main disadvantage is the difficulty in developing group cohesion and trust.

Some Ground Rules

During the initial interview members are told of the group rule of abstinence from drugs prior to meetings. If someone arrives intoxicated, he is not allowed into the group. Two such occurrences means termination. The only other requirement is attendance, and members can be terminated for missing more than the allowable three sessions.

Developing Topics for Group Interaction

Meetings are structured around topics deemed relevant to group goals. Topic discussions are designed to educate, gain involvement, convey information, and confront issues relevant to this population. The topics presented to the groups are loosely divided into areas of interpersonal and intrapersonal experience. *Intrapersonal topics* include education concerning human physiology and endocrine systems functioning, cognitive techniques for emotional processing, relaxation methods, drug and alcohol effects, stress and stress reduction, and anger. The *interpersonal topics* involving relationships include communication theories, problem-solving techniques, sex roles, relational expectations, human needs and differences, values, and family experiences.

Group Outcomes

Some of the group goals are broad and more suited for long-term treatment, yet many members show observable progress. Others continue to blame their partners for their situation throughout the group. For me, working with this population is difficult, trying, frustrating, and yet also rewarding. To remain personally invested, it becomes necessary to notice small incremental changes and regard these as signs of success and progress. One source of reinforcement is through observing improvement. I am continually forced to evaluate my statements, style, countertransference, and motivations. Developing this program helped me to examine my theoretical assumptions and assess my therapeutic skills.

Looking Back on This Group

Designing this group was a creative exercise in which I applied commonsense principles I'd learned through my most significant college classes and had applied to group work with other populations. I tried to anticipate what could be helpful with this population, and it was meaningful to develop a group that served this unmet need in my community.

If I could replay facilitating this group I would now use the research-driven handouts, worksheets, and questionnaires developed by Wexler (2000, 2004, 2005, 2006) and other more complete anger management programs for both education and feedback purposes. It is possible to obtain a more accurate picture of what works if you use worksheets at the initial, midgroup, and later stages to evaluate members' progress. For further information, see Morgan, Romani, and Gross (2014).

Group Treatment for People With Substance Use Disorders

LO5

As the problems of drug and alcohol use increase in our society, so does the demand for treatment of people with substance use disorders. Group work is the treatment of choice for dealing with substance use issues. Substance use treatment groups are usually open and have revolving membership. It is likely that some members will be entering treatment as others are "graduating" and ending this phase of their treatment.

Different types of groups meet clients' needs during the various phases of the recovery process (Substance Abuse and Mental Health Services Administration, 2012). *Psychoeducational groups* provide accurate information on the harmful effects of drugs and alcohol on the brain and body, withdrawal syndromes associated with specific drugs, cravings and relapse triggers, and the role of support groups in the recovery process. *Skills groups* combine an educational component with role-playing activities so clients can practice assertiveness skills, relapse prevention, and effective communication. *Cognitive behavioral groups* help clients become aware of the connection between their thoughts, feelings, and behaviors in making choices that will support their drug-free lifestyle. Some topics include cognitive errors, challenging faulty beliefs, and learning effective ways of thinking. Cognitive behavioral groups are especially important in relapse-prevention groups as clients practice making and maintaining the changes in their lives without their drug of choice. It is common for individuals to terminate treatment because they believe they have their issues under control or because they relapse into active use.

Treatment in the field of chemical dependency counseling tends to be highly structured. Substance abuse treatment is broken into stages containing structural components that may not be needed when working with other populations. Most intensive outpatient programming services are delivered in the group format and may include a weekly 2-hour group focused on events of the past week. Aftercare groups are also common. These groups provide drop-in services for graduates of treatment programs to offer ongoing support as clients maintain their new drug-free lifestyle. Education, skills training, and interpersonal process analysis may be an integral part of these aftercare groups. From detoxification through aftercare, group work provides support and helps remove the sense of isolation throughout the recovery process.

Especially in the early stages of recovery, the focus of treatment is on abstinence, stabilization, and learning skills necessary to progress in the recovery process. Most early stage drug and alcohol treatment groups are focused on assisting individuals in staying alive and living life "one day at a time." Long-term quality of life issues may be addressed but are often secondary to the tasks of restructuring life while abstaining from one's substance of choice and developing new ways of living.

Most human service agencies that work with individuals struggling with substance abuse encourage drug-free connections and sober supports outside of the formal treatment process. Twelve-step support and self-help groups such as Alcoholics Anonymous (AA) and Narcotics Anonymous (NA) are not considered treatment, but they often supplement group treatments. AA and NA are the most widely known support groups working with substance using and abusing individuals. Having an outside support system in place during treatment helps in the transition from formal treatment to termination to living a drug-free lifestyle.

A Substance Use Disorder Treatment Group Using the Payoff Matrix

This section is written from the perspective of Kathy A. Elson, LPCC-S, LICDC-CS, SAP. She works in the direct service of treatment for individuals diagnosed with substance use disorders and is an associate professor of Human Services and Behavioral Health at Sinclair Community College in Dayton, Ohio. (For further information about this group, contact Kathy Elson; telephone: 937-512-5332; email: Kathy.Elson@sinclair.edu.)

Organization of the Group

Group treatment is the treatment of choice for dealing with addictive issues (Substance Abuse and Mental Health Services Administration, 2012.) Working with individuals in drug and alcohol treatment requires flexibility because most groups are open, with some members getting ready to "graduate" and others just starting treatment. Individuals tend to have their own level of awareness and are often in different stages of change. Members in substance use groups may be court referred, other referred, and sometimes are self-referred.

Residential treatment is an intensive level of care that is necessary for individuals who have demonstrated an inability to successfully work a recovery program on an outpatient basis. The group described is part of a 90-day residential program for individuals who have been diagnosed with substance use disorders (SUDs). In this group, the Payoff Matrix is used as an ongoing tool for change.

The Payoff Matrix has tremendous benefits for clients during their stay in residential treatment, and it is an effective tool in assisting clients in the recovery process (Mueser, Noordsy, Drake, & Fox, 2003). It is especially useful in facilitating development of insight and awareness of one's use and the consequences incurred. Members learn to make informed choices and begin to predict the consequences of their choices. An overall goal during this group activity is to assist clients in increasing their level of motivation, which is helpful in sustaining the recovery process.

Group Structure

This is an open group held for 8 consecutive weeks in a 90-day residential treatment center. It is comprised of individuals who have been formally assessed and diagnosed with a substance use disorder.

- Group consists of up to 20 members.
- Members participate weekly for 8 weeks during weeks 4 through 11 of their 13-week stay.
- Sessions last 2 hours with a 10-minute break after the first 50 to 60 minutes.
- Group sessions begin with introductions, a check-in, and a brief discussion of previous homework assignments.
- Topics for discussion include communication skills, drug and alcohol use, saying "no," relapse prevention, and changing friends. The main focus is on the underlying concept of the advantages and disadvantages of the identified topic.
- Once a topic is identified, members write down their thoughts and experiences related to the topic. The Payoff Matrix sheet is provided to the members at each group session for use in the session and to take with them for homework.
- The group utilizes individual and small group activities and large group discussions.
- Time for questions and answers is allotted.
- Group ends with a check out and an assignment focused on writing about new awareness or changes in thinking or behaviors that resulted from this experience.

Basic Group Rules

This group is held in a residential setting, and all of the rules for the residential program apply. Specific rules for this group include:

- Be on time and stay the entire group session. Return from breaks on time.
- Homework must be complete upon arrival to the session.
- Participation is expected within large and small groups.
- Be respectful of members and facilitators.
- Focus on yourself and listen to others when they speak.

Format of the Group

Individuals need a few weeks to acclimate themselves to the residential treatment process. In week 3 of residential care, the Payoff Matrix is introduced to clients during a psychoeducational group. Prospective group members are given information about the purpose of the exercise and how it is utilized to facilitate change and decision making. Members of the Payoff Matrix group begin their participation in week 4 of their residential care.

In early recovery clients tend to be ambivalent about change. These individuals often have made frequent attempts to change but have been unable to sustain these changes. They begin by evaluating and understanding their behavior and their symptoms. They are in the process of evaluating the pros and cons of their behavior and of making behavioral changes. Although clients are often distressed by the thought of change, they do want to gain a sense of control and confidence in their ability to change.

The Payoff Matrix assists clients in identifying the possible advantages of using substances, the possible disadvantages of using, the possible advantages of refraining from use, and the possible disadvantages of refraining from use (Mueser et al., 2003). During this activity, group members are asked to provide thoughts, beliefs, and ideas consistent with the quadrant under discussion. This tool can be used for other behavioral issues as well.

The way the quadrants are organized is important. I work to determine what the main "buy-in" is for the clients in that particular group; that is, the behavior in which most members are invested. The matrix is constructed starting in the upper left quadrant with the advantages of continuing that particular behavior. The upper right quadrant is designed to record the disadvantages of refraining from the same behavior. This is followed by completing, in the lower left quadrant, the disadvantages of continuing the behavior and, finally, recording the advantages of refraining from the behavior in the lower right quadrant.

Advantages of Continuing the Behavior	Disadvantages of Refraining from the Behavior
Disadvantages of Continuing the Behavior	Advantages of Refraining from the Behavior

This order is purposeful and gives clients a chance to share the reasons they have continued a problematic behavior despite being confronted by others about the consequences of their behavior. This activity engages the clients who are typically unmotivated or are new in the treatment process.

After an initial check-in, group members review homework from the previous group session. Members are asked to participate in the Payoff Matrix activity. One example is use of drugs and alcohol. Other topics may include going to meetings or adhering to probation requirements. It is important that any beliefs the group members provide be included within the quadrants that are the focus of attention at that time, or are redirected to be included in a different quadrant. Facilitators must deal effectively with clients' resistance related to the behavior, display a nonjudgmental attitude, and be comfortable with answers that may be perceived as rough or controversial. There is also an opportunity for facilitators to ask open-ended questions and to clarify issues they want to highlight. For example, when a group member identifies "losing my home" as one disadvantage of using drugs and alcohol, I may ask this person to explain further what that experience was like. Also, if a client reports "improved relationship with children" as an advantage of discontinuing use, I may prompt him or her to keep talking about what that was like. These are opportunities for the skilled clinician to assist the client in building awareness and insight, which we hope will increase the client's motivation toward change. It is important to fill all four areas of the matrix prior to the first 10-minute break so members have time to process what was written. After the break, I start by asking if anyone has anything else they want to include in the quadrants. Once the advantages and disadvantages are listed, we open the floor for discussion.

Peer-to-peer interactions are important in a group. Although I guide the discussions, the most helpful interventions come from the members themselves. Members are notified when there are 5 minutes left for the discussion, and they are asked to think about what behavior they will use to complete a Payoff Matrix as a homework assignment. They can choose the topic discussed in the group that day or something related to it. Directions for the homework are given before the group closes. Group members complete a Payoff Matrix on the topic they chose and bring this homework to the next session. The results of the Payoff Matrix can also be discussed in individual sessions with primary therapists to assist in identifying areas that need further attention.

Group Outcomes

The Payoff Matrix group is a small part of the recovery process in a 90-day residential program. However, it plays a large part in identifying barriers to successful abstinence and recovery. The ultimate goal of this group is to increase levels of motivation to change. Although the main goal is abstinence and the main change is from *use* to *no use*, many other areas of life also require change to support the new behaviors. Discussing the realities of choices and consequences systematically assists clients in moving toward their goals. Awareness gained during this group process is helpful to the client and primary clinician because this insight can be the groundwork for investigating stagnant areas and to support areas of positive change and increased motivation.

There is a popular saying in the field of substance use counseling: "another tool for my toolbox." We assist clients in collecting tools that support recovery, and they can utilize these tools during their lifelong recovery process.

Group Work With Older Adults

We now turn our attention to topics related to designing and facilitating groups for older adults in community settings. Group work with older adults is one way to promote the positive aspects of aging and to help participants cope with the developmental tasks of aging. Older people have a range of life experiences and personal strengths that are often overlooked. Counselors need to develop special programs for older people and to continue their efforts to find the means to reach this clientele. Group workers will increasingly be held accountable for developing programs to help older individuals find meaning in their lives and be productive after retirement. As mental health professionals become involved with older people, their challenge is to do more than add years to a person's life—they must help individuals lead fuller and better lives.

We begin by identifying attitudes, knowledge, and skills required of those who are interested in conducting groups with older adults. Then we offer suggestions for those of you who are interested in doing group work with older adults.

Attitudes, Knowledge, and Skills of Leaders

Just as specialized knowledge is required for therapists who work with children and adolescents, so too is specialized knowledge required to treat the unique problems that older adults face. Mental health practitioners need to know more about working with older adults because this is one of the fastest growing groups in the United States (Kampfe, 2015), and clinicians are faced with the challenge of providing effective psychological services to this age group. Both individual and group therapy seem to be effective in treating the psychological problems of older adults. However, as with younger people, differences in culture, race, gender, sexual orientation, and social class need to be understood in making interventions with older people (APA Working Group on the Older Adult, 1998).

Christensen and colleagues (2006) found that group leaders who facilitate reminiscence groups increase their effectiveness when they utilize a slower pace, are more flexible with group process issues, are more accepting of potential distractions, and are more understanding of differing worldviews. Findings of Christensen and her colleagues indicate the importance of leaders providing the space and time for members to share their stories. Although specialized knowledge and training are required, many of the skills and methods used in leading reminiscence groups are similar to those used in a variety of different groups and settings and with diverse populations.

Your range of life experiences, as well as your basic personality characteristics, can either help or hinder you in your work. (This would be a good time to review the personal characteristics of effective group leaders discussed in Chapter 2.) We consider the following to be important assets for group work with older people:

- Genuine respect
- Positive experiences with older people
- A deep sense of caring
- Respect for the person's cultural values
- An understanding of how the individual's cultural background continues to influence present attitudes and behaviors
- An ability and desire to learn from older people
- The conviction that the last years of life can be both challenging and rewarding
- Patience, especially with repetition of stories
- Knowledge of the special physiological, psychological, spiritual, and social needs of older people
- Sensitivity to the burdens and anxieties of older people
- The ability to get older people to challenge many of the myths about old age
- A willingness to touch or be touched, if doing so is culturally appropriate
- A healthy attitude regarding one's own aging
- A background in the pathology of aging
- The ability to deal with extreme feelings of loss, depression, isolation, hopelessness, grief, hostility, and despair
- A working knowledge of the special skills needed for group work with older adults

Preparing Yourself to Work With Older Adults

If you are interested in working with older adults, you can gain valuable experience by becoming involved with older people and their families. It is important that you explore your feelings about responsibilities toward older family members, which can help you understand the struggles of the members of the groups you lead. Examine your attitudes about aging and challenge your negative views about older people. This self-evaluation is likely to be a lifelong task that involves reflection, supervision, training, and perhaps personal counseling (Kampfe, 2015). Here are a number of other steps you can take to better prepare yourself to work with this population:

- Take courses dealing with the problems of older people.
- Get involved in fieldwork and internship experiences working with older individuals.
- Visit agencies for the care of older adults, both in your own country and on any trips you take abroad.
- Attend conventions on gerontology, a mushrooming field.
- Investigate institutes and special workshops that provide training in leading groups for older adults.
- Become aware of your judgments or stereotypes against people based on perceiving them as old. Explore your feelings toward your own aging and toward older people in your life.
- Visit some homes for older people that represent a particular cultural or religious group, which will give you some insight into how old people are perceived and treated by different groups.
- Create a list of what you would like to see for yourself when you reach older adulthood. How would you like to be viewed? How would you like to be attended to? How do you hope you could perceive yourself? If you can identify a list of traits and qualities you hope you will have as an older person, you may get some idea of the needs of older people in your groups.
- You can learn a great deal by talking with older people about their experiences. Based on your discussions with them, create a needs assessment as a basis for a group that you may be interested in designing.

LO7

Practical and Professional Considerations for Group Work With Older Adults

Guidelines for the Group Process

Refer to Part Two of this book, pertaining to stages in the development of a group, as you begin to think about designing and conducting groups for older people in a community setting. This section provides brief examples of practical issues for you to think about in forming specialized groups for older people.

The Group Proposal It is especially important to develop a sound proposal because you may encounter resistance from community agencies that deal with older people. Include practical considerations regarding the size, duration, setting, and techniques to be used based on the level of functioning of your target group. Refer to Chapter 5 for the specific elements that might be included in a proposal for groups for older adults.

Screening and Selection Issues The needs of older people are diverse. Carefully consider the purposes of the group in determining who will or will not benefit from the experience. Older people generally need a clear, organized explanation of the specific purposes of a group and why they can benefit from it. It is important to present a positive approach to potential group members. The anxiety level may be high among a group with older adults, which calls for a clear structure and repetition of the goals and procedures of the group. The decision to include or exclude members must be made appropriately and sensitively. For example, to mix regressed patients (such as people with Alzheimer's disease) with relatively well-functioning older people is to invite fragmentation. There may be a rationale for excluding people who are highly agitated, are delusional, have severe physical problems that could inhibit their benefiting from the group, or display other behaviors that are likely to be counterproductive to the group as a whole.

Confidentiality Institutional life is often not conducive to privacy. Older group members may be suspicious when they are asked to talk about themselves, and they may fear some sort of retaliation by the staff or fellow members. Exert care in defining the boundaries of confidentiality to ensure that confidences will not be broken and to provide a safe and nonthreatening environment.

Labeling and Prejudging Group Members Institutions are quick to diagnose and categorize people, and they are slow to remove such labels when they no longer fit. In working with older people, be careful not to be overly influenced by what you hear or read about a given member. Remain open to forming your own impressions and be willing to challenge any limiting labels imposed on your older adult clients.

Value Differences A good understanding of the social and cultural background of your members will enable you to work with their concerns in a sensitive way. You may be younger than the members, and this age difference may signal significant value differences. For example, a group leader is likely to assume that there is therapeutic value in discussing personal problems and conflicts openly. However, revealing personal matters may be extremely difficult for some older people because of their cultural values. Respect members' decisions to proceed at their own pace in revealing themselves.

Some Cautions Here are some *do's* and *don'ts* in your practice of group work with older adults:

- Do not treat people as if they are frail when they are not.
- Avoid keeping members busy with meaningless activities.
- Affirm the dignity, intelligence, and pride of older group members.
- Do not assume that every old person likes being called by his or her first name or "honey" or "sweetie."
- Make use of humor appropriately. Avoid laughing at your members for failing to accomplish tasks, but laugh with them when, for instance, they have created a funny poem.

- Avoid talking to them as if they were small children, no matter how severely impaired they may be.
- Allow your members to complain, even if there is nothing you can do about their complaints. Do not burden yourself with the feeling that you should do something about all of their grievances; sometimes venting can be sufficient.
- Avoid probing for the release of strong emotions that neither you nor they can handle effectively in the group sessions.
- Determine how much you can do without feeling depleted, and find avenues for staying vital and enthusiastic.

LO8

Working With Healthy Aging People in Groups

Groups are a most effective approach in addressing developmental issues of aging and the key task of finding meaning in later life. In working with the *well* older adult, the social support mechanisms of a group help members understand the universality of their struggles. Many older people have problems coping with the aging process. They have to deal with the many losses associated with old age in addition to the pressures and conflicts that younger generations experience; they can profit from interpersonal groups or personal-growth groups that serve people of all ages. Kampfe (2015) suggests that group work is particularly appropriate with older people "both because this population often experiences loneliness and isolation and because interpersonal interaction is vital for physical and psychological well-being" (p. 21). The increasing demands of serving diverse populations in the community, as well as the mounting evidence of the value of group work with older adults, have fostered this emerging area of practice (Vacha-Haase, 2014).

Jamie Bludworth designed a group that focuses on successful aging and found the following references to be helpful: Erber, Szuchman, and Rothberg (1990, 1991), Kampfe (2015), Levy (1996), and Rowe and Kahn (1998).

GROUP PROPOSAL

A Successful Aging Group

This section is written from the perspective of Jamie Bludworth, PhD, a licensed psychologist and an instructor at Arizona State University. (For further information about this group, contact Jamie via email at Jamieblud@hotmail.com.)

Organizing the Group

During my time as a trainee (and later as a staff member) at a large hospital, I facilitated many groups for older adults: arthritis support groups, Parkinson support groups, dementia caregivers' support groups, bereavement groups, and a reminiscence group. These groups seemed to focus on what was "wrong" in members' lives. When group members were frustrated about setbacks in their lives, they often attributed their difficulties solely to the fact that they were aging, without considering other possible intervening factors.

It seemed to me that many of the older people with whom I worked had bought into various negative myths and stereotypes about what it means to get older and that these beliefs were preventing them from leading more satisfying and socially engaged lives. I also encountered group members who did not appear to believe the stereotypes and myths about growing older and who were active and thoroughly engaged in their communities. They were an inspiration to the groups in which they participated. They were also a touchstone for me in the creation of a group for older adults focused solely on debunking the commonly held myths about aging and encouraging healthy lifestyle changes. I developed a group around the concept of successful aging, which was offered at the local senior center. This group became very popular among the guests of the center and was effective in meeting many of its stated goals.

Basic Components of the Group

Type of Group

The Successful Aging Group was a psychoeducational group with a developmental focus on the issues that older adults must confront in the challenging task of maintaining physical and mental strength as they move further along the continuum of aging. The group was held at the local senior center. Publicity for the group was in the form of flyers posted on the premises as well as advertisements in the senior center newsletter.

Population

Although the group was designed primarily for older adults (ages 65 and up), individuals of any age were encouraged to participate. Group members were especially encouraged to bring family members to the group to facilitate a deeper understanding of aging among and between family members.

Rationale and Basic Assumptions

Traditionally, older adults have been portrayed in a stereotypical manner by the American media. Examples of the doddering old grandfather or the memory lapsed, hearing impaired grandmother have been the butt of countless jokes in commercials and situation comedies. These images are but a miniscule sample of the misconceptions and overly simplified views that many people hold about older adults.

Although my personal experience with the members of my groups was informative, I consulted the research literature to gain a more thorough understanding of what might have been occurring. Moreover, having empirical support for the rationale of the proposed group served to lend credibility to my argument that a successful aging group would be beneficial for the clients served by the hospital.

Resources and Methods

The primary resource for this group was *Successful Aging* (Rowe & Kahn, 1998), which chronicles the MacArthur Foundation longitudinal study on aging begun in 1984 that includes several research projects in the domains of general medicine, psychology, neurobiology, sociology, and several other disciplines to create a "new gerontology." In the opening session I suggested that group members purchase a copy of *Successful Aging* to facilitate discussion and to encourage them to remain in the successful aging conversation outside of group. Supplemental literature, such as magazine, newspaper, and journal articles, was also utilized.

Group Goals

I set out to design a group that not only challenged members' belief systems regarding aging but also presented them with alternative information that was accurate, based in science, and of a positive and encouraging nature. I hoped that educational intervention, presented in an interactional group format, would affect a shift in group members' schemas regarding aging. I believed that if a shift in this domain could occur, then group members would be more likely to make changes in their lifestyle choices that could not only "add years to their lives but also add life to their years." The goals of the group were as follows:

- To foster an increased awareness of the existence of stereotypes and myths regarding older adults among group members.

- For group members to gain an understanding of the ways in which belief in stereotypes or limiting thoughts have a discernable negative effect on their lives.
- To increase members' knowledge in the domains of physical, intellectual, and emotional health.
- For members to utilize knowledge acquired in the group to challenge and debunk the myths and stereotypes of aging.
- To create a social support network among members.
- For members to make informed lifestyle choices that would reduce the risks of age-related disease and disability while fostering greater engagement with life.

Group Format

The first half of each session consisted primarily of a psychoeducational presentation. The second half was more interactional in nature with group members sharing their personal reactions and experiences regarding the session topic. Although this group was limited to 12 sessions, it was open for new members throughout its duration. At the end of 12 sessions there was a break of 2 weeks and then the sessions resumed, recycling back to Session 1.

Session 1: Introduction

- Introduce the goals and nature of the group. Obtain informed consent.
- Introduce the concept of myths and stereotypes about aging. This can be done by asking group members to respond to the question: "What comes to your mind in response to the following words: elderly, aged, or older adult." The responses can be written on the board.
- Choose a few of these salient, popular myths and refute them with evidence. Engage members in discussion about the beliefs and attitudes they hold about the elderly and about the attitudes they believe others hold about them.

Session 2: Usual Aging Versus Successful Aging

- "Usual aging" describes older adults who are relatively high functioning but are also at a significant risk for disease or disability. Provide details and examples such as "syndrome X."
- "Successful aging" describes older adults who have the ability to maintain the following key behaviors: (a) low risk of diseases and disabilities, (b) high levels of physical and mental functioning, and (c) active engagement with life or social vitality.
- Explore any myths or stereotypes about these topics.

Session 3: Environment Versus Genetics

- Present evidence that explains how lifestyle choices are the key to successful aging and how many chronic illnesses may be prevented or treated through lifestyle changes. Some examples are smoking cessation, diet, and exercise.
- This session provides a foundation for the basic premise of the group, which states that lifestyle choices have a greater effect on one's experience of aging than do genetics.
- It is important to explain that lifestyle change is not an easy process.

Session 4: Detection, Treatment, and Prevention of Disease

- Develop strategies for the early detection of disease and encourage a self-monitoring process.
- Make the distinction between diseases that are primarily due to lifestyle (for example, hypertension, diabetes, lung cancer, and heart disease) and other kinds of genetically linked diseases such as Parkinson's and rheumatoid arthritis.
- Provide evidence (both empirical and anecdotal) for the importance of early detection in most diseases.
- Discuss the commonly recommended strategies for the prevention of disease (diet, exercise, and social engagement).

Session 5: Exercise and Nutrition

- Present the latest findings on this topic and its relationship to healthy aging.
- Discuss community resources tailored to the nutritional and exercise regimens for older adults such as walking clubs, aquatic programs, and strength and balance programs.
- Provide a guest speaker who has knowledge of and can demonstrate appropriate exercise regimens for older adults.
- Make it clear that group members should consult their physicians before embarking on any lifestyle changes.

Session 6: Aging and Memory

- Present and discuss the latest information about the aging process and normal memory function.
- Provide detailed information about dementia and Alzheimer's disease with community resources such as the National Alzheimer's Association. Also provide information regarding the latest methods of treating dementia.
- Educate members about possible interaction effects of multiple medications and the implications for negative side effects in cognitive functioning.
- Present strategies for maintaining and enhancing memory and mental functioning such as mnemonics, appointment books, and calendars.
- Help to normalize members' experiences of minor memory losses, such as forgetting where their keys are or having brief difficulty remembering where the car is parked when shopping.

Session 7: Mental Health

- Present and discuss the topics of depression, anxiety, and possible mental health concerns with which group members might be faced.
- Many older people have negative attitudes about mental health issues and see depression or anxiety as a sign of weakness. It is important to provide education about such issues that presents a more balanced view.
- Discuss the environmental and developmental factors involved in mental health issues of older adults (death of loved ones, coping with disease or disability, and interactions of multiple medications).
- Provide a comprehensive list of community resources and be prepared to make referrals for members when appropriate.

Session 8: Relationships

- Discuss the connection between social engagement and overall health in later life. Research findings suggest that social support is a key element in successful aging, which is often overlooked.
- Describe various kinds of social support. It is especially important to mention the health monitoring function of a social support network, wherein friends encourage an individual to seek medical attention when that individual may not otherwise do so.
- Link this topic with any relationships that may be developing in the group.

Sessions 9–11: Consolidation of Learning and Preparation for Termination

Consolidation typically occurs through a review of material presented in earlier sessions. For example, in Session 9 we reviewed information presented in Sessions 1–3; Session 10 reviewed Sessions 4–6; and in Session 11 a review of Sessions 7 and 8 was the focus.

It is important to note, however, that the review sessions should not simply consist of the facilitator reciting information in a lecture type format. One exercise I used to make the consolidation sessions more interactive was "Successful Aging Jeopardy." In this exercise, I generated questions of varying difficulty that corresponded to the topics to be reviewed. For example, in Session 10 the categories were disease prevention, exercise and nutrition, and aging and memory. I then organized the questions within each category based on the difficulty of the question (difficult questions were worth more points, much like the television game show). The group was divided into two teams, with each team having an equal opportunity to answer a question.

At first, members appeared to be reluctant to play this game. Nevertheless, after encouragement from me, and a little bit of coaxing by some of the more outgoing group members, they engaged in the exercise. It took only a few minutes before a friendly competition developed and the group as a whole became enthusiastic. This exercise provided an opening wherein group members could review information while simultaneously engaging in spirited interaction regarding the session topics and associated myths about aging.

The facilitator of this exercise needs to provide clear ground rules as to how the game will be played. Most of the ground rules that I insisted upon were interpersonal in nature. For example, members were not allowed to criticize a person if he or she could not answer a question correctly. The "Successful Aging Jeopardy" sessions tended to be the most energy infused of all the meetings. Although the game can be fun for the group, it is vital that the facilitator maintains the topical focus and continues to intervene in ways that encourage the deepening of group members' knowledge and awareness.

The topic of termination was introduced in Session 9 and briefly revisited in Sessions 10 and 11 with statements like the following: "Our meetings will be coming to an end in three sessions. It is important for each of you to take a look at how you would best like to use the time that we have remaining."

Session 12: Termination

Session 12 was devoted solely to termination. In this session, each member was encouraged to share what he or she experienced over the course of the 12 weeks spent together. Additionally, members were encouraged to discuss any changes they had made in their lifestyles and to brainstorm with each other about ways in which they might maintain such changes. Because of the epidemic proportions of isolation among the elderly, I placed great emphasis on fostering social interaction and support outside of the group, prevailing upon members to continue their interpersonal connections after termination.

Special Considerations

Group facilitators must be vigilant not to practice outside their area of expertise. Group members will often ask for medical advice. *Always* refer them to their physician for such advice. Beyond that, each group should end with a disclaimer that says something to this effect: "This group is designed to provide the latest information about aging. The group is not intended to provide medical or other professional advice. Always consult your physician or other medical professional before making any changes in your health-related behaviors."

The age of the facilitator also can be a factor in the development of trust and credibility with older adult group members. The difference in ages between the group members and me was quite obvious. By addressing this issue in the first session in a nondefensive manner, group members were able to trust me, and my credibility with them increased. It was also important for me to mention my qualifications to facilitate such a group. Moreover, I explained my interest in working with older adults in an open and honest manner, mentioning the importance of my grandparents in my life and my struggle to understand and cope with the declining health of my beloved grandmother. Group members seemed to accept my role as facilitator of the group even though I was less than half their age in many cases. I believe my genuine respect for them and honesty and openness about my motivation to lead the group created the space for this to occur.

Many group members had significant physical limitations, and it was vitally important to accommodate these limitations. For example, members who had hearing loss were seated closer to me so that they could hear what was being said. Other group members were encouraged to speak loudly so that everyone could hear. Space was made to accommodate people in wheelchairs. When I wrote on the board, I used large letters to assist those members who had visual difficulties. It was essential to be flexible in facilitating the safety and comfort of members with special needs.

Group Outcomes

Several members of this group made significant lifestyle changes. One woman in her late 70s took up swimming again. She had been a competitive swimmer for many years but had stopped when she "got old." After several weeks of swimming at the YWCA she was invited to compete on a masters swim team. When she told the group, she was clearly very proud, and it appeared that she had a newfound confidence. Later, several of the group members went to cheer her on in her first competition in more than 40 years!

In similar fashion, a 92-year-old man had always wanted to write a book. Somehow he had never done it. Through the support he gained in the group (and some good old cajoling by group members), he started writing his memoir. He often gave the group updates about how many pages he had written. Toward the end of the group he read a passage aloud and was very moved by the experience, as was the rest of the group.

One woman in her 70s started a monthly outing group, organizing trips to museums, a flea market, a wine tasting, or other such events. The group chartered a small bus and took photographs of their adventures that they would later share with the rest of the group. This motivated other group members to join them. Many people in the monthly outing group reported that it had been years since they had been out with a group of people and that they felt more vital and alive from doing something that they simply had "let slip."

Many members of the group made new social connections and were able to provide support for each other outside of the group. In one instance, members of the group noticed something different about another member and encouraged her to see a doctor. This led to early detection of a potentially life-threatening disease that was treated before it became unmanageable.

Finally, the older group members were not the only beneficiaries of the successful aging group. I was deeply moved and inspired by many of the members. I saw firsthand the resiliency and dignity of older women and men who often were overlooked by society and their families alike. I learned that a sense of humor goes a long way when things get tough. Most of all, I learned the value of true mutual respect. Some of the members of those first successful aging groups have since died. Although I have been saddened by their deaths, I have also taken great solace from knowing that they were known and cared for by the members of their group and that in some cases they had taken the opportunity to reclaim something that they had lost.

LO8

The Therapeutic Value of Grief Work in Groups

Grief work, or *bereavement*, refers to the exploration of feelings generated by a significant loss. The loss of family members, friends, and intimate relationships brings out human wounds that need to be healed. After a loss, some common feelings include sadness, sorrow, fear, hurt, confusion, depression, resentment, relief, loneliness, anger, despair, shame, and guilt. *Mourning* involves recognizing our internal grief and expressing it externally. There is therapeutic value in the process of mourning, which entails dealing with grief on both an emotional and an intellectual level. Grief is a necessary and natural process after a significant loss, but far too often grief is pathologized. Unresolved grief may linger in the background, preventing people from learning to live with their losses and delaying their interest in forming new relationships. Grief may be over many types of losses besides a death, such as the breakup of a relationship, the loss of one's career, or children leaving home. Wolfelt (2015) recognizes the value of leaning *toward*, not *away from*, grief. If we hope to heal, we must directly experience our grief. When people deny sadness and the pain associated with loss, they inevitably suffer more in the long run and are less able to express a range of feelings. This unexpressed pain can be physically and psychologically immobilizing and can prevent accepting the reality of the death of a loved one.

Groups can be instrumental in helping people feel less isolated as they move at their own pace in their own way in attending to their pain and grief. Older adults struggling to adjust to the many changes that confront them through loss can benefit from having an opportunity to grieve and to recognize the significance of their loss. Increased loneliness is often a key factor following the death of a loved one, and a group can offer the older person much needed support and socialization (Vacha-Haase, 2014). Although addressing issues such as loss and pain in grief groups is important, the possibility of developing new relationships is critical and can be explored in these groups.

Bereavement is a particularly critical developmental task for older people, not only because of the loss of others who are close to them but also because of the loss of some of their capacities. Although death strikes at children as well as older people, facing one's own death and the death of significant others takes on special significance with aging. If people who are experiencing bereavement are able to express the full range of their thoughts and feelings, they stand a better chance of adjusting to a new environment. Indeed, part of the grief process involves making basic life changes and experiencing new growth. Group counseling can be especially helpful to people at this time.

Many forces in our society make it difficult for people to experience grief. Social norms demand a "quick cure," and other people often cannot understand why it is taking "such a long time" for a grieving person to "get back to normal." In our fast-paced world today, people are urged to "get over it and move ahead." Hedtke and Winslade (2004) provide a strikingly different perspective on working through losses and moving ahead. They believe people are born into networks of relationships and remain woven into those networks long after they die. Those who experience the loss of someone they love can find comfort in developing a new relationship with the person who died. This relational approach to grief work is based on a process of "re-membering," which is about continuing to foster the memory of a person's life even after he or she dies. By keeping this person's voice and thoughts alive, we have gained an ongoing resource that helps us move forward in life. We can consistently renew a dead person's presence in our lives by remembering the stories and imagining the voice of the loved one as we reflect on what he or she might say to us as we face difficult times. Those who lead bereavement groups can glean some very useful ideas on grief and bereavement from Hedtke and Winslade's (2004) *Re-membering Lives: Conversations With the Dying and the Bereaved*.

If you would like to learn more about designing and conducting bereavement groups with older people, Alan Forrest, who designed an older adult bereavement group, recommends Capuzzi (2003), Christensen et al. (2006), Evans and Garner (2004), Fitzgerald (1994), Freeman (2005), Hedkte and Winslade (2004), James and Friedman (1998), Tedeschi and Calhoun (1993), Wolfelt (2003, 2015), Worden (2002), and Yalom and Vinogradov (1988).

An Older Adult Bereavement Group

This section is written from the perspective of Alan Forrest, EdD, a professor of counseling at Radford University. (For more information on this group, contact Alan at Radford University, Department of Counselor Education, P.O. Box 6994, Radford, VA 24142; telephone: 540-831-5214; email: aforrest@radford.edu.)

Introduction

Before I began facilitating loss and bereavement groups, I was filled with enthusiasm, excitement, and altruism, tempered somewhat by numerous fears, anxieties, and insecurities. At times words are inadequate to express the intensity of feelings in the group; that is how I learned the value of therapeutic silence and how one's presence can be healing. To hear and truly feel another person's pain is not without effort, and knowing you cannot take away that pain can be frustrating and depressing. The first group session is usually the most difficult because each group member relates the circumstance of his or her loss. The hurt, suffering, and pain can be overwhelming, but there is also comfort in knowing that one does not have to be alone.

With age comes an increased number of losses: friends, family, and other losses such as retirement, declining health, home, and for some, mental and cognitive functioning. All of these life transitions, in addition to losses through death, need to be grieved and can be addressed in a bereavement group. The goal of an older adult bereavement group is to facilitate movement through the stages and the tasks of grief by providing an open and supportive environment that promotes emotional recovery. Group participants are encouraged to express their needs, wants, and wishes in addressing their grief and to identify goals they would like to accomplish in the group.

Organizing the Group

One of the primary goals of a bereavement group is to educate the mourner to the reality that grief is a process that is measured in years, not months. It does not proceed the same for everyone; as one widow stated, "You never really get over the loss, but the challenge is learning how to live with it." I strive to be clear about the purpose and structure of the group and focus on creating a group culture of mutual support.

This group has a psychoeducational focus, including elements of education, emotional support, and encouragement for social interaction. The group serves as a catalyst for meeting the members' emotional needs, for dispelling myths and misconceptions of loss responses, and for enhancing the ability to develop new relationships outside the group. To achieve a high level of group cohesion and trust, I have designed a closed, time-limited group. The group meets for 8 to 10 sessions, each lasting for 2 hours, and is limited to no more than eight members.

Screening

The screening and selection process is an essential variable contributing to the success of the group. It is necessary to have a clear sense of who will likely benefit from a group in making the determination of whom to include. One consideration is how much time had passed since the individual experienced the loss. Most people whose loss had occurred less than 12 weeks prior to seeking treatment are too early into their bereavement and are not ready for a group experience. Individuals who are experiencing additional psychological, emotional, interpersonal, or crisis problems are poor candidates for this type of group and may serve to defocus the group away from exploring and working on the grieving process. It is essential to rule out candidates who exhibit serious pathology as they are likely to impede the group process and take precious time from the other group members. I have discovered that individuals who possess basic social skills and who are comfortable with self-disclosure contribute most to making the group both satisfying and beneficial.

Counselor Self-Awareness

To function successfully as a grief counselor requires an awareness of self and one's own experiences of loss. The issues that encompass grief and loss are very emotional and touch our deepest fears as human beings. If the counselor is not aware of personal loss issues, the grief work with clients experiencing loss will be seriously affected and compromised.

The experience of bereavement necessitates that the counselor examine, at least minimally, three personal areas. First, working with bereaved individuals increases one's awareness of one's own losses. Examining personal issues (past and present) surrounding loss and bereavement is a difficult task, filled with profound sentiments. Counselors need not to have fully resolved all the loss issues they have experienced, but they should be aware and actively involved in working on them. If a client is experiencing a loss similar to that of a recent loss in the life of the counselor, it may be difficult to therapeutically help the client.

Second, grief may interfere in working with clients with regard to a counselor's own feared losses. Although all counselors have experienced losses in the past, there may be apprehension over future losses. Counselors may encounter personal anxiety when thoughts of losing their own children, partners, or parents enter into their work with clients. This is usually not problematic unless the loss a client presents is similar to the one we most fear. For example, if the counselor has an elderly parent, he or she may have difficulty facilitating an elderly bereavement group.

A third area involves the counselor's existential anxiety and personal death awareness. Death is a part of the cycle of life, and working with older adult bereaved individuals is a constant reminder of the inevitability of loss in one's own life and in the lives of those we care for deeply. Most of us think about our own mortality and, in varying degrees, experience anxiety about it. However, it is possible to acknowledge this reality and not allow it to impede our work with clients. How we choose to respond to the losses in our own lives will determine how effective we are in providing comfort and growth experiences in the lives of others.

Leadership Issues

Leadership style and the activity level of the leader are important considerations for a bereavement group. A high degree of leader involvement is effective during the early stages of group. But as the group evolves into a cohesive unit, I tend to become less active. I recommend a coleader format. One coleader can concentrate on helping an individual express and work through a painful experience while the other coleader attends to members reacting to this pain.

Disruptive behaviors can impede the group process. It is important to address disruptive behavior as soon as it occurs. For example, it is not unusual for a group member to express the attitude that "my loss is greater than your loss." I handle this by saying, "We are not here to compare losses. Everyone's loss is unique. We are here because of losing someone, and everyone's loss is important in this group." Other disruptive behaviors to be aware of include the person who habitually gives advice but rarely engages in personal sharing; the person who gives moralistic advice and uses "shoulds," "musts," and "have tos"; the member who observes but seldom participates in personal sharing; the person who makes irrelevant comments; the individual who habitually self-discloses and monopolizes the group; and the person who continually interrupts other group members when they are working on their loss issues.

Group Format

Norms and Expectations

During the initial session of the group, I discuss group norms and expectations, including beginning and ending on time and socializing outside of the group. I also address members' questions about how the group functions. Ending sessions on time can be difficult because it is hard to accurately gauge the length of time it takes for the expression of the intense emotions that are elicited.

Socializing outside of group is generally discouraged because subgroups may form, which can have a negative effect on the cohesion and process of the group. However, I do not adhere to this norm when leading bereavement groups for older adults. There are advantages to outside contact among members, such as helping them deal with the loneliness and social isolation that are a part of their bereavement experience.

I try to identify common themes in group members' narratives in an effort to link common experiences and feelings of the group participants. It is important that group members become aware of the similarities and common elements of their loss so they do not experience a sense of isolation and aloneness. The therapeutic factors of universality and instillation of hope are present and can serve as an incentive for group members to continue to participate in the group despite an upsurge of painful emotions.

Participant Introductions

At the first group meeting I ask participants to introduce themselves and share something personal about themselves. I monitor these disclosures so that each member has approximately equal time to share. The introductions provide each member with the opportunity to be the focal point of the group and also facilitate the universality of the feelings and expression of grief. Introductions are generally limited to name, circumstances of the loss, fears and anxieties participants have, and anything else they want others to know about them. One useful technique is to have group members share what they were thinking and feeling while they were on their way to this first meeting. The commonalities are noted, which begins a linking process. Due to the excessive anxiety many individuals experience, it is sometimes necessary to do this exercise in dyads prior to introductions to the entire group.

Sharing Personal Loss and Bereavement Experiences

At some point in the first group session each participant is given the opportunity to discuss in detail his or her loss and bereavement experiences up to this point in life. Introductions allow for some of this to occur, and as group members become more comfortable with one another, they are more receptive to discussing their losses in greater detail and in more personal ways.

Also, group members are not discouraged from talking about other concerns that they need to bring to the group. Often these other issues are related to their life as a result of their loss. A sampling of such topical concerns may include family realignments, role adjustments, finances, managing a household, relocation, and even dating once again.

Understanding the Grief Process

Perhaps the single most important gift counselors can offer bereaved individuals is an accurate understanding of the grief process so individuals no longer believe their grieving is abnormal or that they are "going crazy." Areas typically discussed are descriptions of the grief process, possible reactions such as physical symptoms, suicidal ideation, increased dependence on medication, depression, typical behaviors, and the reactions of others to one's loss.

Wolfelt (2003) describes a model of understanding grief that includes 10 "touchstones" or trail markers that one can use to navigate through the oftentimes confusing process of grief and bereavement. Wolfelt refers to the touchstones as "wisdom teachings" that can assist group members to better understand the grief process and better understand themselves. The touchstones are opening to the presence of loss, dispelling misconceptions about grief, embracing the uniqueness of grief, exploring the feelings of loss, recognizing one is not crazy, understanding the needs of mourning, nurturing oneself, reaching out to others, seeking reconciliation, and coming to appreciate one's transformation. These touchstones can be incorporated into the group process and can even be used as an outline for a 10-week group format.

Topical Issues

Topics generally addressed in the group include guilt, loneliness, a changing identity, fear of letting go of the deceased, interdependence, multiple losses, an increased personal death awareness, changed social and interpersonal roles, important dates such as birthdays and anniversaries, religion and spirituality, rituals, the influence of family members on the grieving process, nutrition and physical exercise, and termination of the group itself, which is another loss that participants will need to address. Although the group facilitator may suggest any of these themes for discussion, it is important to be receptive to the topics group members want to explore.

Photographs and Memories

In an effort to make the deceased real and concrete to the other group members, I encourage members to bring in and share photographs. This facilitates the reminiscing process, which may serve as a form of life review. Each group member is given the opportunity to tell the group about the person in the photograph. This exercise assists group members to feel a deeper sense of each other's loss and gives each mourner the chance to reminisce and share a memory, thereby reaffirming his or her relationship with the deceased.

Addressing Secondary Losses

Secondary losses are frequently ignored in the bereavement process despite the fact that they can be as powerful as the loss itself. A secondary loss—a loss that occurs as a consequence of a death—may take many forms and can affect a group in dramatic fashion. For example, one widow, whose husband had died very suddenly and unexpectedly shortly after taking early retirement, was struggling not only with him physically being gone but also with the loss of all the hopes, plans, and dreams they had shared. It was difficult for her to discuss moving on with her life because her future plans were so intertwined with those of her husband. It was not until she examined her secondary losses that she could open up, engage in the group, and receive group support. Clients need to identify and anticipate secondary losses so they can be prepared for and grieved.

Emotional Intensity

A bereavement group contains a high level of emotional intensity, but many clients are unable or ill prepared to deal with the breadth and depth of emotions they will encounter in themselves or in others. A degree of vulnerability accompanies the expression of emotions, and many participants may not be ready for it. Others may perceive this vulnerability as a sign of weakness. Therefore, these concerns must be addressed repeatedly throughout the group experience. Some group members will weep from the start to the end of each group session, which clearly communicates how difficult the group is for them. This emotion is acknowledged, but it may not be immediately addressed. Members may require time to process their emotions before feeling comfortable in verbally expressing them. These individuals receive support from the group by others respecting their need, for a period of time, to maintain some emotional distance.

Confidence and Skill Building

Many of the bereaved older people, particularly widows, had been very dependent on their spouses. It is possible that some of this dependency may be transferred to their adult children. Although these individuals are grieving and are in emotional pain, they have the capacity to develop new skills. Doing so can bring increased confidence and self-esteem. One group participant whose husband died disclosed that she was having difficulty balancing her checkbook because her husband had always attended to family financial matters. When others in the group shared similar situations of being dependent on their spouses, she was encouraged and went to her bank to learn how to balance the checkbook. This particular woman gained so much confidence in herself that by the final group session she shared that she had bought a new car, something that her husband had always done for her. It is important to remember that confidence and self-esteem are just as essential for an older adult as for anyone else.

The Use of Touch

Many older adults, particularly those who have lost a spouse, have a strong need to be touched. Without a spouse, it is difficult to get this need met. If a counselor is comfortable with the use of therapeutic touching, it is a way to meet the need of being touched on the part of the client and also a way for the counselor, or other group member, to physically make contact with another. It is paramount that the counselor is clear as to the appropriateness of the touching and whether or not the client is willing to be touched. A word of caution in using touch with a grieving individual: the touch may be countertherapeutic if it is used to communicate or is interpreted as "Don't cry, everything's going to be all right." Crying is part of the healing process, so group facilitators need to carefully attend to the participants and take their lead from them.

Religion and Spirituality

The religious and spiritual domains have often been overlooked or ignored by counselors. However, bereaved older adults need to examine their adjustment to the world, particularly to their assumptive world. A person's core beliefs and values can be shaken by losing a loved one or a valued friend. It is not uncommon for an older bereaved individual to feel that he or she has lost direction, purpose, and confidence in life. Group members often search for meaning or purpose in their life, experience a loss of a sense of connection, have feelings of guilt or unworthiness, question their faith, have a desire for forgiveness, and may experience a sense of abandonment by God. Meaning, faith, and connection with God (or a Higher Power) may be called into question when an older person responds to the death of a close loved one. The group can serve as an opportunity to examine such issues that frequently are not discussed and shared with others out of fear, shame, guilt, or embarrassment.

It is normal and reasonable to expect that many bereaved older adults who have experienced a loss are suffering, to some degree, from the anguish caused by questions of meaning, faith, or specific religious or spiritual issues. Asking questions about how people are doing spiritually, how they are coping with their loss, and listening for broader meanings can create an atmosphere of openness and receptivity to talk more about their loss from a spiritual perspective.

One group member expressed her anger at God for allowing her husband of over 40 years to be killed in an automobile accident. Although she was a woman of faith and had previously attended church on a regular basis, she expressed her anger at God and discontinued her church attendance and involvement, thereby cutting out a likely source of spiritual, social, and interpersonal support.

Termination

Some group members have terminated prematurely and suddenly after two or three group sessions. Follow-up interviews indicated a number of reasons for leaving, some of which include members' perceptions that the group is too emotionally threatening, too intimate, too sad, or that they "should" be able to cope with their loss on their own. It is important to be cognizant of generational, cultural, and gender differences when working with an older adult population. Separately, or together, each will have an effect on whether or not one chooses to remain in the group.

What are some lessons that can be learned from the termination of the group as a whole? Termination of the bereavement group provides participants with another opportunity to learn how to deal with loss in a healthy manner. Members are encouraged to address any unfinished business toward the deceased or toward other group members or the facilitators. Group participants are also encouraged to provide each other with feedback on their experience in the group and to say good-bye. The members can anticipate how it will be to no longer have a group, explore what the group experience has meant to them, and examine their plans for continued support.

Rituals

A ritual is a set of actions, performed primarily for symbolic value, designed to preserve the traditions of a community. Grief rituals may provide a process for people to reach a level of accommodation to a different way of living. Most cultures have prescribed rites of passage that honor transitions into the different stages of the life cycle. Bereavement rituals can serve to separate the bereaved from the rest of society and assist the bereaved in a reintegration and return to society as a changed person. Funerals and memorial services are perhaps the best known examples of bereavement rituals.

Rituals can be used effectively throughout the group experience and can be powerful tools to increase self-awareness, especially during the termination process. One technique that has proved to be a powerful group ending experience is to have each participant light a candle that represents the deceased. Participants share with the group any thoughts about what they learned or about their deceased or what the group has meant to them. This exercise engages the group in a final shared experience, provides an ending ritual, uses light as a metaphor for insight and illumination, and leaves each participant with something concrete (the candle) to take home. Group members have found this to be a highly emotional and healing experience.

Group Outcomes

How effective are older adult bereavement groups? Although no empirical outcome studies have been done on the older adult bereavement groups I have facilitated, there is some interesting anecdotal information that supports the value of these groups.

A primary goal of an older adult bereavement group is to reduce the isolation and loneliness that may be the result of a loss, particularly when someone has lost his or her spouse of many years. At the conclusion of one of the groups, all the participants exchanged phone numbers and would periodically meet informally for emotional and social support. Another group contracted with me to meet once a month, for 3 months, in what we referred to as an "aftercare group" following formal termination of the group. In each of these groups, all members had been strangers at the beginning of the group.

What have I learned from facilitating these groups? I have shared tears, and I have shared laughter working with bereaved older adult groups. It may seem paradoxical, but I have learned more about the process of living than about dying and grieving from facilitating these groups. Facilitating an older adult bereavement group is life affirming and personally enriching. I have learned to celebrate each day as a precious gift and to deeply value my personal relationships. Wisdom, courage, and strength of character cannot be taught in graduate school, but I have profited from some wise, courageous, and strong individuals—my clients.

A Group Treatment Program for Institutionalized Older Adults

This proposal is written from the perspective of Marianne Schneider Corey.

Introduction

Many different types of groups are suitable for older people. The number and types of groups possible are limited only by the imagination of the counselor and the counselor's willingness to create groups to meet the special needs of older clients. The group described here is a preplacement group in a psychiatric facility for older people who will be returning to their home or going to another kind of residential living facility in the community.

Organizing the Group

The preplacement group consisted of individuals currently in an institutional setting who were going to be released into community settings—either returning home or going to board-and-care residential facilities. As with other group populations, it is necessary to give careful consideration to the selection of members. A group is not likely to function well if severely disturbed and hallucinating members are mixed with clients who are psychologically intact. It is a good practice, however, to combine talkative and quiet people, depressed and ebullient types, excitable with calmer clients, suspicious with more trusting individuals, and people with different backgrounds. The size of the group is determined by the level of psychological and social functioning of the participants.

The preplacement group that my coleader and I formed consisted of three men and four women—a good balance of the sexes and a workable number for two leaders. Before the first meeting I contacted the members individually and gave them a basic orientation to the group. I told them the purpose of the group, what the activities might be, and where, when, and for how long the group would meet. I let each person know that membership was voluntary. When people seemed hesitant to attend, I suggested that they come to the initial session and then decide whether they wanted to continue.

Group Goals and Group Format

Before the first session my coleader and I decided on a few general goals for the group. Our primary goal was to provide an atmosphere in which common concerns could be freely discussed and in which members could interact with one another. We wanted to provide an opportunity for members to voice complaints and to be included in a decision-making process. We felt strongly that these people could make changes and that the group process could stimulate them to do so.

The group met once a week for an hour in the visitors' room. Before each group session I contacted all the members, reminded them that the group would meet shortly, invited them to attend, and accompanied them to the group room. I learned that it was difficult for them to remember the time of the meetings, so individual assistance would be important in ensuring regular attendance. Those who were absent were either ill or involved in an activity that could not be rescheduled, such as physical therapy. The group was open; members would occasionally be discharged, and we encouraged newly admitted patients to join. This did not seem to bother the members, and it did not affect the cohesion of the group. As leaders, we also attempted to make entrance into the group as easy as possible.

We always allowed some time for the new members to be introduced and to say anything they wanted to about being new to the group, and we asked current group members to welcome them.

The Initial Stage

During the initial sessions, members showed a tendency to direct all of their statements to the two leaders. In the hope that we could break the shell that isolated each person in a private and detached world, my coleader and I immediately began to encourage the members to talk to one another, not to us. When members talked about a member, we asked them to speak directly to that member. When members discussed a particular problem or concern, we encouraged others to share similar difficulties.

In the beginning members avoided talking about themselves, voicing complaints, or discussing what they expected after their release from the institution. Their usual comment reflected their hopelessness: "What good will it do? No one will listen to us anyway." Our task was to teach them to listen to one another.

The Importance of Listening and Acting

My coleader and I felt that one way of teaching these people to listen would be by modeling—by demonstrating that we were really listening to them. Thus, when members spoke of problems related to life on the ward, my coleader and I became actively involved with them in solving some of these conflicts. For example, one member complained that one of the patients in his room shouted for much of the night. We were able to get the unhappy member placed in another room. When some members shared their fears about the board-and-care homes they were to be released to, we arranged to take them to several such homes so that they could make an informed choice of placement. One woman complained that her husband did not visit her enough and that, when he did take her home, he was uncaring and uninterested in her sexually. On several occasions my coleader and I held private sessions with the couple.

Some men complained that there was nothing to do, so we arranged for them to get involved in planting a garden. Another group member shared the fact that she was an artist, so we asked her to lead some people in the group and on the unit in art projects. She reacted enthusiastically and succeeded in involving several other members.

Our philosophy was to encourage the members to again become active, even in a small way, in making decisions about their lives. We learned *not* to do two things: (1) encourage a patient to participate in an activity that would be frustrating and thereby further erode an already poor self-image or (2) make promises we could not keep.

Listening to Reminiscences

In addition to dealing with the day-to-day problems of the members, we spent much time listening as they reminisced about sadness and guilt they had experienced, their many losses, the places they had lived and visited, the mistakes they had made, and so on. By remembering and actively reconstructing their past, older people can work to resolve the conflicts affecting them and decide how to use the time left to them. In addition, members enjoy remembering happy times when they were more productive and powerful than they are now.

The Use of Exercises

My coleader and I designed a variety of exercises to catalyze member interaction. We used these exercises as simple means of getting group interaction going. We always began by showing how an exercise could be done. Here are some exercises we used in this group:

- Go on an imaginary trip, and pick a couple of the other group members to accompany you. (Although you may have to deal with feelings of rejection expressed by those not chosen, this exercise is very helpful for people who are reluctant to reach out to one another and make friends.)
- If you could do anything you wanted, what would it be?
- Bring a picture of you and your family, and talk about your family.
- Describe some of the memories that are important to you.
- Tell what your favorite holiday is and what you enjoy doing on that day.

Another exercise that helped older people focus and contributed to member interaction is the sentence-completion method for low-level clients (Yalom, 1983). Incomplete sentences can be structured around a variety of themes. Here are a few examples:

- Self-disclosure (One thing about me that people would be surprised to know is . . .)
- Separation (The hardest separation that I have ever had is . . .)

- Anger (One thing that really irritates me is . . .)
- Isolation (The time in my life when I felt most alone was . . .)
- Ward events (The fight on the ward last night made me feel . . .)
- Empathy (I feel touched by others when . . .)
- Here-and-now interactions (The person whom I am most like in this room is . . .)
- Personal change (Something I want to change about myself is . . .)
- Stress (I experience tension when . . .)

Working with incomplete sentences can trigger intense emotions, and the group leader needs to be skilled in dealing with these feelings.

By encouraging the members to express themselves, these exercises led to their getting to know one another, which led in turn to a lessening of the "what's the use" feeling that was universal in the beginning.

Debunking Myths

My coleader and I explored some myths and attitudes that prevail regarding the aged and challenged the members' acceptance of these myths. Anyone working with older people needs to differentiate between myths and facts surrounding what it means to grow old. The facts are that older people can and do learn and are able to make changes in their lives. Creative and informed professionals can do much to enhance the lives of their older clients, thereby helping to dispel the myths that have acted as a barrier to providing quality services for older adults.

Termination

I was to be coleader of this group for only 3 months, and I prepared the members for my departure several weeks in advance. After I left, my coleader continued the group by himself. On occasion I visited the group, and when I did I was remembered and I felt very welcome.

Group Outcomes

To work successfully with older adults, one must take into account the basic limitations in their resources for change yet not adopt a fatalistic attitude that will only reinforce their sense of hopelessness. Had my coleader and I expected to bring about dramatic personality changes, we would soon have been frustrated. The changes that occurred were small and came slowly. Instead, we expected to have only a modest impact, and so the subtle changes that took place were enough to give us the incentive and energy to continue. Here are some of the outcomes we observed:

- Members realized that they were not alone in experiencing problems.
- People in the group felt an acceptance of their feelings and realized that they had a right to express them.
- The group atmosphere became one of trust, caring, and friendliness.
- The members continued the socializing that had begun in the group outside group sessions.
- The members learned one another's names, which contributed to increased interaction on the ward.
- Participants engaged in activities that stimulated them rather than merely waiting for their release.
- The members began to talk more personally about their sorrows, losses, hopes, joys, memories, fears, regrets, and so on, saying that it felt good to be listened to and to talk.
- Staff members became involved in thinking of appropriate activities for different members and helped the members carry them out.

My coleader and I also encountered some frustrating circumstances during the course of the group. For instance, the members occasionally seemed lethargic. We later discovered that this occurred when the participants had received medication just before the group session. Still, it was difficult to discern whether a member's condition was due to the medication or to psychological factors. It was not uncommon to find a member functioning well one week and feeling good about herself and then to discover, the next week, that she had had a psychotic episode and was unable to respond to anyone.

Some small changes that occurred in the group sessions were undone by the routine of residential life. Some of the members resisted making their life on the unit more pleasant for fear of giving the impression that their stay would be a long one. It was as though they were saying, "If I communicate that I like it here, you might not let me go." Other members resigned themselves to institutional life and saw the facility as their home, expressing very directly that they did not want to leave.

Working with older adults can be very rewarding, but it also can be draining and demanding. Sometimes I felt depressed, hopeless, and angry. These feelings were seldom directly connected with my activities with the patients; the smallest changes I observed in them were rewarding and gave me an incentive to go on. I felt annoyed when I saw student psychiatric technicians or other staff members show disrespect for the patients. These students often called an elderly person by his or her first name yet insisted that they themselves be addressed by their surname. Occasionally, an agitated patient would be restrained physically or with medication without ever being asked what had made him or her so upset in the first place. Another upsetting sight was a patient in a wheelchair being pushed around and not being told where he or she was going.

Sometimes the behavior of patients was treated as crazy when in reality there was a good reason for it that could have been discovered if anybody had tried. One day a student brought a blind person to the meeting, and the blind man proceeded to take off his shoes. The student shouted at him to put them back on. I approached Mr. W. and kneeled in front of him. "Mr. W., you are taking your shoes off in our group session," I said, "How come?" He apologized, saying he thought he was being taken to the physical therapy room.

In another case, a 75-year-old patient kept taking his shoes off all day long, always gathering up newspaper to put around his feet. Everyone considered this behavior bizarre. I remembered that during my childhood in Germany I was often told in the winter to put newspaper into my shoes to keep my feet warm. After spending some time with this man, I found that this "strange" behavior was based on the same experience. I learned to be careful not to judge a patient as bizarre or delusional too quickly but rather to take the time to find out whether there was a logical reason for a peculiar behavior.

Patients were sometimes discouraged or made to feel shameful when they physically expressed affection for another member on the unit. Sensuality was perceived by the staff as bad because of "what it could lead to." I had several very good discussions with staff members about our attitudes toward the sexuality of the aged. By dealing with our own attitudes, misperceptions, and fears, we were able to be more understanding and helpful to the patients.

Points to Remember

Groups in Community Settings

Groups Designed for Community Settings

- In any kind of group for adults it is essential to be sensitive to diversity. Techniques should be appropriate for the life experiences of the members and should not be forced on members.
- A good understanding of the social, cultural, and spiritual backgrounds of your members will enable you to work with their concerns in a sensitive way.
- Groups can help adults integrate current life changes into an overall developmental perspective. In such a group the members can be encouraged to reflect on who they are, where they have been, and to identify future goals.
- Domestic violence groups and groups for people who abuse substances are increasing in prominence. Conducting such groups demands a great deal of patience and competence in dealing with difficult, often involuntary clients.
- Group workers will increasingly be challenged to develop programs to help older adults find meaning in their lives and be productive after retirement.
- Group counselors often encounter obstacles in their attempts to organize and conduct groups for older adults. Some of the barriers are due to the unique characteristics of this population, yet other obstacles are found within the system that does not support group work for older adults.
- Groups offer unique advantages for older people who have a great need to be listened to and understood. The group process encourages sharing and relating, which has a therapeutic value for the older person.

Exercises

In-Class Activities

1. **Critique Group Proposals.** After reading the various proposals for groups with adults in this chapter, which specific proposal most captures your interest? Form small discussion groups in class to analyze and critique the special types of groups for adults and older adults that are described in this chapter. As you look at each group proposal, discuss what features you find to be the most innovative, interesting, and useful. If you were going to design a similar group, what changes might you want to make from the proposal? What are you learning about designing a particular group from studying these proposals?
2. **A Group for Women.** Review the women's support group for survivors of incest described in this chapter. What do you see as the unique therapeutic factors that can promote healing in this kind of group?
3. **A Group for Men.** Review the men's group in a community agency. Would you be inclined to join this group? Why or why not?
4. **A Substance Use Disorder Group**. Review the substance use disorder group proposal. What are some unique features of this group that most interest you? If you were asked to design and facilitate a group for people with substance abuse problems, how useful would this proposal be to you?

5. **Groups in a Community Agency.** If you worked in a community agency and were asked to organize a group for either women or men, what steps would you take in designing a men's or a women's group? Assume that you were expected to form a psychoeducational group. What topics would you build into your group with either men or women?
6. **Organizing a Group for Healthy Older People.** Review the description given of the successful aging group. What did you learn from reading this proposal? If you were asked to form a group for healthy aging people in a community center, what steps would you take to organize this group and to get members? What are some things you would want to tell potential members about this particular group?
7. **Organizing a Bereavement Group.** Review the description given of a bereavement group. What are the main elements that account for the therapeutic value of grief work? What are some advantages of using a group format for dealing with loss with older adults? If you were to form a similar group, what changes might you make in organizing and conducting such a group? What challenges do you expect to face in conducting this kind of group?
8. **Techniques for Institutional Groups.** Review the group proposal for institutionalized older people described in this chapter. What specific techniques and exercises do you think are most useful with this particular group?
9. **Community Groups for Older People.** Assume you are doing an internship or are employed in a community mental health center and have been asked to develop strategies for reaching and serving the needs of older people in the community. What steps would you take in assessing community needs and developing appropriate group programs? What kinds of personal issues might either help or hinder you in being able to effectively facilitate a group for older people?

MindTap for Counseling

Additional resources can be found on CengageBrain.com and by logging into the MindTap course created by your professor. There you will find a variety of study tools and useful resources that include quizzes, videos, interactive exercises, and more.

REFERENCES AND SUGGESTED READINGS

*An asterisk before an entry indicates a source that we recommend as supplementary reading. (This list contains both references cited within the text and suggested readings).

Akos, P., Hamm, J.V., Mack, S. G., & Dunaway, M. (2007). Utilizing the developmental influence of peers in middle school groups. *Journal for Specialists in Group Work, 32*(1), 51–60.

American Counseling Association. (2014). *ACA code of ethics.* Alexandria, VA: Author.

American Group Psychotherapy Association. (2002). *AGPA and NRCGP guidelines for ethics.* Retrieved from http://www.groupsinc.org/group/ethicalguide.html

American Group Psychotherapy Association. (2007). *Practice guidelines for group psychotherapy.* New York, NY: Author.

American Psychological Association. (2003). Guidelines on multicultural education, training, research, practice, and organizational change for psychologists. *American Psychologist, 58*(5), 377–402.

American Psychological Association. (2010). *Ethical principles of psychologists and code of conduct* (2002, amended June 1, 2010). Retrieved from http://www.apa.org/ethics/code/index.aspx

American Psychological Association. Division 44. (2000). Guidelines for psychotherapy with lesbian, gay, and bisexual clients. *American Psychologist, 55*(12), 1440–1451.

American School Counselors Association. (2010). *Ethical standards for school counselors.* Alexandria, VA: Author.

Anderson, D. (2007). Multicultural group work: A force for developing and healing. *Journal for Specialists in Group Work, 32*(3), 224–244.

APA Presidential Task Force on Evidence-Based Practice. (2006). Evidence-based practice in psychology. *American Psychologist, 61*(4), 271–285.

APA Working Group on the Older Adult. (1998). What practitioners should know about working with older adults. *Professional Psychology: Research and Practice, 29,* 413–427.

Arredondo, P., Toporek, R., Brown, S. P., Jones, J., Locke, D. C., Sanchez, J., & Stadler, H. (1996). Operationalization of the multicultural counseling competencies. *Journal of Multicultural Counseling and Development, 24*(1), 42–78.

*Ashby, J. S., Kottman, T., & DeGraaf, D. (2008). *Active interventions for kids and teens: Adding adventure and fun to counseling!* Alexandria, VA: American Counseling Association.

Association for Lesbian, Gay, Bisexual and Transgender Issues in Counseling. (2008). *Competencies for counseling gay, lesbian, bisexual and transgendered (GLBT) clients.* Retrieved from www.algbtic.org/resources/competencies.html

Association for Multicultural Counseling and Development. (2015). *Multicultural and social justice counseling competencies.* Alexandria, VA: American Counseling Association.

Association for Play Therapy. (2008). *Welcome to the Association for Play Therapy!* Retrieved from http://www.a4pt.org

Association for Specialists in Group Work. (1999). Principles for diversity-competent group workers. *Journal for Specialists in Group Work, 24*(1), 7–14. Retrieved from http://www.asgw.org/diversity.htm

Association for Specialists in Group Work. (2000). Professional standards for the training of group workers. *Group Worker, 29*(3), 1–10. Retrieved from http://www.asgw.org/training_standards.htm

Association for Specialists in Group Work. (2008). Best practice guidelines. *Journal for Specialists in Group Work, 33*(2), 111–117. Retrieved from http://www.asgw.org/pdf/Best_Practices.pdf

Association for Specialists in Group Work. (2012). *Multicultural and social justice competence principles for group workers.* Retrieved from http://www.asgw.org/

Badenoch, B. (2008). *Being a brain-wise therapist: A practical guide to interpersonal neurobiology.* New York, NY: Norton.

Baker, E. K. (2003). *Caring for ourselves: A therapist's guide to personal and professional well-being.* Washington, DC: American Psychological Association.

Barlow, S. H. (2008). Group psychotherapy specialty practice. *Professional Psychology: Research and Practice, 39*(2), 240–244.

REFERENCES AND SUGGESTED READINGS

Barlow, S. H., Fuhriman, A. J., & Burlingame, G. M. (2004). The history of group counseling and psychotherapy. In J. L. DeLucia-Waack, D. Gerrity, C. R. Kalodner, & M. T. Riva (Eds.), *Handbook of group counseling and psychotherapy* (pp. 3–22). Thousand Oaks, CA: Sage.

Barnett, J. E., Wise, E. H., Johnson-Greene, D., & Bucky, S. F. (2007). Informed consent: Too much of a good thing or not enough? *Professional Psychology: Research and Practice, 38*(2), 179–186.

*Bauman, S., & Shaw, L. R. (2016). *Group work with persons with disabilities*. Alexandria, VA: American Counseling Association.

*Bauman, S., & Steen, S. (2009). *DVD celebrating cultural diversity: A group for fifth graders*. Alexandria, VA: ASGW (A Division of the American Counseling Association).

*Bauman, S., & Steen, S. (2012). *DVD celebrating diversity: Leading multicultural groups for middle school students*. Tucson, AZ: Sierra Moon Productions.

*Beck, J. S. (2005). *Cognitive therapy for challenging problems: What to do when the basics don't work*. New York, NY: Guilford Press.

*Beck, J. S. (2011). *Cognitive behavior therapy: Basics and beyond* (2nd ed.). New York: Guilford Press.

Bemak, F., & Chung, R. (2014). Post-disaster group counseling: A multicultural perspective. In J. DeLucia-Waack, C. R. Kalodner, & M. T. Riva (Eds.), *Handbook of group counseling and psychotherapy* (2nd ed., pp. 571–584). Thousand Oaks, CA: Sage.

Bennett, B. E., Bricklin, P. M., Harris, E., Knapp, S., VandeCreek, L., & Younggren, J. N. (2006). *Assessing and managing risk in psychological practice: An individualized approach*. Rockville, MD: The Trust.

Berg, R. C., Landreth, G. L., & Fall, K. A. (2013). *Group counseling: Concepts and procedures* (5th ed.). New York, NY: Routledge (Taylor & Francis).

*Bertram, B. (2011). Ethics and legal issues for group work. In T. Fitch & J. L. Marshall (Eds.), *Group work and outreach plans for college counselors* (pp. 9–17). Alexandria, VA: American Counseling Association.

*Bieling, P. J., McCabe, R. E., & Antony, M. M. (2006). *Cognitive-behavioral therapy in groups*. New York, NY: Guilford Press.

Bieschke, R. M., Perez, K. A., & DeBord, K. A. (Eds.). (2006). *The handbook of counseling and psychotherapy with lesbian, gay, bisexual, and transgender clients*. Washington, DC: American Psychological Association.

*Blatner, A. (1996). *Acting-in: Practical applications of psychodramatic methods* (3rd ed.). New York, NY: Springer.

*Blatner, A. (2000). *Foundations of psychodrama: History, theory, and practice* (4th ed.). New York, NY: Springer.

Briere, J. (1996). *Therapy for adults molested as children: Beyond survival*. New York, NY: Springer.

*Brown, L. S. (2010). *Feminist therapy*. Washington, DC: American Psychological Association.

Burlingame, G. M., & Fuhriman, A. (1990). Time-limited group therapy. *Counseling Psychologist, 18*(1), 93–118.

Burlingame, G. M., Fuhriman, A. J., & Johnson, J. (2002). Cohesion in group psychotherapy. In J. C. Norcross (Ed.), *A guide to psychotherapy relationships that work*. Oxford, England: Oxford University Press.

Burlingame, G. M., Fuhriman, A. J., & Johnson, J. (2004a). Current status and future directions of group therapy research. In J. L. DeLucia-Waack, D. Gerrity, C. R. Kalodner, & M. T. Riva (Eds.), *Handbook of group counseling and psychotherapy* (pp. 651–660). Thousand Oaks, CA: Sage.

Burlingame, G. M., Fuhriman, A. J., & Johnson, J. (2004b). Process and outcome in group counseling and psychotherapy: A perspective. In J. L. DeLucia-Waack, D. Gerrity, C. R. Kalodner, & M. T. Riva (Eds.), *Handbook of group counseling and psychotherapy* (pp. 49–61). Thousand Oaks, CA: Sage.

Burlingame, G. M., MacKenzie, K. R., & Strauss, B. (2004). Small group treatment: Evidence for effectiveness and mechanisms of change. In M. Lambert (Ed.), *Bergin & Garfield's handbook of psychotherapy and behavior change* (5th ed., pp. 647–696). New York, NY: Wiley.

Burlingame, G. M., Whitcomb, K., & Woodland, S. (2014). Process and outcome in group counseling and psychotherapy: A perspective. In J. DeLucia-Waack, C. R. Kalodner, & M. T. Riva (Eds.), *Handbook of group counseling and psychotherapy* (2nd ed., pp. 55–67). Thousand Oaks, CA: Sage.

*Cain, D. J. (2010). *Person-centered psychotherapies*. Washington, DC: American Psychological Association.

*Cain, D. J., Keenan, K., & Rubin, S. (Eds.). (2016). *Humanistic psychotherapies: Handbook of research and practice* (2nd ed.). Washington, DC: American Psychological Association.

Capuzzi, D. (2003). *Approaches to group work: A handbook for group practitioners*. Upper Saddle River, NJ: Merrill/Prentice-Hall.

Capuzzi, D., & Stauffer, M. D. (2016). *Counseling and psychotherapy: Theories and interventions* (6th ed.). Alexandria, VA: American Counseling Association.

Cardemil, E. V., & Battle, C. L. (2003). Guess who's coming to therapy? Getting comfortable with conversations about race and ethnicity in psychotherapy. *Professional Psychology: Research and Practice, 34*(3), 278–286.

Carlson, R. G., Barden, S. M., Daire, A. P., & Greene, J. (2014). Influence of relationship education on relationship satisfaction for low-income couples. *Journal of Counseling and Development, 92*(4), 418–427.

Carter, S. (1998). *Combating teen delinquency in an apartment setting through village building*. Los Angeles, CA: South Central Training Consortium, Inc.

*Cashwell, C. S., & Young, J. S. (Eds.). (2011). *Integrating spirituality and religion into counseling: A guide to competent practice* (2nd ed.). Alexandria, VA: American Counseling Association.

Christensen, T. M., Hulse-Killacky, D., Salgado, R. A., Thornton, M. D., & Miller, J. L. (2006). Facilitating reminiscence groups: Perceptions of group leaders. *Journal for Specialists in Group Work, 31*(1), 73–88.

Christensen, T. M., & Kline, W. B. (2000). A qualitative investigation of the process of group supervision with group counselors. *Journal for Specialists in Group Work, 25*(4), 376–393.

*Chung, R. C., & Bemak, F. P. (2012). *Social justice counseling: The next steps beyond multiculturalism*. Thousand Oaks, CA: Sage.

Chung, R. C., & Bemak, F. (2014). Group counseling with Asians. In J. DeLucia-Waack, C. R. Kalodner, & M. T. Riva (Eds.), *Handbook of group counseling and psychotherapy* (2nd ed., pp. 231–241). Thousand Oaks, CA: Sage.

Corey, G. (2013a). *The art of integrative counseling* (3rd ed.). Belmont, CA: Brooks/Cole, Cengage Learning.

Corey, G. (2013b). *Case approach to counseling and psychotherapy* (8th ed.). Belmont, CA: Brooks/Cole, Cengage Learning.

Corey, G. (2015). Combining didactic and experiential approaches to teaching a group counseling course. In B. Herlihy & G. Corey, *Boundary issues in counseling: Multiple roles and responsibilities* (3rd ed., pp. 177–183). Alexandria, VA: American Counseling Association.

*Corey, G. (2016). *Theory and practice of group counseling* (9th ed.) and *Manual*. Boston, MA: Cengage Learning.

*Corey, G. (2017). *Theory and practice of counseling and psychotherapy* (10th ed.) and *Manual*. Boston, MA: Cengage Learning.

*Corey, G., & Corey, M. (2016). Group psychotherapy (Chapter 15, pp. 289–306). In J. Norcross, G. R. VandenBos, & D. K. Freedheim (Eds.). *APA Handbook of Clinical Psychology* (Volume 3, Application and Methods). Washington, DC: American Psychological Association.

Corey, G., Corey, M., Corey, C., & Callanan, P. (2015). *Issues and ethics in the helping professions* (9th ed.). Belmont, CA: Cengage Learning.

*Corey, G., Corey, M., Callanan, P., & Russell, J. M. (2015). *Group techniques* (4th ed.). Boston, MA: Cengage Learning.

*Corey, G., Corey, M. S., & Haynes, R. (2014). *Groups in action: Evolution and challenges, DVD and workbook* (2nd ed.). Belmont, CA: Brooks/Cole, Cengage Learning.

*Corey, G., Corey, M., & Muratori, M. (2018). *I never knew I had a choice* (11th ed.). Boston, MA: Cengage Learning.

*Corey, M., & Corey, G. (2016). *Becoming a helper* (7th ed.). Boston, MA: Cengage Learning.

Cornish, M. A., & Wade, N. G. (2010). Spirituality and religion in group counseling: A literature review with practice guidelines. *Professional Psychology: Research and Practice, 41*(5), 398–404.

Council for Accreditation of Counseling and Related Educational Programs. (2016). Council for Accreditation of Counseling and Related Educational Programs (CACREP) 2016 standards. Retrieved from http://www.cacrep.org/wp-content/uploads/2015/05/2016-CACREP-Standards.pdf

REFERENCES AND SUGGESTED READINGS

*Courtois, C. A. (2010). *Healing the incest wound: Adult survivors in therapy* (2nd ed.). New York, NY: Norton.

*Curtis, R. C., & Hirsch, I. (2011). Relational psychoanalytic psychotherapy. In S. B. Messer & A. S. Gurman (Eds.), *Essential psychotherapies: Theory and practice* (3rd ed., pp. 72–104). New York, NY: Guilford Press.

de Shazer, S. (1984). The death of resistance. *Family Process, 23*, 79–93.

Debiak, D. (2007). Attending to diversity in group psychotherapy: An ethical imperative. *International Journal of Group Psychotherapy, 57*(1), 1–12.

DeLucia-Waack, J. L. (2001). *Using music in children of divorce groups: A session-by-session manual for counselors.* Alexandria, VA: American Counseling Association.

DeLucia-Waack, J. L. (2006a). Closing: Thanking others. In J. L. DeLucia-Waack, K. H. Bridbord, J. S. Kleiner, & Nitza, A. (Eds.), *Group work experts share their favorite activities: A guide to choosing, planning, conducting, and processing* (Rev. ed., pp. 159–161). Alexandria, VA: Association for Specialists in Group Work.

DeLucia-Waack, J. L. (2006b). Closing: What have we learned about ourselves? In J. L. DeLucia-Waack, K. H. Bridbord, J. S. Kleiner, & A. G. Nitza (Eds.), *Group work experts share their favorite activities: A guide to choosing, planning, conducting, and processing* (Rev. ed., pp. 152–154). Alexandria, VA: Association for Specialists in Group Work.

DeLucia-Waack, J. L. (2006c). *Leading psychoeducational groups for children and adolescents.* Thousand Oaks, CA: Sage.

DeLucia-Waack, J. L (2010). Diversity in groups. In R. K. Conyne (Ed.), *The Oxford handbook of group counseling* (pp. 83–101). New York, NY: Oxford University Press.

DeLucia-Waack, J. L. (2011). Children of divorce groups. In G. Greif & P. Ephross (Eds.), *Group work with at-risk populations* (3rd ed., pp. 93–114). New York, NY: Oxford University Press.

DeLucia-Waack, J. L. (2014). Introduction to multicultural and diverse counseling and psychotherapy groups. In J. L. DeLucia-Waack, D. Kalodner, & M. T. Riva (Eds.), *Handbook of group counseling and psychotherapy* (2nd ed., pp. 193–195). Thousand Oaks, CA: Sage.

*DeLucia-Waack, J. L., Bridbord, K. H., Kleiner, J. S., & Nitza, A. (Eds.). (2006). *Group work experts share their favorite activities: A guide to choosing, planning, conducting, and processing* (Rev. ed.). Alexandria, VA: Association for Specialists in Group Work.

DeLucia-Waack, J. L., & Donigian, J. (2004). *The practice of multicultural group work: Visions and perspectives from the field.* Belmont, CA: Brooks/Cole, Cengage Learning.

*DeLucia-Waack, J. L., Kalodner, C. R., & Riva, M. T. (Eds.). (2014). *Handbook of group counseling and psychotherapy* (2nd ed.). Thousand Oaks, CA: Sage.

*DeLucia-Waack, J. L., Segrist, A., & Horne, A. M. (2007). *DVD leading groups with adolescents.* Alexandria, VA: ASGW (A Division of the American Counseling Association).

Dies, R. R. (1994). Therapist variable in group psychotherapy research. In A. Fuhriman & G. M. Burlingame (Eds.), *Handbook of group psychotherapy: An empirical and clinical synthesis* (pp. 114–154). New York: Wiley.

Drum, D., Becker, M. S., & Hess, E. (2011). Expanding the application of group interventions: Emergence of groups in health care settings. *Journal for Specialists in Group Work, 36*(4), 247–263.

*Duncan, B. L., Miller, S. D., & Sparks, J. A. (2004). *The heroic client: A revolutionary way to improve effectiveness through client-directed, outcome-informed therapy* (Rev. ed.). San Francisco, CA: Jossey-Bass.

*Duncan, B. L., Miller, S. D., Wampold, B. E., & Hubble, M. A. (Eds.). (2010). *The heart and soul of change: Delivering what works in therapy* (2nd ed.). Washington DC: American Psychological Association.

*Dworkin, S. H., & Pope, M. (Eds.). (2012). *Casebook for counseling lesbian, gay, bisexual, and transgender persons and their families.* Alexandria, VA: American Counseling Association.

Edleson, J. L., & Tolman, R. M. (1994). Group intervention strategies for men who batter. *Directions in Mental Health Counseling, 4*(7), 3–16.

*Elkins, D. N. (2016). *Elements of psychotherapy: A nonmedical model of emotional healing.* Washington, DC: American Psychological Association.

*Ellis, A., & Ellis, D. J. (2011). *Rational emotive behavior therapy*. Washington, DC: American Psychological Association.

Englar-Carlson, M. (2014, November 8). *Deepening group work with men*. Presentation at Western Association for Counselor Education and Supervision conference, Anaheim, CA.

Englar-Carlson, M., & Kisalica, M. S. (2013). Affirming the strengths in men: A positive masculinity approach to assisting male clients. *Journal of Counseling & Development, 91*(4), 399–409.

*Enns, C. Z. (2004). *Feminist theories and feminist psychotherapies: Origins, themes, and diversity* (2nd ed.). New York, NY: Haworth.

Erber, J., Szuchman, L. T., & Rothberg, S. T. (1990). Everyday memory failure: Age differences in appraisal and attribution. *Psychology and Aging, 5*(2), 236–241.

Erber, J., Szuchman, L. T., & Rothberg, S. T. (1991). Age, gender, and individual differences in memory failure appraisal. *Psychology and Aging, 5*(4), 600–603.

*Evans, K. M., Kincade, E. A., & Seem, S. R. (2011). *Introduction to feminist therapy: Strategies for social and individual change*. Thousand Oaks, CA: Sage.

Evans, S., & Garner, J. (Eds.). (2004). *Talking over the years: A handbook of dynamic psychotherapy with older adults*. New York, NY: Bruner-Routledge.

Falco, L. D., & Bauman, S. (2014). Group work in schools. In J. L. DeLucia-Waack, C. R. Kalodner, & M. T. Riva (Eds.), *Handbook of group counseling and psychotherapy* (2nd ed., pp. 318–328). Thousand Oaks, CA: Sage.

Fallon, A. (2006). Informed consent in the practice of group psychotherapy. *International Journal of Group Psychotherapy, 56*(4), 431–453.

*Feder, B. (2006). *Gestalt group therapy: A practical guide*. Metairie/New Orleans, LA: Gestalt Institute Press.

*Feder, B., & Frew, J. (Eds.). (2008). *Beyond the hot seat revisited: Gestalt approaches to groups*. Metairie/New Orleans, LA: Gestalt Institute Press.

Fitch, T., & Marshall, J. L. (Eds.). (2011). *Group work and outreach plans for college counselors*. Alexandria, VA: American Counseling Association.

Fitzgerald, H. (1994). *The mourning handbook*. New York, NY: Simon & Schuster.

Flahive, M. W., & Ray, D. (2007). Effect of group sandtray therapy with preadolescents. *Journal for Specialists in Group Work, 32*(4), 362–382.

Fosha, D., Siegel, D., & Solomon, M. (Eds.). (2009). *The healing power of emotion: Affective neuroscience, development & clinical practice*. New York, NY: Norton.

*Foss, L. L., Green, J., Wolfe-Stiltner, K., & DeLucia-Waack, J. L. (Eds.). (2008). *School counselors share their favorite group activities: A guide to choosing, planning, conducting, and processing*. Alexandria, VA: Association for Specialists in Group Work.

Francis, P. C., & Dugger, S. M. (2014). Professionalism, ethics, and value-based conflicts in counseling: An introduction to the special section [Special section]. *Journal of Counseling & Development 92*(2), 131–134.

Freeman, S. J. (2005). *Grief and loss: Understanding the journey*. Belmont, CA: Brooks/Cole, Cengage Learning.

Frew, J., & Spiegler, M. (Eds.). (2013). *Contemporary psychotherapies for a diverse world*. New York, NY: Routledge (Taylor & Francis).

Fuhriman, A., & Burlingame, G. M. (1990). Consistency of matter: A comparative analysis of individual and group process variables. *Counseling Psychologist, 18*(1), 6–63.

Fuhriman, A., & Burlingame, G. M. (1994). Group psychotherapy: Research and practice. In A. Fuhriman & G. M. Burlingame (Eds.), *Handbook of group psychotherapy: An empirical and clinical synthesis* (pp. 3–40). New York, NY: Wiley.

Gerrity, D. A. (2014). Groups for survivors of childhood sexual abuse. In J. L. DeLucia-Waack, D. Kalodner, & M. T. Riva (Eds.), *Handbook of group counseling and psychotherapy* (2nd ed., pp. 463–473). Thousand Oaks, CA: Sage.

Giannone, F., Giordano, C., & Di Blasé, M. (2015). Group psychotherapy in Italy. *International Journal of Group Psychotherapy, 65*(4), 501–511.

Gil, E. (1991). *The healing power of play: Work with abused children*. New York, NY: Guilford Press.

Gil, E. (2006). *Helping abused and traumatized children: Integrating directive and nondirective approaches*. New York, NY: Guilford Press.

REFERENCES AND SUGGESTED READINGS

Gil, E. (2010). *Working with children to heal interpersonal trauma: The power of play*. New York, NY: Guilford Press.

Gladding, S. (2012). *Group work: A counseling specialty* (6th ed.). Upper Saddle River, NJ: Pearson.

*Gladding, S. T. (2016). *The creative arts in counseling* (5th ed.). Alexandria, VA: American Counseling Association.

Goodrich, K. M. (2008). Dual relationships in group training. *Journal for Specialists in Group Work, 33*(3), 221–235.

Goodrich, K. M., & Luke, M. (2012). Problematic students in the experiential group: Professional and ethical challenges for counselor educators. *Journal for Specialists in Group Work, 37*, 326–346.

*Goodrich, K. M., & Luke, M. (2015). *Group counseling with LGBTQI persons*. Alexandria, VA: American Counseling Association.

Green, E. J. (2014). *The handbook of Jungian play therapy with children and adolescents*. Baltimore, MD: Johns Hopkins University Press.

Hage, S. M., Mason, M., & Kim, J. (2010). A social justice approach to group counseling. In R. K. Conyne (Ed.), *The Oxford handbook of group counseling* (pp. 102–117). New York, NY: Oxford University Press.

Halstead, R. W., Pehrsson, D., & Mullen J. A. (2011). *Counseling children: Core issues approach*. Alexandria, VA: American Counseling Association.

Hayes, J. A., Gelso, C. J., & Hummel, A. M. (2011). Management of countertransference. In J. C. Norcross (Ed.), *Psychotherapy relationships that work: Evidence-based responsiveness* (2nd ed., pp. 239–258). New York, NY: Oxford University Press.

Hays, D. G., Arredondo, P., Gladding, S. T., & Toporek, R. L. (2010). Integrating social justice in group work: The next decade. *Journal for Specialists in Group Work, 35*(2), 177–206.

*Hedtke, L., & Winslade, J. (2004). *Re-membering conversations: Conversations with the dying and bereaved*. Amityville, NY: Baywood.

*Herlihy, B., & Corey, G. (2015a). *ACA ethical standards casebook* (7th ed.). Alexandria, VA: American Counseling Association.

*Herlihy, B., & Corey, G. (2015b). *Boundary issues in counseling: Multiple roles and relationships* (3rd ed.). Alexandria, VA: American Counseling Association.

Herman, J. (1992). *Trauma and recovery*. New York, NY: Basic Books.

Herman, J., & Schatzow, E. (1984). Time-limited group therapy for women with a history of incest. *International Journal of Group Psychotherapy, 35*(4), 605–616.

Hindman, J. (1993). *A touching book: ... for little people and for big people*. Ontario, OR: AlexAndria Assoc.

*Hubble, M. A., Duncan, B. L., Miller, S. D., & Wampold, B. E. (2010). Introduction. In B. L. Duncan, S. D. Miller, B. E. Wampold, & M. A. Hubble (Eds.), *The heart and soul of change: Delivering what works in therapy* (2nd ed., pp. 23–46). Washington, DC: American Psychological Association.

Hulse-Killacky, D., Killacky, J., & Donigian, J. (2001). *Making task groups work in your world*. Upper Saddle River, NJ: Merrill/Prentice-Hall.

Hulse-Killacky, D., Orr, J. J., & Paradise, L. V. (2006). The corrective feedback instrument–revised. *Journal for Specialists in Group Work, 31*(3), 263–281.

Ibrahim, F. A. (2010). Social justice and cultural responsiveness: Innovative teaching strategies for group work. *Journal for Specialists in Group Work, 35*(3), 271–280.

Ieva, K. P., Ohrt, J. H., Swank, J. M., & Young, T. (2009). The impact of experiential groups on master's students counselor and personal development: A qualitative investigation. *Journal for Specialists in Group Work, 34*(4), 351–368.

International Journal of Group Psychotherapy. (2015). Special issue on group therapy around the world. *International Journal of Group Psychotherapy, 65*(4), 483–646.

Ivey, A. E., Pedersen, P. B., & Ivey, M. B. (2008). *Group microskills: Culture-centered group process and strategies*. Hanover, MA: Microtraining Associates.

Jackson, T. (2012). *Dreamchild adventures in relaxation and sleep*. Idyllwild, CA: Circadian.

Jacobs, E. E., Schimmel, C. J., Masson, R. L., & Harvill, R. L. (2016). *Group counseling: Strategies and skills* (8th ed.). Boston, MA: Cengage Learning.

James, J. W., & Friedman, R. (1998). *The grief recovery handbook*. New York, NY: HarperCollins.

Jensen, D. R., Abbott, M. K., Beecher, M. E., Griner, D., Golightly, T. R., & Cannon, J. A. N. (2012). Taking the pulse of the group: The utilization of practice-based evidence in group psychotherapy. *Professional Psychology: Research and Practice, 43*(4), 388–394.

Joyce, A. S., Piper, W. E., & Orgrodniczuk, J. S. (2007). Therapeutic alliance and cohesion variables as predictors of outcome of short-term group psychotherapy. *International Journal of Group Psychotherapy, 57*, 269–296.

Joyce, A. S., Piper, W. E., Orgrodniczuk, J. S., & Klein, R. H. (2007). *Termination in psychotherapy: A psychodynamic model of processes and outcomes*. Washington, DC: American Psychological Association Press.

Kampfe, C. M. (2015). *Counseling older people: Opportunities and challenges*. Alexandria, VA: American Counseling Association.

Kees, N., & Leech, N. (2014). Women's groups: Research and practice trends. In J. DeLucia-Waack, C. R. Kalodner, & M. T. Riva (Eds.), *Handbook of group counseling and psychotherapy* (2nd ed., pp. 506–520). Thousand Oaks, CA: Sage.

Kennedy, P. F., Vandehey, M., Norman, W. B., & Diekhoff, G. M. (2003). Recommendations for risk-management practices. *Professional Psychology: Research and Practice, 34*(3), 309–311.

*Kirschenbaum, H. (2009). *The life and work of Carl Rogers*. Alexandria, VA: American Counseling Association.

Kiselica, M. S., & Englar-Carlson, M. (2010). Identifying, affirming, and building upon male strengths: The positive psychology/positive masculinity model of psychotherapy with boys and men. *Psychotherapy: Theory, Research, Practice, Training. 47*(3) 276–287.

Kiselica, A. M., & Kiselica, M. S. (2014). Gender-sensitive group counseling and psychotherapy with men. In J. DeLucia-Waack, C. R. Kalodner, & M. T. Riva (Eds.), *Handbook of group counseling and psychotherapy* (2nd ed., pp. 521–530). Thousand Oaks, CA: Sage.

Kleven, S. (1997). *The right touch: A read-aloud story to help prevent child abuse*. Bellevue, WA: Illumination Arts.

Knauss, L. K. (2006). Ethical issues in recordkeeping in group psychotherapy. *International Journal of Group Psychotherapy, 56*(4), 415–430.

Kocet, M. M., & Herlihy, B. J. (2014). Addressing value-based conflicts within the counseling relationship: A decision-making model. *Journal of Counseling & Development, 92*(2), 180–186.

Kottler, J. A., & Englar-Carlson, M. (2015). *Learning group leadership: An experiential approach* (3rd ed.). Thousand Oaks, CA: Sage.

*Kottman, T. (2011). *Play therapy: Basics and beyond* (2nd ed.). Alexandria, VA: American Counseling Association.

Kottman, T., & Meany-Walen, K. (2016). *Partners in play: An Adlerian approach to play therapy* (3rd ed.). Alexandria, VA: American Counseling Association.

Lambert, M. J. (2011). Psychotherapy research and its achievements. In J. C. Norcross, G. R. Vandenbos, & D. K. Freedheim (Eds.), *History of psychotherapy* (2nd ed., pp. 299–332). Washington, DC: American Psychological Association.

Landreth, G. L. (2002). *Play therapy and the art of the relationship* (2nd ed.). New York, NY: Brunner-Routledge.

Lasky, G. B., & Riva, M. T. (2006). Confidentiality and privileged communication in group psychotherapy. *International Journal of Group Psychotherapy, 56*(4), 455–476.

Lau, M. A., Ogrodniczuk, J., Joyce, A. S., & Sochting, I. (2010). Bridging the practitioner-scientist gap in group psychotherapy research. *International Journal of Group Psychotherapy, 60*(2), 177–196.

*Ledley, D. R., Marx, B. P., & Heimberg, R. G. (2010). *Making cognitive-behavioral therapy work: Clinical processes for new practitioners* (2nd ed.). New York, NY: Guilford Press.

Lee, M. Y., Sebold, J., & Uken, A. (2003). *Solution-focused treatment of domestic violence offenders: Accountability for change*. New York, NY: Oxford University Press.

Leslie, R. S. (2010). Treatment of minors without parental consent. *Legal Resources, Avoiding Liability Bulletin*.

Retrieved from http://cphins.com/LegalResources/tabid/65/

Levy, B. (1996). Improving memory in old age through implicit self-stereotyping. *Journal of Personality and Social Psychology, 71*(6), 1092–1107.

Lowenstein, L. (1999). *Creative interventions for troubled children and youth.* Toronto, Ontario, Canada: Champion Press.

Lubin, H. (2007). Group and individual therapy for childhood sexual abuse survivors. *International Journal of Group Psychotherapy, 57*(2), 257–262.

Luke, M., & Hackney, H. (2007). Group coleadership: A critical review. *Counselor Education and Supervision, 46*(4), 280–293.

Luke, M., & Kiweewa, J. M. (2010). Personal growth and awareness of counseling trainees in an experiential group. *Journal for Specialists in Group Work, 35*(4), 365–388.

MacNair-Semands, R. R. (2007). Attending to the spirit of social justice as an ethical approach in group therapy. *International Journal of Group Psychotherapy, 57*(1), 61–66.

Mangione, L., Forti, R., & Iacuzzi, C. M. (2007). Ethics and endings in group psychotherapy: Saying good-bye and saying it well. *International Journal of Group Psychotherapy, 57*(1), 25–40.

McCarthy, C. J., Falco, L. D., & Villalba, J. (2014). Ethical and professional issues in experiential growth groups: Moving forward. *Journal for Specialists in Group Work, 39*(3), 186–193.

McCarthy, C. J., & Hart, S. (2011). Designing groups to meet evolving challenges in health care settings. *Journal for Specialists in Group Work, 36*(4), 352–367.

McWhirter, P., & Robbins, R. (2014). Group therapy with Native people. In J. DeLucia-Waack, C. R. Kalodner, & M. T. Riva (Eds.), *Handbook of group counseling and psychotherapy* (2nd ed., pp. 209–219). Thousand Oaks, CA: Sage.

*Metcalf, L. (1998). *Solution-focused group therapy: Ideas for groups in private practice, schools, agencies and treatment programs.* New York, NY: Free Press.

*Miller, S. D., Hubble, M. A., Duncan, B. L., & Wampold, B. E. (2010). Delivering what works. In B. L. Duncan, S. D. Miller, B. E. Wampold, & M. A. Hubble (Eds.), *The heart and soul of change: Delivering what works in therapy* (2nd ed., pp. 421–429). Washington, DC: American Psychological Association.

*Miller, S. D., Hubble, M. A., & Seidel, J. (2015). Feedback-informed treatment. In E. Neukrug (Ed.), *The Sage encyclopedia of theory in counseling and psychotherapy* (Vol. 1, pp. 401–403). Thousand Oaks, CA: Sage.

*Miller, W. R., & Rollnick, S. (2013). *Motivational interviewing: Helping people change* (3rd ed.). New York, NY: Guilford Press.

Morgan, R. D., Romani, C. J., & Gross, N. R. (2014). Group work with offenders and mandated clients. In J. DeLucia-Waack, C. R. Kalodner, & M. T. Riva (Eds.), *Handbook of group counseling and psychotherapy* (2nd ed., pp. 441–449). Thousand Oaks, CA: Sage.

Morran, D. K., Stockton, R., & Whittingham, M. H. (2004). Effective leader interventions for counseling and psychotherapy groups. In J. L. DeLucia-Waack, D. Gerrity, C. R. Kalodner, & M. T. Riva (Eds.), *Handbook of group counseling and psychotherapy* (pp. 91–103). Thousand Oaks, CA: Sage.

Mueser, K. T., Noordsy, D. L., Drake, R. E., & Fox, L. (2003). *Integrated treatment for dual disorders: A guide to effective practice.* New York, NY: Guilford Press.

*Murphy, J. (2015). *Solution-focused counseling in schools* (3rd ed.). Alexandria, VA: American Counseling Association.

Neukrug, E. (2011). *Counseling theory and practice.* Belmont, CA: Brooks/Cole, Cengage Learning.

Norcross, J. C., & Beutler, L. E. (2014). Integrative psychotherapies. In D. Wedding & R. J. Corsini (Eds.), *Current psychotherapies* (10th ed., pp. 499–532). Belmont, CA: Brooks/Cole, Cengage Learning.

*Norcross, J. C., & Guy, J. D. (2007). *Leaving it at the office: A guide to psychotherapist self-care.* New York, NY: Guilford Press.

Norcross, J. C., Krebs, P. M., & Prochaska, J. O. (2011). Stages of change. In J. C. Norcross (Ed.), *Psychotherapy relationships that work: Evidence-based responsiveness* (2nd ed., pp. 279–300). New York, NY: Oxford University Press.

Norcross, J. C., & Lambert, M. J. (2011). Evidence-based therapy relationships. In J. C. Norcross (Ed.), *Psychotherapy relationships that work: Evidence-based responsiveness* (2nd ed., pp. 3–31). New York, NY: Oxford University Press.

O'Hanlon, B. (2003). *A guide to inclusive therapy: 26 methods of respectful, resistance-dissolving therapy*. New York, NY: Norton.

O'Hanlon W. H., & Weiner-Davis, M. (2003). *In search of solutions: A new direction in psychotherapy* (Rev. ed.). New York, NY: Norton.

Ohrt, J. H., Frier, E., Porter, J., & Young, T. (2014). Group leader reflection on their training and experience: Implications for group counselor educators and supervisors. *Journal for Specialists in Group Work, 39*(2), 95–124.

Ohrt, J. H., Prochenko, Y., Stulmaker, H., Huffman, D., Fernando, D., & Swan, K. (2014). An exploration of group and member development in experiential groups. *Journal for Specialists in Group Work, 39*(3), 212–235.

Parcover, J. A., Dunton, E. C., Gehlert, K. M., & Mitchell, S. L. (2006). Getting the most from group counseling in college counseling centers. *Journal for Specialists in Group Work, 31*(1), 37–49.

Piper, W. E., & Ogrodniczuk, J. S. (2004). Brief group therapy. In J. L. DeLucia-Waack, D. Gerrity, C. R. Kalodner, & M. T. Riva (Eds.), *Handbook of group counseling and psychotherapy* (pp. 641–650). Thousand Oaks, CA: Sage.

Polster, E. (1995). *A population of selves: A therapeutic exploration of personal diversity*. San Francisco, CA: Jossey-Bass.

Polster, E., & Polster, M. (1973). *Gestalt therapy integrated.* New York, NY: Brunner/Mazel.

Polster, E., & Polster, M. (1976). Therapy without resistance: Gestalt therapy. In A. Burton (Ed.), *What makes behavior change possible?* New York, NY: Brunner/Mazel.

Pope, M., Pangelinan, J. S., & Coker, A. D. (Eds.). (2011). *Experiential activities for teaching multicultural competence in counseling.* Alexandria, VA: American Counseling Association.

*Prochaska J. O., & Norcross, J. C. (2014). *Systems of psychotherapy: A transtheoretical analysis* (8th ed.). Belmont, CA: Cengage Learning.

Rabinowitz, F. E. (2014). Counseling men in groups. In M. Englar-Carlson, M. P. Evans, & T. Duffey (Eds.), *A counselor's guide to working with men* (pp. 55–70). Alexandria, VA: American Counseling Association.

Rabinowitz, F. E., & Cochran, S. V. (2002). *Deepening psychotherapy with men.* Washington, DC: American Psychological Association.

Rapin, L. S. (2010). Ethics, best practices, and law in group counseling. In R. K. Conyne (Ed.), *The Oxford handbook of group counseling* (pp. 61–82). New York, NY: Oxford University Press.

Rapin, L. S. (2014). Guidelines for ethical and legal practice in counseling and psychotherapy groups. In J. L. DeLucia-Waack, C. R. Kalodner, & M. T. Riva (Eds.), *Handbook of group counseling and psychotherapy* (2nd ed., pp. 71–83). Thousand Oaks, CA: Sage.

Reese, M. K. (2011). Interpersonal process groups in college and university settings. In T. Fitch & J. L. Marshall (Eds.), *Group work and outreach plans for college counselors* (pp. 87–92). Alexandria, VA: American Counseling Association.

Riva, M. T. (2014). Supervision of group leaders. In J. DeLucia-Waack, C. R. Kalodner, & M. T. Riva (Eds.), *Handbook of group counseling and psychotherapy* (2nd ed., pp. 146–158). Thousand Oaks, CA: Sage.

*Rogers, N. (2011). *The creative connection for groups: Person-centered expressive arts for healing and social change.* Palo Alto, CA: Science and Behavior Books.

Rowe, J. W., & Kahn, R. L. (1998). *Successful aging.* New York, NY: Pantheon Books.

*Rutan, J. S., Stone, W. N., & Shay, J. J. (2014). *Psychodynamic group psychotherapy* (5th ed.). New York, NY: Guilford Press.

*Salazar, C. F. (Ed.). (2009). *Group work experts share their favorite multicultural activities: A guide to diversity-competent choosing, planning, conducting, and processing.* Alexandria, VA: Association for Specialists in Group Work.

REFERENCES AND SUGGESTED READINGS

*Schneider, K. J., & Krug, O. T. (2010). *Existential-humanistic therapy*. Washington, DC: American Psychological Association.

Schwartz, J. P., & Waldo, M. (2004). Group work with men who have committed partner abuse. In J. L. DeLucia-Waack, D. Gerrity, C. R. Kalodner, & M. T. Riva (Eds.), *Handbook of group counseling and psychotherapy* (pp. 576–592). Thousand Oaks, CA: Sage.

Shapiro, J. L. (2010). Brief group treatment. In R. K. Conyne (Ed.), *The Oxford handbook of group counseling* (pp. 487–510). New York, NY: Oxford University Press.

Shapiro, J. L., Peltz, L. S., & Bernadett-Shapiro, S. (1998). *Brief group treatment: Practical training for therapists and counselors*. Pacific Grove, CA: Brooks/Cole.

*Sharf, R. S. (2016). *Theories of psychotherapy and counseling: Concepts and cases* (6th ed.). Boston, MA: Cengage Learning.

Shechtman, Z. (2014). Group counseling and psychotherapy with children and adolescents. In J. DeLucia-Waack, C. R. Kalodner, & M. T. Riva (Eds.), *Handbook of group counseling and psychotherapy* (2nd ed., pp. 585–596). Thousand Oaks, CA: Sage.

Shumaker, D., Ortiz, C., & Brenninkmeyer, L. (2011). Revisiting experiential group training in counselor education: A survey of master's-level programs. *Journal for Specialists in Group Work, 36*(2), 111–128.

Siegel, D. (2010). *The mindful therapist*. New York, NY: Norton.

Siegel, R. D. (2010). *The mindfulness solution: Everyday practices for everyday problems*. New York, NY: Guilford Press.

Singh, A. A., & Salazar, C. F. (2010a). Process in action in social justice group work practice, training, and supervision: Introduction to the second special issue. *Journal for Specialists in Group Work, 35*(3), 209–211.

Singh, A. A., & Salazar, C. F. (2010b). The roots of social justice in group work. *Journal for Specialists in Group Work, 35*(2), 97–104.

Singh, A. A., & Salazar, C. F. (2010c). Six considerations for social justice group work. *Journal for Specialists in Group Work, 35*(3), 308–319.

*Sink, C. A., Edwards, C. N., & Eppler, C. (2012). *School based group counseling*. Belmont, CA: Brooks/Cole, Cengage Learning.

*Sklare, G. B. (2005). *Brief counseling that works: A solution-focused approach for school counselors and administrators* (2nd ed.). Thousand Oaks, CA: Corwin Press.

*Sonstegard, M. A., & Bitter, J. R. (with Pelonis, P.). (2004). *Adlerian group counseling and therapy: Step-by-step*. New York, NY: Brunner-Routledge (Tayler & Francis).

Spinal-Robinson, P., & Wickham, R. E. (1992a). *Flips flops: A workbook for children who have been sexually abused.* Notre Dame, IN: Jalice.

Spinal-Robinson, P., & Wickham, R. E. (1992b). *Cartwheels: A workbook for children who have been sexually abused.* Notre Dame, IN: Jalice.

Spinal-Robinson, P., & Wickham, R. E. (1993). *High tops: A workbook for teens who have been sexually abused.* Notre Dame, IN: Jalice.

St. Pierre, B. K. (2014). Student attitudes and instructor participation in experiential groups. *Journal for Specialists in Group Work, 39*(3), 194–211.

Steen, S. (2009). Group counseling for African American elementary students: An exploratory study. *Journal for Specialists in Group Work, 34*(2), 101–117.

Steen, S., Bauman, S., & Smith, J. (2007). Professional school counselors and the practice of group work. *Professional School Counselors, 11*, 72–80.

Steen, S., Bauman, S., & Smith, J. (2008). The preparation of professional school counselors for group work. *Journal for Specialists in Group Work, 33*(3), 253–269.

Steen, S., & Bemak, F. (2008). Group work with high school students at risk of school failure: A pilot study. *Journal for Specialists in Group Work, 33*(4), 335–350.

Steen, S., Griffin, D., & Shi, Q. (2011). Supporting students of color on campus. In T. Fitch & J. L. Marshall (Eds.), *Group work and outreach plans for college counselors* (pp. 111–122). Alexandria, VA: American Counseling Association.

Steen, S., Henfield, M. S., & Booker, B. (2014). The achieving success everyday group counseling model: Implications for professional school counselors. *Journal for Specialists in Group Work, 39*(1), 29–46.

Steen, S., Shi, Q., & Hockersmith, W. (2014). Group counseling for African Americans: Research and practice considerations. In J. DeLucia-Waack, C. R. Kalodner, & M. T. Riva (Eds.), *Handbook of group counseling and psychotherapy* (2nd ed., pp. 220–230). Thousand Oaks, CA: Sage.

Stockton, R., & Morran, D. K. (2010). Reflections on practitioner-researcher collaborative inquiry. *International Journal of Group Psychotherapy, 60*(2), 295–305.

Stockton, R., Morran, K., & Chang, S. (2014). An overview of current research and best practices for training beginning group leaders. In J. DeLucia-Waack, C. R. Kalodner, & M. T. Riva (Eds.), *Handbook of group counseling and psychotherapy* (2nd ed., pp.133–145). Thousand Oaks, CA: Sage.

Stockton, R., Morran, D. K., & Krieger, K. M. (2004). An overview of current research and best practices for training beginning group leaders. In J. L. DeLucia-Waack, D. Gerrity, C. R. Kalodner, & M. T. Riva (Eds.), *Handbook of group counseling and psychotherapy* (pp. 65–75). Thousand Oaks, CA: Sage.

Stockton, R., & Toth, P. L. (1997). Applying a general research training model to group work. *Journal for Specialists in Group Work, 22*(4), 241–252.

Substance Abuse and Mental Health Services Administration. (2012). *Substance abuse treatment: Group therapy in-service training*. Rockville, MD: Author.

Sue, D. W. (2016). Race talk and facilitating difficult racial dialogues. *Counseling Today, 58*(7), 42–47.

Sue, D. W., Arredondo, P., & McDavis, R. J. (1992). Multicultural counseling competencies and standards: A call to the profession. *Journal of Counseling and Development, 70*(4), 477–486.

Sue, D. W., Ivey, A. E., & Pedersen, P. (1996). *Multicultural counseling and therapy*. Pacific Grove, CA: Brooks/Cole.

Sue, D. W., & Sue, D. (2013). *Counseling the culturally diverse: Theory and practice* (6th ed.). New York, NY: Wiley.

*Sweeney, D. S., Baggerly, J. N., & Ray, D. C. (2014). *Group play therapy: A dynamic approach*. New York, NY: Routledge (Taylor & Francis).

Tedeschi, R. G., & Calhoun, L. G. (1993). Using the support group to respond to the isolation of bereavement. *Journal of Mental Health Counseling, 15*(1), 47.

Terr, L. C. (1990). *Too scared to cry*. New York, NY: Harper & Row.

Terr, L. C. (1991). Childhood traumas: An outline and overview. *American Journal of Psychiatry, 148*, 10–20.

Terr, L. C. (2008). *Magical moments of change*. New York, NY: Norton.

Terr, L. C. (2009). The use of context in the treatment of traumatized children. *Psychoanalytic Study of the Child, 64*, 275–298.

Thomas, M. C., & Hard, P. F. (2011). Support groups for gay and lesbian students. In T. Fitch & J. L. Marshall (Eds.), *Group work and outreach plans for college counselors* (pp. 123–136). Alexandria, VA: American Counseling Association.

Torres-Rivera, E., Torres Fernandez, I., & Hendricks, W. A. (2014). Psychoeducational and counseling groups with Latinos/as. In J. DeLucia-Waack, C. R. Kalodner, & M. T. Riva (Eds.), *Handbook of group counseling and psychotherapy* (2nd ed., pp. 242–252). Thousand Oaks, CA: Sage.

Vacha-Haase, T. (2014). Group work with those in later life. In J. DeLucia-Waack, C. R. Kalodner, & M. T. Riva (Eds.), *Handbook of group counseling and psychotherapy* (2nd ed., pp. 276–287). Thousand Oaks, CA: Sage.

VanderSchaaf, J. C. (2013). *Integrating yoga and psychotherapy: A doctoral dissertation*. Sarasota, FL: Argosy University.

Veach, L. J., & Gladding, S. T. (2007). Using creative group techniques in high schools. *Journal for Specialists in Group Work, 32*(1), 71–81.

Villalba, J. A. (2007). Incorporating wellness into group work in elementary schools. *Journal for Specialists in Group Work, 32*(1), 31–40.

*Wagner, C. C., & Ingersoll, K. S. (2013). *Motivational interviewing in groups*. New York, NY: Guilford Press.

Waldo, M., Kerne, P. A., & Kerne, V. (2007). Therapeutic factors in guidance versus counseling sessions of domestic violence groups. *Journal for Specialists in Group Work, 32*(4), 346–361.

Weber, R., & Weinberg, H. (2015). Group therapy around the world. *International Journal of Group Psychotherapy, 65*(4), 483–489.

Wedding, D., & Corsini, R. J. (Eds.). (2014). *Current psychotherapies* (10th ed.). Belmont, CA: Brooks/Cole, Cengage Learning.

Wexler, D. B. (2000). *Domestic violence 2000: Group leader's manual*. New York, NY: Norton.

Wexler, D. B. (2004). *Why good men behave badly: Change your behavior, change your relationship*. Oakland, CA: New Harbinger.

Wexler, D. B. (2005). *Is he depressed or what?* Oakland, CA: New Harbinger.

Wexler, D. B. (2006). *STOP domestic violence: Innovative skills, techniques, options, and plans for better relationships*. New York, NY: Norton.

*Wheeler, N., & Bertram, B. (2015). *The counselor and the law: A guide to legal and ethical practice* (7th ed.). Alexandria, VA: American Counseling Association.

Whittingham, M. (2014). Group work in colleges and university counseling centers. In J. L. DeLucia-Waack, C. R. Kalodner, & M. T. Riva (Eds.), *Handbook of group counseling and psychotherapy* (2nd ed., pp. 329–339). Thousand Oaks, CA: Sage.

Winslade J., Crocket, K., & Monk, G. (1997). The therapeutic relationship. In G. Monk, J. Winslade, K. Crocket, & D. Epston (Eds.), *Narrative therapy in practice: The archaeology of hope* (pp. 53–81). San Francisco, CA: Jossey-Bass.

Winslade, J., & Monk, G. (2007). *Narrative counseling in schools: Powerful and brief* (2nd ed.). Thousand Oaks, CA: Corwin Press (Sage).

Wolfelt, A. D. (2003). *Understanding your grief: Ten essential touchstones for finding hope and healing your heart*. Fort Collins, CO: Companion Press.

Wolfelt, A. D. (2015). 5 toxic misconceptions about grief. *Bottom Line Health, 29*(5), 13–14.

Wolitzsky, D. L. (2011a). Contemporary Freudian psychoanalytic psychotherapy. In S. B. Messer & A. S. Gurman (Eds.), *Essential psychotherapies: Theory and practice* (3rd ed., pp. 33–71). New York, NY: Guilford Press.

Wolitzsky, D. L. (2011b). Psychoanalytic theories in psychotherapy. In J. C. Norcross, G. R. Vandenbos, & D. K. Freedheim (Eds.), *History of psychotherapy* (2nd ed., pp. 65–100). Washington, DC: American Psychological Association.

Worden, J. W. (2002). *Grief counseling and grief therapy: A handbook for the mental health practitioner* (3rd ed.). New York, NY: Springer.

*Wubbolding, R. (2011). *Reality therapy: Theories of psychotherapy series*. Washington, DC: American Psychological Association.

*Yalom, I. D. (1980). *Existential psychotherapy*. New York, NY: Basic Books.

Yalom, I. D. (1983). *Inpatient group psychotherapy*. New York, NY: Basic Books.

*Yalom, I. D. (2005a). *The Schopenhauer cure: A novel*. New York, NY: HarperCollins.

*Yalom, I. D., (with Leszcz, M.). (2005b). *The theory and practice of group psychotherapy* (5th ed.). New York, NY: Basic Books.

Yalom, I. D., & Vinogradov, S. (1988). Bereavement groups: Techniques and themes. *International Journal of Group Psychotherapy, 38*(4), 419–446.

Zur, O. (2007). *Boundaries in psychotherapy: Ethical and clinical explorations*. Washington, DC: American Psychological Association.

NAME INDEX

NAME INDEX

SUBJECT INDEX

SUBJECT INDEX